THE SCHOOL LIBRARY MEDIA PROGRAM

Instructional Force for Excellence

THE SCHOOL LIBRARY MEDIA PROGRAM

Instructional Force for Excellence

Third Edition

Ruth Ann Davies

R. R. BOWKER COMPANY
New York & London, 1979

To Frances Henne
Profound scholar
Wise counselor
Intrepid leader
Master teacher

Published by R. R. Bowker Company
1180 Avenue of the Americas, New York, N.Y. 10036
Copyright © 1979 by Xerox Corporation
All rights reserved
Printed and bound in the United States of America

Library of Congress Cataloging in Publication Data
Davies, Ruth Ann.
    The school library media program.

    Second ed. published in 1973 under title: The
school library media center.
    Bibliography: p.
    Includes index.
    1. School libraries. 2. Instructional materials
centers. I. Title.
Z675.S3D35 1979   027.8   79-20358
ISBN 0-8352-1244-0

Contents

Foreword   ix

Preface   xi

1. Crisis in Confidence: The Educational Profession under Siege   1
2. Public Education in a Free Society: Past, Present, and Future Expectations   13
3. The School Library Media Program: Instructional Force for Excellence   35
4. The School Library Media Program: Actualizing Force for Self-Realization   49
5. The Teaching Role of the Library Media Specialist   63
6. The Curriculum Support Role of the Library Media Specialist   71
7. The Library Media Specialist's Role as Instructional Technologist   95
8. The Library Media Program Supports the English Program   135
9. The Library Media Program Supports the Social Studies Program   185
10. The Library Media Program Supports the Science and Mathematics Programs   235
11. The Library Media Program Supports the Humanities Program   277
12. The Library Media Program Implements the Developmental Skills Program   303
13. Evaluating the Effectiveness of the School Library Media Program   313
14. The Supervisor of the Library Media Program   359

Epilogue: What of the Future?   379

APPENDIXES

A. Basic Background Readings   383
B. The Students' Right to Read   406
C. A Sample Interdisciplinary Unit   413
D. Sample Resource Unit: The Civil War and Reconstruction   425
E. A Guide for Constructing Mini-Courses   439
F. Checklists for District and Building Library Policy and Routine Manual Inclusion   444
G. A Faculty Self-Study of the Elementary School Library Media Center   448
H. Media Evaluation Guidelines   457
I. Model School Library Policy Statement   467
J. Elementary Reading Interest Inventory   471
K. How to Use ERIC   474
L. Thinking-Learning-Communicating Skills Continuum, K–12   478
M. Facilities Planning   535
N. Learning to Learn in School Libraries   548

Terminology   557
Bibliography   561
Index   569

FIGURES

1. Individualizing the Teaching Design   53
2. Pilot Projects   82
3. Flowchart of the Acquisitions Process   122

FIGURES (cont.)

4. Flowchart of the Cataloging Process   123
5. Social Studies: Conceptual Components   186
6. Cybernetic-Decisional Model of Social Change   250
7. Continuum of Leader Behavior   363

TABLES

1. Industry by Industry: Who's Ahead in Real Pay   3
2. Diversification for Individualization of Instruction   92
3. Language Processes and Skills   169
4. Table of Specifications for the Language Arts   171
5. Major Emphases as Conceptualized in Selected Social Studies Textbooks
   Published in the United States, 1966–1976   194

CHECKLISTS

 1. Media Programming Components   112
 2. Form for Selecting Resources to Support a Reading Unit   149
 3. Checklist of Instructional Media   201
 4. Checklist of Variations and Adjustments to Meet Individual Differences   202
 5. Planning for Less Able or Slower Learning Students   204
 6. Variations and Adjustments for Gifted Students   204
 7. Selected Criteria for Evaluating Social Studies Materials   227
 8. The Multiethnic Education Program Evaluation Checklist   280
 9. Media Program Checklist   317
10. Planning and Strategy of Change   361

EXAMPLES

 1. Law and Justice Pilot Project Integration Activities   78
 2. Mexico—Its History, Its Land, and Its People   81
 3. Pilot Project Design and Analysis Guide   83
 4. Learning Project: Orientation to the GATE Program   85
 5. The White Men Doom and Then Save the Buffalo   114
 6. The Tasaday: A Study of a Primitive Culture Frozen in Time   116
 7. Learning Guide in U.S. History   119
 8. An Itemized Media Budget   127
 9. A Typical Day in an Elementary and a Secondary Library Media Center   129
10. Literature Enrichment Unit, "Call It Courage"   158
11. Literature Enrichment Unit, "The Rain Forest"   159
12. Literature Enrichment Unit, "The Old Man and the Sea"   160
13. Pittman Literature Learning Guide, "No Man Is an Island"   161
14. Book Summary Form: Grades 3–4   163
15. Personal Reading Notebook   164
16. Biography Report Form ·   164
17. Model Parent Permission to Read Form   168
18. Linguistics Study Unit, "Fun with Words"   172
19. Linguistics Study Unit, "The Wizardry of Words"   175
20. Linguistics Study Unit, "American English: Inherited, Manufactured,
    and Fractured"   177
21. Social Studies Unit Planning   199
22. Teacher-Library Media Specialist Unit Planning Guide:
    Topic and Fundamental Analysis Form   200
23. Westward Ho! The Wagons, or, If I Had Been a Pioneer Trailblazer   206
24. If I Had Lived During the Middle Ages   213
25. Integrated English-Social Studies Unit   222
26. Biography Summary   224

EXAMPLES (cont.)

27. Historical Novel Summary   225
28. Unit Pretest: The Civil War and Reconstruction   230
29. Pros and Cons of Space Colonization   241
30. A Multidisciplinary Science Mini-Unit   243
31. Lesson Plan: Alternate Sources of Energy   246
32. Our Wonderful World of Animals   251
33. Our Wonderful World of Plants   259
34. Test Your City's Quotient   268
35. Great Mathematicians Prior to the Twentieth Century   271
36. Mathematics as a Communication Tool   272
37. Pittman Learning Guide: Roman Numerals   274
38. American Humanities: Tentative Schedule for the 1920s Unit   288
39. American Humanities: Names and Terms of the 1920s   289
40. Book Illustrators and Their Art   290
41. The Introduction, Reinforcement, and Extension of Chronology and Time Line Skills   307
42. Find Your Media Center Service Profile   318
43. Criteria of Excellence Checklist   320
44. New York State Education Department Cooperative Review Service Self-Study Guide: School Library   322
45. Illinois Standards for School Media Programs and the School Evaluation Form   330
46. Illinois Self-Evaluation Form: School Media Programs   347
47. Job Description: Head, Elementary Library Team   369
48. Job Description: Head, Secondary Library Team   369
49. Job Description: Supervisor of Library Media Service   370
50. Evaluation of Media Specialist Services   372
51. Administrative and Supervisory Personnel Evaluation Form   375
52. Administrative Personnel Evaluation Form, Pueblo, Colorado   376

Foreword

The modern school library or educational media program has long lacked a full-length interpretive portrait. Skillfully executed sketches abound—bits and pieces of the total picture have been painted, but until now, they have not been portrayed in a single panoramic format.

This has been unfortunate for the media practitioner who has attempted to keep on top of a rapidly developing and highly complex profession. It is even more difficult for the student being introduced to and involved in learning the profession.

There are understandable reasons for this unfortunate situation. The proliferation of theories and practices in educational purpose and technique have created new demands on the school library's performance. New educational materials—new in content and format, use and expected result—have required new competencies of the school library's personnel. Even the rapid acceptance of the fact that physical facilities be reshaped, component by component, to emancipate the new functions of educational change have originated new forms of libraries and media systems centers. And all of this newness, this change, these theoretical *and* actual processes created, developed, and directed for the most part by gifted leadership have been too many, too quick, too incohesive, too independent to have permitted sitting still long enough for that sharply defined portrait. Until now, we have merely had a blurred picture of the school library.

Ruth Ann Davies has come to terms with the problem in this book. Not in over twenty years has school librarianship been as carefully detailed in a book available to everyone who cares. Ms. Davies is well known as a librarian, a scholar, a library administrator, an educator. She is also an artist: a person of

Note: Adapted from the Preface to the first edition, *The School Library: A Force for Educational Excellence.*

enormous creativity who has known the landscapes of the past and onto them paints the pictures of the future. But perhaps more importantly, she recognizes the present and is able to interpret its design, color, proportion, balance.

Her book is at once historical and visionary, theoretical and highly practical, offering a comprehensive picture of school librarianship in the United States as it enters the 1980s. It should be valued for its perceptive archival content. It should be considered as a rational and defensible position paper. It will be increasingly important as the biography of a young and swiftly growing profession. It is a how-to-do-it handbook; it is philosophy in action; it is an inspiration!

Pre-service and in-service school librarians, library educationists, school administrators, classroom teachers, and the great variety of education specialists will be able to distinguish the school library as portrayed here. If, as may be claimed by some, it is *not* the whole picture, the counterclaim can be made that it is the sharpest, most complete picture we have extant.

The profession of school librarianship is both vertically and horizontally mobile. It moves. To catch its picture in a book is to freeze it unnaturally at one point in space and time. If all the aspects of this developing institution could be filmed, edited, and viewed simultaneously and continually, perhaps we could keep current. That is impossible, of course, but revision is not.

In the meantime, the taut canvas upon which changes will be ordered is available here. *The School Library Media Program: Instructional Force for Excellence* is an impressive and important addition to our professional gallery.

JOHN ROWELL
Director, School Library Media
 and Instructional Publishing Programs
Graduate School of Library Service
Case Western Reserve University, Cleveland, Ohio

Preface

The millennial year 2000 is but twenty years in the future as this, the third edition, goes to press. The decade since the first edition has brought forth radical social, economic, and political changes. Many of these changes have had dynamic impact on education. This revision identifies and explores these changes and examines in detail their resultant impact on the educational program and the accommodating changes within the school library media program. *What of the future*—in the light of the contemporary crisis of confidence in education and in the light of emerging social, economic, and political trends —is a major theme examined throughout this new edition.

Believing that professional preparation for the future is of consummate importance, the National Education Association prepared a report, *Curriculum Change Toward the 21st Century*,[1] to guide curriculum development. Carefully woven into the fabric of this edition within each chapter dealing with the various curricular subject areas are the specific recommendations for future curriculum building stressed by the NEA:

Polyethnic, polycultural, and multilingual education as a force for peace

Learning as a lifelong process

Flexible educational processes

Emphasis on standards and values

Increased emphasis on self-directed learning

Respect for individual differences

Personalization of instruction

Education as a seamless learning continuum

---

[1] Harold G. Shane, *Curriculum Change Toward the 21st Century*, Curriculum Series (Washington, D.C.: National Education Association, 1977).

Application of instructional systems and technologies

Ability, motivation, and readiness serving as the learner's prime credentials

Career education of greater versatility

Emphasis on basic communication skills

Greater emphasis on problem solving and valuing

Accentuated interdisciplinary learning

Introduction to the concept of alternative futures

Sharpened emphasis on human geography and planetary cultures

Furthering the recommendations offered by the NEA, current standards and guidelines from the National Council of Teachers of English, from the National Council for the Social Studies, from the National Science Teachers Association, and from the National Council of Teachers of Mathematics have been included for study and implementation. Throughout, the role of the library media specialist as teacher and that of the school library media program in the implementation of instructional excellence is not only enunciated but also clearly spelled out to preclude any ambiguity or hesitancy!

Fifty-two examples of curriculum support projects bring attainable reality to the theory of instructional excellence. A new chapter, "The School Library Media Program: Actualizing Force for Self-Realization," reflects determination to *humanize education on all levels in all subjects*. The epiloque, "What of the Future?" calls to action all library media specialists committed to the symbiotic welfare of education and the school library profession.

The central purpose, then, of this edition still remains constant with that of the first—to get the static out of the educational intercom so the message can clearly be heard that today's school library (regardless of whether it is called an instructional media center, a resource center, a communications center, or by any other name) is a source and a force for educational excellence and that today's school librarian (regardless of whether he or she is called a media specialist, a resource specialist, a communications specialist, or by any other name) "is a teacher whose subject is learning itself."[2]

As to what lies ahead, I join with Harold G. Shane in believing that despite the alarming uncertainties of the future, "The United States is not a fatigued society sustained by fading and inaccurate remembrances."[3] I, too, believe that we can and will meet current and future threats with renewed vigor, dedication, and determination. I concur in the poignancy of Shane's vision that:

> Historians writing a century hence . . . may well describe the interval between 1976 and 2001 as one of the most portentous in human story. As these years unwind, there is an opportunity for humankind to approach both its age-old dreams and true greatness as its draws near the threshold of the millennium.[4]

> Hopefully . . . by the year 2001 A.D. we will have verified the hope that the fundamental problems now facing us are occurring in the dusk before the cockcrow rather than in the gathering gloom of a long twilight.[5]

---

[2]Douglas M. Knight, "Foreword," in *Library Services for the Nation's Needs: Toward Fulfillment of a National Policy* (Washington, D.C.: National Advisory Commission on Libraries, 1968).
[3]Harold G. Shane, *Curriculum Change Toward the 21st Century*, p. 56.
[4]Ibid., p. 9.
[5]Ibid., p. 128.

1 Crisis in Confidence: The Educational Profession under Siege

With all the multitude of changes under way, ours is a time of doubts, expectations and debate about what is happening or may eventually happen in the world.

Aurelio Peccei*

The roaring current of change is so powerful today that it overturns institutions, shifts our values, and shrivels our roots.

Alvin Toffler†

It is evident to all that the learned professions are not the splendid companies, held in awe and respect, that they once were. . . . The status of any profession . . . goes up and down like the stock market, in response to things other than net worth.

Jacques Barzun‡

Just as a seismograph registers the direction and intensity of earthquakes, schools register both the kinds and severity of social upheaval. As our nation enters its third century, pressures generated by economic, political, and social changes threaten to explode. One has the uneasy feeling that the metaphorical clock of history is about to be replaced by a time bomb. There is a pervading climate of contention and confrontation. With or without justification, the public has lost confidence in the professions and views education, law, and medicine with a jaundiced eye.[1] Dissatisfaction with education is widespread and continues to grow in intensity. In an article carrying as its title "The Great Anti-School Campaign," Robert Hutchins stated:

> In the last few years a flood of books has appeared purporting to show that public education in the United States is a delusion and a fraud, that it is not merely defective, it is positively damaging to the children who have to submit to it. The more extreme critics propose, therefore, not to reform public education but to abolish it.[2]

In summarizing the public's deteriorating attitude toward education during the decade 1969–1978, a Gallup Poll reported, "The public schools have lost favor with the American public during recent years. Therefore, heroic efforts must be devoted to restoring this lost confidence and respect."[3]

From the present vantage point, the future of education is far from assured. Inasmuch as the school library media program is an integral component of education itself, that which threatens education in general likewise immedi-

---

*Aurelio Peccei, "Commentary," in Ervin Laszlo, *The Inner Limits of Mankind: Heretical Reflections on Today's Values, Culture, and Politics* (New York: Pergamon, 1978), p. vii.

†Alvin Toffler, *Future Shock* (New York: Random, 1970), p. 3.

‡Jacques Barzun, "The Professions under Siege," *Harper's Magazine* 257 (Oct. 1978): 61.

ately places in jeopardy the school library media program. It behooves all educators—administrators, classroom teachers, and school library media specialists—to examine the complexity of the forces arrayed against education, to identify valid criticisms, and then to make "heroic efforts" to achieve excellence in all aspects of the profession.

SOCIETAL CHANGES

The reason why the public schools have lost favor with the American public is as complex as society itself. Radical shifts and changes of crisis proportion that have been occurring with shocking regularity have contemporary society reeling from shattering stress and disorientation. During the sixties, the civil rights movements, urban rioting, student demonstrations, and opposition to the Vietnam War shook the nation. During the seventies, corruption in government rocked and shocked the nation. Almost daily the media made new disclosures of vice in high places. In quick succession the public learned of the Watergate break-in and cover-up; of the resignation of a vice president charged with receiving kickbacks; of the resignation of a president to forestall congressional impeachment proceedings; of the trial and sentencing of an attorney general and top presidential aides for conspiracy; of abuse of power by the Central Intelligence Agency (CIA) and the Federal Bureau of Investigation (FBI); of congressional wrongdoing ranging from drunkenness and influence peddling to sex underwritten by the congressional payroll; and of fraud in federal agencies draining more than 5 percent from the annual federal budget.

DOUBLE-DIGIT INFLATION

With the approach of the eighties, all segments of society in all sections of the country are suffering from the shattering impact of uncontrolled, double-digit inflation. Economic survival has become the single most compelling public, personal, and institutional concern, and education is fighting for its life. For example, during the period 1939–1979, prices skyrocketed by better than 373 percent and the purchasing power of the dollar dwindled to but 20 cents.* In fact, 88.4 million Americans—40 percent of the population—lived their lives during a time of unbroken inflation.

MULTIPLE TAXATION

The ever-increasing burden of multiple taxation coupled with the eroding value of the dollar reached the critical stage by the close of the seventies. The federal income tax alone had increased 676 percent since its inception in 1914 when it collected but $380 million in revenue. In 1979, the Internal Revenue Service collected $421 billion and was predicting that by the year 1982 it would be collecting at least $620 billion. State, county, and municipal income taxes likewise had relentlessly escalated, adding billions to the income tax burden. In addition, state sales taxes on commodities and services also continued to soar, serving as daily reminders of the ever-increasing cost of just existing.

*To update these statistics contact the U.S. Bureau of Labor Statistics, 200 Constitution Ave. N.W., Washington, D.C. 20210, tel. 202-523-7827.

PROPOSITION 13

Property taxes during the 10-year period 1966–1976 also increased by a frightening 115 percent. This excessive tax burden led to a nationwide taxpayers' revolt with the first shot being fired in California on June 6, 1978. On this historic date the California voters by a two-to-one margin approved Proposition 13, thereby amending their state constitution to slash property taxes by 57 percent and to erect high barriers against major increases in state and local levies for years to come. This was but the first shot in a national voters' war to curtail government spending and to lower taxes. Immediately throughout the nation demands were made that the federal government be forced by constitutional amendment to place a limit both on debt and on taxation. Just nine months after the California mandate, 24 state legislatures had already passed resolutions calling for a constitutional convention to amend the U.S. Constitution and, thereby, impose a ceiling on federal debt and taxation. Fear and anger had forged a formidable coalition. The voters were on the warpath.

Schools, because they are primarily supported by property taxes, suffered from the punitive action taken by the voters. As a result of Proposition 13, California schools lost more than $3 billion in tax support. All over the country similar tax revolts erupted, leading to what one observer termed "legislation by tantrum." Bond issue after bond issue was defeated. School budgets were slashed and school programs drastically curtailed; the school year was shortened; academic as well as nonacademic subjects were dropped from the curriculum; school library programs were phased out; teaching and custodial staffs were reduced; class size was increased; moratoriums were declared on school construction; and teachers' salaries lagged well behind the rate of inflationary price increases (see Table 1).

TABLE 1 INDUSTRY BY INDUSTRY: WHO'S AHEAD IN REAL PAY*

	AVERAGE WEEKLY PAY BEFORE TAXES (IN DOLLARS)	GAIN IN PAY FROM YEAR AGO (IN DOLLARS)	CHANGE IN REAL PAY— ALLOWING FOR HIGHER PRICES, TAXES† (IN DOLLARS)
Those Ahead . . .			
Farm operators	230.38	49.23	+21.45
Tire-factory workers	372.22	56.68	+19.17
Metal-can makers	368.94	57.06	+18.02
Steelworkers	412.16	60.01	+16.61
Metal miners	364.04	54.94	+16.52
Petroleum-refinery workers	411.65	44.00	+ 3.55
Bank clerks	155.73	9.73	+ 2.92
Aluminum workers	399.81	41.72	+ 2.48
Oil, gas-field workers	388.07	40.07	+ 1.99
Aircraft workers	335.91	33.31	+ .38
Laundry workers	132.86	11.41	+ .18

(cont. on next page)

*Here is how buying power of workers' weekly paychecks—real pay—has changed during the last year. Changes are affected by average hours worked as well as by wage rates, taxes and inflation.

†After federal income and Social Security taxes and adjustment for the rise in consumer prices. Assumes a family of four for tax purposes, except for retired federal workers, who are assumed to be married couples.

Note: Latest available weekly pay usually December 1978. Farm operators often include family members instead of individual workers.

TABLE 1 (cont.)

	AVERAGE WEEKLY PAY BEFORE TAXES (IN DOLLARS)	GAIN IN PAY FROM YEAR AGO (IN DOLLARS)	CHANGE IN REAL PAY— ALLOWING FOR HIGHER PRICES, TAXES† (IN DOLLARS)
. . . And Behind			
Social Security pensioners	58.62	3.47	- 1.49
Construction workers	328.99	29.72	- 1.97
Wholesale-trade workers	239.68	20.89	- 2.10
Clothing workers	146.52	10.78	- 2.12
Auto workers	395.60	35.74	- 2.13
Retired federal workers	163.62	12.70	- 2.36
Retail clerks	133.42	8.84	- 2.50
Leather-goods workers	148.40	10.39	- 3.16
Local bus drivers	286.86	23.12	- 3.54
Instrument workers	247.28	19.72	- 3.58
Paper-mill workers	296.24	24.18	- 3.68
Textile workers	182.78	13.45	- 3.82
Shoe-factory workers	140.91	8.14	- 3.87
Machinery workers (nonelectrical)	305.86	24.64	- 4.18
Veterans on full disability	211.48	13.58	- 4.23
Lumber workers	227.48	16.68	- 4.70
Metal-product workers	277.62	20.58	- 4.74
Sporting-goods workers	176.33	11.75	- 4.76
Rubber workers, except tires	221.40	15.99	- 4.85
Chemical workers	305.95	22.37	- 6.03
Furniture workers	194.57	11.91	- 6.05
Meatpackers	309.33	22.71	- 6.06
Electric, gas-company workers	329.80	24.56	- 6.09
Food processors	241.80	16.12	- 6.16
Electrical-equipment workers	249.48	16.13	- 6.68
Printing and publishing workers	255.46	15.95	- 7.20
Schoolteachers	282.10	14.77	-10.08
Federal-government workers	348.65	18.17	-11.58
Cigarette-factory workers	288.79	9.69	-14.82
Telephone workers	311.24	9.40	-16.77

Source: U.S. Depts. of Labor, Agriculture and HEW, Civil Service Commission, Veterans Administration, National Education Association.

Reprinted from *U.S. News & World Report.* Copyright © 1979 by U.S. News & World Report, Inc.

FRACTURED FAMILIES

The single most profound societal change affecting the schools is the weakening of the American family unit. The so-called typical family—the two-parent family with the father as wage earner and the mother as full-time homemaker caring for the children—is no longer typical. In fact, the "ideal" family may be fast on its way to becoming extinct. By 1979, this stereotype represented but 1 out of every 16 American families.

A statistical analysis of today's family unit reveals drastic changes:‡

The failure rate of marriage doubled in the period 1960–1979; the divorce rate had reached the ratio of two out of every four marriages.

‡For information update contact: Children's Defense Fund, 1520 New Hampshire Ave. N.W., Washington, D.C. 20036, tel. 202-483-1470; National Center for Social Statistics, Rm. 2614, 330 C St. S.W., Washington, D.C. 20201, tel. 202-245-0488; National Commission on Working Women,

In 1979, there were 9.2 million single-parent families; 940,000 mothers were unmarried.

Fifty percent of all mothers were gainfully employed outside the home; 6.4 million children under six years of age had working mothers; 20,000 pre-school children were left alone while their mothers were working; there were 22.4 million children from ages 6–17 whose mothers worked; 2 million of these children were left alone while their mothers were working.

Ten million children were getting virtually no health care; 20 million children under age 15—almost 40 percent of all children—were not immunized against one or more of the major childhood diseases.

Eighteen percent of all children under 3 years of age and 17.4 percent of all children ages 3 to 5 lived in poverty.

"What impact have these radical family changes had on the parents' attitude toward children?" is the question being asked not only by teachers but by the clergy, doctors, sociologists, social workers, lawyers, criminologists, the media, and countless others. Professor Sarane Spence Boocock, of the Department of Sociology at Rutgers University, has answered the question as follows:

> The responsibilities and skills involved in caring for young children are increasingly incompatible with other things adults value, both within and outside marriage. Certainly the self-development that is an important component of an individualistic society is at variance with the constant attention and the frequent selflessness required in the nurturance of babies and young children. . . .
> Indeed, recent surveys indicate that the presence of children has a negative rather than a positive effect on husband-wife relationships. Members of childless marriages report greater marital satisfaction than those with children. They in turn report less marital satisfaction the more children they have. On a variety of marital satisfaction indices, moreover, satisfaction drops sharply with the birth of the first child, sinks even lower during the school years, and goes up markedly only after the last child leaves home.[4]

Parents are unhappy with the schools; paradoxically, they are unhappy even with their own children.

The "me" generation of the sixties are the parents of today. Dr. Robert B. Taylor, specialist in family medicine, believes that the me philosophy has contributed directly to the high divorce rate and the breakdown of the family.[5] A *Time* magazine editorial, "Wondering If Children Are Necessary," reflects the same conviction that an overwhelming number of today's parents are too self-centered to put the welfare of their children before their own. The editorial reported the findings of a survey of 50,000 parents. When responding to the question "If given the chance again would you have children?" 70 percent answered no. The reason the respondents gave for their negative answer was, "It just isn't worth it!"[6]

The degree and overt display of active dislike of children by their parents are evidenced by the fact that at least two million cases of child abuse and neglect occur each year,[7] with the annual toll of 2,000 children dying from physical abuse.* One of the most shocking disclosures of child abuse is the report by the

---

Suite 400, 1211 Connecticut Ave. N.W., Washington, D.C. 20036, tel. 202-466-6770; Urban Institute, 2100 M St., Washington, D.C. 20037, tel. 202-223-1950; Women's Bureau, Dept. of Labor, 200 Constitution Ave. N.W., Washington, D.C. 20210, tel. 202-523-8914.

*For information update contact the National Committee for Prevention of Child Abuse, Box 2866, Chicago, Ill. 60690, tel. 312-565-1100.

Los Angeles police that "30,000 children, many of them under the age of 5, are used each year as objects of pornography. A number of them are actually sold or rented for pornography purposes by their parents."[8]

"What impact have these radical family changes had on the children?" likewise demands attention. The family in the past has been the bedrock of our Judeo-Christian society. The family traditionally has shaped, nurtured, and guided the child. Love of God and country, respect for others, adherence to a moral code, and a positive attitude toward life itself were learned at the mother's knee. In the past, we believed that the hand that rocked the cradle ruled the nation. Juvenile crime and drug and alcohol abuse have reached crisis proportions—convincing evidence that the fractured family has had devastating effect on today's children.

JUVENILE CRIME

The FBI reports that arrests of juveniles for violent crimes shot up 28 percent in the period 1960–1979; this was more than twice the increase in arrests for violent crimes committed by adults.* For example, violent crimes committed by youngsters 17 years of age or *younger* included:

Crimes	Percent
Property crimes	
Burglary	52
Larceny, theft	43
Motor-vehicle theft	53
Violent crimes	
Assault	16
Murder	10
Rape	17
Robbery	32

So widespread is juvenile contempt for the law that the President's Commission on Law Enforcement and Administration of Justice found that 90 percent of all young people admitted to having committed at least one act for which they could be taken to Juvenile Court.[9]

Physical violence against teachers by students has become a major professional concern. The National Education Association (NEA) conducted a national survey in 1978 that revealed that:

Seventy thousand teachers (1 in 33) were physically attacked at least once.

More than 3,000 of the teachers who had been attacked required medical attention in a hospital emergency room; more than 9,000 required attention either in a school clinic or a doctor's office; about 10,000 had to miss one or more days of school to recuperate.

Seventeen percent said they were afraid that they might be personally attacked.

Two hundred and fifty thousand teachers (1 in 8) had personal property damaged.

Five hundred thousand teachers (1 in 4) had personal property stolen.[10]

*For information update contact the Uniform Crime Reporting Section, U.S. Dept. of Justice, J. E. Hoover Building, Washington, D.C. 20535, tel. 202-324-3000.

Disrespect for authority, evidenced by physical violence against teachers, has led to a general breakdown in discipline. It is not unusual to find police stationed in the corridors of schools in the larger cities. The *Gallup Polls of Attitudes toward Education, 1969-1978*, identified the lack of discipline as the "greatest complaint against the schools of the country, at the present time."[11]

DRUG ABUSE

Illegal drug use, once confined to the adult population, has become a problem for today's youth. The National Institute on Drug Abuse conducted a survey in 1972 and again in 1977 to determine the incidence of drug use among youths (18 years or younger) and adults; the institute report follows:*

		Percent			Percent
Marijuana/Hashish			Prescription stimulants		
Youths:	1972	14.0	(nonmedical use)		
	1977	28.2	Youths:	1972	4.0
Adults:	1972	16.0		1977	5.2
	1977	24.5	Adults:	1972	5.0
Inhalants				1977	8.1
Youths:	1972	6.4	Heroin		
	1977	9.0	Youths:	1972	0.6
Adults:	1972	2.1		1977	1.1
	1977	3.7	Adults:	1972	1.3
Cocaine				1977	1.4
Youths:	1972	1.5			
	1977	4.0			
Adults:	1972	3.2			
	1977	6.0			

According to the National Institute on Drug Abuse, the use of marijuana among young people has become epidemic. By 1979, 1 out of 11 high school seniors smoked marijuana daily; 25 percent of these had begun smoking "pot" before tenth grade. This prevalent drug use poses a serious problem for schools. Smoking but one marijuana cigarette a day causes some to become dreamy, others to become talkative and giddy; "thoughts become disconnected. Time seems to pass more slowly. Surroundings and people . . . seem strange and unreal. . . . Remembering things and doing tasks become difficult."[12] How can learning take place when it is physically impossible for the student to concentrate, remember, or respond—let alone think?

ALCOHOL ABUSE

Alcohol use and abuse has become a grave problem not only for adults but for today's youth as well. The National Institute on Alcohol Abuse and Alcoholism in its third special report to Congress, June 1978,† summarized the drinking patterns of young people as follows:[13]

*For information update contact the National Institute on Drug Abuse, 5600 Fishers La., Rockville, Md. 20857, tel. 301-443-4577.
†For information update contact the National Institute on Alcohol Abuse and Alcoholism, Box 2345, Rockville, Md. 20852, tel. 301-468-2600.

	Percent		Percent
Seventh grade		Tenth grade	
Male drinkers	60.3	Male drinkers	84.2
Male problem drinkers	5.0	Male problem drinkers	27.2
Female drinkers	47.4	Female drinkers	76.3
Female problem drinkers	4.4	Female problem drinkers	18.9
Eighth grade		Eleventh grade	
Male drinkers	75.3	Male drinkers	88.5
Male problem drinkers	15.6	Male problem drinkers	33.9
Female drinkers	64.3	Female drinkers	79.0
Female problem drinkers	9.1	Female problem drinkers	19.9
Ninth grade		Twelfth grade	
Male drinkers	77.4	Male drinkers	89.9
Male problem drinkers	20.9	Male problem drinkers	39.9
Female drinkers	72.1	Female drinkers	83.2
Female problem drinkers	16.2	Female problem drinkers	20.6

The National Institute on Alcohol Abuse and Alcoholism defines problem drinking as "drunkenness at least six times in the past year; or presence of negative consequences from drinking two or more times in at least three of five specified situations in the past year or both."[14] The institute estimated that in 1978 there were 3.3 million problem drinkers among youth in the 14–17 age range—19 percent of the 17 million persons in this age group.[15]

The adolescent who uses marijuana tends also to drink; and it appears that the heavier marijuana users, as a group, are heavier drinkers.[16] Problem drinkers often use other drugs and suffer from a variety of adjustment or personality problems, exhibiting such characteristics as physical aggression and defiance of parents and other authority figures. How can the school cope with the disruptive behavior of the problem drinker who is also hooked on drugs? So far there is no answer.

EDUCATION AS SCAPEGOAT

Unrealistically, the sharp increase in juvenile crime, drug addiction, and alcoholism has contributed to the public's lack of confidence in the public schools. The schools have become a scapegoat for the failure of society itself to regulate its youth. Certain groups have voiced unrealistic demands showing that they expect from schools "nothing less than divination and infallibility."[17] Jacques Barzun in *Teacher in America*[18] aptly sums up the problem of unwarranted public expectations. Barzun's summation points out that it is absurd for the general public to expect schools to generate a classless society, do away with racial prejudice, make happy marriages, end the housing shortage, and produce patriotic and religious citizens who abstain from crime, drugs, and alcohol.

Criticism of the schools is as old as the schools themselves. As Walter Kolesnik of the University of Detroit said, "No one knows precisely when or where the first 'school' was established . . . but it would be a safe bet that fifteen minutes after the first school came into existence, at least a few critics were already pecking away at it."[19]

Contention and confrontation are here to stay. History is testimony to this. Human nature is an all too generous blend of the negative with the positive, the bitter with the sweet, and the nasty with the nice. This is a fact of life. Will and Ariel Durant in their *Lessons of History* remind us that we are but one generation away from the cave, for each of us is born with the same base emotions and drives as was primitive man. Progress, though painful and tortuously slow, has been made by those who have banded together to thwart the spoilers.

STRATEGIES FOR PROFESSIONAL SURVIVAL

Because there has been a persistent downgrading of education, the profession itself must make a value judgment as to which criticisms from without the profession and which criticisms from within it are justified. Having identified the legitimate criticisms, the profession must then painstakingly set about to correct what is wrong, to strengthen what is weak, and to safeguard what is excellent. "The whole aim is to lift the critique from a set of complaints to a set of purposes."[20] Only then can a plan for action be formulated and disaster, always lurking in the wings, be forestalled.

Professional gains are the direct result of those teachers, school librarians, administrators, parents, and other members of the community who share the dream and work together to realize it. Unfortunately, the sacrifices and efforts of those who have labored to thrust the profession forward have largely gone unnamed, unchronicled, and unsung. The drafting and enacting of Title II of the Elementary and Secondary Education Act (ESEA) of 1965 is a prime example of a landmark professional advancement that came about only because so many school librarians, teachers, administrators, and legislators cared so deeply and worked so hard. Regrettably, a search of the literature does not tell the story of the behind-the-scenes labors of those who planned the strategy, went to Washington, oversaw the writing of the bill, gave testimony, lobbied tirelessly, and finally brought it to enactment. This writer, as a member of the American Association of School Librarians' Legislative Committee and a member of the Standards Implementation Committee, was privileged to witness the actual drama as it was acted out at the American Library Association headquarters in Chicago and Washington, and then on Capitol Hill.

Although enacted in 1965, Title II of ESEA actually began with the publication in 1960 of the magnificent landmark document *Standards for School Library Programs*. In that timely and eloquent document, Frances Henne and Ruth Ersted, the coeditors, had with convincing logic set forth the philosophy that the school library is a force for educational excellence—a means of enabling each child and youth to achieve full potential as a person, as a learner, and as a citizen. These standards proclaimed that it was important "to all citizens that our schools have the resources needed for teaching and learning," and "that all schools have functional programs of library service."[21] They charged the profession itself with the responsibility for working to attain "excellence in providing school libraries for the youth of our country."[22] No empty rhetoric this! Even before the standards went to the printing press, Henne and Ersted together with the American Association of School Librarians (AASL) Headquarters Staff had a Standards Implementation Program under way. They had obtained funding for the program from the Knapp Foundation, had appointed an Implementation Project Staff, and had organized state, regional, and national task forces.

One major thrust of the Implementation Program was to obtain federal funds to translate the standards into practice. The battle cry of the 1950s had been, "A penny per day per child for library books." This plea went unheeded. Rare indeed was the school board that would appropriate as much as fifty cents per child per school year. All too many school libraries were limping along on funds raised by skating parties and candy sales at football games. Therefore, the plan of action was to petition Congress to extend the National Defense Education Act of 1958 to include funding for school libraries.

John Rowell, then Director of Pennsylvania School Libraries,* and this writer went to Washington, D.C., to petition Congressman Elmer J. Holland (representative from Pennsylvania's twentieth district) to introduce the needed legislation for federal funding. After having read *Standards for School Library Programs*, Congressman Holland was so impressed by this document that he drafted a bill (87th Cong., 2d sess., H.R. 11680) "to amend the National Defense Education Act of 1958 in order to provide a program to improve school library resources needed for teaching and learning." Although this bill initially died in committee, Congressman Holland reintroduced it in January 1963 (88th Cong., 1st sess., H.R. 629). This bill also died in committee. During the first week of January 1965, Congressman Holland notified AASL headquarters that his bill H.R. 629 was being written into the proposed Title II of ESEA, which act was signed into law by President Johnson in April. This act during the period 1966–1979 provided the school libraries of the United States with $1,031,453,553.†

The writing of the 1960 *Standards for School Library Programs* and the subsequent Standards Implementation Program culminating in the passage of ESEA Title II are proof of the effectiveness of professional leadership and commitment that lead to new heights of professional achievement. This successful endeavor emerges as a prototype of professional vision and self-determination. Though currently under siege, both the educational profession and the library profession can, nevertheless, by exercising vision, by exhibiting leadership, and by eliciting commitment not only survive this crisis- and shock-ridden world, but surmount problems and flourish. Jonas Salk reminds us that the outcome in any crisis situation will be gloomy only if we fail to act with vigor and imagination. He points out that half the Chinese ideography for the word *crisis* means "challenge."[23]

Already exercising desperately needed leadership and vision, NEA has set about charting the course for the educational profession to follow as it enters the 21st century (see Chapter 2). As spokesman for NEA in *Curriculum Change Toward the 21st Century*, Harold Shane warns that while we live in "a time rife with uncertainties, a time of relativism and 'permissiveness' when old values are being severely questioned and new ones have not yet clearly replaced them, the teaching profession in the United States—and indeed the world—has enormous opportunities and responsibilities."[24] He predicts that teachers and

---

*John Rowell currently is Professor and Director of School Library Media and Publishing Programs in the Case Western Reserve University Graduate School of Library Science.

†For information update on school library development and ESEA programs and funding contact Dr. Milbrey Jones, Chief, School Media Resources Branch, Offices of Libraries and Learning Resources, U.S. Office of Education, 400 Maryland Ave. S.W., Washington, D.C. 20202, tel. 202-254-2488.

their schools in coming decades will not be operating in a moral, social, and political utopia. "In other words, there will continue to be limits to the kinds of ideal situations that one might wish for. Schools in some instances will continue to operate on limited budgets, in aging plants . . ., and to work with students some of whom will be obstinate, hyperactive, slow to learn, and . . . badly battered."[25]

There has never been a period in history when people were not beset by problems—our time is no exception. We must not be overly intimidated by the contradictory nature of the world in which we live. It is probable that at some future time we, too, shall look back and more objectively assess our times as did Charles Dickens when he wrote:

> It was the best of times, it was the worst of times, it was the age of wisdom, it was the age of foolishness, it was the epoch of belief, it was the epoch of incredulity, it was the season of Light, it was the season of Darkness, it was the spring of hope, it was the winter of despair.[26]

NOTES

1. Jacques Barzun, "The Professions under Siege," *Harpers* 257 (Oct. 1978): 61–68.
2. Robert M. Hutchins, "The Great Anti-School Campaign," *The Center Magazine*, Jan./Feb. 1975, p. 7.
3. Stanley M. Elam, ed., *A Decade of Gallup Polls of Attitudes toward Education, 1969–1978* (Bloomington, Ind.: Phi Delta Kappa, 1978), p. 6.
4. Sarane Spence Boocock, "Today's Childhood—A Unique Condition," *Today's Education* 68 (Feb./Mar. 1979): 52.
5. Robert B. Taylor, "Behind the Surge in Broken Marriages," *U.S. News & World Report* 86 (Jan. 1979): 53.
6. Lance Morrow, "Wondering If Children Are Necessary," *Time* 113 (Mar. 5, 1979): 42.
7. Ibid.
8. Ibid.
9. Special Committee on Youth Education for Citizenship, *Law-Related Education in America* (Chicago: American Bar Association, 1975), p. 3.
10. National Education Association, "Teacher Opinion Poll," *Today's Education* 68 (Feb./Mar. 1979): 20.
11. Elam, *A Decade of Gallup Polls*, p. 12.
12. Maureen H. Cook and Carol Newman, *This Side Up: Making Decisions about Drugs* (Rockville, Md.: National Institute on Drug Abuse, 1978), p. 12.
13. Ernest P. Noble, ed., *Third Special Report to the U.S. Congress on Alcohol and Health* from the Secretary of Health, Education, and Welfare, U.S. Department of Health, Education, and Welfare (Washington, D.C.: Government Printing Office, 1978), p. 18.
14. Ibid., p. 17.
15. Ibid., p. xi.
16. *Summary of Final Report: A National Study of Adolescent Drinking Behavior, Attitudes and Correlates* (Rockville, Md.: National Clearinghouse for Alcoholic Information, 1975), p. 152.
17. Barzun, "The Professions under Siege," p. 66.
18. Jacques Barzun, *Teacher in America* (Boston: Little, 1945).
19. Walter B. Kolesnik, *Humanism and/or Behaviorism in Education* (Boston: Allyn & Bacon, 1975), p. 8.
20. Barzun, "The Professions under Siege," p. 68.
21. American Association of School Librarians, *Standards for School Library Programs* (Chicago: American Library Association, 1960) pp. 3–4.
22. Ibid., p. 6.

23. Jonas Salk quoted in Albert Rosenfeld, "Good News on Population," *Saturday Review* 6 (Mar. 3, 1979): 19.
24. Harold G. Shane, *Curriculum Change Toward the 21st Century*, Curriculum Series (Washington, D.C.: National Education Association, 1977), p. 10.
25. Ibid., p. 11.
26. Charles Dickens, *A Tale of Two Cities* (New York: Macmillan, 1962), p. 1.

2 Public Education in a Free Society: Past, Present, and Future Expectations

If we lack a clear vision of the future we seek, we lack both goals and the guidelines that help us to reach them.

Harold G. Shane*

Following a star does not imply interplanetary travel; it also means having a good compass. Ideals and positive visions are important not because they can be immediately and fully attained, but because they can set standards by which we can direct our steps.

Ervin Laszlo†

Lend me the stone strength of the past and I will lend you the wings of the future.

Robinson Jeffers‡

The school library media program becomes an instructional source and force for excellence only when it functions as an integral support component of the total teaching-learning enterprise. The library media program and the educational program are interdependent and inseparable. To attempt to understand the library media program in isolation from the educational program would be comparable to an attempt to construct a school without blueprint or specifications. It is the educational program—its philosophy, goals, purpose, and objectives—that gives purpose and direction, scope and dimension, form and substance, significance and value to the school library media program. Therefore, perspective in viewing the function and role of the school library media program begins logically by building a historical understanding of education itself.

HISTORICAL PERSPECTIVE

Education is an instrument that our society has designed and employs to strengthen, to perpetuate, and to safeguard the American way of life. In our democracy direct participation by the citizen in governmental policymaking holds both the promise of freedom and the threat of enslavement. Historically, democratic concern for education has been predicated on the assumption that an educated citizenry should be competent to act intelligently and thereby pre-

---

*Harold G. Shane, *Curriculum Change Toward the 21st Century*, Curriculum Series (Washington, D.C.: National Education Association, 1977), p. 14.

†Ervin Laszlo, *The Inner Limits of Mankind: Heretical Reflections on Today's Values, Culture and Politics* (New York: Pergamon Press, 1978), p. 28.

‡Warren B. Hicks and Alma M. Tillin, *Developing Multi-Media Libraries* (New York: R. R. Bowker, 1970), p. xi.

serve its freedom. Conversely, an uneducated electorate, not perceiving dangers inherent in unwise decisions, could embrace false doctrines and as a result lose its freedom.

Our Founding Fathers believed that an enlightened government had to have as a corollary an enlightened citizenry. Thomas Jefferson considered education to be "the most legitimate engine of government."[1] He warned that "if a nation expects to be ignorant and free . . . it expects what never has and never will be."[2] Likewise, James Madison held a deep personal conviction that education was the sure bulwark against self-elected enslavement due to ignorance. Madison said, "Popular government, without popular information or the means of acquiring it, is but a Prologue to a Farce or Tragedy; or, perhaps, to both."[3] America's public schools were established to spread literacy and general knowledge throughout the population, making possible an informed electorate that could not have been achieved in any other way.

Each generation has the obligation to evaluate critically the adequacy of traditional educational goals and practices in the light of its own survival needs. Since society is a living and dynamically changing organism, education dare not be static. An educational program designed to prepare the past generation for productive living in the horseless carriage age will not suffice to prepare today's youth for space exploration and tomorrow's youth for space colonization.

GOALS OF EDUCATION

Goals are general statements that give purpose and direction to education. Basic educational goals that affirm the aspirations of our free society are found in three landmark documents: the Harvard Report, the Rockefeller Report, and the National Goals Report.

THE HARVARD REPORT, 1945

Dr. James Conant, when president of Harvard University, recognized the necessity for rethinking critically the very purpose and nature of education in a free society. Dr. Conant appointed the Committee on the Objectives of Education in a Free Society and commissioned its members to "venture into the vast field of American educational experience in quest of a concept of general education that would have validity for the free society we cherish."[4] In 1945, the committee, after months of soul-searching, submitted its report, *General Education in a Free Society*, to Dr. Conant. The Harvard Report, as it is popularly called, is a classic—required reading for all who would understand the import of education in a free society (see Appendix A for excerpts). Here in extremely readable prose is presented a searching analysis of American education—background, theory, and philosophy.

The Harvard Report brought a new dimension to the Bill of Rights. It stated without qualification that a quality education is the birthright of each American citizen regardless of race, creed, economic condition, or geographic location. It charged that a democracy did not meet its obligation to the citizen by providing schools for the masses; rather, a democracy met its obligation only when it had provided *equal opportunity* for all citizens to experience quality education uniquely reflective of their needs, interests, goals, and abilities. The report's concern for equality of opportunity presaged the civil rights movement of the 1960s.

THE ROCKEFELLER REPORT, 1958

Unfortunately, Americans did not read and heed the Harvard Report. Indeed, America was not ready to bring seriousness of purpose to general education until Russia launched its first successful Sputnik in 1957.[5] At long last the American people became dissatisfied with educational drifting and dreaming. Sputnik changed the climate and fortunately America became receptive to the recommendations set forth in a second significant educational document, *The Pursuit of Excellence: Education and the Future of America*, published in 1958 by the Rockefeller Brothers Fund[6] (see Appendix A for excerpts). Here America found reiterated the basic tenet of the Harvard Report—excellence in all aspects of the educational endeavor is the only goal worthy of our free society. Here were reflected the same concern for equality of opportunity and the same concern for optimum achievement evidenced in the Harvard Report. Here was stated the same urgent plea that Americans realize that excellence cannot be left to chance but must be planned for, worked for, and paid for. Analyzing and evaluating the findings and recommendations of the Rockefeller Report give insight and perspective, for the report clearly outlines the road to be traveled in carrying American education from traditional mediocrity to innovative excellence.

The Rockefeller Report stressed, as did the Harvard Report, that it is the birthright of all American citizens to have their individuality respected. It stated that there could be no excellence in America's educational endeavor until individuals were rescued from the faceless anonymity of impersonal mass education. The report correlated the optimum development of the individual with the health of society itself, for enabling each citizen to achieve to the optimum potential is a means of society's reinvigorating itself.

THE NATIONAL GOALS REPORT, 1960

The Harvard and the Rockefeller reports serve as foundation stones in building an understanding of American education. A third report, *Goals for Americans*, published in 1960 by the U.S. Commission on National Goals,[7] serves as the keystone, for it relates education to the totality of the American enterprise (see Appendix A for excerpts). The commission endorsed the philosophy set forth in the Harvard and Rockefeller reports and stated that equality of opportunity for all citizens to experience an educational program of excellence uniquely reflective of the individual citizen's capabilities, needs, and goals was the only goal worthy of a free society. Attaining that goal, the commission maintained, was the challenge of the 1960s.

The Harvard Report, the Rockefeller Report, and the Report of the U.S. Commission on National Goals bring the American educational ideal into sharp, clear focus. They translate the obligation of our free society into a basic directional goal—to provide a *quality* education and an *optimum* education for each citizen so that all will be encouraged to achieve to the maximum of their potential as learners, as citizens, and as human beings. They have focused attention on the necessity of educating citizens in the art of competent thinking and competent social participation, i.e., being capable of translating knowledge into a pattern of constructive, reasoned, rational, purposeful, and positive behavior. These reports have extended the responsibility of education beyond preparing each citizen for intelligent political participation to encompass preparation for purposeful living, for economic effectiveness, for responsible individualism, for successful intergroup relations, for world consciousness, and, above all, for self-realization and self-fulfillment.

HIERARCHY OF EDUCATIONAL GOALS

Educational excellence is not a gift from the gods. Attainment must be planned for, worked for, and paid for. If not translated into action plans and substantive changes, the promise of excellence is but a myth, a hoax, and a cruel delusion. In the hierarchy of educational goals, the societal aspiration of providing a quality, optimum education for each citizen is the basic national bedrock goal. Like the Bill of Rights, this goal is both timeless and enduring, a constant in an ever-changing world. Immediately below and directly supportive of it are the national and state goals promulgated by the education profession to implement the attainment of the basic bedrock goal.

TWENTIETH-CENTURY IMPLEMENTATION GOALS: NATIONAL LEVEL

The national implementation goals of the greatest import during the twentieth century have been: the Seven Cardinal Principles, 1918; the Purpose of Education, 1938; the Central Purpose of Education, 1961; the Eighteen Goals of Education, 1973.

THE SEVEN CARDINAL PRINCIPLES (1918)

Although the Seven Cardinal Principles were proposed as major goals for secondary education, they had profound influence on elementary education as well. These statements reflect the concern of national educational leaders that education reflect the emerging needs of society and individuals in that society. The principles were presented under seven main headings:

HEALTH

Health needs cannot be neglected . . . without serious danger to the individual and the race.

Schools should provide health instruction, inculcate health habits, organize an effective program of physical activities, regard health needs in planning work and play, and cooperate with home and community in safeguarding and promoting health interests.

COMMAND OF FUNDAMENTAL PROCESSES

Much of the energy of the elementary school is properly devoted to teaching certain fundamental processes. The facility that a child of 12 or 14 may acquire in the use of these tools is not sufficient for the needs of modern life. This is particularly true of the mother tongue.

Proficiency in many of these processes may be increased more effectively by their application to new material than by the formal reviews commonly employed.

WORTHY HOME MEMBERSHIP

Home membership as an objective should not be thought of solely with reference to future duties. These are the better guaranteed if the school helps the pupils to take the right attitude toward present home responsibilities and interprets to them the contribution of the home to their development.

VOCATION

Vocational education should equip the individual to secure a livelihood for himself and those dependent on him, to serve society well through his vocation, to maintain right relationships toward his fellow workers and society, and, as far as possible, to find in that vocation, his own best development.

CIVIC EDUCATION

Civic education should develop in the individual those qualities whereby he will act well his part as a member of neighborhood, town or city, state or nation, and give him a basis for understanding international problems.

WORTHY USE OF LEISURE

Education should equip the individual to secure from his leisure the recreation of body, mind, and spirit, and the enrichment and enlargement of his personality.

ETHICAL CHARACTER

In a democratic society, ethical character becomes paramount among the objectives of the secondary school. Among the means of developing ethical character may be mentioned the wise selection of content and methods of instruction in all subjects of study, the social contacts of pupils with one another and with their teachers, the opportunities afforded by the organization and administration of the school for the development on the part of pupils of the sense of personal responsibility and initiative, and, above all, the spirit of service and the principles of true democracy which should permeate the entire school—principal, teachers, and pupils.[8]

THE PURPOSE OF EDUCATION (1938)

The Educational Policies Commission of the National Education Association (NEA) prepared *The Purpose of Education in American Democracy*, which postulated the fullest possible development of the individual within the framework of our democratic society as the basic goal of education.

SELF-REALIZATION

The inquiring mind.   The educated person has an appetite for learning.

Speech.   The educated person can speak the mother tongue clearly.

Reading.   The educated person reads the mother tongue efficiently.

Writing.   The educated person writes the mother tongue effectively.

Number.   The educated person solves his problems of counting and calculating.

Sight and hearing.   The educated person is skilled in listening and observing.

Health knowledge.   The educated person understands the basic facts concerning health and disease.

Health habits.   The educated person protects his own health and that of his dependents.

Public health.   The educated person works to improve the health of the community.

Recreation.   The educated person is a participant and spectator in many sports and other pastimes.

Intellectual interests.   The educated person has mental resources for the use of leisure.

Esthetic interests.   The educated person appreciates beauty.

Character.   The educated person gives responsible direction to his own life.

HUMAN RELATIONSHIPS

Respect for humanity.   The educated person puts human relationships first.

Friendships.   The educated person enjoys a rich, sincere, and varied social life.

Cooperation.   The educated person can work and play with others.

Courtesy.   The educated person observes the amenities of social behavior.

Appreciation of the home.   The educated person appreciates the family as a social institution.

Conservation of the home.   The educated person conserves family ideals.

Homemaking.   The educated person is skilled in homemaking.

Democracy in the home.   The educated person maintains democratic family relationships.

ECONOMIC EFFICIENCY

Work.   The educated producer knows the satisfaction of good workmanship.

Occupational information.   The educated producer understands the requirements and opportunities for various jobs.

Occupational choice.   The educated producer has *selected* his occupation.

Occupational efficiency.   The educated producer succeeds in his chosen vocation.

Occupational adjustment.   The educated producer maintains and improves his efficiency.

Occupational appreciation.   The educated producer appreciates the social value of his work.

Personal economics.   The educated consumer plans the economics of his own life.

Consumer judgment.   The educated consumer develops standards for guiding his expenditures.

Efficiency in buying.   The educated consumer is an informed and skillful buyer.

Consumer protection.   The educated consumer takes appropriate measures to safeguard his interests.

CIVIC RESPONSIBILITY

Social justice.   The educated citizen is sensitive to the disparities of human circumstance.

Social activity.   The educated citizen acts to correct unsatisfactory conditions.

Social understanding.   The educated citizen seeks to understand social structures and social processes.

Critical judgment.   The educated citizen has defenses against propaganda.

Tolerance.   The educated citizen respects honest differences of opinion.

Conservation.   The educated citizen has a regard for the nation's resources.

Social applications of science.   The educated citizen measures scientific advance by its contribution to the general welfare.

World citizenship.   The educated citizen is a cooperating member of the world community.

Law observance. The educated citizen respects the law.

Economic literacy. The educated citizen is economically literate.

Political citizenship. The educated citizen accepts his civic duties.

Devotion to democracy. The educated citizen acts upon an answering loyalty to democratic ideas.[9]

THE CENTRAL PURPOSE OF EDUCATION (1961)

In 1961, the NEA Educational Policies Commission addressed itself to answering the question, "What is the central purpose of American education?" After research and deliberation, the commission provided the following statement respected today as basic and intrinsic to educational planning:

The purpose which runs through and strengthens all other educational purposes— the common thread of education—is the development of the ability to think. This is the central purpose to which the school must be oriented if it is to accomplish either its traditional tasks or those newly accentuated by recent changes in the world. To say that it is central is not to say that it is the sole purpose or in all circumstances the most important purpose, but that it must be a pervasive concern in the work of the school. Many agencies contribute to achieving educational objectives, but this particular objective will not be generally attained unless the school focuses on it. In this context, therefore, the development of every student's rational powers must be recognized as centrally important.[10]

THE EIGHTEEN GOALS OF EDUCATION (1973)

In a survey conducted by Phi Delta Kappa, an honorary educational fraternity, a random sample of over 1,000 members was asked to rank 18 educational goals as to importance. Following are the 18 goals as ranked according to importance with descriptive phrases excerpted from the more detailed statements.

1. Develop reading, writing, speaking, and listening skills
   Communication of ideas and feelings
   Skill in oral and written English
2. Develop pride in work and a feeling of self-worth
   Achievement and progress
   Self-understanding
   Self-assurance
3. Develop good character and self-respect
   Ethical and moral behavior
   Self-discipline
   Work, study, and play constructively
   Values, goals, and processes of a free society
   Standards of personal character and ideas
4. Develop a desire for learning now and in the future
   Curiosity and eagerness for lifelong learning
   Positive attitude toward learning and continuing independent education
5. Learn to respect and get along with people with whom we work and live
   Worth and dignity of individuals
   Minority opinion, majority decision
   Cooperative attitude
6. Learn how to examine and use information
   Constructive and creative examination
   Scientific methods
   Reasoning abilities
   Logical thinking and proceeding

7. Gain a general education
   Numbers, science, mathematics, social sciences
   Information and concepts
   Special interests and abilities
8. Learn how to be a good citizen
   Civic rights and responsibilities
   Attitudes for citizenship in a democracy
   Respect for personal and private property
   Obligations and responsibility of citizenship
9. Learn about and try to understand changes that take place in the world
   Adjust to changing societal demands and a changing world and its problems
   Understand the past, identify with the present, meet the future
10. Understand and practice democratic ideas and ideals
    Loyalty to ideals
    Patriotism and loyalty to democratic ideas
    Rights and privileges in our democracy
    Appreciation of the American heritage
11. Learn how to respect and get along with people who think, dress, and act differently
    Understanding of other people and cultures, other political, economic, and social patterns
    Awareness of interdependence and processes of group relationships
12. Understand and practice skills of family living
    Group living principles
    Attitudes of acceptance of responsibility
    Awareness of future family responsibilities and skills needed to carry them out
13. Gain information needed to make job selections
    Self-understanding and self-direction in relation to occupational interests
    Use of information and counseling services
    Vocational information
14. Learn how to be a good manager of money, property, and resources
    Economic principles and responsibilities
    Personal buying, selling, investment
    Management of resources and the environment
15. Practice and understand the ideas of health and safety
    Individual physical fitness
    Understanding of good health and well-being
    Sound personal habits
    Public health and safety
16. Develop skills to enter a specific type of work
    Skills for immediate employment
    Requirements for a specific type of work
    Appreciation of good workmanship
17. Learn how to use leisure time
    Productive use of leisure
    Variety of intellectual, physical, and creative activities
    Interests that lead to wise and enjoyable use of leisure
18. Appreciate culture and beauty in the world
    Expression of ideas
    Beauty in various forms
    Self-expression through art, music, writing
    Special talents in art, music, literature, foreign language[11]

Twentieth-Century Implementation Goals: State Level

Responsibility for education is vested in the separate states. Each state defines its own goals; sets its own priorities, rules, and regulations; spells out its own curriculum requirements; and determines certification requirements. *The Common Goals of Michigan Education* (1971) and Pennsylvania's *Goals of Quality Education* (1979) are typical state goal statements.

THE COMMON GOALS OF MICHIGAN EDUCATION (1971)

1. *Basic skills.* The four basic skills are:

   The ability to comprehend ideas through reading and listening.

   The ability to communicate ideas through writing and speaking.

   The ability to handle mathematical operations and concepts.

   The ability to apply rational intellectual processes to the identification, consideration, and solution of problems.

2. *Preparation for a changing society.* Education must encourage and prepare the individual to become responsive to the needs created and the opportunities afforded by an ever-changing social, economic, and political environment both here and throughout the world.

3. *Career preparation.* Education must provide each individual the opportunity to select and prepare for a career of his choice consistent to the optimum degree with his capabilities, aptitudes, and desires, and the needs of society.

4. *Creative, constructive, critical thinking.* Education must . . . enable the individual to deal effectively with situations and problems which are new to his experience in ways which encourage him to think and act in an independent, self-fulfilling, and responsible manner.

5. *Sciences, arts, and humanities.* Education must enable the individual . . . to gain knowledge and experience in the area of the natural sciences, the social sciences, the humanities, and the creative and fine arts so that his personal values and approach to living may be enriched by these experiences.

6. *Physical and mental well-being.* Education must promote the acquisition of good health and safety habits and an understanding of the conditions necessary for physical and mental well-being.

7. *Self-worth.* Education must respond to each person's need to develop a positive self-image within the context of his own heritage and within the larger context of the total society.[12]

PENNSYLVANIA'S GOALS OF QUALITY EDUCATION (1979)

Preamble: The constitution of the Commonwealth of Pennsylvania states, "The General Assembly shall provide for the maintenance and support of a thorough and efficient system of public education to serve the needs of the Commonwealth." This provision mandates a quality education for each child in the Commonwealth.

The schools have the primary responsibility for the achievement of the goals of quality education as established by the State Board of Education, but they must work in close and continuous cooperation with the family, community and other appropriate social, religious and governmental institutions to insure the highest possible achievement of the goals.

To foster achievement of a quality education, the school environment should be safe, attractive and orderly, promote a willingness to work for objectives, stimulate a readiness to continue learning throughout life, and encourage the fullest possible educational development of each student.

To foster achievement of a quality education, the school program should reflect the following goals:

GOALS OF QUALITY EDUCATION

Communication Skills. Quality education should help every student acquire communication skills of understanding, speaking, reading and writing.

Mathematics. Quality education should help every student acquire skills in mathematics.

Self-Esteem.   Quality education should help every student develop self-understanding and a feeling of self-worth.

Analytical Thinking.   Quality education should help every student develop analytical thinking skills.

Understanding Others.   Quality education should help every student acquire knowledge of different cultures and an appreciation of the worth of all people.

Citizenship.   Quality education should help every student learn the history of the nation, understand its systems of government and economics and acquire the values and attitudes necessary for responsible citizenship.

Arts and the Humanities.   Quality education should help every student acquire knowledge, appreciation and skills in the arts and the humanities.

Science and Technology.   Quality education should help every student acquire knowledge, understanding and appreciation of science and technology.

Work.   Quality education should help every student acquire knowledge, skills and attitudes necessary to become a self-supporting member of society.

Family Living.   Quality education should help every student acquire the knowledge, skills and attitudes necessary for successful personal and family living.

Health.   Quality education should help every student acquire knowledge and develop practices necessary to maintain physical and emotional well-being.

Environment.   Quality education should help every student acquire the knowledge and attitudes necessary to maintain the quality of life in a balanced environment.[13]

The Michigan and Pennsylvania Goals are representative of typical state educational goal statements. While they are phrased differently, they are, nonetheless, compatible each with the other, and are reflective of the national bedrock goal of providing a quality, optimum education for each citizen.

PRINCIPLES AND PREMISES
FOR 21st-CENTURY EDUCATION

In *Curriculum Change Toward the 21st Century*, Harold G. Shane examines the responses of an international panel of educators and other leaders to questions regarding the content and direction of education in the next hundred years. The questions asked the panelists grew out of the assumptions of the NEA Bicentennial Committee that "most policy statements about education are obsolete; education, taken as a whole, is not adequate to the times and too seldom anticipates the future," and that it has become necessary, therefore, to reframe the Seven Cardinal Principles of education first published in 1918.[14]

THE SEVEN CARDINAL PRINCIPLES REINTERPRETED

The international panel felt that the seven goals had retained their usefulness and their importance, and should not be discarded but should be updated. The following are changes recommended by the international panel:

HEALTH

The need for healthy interpersonal and intercultural attitudes is to be stressed.

Children and youth need to be made aware that overconsumption can be as debilitating as underconsumption, and that both can affect one's behavior in similarly adverse ways.

Schools should direct learners' attention to the unhealthful aspects of imperfect U.S. life-styles and to environmental dangers such as air pollution.

A knowledge of "stress points" should be part of health education.

Extend an understanding of dietary needs to include dangers in food additives, in pollution, in faulty city planning, and in sanitary standards.

The goal is total mental, physical and emotional health for the total person [see Chapter 4].

Command of Fundamental Processes

The new and additional fundamental processes are:

Skill in humanistic processes, including human relations, group processes, and those skills based on cross-cultural and multiethnic insights.

Neo-academic skills, including a knowledge of sources, the understanding and use of computer languages, and improved ability to cope with increasing specialization through a command of cross-disciplinary understandings.

Anticipatory skills represented by (a) the ability to see relationships and to make correlations, (b) the skills of sorting, weighing, and then acting on data, (c) evaluating choices and making decisions wisely despite the current information and misinformation glut, and (d) understanding how power functions at various levels from neighborhoods to international capitals.

Worthy Home Membership

This principle should be rephrased "worthy *family* membership."

Family-type groups are "a close ecosystem for rewarding, mutual interdependence."

Heretofore . . . the educational system has been a system comprised of the home, the workplace, the church, and the school. At present only the school continues to provide the same number of hours of educational experience. The home has reduced its contribution.

Vocation

The problem in a changing society is to know what vocations are going to be required in the next 10 or 15 years.

A good general education should then be followed by teaching of specific skills.

The habit of *lifelong* learning is now, in a sense, a vocational skill.

Most vocational education can best be acquired outside of school.

Competence in problem solving has now become a requisite for vocational efficiency [see Chapter 12 and Appendix L].

We need a "new vocational breed" that sees the implications *in their vocations* for combating pollution and other ecological problems.

Schools should focus on general requirements of all vocations and on serial or recurring preparation.

Vocational preparation must avoid locking people in the wrong jobs.

Effective citizenship, vocational skills, and general education are interrelated and more complex because life has become more complex and, therefore, more demanding.

Civic Education

We must work to build respect and support for leadership of integrity, "leadership that will not abdicate its responsibilities."

Civic education should encourage active, constructive participation in politics and should help people understand how to make positive use of power.

Skills of interaction among the young should become a new, vigorous dimension for the future [see Chapter 4].

Schools are a microcosm of democracy where people care, or are learning to care, about others.

Our efforts to make our society more democratic beyond the schools' walls and playgrounds is going to be aided tremendously by maintaining a school environment in which teachers try to be democratic in their relations with students and with one another.

WORTHY USE OF LEISURE

The line between work and leisure is beginning to blur because there is more time for relaxation available to more people and because an energy-intensive as opposed to labor-intensive economy leaves them less fatigued.

Schools and other educational agencies are challenged to develop the skills and to encourage the productivity that permit the attainment of economic levels at which leisure time is available.

There is a new role for education: helping young and old alike to wrestle with complexity in order to prevent its completely eroding their leisure time.

ETHICAL CHARACTER

The task of developing ethical character is more important during the present era of moral and spiritual crises than it has been in the past.

To strengthen and build ethical character is an educational imperative.

Young and old alike need ethical models—models that leaders often provide, whether they be in government, labor, industry, the church, education, or the world of entertainment [see Chapters 8, 9, 10, and 11].

We need a renewal of respect—merited respect—for the institutions that give democracy, the human conscience, and the individual life their meanings.

We need to develop, through group consensus, basic guideposts that will give strength and meaning to social and educational policies.

Ethical character grows from *within* as wholesome personhood is achieved. It cannot be *imposed*.

Ethical character also calls for an awareness of right and wrong and for a rejection of a relativism that denies, if only by implication, that there are such things as the common good and the general welfare.[15]

CARDINAL PRINCIPLES FOR EDUCATIONAL CHANGE: 1976–2001

General Premises: While all of the proposals for improving teaching and learning are roughly of coordinated importance, they differ somewhat in focus. The general premises are broad ones and tend to permeate process, organization, and the content of instruction.

1. The need to develop a spirit of "global community" in an increasingly interdependent world has reaffirmed an important task for education: to recognize and to respect the multiethnic, polycultural, and multilingual education in pluralistic societies both in the United States and abroad [see Chapters 9 and 11].
2. Education has assumed new significance as a positive force for peace in a world capable of destroying itself.
3. Learning is a lifelong process, and education, therefore, should be seen as a seamless continuum of experiences from early childhood to old age [see Chapter 6].
4. The value to the learners of their experiences obtained through education is more important than the routes they may follow in obtaining those experiences.
5. There are standards that are essential to life on a planet sometimes imperiled by the less thoughtful of its human population.

Premises Pertaining to Process: The second group of cardinal premises is based on a phenomenon of which most teachers are aware: it isn't just *what* you do, but also *how* you do it that makes a difference. In other words, the *processes* one follows are likely to determine to a considerable degree the success or failure of a given venture. Opportunities to work closely with others on matters of common concern bring satisfaction through involvement, clarify and refine interpersonal relations, deepen understanding of what is involved in a project, and are consistent with Carl Sandburg's pointed reminder that *"every*body is smarter than *any*body"

6. The aspirations and abilities of the student are best served when the student's learning experiences are at least partly self-directed rather than selected entirely by teachers [see Chapters 3, 4, 5, 6, and 15].

7. Because of the impact of the attitudes, comments, and actions of teachers (the "hidden curriculum," reflecting what teachers really value), greater efforts should be made to insure that this latent curriculum becomes clear and provides wholesome input for the learner.

8. Because the experiences of each learner are unique, teachers should expect a wide range of performance from children, youth, and adults.

9. Good instruction is personalized rather than individualized [see Chapters 3, 4, 5, 6, and 15].

10. The opportunity for universal early childhood education should be an integral part of the structure of education in a seamless learning continuum.

11. Adult education that exceeds mere literacy should receive worldwide emphasis.

12. Continuing educational opportunities should be designed to serve both mature (past 30) and senior (past 60) learners.

13. Particularly at the transnational level, the application of instructional systems and technologies can make important contributions to education as ideas, knowledge, and know-how are shared with the illiterate and the semiliterate in order to further their education. However, the use of systems and of media must be consonant with carefully reasoned human values [see Chapter 7].

14. Sharply delineated segments of education based on K–6–12 type grade levels ought to be eliminated as soon as feasible. Ability, motivation, and readiness rather than certificates and diplomas should serve as the learner's prime credentials.

15. When and where teaching and learning occur must not be bounded either by the school's walls or by our preconceived idea as to what should be learned at the once traditional age for learning it [see Chapter 4].

16. Persons in the field of career or occupational education should develop their programs in ways which recognize even more fully that vocational activity— the jobs held and services performed—often is sequential and will require greater versatility from members of the work force in the years ahead.

17. Traditional patterns of home-school relations need to be reconsidered and perhaps sharply modified in recognition of changes in the family which, in many instances today, is often an "affinity group" rather than the nuclear family consisting of mother, father, and children [see Chapter 1].

Premises with a Bearing on Content and Instruction: *Content*, in the premises that follow, refers to the substance of experiences designed to help the learner control and contribute to his/her environment for worthy purposes. *Instruction* is defined as those strategies that facilitate or serve as a lubricant for the processes involved in teaching and in learning

18. Present social trends, which are characterized by accelerating change and increasing complexity, have enhanced the need for basic communication skills such as the ability to handle the written and spoken word and to deal with number concepts [see Chapters 8, 9, 10, 11, and 12].

19. Valid methods of instruction vary from one learner to another, hence the goal of equitable educational opportunity can be approached only when schooling provides—at least in some respects—experiences that are different for each student [see Chapters 3, 4, and 5].

20. Traditional instructional methods should be expanded to include problem-solving approaches, and their emphasis on cognition and on valuing should be renewed [see Chapter 4 and Appendix L].
21. Interdisciplinary learning should be stressed and the art of comprehending and anticipating complex relationships should be fostered [see Chapters 6 and 11].
22. Good vocational or occupational education should be more thoroughly permeated by the content of a general or "liberalizing" education; conversely, it should be recognized that a sound liberal education also will be inherently vocational in the years ahead.
23. Because human differences and educational uniformity cannot be reconciled, the testing and measurement of content skills should be evaluated on an individual basis.
24. There is a need to teach the concept of alternative futures since, lacking a desirable image of tomorrow's possible worlds, one lacks purpose, goals, and the motivating spirit of community that are needed to serve as guides to action.
25. Instruction in subject matter fields should develop a deepening understanding of contemporary threats to the biosphere, include socially useful service in its maintenance, and communicate to youth the need for achieving balance or equilibrium between humans and their environment.
26. So that desirable alternative futures can be envisioned, work in the social studies should be redesigned so as to promote a grasp of human geography and of planetary cultures as they exist today [see Chapter 9].
27. In studying possible futures the natural and physical sciences, both in content and methodology, should serve as illustrations of truth-validating inquiry [see Chapter 10].
28. In the symbolic sciences—language arts, foreign language, mathematics, linguistics, and the like—more heed should be given both to basic communication skills as well as to the ability to recognize propaganda, shoddy advertising, and political double-talk [see Chapters 8, 10, 11, and 12 and Appendix L].[16]

Shane warns that the reinterpretation of the Seven Cardinal Principles and the newly formulated 28 premises will be but "an exercise in futility" unless they are translated into "emerging educational policies and improved practices."[17] The foregoing are guides to action—action that must begin immediately and continue at an accelerated rate. We can no longer put off educational improvement and innovation for the future, for the future of education begins today.

EDUCATIONAL RESISTANCE TO CHANGE

Educators have proven to be inept as change managers; valid expectations for innovation during the sixties and seventies generally did not come to fruition. Even the most kindly critics and reformers, such as John Goodlad, found education at the close of the seventies still in desperate need of renovation and innovation. If the Seven Cardinal Principles and the 28 premises are ever to permeate and direct education, specific implementation plans must be formulated and then carried out in each school district and in each school within the district.

Judicious renovation is the first step to be taken in changing a district's and/or school's educational program for the better. Renovation should be the educator's way of life: "The elimination of useless ideas and practices is as important as the acceptance of good ones."[18] The dry rot that permeates the "bloated curriculum" must be dug out and thrown away. Harold Benjamin in *The Saber-Tooth Curriculum* satirized the sorry waste of human effort and human potential that results when an educational program is chained to the needs of past generations rather than geared to meeting the needs of contemporary society.[19] He recounts the story of a primitive tribe that organized a school to teach fish grabbing, horse clubbing, and saber-toothed tiger scaring, for these were the three skills basic to the survival of the tribe. As generation followed generation, a better method of fishing was devised; the horses moved to far-off grazing grounds; and the saber-toothed tiger died off. Yet the three original curricular skills continued to be taught to the young; they were traditional and, therefore, sacred.

THE SABER-TOOTH SYNDROME: ARCHAIC EDUCATIONAL PRACTICES

NEW LABEL, SAME OLD PRACTICE

Goodlad, reviewing the lack of progress made in reforming education during the sixties and seventies stated, "Unfortunately, the implementation of proposed . . . change was more apparent than real. It was easy to apply the labels of the new practices and everyone employed the rhetoric of change. . . . In essence, this was an effort to innovate without really changing anything."[20] The following two case studies are typical of the tendency of educators to reach for the innovative label while continuing the same traditional practices.

CASE STUDY 1

In September 1972, much publicity was given to the opening of a new multimillion-dollar elementary school reportedly designed to support the open-school concept. According to the news media, there were no walls in the school and, therefore, there would be no barriers to learning. Free access to all instructional resources and faculty was the basic principle on which the building and the teaching-learning program had been designed.

The first day of school the librarian received her schedule. Far from being open every period, the library was closed every period! The principal defended the scheduled use of the library by saying that the only way he could provide each classroom teacher with a free period was to schedule classes into the library. Pathetically, the principal, by instituting the traditional scheduled use of the library as a study hall, had negated the entire open school concept.

CASE STUDY 2

An elementary school in one of the wealthiest suburbs in the United States claims to be using team teaching in its fifth grade. What this means is that some teachers are handling math and science, others English and social studies. It is called team teaching because the teachers allegedly "get together and discuss all the children." "Isn't that kind of conference difficult to fit into a full teaching schedule?" a visitor asks with feigned innocence. "Well, you know how it is," comes the reply. "We fit it in during lunch hour, or we stay around after three for a few minutes."[21]

VENERATION OF THE TEXTBOOK

All too often today's children and youth are chained like Prometheus to an archaic instructional practice. One paleolithic shibboleth condemning students to an education that is less than excellent is the traditional veneration of the textbook. Traditionally the textbook has served as the sole source of knowledge, the alpha and the omega of classroom teaching. And as long as outlining the textbook paragraph by paragraph and page by page is the accepted method of teaching, and verbatim memorization and feedback the accepted method of learning, the textbook more than suffices.

The reluctance of schools to change is all too evident when one considers the time lag between recognizing and compensating for the inadequacies of the textbook. As early as 1839, Horace Mann warned that students limited to a textbook would "contract the habit of being content with ignorance."[22] The limitations of the textbook were highlighted in the Harvard Report, which stated that:

> Texts often fail. They sum up too soon. It is right to let a student know roughly where he is going, but wrong to save him the journey. Too many courses tell him throughout what he is seeing, so that he memorizes the account of a trip which he never took. His head was buried in the guidebook.[23]

Nevertheless, twenty years later Goodlad observed that "the textbook was the most visible instrument of learning and teaching" when he visited classrooms.[24]

A textbook is not the most but the least that can be said on any subject. Therefore, an educational program of excellence employs the textbook only as a possible tool for orientation and departure, as an outline identifying concepts and topics worthy of further consideration and exploration by the student. The textbook in a program designed to provide a quality, optimum education can serve as a beginning but never as an end of learning.

WORSHIP OF PRINT

Another archaic practice chaining today's students to a less than adequate education is the reluctance to embrace the multimedia approach to teaching and learning. Just as the textbook cannot be the means and end of knowledge building, so printed resources cannot provide the totality of understanding. A quality, optimum educational program will provide all the essential carriers of information regardless of format, wrapper, or container. When listening is essential (the song of the thrush, the sound of a harpsichord, the Mendelssohn Violin Concerto, Robert Frost reading his poetry), then a disc or tape recording must be provided. When seeing is essential (an iceberg, a volcano, a Depression-era soup line or shantytown, the raising of the flag at Iwo Jima, the Taj Mahal, the La Brea Tar Pits, Leonardo da Vinci's painting *The Last Supper*), then a filmstrip, a slide, an art or study print must be provided. When listening in combination with seeing is essential (the sights and sounds of a Mexican fiesta, the *Swan Lake* ballet, Hitler haranguing the German people), then a sound filmstrip or a motion picture must be provided. When reality is essential (petrified wood, a piñata, an abacus, a magnet, a model of the human eye), then an actual object must be provided.

Educational impact is made by the ideas in the package, not by the package. Excellence in education demands that all types and kinds of instructional media essential to the teaching and learning program be made available when uniquely appropriate to the learning task at hand. Today's student should be as accustomed to using nonprint media as students traditionally have been accustomed to using the textbook. Here again, the observations of the experts are disappointing. The Commission on Instructional Technology reported in its comprehensive study *To Improve Learning*[25] that the use of most instructional media was spasmodic and unplanned (see Chapter 7).

CLASS APPROACH

The time-hallowed impersonal class approach to teaching also chains today's children to an educational experience of limited effectiveness. Traditionally all children in a given classroom are taught the same content, in the same way, and at the same rate. All children, regardless of ability and promise, study the same textbook, complete the same assignments, take the same tests. All experience a program designed to fit no one in particular. The class approach to teaching—that lockstep, never look to the right or to the left, keep eyes glued to the textbook, hurry to complete the text before the end of the semester approach—has been designed to move the bright, the average, and the slow through the textbook at the same rate. And if the teacher can gauge the rate just right, the average can walk through the text, the slow can stumble through, and the bright, who could have run through so easily, can just stand around and wait.

The class approach has been defended in the past as a means of perpetuating the oneness of society—one way for all. This philosophy implies that democracy is obligated to provide for "colorless egalitarianism" in its schools. This practice is contrary to the very promise of democracy that all citizens will have as their birthright respect and concern for their individuality. All students when guaranteed an optimum education are being guaranteed the right to be taught as individuals, the right to learn in their own special ways, the right to achieve self-realization and self-fulfillment. The class-oriented program is not democratic, for it denies the rights of the individual student, limiting "the development of individual excellence in exchange for a uniformity of external treatment."[26] The promise of an optimum education demands that teaching and learning be individualized, that students receive their education commensurate with their special needs, interests, goals, abilities, and concerns.

TALK, CHALK, CELLS, AND BELLS

Despite the fact that many schools boast of having individualized instruction, the Commission on Instructional Technology observes that instruction is still largely confined to the classroom and is restricted to the teacher talking, and the students listening to the teacher or reading their textbooks. The most popular instructional aid is still the chalkboard. The commission states that "the media by which information transmission takes place and the student reacts with the subject matter . . . are the teacher and the textbook."[27] Most educational reformers agree that instruction must be individualized, for "a society hurtling into the age of the computer and the satellite can no longer be held back by an educational system which is limping along at the blackboard-and-textbook stage of communication."[28]

Innovations developed to facilitate individualizing instruction are numerous; they include nongraded schools, flexible scheduling, flexible grouping, more relevant curriculum, open classrooms, and the open plan school. There is no one pattern consistently discernible in the schools' approach to individualizing instruction. While the innovative label may be the same, the manner in which the innovation is implemented varies from school to school. Just as each student is a unique learner so is each school uniquely different from all others. Even the most traditional school can have islands of innovative excellence where the individuality of the students is respected and students are encouraged to learn in their own special ways.

One traditional barrier to instructional improvement has been the lack of opportunity during the school day for teachers to plan together, to work together, and to exchange ideas. In the past, teachers as well as students have been confined to classrooms. Regrettably, some administrators deliberately create a climate that discourages teachers from communicating with each other. Goodlad observes that "schools reflect the strange notion that . . . teachers are not to converse with each other."[29] In other words, teachers are to teach communication, but not practice it.

Team teaching is an innovative approach to utilizing teacher time, energies, talents, and special competencies as they plan and work together as members of a group. Informal team teaching is on a voluntary basis. An innovative principal frequently will encourage his faculty to work cooperatively in order to meet more effectively the implementation needs of the curriculum and the developmental needs of the students. For example, a teacher of reading might invite the art teacher and the library media specialist to help develop a reading enrichment unit (see model teaching unit, "Book Illustrators and Their Art," Chapter 11, Example 40).

Formal team teaching involves two or more teachers who are requested by the principal to share the responsibility for teaching a subject or subjects to a group of students. The teaching team cooperatively defines the objectives, determines the scope and sequence of topic coverage, designs teaching strategies, selects materials, and agrees on which part of the teaching process will be the special responsibility of each team member. Team teaching, whether formal or informal, brings greater depth, breadth, and vitality to the teaching-learning program. Cutting across subject lines breaks the barriers imposed by tight compartmentalization of subjects. When teachers, media specialists, and administrators no longer work in isolation one from the other but rather pool their specialized knowledge, professional skills, special competencies, and personal creative talents, then the students are freed from the straitjacket of restrictive teaching and fragmentary learning.

ROTE RECALL IS ALL

There are students today, unfortunately, who are still being plagued by the outmoded practice of rote memorization coupled with rote recall. Here again is evidence of the persistence of an archaic practice. Ralph Waldo Emerson more than 130 years ago made it quite clear that memorization was not synonymous with understanding. He said:

> We are students of words. We are shut up in schools and colleges and recitation rooms for ten or fifteen years, and come out at last with a bag of wind, a memory of words, and do not know a thing.[30]

Likewise in 1860 Herbert Spencer echoed Emerson's distrust of memorization, noting that "pervading the whole [of education] is the vicious system of rote learning—a system of sacrificing the spirit to the letter."[31]

In *The Process of Education*, Bruner advocates the discovery method of learning, a practice in sharp contrast to rote memorization and recall. Discovery, Bruner says, adds *zest* to learning. "There should be a sense of excitement about discovery—discovery of regularities, of previously unrecognized relations and similarities between ideas, with a resulting sense of self-confidence in one's abilities."[32] Students should have every opportunity to learn how to solve problems on their own and to develop a positive attitude toward learning and inquiry.

LACK OF AN OVERALL PLAN

The lack of an overall directional plan for the sequential development of a fundamental body of knowledge, grade by grade and subject by subject, is yet another hereditary educational deficiency. Traditionally, from the days of the one-room school, teachers have been given latitude in determining what will and what will not be taught in the classroom. What the student has been taught, in large measure, has been reflective of teacher interest rather than the developmental needs of the student.

CASE STUDY 3

A principal in a large urban junior high school over a period of two years kept a checklist of units taught by the eleven teachers of seventh-grade science. To his amazement, he discovered that there was little or no congruity in the seventh-grade science program. Each of the eleven teachers was teaching a program uniquely different from the others. For example, one man taught a unit in depth on electricity; one woman taught an in-depth unit on birds. The man did not even mention birds in his entire year's program; the woman never mentioned electricity in hers. The principal met with the eleven teachers individually and asked what prompted each to select the major topics taught. Each teacher said that what was taught was determined on the basis of specialized knowledge and personal preference, i.e., what one knew a great deal about and personally enjoyed. Not a single teacher mentioned considering student interest or student scientific growth needs.

There has been little continuity experienced by the learner as he moves from room to room and from grade to grade. The lack of continuity and articulation in the educational program has condemned the learner in the past to a fragmented education of bits and pieces, a collection of disjointed, skeletal facts lacking interconnectedness, cohesiveness, form, and substance.

A quality educational program cannot be left to whim or chance. Quality must be both planned and worked for. A quality program begins with a quality blueprint which identifies the scope and dimension of the total program, kindergarten through grade 12. A blueprint for excellence clearly identifies all elements basic to the program, and having identified the elements, orders them into patterns of logical, progressive sequence. An educational program of excellence is strongly structured to guard against any inadequacies occurring in the plan. How can understanding be complete if basic structure be misplaced or missing? (See Chapter 6.)

THE LIBRARY: STUDY HALL–BOOK DISPERSAL CENTER

In the past, direct involvement of the library in the instructional process was the exception, not the rule. So long as teaching and learning were restricted to the "two-by-four" concept of education (the information contained between the two covers of the textbook and the four walls of the classroom), the school library was required to serve in no other way than as a studyhall–book dispersal center. It is only when the educational program evolves from traditional mediocrity to innovative excellence that the function of the library must change to that of a learning laboratory; from a collection limited to printed materials to a collection embracing all types and kinds of appropriate media carriers essential for a bonus-rich instructional environment; from the sporadic use of media to the planned and purposeful integration of library resources and services with the ongoing teaching and learning enterprise. Direct involvement in the instructional process requires that the school library media specialist become directly involved in the total teaching and learning enterprise. Such involvement requires that the library media specialist develop and maintain a library media program that will serve as the launching pad for learning takeoff, will provide not only the fuel to power the thrust for learning but also the flight plan, and then provide the needed expertise in readjusting the flight plan to accommodate unexpected adventurous flights of fancy. "The heart of education is the student learning," and the responsibility of the library media specialist is to humanely and creatively manage the library media program so that learning will become more lastingly significant, more permanently meaningful, and more personally satisfying. Only then will the Seven Cardinal Principles and the 28 premises become actuality. The concept of the school library media program as an instructional force for excellence is detailed in the chapters that follow.

NOTES

1. Thomas Jefferson, *The Writings of Thomas Jefferson*, ed. by Albert Ellery Bergh, vol. 6 (Washington, D.C.: Thomas Jefferson Memorial Association, 1970), p. 392.
2. Ibid., vol. 14, p. 384.
3. James Madison, *The Complete Madison: His Basic Writings*, ed. by Saul K. Podover (New York: Harper, 1953), p. 337.
4. *General Education in a Free Society: A Report of the Harvard Committee* (Cambridge: Harvard University Press, 1945), p. xiii.
5. Paul H. Douglas, *In the Fullness of Time* (New York: Harcourt, 1972), p. 418.
6. *The Pursuit of Excellence: Education and the Future of America*, America at Mid-Century Series, Special Studies Project Report V, Rockefeller Brothers Fund (Garden City, N.Y.: Doubleday, 1958).
7. The Report of the President's Commission on National Goals, *Goals for Americans*, The American Assembly, Columbia University, New York (Englewood Cliffs, N.J.: Prentice-Hall, 1960).
8. Commission on Reorganization of Secondary Education, *The Seven Cardinal Principles* (Washington, D.C.: U.S. Bureau of Education, 1918).
9. Educational Policies Commission, *The Purpose of Education in American Democracy* (Washington, D.C.: National Education Association, 1938), p. 41.

10. Educational Policies Commission, *The Central Purpose of American Education* (Washington, D.C.: National Education Association, 1961).
11. Harold Spears, "Kappans Ponder the Goals of Education," *Phi Delta Kappan* 55 (Sept. 1973): 29–32.
12. *The Common Goals of Michigan Education* (Lansing, Mich.: Michigan Department of Education, 1971).
13. *Goals of Quality Education* (Harrisburg, Pa.: Pennsylvania Department of Education, 1979).
14. Harold G. Shane, *Curriculum Change Toward the 21st Century*, Curriculum Series (Washington, D.C.: National Education Association, 1977), p. 7.
15. Ibid., pp. 43–55.
16. Ibid., pp. 59–68.
17. Ibid., pp. 69–70.
18. Research and Policy Committee of the Committee for Economic Development, *Innovation in Education: New Directions for the American School* (New York: Committee for Economic Development, 1968), p. 29.
19. Harold Benjamin, *The Saber-Tooth Curriculum*, Memorial ed. (New York: McGraw-Hill, 1972).
20. John I. Goodlad, *The Dynamics of Educational Change: Toward Responsive Schools*, a Charles F. Kettering Foundation Program (New York: McGraw-Hill, 1975), p. 35.
21. Charles E. Silberman, *Crisis in the Classroom: The Remaking of American Education* (New York: Random House, 1970), p. 162.
22. Horace Mann, *Life and Works of Horace Mann*, vol. 3, "Annual Reports of the Secretary of the Board of Education of Massachusetts, 1839–1844" (Boston: Lee and Shepard, 1891), p. 49.
23. *General Education in a Free Society*, p. 109.
24. John I. Goodlad, "The Schools vs. Education," *Saturday Review of Literature* 50 (Apr. 19, 1969): 60.
25. Sidney G. Tickton, ed., *To Improve Learning: An Evaluation of Instructional Technology*, 2 vols. (New York: R. R. Bowker, 1971).
26. *The Pursuit of Excellence*, p. 22.
27. Tickton, *To Improve Learning*, vol. 2, p. 144.
28. Ibid., vol. 1, p. 10.
29. Goodlad, *The Dynamics of Educational Change*, p. 61.
30. Dean Acheson, *Fragments of My Fleece* (New York: Norton, 1971), p. 36.
31. Herbert Spencer, *Herbert Spencer on Education*, ed. by Andreas M. Kazamias (New York: Teachers College Press, Columbia University, 1966), p. 142.
32. Jerome S. Bruner, *The Process of Education* (Cambridge: Harvard University Press, 1960), p. 20.

3 The School Library Media Program: Instructional Force for Excellence

The "educational program is strengthened in direct proportion to the quality of the school's library service," for the school library is the "keystone of a quality educational program."
Pennsylvania Governor's Committee on Education*

As a library program becomes more meaningful, it is more closely identified with the total instructional program, so that its ultimate success is really to put itself, as a separate program, out of business.
Marguerite Murray†

The concept of the school library media program as an instructional force for educational excellence is far from being a new one. Here again, history proves that educators have been inept as change managers. The educational necessity of employing library materials to extend learning beyond textbook and classroom has long been recognized as essential for effective learning. The concept of the school library serving as an instructional media center can be traced back to approximately 200 years before the American Declaration of Independence. In Shrewsbury, England, an ordinance was passed in 1578 stating that schools should include "a library and gallerie . . . furnished with all manner of books, mappes, spheres, instruments of astronomye and all other things apperteyninge to learning which may either be given to the schools or procured with school money."[1]

BREAKING THE TEXTBOOK BARRIER

Horace Mann in 1839 recommended establishing school libraries to compensate for the informational limitations of the textbook.[2] The Madison Conference in 1892 wrote in its report, "Recitation alone cannot possibly make up proper teaching. . . . It is absolutely necessary from the earliest to the latest grades, that there should be parallel reading."[3] Bessie Smith, speaking before the National Education Association (NEA) Convention in New York

*Pennsylvania Governor's Committee on Education, 1960, Task Force on Curriculum, "The School Library—Keystone of Quality Education," in *The Pennsylvania Guide for School Library Media Specialists,* ed. by Shirley A. Pittman (Pittsburgh, Pa.: Pennsylvania School Librarians Association, 1978), p. 9.

†Marguerite Murray, "Knapp Project Evaluated," *Library Journal* 92 (Sept. 15, 1967): 3127.

City in 1916, linked the inadequacies of the textbook with the need to establish school libraries:

> It is within the memory of many of us that public-school education consisted in learning facts which were between the covers of given textbooks no matter how dry and seemingly without meaning for the present they might be. The pupil who most accurately and quickly learned those facts was held as the best student, and the pupil whose gift of imagination led him to venture on a new expression of the subject-matter of the textbook was reproved.
>
> Happily for the child of today, teaching from the textbook has expanded into wide fields, and supplementary reading has grown to be a large part of the work which all progressive teachers require. This change in method has necessitated collections of books in the schools to furnish the child with supplementary material. As this demand for supplementary reading has developt in all grades, the school library has followed of necessity.[4]

LEARNING LABORATORY ROLE OF THE LIBRARY

The concept of the school library serving as a laboratory for effective learning is likewise not a recent one. In 1913 Lucille Fargo, speaking before the NEA Convention, presented the concept of the school library functioning as "a laboratory and a workshop, [a means of] putting into the hands of the pupils the necessary tools for further achievement."[5] In 1915 Mary E. Hall, writing in the *Library Journal,* quoted a Grand Rapids high school principal as saying:

> The school library of the future will be the proof of the extent of the transformation of a high school from the medieval system of the past to the new standards and ideals in high school education of this twentieth century. I believe I am safe in saying that the school library will be the proof of the educational value of the new curriculum. When our schools have outgrown their cloister days and are aiming to prepare our boys and girls for the life they must live in a work-a-day world the library will be the open door to the opportunity of the present.[6]

Miss Hall then explained how the "new" library differed from the "old" in supporting the curriculum:

> The old high school library was static. The new is dynamic. The old was largely for reference and required reading in history and English; the new is all things to all departments, if in any way it may serve the school. It is not only a reference library, but a *training school* in the best methods of using library aids in looking up a topic. . . . The new library is dynamic, because it is not content with storing, and organizing and recording the loan of books and other material, but because it uses every method known to the best college and public libraries for encouraging their use, *stimulating interest in good reading, arousing intellectual curiosity,* and *broadening the horizon of the students.*[7]

The necessity for the new library to provide both print and nonprint materials was also specified by Miss Hall:

> In the new high school library many of our schools have found it well worthwhile to bring together all lantern slides, pictures, victrola records and post cards, and to organize them according to modern methods of classification and cataloging so that they may be available for all departments and at all times as they are not available when kept in departmental collections.[8]

Many educators advocated what we now call the multimedia approach to teaching at the turn of the century. Henry Johnson, Columbia University professor of history, wrote in 1915 that casts, models, pictures, maps, charts, and diagrams as well as printed materials were essential to teaching history effectively. He deplored the reluctance of American administrators to provide an organized school program for instructional media acquisition and use:

> The need of such aids was clearly set forth as long ago as the eighteenth century, and has been almost continuously emphasized ever since. In Europe the response has been so generous that there is now scarcely any known phase of past civilization which is not represented. In the United States, until recently, the chief reliance has been on maps and pictures, but other aids are now coming into use. The American Historical Association led the way with an exhibit in New York in 1909. The *History Teacher's Magazine* for February, 1910, carried an account of this exhibit to teachers in every section of the country and thus spread information which up to that time has been mainly confined to observers of history teaching in Europe. . . . Two important pieces of work remain to be done. The first is to prepare a really exhaustive guide to aids especially adapted to American schools. The second is to provide a series of illustrated exercises showing definitely when and how the aids ought to be used. As matters now stand at present many schools seem to be wasting their substance in the acquisition of unsuitable material and wasting their time in unsuitable use even of suitable material.[9]

Professor Johnson's observation in 1915 that schools were "wasting their substance in the acquisition of unsuitable material and wasting their time" even in the use "of suitable material" foretold the need to organize a functional multimedia library program. Unfortunately, the typical 50-year lag between recognizing an educational need and adequately meeting that need has been all too apparent in the history of the evolution of the public school library.

STANDARDS DEFINE LIBRARY'S INSTRUCTIONAL ROLE

SECONDARY SCHOOL LIBRARY STANDARDS (1918)

NEA formally endorsed the concept of the secondary school library as "the very heart of the school" when it adopted in 1918 the report of the Committee on Library Organization and Equipment, *Standard Library Organization and Equipment for Secondary Schools of Different Sizes*.[10] These historic standards, popularly known as the "Certain Standards" in honor of the chairman, Charles C. Certain, were subsequently adopted by the American Library Association (ALA) and published by that association in 1920. This document not only provided comprehensive and quantitative requisite standards for high school library organization and development but also set forth the professional qualifications and status of the school librarian as a teacher when it stated, "The librarian . . . should combine the good qualities of both the librarian and the teacher and must be able to think clearly and sympathetically in terms of the needs and interests of high-school students."[11] These Certain Standards are so significant that they deserve a fuller reading; therefore, excerpts from this document have been included in Appendix A.

ELEMENTARY SCHOOL LIBRARY STANDARDS (1925)

In 1925, the National Education Association, the Department of Elementary School Principals, and the School Librarians Section of the American

Library Association adopted the report of the Joint Committee on Elementary School Library Standards.[12] In the foreword, Charles C. Certain, the chairman of the committee, clearly related the emergence of the elementary school library as an instructional support agency to the changes in methodology taking place in the elementary school:

> Modern demands upon the public school presuppose adequate library service. Significant changes in methods of teaching require that the school library supplement the single textbook course of instruction and provide for the enrichment of the school curriculum. Children in the school are actively engaged in interests which make it necessary for them to have the use of many books and a wide variety of materials, such as pictures and lantern slides. An essential consideration is that the books and materials be readily available when needed, and under the direction of a library staff which is part of the school organization.[13]

Because this document, too, deserves fuller reading, excerpts have been included in Appendix A.

SCHOOL LIBRARY STANDARDS (1945)

ALA in 1945 published *School Libraries for Today and Tomorrow*, which defined the educational purposes of the library as follows:

Participate effectively in the school program as it strives to meet the needs of pupils, teachers, parents, and other community members.

Provide boys and girls with the library materials and services most appropriate and most meaningful in their growth and development as individuals.

Stimulate and guide pupils in all phases of their reading so that they may find increasing enjoyment and satisfaction and may grow in critical judgment and appreciation.

Provide an opportunity through library experiences for boys and girls to develop helpful interests, to make satisfactory personal adjustments, and to acquire desirable social attitudes.

Help children and young people to become skillful and discriminating users of libraries and of printed and audiovisual materials.

Introduce pupils to community libraries as early as possible and cooperate with those libraries in their efforts to encourage continuing education and cultural growth.

Participate with teachers and administrators in programs for continuing professional and cultural growth of the school staff.[14]

These standards tied the quality of school library service to the quantitative requirements of qualified personnel in sufficient numbers, an abundance of appropriate printed and audiovisual materials, adequate facilities, sufficient equipment, and a planned procedure for making the resources and the services of the school library readily available.

SCHOOL LIBRARY STANDARDS (1960)

The American Association of School Librarians (AASL) published in 1960 the single most important document in the history of school library development, *Standards for School Library Programs*.[15] These standards, prepared under the joint chairmanship of Frances Henne and Ruth Ersted, are much more than a statement of the quantitative and qualitative requirements for school library programs; this document, in actuality, is an educational "bill of rights" for all children and youth of the United States. Part 1 of these standards is captioned "The School Library as an Educational Force" and clearly states that the school library should serve as both a source and a force for educational excellence:

> [It is] of importance to all citizens . . . that our schools have the resources needed for teaching and learning.
>
> Whatever form the soul-searching regarding the education of youth may take, sooner or later it has to reckon with the adequacy of the library resources in the schools. Any of the recommendations for the improvement of schools . . . can be fully achieved only when the school has the full complement of library resources, personnel, and services. . . .
>
> In the education of all youth, from the slowest learner in kindergarten to the most intelligent senior in the high school, an abundance of printed and audiovisual material is essential. These resources are the basic tools needed for the purpose of effective teaching and learning. . . . The scope of knowledge has become too vast to be covered extensively within the boundaries of classroom instruction, superior though that instruction may be. Through the school library these boundaries can be extended immeasurably in all areas of knowledge and in all forms of creative expression, and the means provided to meet and to stimulate the many interests, appreciations, and curiosities of youth. . . .
>
> Educational leaders stress the point that the school library is one of the requirements for quality education . . . the school library program, embracing teaching, guidance, and advisory services, forms a unique and vital part of quality education.[16]

STANDARDS FOR SCHOOL MEDIA PROGRAMS (1969)

The 1960 standards stressed that "good school library programs make audiovisual materials easily accessible for use in the library, regardless of the prevailing administrative pattern of these materials";[17] yet, these standards did not advocate that the school library change its traditional name in order to indicate the multimedia approach to instructional support. In 1969, AASL and the NEA Department of Audiovisual Instruction issued joint standards entitled *Standards for School Media Programs*. These standards adopted new professional terminology, which follows:

> In this publication, the term *media* refers to printed and audiovisual forms of communication and their accompanying technology. Other basic terms include *media program, media specialist, media center*. When reference is made to the next larger organizational unit, *system media center* is used.
>
> The terms *media program, media specialist,* and *media center* are used in this publication for purposes of convenience, consistency, and clarification within the context of the standards, and are not employed with an intent to mandate any particular title or terminology.[18]

The 1969 standards endorsed the philosophy of the school library media center playing a vital instructional role:

> In this entire [educational] process the media program, its staff and its center play vital roles. Media convey information, affect the message, control what is learned, and establish the learning environment. They will help to determine what the pupil sees and what his attitude will be toward the world in which he lives. Therefore, it is important that every media specialist participate actively in shaping the learning environment and the design of instruction, and that every media facility, piece of equipment, book, or material be selected, produced, and used so that the students in our schools are challenged to a dynamic participation in a free, exciting, and enriched life. . . .

Today, educators and other citizens realize that educational programs of vitality, worth, and significance to students and to society depend upon excellent media services and resources in the schools.[19]

STANDARDS FOR MEDIA PROGRAMS (1975)

In 1975, AASL and the Association for Educational Communications and Technology (AECT; formerly the Department of Audiovisual Instruction, NEA) published revised standards, *Media Programs: District and School.* These standards "call for media programs that are user-centered, that promote flexibility in practice based on intelligent selection from many alternatives, and are derived from well-articulated learning and program objectives."[20] The major purpose of the school library media program as articulated in these standards is to improve the educational experience of all learners by building "bridges between content and context, purpose and procedure, self and society."[21]

IMPERATIVES OF INSTRUCTIONAL EXCELLENCE

The school library media program must be a partner directly involved in realizing the curriculum envisioned for the 21st century (see Chapter 2). Realization of these goals encompasses imperative changes in content, process, and product. In an instructional program of excellence, content no longer restricted to textbook and classroom must provide a greater dimension of depth, breadth, and relevance. *Depth* of understanding develops more fully and adequately the topics, concepts, experiences, and activities merely introduced in the classroom. *Breadth* of understanding introduces significant topics, concepts, experiences, and activities not mentioned in the classroom but directly related to the learning task at hand. *Relevance* by personalizing and/or contemporizing learning compensates for the limitations of textbook and course of study in two distinct ways: first, by providing significant and directly related learning experiences that are uniquely reflective of the individual student's own needs, interests, goals, abilities, and background experiences; and, second, by providing those learning experiences which are significant and directly related to the contemporary world—current happenings and events, socioeconomic and political concerns, technological and scientific advancements, cultural developments and achievements, and emerging patterns of change here, there, and beyond.

Case studies 4–15 are examples of depth, breadth, and relevance; they are neither fabricated nor contrived; they are actual case studies of how a library media program compensates for inadequate textbook and classroom information.

DEPTH OF UNDERSTANDING

CASE STUDY 4   PREPARING A MINI-PROGRAM FOR INDEPENDENT STUDY

An eleventh-grade social studies teacher requests that the senior high school librarians prepare a mini-program on "Appomattox and the End of the Civil War" as an independent study project for a gifted student with a consuming interest in General Robert E. Lee (see Chapter 7, Example 7). The classroom teacher suggests that the program include primary sources such as eyewitness accounts and historical documents. She also recommends that the program be "open-ended" and that the learning opportunities extend well beyond the optional activities included in the program itself.

CASE STUDY 5　VISITING THE PARTHENON IN NASHVILLE, TENNESSEE

In the seventh-grade history textbook the Parthenon is described in detail but no mention is made that only one full-sized replica of the Parthenon exists in the world today. If limited to the textbook the students would never discover that in Nashville, Tennessee, there is an exact replica in size, design, and materials and that the Nashville Parthenon is open to the public, free of charge, every day of the year except Christmas. Through the use of the American Automobile Association *Tour Book*, the students not only discover a complete description of the Parthenon and its exact location, but also discover the value of using the AAA *Tour Book* to determine distances, accommodations, and what to see and visit. This is an example of being introduced in school to a basic tool for lifelong use and value.

CASE STUDY 6　PREPARING A MOCK TRIAL FOR AMERICAN HISTORY

In the eleventh-grade U.S. history class reference is made to John Brown's raid at Harpers Ferry. The textbook merely states that he was arrested, tried, and convicted of treason and no further particulars are given. If limited to the textbook the students will have but little insight into the actual happenings that prompted the arrest, trial, conviction, and hanging of John Brown. The class decides to hold a mock trial and to present in an objective, unemotional manner the facts as recorded in the court records and in contemporary newspapers. The lawyer for the defense and the lawyer for the plaintiff work in the library media center listening to the Tufts University tape of the reenactment of the trial of John Brown and reading the microfilmed reprints of *Harper's Weekly*. The judge works in the media center building his knowledge of the laws governing treason and his understanding of how to conduct a federal court trial. If limited to the textbook and classroom resources a socio-drama of this impact and validity could never be experienced, could never be hoped for.

BREADTH OF UNDERSTANDING

CASE STUDY 7　RESEARCHING THE SCOPES TRIAL

A tenth-grade biology teacher plans with the senior high school media specialists for a group of interested students to work in the library media center, building background information about the Scopes Trial. The teacher, wishing to use this information as a motivational introduction to the forthcoming unit on evolution, requests that the following topics be researched by the group: the 1925 Tennessee Statute prohibiting the teaching of evolution; John Thomas Scopes, teacher convicted and fined for teaching the theory of organic evolution in Tennessee; Clarence Seward Darrow, counsel for the defense; and William Jennings Bryan, witness for the plaintiff. The school library media specialists share with the biology teacher two comprehensive sources of information, *The World's Most Famous Court Trial* (Civil Liberties in American History Series), a 1971 reprint of the 1925 account of the trial; and *Center of the Storm, Memoirs of John C. Scopes,* published in 1967. They also suggest the Broadway stage play *Inherit the Wind* by Jerome Lawrence and Robert E. Lee.

CASE STUDY 8   A READING ENRICHMENT EXPERIENCE

The sixth-grade New Basic Reader *Cavalcades* includes as its last reading unit the adventure novel *The Rain Forest* by Armstrong Sperry. This reading experience serves as a springboard to further reading, viewing, and listening experiences including other novels written by Armstrong Sperry and other adventure novels with parallel plot, theme, or locale written by other authors (see Chapter 8, Example 11).

CASE STUDY 9   EXPLORING THE LIBRARY MEDIA CENTER'S DICTIONARY COLLECTION

An eighth-grade student currently studying the unit "The Wizardry of Words" (see Chapter 8) becomes interested in exploring the various kinds of dictionaries in his school library media center. The library media specialist, delighting in his sincere interest, brings to his attention *An Egyptian Hieroglyphic Dictionary* by E. A. Wallis Budge, which contains nearly 28,000 words or terms occurring in ancient Egyptian texts. The student, an accomplished artist, is fascinated by the hieroglyphic designs, which he in turn uses as design motifs for bookplates.

RELEVANCE—PERSONALIZED

CASE STUDY 10   DESIGNING A METAL-SHOP PROJECT

A senior has seen in a local gift shop a collection of Otagiri kinetics (chrome-finished, delicate balances that glisten and sway with each current of air). Seeing these mobiles and "desk flyers" has given him an idea for his final metal-shop project. He would like to design and construct a mobile merry-go-round and a desk flyer of hunting dogs chasing a fox. He asks the school media specialist to help him search out appropriate designs.

CASE STUDY 11   SELECTING A SKIT FOR DRAMATIC CLUB

A student trying out for membership in the junior high school dramatic club comes to the library media center for help in identifying a three-minute skit requiring but one actor and offering sufficient variety in action that the club sponsor will be able to assess her acting ability and hopefully admit her to club membership.

CASE STUDY 12 COMPENSATING FOR READING DISABILITIES

A student with a reading disability comes to the library media center to use sound filmstrips to build his understanding of science and social studies topics. The fact that the filmstrip text is minimal and is illustrated frame by frame enables him to gain sufficient understanding to contribute to class discussions.

RELEVANCE—CONTEMPORIZED

CASE STUDY 13 AN INDIVIDUALIZED LEARNING PROGRAM

During the seventh-grade unit "Primitive Man," a student comes to the library media center to build her knowledge of a contemporary stone-age society. In building her knowledge, she employs the individual learning program *The Tasaday: A Study of a Primitive Culture Frozen in Time*, which had been prepared in anticipation of her visit (see Chapter 7, Example 6).

CASE STUDY 14 PREPARING A SCIENCE DEBATE

The debate coach plans with the library media specialist to develop a collection of media to support the current debate topic "Resolved: The United States should undertake a space colonization project immediately" (see Chapter 10, Example 29).

CASE STUDY 15 THE NIXON IMPEACHMENT PROCEEDINGS

The twelfth-grade political science textbook when discussing the power of Congress to impeach the president of the United States refers only to the impeachment of President Andrew Johnson. No mention is made of the congressional impeachment proceedings against President Nixon. After preplanning with the library media specialist, the teacher schedules the class to work in the library media center building their knowledge of the Watergate scandal and the events that precipitated congressional action against President Nixon.

COGNITIVE AND AFFECTIVE OBJECTIVES

The educational objective of bringing depth, breadth, and relevance to education demands that learning go beyond facts per se to embrace the total cognitive and affective domains. *Taxonomy of Educational Objectives: Handbook I, Cognitive Domain*[22] classifies the cognitive educational objectives in the following hierarchy:

1. Knowledge
2. Comprehension
3. Application
4. Analysis
5. Synthesis
6. Evaluation

This hierarchy grouping learning experiences from the lowest to the highest mental process is based on the theory that knowledge is but the first step along the road to learning.

Taxonomy of Educational Objectives: Handbook II, Affective Domain[23] classifies the affective educational objectives in this continuum:

1. Receiving (Attending)
2. Responding
3. Valuing
4. Organization
5. Characterization by a value or value complex

The affective objectives ascend from the simple to the complex with each level demanding of the learner an ever-greater sense of personal involvement and commitment. Intellectual survival requires that the schools consistently and consciously incorporate in the basic teaching and learning process opportunities for the student to learn how to be a competent learner; how to make value judgments; and how to run the thought maze with positive direction, disciplined imagination, efficiency, and effectiveness, as well as with challenge and delight.

Another imperative of educational excellence involves both the process of teaching and the process of learning. The role of the teacher has changed from that of lecturer and fountainhead of knowledge to that of facilitator of learning. As facilitator of learning, the major responsibility of the teacher is to personalize instruction so that each student is encouraged and enabled to achieve to the optimum of his or her potential. The role of the student has changed from passive to active participation. The emphasis has shifted from fact memorization to learning how to learn. The inquiry method of learning, which is specifically designed to nurture the student's ability to be a competent, independent learner, demands a stimulating environment that encourages the learner to think, to feel, to behave, and to become a self-actualizing person (see Chapter 4).

SCIENTIFIC DESIGN OF THE SCHOOL LIBRARY MEDIA PROGRAM

Excellence in the instructional program demands commensurate excellence in the library media program; such excellence is never the result of chance but must be built into the very fabric of the library media program itself. Just as the process of education must be designed scientifically, so must the library media program be designed scientifically to function efficiently and effectively as an integral support component of the total instructional program.

The first step in scientific program design is to blueprint a master plan for the development of a district library program, K–12. Designing a master plan either to initiate or to strengthen an existing district library media program should be a cooperative team enterprise involving library media specialists, representatives from the administrative and teaching staffs, and representatives from school-affiliated parent organizations. Ideally, this is the appropriate time for the chief school administrator to appoint a supervisor or coordinator of district library media programs, if one has not previously been appointed. The supervisor or coordinator of the district library media program should serve as chairperson of the planning-steering committee and should, in this capacity, provide leadership in designing, structuring, and implementing the master plan for library media program development (see Chapter 14).

The following procedure is recommended for blueprinting a district library media program, K–12. First, the chief school administrator appoints a planning-steering committee to be chaired by the supervisor of the library media program. This committee is charged with the responsibility for developing the master plan that blueprints the basic elements of the district library media program.

The committee builds its background knowledge by:

Reading and discussing pertinent professional literature. (*Note:* If your state publishes standards, guidelines, or criteria for school library media programs, these publications are your basic reference tools and should be used either in place of or in conjunction with the publications listed below.)

American Association of School Librarians and the Association of Educational Communications and Technology. *Media Programs: District and School*. Chicago: American Library Association, 1975. Obtain most recent edition.

Chisholm, Margaret E., and Ely, Donald P. *Media Personnel in Education*. Englewood Cliffs, N.J.: Prentice-Hall, 1976.

Darling, Richard. *Teams for Better Education: The Teacher and the Librarian*. Champaign, Ill.: Garrard, n.d.*

Davies, Ruth Ann. *The School Library Media Program: Instructional Force for Excellence*, 3rd ed. New York: R. R. Bowker, 1979.

Maryland State Department of Education. *Criteria for Modern School Media Programs*. Baltimore, Md.: State Department of Education, 1975.

Pearson, Neville, and Butler, Lucius, eds. *Learning Resource Centers: Selected Readings*. Minneapolis, Minn.: Burgess, 1973.

Pittman, Shirley A., ed. *The Pennsylvania Guide for School Library Media Specialists*. Pittsburgh, Pa.: Pennsylvania School Librarians Association, 1978.†

School Library Manpower Project. *Occupational Definitions for School Library Media Personnel*. Chicago: American Library Association, 1971.

Consulting with state, regional, or county school library media supervisors or members of their staff to identify the basic ingredients of a quality library media program.

Consulting with the staff at AASL headquarters‡ either by letter or by telephone to request recommendations as to procedures to follow.

---

*Multiple copies of Richard Darling's monograph *Teams for Better Education* are available at no cost on request from the Garrard Publishing Co., Champaign, Ill. 61820.

†*The Pennsylvania Guide for School Library Media Specialists* is available from Shirley A. Pittman, 186 McIntyre Rd., Pittsburgh, Pa. 15237, $5.50 per copy.

‡American Association of School Librarians, 50 E. Huron St., Chicago, Ill. 60611, tel. 312-944-6780.

Consulting with the officers of the state school library association either by letter or by telephone to request recommendations as to exemplary programs or persons to consult.

Visiting school districts reputed to have library media programs of functional excellence.

The committee defines and endorses basic philosophy such as:

District library media program—a plan, both developmental and operational, designed and structured to achieve the fullest realization of district educational goals and objectives through the integration of library media service and the instructional process.

Building library media program—a developmental and operational plan wherein the building library media center functions as a learning laboratory where the use of all media, print and nonprint, is purposeful, planned, and integrated with the educational program and instructional processes to widen, deepen, intensify, and personalize learning.

Library media specialist—a member of the teaching faculty who has broad professional preparation in educational media, is certified as a teacher, and is knowledgeable about educational processes, methodology, strategies, and designs; is conversant with curriculum and media content; and is expert in programming for the most effective use of media to make teaching and learning more effective, efficient, and rewarding.

The committee prepares for faculty and administrative consideration, modification, and adoption:

A statement of philosophy, goals, and objectives to undergird the district library media program (see Appendix I).

A statement endorsing the School Library Bill of Rights for School Library Media Programs (see Chapter 7).

A statement of policy pertaining to the procedure for integrating the library media program with the instructional program (see Chapter 7).

A statement of policy recommending the establishment of a district instructional materials center and the centralization in that facility of all technical processing (see Chapter 7).

A statement of policy and procedures for selecting instructional media including criteria for selection (see Chapter 7 and Appendix H).

A statement of routine procedures for handling complaints about questioned media (see Chapters 7 and 8).

A statement of recommended procedure to follow in working cooperatively with the public library.

A five-year plan for initiating and/or strengthening the library media program on the district and individual school level including specific recommendations concerning: staff, facilities, materials, production services, budget, program development, and program evaluation (see Chapter 13).

The committee compiles a district policy and routine manual for the district library media program (see Appendix F).

The committee prepares, in cooperation with the administration, job descriptions for the library media staff that are reflective of those in *Occupational Definitions for School Library Media Personnel* and *Media Personnel in Education;* these job descriptions are included in the district policy and routine manual (see Chapter 14 and Appendix F).

The second step in scientific program development is to translate the master plan into supportive library media programs on the individual school building level. Just as the educational philosophy, goals, and objectives of the district serve as hallmarks in structuring the educational program on the school building level, so the district philosophy, goals, and objectives of library media service provide the basic structure for the library media program in individual schools. The following procedure is recommended for either initiating or strengthening the library media program on the building level:

The principal appoints a faculty advisory committee to work with the building library media center staff and the district library media program supervisor in blueprinting a building library media program.

The committee studies the district master plan for library media programs and makes recommendations to the principal as to how best to implement the program.

The committee evaluates the existing library media program using a recognized evaluation instrument to determine areas of strength and areas of weakness (see Chapter 13).

The committee constructs a library media program evaluation profile, setting priorities for attaining excellence in each category of service (see "Criteria of Excellence Checklist," Chapter 13, Example 43).

The library media center staff compiles a building policy and routine manual for the school's library media program (see Appendix F).

The library media specialists invite teachers and students to participate in media evaluation and selection (see Chapter 7).

The library media specialists invite department chairpersons and faculty members to discuss ways and means of integrating the library media program with the instructional program.

The library media program that is educationally economic, efficient, and effective is much more than the sum of its parts—philosophy, goals, objectives, procedures, media, equipment, facilities, and staff. It is both an instructional source and an instructional force permeating, activating, and motivating learning—a means of managing knowledge in a media-rich learning laboratory environment so that the school and its faculty can achieve their common goal of equalizing educational opportunity in a context of excellence while personalizing and humanizing the processes of instruction.

NOTES

1. Dorothy McGinnis, "Instructional Materials Centers—Something New?" *California School Libraries* 34, no. 1 (Nov. 1962): 4–6.
2. Horace Mann, *Life and Works of Horace Mann*, vol. 3, "Annual Reports of the Secretary of the Board of Education of Massachusetts, 1839–1844" (Boston: Lee and Shepard, 1891), p. 49.
3. Committee of Ten, Madison Conference Report, 1892, as quoted in *Teaching of*

History in Elementary and Secondary Schools by Henry Johnson (New York: Macmillan, 1915), p. 323.

4. Bessie Smith, "Joint Administration of the High-School Library by the Board of Education and the Public Library," in *Addresses and Proceedings, 1916*, vol. 54 (Ann Arbor, Mich.: National Education Association, 1916), pp. 656–657.

5. Lucille F. Fargo, "Training High School Students in the Use of the Library," in *Addresses and Proceedings, 1913*, vol. 51 (Ann Arbor, Mich.: National Education Association, 1913), p. 760.

6. Mary E. Hall, "The Development of the Modern School Library," as quoted in Mary Wilson, *Selected Articles on School Library Experience* (New York: H. W. Wilson, 1925), p. 70.

7. Ibid., p. 72.

8. Ibid., p. 75.

9. Johnson, *Teaching of History*, pp. 208–209.

10. Committee on Library Organization and Equipment of the National Education Association and of the North Central Association of Colleges and Secondary Schools, *Standard Library Organization and Equipment for Secondary Schools of Different Sizes* (Chicago: American Library Association, 1920).

11. Ibid., p. 16.

12. Joint Committee of the National Education Association and the American Library Association, *Elementary School Library Standards* (Chicago: American Library Association, 1925).

13. Ibid., p. 1.

14. Committee on Post-War Planning of the American Library Association, *School Libraries for Today and Tomorrow* (Chicago: American Library Association, 1945), pp. 9–10.

15. American Association of School Librarians, *Standards for School Library Programs* (Chicago: American Library Association, 1960).

16. Ibid., pp. 1, 3–4.

17. Ibid., p. 12.

18. American Association of School Librarians and the Department of Audiovisual Instruction of the National Education Association, *Standards for School Media Programs* (Chicago: American Library Association, 1969), pp. xi–xii.

19. Ibid., pp. 1–2, 5.

20. American Association of School Librarians and the Association for Educational Communications and Technology, *Media Programs: District and School* (Chicago: American Library Association, 1975), p. 107.

21. Ibid., p. 4.

22. Benjamin S. Bloom, ed., *Taxonomy of Educational Objectives: The Classification of Educational Goals—Handbook I, Cognitive Domain* (New York: David McKay, 1956).

23. David R. Krathwohl et al., *Taxonomy of Educational Objectives: The Classification of Educational Goals—Handbook II, Affective Domain* (New York: David McKay, 1964).

4 The School Library Media Program: Actualizing Force for Self-Realization

When I say I believe in helping children experience joy and happiness in learning, I do not mean protecting them artificially against the crises of life or from all experiences of fear, anxiety, and unhappiness. When I say I want children to feel free to ask questions, to explore, to experiment, to be spontaneous, I am not advocating license in a classroom that is unsupervised or led by a teacher who is incompetent or irresponsible. I expect teachers to be informed about appropriate curricular materials, but also to know how to incite the deep interest of children through their teaching skill and their relationship with pupils, without resorting to pedagogical tricks. I expect educational programs to help children find themselves as individuals—learners, thinkers, doers, persons with feelings, increasing clarity as to their identities, and appropriate roles in life. Such programs can be based on sound experimental studies of learning and teaching and the results evaluated by rigorous methods that go beyond the measurement of changes in IQ.

Milton J. E. Senn, M.D.*

One profound ideological difference between democracy and communism is the place of the citizen in the political scheme of things. In a democracy, the state exists for the health, benefit, and welfare of the citizens, individually and collectively. The place of the citizen in a communist state is diametrically opposite. In communism the state itself is paramount and the citizens, individually and collectively, exist for the benefit of the state. In assessing educational priorities as we approach the 21st century, personalized education has been identified by the National Education Association (NEA) as a basic concern. This priority demands that teaching be humanized and that learning be individualized. In theory, the promise that each citizen will have the opportunity to experience an optimum education demands that in practice all citizens be guaranteed that their individuality will be respected, that they will be taught as individuals, and that they will be encouraged to achieve their full potential as learners, as citizens, and as human beings. Actualization of the promise of self-realization is what the American dream is all about.

INDIVIDUALIZING, HUMANIZING, AND PERSONALIZING INSTRUCTION

Though it is plain common sense to recognize and to accommodate the vast actual differences among learners, the saber-toothed tiger, one-way-for-all class approach is alive and flourishing as we approach the 21st century. In 1916, psychologist Lewis Terman spoke out against class-paced learning. He recommended that courses of study be differentiated to permit each student

---

*Milton J. E. Senn, "Early Childhood Education: For What Goals?" in Glen Hass, Joseph Bondi, and Jon Wiles, *Curriculum Planning: A New Approach* (Boston: Allyn and Bacon, 1974), p. 273.

"to progress at the rate which is normal for him, whether that rate be rapid or slow." He also recommended that teachers "measure out the work for each child in proportion to his mental ability."[1] Though the injustice of impersonal education has been recognized for over threescore years, individualization is the exception and not the rule in modern education.

In 1944, Stephen Corey wrote an article for *Childhood Education* titled "The Poor Scholar's Soliloquy."[2] Corey's case study of an alienated seventh-grade repeater is eloquent testimony to the tyranny of impersonal education. The youngster reported his inner thoughts about himself and his schooling as follows:

No I'm not very good in school. This is my second year in seventh grade and I'm bigger and taller than the other kids. They like me all right, though, even if I don't say much in the schoolroom, because outside I can tell them how to do a lot of things. They tag me around and that sort of makes up for what goes on in school.

I don't know why the teachers don't like me. They never have very much. Seems like they don't think you know anything unless they can name the book it came out of. I've got a lot of books up in my own room at home—books like *Popular Science Mechanical Encyclopedia*, and the Sears' and Ward's catalogues, but I don't very often just sit down and read them through like they make us do in school. I use my books when I want to find something out, like whenever Mom buys anything secondhand I look it up in Sears' or Ward's first and tell her if she's getting stung or not. I can use the index in a hurry to find the things I want.

In school, though, we've got to learn whatever is in the book and I just can't memorize the stuff. Last year I stayed after school every night for two weeks trying to learn the names of the Presidents. Of course I knew some of them like Washington, Jefferson and Lincoln, but there must have been thirty altogether and I never did get them straight.

I'm not too sorry though because the kids who learned the Presidents had to turn right around and learn all the Vice Presidents. I am taking the seventh grade over but our teacher this year isn't so interested in the names of the Presidents. She has us trying to learn the names of all the great American inventors.

I guess I just can't remember names in history. Anyway, this year I've been trying to learn about trucks because my uncle owns three and he says I can drive one when I'm sixteen. I already know the horsepower and number of forward and backward speeds of twenty-six American trucks, some of them Diesels, and I can spot each make a long way off. It's funny how that Diesel works. I started to tell my teacher about it last Wednesday in science class when the pump we were using to make a vacuum in a bell jar got hot, but she said she didn't see what a Diesel engine had to do with our experiment so I just kept still. The kids seemed interested though. I took four of them around to my uncle's garage after school and we saw the mechanic, Gus, tearing a big truck Diesel down. Boy, does he know his stuff!

I'm not very good in geography either. They call it economic geography this year. We've been studying the imports and exports of Chile all week but I couldn't tell you what they are. Maybe the reason is I had to miss school yesterday because my uncle took me and his big trailer truck down state about two hundred miles and we brought almost ten tons of stock to the Chicago market.

He had told me where we were going and I had to figure out the highways to take and also the mileage. He didn't do anything but drive and turn where I told him to. Was that fun! I sat with a map in my lap and told him to turn south or southeast or some other direction. We made seven stops and drove over five hundred miles round trip. I'm figuring now what his oil cost and also the wear and tear on the truck—he calls it depreciation—so we'll know how much we made.

I even write out all the bills and send letters to the farmers about what their pigs and beef cattle brought at the stockyards. I only made three mistakes in 17 letters last time, my aunt said—all commas. She's been through high school and reads them over. I wish I could write school themes that way. The last one I had to write was on, "What a Daffodil Thinks of Spring," and I just couldn't get going.

I don't do very well in school in arithmetic either. Seems I just can't keep my mind on the problems. We had one the other day like this: if a 57 foot telephone pole falls across a cement highway so that $17\frac{3}{6}$ feet extend from one side and $14\frac{9}{17}$ feet from the other, how wide is the highway? That seemed to me like an awfully silly way to get the width of a highway. I didn't even try to answer it because it didn't say whether the pole had fallen straight across or not.

Even in shop I don't get very good grades. All of us kids made a broom holder and a bookend this term and mine were sloppy. I just couldn't get interested. Mom doesn't use a broom anymore with her new vacuum cleaner and all our books are in a bookcase with glass doors in the parlor. Anyway, I wanted to make an end gate for my uncle's trailer but the shop teacher said that meant using metal and wood both and I'd have to learn how to work with wood first. I didn't see why but I kept still and made a tie rack at school and the tail gate after school at my uncle's garage. He said I saved him $10.

Civics is hard for me, too. I've been staying after school trying to learn the "Articles of Confederation" for almost a week because the teacher said we couldn't be good citizens unless we did. I really tried, because I want to be a good citizen. I did hate to stay after school, though, because a bunch of us boys from the south end of town have been cleaning up the old lot across from Taylor's Machine Shop to make a playground out of it for the little kids from the Methodist home. I made the jungle gym from old pipe and the guys made me Grand Mogul to keep the playground going. We raised enough money collecting scrap this month to build a wire fence clear around the lot.

Dad says I can quit school when I'm fifteen and I'm sort of anxious to because there are a lot of things I want to learn how to do and as my uncle says, I'm not getting any younger.

Lest the reader have a tendency to excuse the frustration and alienation of the student described above on the basis of his being a repeater and "obviously not being too swift mentally," case studies abound testifying to the tyranny and abuse of impersonal education experienced by children and youth from all levels of the ability spectrum. Elizabeth Drews, clinical psychologist and recognized authority on creativity, documents a number of such cases in her book *Learning Together: How to Foster Creativity, Self-Fulfillment, and Social Awareness in Today's Students and Teachers.*[3] Her book contains case studies of students whose spirit has been maimed by teachers who resented them because they were creative human beings. Her case study of Don Saxon, a sensitive, brilliant, creative youngster, is a classic and should be required reading for all who teach, for Don from his first day in school was embarrassed, harassed, thwarted, and resented by some of his teachers simply because he was brilliant and did not fit into the one-way-for-all approach. Don became so desperate that at one point he contemplated suicide, and finally saved his sanity by withdrawing from school. His school had effectively mutilated his joy in learning, his pleasure in creating, and his sense of self—in reality the school was the killer of Don's dreams.

In 1971, NEA published *Schools for the 70's and Beyond: A Call to Action,* which stated that the major goal for educational reform during the 1970s was "that of *making the schools humane institutions.*"[4] Such a reform, stated NEA, required that "the schools must now go beyond their previous role of preparing children for social functions" and prepare "children to become totally realized individuals—humane, self-renewing, self-directed individuals

—who will not only survive in society, but will take a conscious role in shaping it for the better."[5]

The goal of making the schools humane institutions requires that the focus of attention be placed not on teaching but on learning; not on facts alone but on understanding; not on intellect alone but on the learner's emotional, social, aesthetic, spiritual, and physical well-being and development. Nurturing humaneness encompasses not only feelings, beliefs, values, and understanding, but also self-perception, self-discipline, self-fulfillment, and self-realization. Beyond things of an academic nature, the instructional program is also concerned with each student's developing the warm human qualities of compassion, caring, concerned involvement, striving for justice, and sensitivity to the rights and needs of others. "Fully functioning individuals become that way by maximizing their own capabilities and aspirations through interchange with other persons. In the process of becoming humane, growth achieved through sensitive responses to others is as significant as gains resulting from personal initiative."[6] The continuing concern of humane education is the release of human potential, that "multidimensional, many-faceted, personal possession of the human spirit"[7] which is the source for creative insights and unlimited aspirations. "Few possessions are more utilitarian than an education that allows one to distill from life some interior joy despite a boring job, a tedious marriage, or the sudden advent of tragedy."[8]

Individualization of instruction is the most important single component of an educational program designed to promote humaneness. The term *individualized instruction* as used in this context means instruction that is designed for the individual student and that recognizes and accommodates the learner's uniqueness in learning style, level of intellectual and skill competence, emotional maturity, likes and dislikes, social adequacies and inadequacies, frustration threshold, motivational reactions, need for encouragement and/or challenge, level of academic sophistication, and personal hopes and aspirations. Shane in *Curriculum Change Toward the 21st Century* states in Premise IX: "Good instruction is personalized rather than individualized. Classical *individualized* instruction was designed to help learners reach or exceed grade level," while *"personalized* instruction recognizes that children and youth mature at different rates and is designed to help them reach whatever competency level they can reach without undue pressure."[9] The term *individualization* is synonymous with personalization as used by most modern writers and the difference between the terms as stressed by Shane is for purposes of emphasis only.

Individualized instruction can take place in a conventional self-contained classroom in a conventional school building. It does not require special facilities such as the open plan school, which is designed to support informal teaching and individualized learning. Such an open plan school is usually built with large open spaces rather than with separate classrooms, frequently with the library media center in the geographic center of the building. Some schools have been built without walls; others have portable partitions; some have seminar rooms, laboratories, offices, and quiet study rooms; others have no separate rooms with all special facilities assigned an area in the open complex. Facilities alone do not establish a climate that is conducive to individualizing learning. Rather, it is the openness of the teacher to student needs and the teacher's willingness to shift teaching emphasis from the class to meeting the needs of the students in the class (see Fig. 1).

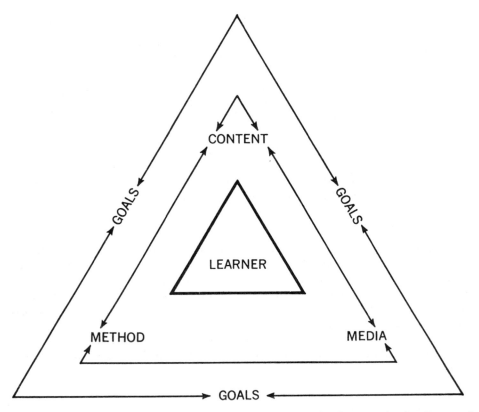

FIGURE 1. Individualizing the Teaching Design. The learner is the focus of instructional activities. Content, method, media, and goals are related to the developmental needs of the individual learner.

Individualized instruction requires "instructional methods and materials of such scope and flexibility as to reasonably fit the diverse requirements of different individuals."[10] Diversification is the solution to the problem of how to individualize instruction (see Chapter 6, Table 2). Individualization of instruction requires that the teacher be especially proficient in utilizing the small-group process in teaching. The aim of having students become independent learners "will never be fulfilled if the child only learns how to solve problems individually; he must be prepared to approach learning in cooperation with others."[11] Learning how to work productively and in harmony with others is a vital part of preparing today's youth for their future roles as wage-earners and as cooperative, contributing members of a family, a community, a nation, and the world. Individualized instruction should be an effective means of enhancing students' awareness of their responsibility to their fellowmen—an important behavioral objective to be accomplished by humanizing instruction.

TEACHING TOWARD INQUIRY

When instruction is individualized, the emphasis shifts from teaching to learning; from the teacher telling to the teacher encouraging the student to quest for understanding; from learning restricted to reading the textbook to learning generated through and by problem solving, by group interaction, and by imaginative, informed, constructive, divergent thinking. Learning by inquiry is a basic part of an instructional program designed to enable students to learn how to think rather than by telling them what to think.

> Inquiry environment . . . means creating an environment that gives the highest possible priority to inquiry behavior. It is an environment that values above all else the development of such survival attitudes as objectivity, tentativeness, self-sufficiency, contingency, open-endedness, flexibility, inventiveness, and resourcefulness.[12]

The inquiry approach provides, in myriad context patterns, opportunity for the student to engage in and practice the fundamental thinking skills of question asking, defining, observing, classifying, generalizing, verifying, drawing conclusions, making judgments, and communicating findings (see Chapter 12).

NURTURING CREATIVITY

Creative learning extends beyond the skills of inquiry to embrace the highly personal process of imagining, incubating, and expressing. It "occurs when a person responds constructively to a situation that calls for nonhabitual behavior, solutions for which the behaver has no learned response."[13] "Creativity, the most distinctively human of all our attributes, . . . is the union of independence, spontaneity, and originality."[14]

Paul Torrance, a leading authority in the field of creativity, believes that schools should develop strategies for nurturing the following humane characteristics in contemporary youth:

WANTING TO KNOW

   Asking questions

   Engaging in the absorbed search for truth

   Testing guesses

   Finding better ways of finding out

   Preparing for the use and extension of learning skills throughout life

DIGGING DEEPER

   Attempting more difficult tasks

   Shunning mediocrity and the quick easy way

   Hungering for excellence and working hard to achieve it

   Keeping open the capacity for genuine affection, love, empathy, and honesty of feeling

LOOKING TWICE AND LISTENING FOR SMELLS

   Looking from different angles

   Taking a closer look

   Experiencing with all senses

   Investigating fully and independently

   Submerging self in ideas and projects

   Enjoying working alone at times

LISTENING TO A CAT

   Learning to listen and communicate with understanding

   Trying to find out what really matters to others

Developing skills of empathy

Expressing ideas and feelings accurately and honestly through nonverbal means

Expressing self through creative movements, creative dramatics, visual art, and creative reading

CROSSING OUT MISTAKES

Gathering courage to attempt something difficult and important, even with the expectation of making mistakes

Using mistakes constructively to move forward to new levels of skills and dignity

Learning reality through direct, personal experience

GETTING INTO AND OUT OF DEEP WATER

Testing one's skills and abilities

Testing the situation

Testing one's resources

Taking calculated risks

Asking questions for which no ready answers exist

Making choices

Seeing defects in the existing order

Gaining confidence in the ability to "get out of deep water"

HAVING A BALL

Enjoying bursting forth to a new level of knowing and functioning

Being able to laugh, play, fantasize, and loaf

Being careful but not overcautious or fearful

Finding fun and pleasure in work and learning

CUTTING HOLES TO SEE THROUGH

Tolerating complexity

Manipulating complexity, incompleteness, and imperfections to achieve breakthroughs and genuine innovations[15]

The following behavior patterns, reminiscent of Torrance's conception of humane characteristics, are evidence of creative thinking:

Sensitivity to problems, attitudes, and feelings of others and to life itself.

Fluency in producing ideas and in the ability to think rapidly and freely.

Flexibility in adjusting quickly to new situations.

Originality in thinking of new or novel responses.

Capacity to redefine or reorganize by utilizing what is known but for new and different reasons.

Ability to abstract by analyzing the component parts of a problem or in seeing specific relationships between and among the parts of a problem.

Ability to synthesize by combining several elements into a new form or whole.

Ability to organize by putting parts together in a meaningful way.[16]

Creative learning provides the fertile environment that greatly increases the possibility of the student's projecting beyond the usual and the obvious to generate new thought patterns.

Research has produced convincing evidence that creativity is not an offshoot of native intelligence. "It simply is not true that the more intelligent person is necessarily the more creative one."[17] Consistently it has been proven that creativity is a separate factor and is not linked to intelligence. Some brilliant people, academically speaking, lack the spark of creativity altogether. On the other hand, Getzels and Jackson, research pioneers in the field of creativity and learning, found that a student with a high creativity factor and an average IQ (around 100) frequently achieved as high as or even higher than the student with the high IQ (around 150) but lower creativity factor.[18]

In determining creativity the following characteristics have been identified by Donald MacKinnon, director of the Institute of Personality Assessment and Research at the University of California, as being more important as predictors of creativity than the IQ:

> The person's personality
> His enduring interests
> His values
> His motives
> His cognitive style
> His whole-hearted commitment to the creative enterprise
> His spirit is free from crippling restraints and impoverishing inhibitions[19]

A truly creative thinker breaks away from the conventional or usual sequence of thought and is not shackled by the fear of failure.

Problem solving, an essential skill for lifelong learning, is a creative enterprise if one or more of the following conditions is satisfied:

> The product of the thinking has novelty and value. . . .
>
> The thinking is unconventional, in a sense that it requires modification or rejection of previously accepted ideas.
>
> The thinking requires high motivation and persistence, taking place either over a considerable span of time or at high intensity.
>
> The problem as initially posed was vague and undefined, so that part of the task was to formulate the problem itself.[20]

Such creative problem solving is not limited to things academic but encompasses art, music, dance, and composition. Likewise, creative problem solving is not limited to school but is especially evident in how individuals approach and proceed to solve their own personal problems. Coping with the day-to-day problems of home and job in a constructive, creative manner is all too often "unhonored and unsung." Yet these creative efforts bearing the "handprints of necessity" raise the life of the creator above the level of a humdrum existence to the level of zestful living.*

INSTRUCTIONAL RELEVANCE

A humane curriculum is responsive not only to the educational and personal growth needs of the students but especially to student interests and student concerns; this is a major thrust in an instructional program designed for relevance. Developing a relevant curriculum does not mean that the teacher abdicates educational responsibility in favor of letting youngsters do "what

---

*The term "handprints of necessity" was used by James Dickey in his article "The Many Ways of Speaking in Verse," *The New York Times Book Review*, December 22, 1963, p. 4.

comes naturally." Far from it. Relevant educational experiences are "developed by teachers after intensive study of the students, their interests and aspirations, the immediate community, and the broader concerns of the total society."[21] Teachers frequently involve students in developing relevant learning experiences; nonetheless, it is largely the teacher's responsibility to build relevancy into the instructional program.

Harvey Goldman, Association Professor of Educational Administration at the University of Maryland, suggests using the following criteria as a conceptual framework on which to base a relevant curriculum:

> A relevant curriculum is active rather than passive.
>
> A relevant curriculum will deal with values.
>
> A relevant curriculum should be based on experiences with which children are familiar and in which they are interested.
>
> The learners must be guided into new areas of concern.
>
> A teacher can present the same concepts to children within the framework of a relevant curriculum as are offered through more conventional curricula.[22]

Relevance in the curriculum is mandatory, for unless a learning experience is perceived to be of value it will be approached with reluctance, if not resentment.

Postman and Weingartner suggest that teachers determine what is relevant by measuring the questions they pose against these standards:

> Will your questions increase the learner's *will* as well as his capacity to learn?
>
> Will they give him a sense of joy in learning?
>
> Will they help to provide the learner with confidence in his ability to learn?
>
> In order to get answers, will the learner be required to make inquiries?
>
> Does each question allow for alternative answers?
>
> Will the process of answering the questions tend to stress the uniqueness of the learner?
>
> Would the questions produce different answers if asked at different stages of the learner's development?
>
> Will the answers help the learner to sense and understand the universals in the human condition and so enhance his ability to draw closer to other people?[23]

The answer to each of the above questions is an unqualified "yes" if what is being taught is relevant to the learners' world and to their need to perceive their roles in that world. Question asking and answering go hand in hand with teaching for relevance, providing the questions are significant and bring into play the student's ability to solve problems and discover that which is relevant.

STRESSING VALUES

A relevant curriculum deals with values, that most important area of the affective domain. "A value is a standard or yardstick to guide actions, attitudes, comparisons, evaluations, and justification of self to others."[24] Values are demonstrated through action that encompasses choosing, prizing, and acting. The process of valuing includes the following basic steps:

> Choosing: (1) freely, (2) from alternatives, (3) after thoughtful consideration of the consequences of each alternative.

Prizing: (4) cherishing, being happy with the choice, (5) willing to affirm the choice publicly.

Acting: (6) doing something with the choice repeatedly, in some pattern of life.[25]

A primary instructional goal of an educational program designed to stress values is to cultivate the ability to make judgments, exercise self-direction, and achieve self-fulfillment. The traditional emphasis of the intellectual to the exclusion of the emotional development of the learner is contrary to human nature; we think not only with our minds but also with our emotions. School should be a place where students build a positive set of values that they prize highly and demonstrate in their behavior.

A consistent goal of education is to develop the student's capability to think and to act in a rational manner. Rationality, which is an integrated activity, means more than applying knowledge and logic when solving a problem. Rationality "means thinking with values and commitments."[26]

> The modern dilemma, says John McMurray, is that we have set the intellect free and kept emotion in chains. "Knowledge is power, but emotion is the master of our values and of the uses, therefore, to which we put power. . . . unless the emotions and the intellect are in harmony, rational action will be paralyzed."[27]

Basic values and commitments are the launching pads for constructive, purposeful behavior. School is the civilizing agent that, if it is humane in intent and in method, will provide the climate conducive to positive value choosing and judgment making.

In addition to the moral values traditionally honored by the Judeo-Christian culture—integrity, truthfulness, honesty, filial respect, sobriety, selflessness, compassion—there is a pressing need for the schools to stress the necessity of putting forth maximum effort to learn. In striving to be humane it is imperative that the "easygoing way" not replace the "strenuous mood" as distinguished by William James.[28] The strenuous mood means being willing to work hard, taking things seriously, making free choices, and taking responsibility for one's actions. The easygoing way is sitting back being a passive recorder of facts and doing no more than absolutely necessary.

In assessing educational priorities, the concern that surpasses all others in importance is concern for the personal quality of the student as a citizen and as a human being. Personal excellence of the citizen, which is characterized by self-discipline, authentic concern for the well-being of one's fellowman, respect for law and order, and a deep abiding love of nation, is the unique ingredient alone preventing democracy from becoming merely "a prologue to a tragedy or a farce." The very survival of this nation as a free society is inextricably interwoven with the quality of the individual citizen.

When equating personal excellence in action with the expectation of attainment, today's schools are less than successful. Goodlad laments that contemporary man still has far to go in achieving personal excellence.

> Man has rocketed his kind into space. He has brought back into pulsating life human beings already pronounced dead. He has fashioned in his own likeness robots that remember, file, sort and then answer in moments problems that would tax a hundred men for a thousand days. But men still cheat and steal and kill as they did a thousand years ago and thousands of years before that.
>
> These are not always trapped men or hungry men or threatened men who cheat and steal and kill. Some men pronounced learned cheat because they are

vain. Some men pronounced holy steal because they are greedy. Some men pronounced wise kill because they have established no identity with their fellowmen.
The people who soon may bring down upon themselves a holocaust are—or
will have been—the most educated of all time.[29]

Alvin Eurich echoes Goodlad's concern for the upgrading of the quality of
the citizen. He warns:

> We cannot tolerate another generation that knows so much about preserving and
> destroying life, but so little about enhancing it. We cannot permit our children
> to come into their maturity as masters of the atom and the gene, but ignorant and
> barbarous about the ways of the human mind and heart.[30]

If development of personal excellence is truly to transcend all other educational commitments and concerns, the affective area of learning—the area concerned with developing interests, attitudes, appreciations, values, and emotions
—must assert its preeminence in the curriculum and receive emphasis commensurate with its importance to the well-being of the individual and the continuing health and vigor of the nation. Twenty-one civilizations have come
and gone on the stage of history; nineteen have perished because large segments of the citizenry became morally impoverished and sacrificed their nation on the altar of myopic self-interest. Lawrence M. Gould puts it this way:

> I do not believe the greatest threat to our future is from bombs or missiles. I do
> not think our civilization will die that way. I think it will die when we no longer
> care, when the spiritual forces that make us wish to be right and noble die in the
> hearts of men. Toynbee has pointed out that nineteen of twenty-one notable
> civilizations have died from within and not from conquest from without. There
> were no bands playing, and no flags waving when these civilizations decayed. It
> happened slowly in the quiet and dark, when no one was aware.[31]

The affective area of learning must not be eclipsed by the cognitive area—that
justifiably respected area of learning devoted to building what Jacques Barzun
refers to as the student's "house of intellect."[32] Rather, the affective and the
cognitive areas must work in tandem, each nurturing and enhancing the other.

The goal of educational excellence must transcend things of a merely academic nature and embrace "the inner life of feeling and appreciation, and the
moral, esthetic and spiritual values associated with the life."[33] School should
be a civilizing agent and should militate against self-destruction. For "civilization is not inherited; it has to be learned and earned by each generation anew;
if the transmission should be interrupted one century, civilization would die,
and we should be savages."[34] Therefore, the goal of educational excellence
must encompass the total person—mind, body, heart, spirit, and soul. Intellectual excellence coupled with personal excellence is the ideal whose time
has come.

NOTES

1. Lewis M. Terman, *The Measurement of Intelligence* (Boston: Houghton, 1916),
   p. 4.
2. Stephen M. Corey, "The Poor Scholar's Soliloquy," *Childhood Education* 20, no. 5
   (Jan. 1944): 219–220.
3. Elizabeth M. Drews, *Learning Together: How to Foster Creativity, Self-Fulfillment,
   and Social Awareness in Today's Students and Teachers* (Englewood Cliffs, N.J.:
   Prentice-Hall, 1972).

4. *Schools for the 70's and Beyond: A Call to Action*, A Staff Report from the Center for the Study of Instruction (Washington, D.C.: National Education Association, 1971), p. 17.
5. Ibid., p. 20.
6. Raphael O. Nystrand and Luvern L. Cunningham, "Organizing Schools to Develop Humane Capabilities," in *To Nurture Humaneness: Commitment for the 70's*, ed. by Mary-Margaret Scobey and Grace Graham (Washington, D.C.: Association for Supervision and Curriculum Development, National Education Association, 1970), p. 120.
7. Robert F. De Haan and Ronald C. Doll, "Individualization and Human Potential," in *Individualizing Instruction*, Association for Supervision and Curriculum Development Yearbook (Washington, D.C.: Association for Supervision and Curriculum Development, National Education Association, 1964), p. 16.
8. *Schools for the 70's and Beyond*, p. 42.
9. Harold G. Shane, *Curriculum Change Toward the 21st Century*, Curriculum Series (Washington, D.C.: National Education Association, 1977), p. 62.
10. *Innovations in the Elementary School*, Report of a National Seminar (Dayton, Ohio: Institute for Development of Educational Activities, 1971), p. 11.
11. *How to Enhance Individuality in Learning*, The Report of an International Seminar sponsored by the National Association of Secondary School Principals and /I/D/E/A/ (Dayton, Ohio: Institute for Development of Educational Activities, n.d.), p. 10.
12. Neil Postman and Charles Weingartner, *Teaching as a Subversive Activity* (New York: Delacorte Press, 1969), p. 54.
13. Robert R. Leeper, ed., *Curricular Concerns in a Revolutionary Era* (Washington, D.C.: Association for Supervision and Curriculum Development, National Education Association, 1971), p. 50.
14. Drews, *Learning Together*, p. 1.
15. Adapted from E. Paul Torrance, "What It Means to Become Human," in Scobey and Graham, *To Nurture Humaneness*, pp. 3-7.
16. Adapted from Viktor Lowenfeld and W. Lambert Brittain, *Creative and Mental Growth*, 4th ed. (New York: Macmillan, 1964), pp. 7-9.
17. Donald W. MacKinnon, "The Study of Creative Persons," in *Creativity and Learning*, ed. by Jerome Kagan (Boston: Houghton, 1967), p. 33. Reprinted by permission, *Daedalus*, Journal of the American Academy of Arts and Sciences, Boston, Mass., Summer 1965.
18. Jacob W. Getzels and Philip W. Jackson, *Creativity and Intelligence* (New York: Wiley, 1962).
19. MacKinnon, "The Study of Creative Persons," p. 33. Reprinted by permission, *Daedalus*, Journal of the American Academy of Arts and Sciences, Boston, Mass., Summer 1965.
20. E. Paul Torrance, "Scientific Views of Creativity," in Kagan, *Creativity and Learning*, p. 76. Reprinted by permission, *Daedalus*, Journal of the American Academy of Arts and Sciences, Boston, Mass., Summer 1965.
21. Harvey Goldman, "The Nature of Curricular Relevance," in Leeper, *Curricular Concerns in a Revolutionary Era*, p. 225.
22. Ibid., pp. 225-226.
23. Postman and Weingartner, *Teaching as a Subversive Activity*, p. 66.
24. Milton Rokeach, *Beliefs, Attitudes and Values* (San Francisco: Jossey-Bass, 1969).
25. Louis E. Raths et al., *Values and Teaching* (Columbus, Ohio: Charles E. Merrill Books, 1966).
26. J. Galen Saylor and Joshua L. Smith, eds., *Removing Barriers to Humaneness in the High School* (Washington, D.C.: Association for Supervision and Curriculum Development, National Education Association, 1971), p. 10.
27. Ibid., p. 10.
28. William James, "The Moral Philosopher and the Moral Life," in *Pragmatism and Other Essays*, ed. by J. L. Blau (New York: Washington Square Press, 1963), pp. 214-235.
29. John I. Goodlad as quoted in National Education Association Project on Instruction, *Schools for the Sixties* (New York: McGraw-Hill, 1963), p. 2.

30. Alvin C. Eurich as quoted in *Toward a More Relevant Curriculum* (Dayton, Ohio: Institute for the Development of Educational Activities, 1972), p. 1.
31. Lawrence M. Gould as quoted in Alvin D. Loving, "Leadership for Survival," *New Development, Research and Experimentation in Professional Laboratory Experiences*, bulletin, no. 22 (Washington, D.C.: Association for Student Teaching, 1964), p. 48.
32. Jacques Barzun, *House of Intellect* (New York: Harper, 1959).
33. Sidney G. Tickton, ed., *To Improve Learning: An Evaluation of Instructional Technology*, vol. 1 (New York: R. R. Bowker, 1971), p. 15.
34. Will and Ariel Durant, *The Lessons of History* (New York: Simon and Schuster, 1968), p. 101.

5 The Teaching Role of the Library Media Specialist

*Then said a teacher, Speak to us of Teaching. And he said: No man
can reveal to you aught but that which already lies half asleep in
the dawning of your knowledge. The teacher who walks in the
shadow of the temple, among his followers, gives not of his wisdom
but rather of his faith and lovingness. If he is indeed wise he does not
bid you enter the house of his wisdom, but rather leads you to the
threshold of your own mind.*

Kahlil Gibran*

*The teacher stands, in many ways, at the crossroads of meaning in
the life of the pupil.*

James B. Macdonald†

*The librarian of today and tomorrow must have many technical
and professional skills, but above all he must have skill with people.
He is a teacher whose subject is learning itself.*

Douglas M. Knight‡

The school library media specialist is the energizing force that powers the
educational thrust of the instructional media program. No matter how vast the
media collection, the media program lacks educational significance and
"clout" until its resources and services are synchronized and intermeshed with
the ongoing, day-to-day instructional program. The library media program
has a vital job to do and it is the responsibility of the library media specialist
to see that the job is expeditiously accomplished.

Direct involvement of the school library media program in the instructional
process has changed the status of the library media specialist from passive spectator to active participant in the drama of teaching and learning. As study
hall monitor and book curator back in the days of the saber-toothed tiger curriculum, the school librarian was little more than "a hatcheck boy in the halls
of culture." Today's school library media specialist is a teacher in the broad-
est sense of the term—in training, in certification, in attitude, in function,
and in commitment. The responsibility of this position extends far beyond
organizing and maintaining a media collection, important and basic though
these services surely are. The major responsibility and prime function are
to implement the educational program by working directly with teachers to
facilitate and expedite their teaching and by working directly with students
to effectualize and enhance their learning.

*Kahlil Gibran, *The Prophet* (New York: Knopf, 1923, 1951), p. 56.

†James B. Macdonald, "An Image of Man: The Learner Himself," in *Individualizing Instruction*,
Association for Supervision and Curriculum Development Yearbook (Washington, D.C.: Association for Supervision and Curriculum Development, 1964), p. 42.

‡National Advisory Commission on Libraries, *Library Services for the Nation's Needs: Toward
Fulfillment of a National Policy* (Washington, D.C.: National Advisory Commission on Libraries,
1968), Foreword.

PROFILE OF THE LIBRARY MEDIA SPECIALIST

PERFORMANCE REQUISITES

Since the services of the library media program permeate the entire instructional process, the quality of leadership, guidance, and instruction provided by the library media specialist directly influences and affects the quality of the educational program. "The school library media specialist fills an active teaching role in the instructional program of the school";[1] therefore, the school library media specialist is a teacher in service. Inasmuch as "no educational program can be better than its teachers"[2] and because "one of the key factors in achieving our (national) goals (is) the quality of teaching,"[3] the quality of the library media specialist as a teacher is of grave importance.

What then is a quality library media specialist?* Above all a quality library media specialist is a competent and effective member of the teaching faculty who brings to this position:

Knowledge of teaching theories, methods, and practices

Knowledge of subject content and curriculum design and implementation

Knowledge of how to select, organize, administer, and utilize instructional media and equipment

Knowledge in depth of types and kinds of instructional media and media content

Knowledge of the science and art of communication

Knowledge of how to integrate the resources and services of the library media program with the ongoing instructional program

Knowledge of how to make instructional technology a viable art

The library media specialist holds membership in both the teaching and library professions, and is both an educational generalist and a media specialist. Respecting the duality of this professional role, the library media specialist places equal significance on each aspect, realizing that, like the two sides of a coin, neither role has value without the other.

TEACHING REQUISITES

As a teacher, the school library media specialist must bring to this position respect for the professional nature of the calling as set forth in the following definition found in Webster's *Third New International Dictionary:*

> *profession:* A calling requiring specialized knowledge and often long and intensive preparation including instruction in skills and methods as well as in the scientific, historical, or scholarly principles underlying such skills and methods, maintaining by force of organization or concerted opinion high standards of achievement and conduct, and committing its members to continued study and to a kind of work which has for its prime purpose the rendering of a public service.

*For a comprehensive survey of the basic knowledge and abilities required of a school library media specialist, see School Library Manpower Project, *Occupational Definitions for School Library Media Personnel* (Chicago: American Library Association, 1971); and Margaret E. Chisholm and Donald P. Ely, *Media Personnel in Education: A Competency Approach* (Englewood Cliffs, N.J.: Prentice-Hall, 1976).

A library media specialist of true professional stature will realize the necessity for continuous in-service study and growth and will possess the rigorous self-discipline essential for persistent self-directed knowledge building.

As a teacher, the school library media specialist must appreciate that teaching is both a science and an art and that the teacher must be original, inventive, and creative, not merely informed. William H. Burton in *The Guidance of Learning Activities* characterizes teaching as follows:

> Teaching is not a routine or rule-of-thumb process; it is a genuine intellectual adventure. . . . Teaching demands . . . the ability to adapt boldly, to invent, to create procedures to meet the ever changing demands of a given learning situation. Teaching demands continuous, imaginative anticipation of the mental processes of others, the ability to think quickly, to phrase questions and answers so as to stimulate thinking, the ability to keep intricate and subtle learning activities organized and moving toward a desirable outcome without at the same time dominating or coercing. Teaching necessitates a broad background of technological information.
>
> Teaching cannot possibly be done on the basis of common sense or experience alone. A surgeon could not possibly learn how to operate for appendicitis on the basis of common sense and raw experience. Engineers do not build tunnels from two sides of a mountain to meet squarely in the middle on the basis of common sense or raw trial and error. To do either of these things on the basis of common sense or experience alone would result in many deaths and in huge waste of money. These things are done successfully on the basis of lengthy, difficult professional training which includes a period of experience under guidance. Naturally, later experience and critical analysis of that experience play a large part in improving skill, but this experience and analysis are enlightened by the preparatory training in basic technology. Furthermore, there is demanded in addition the ability to make courageous adaptations of known procedures to unexpected conditions and unusual variations, and the ability to invent new procedures. So it is with teaching. A teacher can no more teach little children to read on the basis of her common sense or uncritical experience than can the surgeon operate or the engineer carry out projects. An even closer parallel can be drawn between the diagnosis of illness by the physician and the diagnosis of learning difficulty by the teacher.
>
> How then will the actual necessary skills be developed? Largely through the resolute critical analysis of one's own experience. This analysis is possible only with teachers who see clearly that teaching is in fact dynamic instead of static, an exciting intellectual enterprise, and whose self-analysis is illuminated by adequate general and technological background. Teaching, more than most human activities, demands the use of judgment, imagination, initiative, and enthusiasm. Particularly does it demand the use of freely working, creative imagination.[4]

The librarian who would serve as a teacher must respect and value teaching as an adventure of the spirit as well as an adventure of the mind.

Research has identified certain characteristics as basic for effective teaching. The school library media specialist must possess and demonstrate the following traits identified by Don Hamachek as basic:

1. They view teaching as basically—first and last—a human process. Such teachers have a sense of humor; they can empathize with students; they are fair; they are flexible; they are more democratic than autocratic; and they relate naturally and easily with pupils and peers. Their classrooms reflect an openness and a sense of mutual trust.
2. They feel good about themselves and they have a positive view of others. Thus, they identify with people rather than withdrawing from them. They feel adequate; they feel wanted; they are trustworthy, and they feel worthy in what they believe to be a significant human service.

3. They are knowledgeable and well informed on a wide range of subjects. They have a respect for knowledge, and they believe strongly that their pupils must also learn to respect it as a vital force in a happy and a productive life.
4. They are able to communicate effectively. They understand that the communication process includes more than presentation—it also provides for discovery and interaction with others as it provides for the development of personal meanings. They employ a comprehensive repertoire of teaching modes that produce affective as well as cognitive gains in their pupils.[5]

Although teaching is a multidimensional, multifaceted role, the basic all-encompassing role is instruction. Instruction is likewise the school library media specialist's *raison d'être*. *Instruction*, according to John Jarolimek and Clifford Foster, includes three generic roles:

1. Planning for learning and instruction
2. Facilitation of learning and instruction
3. Evaluation of learning and instruction[6]

APPLYING LEARNING PRINCIPLES

As a teacher directly involved in planning, facilitating, and evaluating instruction, the school library media specialist must understand and apply the principles undergirding the learning process. The following techniques are applied by the school library media specialist when planning and working with teachers and students:

1. *Motivating.*   Just as the textbook is not self-motivating and requires inspiration and guidance from the classroom teacher, so the card catalog and other library keys and resources lack motivational impact of and by themselves. The library media specialist is the motivational force that personalizes the services of the library media center and helps the student not only to see purpose in what is being done but also to know how to proceed with the learning task at hand.
2. *Minimizing Frustration.*   Realizing that assignments are frequently misunderstood, the library media specialist can minimize student frustration and waste of time and energy by helping the student to clarify the assignment or define the problem and then to determine the most efficient and effective method of proceeding.
3. *Providing Learning Guides.*   When planning with teachers, the library media specialist can suggest and/or help design learning guides, checklists, models, and evaluation forms. When working with students, the library media specialist can suggest the use of appropriate learning guides and other evaluation and summary forms, and can provide verbal guidance and cues that will facilitate student understanding and progress.
4. *Individualizing.*   When planning with the teacher, the library media specialist designs strategies for stimulating student interest, for encouraging student exploration, for accommodating student progress, rate, and learning style. When guiding students, the library media specialist maintains a climate conducive to student self-exploration, experimentation, and self-fulfillment.
5. *Evaluating.*   When planning with classroom teachers, the library media specialist can follow up library media center based learned experiences to discover their effectiveness. The library media specialist can encourage

students to evaluate the adequacy of accomplished tasks and then encourage them to strengthen noted weaknesses.

BECOMING INVOLVED IN THE INSTRUCTIONAL PROCESS

No longer is the library media specialist isolated from the drama of teaching and the business of learning. Whether the school program be organized for formal or informal teaming,* teacher–library media specialist cooperation is basic to actualizing an educational program of excellence. Direct communication and cooperation are the operational bases for meaningful, effective, and efficient integration of media center resources and service with the instructional program. The library media specialist isolated from the planning of instruction can never provide for teacher, class, group, or student the degree of effectiveness possible when preplanning and direct communication exist. Just as adequate preplanning is basic to effective classroom teaching, so is adequate preplanning essential to successful integration of the supportive resources, facilities, and services afforded by the school library media center. It is only logical that the library media specialist who is charged with the responsibility for implementing the instructional program be informed as to what is to be taught, when it is to be taught, in what sequence it is to be taught, to whom it is to be taught, with what it is to be taught, where it is to be taught, and with what anticipated results.

The library media specialist, when planning with one teacher, a group or committee of teachers, or a teaching team:

Determines the contribution the library media center is to make to the overall teaching plan (see Chapter 6).

Determines specific teaching objectives to be accomplished through the use of library media center resources and guidance (see Chapter 6).

Identifies basic concepts and skills to be introduced, reinforced, or extended (see Chapter 6).

Structures learning guides; reading, viewing, listening checklists; summary forms; reaction charts; critical evaluation scorecards; etc.

Determines appropriateness of assignments and the availability of suitable materials: filmstrips, motion pictures, slides, videotapes, transparencies, art prints, study prints, graphics, maps, charts, recordings, realia, resource kits, etc. (see Chapters 6 and 7).

Sets target dates for each phase of the library media center support program.

Designs specific teaching strategies requiring library media center support (see Chapters 6 and 7).

Designs specific learning experiences and activities requiring library resources (see Chapters 6 and 7).

Designs specific unit and support activities (see Chapters 6 and 7).

Designs strategies for meeting student needs, interests, goals, abilities, progress rate, concerns, and potential (see Chapters 6 and 7).

---

*Multiple copies of Richard Darling's monograph *Teams for Better Education: The Teacher and The Librarian* are available at no cost on request from the Garrard Publishing Company, Champaign, Ill. 61820.

Identifies specific media uniquely appropriate for each of the teaching and learning designs (see Chapters 6 and 7).

Designs appropriate culminating teaching and learning activities (see Chapter 6).

Designs appropriate evaluating activities to determine the effectiveness of the library media center support program (see Chapter 6).

A step-by-step procedure to be followed when teachers and library media specialists sit down to preplan instructional support activities is developed in Chapter 6.

HUMANIZING INSTRUCTION

As teachers, library media specialists must bring to their position authentic respect and genuine concern for the individuality of students. They must understand that each learner is a unique and complex blend of myriad physical, intellectual, emotional, social, cultural, and environmental factors. No matter how homogeneous the community, whether it be ghetto or affluent suburb, the student body is made up of individuals with:

Varying family patterns and relationships	Varying degrees of receptivity to learning
Varying cultural backgrounds	Varying degrees of creativity
Varying social backgrounds	Varying degrees of skill attainment
Varying environmental influences	Varying intellectual capacities
Varying degrees of sensitivity	Varying cognitive styles
Varying degrees of incentive	Varying perception patterns
Varying degrees of drive	Varying emotional patterns
Varying degrees of awareness	Varying reaction patterns
Varying degrees of stability	Varying interests, goals, and aspirations

The library media specialist has the professional obligation to deal realistically but humanely with each student and to provide learning resources and to design learning experiences that will be compatible with the needs, interests, abilities, goals, concerns, and learning styles of each individual student.

The library media specialist must be accessible, approachable, and responsive; must establish a climate conducive to maximum learning—a warm, happy, inviting place where students may taste success, where their disabilities are not on public display, where they can work at their own speed, in their own private way, and where there is a rich reservoir of appropriate media readily available. The library media specialist, valuing the individuality of the students, realizes that the library media center serves as an avenue of escape from the pressures of impersonal, mass education. Here students can choose their own areas of specialization, define their own limits, and set their own pace; here they are in competition only with themselves, and the pressures of group, class, and ability competition are mercifully absent; here students can find an outlet for their own interests, inventiveness, and creativity; here they can bring substance to their dreams, their love of poetry, music, drama, art;

here they can improvise, experiment, and explore without fear of ridicule from peers.

Library media specialists who would humanize their teaching must personalize the services of the library media center. They must hold and demonstrate authentic concern for the intellectual, moral, spiritual, social, and cultural well-being of each student no matter how rich or how poor, how brilliant or how dull. They must consistently build their knowledge of the students, not by studying IQ and achievement scores, but by face-to-face communication with students as they work with them as mentors, counselors, and friends. Library media specialists who would personalize and humanize the services of the library media center must have as their constant goal the desire to make learning to learn in the library media center a totally satisfying experience. (Humanizing instruction is further explored and developed in Chapter 4.)

Library media specialists who would serve effectively as teachers must be self-motivated by a continuous compelling zest for learning. They must regard their service as a creative challenge—a never-ending quest for added understanding and deepened insight. They must possess an infectious enthusiasm for learning that permeates their work with teachers and students. They must derive satisfaction from exploring the new, the untried, the unfamiliar, as well as from uncovering in the familiar something new, significant, and unsuspected. They must possess an insatiable curiosity about the hidden value and potential utility of every library resource. They must value media not as things but as ideas, delighting in searching for, identifying, analyzing, grouping, and organizing ideas into patterns of logical, cohesive interrelatedness. They must derive stimulation and satisfaction from the realization that their work is never done: New materials must be searched for and evaluated; old materials must be reevaluated in the light of current needs; new curricular trends, content, and methods must be studied and reflected in the library program; new faculty and students must be welcomed and their interests and concerns discovered and translated into commensurate patterns of library support service. Library media specialists who elect to serve in an educational environment should be capable of finding challenge and satisfaction in learning and in helping others to learn. They must view their service as an adventure of the mind and of the spirit, a demanding but rewarding adventure in creative self-realization, self-expression, and professional self-fulfillment.

NOTES

1. School Library Manpower Project, *Occupational Definitions for School Library Personnel* (Chicago: American Library Association, 1971), p. 10.
2. *The Pursuit of Excellence: Education and the Future of America*, America at Mid-Century Series, Special Studies Project Report V, Rockefeller Brothers Fund (Garden City, N.Y.: Doubleday, 1957), p. 23.
3. Paul R. Hanna, ed., *Education: An Instrument of National Goals* (New York: McGraw-Hill, 1962), p. 22.
4. William H. Burton, *The Guidance of Learning Activities: A Summary of the Principles of Teaching Based on the Growth of the Learner*, 3rd ed. (New York: Appleton-Century-Crofts, Educational Division, Meredith Corp., 1962), pp. 267–268. Reprinted by permission of Prentice-Hall, Inc.
5. Hamachek in John Jarolimek and Clifford D. Foster, *Teaching and Learning in the Elementary School* (New York: Macmillan, 1976), pp. 31–32.
6. Ibid., p. 44.

6 The Curriculum Support Role of the Library Media Specialist

The tasks I have suggested for the librarian require a person with high-level professional training. They make the library an educational environment for maximal learning. They require a librarian who understands the broader range of materials of instruction now available and who is sensitive to the total curriculum of the school.

Edgar Dale*

It is good to learn how to learn, but what do you learn after you have learned how to learn?

Edgar Dale†

It is very easy for enthusiastic curriculum developers to climb on the bandwagon of new educational approaches without giving due consideration to their implementability in the existing school framework.

Chew Tow Yow‡

Traditionally, from the days of the one-room school, the textbook and the teacher determined what would and what would not be taught in the classroom. During the forties and fifties the extremists in progressive education were being heard and heeded; this "happiness cult" frowned on intellectualism as a primary educational goal. Indeed, America was not ready to stress seriousness of purpose in content design until Russia launched its first successful Sputnik in 1957. Seeing Russia's scientific superiority in the field of space alarmed and acutely embarrassed Americans. The man in the street raised the question, "Is America lagging behind Russia in her educational program as well as in her space program?" This question was followed by a second, "Is it not time to evaluate critically what we are doing educationally, and then immediately set about strengthening the educational program on all levels?"

Jerome Bruner, Harvard professor of educational psychology, distressed at the aimlessness of American education, advocated scientific planning of curriculum in his book *The Process of Education* published in 1960.[1] So influential has this book proven to be that Charles Silberman, director of the Carnegie Foundation, acclaims it "the most influential contemporary work on curriculum."[2]

Bruner advocates that the scientific design and structure of the educational program provide "continuity, unity, balance and harmony" in the total educational experience. He recommends that the teaching and learning processes continually broaden and deepen knowledge in terms of basic and general ideas. This requires written courses of study for each discipline that identify

*Edgar Dale, "Educating for Flexibility," *ALA Bulletin* 57, no. 2 (Feb. 1963): 134.
†Edgar Dale, *Building a Learning Environment* (Bloomington, Ind.: Phi Delta Kappa, 1972), p. 80.
‡Chew Tow Yow, "Evaluation at the Planning Stage," in *Handbook of Curriculum Evaluation*, ed. by Arieh Lewy (Paris: UNESCO, 1977 and New York: Longman, 1977), p. 72.

"the pervading and powerful ideas and attitudes."[3] The educational program, he states, must be designed to introduce and reintroduce at each grade level the appropriate fundamentals. And the entire program must be organized so as to relate the parts to the whole, for "unless detail is placed into a structural pattern [of interrelatedness] it is rapidly forgotten."[4] The key to retrieval is organization. An educational program of excellence is so designed and structured ever to broaden, ever to widen, ever to relate, and ever to extend understanding through a logical progression of interlocking, cohesive, and mutually supportive experiences. So influential has Jerome Bruner's *The Process of Education* been that it has been translated into 21 languages, with the Russians being the first to seize on it. The sale in Japan has been enormous, and it is also available in Hebrew and Arabic.[5]

Planning for meaningful curricular change at the school district level is a professional way of life. The tempo of curriculum revision must match the rate of societal change. There is too much that needs to be taught and too much that must be learned to permit the worshipful continuance of the educational status quo. Heeding the warning of the historian Arnold Toynbee that "the nemesis of creativity is the idolization of an ephemeral technique,"[6] the competent educator thoughtfully discards the outmoded when better ways of meeting the needs of society and the future needs of citizens in that society are discovered. Planning for meaningful change is a professional way of life, for "competency in teaching is not possible at all without an ardent desire to grow and to improve both personally and in professional knowledge and skill; willingness to give up easy, well-known routines; willingness to study the new and go through the arduous and difficult process of learning new ways."[7]

THE LIBRARY MEDIA SPECIALIST IN CURRICULUM DESIGN, IMPLEMENTATION, AND EVALUATION

Direct involvement of the library media specialist in each phase of curriculum development—study, revision, implementation, and evaluation—is to be expected by the building principal and by the chief school administrator and welcomed by the library media specialist. Such involvement is clearly implied by the following contemporary definition of the term *curriculum:*

> the *curriculum* is considered to encompass the instructional activities planned and provided for pupils by the school or school system. The curriculum, therefore, is the planned interaction of pupils with instructional *content*, instructional *resources*, and instructional *processes* for the attainment of educational objectives.[8]

Resources are the library media specialist's stock in trade; bringing depth, breadth, and relevance to instructional *content* is the library media specialist's unique contribution to the teaching and learning program; and designing and implementing instructional *processes* are two of the library media specialist's specialized competencies; therefore, the library media specialist is a key figure and has a major role in curriculum development.

The International Institute for Educational Planning designed its publication *Handbook of Curriculum Evaluation* "to meet the needs of experts working on the planning and evaluation of curriculum throughout the world."[9]

In this basic handbook, curriculum development activities are identified as follows:

1. Identification and formulation of instructional objectives
2. Specification of the scope and sequence of the content of instruction
3. Selection of teaching-learning strategies
4. Development of instructional materials[10]

Again, these curricular activities mandate the direct involvement of the library media specialist in each phase of curriculum development.

BASIC UNDERSTANDINGS FOR CURRICULUM SUPPORT

In order to serve competently as a curriculum design and support agent the library media specialist must have a working knowledge of the basic ingredients of the instructional program: philosophy, goals, objectives, curricular guidelines for each discipline, methods, trends, and evaluative procedure and criteria (see Terminology section at end of this book). In addition to these basics, the library media specialist must be aware of emerging areas of educational emphasis and concern and be able to answer these questions:

1. What are the National Education Association's guidelines for curriculum change as we approach the 21st century? (See "The Seven Cardinal Principles Reinterpreted" and "Cardinal Principles for Educational Change, 1976–2001" in Chapter 2.)
2. How can we individualize, humanize, and personalize instruction? (See "Teaching Toward Inquiry," "Nurturing Creativity," "Instructional Relevance," and "Stressing Values" in Chapter 4.)
3. How can we translate the "Thinking-Learning-Communicating Skills Continuum" into workable instructional teaching and learning experiences? (See Chapter 12 and Appendix L.)
4. How can we provide for continuity, unity, balance, and harmony in the total instructional program, K–12?
5. How can we translate state-mandated programs into instructional programs that directly reflect the unique characteristics and developmental needs of the instructional program; of the students, individually and collectively; and of the community?

WHAT KNOWLEDGE

The purpose of the school in our democracy has been the transmission of knowledge to the young. "Yet, despite this long-standing responsibility, it would be difficult to demonstrate that the school has handled this task well . . . and that their curricula deal effectively with significant and powerful ideas."[11] Edgar Dale, educational philosopher and master teacher, has provided a comprehensive answer to the persistent question "What is worth knowing?" in his essay by the same title, which he included in his essay collection *Building a Learning Environment.*[12]

> Every teacher and every producer and user of materials of instruction must face the perennial and perplexing question: What is worth knowing? By knowledge I mean information, skills, and attitudes incorporated into one's intellectual and emotional habits, mastered and retained by continuing use. . . .

The learning that is of the most worth enables us to get a sense of our individual and social identity—who we are, what we care about, and what we can do. . . .

That knowledge is of most worth which enables a person to do the best that he can, to be fulfilled. The knowledge especially to be prized enables a person to live close to the upper limits of his physical, mental, and emotional powers. . . .

That knowledge is of most worth which generates knowledge. It does this by extending what we already know, by deepening and refining it. . . .

That knowledge is of most worth that enables us to work efficiently and effectively in the organization and application of ideas.

That knowledge is of the most worth which enables us to see the wholeness of our life—the system that is at work whether we realize it or not. . . .

Many studies show that additional time spent on reflection, on thinking about what we have read, heard, seen, or done, is highly profitable, hence the importance of that knowledge which helps us organize, classify, pattern, structure, rearrange, reconstruct, synthesize, and conceptualize what we know. . . .

That knowledge is best which can be learned. . . .

That knowledge is of most worth which enables us to tell the difference between fact and opinion, evidence and propaganda, and the logical and the illogical. This means that schools and colleges need to place heavy emphasis on methods and materials of instruction in critical reading, critical listening, and critical observing. . . .

That knowledge is of high worth which enables students to communicate effectively in reading and writing, speaking and listening, and visualizing and observing. . . .

That knowledge is of most worth which enables us to share ideas with others. . . . The ability to speak well and to listen thoughtfully is paramount in this society. . . .

That knowledge is of most worth which contributes a sense of joy, exhilaration, and poignancy to the life of the learner. . . . The mind illuminates the way, and the heart helps push us ahead on our journey. . . .

That knowledge is of most worth that enables persons and societies to know where it hurts, and know what to do not only to relieve the pain, but also to cure it. Many now try to relieve their pain by thoughtless nonconformity which may turn out to be simply conformity to another point of view. . . .

That knowledge is of most worth which enables an individual to see cause-and-effect relationships between his choices and their consequences, a characteristic of a moral man. Besides asking what happened, people need to ask why it happened, what will happen next, and what difference, if any, that it makes. . . . In other words, the knowledge of most worth is that which enables people to be foresighted in their thinking, to predict the consequences of their choices, and, when necessary, to change their course of action.

That knowledge is of most worth which helps individuals recognize knowledge that is of most worth. This means learning to judge values, and to recognize the difference between the permanent and the ephemeral, the important and the trivial, and the rational and the irrational.

In a world brimming with new knowledge it is not enough to ask whether learning has worth. We must ask rather: what learning is of *most* worth? That knowledge is of most worth which enhances the dignity of persons. To dignify man is to honor, to exalt, to make worthy. It is easy to say this, but to translate it into reality is today's great challenge.

In assigning knowledge priorities, Dale places top priority on self-realization of the student rather than on informational content. Using his guidelines in designing, structuring, implementing, and evaluating curriculum will move education from the saber-toothed tiger days of subject matter concentration to the innovative, 21st-century concept of creating warm, strong school experiences and relationships that will "increase the odds that the learner will be able to live a satisfying, contributive life both in school and in the future."[13] The school library media specialist shares with the classroom teacher the responsibility for translating Dale's guidelines into day-to-day instruction practice.

District Curriculum Study Council

Traditionally, planning the education program has been the responsibility of the local school district. Some states recommend or mandate general course requirements but delegate to local school districts the responsibility for determining course organization and content. All too frequently in the past the local district relied on the textbook as the course of study, letting the contents of the textbook determine what was to be taught in any subject at any grade level. Contemporary concern for excellence requires that the educational program be planned and structured to provide unity, continuity, balance, and harmony in the total program, kindergarten through grade 12. It is increasingly common for local school districts to develop their own comprehensive curriculum guides and to involve their teachers and library media specialists in each phase of curricular study and design.

It is recommended practice that each school district organize an ongoing, district-wide curriculum study and renewal program. Since library media specialists are directly involved in curriculum study and development on both the district and the school building levels, it is essential that they have a working knowledge of how such a district program operates. The basic administrative unit responsible for directing curriculum development is usually the district curriculum council or curriculum steering committee, which is appointed by the chief school administrator and is organized as follows:

I. Membership in the curriculum council includes
   A. Chief school administrator or assistant
   B. Directors of elementary and secondary curriculum
   C. Supervisors, coordinators, and department chairmen (including the supervisors of library media services)
   D. Representatives of elementary and secondary building principals
   E. Representatives of elementary and secondary faculties (including library media specialists)
   F. Representatives of the teachers' organization
   G. Representatives of the school board
   H. Representatives of parent and community organizations
II. Major responsibilities of the curriculum council include
   A. Coordinating all district curricular and instructional programs
   B. Recommending basic policy changes to the chief school administrator
   C. Providing leadership in defining district philosophy, goals, and objectives
   D. Planning and implementing the district in-service study and growth program
   E. Blueprinting a district long-range developmental program and setting priorities to implement it
   F. Organizing subject-area curriculum committees
   G. Preparing a district routine and policy handbook or manual

The responsibility for revising and restructuring courses of study is delegated by the chief school administrator to the subject-area curriculum committees.

These committees are chaired by the department head or chairman from each subject area. A library media specialist can anticipate being asked to serve as a contributing member of each subject-area committee. In addition to participating in course analysis, evaluation, revision, and redesign, the library media specialist is frequently called on to provide the following special services for the subject-area committee:

    I. Supplying basic curricular guides, checklists, criteria, and outlines such as
        A. Criteria for Developing and Evaluating Curriculum Guides (see Chapter 8)
        B. Outline of a Resource Unit (see Appendix D)
        C. Guide for Constructing Mini-Courses (see Appendix E)
        D. Elementary Reading Interest Inventory (see Appendix J)
        E. Thinking-Learning-Communicating Skills Continuum (see Appendix L)
        F. Criteria for Selection of Instructional Materials (see Chapter 7 and Appendix H)
        G. Citizen's Request Form for Reevaluation of Materials (see Chapter 8 and Appendix B)
        H. Criteria for Selection of Curriculum Packages (see Chapter 7)
    II. Obtaining sample courses of study
    III. Obtaining sample resource units (see Appendix D)
    IV. Obtaining for committee consideration professional publications and research studies germane to topics being discussed and explored
    V. Obtaining for committee consideration resources to support new curricular areas of emphasis
    VI. Obtaining for committee consideration sample textbooks to match new curricular areas of emphasis
    VII. Helping to design learning guides to facilitate the integration of skills in new courses of study
    VIII. Helping to design pilot studies to test operationally new content, new techniques, new procedures, new media, and new organizational patterns
    IX. Helping to design library-based units for those curricular areas which demand resources, facilities, equipment, and guidance beyond that available in the classroom
    X. Helping to design optional learning experiences and alternative roads to be followed in achieving behavioral objectives

The library media specialist is not only called on to provide fellow committee members with curricular guides and instructional media but is also directly involved in all aspects of designing, structuring, and testing courses of study. One of the most common and most demanding curricular enterprises is building resource units—these are the backbone of the district's instructional program. The quality of the resource unit in large measure predetermines the resultant quality of the teaching unit. Therefore, it is important that the library media specialist clearly understand the significance, scope, and plan of both kinds of units.

Resource units may properly be thought of as collections of suggested teaching materials and activities organized around large topics such as "Health," "Recreation," "Transportation," and "Conservation." They are frequently prepared by committees of teachers, curriculum workers, state department of education, graduate classes, workshops, institutes, or commercial agencies. Resource units are not developed with any particular group of children in mind. . . . They cover broad areas of content and always contain more information and suggestions than could be used with any one class. Since they represent general rather than specific procedures, they suggest a variety of ways of achieving the same goal. In a very real sense, resource units should serve as a source of material and suggestions for the teacher when he is planning his teaching unit. The teacher may draw from the resource unit what is appropriate in terms of a specific situation and a particular group of children [see Appendix D].[14]

Teaching units differ from resource units in several respects. Ordinarily, the teacher preparing the unit has a specific group of children in mind and has at his disposal a wealth of information about their abilities, interests, levels of reading, special weaknesses, and strengths. The teaching unit is planned in terms of those known characteristics of the particular class which will be involved in the unit. The topic under study in teaching units is not as broad as it is in resource units. While resource units are general in nature, teaching units are specific.[15]

If resource units are field-tested before being incorporated in the course of study, the library media specialist will be directly involved in each phase of the pilot study from inception to evaluation.

DESIGNING TEACHING STRATEGIES AND LEARNING EXPERIENCES FOR NEW STATE-MANDATED PROGRAMS

Frequently state departments of education mandate areas of curricular and/or subject development, inclusion, and emphasis. The state supplies guidelines of a general nature, but delegates to the local district the responsibility for developing the courses of study and/or specific curricular experiences that carry out the state mandate. One such mandated area of concern and emphasis that has been introduced in the last few years is law-related education. In 1974, the Pennsylvania Department of Education declared legal education a curriculum priority and distributed to each school district a list of law-related competencies to be incorporated into each district's instructional program. In the introduction to the competency list, the secretary of education stated, ". . . it is hoped that these competencies will offer a unified core around which individual districts can build the many available resources into their own curriculum offerings."[16]

The first task assigned the curriculum study group for the elementary social studies in a Pennsylvania school district was to scrutinize the existing courses of study to discover appropriate opportunities for integrating law-related competencies. For example, the state list of law-related competencies included: identify how laws are made and changed; discriminate between civil, criminal, and regulatory laws; relate instances where behavior of small groups such as gangs may conflict with what society deems acceptable behavior; and, provided with case studies involving personal and property rights, propose and substantiate a solution. The curriculum committee asked the library media specialist to search out case studies that might be considered for inclusion in the fifth-grade curriculum. Knowing the fifth-grade social studies program, the library media specialist recommended that the committee consider using the book *Mustang: Wild Spirit of the West* by Marguerite Henry as a case study of law enactment when the fifth-grade students were studying the unit "California and the West." Despite the fictional ring of the title, *Mustang* is a factual biography of Annie Johnston who led the legislative fight to save the wild mustangs from extinction. Her fight, which began with the Arizona state legislature, ended in Congress with the passage of H.R. 2725, a regulatory law forbidding the killing of wild mustangs on the public range lands. The committee read the book, was delighted with the wealth of information on how a citizen can become directly involved in the lawmaking process on the state and federal levels, and asked the library media specialist to build a Law and Justice Pilot Project (see Example 1) based on the use of *Mustang* as a case study. The Pilot Project Procedural Outline is included here as Example 3.

EXAMPLE 1 LAW AND JUSTICE PILOT PROJECT INTEGRATION ACTIVITIES*

Grade: 5

Unit: California and the West

Case Study: How a citizen can become directly involved in the lawmaking process on the state and federal levels.

Purpose: To provide a significant, relevant, and appealing learning experience that will dramatize the citizen's role in lawmaking.

Procedure:

    I. A group of students will read *Mustang: Wild Spirit of the West* by Marguerite Henry (Rand McNally, 1966). This biography of Annie Johnston will serve as a case study of how a citizen led the legislative fight to protect the wild mustang from extinction.

        A. Following the reading of the biography, the group will share with the class the understandings it has gained concerning the following concepts:

            1. In a democracy elected representatives are answerable to the voters.

                Evidence:

                "The everyday people are lawmakers." p. 115

                "We must trust the people, the everyday people, Annie, THEY are the law-makers." p. 117

                "Mr. Baring is not just a name in the paper or a picture on a poster. He's a friend. MY FRIEND! My very own voice in Washington."

            2. Public opinion is a powerful influence on lawmakers.

                Evidence:

                "It might be YOUR letter to YOUR Congressman that will help save the mustang." p. 169

                "Write to your Congressman. . . . Ask your friends to write, too. Let's unite in outrage, unite as Americans until the lawmakers are swamped with a sea of mail." pp. 178–179

                "Letters from the People" pages. p. 126

            3. Newspaper editorials are effective in influencing lawmakers.

                Evidence:

                "Passenger pigeons used to darken the heavens with their numbers. They and the buffalo were slaughtered by the millions. For what? For blood money, that's what! The American people will never recover from the shame of it." Lucius Beebe's editorial in the ENTERPRISE. p. 126

            4. Making money prompts some businessmen to argue against protecting America's natural resources.

                Evidence:

                "What have the wild horses done to deserve butchery and mass extinction? The mustangers who make a living at it are savages. They enjoy being filth at 5 cents a pound for live horseflesh!" p. 127

                "We at the ENTERPRISE demand passage of the mustang bill. The only opposition it can possibly provoke is greed, brutality, and a total contempt for wildlife." p. 127

*This Pilot Project was developed by Shirley A. Pittman, Coordinator of Library Services, North Hills School District, Pittsburgh, Pa. 15229.

EXAMPLE 1 (cont.)

5. In America even the children can be heard in the state and federal legislatures.
   Evidence:
   "The Power of Children" pp. 166–179
6. The statue of Justice is frequently portrayed as a woman who is blindfolded
   and holds a sword in one hand and a scale in the other.
   Evidence:
   "Without justice and fairness we are hopelessly lost." p. 202

   "Compassion is mightier than money." p. 168

B. The group will reenact for the class the congressional hearing on H.R. 2725 at
   which Mrs. Annie Johnston gave testimony. pp. 197–218
C. The class as a culminating activity will summarize their learning by defining and
   discussing the following terms:

1. "blood money"
2. congressional committees
3. congressional hearings
4. evidence: historical
   pictorial
   statistical
5. justice vs. injustice

6. "Letters to the Editor" column
7. newspaper editorials
8. petitions
9. public opinion
10. role of the district attorney and judge
11. testimony
12. witnesses

II. Reinforcement and extension of the basic concepts presented in the case study.
   A. Other citizens have successfully influenced state and federal legislators to pass
      laws protecting American wildlife and natural resources.
      1. Scotty Philip was instrumental in getting H.R. 13542 passed in 1906, which set
         aside 3,500 acres of public land for a buffalo pasture.
         By 1900 only a few hundred buffalo existed. It was estimated that by 1910
         they would have disappeared entirely.

         It has been estimated that in the period from 1800 to 1900, the buffalo popu-
         lation had been reduced from 40,000,000 to only a few hundred.

         Scotty Philip gathered together a small herd and cared for them. Because
         he cared he alerted his friends in Congress to the plight of the buffalo, and
         largely through his efforts the buffalo was saved from extinction.
      SOURCE: *The Buffalo King: The Story of Scotty Philip* by Nancy Veglahn (Scribner
               1971).
      2. John Muir led the fight to create national parks to preserve America's forests
         and natural wonders.
         Through articles and speeches he told the nation that the lumber industry was
         destroying a priceless heritage.

         His first two articles in the national magazine *Century*, "Treasures of the
         Yosemite" and "Features of the Proposed Yosemite National Park," pub-
         lished in 1890, created a furious debate between those who wanted to safe-
         guard the forests and the miners, loggers, and herdsmen who wanted to
         exploit the forests for profit.

         Muir became a target of a newspaper smear campaign (see *John Muir:
         Prophet among the Glaciers* by Robert Silverberg, pp. 197–198).

         As a result of Muir's talks with President Theodore Roosevelt, 148,000,000
         acres of national forests were created and the number of national parks was
         doubled.
      SOURCE: *John Muir: Protector of the Wilds* by Madge Haines and Leslie Morrill
               (Abingdon Press 1957).

               John Muir: Father of Our National Parks by Charles Norman (Messner
               1957).

               John Muir: Prophet among the Glaciers by Robert Silverberg (Putnam
               1972).

   B. Annie Johnston organized the International Society for the Protection of Mustangs
      and Burros to help her gain public support in her battle to save the mustang.

EXAMPLE 1 (cont.)

1. In 1974 a group of slaughter houses in Idaho began a series of aerial roundups of wild horses to be processed as pet food.
2. Currently petitions are being circulated by the International Society for the Protection of Mustangs and Burros, 140 Greenstone Drive, Reno, Nevada 89502.
   The class, if interested, should write to this society asking for official petitions to stop this slaughter and also for current information about the plight of the mustang and burros.
C. The Animal Protection Institute of America, P.O. Box 22505, Sacramento, California 95822, is actively engaged in an educational and legislative program to prevent cruelty to animals.
   1. The class, if interested, should write to this society and ask for information concerning its program.
   2. If, when the information is received, the students wish to become involved in the society's work, they can take the responsibility for circulating petitions and sending them to the society's headquarters.

Another curricular mandate legislated by state departments of education in the past few years is that each school district will develop differentiated programs for gifted and talented students. Basic forms taken by programs for the gifted and talented are: (1) enrichment of content, (2) acceleration of content, (3) individualization of instruction, (4) a modified open-ended curriculum, and (5) special goal-directed programs to develop and/or foster such diverse aspects of giftedness as creativity, critical thinking, evaluative thinking, leadership, etc. The organization of the programs may include: full-time regular classes; part-time separate classes; individualized tutorial sessions; laboratory-based learning projects; honors classes; advanced placement classes; and seminars.

An instructional program encompassing enrichment and acceleration of content, individualization of instruction, open-ended curriculum, and critical, creative, evaluative thinking requires the direct involvement of the library media specialist in curriculum planning and implementation. As Florence Cleary stated in her book *Blueprints for Better Reading*, "Nowhere in the school is there to be found a more promising situation for the academically gifted . . . than in the library."[17] The classroom teacher with gifted students in a heterogeneous class welcomes the opportunity to plan with the library media specialist to bring greater depth, breadth, relevance, and challenge to the instructional program by expanding that program with enrichment and acceleration learning experiences based on library media center resources and guidance.* A sample list of research-based enrichment/acceleration learning experiences is included in Example 2, Mexico: Its History, Its Land, and Its People.

When the school district elects to have a separate program for gifted and talented students, the school library media specialists on both the elementary and the secondary level must be involved in course design, pilot testing, and evaluation. Figure 2, Pilot Projects, and Example 3, Pilot Project Design and Analysis Guide, are useful tools for facilitating program design, field testing,

---

*A comprehensive source for instructional programs for the gifted and the talented involving the integration of the resources and services of the library media center is Corinne Clendening and Ruth A. Davies, *Creating Programs for the Gifted: A Guide for Teachers, Librarians, and Students* (New York: R. R. Bowker, 1980).

EXAMPLE 2 MEXICO—ITS HISTORY, ITS LAND, AND ITS PEOPLE

Enrichment/Acceleration Topics
Grade: 6
Unit: Mexico: Its History, Its Land, and Its People
Project Goals:

To bring greater depth, breadth, and relevance to the study of Mexico

To provide opportunity for the student to understand, to appreciate, and to respect the Mexican people—their history, their culture, their literature, their manners and customs, their arts, their music, their government, and their social and economic problems

Possible Research Topics:

1. Acapulco
2. Adobe
3. Agriculture
4. Alamo
5. Aleman, Miguel
6. Anguiano, Lupe
7. Animals
8. Archeological Discoveries
9. Architecture
10. Artists
11. Arts
12. Aztecs
13. Banking and Currency
14. Bartolome, Friar
15. Borda, Jose de la
16. Border Patrol
17. Callen, Plutarco
18. Cardenas, Lazaro
19. Carlota, Empress
20. Castellanos, Julio
21. Cathedrals
22. Ceramics
23. Chavez, Carlos
24. Chicanos
25. Chicle
26. Cities
27. Clothing
28. Commerce and Industry
29. Communications
30. Cooking
31. Cortes, Hernando
32. Covarrubias, Miguel
33. Cowboys
34. Crafts
35. Cuauhtemoc
36. Cuernavaca
37. Dance
38. Diaz, Porfirio
39. Drama and the Theater
40. Education
41. Engineering
42. Exports and Imports
43. Family Life
44. Fiestas and Holidays
45. Fishing
46. Flag
47. Floating Gardens
48. Folklore and Legends
49. Geographic Features
50. Government and Politics
51. Guadalajara
52. Guadalupe Shrine
53. Health and Medicine
54. Hidalgo, Father Miguel
55. History
56. Houston, Sam
57. Indians
58. Ines, Juana
59. Inventions
60. Iturbide, Augustin de
61. Itzcoatl
62. Josefa, Dona
63. Juarez, Benito
64. Lakes
65. Languages
66. Law and Justice
67. Libraries
68. Literature
69. Lorenzo, Agustin
70. Machu Picchu
71. Madero, Francisco
72. Manners and Customs
73. Markets
74. Maximilian, Emperor
75. Mayas
76. Mestizos
77. Mexican-Americans
78. Mexican War
79. Mexico City
80. Minerals
81. Montezuma
82. Morelos, Jose
83. Museums
84. Music
85. Narcotics
86. National Anthem
87. Natural Resources
88. Obregon, Alvaro
89. Orozco, Jose
90. Pan American Highway
91. Paseo de la Reforma
92. Petroleum
93. Plants
94. Posada

EXAMPLE 2 (cont.)

Possible Research Topics (cont.):

95. Pueblo
96. Pyramid in Yucatan
97. Recreation and Sports
98. Relations between Mexico and the United States
99. Religion
100. Rivera, Diego
101. Santa Anna, Antonio Lopez de
102. Science and Technology
103. Sierra Madre
104. Stamps
105. Standard of Living
106. Status of Women
107. Student Exchange Program
108. Tarascans

109. Taxco
110. Textiles
111. Toltecs
112. Transportation
113. UNICEF in Mexico
114. United Nations Membership
115. University City
116. Veracruz
117. Villa, "Pancho"
118. Village Life
119. Volcanoes
120. "Wetbacks"
121. Yucatan
122. Zapata, Emiliano

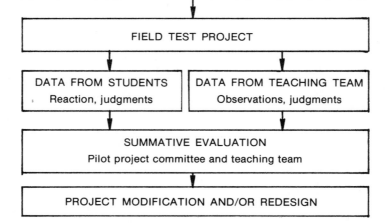

EXPERIMENTAL TEACHING-LEARNING PROJECT
FOR THE GIFTED AND TALENTED PROGRAM

PRELIMINARY PROJECT DESIGN
(Pilot Project Committee)
Goals, objectives, content, skills, products, evaluative criteria

TEACHING TEAM INPUT
Delete/expand/clarify goals and objectives
Define content specifics: concepts, processes, topics, terms
Design teaching-learning strategies, alternatives, guides
Selecting and programming use of instructional media

FIELD TEST PROJECT

DATA FROM STUDENTS
Reaction, judgments

DATA FROM TEACHING TEAM
Observations, judgments

SUMMATIVE EVALUATION
Pilot project committee and teaching team

PROJECT MODIFICATION AND/OR REDESIGN

FIGURE 2. Pilot Projects

EXAMPLE 3 PILOT PROJECT DESIGN AND ANALYSIS GUIDE

Project Title _____

Teachers Involved _____

School _____ Grade Levels _____

Number of Students Involved _____

Number of Class Periods Required _____

Project Began _____ Project Ended _____

Project Goals:

Project Objectives:

Project Content:
    Concepts—

       Persons—

       Places—

       Things—

       Events—

       Processes—

       Terminology—

       Skills—

       Attitudes—

       Appreciations—

       Judgments—

Teaching-Learning Strategies:
    Orientation procedures—

       Motivational procedures—

       Group interaction procedures—

EXAMPLE 3 (cont.)

Divergent thinking experiences—

Culminating activities—

Teaching-Learning Guides:

Field Experiences:

Instructional Media:
    Print—

    Nonprint—

Resource People:

Project Evaluation:
    Student Reactions—

    Teacher Observations—

    Teacher Concerns and Reservations—

    Teacher Recommendations—

Teacher's Signature _____ Date _____

EXAMPLE 4 LEARNING PROJECT: ORIENTATION TO THE GATE PROGRAM*

Grade: 6

Project Goals:

To orient the students to the purpose, scope, and value of the sixth-grade GATE Program

To sharpen and refine the students' ability to think creatively

To extend the students' awareness that the GATE Program is an effective means of self-discovery and self-realization

Teaching Objectives:

This project has been designed and structured to provide learning experiences that will enable the student:

To explore the concept of self-actualization

To experiment with creative and adventurous thinking

To discover new dimensions, greater satisfaction, and challenge in learning to learn

To perceive and value the contributions others have made as a result of creative, adventurous thinking

To perceive and value the school library as a laboratory for self-discovery and self-actualization

Teaching Strategies and Methods:

No time limits are imposed on this project. Number of students and student interest are the two factors that determine the duration of this GATE project and subsequent projects whether the time be two weeks, two months, or longer

A basic part of orienting the students to the GATE Program is to provide an overview of possible group and individual learning experiences. Administering the Interest Inventory and identifying areas of individual student interest can serve as an effective means of individualizing GATE learning experiences

Each student should be encouraged to explore areas of special interest and to suggest individual and/or group learning experiences

Procedural Outline:

I. Group orientation to and overview of the GATE Program

   A. Why a GATE Program?

      1. The GATE Program will provide challenging learning experiences that will stretch the mind and quicken the imagination

         The Russian Language and Culture will be studied throughout the school year

         A number of challenging individual and group learning experiences will be offered, including the following:

         If I Had Lived During the Middle Ages: An Experiment in Adventurous Thinking

         The Wizardry of Words

         Pirates—Real and Imaginary

         Historical Novels: Zestfully Reliving the Past

         Great Books—Past and Present

         They Made the Difference

         Arty Things to Do: Cartooning, Drawing, Painting

         Crafty Things to Do: Ceramics, Puppetry, Model Building, Photography, Carving, Mosaics, Macrame, Needlework, Cookery, Batik

         Chillers and Thrillers

         Mind-Boggling Phenomena

         Interest Zingers and Zappers

         Laughs, Chuckles, and Guffaws

*This learning project is part of the North Hills School District's elementary program for the gifted and talented enrichment program (GATE). For information pertaining to the GATE Program, consult Corinne P. Clendening, North Hills School District, Pittsburgh, Pa. 15229, tel. 412-931-4000.

EXAMPLE 4 (cont.)

Tantalizing Puzzles

Wonderful World of Science

2. The GATE Program will provide opportunities to bring greater depth and breadth to units being studied in the classroom

Depth and breadth require a wealth of appropriate learning resources and a learning laboratory where the student can work with ideas creatively and intensely

The GATE students will have the opportunity to serve as research consultants to the class for each social studies unit, assuming one of the following roles:

Agriculturalist	Dietician	Historian
Anthropologist	Economist	Musician
Archaeologist	Educator	Naturalist
Artist	Folklorist	Sociologist
Biographer	Geographer	Statistician
Book reviewer	Geologist	Travel agent

3. The GATE Program will provide opportunities for each student to learn how to think and to act creatively

Creativity is the power to develop to the fullest all of one's abilities; to see what others have seen and to respond differently; to form new ideas, to invent, and to discover

Margaret Mead, the anthropologist, estimated that most human beings use only 6 percent of their creative potential

A constant goal of the GATE Program is to enable each student to achieve his/her highest level of creativity

B. An excellent introduction to learning how to think creatively is found in *Creativity and Imagination* by Jacolyn Mott (Creative Education, 1973)

1. The magic of the mind is learning to think and to act creatively

2. Psychologists believe that creativity occurs in four steps:

First, preparation

This is a time of action—gathering facts, seeking answers

A time of experimenting with ideas—a period of trial and error

Hard work paves the way for success

Second, incubation

The mind considers and organizes ideas gathered during preparation

The mind combines and compares new ideas with facts and ideas already known

Third, inspiration

Inspiration is a sudden solution to a problem

Examples of inspiration have occurred in every area of creativity

Fourth, verification

Testing the solution to determine if it is true

If the idea fizzles, creative process begins again

3. The desire to create would die without imagination

Imagination is the ability to form in the mind a picture or idea

Such mental pictures or ideas are like kaleidoscopic or teleidoscopic images or designs

We employ imagination: to recreate the past; to wonder about unfamiliar people or places; and to toy with ideas about the future

EXAMPLE 4 (cont.)

Vicarious experience is an experience that is felt or enjoyed through imagined participation in the experience of others

Vicarious imagination helps us understand and sympathize with other people

Vicarious imagination helps people solve problems—role playing is an example of vicarious imagination

Vicarious imagination makes the reader of a story or the audience watching a play become involved in the plot

4. Everyone has creative potential that can be developed

All have seeds of creativity that, if nurtured, will grow

Practice improves creativity

The Book of Think (Or How to Solve a Problem Twice Your Size) by Marilyn Burns (Little, Brown, 1976), provides numerous creative thinking experiences

5. There is growing evidence that intelligence tests identify only a part of mental ability

Creativity and imagination are a vital part of each person's mental potential

6. The first step in developing creativity is to wonder why

Serendipity is the ability to make unexpected discoveries by accident—such an ability is basic to creativity

Examples of serendipity:

Vulcanization of rubber

Discovery of penicillin

Discovery of X-rays

Many discoveries are made as the result of painstaking research

Examples of discoveries resulting from painstaking, exhaustive research:

Radium

Incandescent light bulb

Vaccine for polio

Creative people see with a wonder that blows away the clouds of habit, tradition, and prejudice

II. Curiosity is the heart of creativity

A. Creative people project beyond what is to what might be

1. *New Trail Blazers of Technology* by Harland Manchester (Scribner, 1976) tells about ten twentieth-century inventors whose work has had great impact on modern-day life

Each of these men has made a difference in contemporary life

These creative men are the inventors of the Xerox Copier, Cable TV, the Polaroid Camera, the Wankel Engine, Hovercraft, the Transistor, Masers and Lasers, and FM Radio

At age 14 Frederick Cottrell invented an air pollution precipitator

"Cot sees ahead into that field which most of us do not see. He has to have an army behind him to rake up the things he uncovers." p. 22

2. Leonardo da Vinci, who will be introduced in the learning project If I Had Lived During the Middle Ages, was curious about all manner of things

His contributions include his work as:

Anatomist	Engineer	Naturalist
Architect	Inventor	Painter
Author	Mathematician	Philosopher
Caricaturist	Musician	Sculptor

EXAMPLE 4 (cont.)

3. Benjamin Franklin and Thomas Jefferson were geniuses driven by insatiable curiosity

Research the lives of Franklin and Jefferson

Make a list of their accomplishments and compare with those of Leonardo da Vinci

Would you nominate either or both of these men to the Hall of Fame for Great Americans?

Did Franklin and Jefferson really make a difference?

B. A special sixth-grade ongoing GATE project is to discover men and women whom you would nominate for membership in a Hall of Fame for Creative Thinkers

III. We all perceive differently

A. Perception is the meaning or mental picture that results when sensations (signals from our senses) combine with our storehouse of experiences and emotions

1. The tapestry of patterns supplied by the senses is different for each person
2. No two people perceive alike
3. Interest motivates perception
4. The North Hills School District Interest Inventory is designed to identify each student's major interests and concerns

NOTE: Administer the inventory at this point in the orientation program. Have the GATE students compile their own interest profiles, and share their interests and concerns with the other GATE students in their GATE group

B. Perception is selective

1. The mind automatically screens sights, sounds, information
2. The mind files away in the memory bank information that seems to be important

IV. Openness to experience is the launching pad for creativity

A. The sense of wonder, like a talent, grows with practice
B. Look beyond the familiar
C. To marvel is the beginning of knowledge
D. To quest for the unknown is to go beyond the mundane, to give wings to the imagination
E. To ask yourself the question "What if . . ." is the first step in creative thinking

V. Notetaking helps organize ideas and helps preserve fleeting thoughts

A. The geniuses of the world have commonly been notemakers

1. Leonardo da Vinci's notebooks are available for study
2. Thomas Edison was a conscientious notetaker

B. A well-organized notebook plus conscientious notemaking are the hallmarks of mature, creative thinkers
C. Keeping a journal of what you have done and specifying what needs to be done is recommended by experts in the field of developing creativity

1. The form MY JOURNAL is designed to provide a framework for self-analysis and self-directed knowledge building
2. Rereading the journal at the end of the first semester is not only an effective way to review what has been accomplished but also an effective means of self-evaluation—has the student measured up to scratch. Likewise, rereading the journal at the end of the school year is both an excellent review of the sixth-grade GATE program and an excellent basis for judging personal growth and development

VI. A constant goal throughout the sixth grade is to have the GATE students translate the acronym TARGET into a way of learning how to learn

<u>T</u>hinking

<u>A</u>pplying

<u>R</u>eacting

<u>G</u>rowing

<u>E</u>xploring

<u>T</u>otal learning

and evaluation. Example 4, Learning Project: Orientation to the GATE Program, clearly indicates the direct involvement of the library media center—its resources, facilities, and staff—in the entire year's work for the sixth-grade gifted and talented students. Several of the learning experiences listed in Example 4 are to be found in subsequent chapters of this book; "If I Had Lived During the Middle Ages" is included in Chapter 9, and "The Wizardry of Words" is included in Chapter 8.

COOPERATION OF TEACHERS AND LIBRARY MEDIA SPECIALISTS

The cooperation of teacher and library media specialist is the keystone of an effective media support program. Since curriculum is the *planned interaction* of pupils with content, resources, and instructional processes, face-to-face communication between the teacher or teaching team and the library media specialist is absolutely essential. The following outline suggests a step-by-step procedure that may be followed by teacher and library media specialist when planning together:

I. The teacher and the library media specialist in a scheduled conference determine the development and support needs of the unit or teaching plan by identifying
   A. Unit goals
   B. Behavioral objectives
   C. Special class, group, and individual student needs, interests, goals, abilities, progress rates, and concerns
   D. Specific topics, concepts, skills, and attitudes, to be introduced, reinforced, and extended
II. The teacher and library media specialist analyze the basic components of the unit or teaching plan that require the direct support of instructional media by
   A. Identifying specific topics in the *cognitive area* under the following headings
      1. What persons?
      2. What places?
      3. What things?
      4. What events?
      5. What concepts?
      6. What fundamentals?
   B. Identifying specific topics in the *affective area*
      1. What attitudes?
      2. What appreciations?
      3. What value judgments?
      4. What self-perceptions?
   C. Identifying specific thinking-learning-communicating skills
      1. Listening
      2. Recalling
      3. Observing
      4. Outlining
      5. Comparing
      6. Summarizing
      7. Classifying
      8. Generalizing
      9. Making assumptions
      10. Analyzing
      11. Criticizing
      12. Problem solving
      13. Interpreting
      14. Synthesizing
      15. Communicating

    D. Identifying specific possibilities for tie-ins with previous learnings

    E. Identifying culminating activities

    F. Identifying evaluation procedures and techniques

III. The teacher and the library media specialist share the responsibility for

    A. Determining how each topic can best be developed

    B. Determining which experiences will be required of

       1. The entire class

       2. Special groups

       3. Individual students

    C. Designing strategies for

       1. Introduction of unit

       2. Linking ideas

       3. Stimulating creativity

       4. Encouraging group interaction

       5. Stimulating divergent thinking

       6. Sustaining interest

       7. Encouraging student self-evaluation of progress

    D. Designing appropriate learning guides

    E. Designing optional and/or branching experiences and activities

    F. Determining which learning experiences can best occur

       1. In the classroom

       2. In the library media center

       3. In the large-group instruction room

       4. In the seminar rooms

       5. In other areas of the school

       6. In the community

    G. Giving consideration to the following

       1. How can understanding be facilitated?

       2. How can learning be developed logically?

       3. How can learning be individualized?

       4. How can failure be avoided?

       5. How can boredom and frustration be minimized?

       6. How can interest be motivated, sustained, and rewarded?

       7. How can creativity be stimulated?

       8. How can previous learnings be reinforced and extended?

       9. How can relevancy be assured?

      10. How can open-ended learning be encouraged?

      11. How can learning be extended into other curricular and cocurricular areas?

      12. How can alternative enrichment experiences be provided?

IV. The library media specialist builds a media support program to match the developmental needs of the teacher's unit or plan by

    A. Searching for appropriate media

    B. Determining media usage sequences and patterns

    C. Designing optional learning experiences

    D. Designing and producing or planning to have the students produce media to meet special needs

    E. Assembling and grouping media

V. The teacher and the library media specialist share the responsibility for implementing the library media support plan

A. The teacher preschedules class, group, and individual student
   1. Use of the library media center
   2. Use of other school facilities
   3. Field trips and laboratory experiences
   4. Culminating activities
B. The students work in the library media center
   1. The library media specialist serves as teacher, consultant, and mentor
     a. Orienting the class to new tools, new techniques, and procedures
     b. Working directly with groups and individuals
     c. Encouraging students to explore beyond the prescribed learning experiences
   2. The students in conference with the teacher determine program adjustment and modification

VI. The teacher and the library media specialist determine the effectiveness of the media support program as evidenced in this unit
A. The library media specialist, at the invitation of the teacher, participates in the culminating activities
B. The library media specialist solicits suggestions and criticisms from the students
C. The teacher shares with the library media specialist his or her evaluation of the effectiveness of the unit
   1. Identifying learning experiences and activites that were successful
   2. Identifying learning experiences and activities that were less than successful and need to be deleted or modified
   3. Identifying areas of student interest that emerged during the teaching of the unit and are to become part of the unit when next taught
   4. Suggesting possible changes in content, process, and media usage when unit is next taught
D. The library media specialist makes an anecdotal record of changes to be made in the content of the unit and in the procedure
   1. Files the unit outline, work sheets, bibliographies, learning guides, and anecdotal report in the library media center's curriculum file under the teacher's name
   2. Adds to the "To Be Purchased List" the added copies of titles needed for this unit
   3. Adds to the "Areas and Topics Needing Additional Materials List" those areas and topics not adequately covered in the existing collection.

Frequently in cooperation with the library media specialist, an innovative teacher will design a unit totally based on the services and resources of the library media center. Such a "library-based unit" is taught in its entirety through the utilization of library resources, facilities, and guidance. Each phase of the unit from inception to conclusion is the shared responsibility of the classroom teacher and the library media specialist. A creative teacher transcends the limitations of classroom, textbook, and course of study by utilizing the library media center as a special teaching laboratory. (See the following library-based units: Chapter 8, "Fun with Words," "The Wizardry of Words," and "American English: Inherited, Manufactured, and Fractured"; Chapter 11, "Book Illustrators and Their Art.")

TABLE 2 DIVERSIFICATION FOR INDIVIDUALIZATION OF INSTRUCTION

PROBLEM	SOLUTION
Same goal for all, yet each student is a unique learner	Individualize the teaching–learning program to enable each learner to reach a common goal in a unique way

SUBPROBLEMS	SOLUTIONS
Each student in any given class differs in abilities from every other class member	Devise a variety of appropriate, significant, challenging experiences commensurate with class ability range; wide enough in latitude to challenge and satisfy both the slowest and the quickest learner
Each student in any given class differs in environmental and cultural background from every other class member	Provide learning experiences, activities, guidance, and resources that will compensate for any learner's environmental or cultural disabilities
Each student in any given class differs in progress rate from every other class member	Provide appropriate experiences, activities, guidance, and resources, so that each learner can begin on his or her own maturity level to learn at his or her own comprehension rate
Each student in any given class differs in drive from every other class member	Provide appropriate experiences, activities, guidance, and supporting resources that will create, motivate, and sustain interest in "perceiving, behaving, becoming"
Each student in any given class differs in creativity from every other class member	Provide appropriate experiences, activities, and resources that will encourage the expression and development of each learner's creative potential
Each student in any given class differs in personal goals from every other class member	Provide appropriate experiences, activities, guidance, and resources that will encourage each learner to strive for self-realization, self-fulfillment, and self-understanding
Each student in any given class differs in needs from every other class member	Provide ample opportunity for each learner to find within each school experience assurance of authentic concern for his or her developmental needs as a student, as a future citizen, and as a human being

THE CURRICULAR ROLE OF THE SCHOOL LIBRARY MEDIA SPECIALIST

In designing each instructional program, media as well as goals, objectives, content, and process must be specified; these are the factors giving directions, purpose, and scope to basic instructional design. Yet, in *The Process of Education*, Bruner warns that even after content has been written so that the pervading and powerful ideas are given a central role, two basic problems still remain: how to match "materials to the capacities of the children"[18] and how to "tailor fundamental knowledge to the interests and capacities of children."[19] Solving both of these basic problems mandates the direct involvement of the library media specialist not only in curriculum design but especially in the teaching and learning process itself. As a teacher, the school library media specialist is sensitive to the educational and personal needs of the individual student, with special expertise in designing a great diversity of ways for the student to achieve understanding (see Table 2). It is the school library media specialist's obligation to see that:

> When the curriculum is being planned, each unit of work should be tested to see how many roads to success are built into it—how many ways for individuals to contribute diversely to the common whole. . . . The test then is: Does the youngster go home from school most days, with the feeling of at least some little success lingering in his memory?[20]

Personalizing and customizing instructional strategies to assure student success are unique facets of the curricular role of the school library media specialist. Though frequently taken for granted, the absence of such personalized and customized instructional services provided by the library media specialist will condemn many a child to taste of failure rather than success.

NOTES

1. Jerome S. Bruner, *The Process of Education* (Cambridge: Harvard University Press, 1960).
2. Charles E. Silberman, *Crisis in the Classroom: The Remaking of American Education* (New York: Random House, 1970), p. 326.
3. Bruner, *The Process of Education*, p. 18.
4. Ibid., p. 24.
5. Jerome S. Bruner, "The Process of Education Reconsidered," in *Curriculum Planning: A New Approach*, by Glen Hass, Joseph Bodi, and Jon Wiles (Boston: Allyn and Bacon, 1974), pp. 175-176.
6. Arnold J. Toynbee, *A Study of History*, abr. by D. C. Somervell, vol. 1 (New York: Oxford University Press, 1946), p. 326.
7. William H. Burton, *The Guidance of Learning Activities: A Summary of the Principles of Teaching Based on the Growth of the Learner*, 3rd ed. (New York: Appleton-Century-Crofts, 1962), p. 249.
8. John F. Putnam and W. Dale Chismore, eds., *Standard Terminology for Curriculum and Instruction in Local and State School Systems*, State Educational Records and Report Series: Handbook VI (Washington, D.C.: U.S. Department of Health, Education, and Welfare, 1970), p. 3.
9. Arieh Lewy, ed., *Handbook of Curriculum Evaluation* (Paris: UNESCO and New York: Longman, 1977), p. v.
10. Ibid., p. 62.
11. "Revision of the NCSS Social Studies Curriculum Guidelines," *Social Education* 53, no. 4 (April 1979): 262.
12. Edgar Dale, *Building a Learning Environment* (Bloomington, Ind.: Phi Delta Kappa, 1972), pp. 41-50.
13. Harold G. Shane, *Curriculum Change Toward the 21st Century*, Curriculum Series (Washington, D.C.: National Education Association, 1977), pp. 88-89.
14. John Jarolimek, *Social Studies in Elementary Education* (New York: Macmillan, 1963), p. 61.
15. Ibid., p. 65.
16. *Law-Related Educational Competencies*, Pennsylvania Division of Interdisciplinary Programs, Bureau of Curriculum Services (Harrisburg, Pa.: Department of Education, 1974), p. v.

17. Florence D. Cleary, *Blueprints for Better Reading* (New York: Wilson, 1972), p. 12.
18. Bruner, *The Process of Education*, p. 18.
19. Ibid., p. 22.
20. *A Climate for Individuality* (Washington, D.C.: National Education Association, 1965), pp. 36–37.

7 The Library Media Specialist's Role as Instructional Technologist

Facts, skills, and concepts are battered by change and withered by obsolescence. Factual data are in ever-increasing supply, and specialists are hard put to select, organize, interpret, and communicate the knowledge essential for the young.

National Education Association*

The school library, historically a reading center, became first a media center and later a technology center.

Robert C. Snider†

The memory bank of the human race goes back but 10,000 years. As long as knowledge was recorded manually there was little chance to preserve, accumulate, and profit from what the human mind had discovered. The thoughts of human beings were buried with them and civilization was the poorer for it. It was not until the invention of movable type around 1440 that human memory surmounted the barriers of time, place, and death itself. The following book production statistics portray graphically how technology has exploded the fetters of transient knowledge—proof that what has been learned need no longer perish with the death of individuals. The statistics for the years 1960, 1970, and 1974 have been taken from the UNESCO *Statistical Yearbook, 1975* (Paris: UNESCO, 1976), p. 581.

Year	Titles Produced
1500	1,000
1950	120,000
1960	332,000
1970	521,000
1974	571,000

Information in all areas is compounding at an exponential rate. "Never before has man needed to know so much—just to be ignorant."[1]

Like the fabled apprentice who foolishly commanded the wizard's magic mill to grind salt and then knew not how to stop it with the result that an end-

Instructional Materials: Selection and Purchase, rev. ed. Published in cooperation with the Association of American Publishers (Washington, D.C.: National Education Association, 1976), p. 16.

†Robert C. Snider, *Back to the Basics?* (Washington, D.C.: National Education Association, 1978), p. 6.

less deluge of salt poured forth and filled the sea, so have technological advancements poured forth an ever greater deluge of information, a deluge so great that we are becoming submerged in a quagmire of information. The proliferation of knowledge has reached future shock proportion. Don Swanson, Dean of the Graduate Library School, University of Chicago, foresees that, unless the right countermeasures are taken, each generation will take progressively longer to uncover what has gone before and the law of diminishing returns will prevail.[2]

INSTRUCTIONAL MEDIA MORASS

Knowledge grew slowly at first. It doubled from A.D. 1 to A.D. 1750. It doubled again from 1750 to 1900. It doubled once more from 1900 to 1950. Now it doubles every 8 to 10 years. The knowledge explosion has burst on the educational scene with an ever-increasing number of types and kinds of instructional media. A conservative estimate in 1979 placed the number of print and nonprint media of possible interest to a school system at over 900,000 separate titles. The task of sorting out from this media welter specific titles appropriate to any school's educational needs becomes more difficult with each passing day. The diversity of instructional media carriers (which according to Glenn McMurry, chief of the Informational Branch of the National Audiovisual Center, Washington, D.C., numbers no fewer than 65 different formats) further complicates the media identification and selection process. The sharp increase in the cost of media coupled with the curtailment of school budgets makes it doubly important that each title purchased is a sound instructional investment.

THE MEDIUM IS THE MESSAGE

Schools employ instructional resources not as "things" but as "ideas." The value of each resource lies in its knowledge-building, its knowledge-extending, and its knowledge-imploding potential, i.e., the power to break through the constraints of previous understandings. In coining the phrase "the medium is the message,"[3] Marshall McLuhan dramatized the necessity of looking beyond the wrapper of any carrier of information to the ideas latent within the package itself. For it is *not* in stocking books and pamphlets, newspapers and microfilms, filmstrips and motion pictures, disc and tape recordings, and all other print and nonprint media that the school library media center becomes an agent for educational effectiveness. It is the availability of the appropriate carrier of knowledge-building, knowledge-extending, or knowledge-imploding ideas when that availability is timely, significant, and directly supportive of the learning task at hand that powers the library media center's educational thrust.

INSTRUCTIONAL TECHNOLOGY

On January 24, 1970, Congress received from the Commission on Instructional Technology a report entitled *To Improve Learning: An Evaluation of Instructional Technology.*[4] This report, known as the McMurrin Report in honor of Sterling M. McMurrin, the commission chairman, advocated the employment of instructional technology as an innovative means of improving learning and of coping with the instructional media morass. Instructional technology, as defined by the commission, "is a systematic way of designing, carrying out, and evaluating the total process of learning and teaching in terms of specific objectives based on research in human learning and communication, and employing a combination of human and nonhuman resources to bring about more effective instruction."[5] Through the scientific management of knowledge the Commission on Instructional Technology believes that "education will become more immediate; instruction will have a more scientific base; and access to education will be more equal."[6]

MEDIA MANAGEMENT

Media management, that specialized professional competency demanded of today's school library media specialist, is the *scientific* use of media content to achieve specific teaching goals and desired behavioral objectives.* In function it is the process of converting information into understanding. Management of media extends the responsibility of the library media specialist beyond organizing the media collection for accessibility and availability to encompass utilizing materials in a planned, purposeful, efficient, effective, and humane manner. Today's school library media specialist must be expert in identifying and retrieving those ideas latent in materials which are uniquely appropriate to the learning task at hand. As a media manager the library media specialist joins generalized knowledge of the instructional program and process with specialized knowledge of media content and utilization strategies.

In media management the library media specialist not only selects appropriate materials but also predetermines what combination of materials can best meet a specific support need of the teaching plan or a special learning need of an individual, a group, or a class. As the findings of the Commission on Instructional Technology clearly indicate, material use that is unplanned, unpatterned, or unrelated wastes time, aborts energy, and destroys interest. To need specific information and not be able to locate it is not only a waste of time but frustrating to the point of dissipating interest and patience.

Freedom to learn does not imply the absence of a structured learning plan for knowledge building (see Appendix N). William Burton, eminent authority in the field of educational psychology, warns:

> No one ever learned to think under conditions of uncontrolled, uninhibited freedom. . . . Freedom, like discipline, can become an end in itself, activity for activity's sake. . . . The results of painless freedom are lack of *continuity* and *system*, acceptance of fuzzy, inadequate reasons for one's beliefs and eventually a demand for continual stimulation by new trivia.[7]

Planning is essential even in an informal instructional environment such as is found in the open classroom. The Institute for Development of Educational Activities, in its publication *The Open Classroom: Informal Education in America*, stresses the importance of "extensive planning":

> The properly managed informal classroom is well-structured, albeit in its own way, and the teacher makes specific decisions about who will do what, when it

---

*For assistance in designing and implementing media management systems consult Jack Luskay, Assistant Professor, Clarion State College, Clarion, Pa. 16214, tel. 814-226-2272.

will be done, and where it will take place. The atmosphere of a properly run informal classroom can best be described as controlled but not regulated. Extensive planning and meticulous records are part and parcel of informal education.[8]

Pointless browsing among a wealth of instructional media without plan or purpose is about as educationally effective as playing blindman's bluff in the library media center and stumbling in a haphazard, random manner from resource to resource. The sporadic, unplanned, purposeless use of media is educationally indefensible. Just as planning is basic for developing an effective, viable teaching program, so is planning basic for the effective and dynamic use of instructional media by teacher and by student.

MEDIA MANAGEMENT: POLICIES AND PROCEDURES FOR THE SELECTION AND USE OF MEDIA

Since instructional media are vital to the health and success of the instructional program, the procedure for media selection and use cannot be left to whim or chance. The American Association of School Librarians (AASL) has set forth the following procedural statements:[9]

POLICIES AND PROCEDURES FOR SELECTION OF INSTRUCTIONAL MATERIALS

Policies and Procedures for Selection of Instructional Materials (1976) *is a revision of the former document approved by the Board of Directors of the American Association of School Librarians (AASL) at the ALA Midwinter Meeting in 1970. The following revision, which contains a model for the selection process, was adopted by the AASL Board of Directors on August 15, 1976. A statement of the American Association of School Librarians endorsing the* Library Bill of Rights *of the American Library Association is included within this document.*

I. INTRODUCTION

The human worth that democratic societies seek to protect and develop rests upon commitment to educational programs which meet the individual purposes and developmental needs of students and prepare them to resolve the problems that continually confront them. Social, economic, and political issues, national and international, as well as the changing expectations of individuals and groups, represent the human concerns to which education must respond if it is to perpetuate and improve the society that supports it.

Those who would create better educational opportunities must strive to develop comprehensive systems that meet the needs of students of differing abilities, backgrounds, and interests, enabling them both to adjust to and influence the changing society in which they live. Media programs which reflect applications of educational technology, communication theory, and library and information science contribute at every level, offering essential processes, functions, and resources to accomplish the purposes of the school.*

Committed to the philosophy of school media programs as expressed in *Media Programs: District and School* and the selection of quality media collections which ensure that "learners will have the opportunity to grow in their ability

*American Association of School Librarians, ALA, and Association for Educational Communications and Technology, *Media Programs: District and School* (Chicago: American Library Assn., 1975), p. 1.

to find, generate, evaluate, and apply information that helps them to function effectively as individuals and to participate fully in society," the American Association of School Librarians has prepared this material as a guide for the formulation of selection policies and procedures for the school media program.

The selection of quality instructional materials is one of the most important and controversial tasks performed by school personnel. Often school districts are subject to challenge by individuals or groups who are concerned about what the collection does or does not include. Such action may be based on considerations involving political, social, or personal values, religion, profanity, treatment of matters relating to sex, or other controversial issues.

A selection policy, therefore, should provide a procedure for maintaining a consistent quality of excellence in the materials for use in the teaching-learning process including continuing evaluation of the media collection. The American Association of School Librarians *believes* that such a policy and procedures statement should be adopted formally and approved officially by each school district as a basis for selecting instructional materials, and used as a document to help students, parents and other citizens better understand the purposes and standards used to select instructional materials.

II. GUIDELINES

A. STATEMENT OF POLICY

The governing body of a school district should declare that it is the policy of the school district to provide a wide range of instructional materials on all levels of difficulty, with diversity of appeal, and the presentation of different points of view for all students. Further, the governing body should declare it is their policy to allow the systematic review of existing media collections and to permit the reconsideration of allegedly inappropriate instructional materials through established procedures.

B. STATEMENT OF SELECTION PROCEDURES

Responsibility for Selection of Instructional Materials—The governing body of a school district is legally responsible for all matters relating to the operation of the school district. The responsibility for the selection of instructional materials, however, should be delegated to the certificated library/media personnel employed by the school district.

While selection of instructional materials involves many people (library/media specialists, teachers, students, supervisors, administrators, and community persons), the responsibility for coordinating the selection of most instructional materials and making recommendations for acquisition rests with certificated library/media personnel.

The selection of textbooks* may rest with department chairpersons or with textbook evaluation committees.

Acquisition Procedure—A selection procedure should include provisions for the acquisition of all forms of instructional materials. Consistent criteria for selection should be applied to all acquisitions, including gifts, leased materials, and loans.

Criteria for Selection—The school media program is an integral part of the educational program of the school or district. Criteria for the selection of instructional materials should implement this basic purpose.

Instructional materials should be selected on the basis of the: appropriateness of the medium, varying levels of difficulty, student interests, curriculum needs, and representation of varying points of view.

The selection process should provide for the consideration of requests from students, teachers, administrators and the community. Selection of instructional

*Textbook definition: "any manual of instruction; a book dealing with a definite subject of study systematically arranged, intended for use at a specified level of instruction, and used as a principal source of study material for a given course" (Carter V. Good, ed., *Dictionary of Education* [3rd ed.; McGraw-Hill, 1973]).

materials should be based upon preview or evaluation reviews in professionally prepared selection aids or other appropriate sources.

Recommendations for acquisition will be solicited from faculty and students.

Gift materials should be judged by the criteria listed in the preceding section and should be accepted or rejected on the basis of those criteria.

It should be understood that selection is an ongoing process which should include the removal of instructional materials no longer appropriate and the replacement of lost and worn materials which are still of educational value.

A media advisory committee following local policy for such appointments may be appointed to assist in the selection and evaluation process.

Procedures for Reconsideration of Challenged Materials—Occasional objections to instructional materials will be made despite the quality of the selection process; therefore, the procedure for handling reconsideration of challenged materials in response to questions concerning their appropriateness should be stated. This procedure should establish the framework for registering a complaint that provides for a hearing with appropriate action while defending the principles of freedom of information, the student's right to access of materials, and the professional responsibility and integrity of the certificated library/media personnel. The principles of intellectual freedom are inherent in the First Amendment of the Constitution of the United States and are expressed in the *Library Bill of Rights* adopted by the Council of the American Library Association in 1948 and amended in 1961 and 1967 and in the *Students' Right to Read* a [1972] publication of the National Council of Teachers of English [see Appendix B]. In the event instructional materials are questioned, the principles of intellectual freedom should be defended rather than the materials.

III. Policy and Procedures Model

Policy for Selection of Instructional Materials—The _____ School Board hereby declares it is the policy of the _____ District to provide a wide range of instructional materials on all levels of difficulty, with diversity of appeal, and the presentation of different points of view and to allow the review of allegedly inappropriate instructional materials through established procedures.

Objectives of Selection—In order to assure that the school media program is an integral part of the educational program of the school, the following selection objectives are adopted:

To provide materials that will enrich and support the curriculum and personal needs of the users, taking into consideration their varied interests, abilities, and learning styles;

To provide materials that will stimulate growth in factual knowledge, literary appreciation, aesthetic values, and ethical standards;

To provide a background of information which will enable pupils to make intelligent judgments in their daily lives;

To provide materials on opposing sides of controversial issues so that users may develop under guidance the practice of critical analysis;

To provide materials which realistically represent our pluralistic society and reflect the contributions made by these groups and individuals to our American heritage;

To place principle above personal opinion and reason above prejudice in the selection of materials of the highest quality in order to assure a comprehensive media collection appropriate for the users.

Responsibility for Selection—Although the _____ School Board is legally responsible for the operation of the school, the responsibility for the selection of instructional materials is delegated to the certificated library/media personnel.

While selection of materials involves many people, including library/media specialists, teachers, students, supervisors, administrators, and community persons, the responsibility for coordinating and recommending the selection and purchase of instructional materials rests with the certificated library/media personnel. Responsibility for coordinating the selection and purchase of textbooks may rest with appropriate department chairpersons or with textbook evaluation committees.

Criteria for Selection—Educational goals of the local school district, individual student learning modes, teaching styles, curricula needs, faculty and student needs, existing materials and networking arrangements should be considered in developing the media collection. Guidelines for the evaluation and selection of curricula resources are listed.

Curricula materials should:

Be relevant to today's world;

Represent artistic, historic, and literary qualities;

Reflect problems, aspirations, attitudes and ideals of a society;

Contribute to the objectives of the instructional program;

Be appropriate to the level of the user;

Represent differing viewpoints on controversial subjects;

Provide a stimulus to creativity.

Technical materials should:

Be of acceptable technical quality; clear narration and sound, synchronized pictures and sound;

Be readable; typographically well-balanced.

For specific criteria for various forms of materials and equipment, refer to *Media Programs: District and School,* pp. 70–86.

Procedures for Selection—In selecting materials for school media programs, the certificated library/media personnel in consultation with the selection committee will: evaluate the existing collection; assess curricula needs; examine materials and consult reputable, professionally prepared selection aids. Recommendations for acquisition will be solicited from faculty and students.

Gift materials should be judged by the criteria listed in the preceding section and should be accepted or rejected on the basis of those criteria.

It should be understood that selection is an ongoing process which should include the removal of materials no longer appropriate and the replacement of lost and worn materials still of educational value.

Procedures for Reconsideration of Materials—Occasional objections to instructional materials will be made, despite the quality of the selection process. The _____ School Board supports principles of intellectual freedom inherent in the First Amendment of the Constitution of the United States and expressed in the *Library Bill of Rights* of the American Library Association and *Students' Right to Read* of the National Council of Teachers of English. In the event that materials are questioned, the principles of intellectual freedom, the right to access of materials and the integrity of the certificated library/media personnel must be defended rather than the materials.

If a complaint is made, the following procedures should be followed:

1. Inform the complainant of the selection procedures and make no commitments.
2. Request the complainant to submit a formal "Request for Reconsideration of Instructional Materials" [see later].
3. Inform the superintendent and other appropriate personnel.
4. Keep challenged materials on the shelves during the reconsideration process.
5. Upon receipt of the completed form, the principal requests review of the challenged material by an ad hoc materials review committee within fifteen working days, and notifies the district media director and superintendent that such review is being done. The review committee is appointed by the principal, with the concurrence and assistance of the certificated library/

media personnel, and includes media professionals, representatives from the classroom teachers, one or more parents, and one or more students.
6. The review committee takes the following steps after receiving the challenged materials:
   a. reads, views, or listens to the material in its entirety;
   b. checks general acceptance of the material by reading reviews and consulting recommended lists;
   c. determines the extent to which the material supports the curriculum;
   d. completes the appropriate "Checklist for School Media Advisory Committee's Reconsideration of Instructional Material" [see later], judging the material for its strength and value as a whole and not in part.
7. Present written recommendation of review committee to the superintendent and the school board.
8. Retain or withdraw challenged materials as mandated by the decision of the school board.

(Appointment of committee members and specific procedures to follow should be made in accordance with local policy. The steps listed above are given as a model to be used in development of local policies and are not suggested as the only procedures which are effective. A procedures policy should include these steps.)

REQUEST FOR RECONSIDERATION OF INSTRUCTIONAL MATERIALS (*SAMPLE*)

School _____

Please check type of material:
( ) Book   ( ) Film   ( ) Record
( ) Periodical   ( ) Filmstrip   ( ) Kit
( ) Pamphlet   ( ) Cassette   ( ) Other

Title _____
Author _____
Publisher or Producer _____
Request initiated by _____
Telephone _____ Address _____
City _____ State _____ Zip _____

The following questions are to be answered after the complainant has read, viewed, or listened to the school library material in its entirety. If sufficient space is not provided, attach additional sheets. (Please sign your name to each additional attachment.)

1. To what in the material do you object? (Please be specific, cite pages, frames in a filmstrip, film sequence, et cetera.)
   _____
   _____
   _____
   _____

2. What do you believe is the theme or purpose of this material?
   _____
   _____
   _____
   _____

3. What do you feel might be the result of a student using this material?
   _____
   _____
   _____
   _____

4. For what age group would you recommend this material?
   _____

5. Is there anything good in this material? Please comment.

_____

6. Would you care to recommend other school library material of the same subject and format?

_____
_____

_____   _____
Signature of Complainant   Date
Please return *completed* form to the school principal.

CHECKLIST FOR SCHOOL MEDIA ADVISORY COMMITTEE'S RECONSIDERATION
OF INSTRUCTIONAL MATERIAL—NONFICTION (*SAMPLE*)

Title _____
Author _____
A. Purpose
  1. What is the overall purpose of the material? _____
  _____
  2. Is the purpose accomplished? _____ Yes _____ No.
B. Authenticity
  1. Is the author competent and qualified in the field?
  _____ Yes _____ No.
  2. What is the reputation and significance of the author and publisher/ producer in the field? _____
  _____
  _____
  3. Is the material up-to-date? _____ Yes _____ No.
  4. Are information sources well documented? _____ Yes _____ No.
  5. Are translations and retellings faithful to the original?
  _____ Yes _____ No.
C. Appropriateness
  1. Does the material promote the educational goals and objectives of the curriculum of District Schools? _____ Yes _____ No.
  2. Is it appropriate to the level of instruction intended?
  _____ Yes _____ No.
  3. Are the illustrations appropriate to the subject and age levels?
  _____ Yes _____ No.
D. Content
  1. Is the content of this material well presented by providing adequate scope, range, depth and continuity? _____ Yes _____ No.
  2. Does this material present information not otherwise available?
  _____ Yes _____ No.
  3. Does this material give a new dimension or direction to its subject?
  _____ Yes _____ No.
E. Reviews
  1. Source of review _____
  Favorably reviewed _____ Unfavorably reviewed _____
  2. Does this title appear in one or more reputable selection aids?
  _____ Yes _____ No. If answer is yes, please list titles of selection aids.
  _____
  _____

Additional Comments
_____
_____
_____

Recommendation by School Media Advisory Committee for Treatment of Challenged Materials

_____

_____

_____

_____

Date _____

Signature of Media Advisory Review Committee

_____   _____

_____   _____

_____   _____

CHECKLIST FOR SCHOOL MEDIA ADVISORY COMMITTEE'S RECONSIDERATION OF INSTRUCTIONAL MATERIAL—FICTION AND OTHER LITERARY FORMS (*SAMPLE*)

Title _____

Author _____

A. Purpose
   1. What is the purpose, theme or message of the material? How well does the author/producer/composer accomplish this purpose?

   _____

   _____

   _____

   2. If the story is fantasy, is it the type that has imaginative appeal and is suitable for children? _____ Yes _____ No; for young adults? _____ Yes _____ No. If both are marked no, for what age group would you recommend?
   3. Will the reading and/or viewing and/or listening to material result in more compassionate understanding of human beings? _____ Yes _____ No.
   4. Does it offer an opportunity to better understand and appreciate the aspirations, achievements, and problems of various minority groups? _____ Yes _____ No.
   5. Are any questionable elements of the story an integral part of a worthwhile theme or message? _____ Yes _____ No.

B. Content
   1. Does a story about modern times give a realistic picture of life as it is now? _____ Yes _____ No.
   2. Does the story avoid an oversimplified view of life, one which leaves the reader with the general feeling that life is sweet and rosy or ugly and meaningless? _____ Yes _____ No.
   3. When factual information is part of the story, is it presented accurately? _____ Yes _____ No.
   4. Is prejudicial appeal readily identifiable by the potential reader? _____ Yes _____ No.
   5. Are concepts presented appropriate to the ability and maturity of the potential readers? _____ Yes _____ No.
   6. Do characters speak in a language true to the period and section of the country in which they live? _____ Yes _____ No.
   7. Does the material offend in some special way the sensibilities of women or a minority group by the way it presents either the chief character or any of the minor characters? _____ Yes _____ No.
   8. Is there preoccupation with sex, violence, cruelty, brutality, and aberrant behavior that would make this material inappropriate for children? _____ Yes _____ No; young adults? _____ Yes _____ No.
   9. If there is use of offensive language, is it appropriate to the purpose of the text for children? _____ Yes _____ No; for young adults? _____ Yes _____ No.

10. Is the material free from derisive names and epithets that would offend minority groups? _____ Yes _____ No; children? _____ Yes _____ No; young adults? _____ Yes _____ No.
11. Is the material well written or produced? _____ Yes _____ No.
12. Does the story give a broader understanding of human behavior without stressing differences of class, race, color, sex, education, religion or philosophy in any adverse way? _____ Yes _____ No.
13. Does the material make a significant contribution to the history of literature or ideas? _____ Yes _____ No.
14. Are the illustrations appropriate and in good taste? _____ Yes _____ No.
15. Are the illustrations realistic in relation to the story? _____ Yes _____ No.

Additional Comments

_____

Recommendation by School Media Advisory Committee for Treatment of Challenged Materials

_____

Date _____

Signature of Media Advisory Review Committee

_____   _____
_____   _____
_____   _____

AMERICAN ASSOCIATION OF SCHOOL LIBRARIANS STATEMENT ON *LIBRARY BILL OF RIGHTS*

The American Association of School Librarians endorses the *Library Bill of Rights* of the American Library Association.

LIBRARY BILL OF RIGHTS

The council of the American Library Association reaffirms its belief in the following basic policies which should govern the services of all libraries:

1. As a responsibility of library services, books and other library materials selected should be chosen for values of interest, information, and enlightenment of all the people of the community. In no case should library materials be excluded because of the race or nationality or the social, political, or religious views of the authors.
2. Libraries should provide books and other materials presenting all points of view concerning the problems and issues of our times; no library materials should be proscribed or removed from libraries because of partisan or doctrinal disapproval.
3. Censorship should be challenged by libraries in the maintenance of their responsibility to provide public information and enlightenment.
4. Libraries should cooperate with all persons and groups concerned with resisting abridgment of free expression and free access to ideas.
5. The rights of an individual to the use of a library should not be denied or abridged because of his age, race, religion, national origins, or social or political views.
6. As an institution of education for democratic living, the library should

welcome the use of its meeting rooms for socially useful and cultural activities and discussion of current public questions. Such meeting places
should be available on equal terms to all groups in the community regardless of the beliefs and affiliations of their members, provided that the meetings be open to the public.

Adopted June 18, 1948.
Amended February 2, 1961, and June 27, 1967, by the ALA Council.

These rights are fundamental to the philosophy of school media programs as
stated in *Media Programs: District and School*, Chicago, Ill: AASL, AECT, 1975.

MEDIA MANAGEMENT: SELECTION CRITERIA

To promote uniformity and objectivity in evaluating instructional resources, it is recommended practice that each school district develop specific
criteria with matching checklists to unify and guide media selection. Samples
of book and nonbook selection criteria are offered here and in Appendix H
as models for the district library media staff to consider when designing or
revising its own media selection criteria.

BOOKS

Fiction should conform to the following principles:
1. It should interpret life truly.
2. The characters should be real and vital.
3. Selection should be based on awareness of the world today, an understanding
   of modern youth, and common sense.
4. Dull, didactic books, no matter how informative or how lofty the author's
   intentions, should be excluded. . . .
5. Books written with a bias intended to persuade the reader of a religious or
   political point of view are out of place in recreational collections in . . .
   school libraries.
6. Moralistic writing that seeks to drive home a lesson should be passed over
   in favor of more subtle stories.
7. Interpretive writing that depicts the human heart is more useful in stimulating thinking, developing understanding than is factual information on the
   same subject, though both types of writing may be useful.
8. Titles that seem adequate but are no better than books on the same subject
   already in stock should be rejected unless the demand for that type of book
   exceeds the supply.
9. Books that present any racial or national group in a derogatory manner,
   that consistently use objectionable nicknames for ethnic groups or races, that
   perpetuate stereotyped racial characteristics and ideas, are not acceptable.
10. Fiction written especially for the teen-ager does not need to be judged by the
    standards set up for adult novels.
11. Style that distinguishes a book as literature is very rare. Though it is to be
    cherished when found, it is not essential.
12. The principles and standards of book selection should determine the books
    to be included in the collection rather than one's individual taste or pressure
    from citizens, however well-meaning.

Points to be considered in judging nonfiction:
1. The date of publication is especially important for history, travel, vocational,
   and similar books.
2. How much of an authority is the author?
3. What is the author's point of view?

4. Has the book vitality?
5. As was said of fiction, titles that seem adequate but are no better than those already in stock should be rejected unless there is a need for more books on the subject.
6. A quick evaluation.

Ten tests of sound book-selection practice:
1. Do you read widely, regularly, critically?
2. Do you keep a running file of order cards based on your own reading, suggestions from teachers and students, and needs uncovered by use of the library?
3. Do you check books by reading reviews in accepted sources?
4. Is there a written statement of book-selection policy for your school?
5. Do you apply well-defined criteria for the book that you choose?
6. Do you select books in relation to a well-thought-out plan for the development of the total collection?
7. Do you consider school needs and pupil interests and abilities when choosing books?
8. Do you encourage wide participation in book selection?
9. Do you examine books before buying them whenever possible?
10. Do you compare related books to see which is preferable?[10]

CURRICULUM PACKAGES OR INSTRUCTIONAL UNITS

The Association for Supervision and Curriculum Development, a division of the National Education Association, published in 1971 a brochure entitled *Selecting New Aids to Teaching*, which sets forth specific guides to be followed in selecting instructional units. Instructional units or curriculum packages are packaged and sold as an entity and are usually composed of several related types of media. Such a package might contain books, filmstrips, disc or tape recordings, study prints, learning guides, and teacher's manual. The need for special guidelines was based on the following assumptions:[11]

1. Increasingly, the local decision makers are faced with the task of selecting and curricularizing instructional units rather than beginning from scratch and designing them.
2. The units are becoming increasingly complex and sophisticated, requiring more study and more assistance in their appraisal.
3. The instructional units usually require a substantial financial outlay and usually will need to be used over a period of several years; therefore, careful consideration of these decisions becomes more essential than ever. Also, a growing tendency for local communities to reject increased taxation is turning school officials toward better utilization and accountability procedures.
4. Local school officials need specific guidelines to assist them in reaching educationally sound decisions about such units.

Complexity of the task of selecting instructional units demands that the guidelines be utilized in their entirety. The major headings of the checklist are given here to indicate the scope of this basic selection tool.

Initial probing of proposed unit. Before moving into a detailed plan for assessing the instructional unit, initial consideration should be given to whether the subsequent effort is likely to result in success, asking:

1. Is the unit really needed?
2. What are its anticipated accomplishments?
3. Does the unit represent the best alternative available to achieve stated objectives?
4. At this point, what major obstacles and problems can be anticipated?

Developing a plan of action. The first step is to develop a plan of action, assuming that a decision has been made to undertake a more extensive investigation. Since the unit to be analyzed may represent a sizeable investment of school money, a fairly well-defined plan is highly desirable in order that the study be as effective and as efficient as possible.

1. What, specifically, is the purpose of the investigation of the proposed unit?
2. Who should be involved?
3. When should the investigation take place?
4. How should it be undertaken?

Accomplishing the plan. The plan of action is ready for implementation. . . . some prepared plan of action is a *must* for making effective and efficient decisions about instructional units.

1. Objectives of the unit: those of the producer as well as yours
2. Relevance and validity of unit's content
3. Compliance of unit with principles of human growth and development
4. Time and space (organizational) considerations
5. Personnel factors
6. Community factors
7. Cost analysis of the unit
8. Instructional and curricular factors
9. Evaluative procedures
10. Dissemination
11. Implementation

Decision. If no "abort" decision is reached by this time, a final decision is now in order. This process may be simple or complex, depending upon the variety of circumstances that will be unique to any particular problem.

1. Who will make the decision?
2. How long should be allowed for the final decision?
3. What decision will be made?

Revision and recycling. Unexpected problems may interfere with implementation after a positive decision has been made on the unit under consideration. Factors such as lack of staff availability, unexpected costs, and unanticipated obstacles may force adjustments at the time of implementation or, indeed, in rare cases a reconsideration of the decision itself. . . .

1. What plans are made for a systematic evaluation of the ongoing innovation?
2. What provisions are made for basing revisions upon these evaluations?
3. Who is to do the ongoing evaluation?
4. Are sufficient funds available for it?

To some, the process for decision making outlined above may seem unnecessarily long and involved. "Yet, *in most instances*, the process of making decisions about instructional units suffers because of oversimplified and inadequate procedures."

MULTIETHNIC MATERIALS

The school has been assigned a major responsibility for developing intergroup understanding based on respect for the worth and dignity of every individual, regardless of race, color, creed, or socioeconomic status. In choosing materials to foster positive feelings and attitudes toward minority groups, these criteria give guidance:

1. An accurate, adequate objective presentation of basic concepts of race and culture.
2. Sufficient facts to eradicate the prejudgments and generalizations about minorities.
3. Emphasis on human values—the dignity and worth of each individual.

4. The diversity of American life presented in a meaningful, realistic, unbiased manner with interaction among multicultural, multiracial, and multireligious groups.
5. An objective treatment of the problems and obstacles, as well as the contributions of each minority group.
6. Well-developed content, with the basic concepts and principles of the particular subject expressed adequately.[12]

Truth and art are two basic criteria to be used as guides in selecting materials pertaining to minority groups. Both of these criteria are embodied in the guidelines developed for the selection of materials concerning the American Indian. Because these guidelines are applicable to all minority groups they are offered here with the suggestion that each guideline be expanded to include all minorities. The first three guidelines are considered basic principles. The ten additional guidelines reinforce the basic ones.

BASIC

1. Is the image of the Indian one of a real human being, with strengths and weaknesses, acting in response to his own nature and his own times? If material is fictional, are the characters realistically developed? Are situations true or possibly true to Indian ways of life?
2. Does the material present both sides of the event, issue, problem, or other concern? Is comparable information presented more effectively in other material?
3. Are the contributions of American Indian culture to Western civilization given rightful and accurate representation, and is this culture evaluated in terms of its own values and attitudes rather than in terms of those of another culture?

ADDITIONAL

1. What are the author's or producer's qualifications to write or produce material dealing with American Indians?
2. Does the material contain factual errors or misleading information?
3. Does the material perpetuate stereotypes or myths about the American Indian? Does the material show an obvious or subtle bias?
4. Do illustrations authentically depict Indian ways of life?
5. How might the material affect an Indian person's image of himself?
6. Would the material help an Indian identify with and be proud of his heritage?
7. Does the material express Indian values and might it help an American Indian to reconcile his own values with conflicting ones?
8. Does the material present a positive or negative image of the American Indian and how might the material affect the non-Indian's image of Indian people?
9. Are loaded words (e.g., buck, squaw, redskin, etc.) used in such a way as to be needlessly offensive, insensitive, or inappropriate?
10. Does the material contain much of value but require additional information to make it more relevant or useful?[13]

Because the textbook is the most universally used instructional resource, it has great influence on the instructional program. In the past, many textbooks were grossly inadequate in their treatment of minorities. Close scrutiny is the rule in textbook selection today and requires rigorous application of a well-defined set of criteria. The Pennsylvania Department of Public Instruction, striving to assure a fair and just presentation of minorities and multiethnic problems, developed a checklist to determine the adequacy of a textbook's treatment of minorities (see Appendix H for "Evaluating Textbooks: Treatment of Minorities").

MEDIA MANAGEMENT: THE MATCH

In order to match instructional support materials to the developmental needs of the curriculum, the library media specialist must become conversant with the content and design of the school's instructional program—what is taught, how it is taught, in what sequence it is taught, in what detail it is taught, to whom it is taught, and with what anticipated activities it is taught. In addition to matching media to the developmental needs of the curriculum, the library media specialist must build background knowledge of: faculty support needs; student needs; and support needs of the cocurricular program. In building such insight this procedure is recommended:

1. Confer with the curriculum director and/or building principal.

   Discuss the prevailing educational philosophy, goals, and objectives.

   Discuss the organizational pattern of the teaching program.

   Discuss possible patterns for integrating library usage with the teaching and learning program.

   Request opportunity to schedule visits to classrooms and to participate in class discussions.

   Request the opportunity to meet with each teacher in a scheduled planning conference.

   Request copies of each course of study for the library curriculum file.

   Request, for permanent loan, copies of the teacher's edition of each textbook currently used.

2. Confer with each teacher in a scheduled exploratory planning conference.

   Identify units to be taught throughout the school year.

   Explore topic inclusion and areas of emphasis for each unit.

   Discover teacher's method of presentation.

   Discover textbooks being used for each class.

   Discuss possible patterns of library usage by class, by groups, by individuals.

   Discuss possible patterns for integrating library media support with the classroom teaching and learning program.

   Discuss possible strategies for study skill integration with the classroom teaching and learning program.

   Request teacher's cooperation in evaluating, testing, and selecting library media.

   Request teacher's suggestions as to specific kinds of material to be included in the library collection.

   Request copies of teacher-made guides, outlines, etc.

3. Analyze course content for each subject at each grade level.

   Determine for each unit:
   Scope and sequence of topic inclusion and development;
   Pattern of concept development and linkage;

Specific teaching and learning experiences and activities;

Appropriate patterns for integrating the use of library resources with the teaching and learning program.

4. Analyze textbook coverage.

Determine scope and sequence of topic coverage in each unit.

Determine adequacy of topic development in each unit.

Identify activities recommended for each unit.

Identify supplementary resources recommended for each unit.

5. Structure a master checklist of topics, strategies, and activities included in each unit plan.

Unify textbook inclusion and teacher suggestions.

Provide for specific skill introduction and reinforcement.

Provide for cross subject integration.

Provide for divergent capabilities of students.

6. Build knowledge of the students' needs, interests, goals, abilities, concerns, and progress rates.

Confer with students in scheduled classroom visits:
   Identify student hobbies and/or recreational interests;

   Identify student reading interests (see Appendix J);

   Ask for student help in evaluating, testing, and selecting materials.

Confer with reading consultants, guidance counselors, classroom teachers, and/or homeroom teachers:
   Identify individual student IQ and achievement scores.

Structure a checklist of student interests and needs:
   Indicate special interests, abilities, disabilities, concerns.

7. Build knowledge of the cocurricular program.

Identify types and kinds of student organizations.

Identify types and kinds of activities.

Confer with club sponsors and officers.

8. Select materials to match.

Curricular development needs.

Teacher interest and emphasis needs.

Student personal and educational needs.

Cocurricular program implementation needs.

Having built background knowledge of the school's instructional program, the library media specialist then searches for media to *match* the support needs of the curriculum, the personalized teaching needs of the faculty, and the educational and personal needs of the students. A wise library media specialist will involve both teachers and students in media selection. Direct involvement of teachers in choosing materials serves a dual purpose: It enables the library media specialist to profit from the teachers' specialized knowledge, and enables the teachers to extend their knowledge of new media. Involvement of students in media selection is of inestimable value both to the library media specialist and to the students; it enables the library media specialist to achieve a high degree of objectivity in selection—to look at materials through the eyes of the potential users; it is also an educational experience for the students, providing them with an opportunity to learn and to practice techniques of critical thinking (see Appendix H for a model Student Book Evaluation Guide).

MEDIA MANAGEMENT: THE MIX

Library media specialists systematically build their content knowledge of both print and nonprint media. Since they employ media not as "things" but as "ideas," they respect *all* authentic information carriers regardless of format. The concept of the library as a multimedia center employing the cross-media approach to facilitate teaching and learning is far from recent. There is and can be no competition among materials; adequacy of understanding requires the multimedia approach embracing reading, viewing, listening, and communicating. When selecting media to meet a teaching or learning need, the library media specialist asks which medium or *combination* of media will best achieve the successful completion of the teaching or learning task at hand.

MEDIA MANAGEMENT: MEDIA PROGRAMMING

The library media specialist translates teaching and learning strategies into supportive patterns of media usage. Blueprinting such a plan for the sequential use of appropriate instructional media to support teaching and learning experiences, whether it be for a class, a group, or an individual student, is called media programming. Before being concerned with media, the library media specialist in conference with the teacher or teaching team sets about identifying the basic ingredients of the instructional plan. Only then is one ready to determine with what resource or combination of resources this plan can be most effectively supported (see Checklist 1).

CHECKLIST 1 MEDIA PROGRAMMING COMPONENTS

1. What is to be taught? (Specification of content)

Appreciations	Processes
Attitudes	Skills
Concepts	Structures
Fundamentals	Terms
Generalizations	Theories
Principles	Understandings
Problems	Values

2. When can it best be taught? (Timeliness of topic presentation)

In which grade	Exploration
In what unit	Summarization
Where within the unit	Culmination
Introduction	

CHECKLIST 1 (cont.)

3. To whom can it best be taught? (Appropriateness to learner maturity)
   To above average student   To below average student
   To average student

4. How can it best be taught? (Method of instruction)
   By comparative analysis   By listening
   By demonstration   By manipulative and tactile activity
   By directed observation   By modeling
   By discussion   By practice
   By dramatization   By problem solving
   By drill   By programmed instruction
   By experimentation   By project
   By field experience   By reading
   By a field trip   By recitation
   By group work   By seminar
   By imitation   By testing
   By laboratory experience   By viewing
   By lecture

5. In what sequence can it best be taught? (Sequence of topic presentation)
   In logical progression   In branching concept and interest order
   In motivational order   In summarizing order
   In priority order   In reinforcing order
   In conceptual interlock order   In synthesizing order
   In basic concept development order

6. Where can it best be taught? (Physical environment conducive to learning)
   In the auditorium   In the laboratory
   In the classroom   In the large-group instruction area
   In a community facility   In the library
   In the conference room   In the seminar room
   In the gymnasium   In the small-group instruction area

7. By whom can it best be taught? (Locus of teaching responsibility)
   By the classroom teacher   By the librarian
   By the community resource consultant By a subject specialist
   By the guidance counselor   By a teaching team
   By the head of department

8. With what resource or resources can it best be taught? (Medium of instruction)
   Art print   Microfilm
   Book   Microslide
   Chart   Model
   Community contact   Motion picture (16mm, 8mm)
   Depth study kit   Pamphlet
   Diorama   Periodical
   Disc recording   Programmed instruction
   Filmstrip   Real object
   Flannelgram   Slide
   Globe   Study guide
   Graph   Study point
   Kinescope   Tape recording
   Laboratory manual   Televised program
   Map   Transparency
   Microcard   Videotape

A systems approach to media programming such as that employed in the following Pittman Learning Guide creatively utilizes instructional media in a logically patterned learning sequence. Such a skillfully preplanned, systematic use of media is based on these assumptions:

Learning can be facilitated, expedited, and effectualized by the strategic use of appropriate media if that use is developed in a logical, progressively sequential order of meaningful, balanced interrelatedness.

Learning can be motivated by having the student see the learning task in its entirety, seeing each part as an integral supporting component of a total learning design.

Learning to learn requires that students view a learning experience as a challenging, ongoing, continuous, regenerative process of cohesive inter-relatedness so that they know where they are going and have a reasonable idea of how they are going to get there.

Learning to learn requires guided practice working with significant ideas; resources contain ideas and, therefore, are a means to an end; the learner must perceive clearly the end to be achieved through the use of each resource before beginning the search for understanding.

Learning resources used indiscriminately without plan or purpose have little or no educational significance or value.

Learning that is purposeful, challenging, and pleasurable is more perma-nently meaningful, more lastingly significant.

Zest for learning is motivated by success in learning; a learning program should be designed and structured to promote learner success and to mini-mize learner confusion, frustration, disappointment, and failure.

Learning programs are not impersonal when they build into their design opportunities for student choice of material, student choice of activity, and student reaction.

Innovative learning guides designed by Shirley A. Pittman* employ the systems approach to media usage. Shirley Pittman has had marked success using learning guides with elementary and secondary students in the areas of social studies, mathematics, language arts, reading, science, and health. The Pittman Learning Guides are designed for self-paced learning and employ guide questions, references to specific resources, and optional and branching activities. Each student receives a learning guide on either 8″ × 5″ cards or on 8½″ × 11″ mimeograph paper, punched for inclusion in the student's notebook; the student follows the directions on the program as understanding is built through a series of learning experiences. Examples 5, 6, and 7 illustrate the Pittman Learning Guides.

EXAMPLE 5 THE WHITE MEN DOOM AND THEN SAVE THE BUFFALO

Subject:	Social Studies
Unit:	Midwest and the Great Plains
Topic:	The White Men Doom and Then Save the Buffalo
Subtopic 1:	When the first explorers came to the North American continent, there were as many as 60 million buffalo roaming free. During the

*For further information contact Shirley A. Pittman, Coordinator of Library Media Services, North Hills School District, 200 McIntyre Rd., Pittsburgh, Pa. 15237, tel. 412-931-4000, exts. 314 and 340.

EXAMPLE 5 (cont.)

Subtopic 1 (cont.) period from 1800 to 1900, the buffalo population was reduced from 40 million to less than 800 animals. Can you discover the chain of events that caused the buffalo to be threatened with extinction?

Source A
Mason, George. *The Wildlife of North America.* pp. 22-23.

and

Source B
Barker, Will. *Wildlife in America's History.* pp. 21-28.

and

Source C
McClung, Robert. *Shag, Last of the Plains Buffalo.*

Subtopic 2: Dr. Hungerford devoted the first chapter in his book *Ecology, the Circle of Life* to the wanton destruction of the American buffalo. Do you think this first chapter has a special message for us concerning our obligation to safeguard our natural resources?
What is the significance of "The Great Plains Chain"?

Source
Hungerford, Harold R. *Ecology, the Circle of Life.* pp. 7-14.

Subtopic 3: What contribution did Scotty Philip and William Temple Hornaday make to preventing the total obliteration of the American buffalo?

Source
Veglahn, Nancy. *The Buffalo King: The Story of Scotty Philip.* Chapters 11, 16, and 17.

Subtopic 4: Can you discover what a wildlife sanctuary is and how it differs from a wildlife refuge?
Do you consider wildlife sanctuaries and refuges to be ecologically important?

Source
Harrison, C. W. *The First Book of Wildlife Sanctuaries.* pp. 1-2.

Optional topic 1: Each year, the United States Department of the Interior sells buffalo to reduce the size of a herd which has grown too large for the available public range. Can you discover the current purchase price of a buffalo being offered for sale by the Department of the Interior?

Source
Harrison, C. W. *The First Book of Wildlife Sanctuaries.* p. 40.

Optional topic 2: Because the Plains Indians depended on the buffalo to supply their basic needs, they called the buffalo "The Giver of life." Can you discover the many uses the Plains Indians made of the buffalo?

Source A
Hofsinde, Robert. *The Indian and the Buffalo.* pp. 29-53.

or

Source B
Rounds, Glen. *Buffalo Harvest.* pp. 14-15.

EXAMPLE 5 (cont.)

Optional topic 2 (cont.)
           or
                     Source C
                     American Bison, Studyprint #2, in the Audio Visual Enterprises Set,
                     "Wild Animals, Their Role in American History."

Optional activities:
                     Prepare a transparency or a poster identifying the many products
                     the Plains Indians derived from the buffalo.

                     If you would enjoy learning the Indian Buffalo Dance, the following
                     sources will help you:.

                     Source A
                     Powers, William. *Here Is Your Hobby . . . Indian Dancing and Cos-
                     tumes.* Chapter XVI.

           and
                     Source B
                     Hofmann, Charles. *American Indians Sing.*
                     Note: Music for the Buffalo Dance is available on the recording
                          which you will find in the slipcover attached to the inside of
                          the back cover of the book.

                     The Indians were bewildered when the buffalo disappeared from
                     the plains. Can you discover how the disappearance of the buffalo
                     affected the Indians?

                     Source
                     Bleeker, Sonia. *The Sioux Indians.* pp. 139–155.

EXAMPLE 6   THE TASADAY: A STUDY OF A PRIMITIVE CULTURE FROZEN IN TIME

Grade: 7
Subject: Social Studies
Learning Project: Primitive Man
Individual Learning Program: *The Tasaday: A Study of a Primitive Culture Frozen in Time*

Case Study: In 1971, in the Philippines on the Island of Mindanao, a small group of primitive
     people was discovered deep in the heart of the unexplored rain forest. When these
     people, the Tasaday, were found, it was discovered they were living in a way our ances-
     tors lived more than 50,000 years ago. They had no metal and knew nothing about
     farming or hunting—natural caves providing their only shelter. Yet, strangely enough,
     in view of the constant threat of war in our world today, these primitive people lived in
     total harmony with their environment and with each other—there were no words in their
     vocabulary for enemies, war, or weapons.

Analyzing a Case Study:
     A case study is the gathering and organization of all relevant materials to enable an
     in-depth study and an analysis of a person, an event, a community, a society, or a cul-
     ture. The reader of the case study is invited to apply his own knowledge, observations,
     feelings, and value judgments when analyzing and interpreting the facts.

     In analyzing the culture of the Tasaday, use the Learning Guide: Analysis of a Culture
     [see later].

Build Background Knowledge and Understanding by:

     Reading and analyzing the following:

EXAMPLE 6 (cont.)

Source 1. *The Gentle Tasaday* by John Nance published by Harcourt Brace, 1975.

Source 2: "The Tasaday: Stone Age Cavemen of Mindanao" by Kenneth MacLeish in the *National Geographic*, August 1972, pp. 219-49.

Viewing and analyzing the documentary sound filmstrip set:

The Tasaday: Stone Age People in a Space Age World produced by The Associated Press and distributed by Pathescope Educational Media, 1976.

Part 1—The Cave People
Part 2—Civilization—Curse or Blessing?

Optional Learning Experiences:

Compare and contrast the culture of the Tasaday of the Philippines with that of the aborigines of Australia:

Source 1. *The Aborigines* by B. C. Ross-Larson published by Creative Educational Society, 1972.

Source 2. *Boomerang Hunter* by Jim Kjelgaard published by Holiday House, 1960.

An ethnologist is a scientist who studies the similarities and differences among cultures. You can gain insight into the methods and procedures employed by an ethnologist by viewing the following sound filmstrip from the set entitled "Anthropologists at Work":

The Ethnologist produced by Globe Filmstrips, 1975.

An anthropologist is a scientist who studies people, their behavior and social groups. In the field of anthropology there are four major areas of specialization:

Ethnology: the branch of anthropology dealing with the study of the similarities and differences among cultures

Archeology: the branch of anthropology dealing with the study of prehistoric artifacts and the people who left them

History: the branch of anthropology dealing with the use of historical restoration techniques and archeological methods in the search for understanding of the total way of life of a people

Paleontology: the branch of anthropology dealing with the study of bone remains of people and animals

You can gain insight into the methods and procedures employed by the specialists in each of the above fields by viewing the following sound filmstrips:

The Archeologist produced by Globe Filmstrips, 1975.

The Historian produced by Globe Filmstrips, 1975.

The Paleontologist produced by Globe Filmstrips, 1975.

Continue throughout this school year to build your in-depth understanding of the work of these anthropologists as you explore the civilizations of ancient peoples such as: the Egyptians, Babylonians, Assyrians, Chaldeans, Israelites, Phoenicians, Greeks, Carthaginians, and the Romans.

For a survey of educational requirements and career possibilities in the field of anthropology consult the Career Resource Center at the Senior High School.

LEARNING GUIDE ANALYSIS OF A CULTURE

Student _____

Facts—

Location:

Population:

LEARNING GUIDE ANALYSIS OF A CULTURE (cont.)

Time span:

Arts and crafts:

Ceremonies and rituals:

Clothing:

Communication:

Currency:

Education:

Food:

Government:

Health and medicine:

Laws:

Literature:

Manners and customs:

Mobility:

Mores:

Music and dance:

Place of children:

Place of the elderly:

Place of men:

Place of women:

Records:

Religion:

Shelter:

Social and economic problems:

Superstitions:

Traditions:

Transportation:

Values:

Weapons:

Your Observations and Impressions—

LEARNING GUIDE ANALYSIS OF A CULTURE (cont.)

Your Feelings and Concerns:

Your Attitudes and Judgments:

EXAMPLE 7 LEARNING GUIDE IN U.S. HISTORY*

Unit: The American Civil War
Topic: Appomattox and the End
Grade: 11

Subtopic 1:   As the battered, once-proud Army of Northern Virginia neared final, crushing defeat, what were some of the reactions of those on both sides who participated in these grim days?

Source A
Eisenschiml, Otto. *Eyewitness; the Civil War As We Lived It*. Chapter 20, "The Curtain Falls." pp. 666–688.

or

Source B
Bradford, Ned, ed. *Battles and Leaders of the Civil War*. pp. 601–607.

Subtopic 2:   To set the scene, read a brief description of the bitter fighting waged up to the day of the surrender.

Source A
Fuller, J. F. C. *Grant and Lee; a Study in Personality and Generalship*. pp. 234–241.

or

Source B
Dupuy, R. Ernest. *The Compact History of the Civil War*. pp. 408–413.

Subtopic 3:   What degree of destruction at Petersburg and Richmond immediately preceded Lee's surrender? How would this influence Lee's decision?

Source A
Ellis, Keith. *The American Civil War*. Putnam Pictorial Sources Series. pp. 44–45.

and

Source B
The Civil War (From Gettysburg to Appomattox). Study Prints 6 through 10.

Subtopic 4:   An exchange of notes, under a flag of truce, between the opposing commanders preceded their historic meeting on April 9, 1865. What was the tone of these notes, and what reactions were expressed by officers on either side?

Source A
The Way to Appomattox. Vol. IV of *Battles and Leaders of the Civil War*. pp. 729–747.

*This learning guide was designed by Mrs. Henry Persinger, Head Librarian, North Hills Senior High School, Rochester Rd., Pittsburgh, Pa. 15229.

EXAMPLE 7 (cont.)

Subtopic 4 (cont.)
    and

> Source B
> Henry, Robert Selph. *The Story of the Confederacy*. pp. 459–464.

Subtopic 5:   How are these events reported in secondary sources?

> Source A
> Catton, Bruce. *This Hallowed Ground; the Story of the Union Side of the Civil War*. pp. 385–390.

    and

> Source B
> Dupuy, R. Ernest. *The Compact History of the Civil War*. pp. 408–418.

    or/and

> Source C
> Randall, J. G. *The Divided Union*. pp. 525–529.

Subtopic 6:   Read Grant's account of Lee's surrender. What attitudes toward General Lee and toward the defeated Confederacy does he impart?

> Source
> Davie, Emily, comp. *Profile of America; an Autobiography of the U.S.A.* pp. 282–286.

Subtopic 7:   To the victor goes the privilege of dictating the terms of surrender to the vanquished. In what way would you characterize the terms Grant dictated? His attitude toward the defeated army?

> Source A
> *The Way to Appomattox*. pp. 729–746.

    and

> Source B
> *American History in Sound*. Disc recording. Listen to Record 2, Side 1, Band 1.

Subtopic 8:   On the day following the signing of the surrender, General Lee bade farewell to his troops. How did his address come to be written? How would you characterize it?

> Source A
> *The Way to Appomattox*. p. 747.

    and

> Source B
> *American History in Sound*. Disc recording. Record 2, Side 1, End of Band 1.

Subtopic 9:   Most students of U.S. history are familiar with the course of events in Ulysses S. Grant's life after the tragic conflict, but what became of General Robert E. Lee?

> Source A
> Peattie, Donald Culross. *Parade with Banners*. Read the chapter titled "Lee's Greatest Victory." pp. 147–155.

    or

> Source B
> Carmer, Carl. *Cavalcade of America*. Read "President Robert E. Lee." pp. 130–133.

Optional activity 1:   Review what you have learned by reading pp. 582–589, and viewing the splendid illustrations in:

EXAMPLE 7 (cont.)

Optional activity 1 (cont.)   Source
American Heritage. *The American Heritage Picture History of the Civil War.*

Optional activity 2:   Prepare a report of your findings to share with your classmates. View the filmstrip E-19, *The Road to Appomattox.* Decide whether or not you would like to use the filmstrip to illustrate your report. If you decide yes, would you show the entire strip or select certain frames?

Optional activity 3:   Much is made of the contrasting impressions the two leaders made at the McLean Farm House. Read the parts in Fuller's *Grant & Lee; a Study in Personality and Generalship*, in which the author analyzes the personalities of the two men. With the insights you have already gained and with Fuller's analysis, prepare a comparison of the two men.

Optional activity 4:   If you are interested in a different perspective for understanding the final, tragic, confused, and haunting moments of the Civil War, you might enjoy the diary of a Southern woman who witnessed, at first hand, the collapse of the Confederacy. Her account is bitter. Can you find human reasons for that bitterness?

Source
Le Conte, Emma. *When the World Ended; the Diary of Emma Le Conte.*

Optional activity 5:   At the end of the war, both Grant and Lee, giants of warfare, spoke eloquently on behalf of peace. Read the April 22, 1865, issue of *Harper's Weekly* (on microfilm), specifically, the article on p. 243, which discusses what the attitude of its Northern readers should be in regard to the defeated Lee and the cause he represented. What does this augur for the future and the making of the peace? Examine other issues for more evidence.

Optional activity 6:   If you wish a deeper understanding of Robert E. Lee, the man, try Douglas Southall Freeman's *Lee of Virginia.* Freeman's four-volume life of Robert E. Lee won a Pulitzer Prize. This book was written expressly for young adults and shows the same devotion that made his earlier work a classic.

MEDIA MANAGEMENT: DISTRICT MEDIA SERVICES

In this day and age of the school budget crunch, it is imperative that each traditional practice be scrutinized to determine its cost effectiveness. One innovative way to reduce the cost of media services is to establish a *district* media program. This program, under the direction of a coordinator or supervisor of media services, is responsible for: planning, budget, ordering, processing, productions, access and delivery systems, maintenance, facility design, and program evaluation. Centralized ordering and centralized processing of media will effect savings in both time and money. Even a cursory examination of Fig. 3, Flowchart of the Acquisitions Process, and Fig. 4, Flowchart of the Cataloging Process, proves the merit of centralizing these services rather than continuing the costly drain of energy and time of each library media specialist in each of the district's school library media centers.

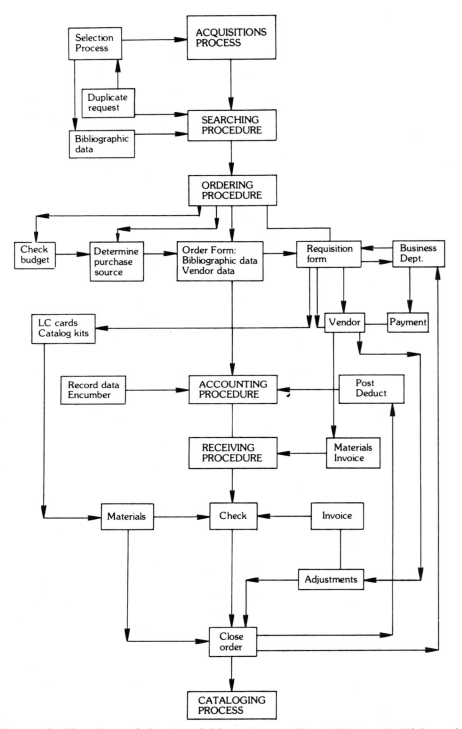

FIGURE 3. Flowchart of the Acquisitions Process. From Warren B. Hicks and Alma M. Tillin, *Managing Multimedia Libraries* (New York: R. R. Bowker, 1977), p. 164.

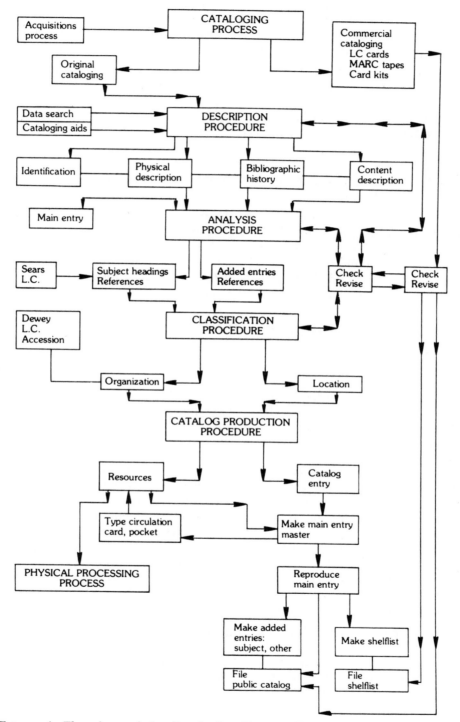

FIGURE 4. Flowchart of the Cataloging Process. From Warren B. Hicks and Alma M. Tillin, *Managing Multimedia Libraries* (New York: R. R. Bowker, 1977), p. 173.

Another means of stretching the media dollar and widening media support services is the establishment of a district instructional materials center (IMC). In the district IMC the following types of materials should be included:

1. Very expensive materials that individual schools cannot afford to buy, e.g., the Alva Museum replica of the Rosetta Stone
2. Materials for classroom learning centers
3. Curriculum support kits
4. Materials for pilot study projects
5. Costly audiovisual materials, e.g., motion pictures, videotapes, dioramas, and models
6. Audiovisual equipment pool to supply extra equipment to buildings when and as needed

Two basic sources providing guidelines for the establishment and maintenance of a district media program are: *Media Programs: District and School* prepared by the American Association of School Librarians and the Association for Educational Communications and Technology (Chicago: American Library Association, 1975) and *A Model School District Media Program* by John T. Gillespie (Chicago: American Library Association, 1977).

MEDIA MANAGEMENT: BUILDING MEDIA SERVICES

PLANNING

A quality library media program requires facilities adequate to support its myriad functions—to house students, staff, and collection comfortably, and to facilitate each investigative and learning activity essential for instructional support. (An outline of the Goals of the Multimedia Library Expressed as Functions follows.) To accommodate its complex educational role, those who design the library media center must plan with each of the basic functions specifically in mind. For example, since today's school library media center is to serve as a laboratory for classes, groups, and individual students, the plans must provide not only the conventional reference room but also library class-rooms, seminar rooms, taping rooms, closed circuit television studios, media production laboratories, and other special areas. Appendix M provides architects, administrators, and library media specialists with objective guidance in relating specific functions, procedures, and facilities to space allocation, to traffic and usage patterns, to faculty and learner needs, to general and specific resources, equipment, and furnishings.

GOALS OF THE MULTIMEDIA LIBRARY EXPRESSED AS FUNCTIONS

I. *Informational Function*
   A. The multimedia library is intended to achieve the following:
      1. Communication of ideas
      2. Confidence and judgment in the handling of information
      3. Utilization of available information to achieve specific ends, change economic, political, and social life conditions
      4. Assist in solving problems of society
   B. The process by which the multimedia library accomplishes these goals is best exemplified by the role of the library as:
      1. A center for reliable information

2. A source of rapid access, retrieval, and transfer of information
3. A locus from which to relate human knowledge to human needs
4. A focal center which emphasizes the importance of information and knowledge toward resolution of human needs

II. *Educational Function*
  A. The multimedia library seeks to implement the following educational goals:
    1. To provide for continuous, lifelong education
    2. To create and sustain broad academic interests, creativity, and independent intellectual activity, and to support intellectual freedom
    3. To encourage perceptual sensitivity and occupational competence
    4. To promote positive social attitudes and a democratic society
  B. The processes by which these ends are accomplished by the multimedia library include the following:
    1. The provision of educational opportunities and an atmosphere of learning
    2. Guidance in the selection and use of materials
    3. Training in perceptual and research skills
    4. The promotion of intellectual freedom as related to the use and meaning of knowledge and the problems of human survival, emotional balance, and social needs

III. *Cultural Function*
  A. The multimedia library has as its goals the need to work toward the achievement of the following:
    1. An improved quality of life
    2. Broadened aesthetic interests and artistic appreciations
    3. The encouragement of artistic creativity and cultural freedom
    4. The development of positive human relations
  B. These goals are supported by processes suggested by the following:
    1. The presentation and support of art forms representative of all cultures
    2. The support of aesthetic experience
    3. Guidance in appreciation of the arts, culturally divergent points of view, and an atmosphere of intercultural understanding
    4. The promotion of artistic and cultural expression as related to daily living, sentient needs, and emotional and interpersonal needs

IV. *Recreational Function*
  A. The multimedia library serves the following goals in the area of human recreational needs:
    1. To support and enhance a balanced and enriched life
    2. To provide for a wide range of recreational interests and the meaningful use of leisure time
    3. To support the creative use of entertainment activity
    4. To support intercultural understanding
  B. These goals are served by the following processes:
    1. The provision of a center for recreational information, the materials for recreation, and programs of recreational value
    2. The support of an atmosphere conducive to relaxation and enjoyment
    3. Guidance in the use of leisure time
    4. The relation of recreation to needs of daily living, education, and culture[14]

BUDGETING

Inevitably, the cost of instructional materials must be interjected into a discussion of media management. It is the responsibility of the library media specialist to convince the administration that a quality media program requires an adequate budget. To build the library media center's collection to functional strength requires an adequate capital investment plus an adequate continuing maintenance budget. The professional qualitative and quantitative standards, as set forth in the most recent edition of *School Library Media Standards*, should be consulted by the school administrator, the business manager, and the school library media specialist as they set about determining the budget requirements of the library media center.

In the past there have been those who have advocated arbitrarily structuring the school's library media budget by predetermining a definite percentage allotment for fiction and for each of the ten major divisions of the Dewey Decimal System. Such an unenlightened approach cannot possibly reflect the actual growth support needs of the instructional program. The law of media supply and educational demand should be the determining factor in setting up a school library media budget. The adequacy of the supply of appropriate print and nonprint media in relation to the support needs (current and anticipated) of the instructional program plus the personal needs, interests, performance level, and learning styles of the students should be the guide to budget planning.

When establishing a new library media center, the cost figure for purchasing the initial collection should be determined by totaling the cost of specific print and nonprint titles essential for teaching each unit in the school's curriculum and for meeting the specific needs and interests of the student body and of the community. The cost of materials when related to specific educational value makes good sense to a school administrator, who can see then what the money is going to buy and can equate the educational potential with the money invested. An itemized media budget is much more effective and convincing than an unspecified "pig-in-a-poke" budget request (see Example 8).

STAFFING

The proper staffing of the library media center is the one factor that determines whether or not the library media program will successfully and effectively support the school's instructional program. A library media program of educational excellence demands the services of sufficient numbers of librarians, technicians, paraprofessionals, and clerical assistants to run the program adequately. Traditionally the school library was the total responsibility of but a single librarian, one whose main obligation was to organize, maintain, and circulate books and whose total sphere of influence was to maintain order while supervising the library study hall. Today's library media specialist is a teacher directly involved in the total teaching and learning process: serving on curriculum study and revision committees; functioning as a planning-working member of teaching teams; planning with individual teachers and committees of teachers for the integration of the resources and services of the library media center with the day-to-day, ongoing teaching and learning program; designing media usage programs; guiding individual students and groups of students in their search for and use of materials; selecting for purchase instructional media uniquely appropriate for the developmental needs of the curriculum and the personal growth needs and interests of the students; evaluating the effectiveness and efficiency of the library media program and communicating to the building principal or school library media services coordinator the growth needs of the program. Because the instructional role of the school library media specialist is so time- and energy-consuming, neither time nor energy is left for performing any task other than instructional tasks.

EXAMPLE 8 AN ITEMIZED MEDIA BUDGET

Budget Request: Part 1

1. Basic media selection tools
    Note: These tools serve as a data bank for the entire district.

Books in Print. 4 vols. Bowker	$ 92.50
Subject Guide to Books in Print. 2 vols. Bowker	69.50
Books in Series in the United States. Bowker	62.50
Children's Books in Print. Bowker	29.95
Subject Guide to Children's Books in Print. Bowker	29.95
El-Hi Textbooks in Print. Bowker	29.95
Feature Films on 8mm and 16mm. Bowker	21.95
Guide to Microforms in Print. Microform Review	35.00
Subject Guide to Microforms in Print. Microform Review	42.50
Index to Educational Audio Tapes. NICEM	47.00
Index to Educational Overhead Transparencies. 2 vols. NICEM	75.50
Index to Educational Records. NICEM	47.00
Index to Educational Slides. NICEM	42.50
Index to Educational Video Tapes. NICEM	29.50
Index to 8mm Motion Cartridges. NICEM	47.00
Index to Free Educational Materials—Multimedia. NICEM	26.50
Index to 16mm Educational Films. 4 vols. NICEM	109.50
Index to 35mm Filmstrips. 3 vols. NICEM	86.50
Magazines for Libraries. Bowker	35.00
Paperbound Books in Print. 2 vols. Bowker	62.50
Publishers' Trade List Annual. 6 vols. Bowker	50.00
U.S. Government Publications: Monthly Catalog. Superintendent of Documents	45.00
Total	$1,117.30

Budget Request: Part 2

Note: The following materials are required to support the teaching of the new twelfth-grade advanced placement unit "American English: Inherited, Manufactured, and Fractured."

1. Books

Book of Pidgin English by John Murphy. AMS Press	$ 10.50
A Civil Tongue by Edwin Newman. Bobbs, Merrill	8.95
Culture, Class, and Language Variety by A. L. Davis. NCTE	7.95
Dictionary of Contemporary Usage by William and Mary Morris. Harper	15.95
Dictionary of Slang & Unconventional English by Eric Partridge. 7th edition. Macmillan	18.50
Double-Speak in America by Mario Pei. Hawthorne. Paper	3.95
First Names First by Leslie Dunkling. Universe Books	10.00
I Hear America Talking by Stuart Flexner. Van Nostrand	18.95
Old Names and New Places by Robert Alotta. Westminster Press	8.95
Slang Today and Yesterday by Eric Partridge. 4th edition. Routledge & Kegan	17.50
Strictly Speaking by Edwin Newman. Bobbs, Merrill	7.95

2. Kit

Dialects and Dialect Learning by Karen Hess. NCTE	55.00

3. Motion Pictures

The English Language: How It Changes. Coronet	165.00
The English Language: Patterns of Usage. Coronet	165.00

4. Recording

Americans Speak. NCTE	6.00
Total	$ 520.15

Media Programs: District and School[15] recommends that the professional staff of the school library media center include one full-time media specialist for every 250 students or major fraction thereof. These standards also recommend that at least one media technician and one media aide be employed for every 250 students or major fraction thereof. Such media technicians provide assistance in the following areas: graphics production and display, information and materials processing, photographic production and equipment operation, scheduling, and maintenance. The media aides do clerical and secretarial work; they are responsible for circulation routines, reading shelves, shelving, and filing; typing correspondence, reports, and bibliographies; inspecting and repairing materials; maintaining records, inventories, and bookkeeping accounts; and general housekeeping duties.

When appraising the staffing needs of the library media center, the building principal and/or the supervisor of library media services should refer to the occupational definitions set forth by the Manpower Project in its publication *Occupational Definitions for School Library Media Personnel* (Chicago: American Library Association, 1971), as well as the last edition of the AASL/AECT media program standards.

SCHEDULING

Flexible scheduling refers to the use of the library media center by teachers and students as their needs dictate. The "open" schedule permits the classroom teacher to schedule class and group use of the library media center on the basis of immediacy of need. In the saber-toothed-curriculum days, the library served as a scheduled study hall where students were required to spend a period in the library at a specified time whether or not they had any need of its resources or services. All too frequently the students who needed to work in the library could not get in—the chairs were jammed with the study hall assignees who did not need to be there.

Just because the schedule of the library media center is an open one it does not follow that its use is not frequently preplanned by teachers and the library media specialist. A catch-as-catch-can policy for the use of the library media center is educationally abortive. The classroom teacher, who is primarily responsible for designing conditions of learning, shares this responsibility with the library media specialist as they cooperatively develop library-media-based learning experiences. How can instructional media possibly support the teaching plans and accommodate the learning needs if the teacher and the library media specialist remain incommunicado?

A close look at the variety of instructional activities taking place during a typical day in an elementary and in a secondary school library media center offers convincing evidence that a flexible scheduling policy not only permits but actually encourages class, group, and individual student use of the center and its resources (see Example 9).

MANAGING MEDIA TO IMPROVE LEARNING: THE ROLE OF THE LIBRARY MEDIA SPECIALIST

Relating and integrating media with the ongoing teaching-learning process is a vital part of instructional technology—the new science of utilizing human and nonhuman resources to bring about more effective instruction. In schools

EXAMPLE 9 A TYPICAL DAY IN AN ELEMENTARY AND A SECONDARY
LIBRARY MEDIA CENTER

Part 1: A Typical Day in an Elementary Library Media Center.
Staff Consists of a Library Media Specialist and a Media Aide.

8:00–8:30

The media aide supervises the return and checkout of materials.
The library media specialist works with:

A group of three cub scouts searching for skits suitable for their father-and-son banquet.

A sixth-grade girl seeking stories suitable for reading to a three- and a five-year-old she is going to babysit.

The sixth-grade Mexican fiesta committee searching for instructions for making a papier-mâché piñata.

A second grader with a note from his mother requesting a book she might read to her three-year-old to help the child overcome his fear of the dark.

The third-grade social studies teacher needing to schedule her class to work in the library media center to complete their study of the cold lands.

The kindergarten teacher who stops by to share her delight over the success of the previous day's field trip to the zoo and to make final plans for the story hour scheduled for the afternoon session.

8:35–8:50

The media aide completes the circulation routines and begins to unpack a shipment of new books received yesterday from the district processing center.

The library media specialist plans with the principal to schedule a new entrant into the library media center for special help in math. The principal leaves the student's cumulative record folder so that the library media specialist can study the student's achievement profile and pinpoint areas needing special help.

8:55–9:10

The media aide and the library media specialist plan together the day's sequence of clerical duties including:

Filing catalog cards for the new books just received.

Writing notes to teachers and students apt to be interested in certain of the new books.

Preparing interlibrary loan requests for materials from the district instructional materials center.

Cutting the stencils and mimeographing individualized learning guides for: the fourth-grade social studies unit "The Lands and People of Australia"; for the third-grade unit "Homes Around the World"; for the sixth-grade science unit "Ecology, the Circle of Life"; and the fith-grade reading unit "When Trails Led West."

Readying the story hour corner for the afternoon kindergarten session.

If time permits, assembling materials for the second-grade science unit "Birds in Our Community."

9:15–9:55

The library media specialist plans with the sixth-grade reading teacher to expand the Scott, Foresman reading unit "The Rain Forest" [see Chapter 8 for the completed unit]. They decide to include: a depth study of the author, Armstrong Sperry, and his writings; an opportunity for the students to compare and contrast the life-style of the aborigines of New Guinea as portrayed in the book *The Rain Forest* with the life-style of the aborigines of Australia as portrayed in *Boomerang Hunter* by Jim Kjelgaard; evaluating the authenticity of the background information on New Guinea by checking the information provided by Armstrong Sperry in the novel with the factual information given in the nonfiction account *New Guinea: A Journey into Yesterday* by Eleanor Baker.

10:00–10:45

The library media specialist works with groups and individual students:

EXAMPLE 9 (cont.)

Teaches a group of fifth-grade social studies students how to make parallel time lines comparing happenings occurring at the same time in different places.

Guides a committee preparing an assembly program for Earth Day.

Helps several sixth-grade math students construct circle and bar graphs to communicate the current world availability and consumption of petroleum.

Suggests that a student who has read *My Friend Flicka* and its two sequels, *Thunderhead* and *The Green Grass of Wyoming*, and who also is a World War II buff, might enjoy reading *The Chestry Oak* by Kate Seredy, for it combines a horse story with a story of the Second World War.

10:50-11:35

The library media specialist, in addition to working with groups and individual students, has a planning session with the district music coordinator to help her design learning experiences that will integrate the music of Stephen Foster and John Philip Sousa with the fifth-grade social studies unit "Life in Northeastern United States, Yesterday and Today."

11:40-12:10

Media aide goes to lunch.
   Library media specialist supervises the circulation of media and guides individuals and groups.

12:15-12:45

Library media specialist goes to lunch.
   Media aide supervises the circulation of media and is available to answer students' questions.

12:50-1:35

Library media specialist in addition to working with groups and individuals builds a media support unit to enrich the second-grade unit "The Circus."

1:40-2:25

Library media specialist "tells" the story *The Little Bear's Pancake Party*, by Janice, to thirty-five kindergarten children, who last week had heard *The Little Bear's Sunday Breakfast*. After telling the story, the library media specialist reinforces the point made in the story that "if you want to know what anything says, you have to read for reading is listening with your eyes."

2:30-3:15

The library media specialist guides a number of individual students in their search for materials. Several are searching for resources and experiments to use in demonstrating magnetism to their fourth-grade science class.

3:20-3:45

Library media specialist introduces a class of third graders to the mysteries of the card catalog so they will be able to locate fairy tales under author, title, and subject.

3:50-4:30

Media aide supervises the circulation of media. Library media specialist attends a building faculty meeting.

Part 2: A Typical Day in a High School Library Media Center.
In This Four-Year High School, the Staff Consists of Two Library Media Specialists and a Media Aide.

7:30-8:30

The media aide supervises the return and checkout of materials.
The head library media specialist works with:

An English student searching for a book paralleling *The Diary of a Young Girl*; the library

EXAMPLE 9 (cont.)

media specialist gives her *The Upstairs Room* by Johanna Reiss, the autobiography of a Dutch girl who went into hiding to escape the Nazis.

The foreign exchange teacher, a young man from Brazil, who asks for help in planning a weekend jaunt to Niagara Falls; the library media specialist provides a road map and an AAA *Tour Book*.

A mother telephoning to ask for help in getting materials for her son, who is recuperating from an operation and does not wish to fall behind in his class work; the library media specialist arranges to have the requested materials for the mother to pick up in the media center later that afternoon.

The assistant library media specialist works with:

A member of the senior debate team who is searching for statistical evidence to bolster his contention that socialized medicine is not a violation of the free enterprise system.

A beginning chemistry student searching for Mendeleev's Periodic Table of Elements.

A committee of eleventh graders from the world cultures class searching for authentic designs of African masks.

A senior political science student searching for a commentary on Thoreau's essay "Civil Disobedience"; from the group of books the library media specialist offers him, the student selects *Books That Changed the World* by Downs to be most adequate for his task.

8:35–9:20

The head library media specialist plans with the media aide for the day's work schedule including:

Following through on the day's circulation routines, including slipping and shelving books, writing overdue notices, notifying teachers and students that requested materials are now available, etc.

Cutting the stencil and mimeographing the Historical Novel Summary form [see Chapter 9, Example 27].

Typing the next week's schedule for the library media center to be sent to the district supervisor of library media services accompanied by a request for additional materials to be sent from the instructional materials center.

Cutting the stencil and mimeographing individual learning guides for a ninth-grade geology unit.

If time permits, filing cards in the card catalog.

The assistant library media specialist, in addition to supervising the general reference activities in the library media center, works with a special ninth-grade civics committee whose assignment is to read or listen to political speeches in order to pinpoint evidence of the seven basic propaganda tricks: name calling, transfer, glittering generalities, testimonial, plain folks, card stacking, and bandwagon.

9:25–10:10

The head library media specialist plans with the eleventh-grade advanced-placement physics teacher for his class to work in the library media center building background knowledge in the field of kinematics during the three days he is away serving on an evaluation team in another school district.

The assistant library media specialist, in addition to supervising the general reference activities in the library media center, works with the dramatic club sponsor and club officers as they select books, filmstrips, and single-concept motion pictures to be used in their club seminar on acting as a career.

10:15–11:00

The head library media specialist plans with the tenth-grade home economics teacher for her classes to work in the library media center to prepare for the upcoming unit "Creative Family Living." They decide, in addition to including the regular range of topics,

EXAMPLE 9 (cont.)

to encourage the students to identify contemporary family problems by reading newspaper columns such as "Dear Ann Landers" and "Dear Abby," which are readily available on microfilm. The assistant library media specialist, in addition to supervising the general reference activities in the library media center, gathers materials in preparation for her next class period, involving the eleventh-grade research paper.

11:05–11:50

The head library media specialist, in addition to supervising the general reference activities in the library media center, builds a special collection of books that are to be introduced to the ninth-grade English class that has just completed *True Grit* by Charles Portis. She includes in her selection the following titles portraying extreme courage and paralleling the theme of *True Grit: Adventure in Survival* by Beam, *John F. Kennedy and PT-109* by Tregaskis, *A Long Vacation* by Verne, *A Night to Remember* by Lord, *Ordeal by Mountains* by Stapp, *Seven Came Through* by Rickenbacker, *White Water, Still Water* by Bosworth, and *Zeb* by Anderson.

The assistant library media specialist, working in the library media center classroom, instructs the eleventh-grade English class in the use of periodical indexes and other basic research tools, including the microfilm guides.

11:55–12:40

The media aide, who has previously been to lunch, supervises the circulation of materials while the head library media specialist goes to lunch and the assistant library media specialist prepares for her afternoon classes. When the head library media specialist returns, the assistant goes to lunch.

12:45–1:30

The head library media specialist and the head of the English department, the head of the social studies department, and the director of secondary education meet to discuss possible development of humanities mini-units [see Chapter 11 and Appendixes C and E]. The head library media specialist introduces for their consideration five commercially available units from The Center for Humanities, Inc., which are: "The American Dream: Myth or Reality?" "An Inquiry into the Nature of Man: His Inhumanity and His Humanity," "Man and His Environment: In Harmony and in Conflict," "Man's Search for Freedom: An Inquiry into the History of Liberty," and "No Man Is an Island: An Inquiry into Alienation."

The assistant library media specialist works in the library media center classroom with an eleventh-grade Spanish class, guiding them as they build their knowledge of the ancient Aztec, Inca, and Mayan civilizations.

1:35–2:25

The head library media specialist continues to work with the committee building the humanities mini-units.

The assistant library media specialist works in the library media center classroom, introducing a class of tenth-grade science students to the techniques and procedures to be utilized in preparing their oral presentation for the unified science and speech unit "We Have Something Important to Say about Ecology" and in acquainting them with the two speech-appraisal guides they are to use in judging the merit of their speech topic and in determining the adequacy of their speech preparation.

2:30–3:15

The head library media specialist consults with the supervisor of library media services by telephone, sharing with her the decisions made that afternoon concerning the humanities mini-kits, and requests help in locating additional kits for examination. After the conference with the supervisor, the head and the assistant library media specialists review together the day's accomplishments and share in thinking through what needs to be done for tomorrow. While the library media specialists are planning together, they are available to students and teachers needing guidance or help.

EXAMPLE 9 (cont.)

3:20–4:05
>The media aide supervises the return and checkout of materials.
>   The head library media specialist and the assistant library media specialist work with groups and individual students requesting their help.

where instruction is learner centered, where content and method extend beyond classroom and textbook, where understanding replaces memorization, where instruction is relevant, and where the process is humane, the direct involvement of the library media program in the teaching-learning process is commonplace. Where the school is still limping along at the teacher-textbook-chalkboard stage of communication, the involvement of the library media program is the exception and not the rule. Unfortunately "technology touches only a small fraction of instruction."[16] Some schools have been able to master the art of using the right media at the right time to implement the instructional program, "while others, after an initial burst of enthusiasm, quickly lose interest."[17] Persistently schools have failed to appreciate the use of instructional hardware and software as teaching-learning tools; they persist in relegating them to the level of educational gadgets, frills, or toys. Their failure to perceive the potential value of these tools is reminiscent of Mark Twain's failure to take the typewriter seriously:

>I played with the toy [the typewriter], repeating and repeating, "The boy stood on the burning deck" until I could turn that boy's adventure out at a rate of 12 words a minute; then I resumed the pen, for business, and only worked the machine to astonish inquiring visitors. They carried off many reams of the boy and his burning deck.[18]

The purpose of instructional technology is to improve learning. As a partner in the instructional process, it is the special function of the library media specialist to provide the type, kind, and quality of media service that will translate into practice the theory that "technology can make education more productive, individual, and powerful, make learning more immediate, give instruction a more scientific base, and make access to education more equal."[19]

NOTES

1. Paul DeHart Hurd, *Science Teaching for a Changing World* (Chicago: Scott, Foresman, 1963), p. 6.
2. Sidney G. Tickton, ed., *To Improve Learning: An Evaluation of Instructional Technology*, vol. 1 (New York: R. R. Bowker, 1971), p. 365.
3. Marshall McLuhan, *Understanding Media: The Extensions of Man* (New York: New American Library, 1964), pp. 23–25. Used with permission of McGraw-Hill (original publishers).
4. Tickton, *To Improve Learning.*
5. Ibid., p. 7.
6. Ibid., p. 10.
7. William H. Burton, Roland B. Kimball, and Richard L. Wing, *Education for Effective Thinking* (New York: Appleton-Century-Crofts, 1960), p. 291.
8. *The Open Classroom: Informal Education in America* (Dayton, Ohio: Institute for Development of Educational Activities, 1972), p. 8.
9. American Association of School Librarians, "Policies and Procedures for Selection of Instructional Materials," in *School Media Quarterly*, Winter 1977, pp. 109–116.
10. Margaret A. Edwards, *The Fair Garden and the Swarm of Beasts: The Library and the Young Adult* (New York: Hawthorn Books, 1974), pp. 143–182.

11. Richard I. Miller, *Selecting New Aids to Teaching* (Washington, D.C.: Association for Supervision and Curriculum Development, 1971), pp. 2–21.
12. M. Lucia James, "Instructional Materials Can Assist Integration," in *Curricular Concerns in a Revolutionary Era: Readings from "Educational Leadership,"* ed. by Robert R. Leeper (Washington, D.C.: Association for Supervision and Curriculum Development, 1971), p. 121.
13. American Library Association, Adult Services Division, Subcommittee on Indian Material, "Guidelines for the Evaluation of Indian Materials for Adults," *ASD Newsletter* 8, no. 3 (Spring 1971): n.p.
14. Warren B. Hicks and Alma M. Tillin, *Managing Multimedia Libraries* (New York: R. R. Bowker, 1977), pp. 13–14.
15. American Association of School Librarians and the Association for Educational Communications and Technology, *Media Programs: District and School* (Chicago: American Library Association, 1975), pp. 33–35.
16. Tickton, *To Improve Learning*, p. 9.
17. Ibid.
18. Mark Twain, *Thirty Thousand Bequests and Other Stories* (New York: Gabriel Wells, 1923), p. 226.
19. Tickton, *To Improve Learning*, p. 10.

8 The Library Media Program Supports the English Program

As a student majoring in English literature, I am frequently harangued by my business and engineering friends who ask with a smirk, "But what are you going to DO with an English degree?" "I'm going to be literate," I reply.

Linda Anne Barrett*

We shall have to become acquainted with many new materials of instruction, with newer methods of utilizing them, with better ways to understand our students, and devices for evaluating our instruction. The English teacher, armed with a grammar, a literature anthology, and a piece of chalk, may have been acceptable in my high school days, though he was rarely popular; but in the demanding days ahead, he will be as out of date as the quill pen.

Joseph Mersand†

Present social trends, which are characterized by accelerating change and increasing complexity, have enhanced the need for basic communication skills such as the ability to handle the written and spoken word. . . .

Harold G. Shane‡

When human beings received the gift of speech they were richly blessed, for speech is the means of our becoming participants in the drama of human events. Our voice has made us social beings capable of communicating with our fellowmen. Speech is the vehicle of self-expression; for through speech we can express our thoughts, our desires, and our emotions. Without the gift of speech we would be dumb animals cursed to suffer the travail of inarticulateness, the pain of unshared thoughts, of unsung songs, and of unspoken prayers.

When writing was devised, humanity was raised to a level little lower than that of the angels. Through writing we have become participants in the total drama of humanity transcending time, place, space, and memory. Because of the gift of spoken and written communication "no man is an island," for language makes universal our kinship with others, joint inheritors of the wealth of the accumulated history and wisdom of the ages.

COMMUNICATION AS A BASIC SKILL

The school with sincere concern for nurturing the individual promise of its students must assign top priority to building excellence into the total

---

*Linda Anne Barrett, "Letter to the Editor," *Saturday Review*, March 3, 1979, p. 4.

†Joseph Mersand, quoted in *The Teaching of High School English*, 4th ed., by J. N. Hook (New York: Ronald Press, 1972), p. 562.

‡Harold G. Shane, *Curriculum Change Toward the 21st Century*, Curriculum Series (Washington, D.C.: National Education Association, 1977), p. 65.

English language arts program. It is largely through experiences provided in formal English teaching that the student will become an effective communicator. If the school fails to enable the student to develop fluency, facility, and integrity both in thinking and in communicating thought, the student will go through life as a functional illiterate, maimed and impoverished.

The library media specialist shares with the teacher of English the responsibility for designing, structuring, and implementing an instructional program for the most efficient and effective teaching of the art and science of communication. To function competently, the library media specialist must be thoroughly conversant with the basics of the English program: philosophy, goals, aims, guiding principles, and trends. Intelligent action on the part of the library media specialist requires in-depth knowledge of the specifics of the English instructional program.

GOAL AND AIMS OF THE ENGLISH PROGRAM

The constant goal of the English program is to enable each student to read with competence, write with competence, speak with competence, listen with competence, think and communicate with competence. In the *Evaluative Criteria*, which is nationally recognized as the basic evaluation tool for secondary school programs, the goal of the English program is set forth in the following guiding principles:

> The English program is designed to improve the students' awareness of the important role that the English language and its literature play in their personal and career development. Essential to the over-all program of studies, the English program emphasizes the development of the powers of comprehension, of critical thinking skills, and of coherence, cogency, and fluency in the expression and communication of ideas.
>
> While the English program stresses competence in skills of reading, writing, speaking, and listening, it also provides experiences and activities that will help students become discriminating users of print and non-print media. Literary and media works, selected for both excellence in content and style and relevance to student interests, will promote humanistic attitudes, aesthetic appreciation, and critical evaluation skills while also providing leisure time activities.[1]

TRENDS

An examination of current language arts programs indicates that they are characterized by such trends as the following:

Recognition of the interrelationships of the language arts including reading and literature

Greater emphasis on oral language and simultaneous instruction in listening and speaking

Development of skills in thinking, independent learning, and self-evaluation in the context of language-learning experiences

Emphasis on varieties of creative expression for all children

Acceptance of different forms of language usage in different situations[2]

NATIONAL COUNCIL OF TEACHERS OF ENGLISH CURRICULUM GUIDELINES

Following are the National Council of Teachers of English (NCTE) Criteria for Planning and Evaluation of English Language Arts Curriculum Guides (Revised).[3]

INTRODUCTION

To perform the task of curriculum evaluating, the Committee on Curriculum Bulletins [of the National Council of Teachers of English—NCTE] has developed and repeatedly revised its "Criteria for Planning and Evaluation of Curriculum Guides," trying to keep up with trends set by the best curriculum practitioners. These criteria were established with several objectives in mind. First, with these criteria each member of the Committee has a uniform tool which he can use to evaluate the curriculum guide. In line with this first objective, the subcommittee that developed the criteria felt that each guide should be evaluated as a unique guide, not directly compared to other guides throughout the United States. Secondly, the criteria serve to help schools and other educational agencies develop and evaluate curricula designed to guide teachers. The Committee also hopes that the criteria will be a possible change agent. The evaluation instrument was designed to apply to many different content emphases within the field of English-language studies, along with the learning process, organization, methodology, and language versatility. The criteria and the annotation are a kind of synthesis set of Utopian standards with definite biases that the Committee readily acknowledges. So far no single guide has "met" the standards for the criteria.

School districts wishing to have guides evaluated should mail one copy to the NCTE Committee on Curriculum Bulletins, 1111 Kenyon Road, Urbana, Illinois 61801. It would help the Committee to have in addition a statement containing information about the development of the guide, the nature of the school population and community, and the guide's relationship to other curriculum materials in use. The evaluation process normally takes from four to eight weeks. There is no charge for this service.

PHILOSOPHY: WHAT WE SUBSCRIBE TO

This guide . . .

1. Has a statement of philosophy that coherently explores the beliefs of teachers about students and subject matter. *Philosophy is what we believe, and it's a good thing to get out in the open.*
2. Has content that follows logically and consistently from its statement of philosophy. *If a philosophy doesn't guide decision-making, it's largely useless.*
3. Promotes a natural, organic integration of language arts experiences. *Things ought to go together.*
4. Encourages teachers to view language both as a subject and as a communicative process central to all human life and learning. *Language is primarily a living process, not an artifact.*
5. Stipulates that individual processes of language development and concept development take precedence over arbitrary grade level expectancies or requirements. *The best chance for stimulating learning is to start where the kids are.*
6. Expresses the belief that the English program should aid students in planning, executing, and evaluating their learning experiences both individually and in groups. *Who's it for anyway? Complete involvement in the process is ideal.*
7. Suggests that teaching and learning are cooperative, not competitive, activities in the classroom. *Nobody ever really wins. The business of the classroom is cooperation: between teachers and students, and students and students.*

8. Indicates that successful experiences in language development are essential for all students. *Success comes in all colors, shapes, and sizes. All kids need to succeed in school.*

POLICIES AND PROCEDURES: HOW WE OPERATE

This plan . . .

1. Helps free teachers by explaining their responsibilities and by suggesting the possibilities open to them. *School systems usually have expectations, and it's a good thing for teachers to know their options.*
2. States procedures for both individual and group decision-making on such matters as selecting and ordering materials, equipment, and services. *The nuts and bolts ought to be specified, not just guessed at.*
3. Supports the view that curriculum building is an ongoing process. *Curriculum, like kids, keeps changing—or at least it should. There ought to be a plan and somebody to make sure it happens.*
4. Reflects the interaction and cooperation of members of the total educational community. *Everybody should have a say, and they ought to be listened to.*
5. Encourages continual inservice training and professional improvement for all teachers. *Change is continuous, as is the learning process.*

OBJECTIVES: WHAT WE HOPE WILL HAPPEN

This guide . . .

1. Has objectives that follow directly from the philosophy. *"What you see is what you get!"*
2. Sets clear objectives for all the major components of the English curriculum. *Say what you want to happen so that it makes sense to you and anybody who reads it.*
3. States objectives in a manner which facilitates recognition and description of progress. *An objective can be a useful thing if it helps you to focus on what kids do.*
4. Distinguishes teacher objectives from student objectives. *What teachers do should be differentiated from what students do.*
5. Recognizes that many objectives are desirable even though progress toward them may not be conveniently observed nor accurately measured. *Restriction to a limited set of precise objectives can unduly inhibit learning and teaching. Some goals are reached only very gradually, almost imperceptibly, and some processes are not easily broken into steps or levels of achievement.*
6. Recognizes that cognitive and affective behavior are inseparable in actual experience. *Thoughts and feelings interact continuously.*
7. Contains objectives for improving language performance, as well as perceiving more clearly what others do with language. *Language is a game for playing as well as watching. You learn to do something by doing it, not by sitting on the sidelines.*

ORGANIZATION: HOW WE CHANNEL THE FLOW OF ENERGY

This plan . . .

1. Makes clear how particular units, lessons, and/or procedures are related to the total English program. *Connections need to be made now and then. It helps if you have some idea how things might fit together and make sense.*
2. Suggests a possible workable sequence of basic communication skills. *A suggested logical order is helpful even if it can't always be followed by particular children.*
3. Organizes major aspects of the language arts to provide directions for planning. *Themes are a pretty good way to organize a curriculum but not the only way.*
4. Regards textbook materials, if used, as resources rather than courses of study.

Textbooks don't equal the curriculum—at least not in the best programs. Teachers and kids and parents are the real resources.

5. Suggests a variety of classroom organizations and activities to accommodate various kinds of learning. *Classrooms are not conveyor belts in the factory of learning. It's the things that happen on the way that count.*
6. Supplies specific procedures which will enable teachers to help their students to become increasingly independent. *Dependency is learned, but so is independence.*
7. Reflects the principle that the students themselves should often generate learning activities. *Kids are natural learners who sometimes learn to be uncurious and unquestioning. They learn when we let them.*

PROCESS AS CONTENT: THE WAYS THAT STUDENTS EXPERIENCE

This guide . . .

1. Distinguishes between conventional "expository" teaching methods and "discovery," "inductive," or "inquiry" methods. *No method is sacred; each is useful for a different purpose. In many schools, however, more emphasis needs to be placed on inquiry.*
2. Contains activities that have a "problems" or "questions" focus. *Documents from the past or problems from the present or future should often be used to promote training in inquiry.*
3. Arranges its inquiry approach so that students gain confidence in their problem-solving abilities. *An "inquiry attitude" is learned through successive and successful encounters with problems that can be solved.*
4. Indicates methods to promote cooperative interaction among students. *Classroom experiences should provide guided practice in group dynamics.*
5. Has strategies to encourage each student to discover and extend his own ways of perceiving and learning. *Because each student has a unique perception of experience, it is essential for him to develop his own growing analytic and creative powers.*
6. Stipulates ways to focus conscious attention on the processes of inquiry and learning. *Inquiry processes—learning how to learn—are probably the most important activities that students and their teachers can engage in.*

LANGUAGE

This guide . . .

1. Suggests that the content of language study often comes from real life. *Language is as real and personal as each individual.*
2. Provides for study of conventional areas of linguistics. *Linguistics, as usually taken up in schools, includes semantics, history of language, grammars, regional dialects, social dialects, lexicography, and kinetics (body language).*
3. Suggests study of unique customs of specific language areas. *The "' n-guages" of advertising, politics, religion, and many other human activitie. .re worth studying. Teachers need to ask the right questions about the way these languages work.*
4. Provides for frequent imaginative use of language in student-created and student-moderated groups. *Improvised drama, role-playing, task groups, and brainstorming are ways that kids can explore language. Imagine what it would be like if. . . . Then talk it out.*
5. Reflects knowledge of current or recent developments in modern language theory. *Some of the new grammars work better than the old ones because they describe our language more precisely.*
6. Suggests activities that help students learn the difference between grammar and usage. *Grammar is primarily the study of language structure; usage is the study of the values we attach to pronunciations, vocabulary, and particular conventions.*

7. Recognizes that analysis of language, as in grammar study, does not necessarily improve performance in composing. *The analysis of grammar is different from processes of composing.*
8. Recognizes the assets of bidialectal, bilingual, and non-English-speaking children in exploring language concepts. *We live in a pluralistic society.*
9. Suggests activities that help students acquire or expand their facility to understand and use the English language. *The basis for all language is experience.*
10. Recognizes the importance of children accepting their "home-rooted" language, as well as that of others. *Positive self-concepts help kids to become more "open" people.*

COMPOSITION: HOW WE SHAPE LANGUAGE AND OURSELVES

This guide . . .

1. Perceives composing as occurring in four ways: speaking, writing, acting, and filming. *Composing requires an orchestration of experience. There are different ways to say things, and all are worthy of investigation.*
2. Emphasizes the significance of composing as a means of self-discovery. *E. M. Forster said, "How can I know what I think 'til I hear what I say?"*
3. Recognizes the importance of the composing processes as ways of bringing order to human experience. *Composing is a way to make sense of our world.*
4. Has activities designed to stimulate composing. *Precomposing experiences, if important to kids, can help stimulate more worthwhile writing.*
5. Recommends that composing should often occur in small groups. *Kids can help each other shape their thinking.*
6. Affirms that composing is always creative.
7. Suggests that composing stems from meaningful precomposing experiences. *The better the input, the better the output. Creation requires stimulation.*
8. Recommends that composition should occur for different purposes and usually for audiences other than the teacher. *Decisions about communication ought to be determined by something more than the teacher's grade book. Authenticity is a function of knowing whom you're talking to and why.*
9. Recommends that composing should occur in an atmosphere of maximum sharing. *Let kids help each other.*

MEDIA: "THE MEDIUM IS THE MESSAGE"

This guide . . .

1. Promotes audiovisual as well as verbal literacy. *Students need to explore the relationships among visual, verbal, and kinesthetic communication.*
2. Acquaints teachers with the characteristics and potential use of various media. *The electronic age is with us. Are we with it?*
3. Suggests ways of involving students in using media. *A pen and ink is just one voice. Kids need the options of communicating with color, motion, and sound.*
4. Suggests specific media supplements for learning activities. *The media are like extension cords; they plug into a wider world.*
5. Lists media resources available to teachers, and specifies procurement procedures. *What's available and how do you get it? Media doesn't get used unless it's accessible.*

READING AND LITERATURE: THE WORLDS STUDENTS EXPERIENCE

This guide . . .

1. Provides ways for the teacher to determine individual degrees of readiness. *Shakespeare said, "The readiness is all."*
2. Suggests procedures to help teachers develop student reading skills. *The "teaching of reading" means more than having a few books around.*
3. Recognizes that a total reading program reaches beyond the developing of basic

reading skills. *A person really never stops learning how to read. There are always new skills to learn.*

4. Relates the skills of reading to a total language program. *Reading, writing, listening, and speaking are more like a web than like four peas in a pod. You touch one strand of language experience, and the whole thing vibrates and responds.*

5. Makes provisions for a comprehensive literature program. *Get a lot of books of all kinds in kids' hands.*

6. Recognizes that it is more important to "engage in" literature than to talk about terms. *Literary terms, conventions, and systems of classification are inventions of the profession. If talk about these externals is substituted for experience with literature, we "murder to dissect," as Wordsworth put it.*

7. Recommends that teachers allow and encourage students to select and read all types of literature, especially contemporary. *Take the lid off the reading list, and let kids explore.*

8. Helps teachers to identify, accept, and explore all varieties of affective and cognitive response. *What kids say about literature is important, and so is how they feel about it. Our efforts should be devoted to helping kids extend and deepen their responses.*

9. Suggests acting and role playing as a means of exploring literature. *Literature is frozen drama. Whenever you get your body into the language of a poem or story, you're interpreting it.*

EVALUATION: DISCOVERING AND DESCRIBING WHERE WE ARE

This guide . . .

1. Has a coherent and useful rationale for evaluation. *The rationale should be related to philosophy and objectives. The reporting policy should be explicit.*

2. Stipulates that reporting procedures describe pupil progress, including growth beyond the scope of stated objectives. *Teachers and students should not feel inhibited by narrowly specified objectives. "The asides are essential to the insides."*

3. Makes clear that grades and standardized tests, if used, do not constitute the major purpose of evaluation. *Marks and scores are not ends; the end of evaluation should be information useful for furthering achievement.*

4. Suggests methods of evaluation which help to encourage a pupil, not to discourage him. *Teachers should encourage and respect any progress a pupil makes rather than punish or badger him for any apparent lack of progress.*

5. Helps teachers diagnose individual learning progress and suggests methods and material to accomplish this. *Each pupil learns in a different way at a differing rate from other pupils.*

6. Suggests that most evaluation be tailored to the students' ability, age, and personality. *Evaluation should be adapted to people, not vice versa. If evaluation is primarily for helping individuals learn, and if differences are at least acknowledged, then evaluation should be individualized.*

7. Recognizes that the student must be involved in all evaluation. *Self-evaluation is crucial to learning.*

8. Suggests ways that teachers and students can use the results of evaluation to change the program as often as necessary. *The ideal curriculum is tentative, flexible, and responsive to the results of continual evaluation.*

DESIGN: FORM, FUNCTION, AND FLAVOR

This guide . . .

1. Is easy to read; the language is clear and effective. *Guide writers should set a good example in communicating; our medium has a message.*

2. Exhibits an appealing form and style. *An attractive and creative guide will stimulate use.*

3. Has a format which makes revision convenient. *A looseleaf format makes a guide more amenable to change.*
4. States its relationship to any other curriculum guides published by the school system. *Sometimes new teachers have a better idea of what's going on when curriculum relationships are explicit.*
5. Suggests as resources a large variety of specific background materials and school services. *A guide, to be useful, has got to have usable things in it.*
6. Identifies people and procedures which will promote interdisciplinary activities. *We can build walls around ourselves with labels like English, social studies, and science.*

THE READING PROGRAM

In no area of the English curriculum is the responsibility of the library media specialist greater than in support of the reading program. Facilitating the optimum development of both the formal and the recreational reading program is a constant concern and a continuing challenge. "Some subjects are more important than others. Reading is the most important of all."[4] Reading is the basic tool for continued self-education and intellectual renewal. "Those who do not learn to read and write effectively are not only deficient in the basic tools for further learning; they are often lost from the mainstream of the educational process."[5]

BASIC ASSUMPTIONS

Blueprints for Better Reading: School Programs for Promoting Skill and Interest in Reading is a monumental work and should be *required reading* for all teachers and all school library media specialists who are involved in reading guidance. Its author, Florence Cleary, Professor Emeritus of Wayne State University, bases her contention that the library media center must be an active participant in the school's reading program on the following assumptions:

During the past decade a number of significant concepts relating to reading programs have emerged. These suggest a philosophical base that school staffs might use to evaluate their current reading programs and to plan for improvement.

1. Reading can be a potent factor in the development of knowledge, understandings, appreciations, values, and beliefs required by the individual in dealing with his own problems and in relating effectively to others. Reading, however, is a complicated skill, and the degree of facility in reading attained by pupils depends on sound basic instruction; on the teacher's understanding of the motivations, drives, and interests of his pupils; and on his skill in encouraging young people to read and to generalize from their reading, to relate and apply the values in many situations and associations.

2. It should not be taken for granted that boys and girls in the middle and upper grades have learned to read and hence have no further need for reading guidance in the content subjects. Reading the words is a basic skill, but discovering what the words mean, relating ideas, utilizing and applying the knowledge gained *is* skill in reading. Moreover, there are a number of intermediate skills such as skimming, outlining, note-taking, and reporting that are essential in the gathering and utilization of knowledge. These are not acquired by chance. They must be taught.

3. The idea that the child will learn to read by reading and that he will develop interest in books if they are made accessible to him is no longer acceptable. School administrators, librarians, and teachers must continue their efforts to

provide reading materials that meet the needs and interests of their pupils. Exposure to books and other nondirective reading guidance techniques are sufficient motivations for large numbers of children. For still larger numbers, *reading periods in the classroom or library, when little guidance is given, produce neither interest nor skill. Only as librarians and teachers provide real learning situations in reading guidance, taking into account such viewpoints about learning as readiness, relatedness, and usefulness of learning experiences, will pupils learn to like to read and develop the skills for reading to learn.*

4. The image of the librarian as a keeper and dispenser of books and other learning materials held by many teachers, administrators, and librarians can and will be dispelled as librarians assume real leadership roles in librarian-centered reading guidance programs in the schools.

5. Skill and interest must be considered interdependent factors in the development of reading tastes and habits. The skillful reader tends to develop and maintain high interest in reading. In turn, high interest motivates the development of greater skill. In planning reading programs teachers and librarians tend to consider these two factors as mutually exclusive. They make a sharp distinction between free, voluntary, or recreational reading, and required or reference reading. The attendant result of compartmentalizing reading, of labeling and categorizing reading activities, is that pupils sometimes gain the impression that free or recreational reading is interesting, while reading for information is dull and difficult.

6. The growing number of research projects in special areas and disciplines has brought about a sharp increase in curriculum offerings in these areas. The additive concept of curriculum change and improvement which is operating at present threatens to produce a curriculum that may topple under its own weight. Many of the new approaches appear promising as teachers and administrators seek to upgrade standards of achievement, but there appears to be no time for leisure reading in school libraries or at least insufficient time for self-learning and investigation on the part of secondary school pupils. The time is approaching when priorities will have to be established as to the relative merits of programs, whether they be driver education or honors courses in literature and reading.

7. Reading does not stand in danger of becoming obsolete although people are increasingly entertained and informed by such mass media of communication as television, radio, movies, the newsreels, tabloids, comics, and pictorial magazines. These media may be competitive users of time but they cannot provide, as books do, the complete record of man's best thinking or the story of his cultural heritage. Moreover, the symbols on the pages of a book are not fleeting and evanescent. The reader may proceed at his own rate, may pause to reflect, to question, to clarify his thinking, to weigh his own values, to agree or disagree. Thus for the skillful reader, books can be a charging of mind and spirit, a pleasure that needs no defense or explanation.[6]

FUNCTIONAL LITERACY AND THE RIGHT TO READ

In summarizing the public's attitude toward education at the close of the seventies, the Gallup Poll report *A Decade of Gallup Polls of Attitudes toward Education 1969–1978* revealed that the "back to basics" movement had wide support throughout the nation, with many people wanting greater emphasis placed on the "fundamentals"—reading, writing, and arithmetic.[7] Close agreement was found regarding reading as a basic requirement among all major groups interviewed.[8] Dissatisfaction with the schools' attainments in the field of reading has been dramatized and publicized by the mass media for the past quarter of a century; *Why Johnny Can't Read* . . . by Rudolf Flesch hit the bestseller list as far back as 1955.[9]

In 1969, the late James E. Allen, then U.S. Commissioner of Education, instituted the federal government's Right to Read program. In announcing this program, Commissioner Allen stated, "We should immediately set for ourselves the goal of assuring that by the end of the 1970s the right to read shall be a reality for all—that no one shall be leaving our schools without the skill and the desire to read to the full limits of his capability." He cited the following statistics as evidence of the widespread reading deficiencies existing in the United States:

> One out of every four students nation-wide has significant reading deficiencies.
>
> In large city school systems up to half of the students read below expectation.
>
> There are more than three million illiterates in our adult population.
>
> About half of the unemployed youths, ages 16–21, are functionally illiterate.
>
> Three-quarters of the juvenile offenders in New York City are two or more years retarded in reading.
>
> In a recent U.S. Armed Forces Program called Project 100,000, 68.2 percent of the young men fell below grade seven in reading and academic ability.[10]

One specific recommendation made by Commissioner Allen was to have relevant books and other materials readily available to children. This, of course, demands the direct support of the library media program if the Right to Read program is to reach its goal of encouraging each student to read to maximum capacity.

David Harman, adult education expert and member of an advisory group assisting the U.S. Office of Education with the Right to Read program, conducted a research study at Harvard University that indicated that as many as half of the adults in the United States may lack the degree of literacy necessary to master the day-to-day required reading matter such as newspapers, driving manuals, and job applications. Writing in the *Harvard Educational Review*, Harman takes issue with the commonly accepted practice of basing literacy judgments on whether or not individuals have completed the fourth or the fifth grade. He, however, endorses the U.S. Office of Education definition of *functional literacy*—"The ability to hold a decent job, to support self and family, to lead a life of dignity and pride."[11] He believes that adult literacy assessments should be made independently of grade equivalent and should be based on whether or not individuals can in fact fulfill adult reading requisites. In his opinion much essential reading material requires at least tenth- and perhaps eleventh-grade education. And for more sophisticated reading material, such as tax returns, the required level is markedly higher.

The Education Department of the State of New York sets forth its endorsement of the Right to Read program in the form of a Bill of Rights,* which states:

> Every child, youth, and adult must be guaranteed certain rights in his pursuit of literacy.
>
> 1. Right to an environment in his pre-school years which stimulates and helps satisfy his desire to understand.
> 2. Right to be accepted as an individual of worth with his own learning styles.
> 3. Right to a teacher adequately trained in reading procedures and informed about latest research and effective methods of teaching reading.
> 4. Right to enough time to develop his reading skills.
> 5. Right to proceed at his own rate of progress and to have his growth evaluated individually.

*Reading Task Force, Bill of Rights, reprinted with permission from the University of the State of New York, the New York State Education Department.

6. Right to special services for learning problems—physical, social, and psychological.
7. *Right to a school library media center staffed by a trained librarian and equipped with an appropriate collection of materials to satisfy his wide range of interests.* [emphasis supplied]
8. Right to a sequential reading program throughout his elementary and secondary schooling.
9. Right to continue upgrading his reading skills after completion of high school or highest grade attended.
10. Right to an opportunity to learn to read or to upgrade reading skills as an adult for occupational advancement and cultural enrichment.

SUPPORT OF THE LIBRARY MEDIA PROGRAM: A BASIC REQUIREMENT

Researchers and experts in the field of reading have frequently stressed the primary importance of the library media program to the success of the school's reading program. These four instances serve as examples:

The most comprehensive survey of the content and practices of reading programs ever to be undertaken was conducted by researchers on the staff of Harvard University in 1962. The survey analyzed reading programs in 1,023 school systems and involved 6,361,139 pupils enrolled in 13,609 elementary schools. In the survey report, *The First R: The Harvard Report on Reading in Elementary Schools*, high tribute is paid to the school library program as a supportive arm of the reading program:

> The extent to which a successful library program will substantially improve the total reading program cannot be overestimated. Children who can choose from a wide range of carefully selected books, and who receive instruction in library and reference skills from a trained teacher-librarian, are likely to become more interested and capable readers than are others without these advantages. . . . Therefore, it is recommended: that a central library be established in every elementary school with the following provisions: (1) at least the minimum number of volumes recommended by the American Library Association; (2) books chosen by a selection committee headed by the teacher-librarian; and (3) a full-time certified teacher-librarian.[12]

Focus on Reading, a joint report of the New England Reading Association and the New England School Development Council, stresses the significance of the school library and its resources. It states that the "characteristics of an effective reading program would include the following: A suitable, stimulating environment in classroom and school; a 'reading atmosphere'; and good library facilities."[13]

In the introduction to the teacher's edition of each of the Harcourt, Brace, and World textbooks in the Bookmark Reading Series there are specific recommendations concerning the role of the school library in implementing the program. *"Teachers and children must have access to a good collection of children's books. . . . In a good program of literature study, the textbook and the library complement each other. . . .* Boys and girls must be introduced as individuals to the riches of a library. Through a variety of planned experiences, they should be encouraged to follow their own interests, to read and to share a variety of books and periodicals, and to learn for themselves the delight, the aid, and the inspiration that reading can bring. *School librarians have specific responsibilities related to the teaching of literature. . . .* Obviously, in good schools, teachers and librarians share their planning, their experiences with children, and their evaluation of children's learning about literature."[14]

Paul Burns, Betty Broman, and Alberta Lowe in the second edition of their book *The Language Arts in Childhood Education* emphasize that "the school librarian can be the teacher's most important assistant." They stress the necessity of the teacher's working and planning with the school librarian in order to meet adequately the needs of all children—the language-gifted, the language-deprived, the underprivileged, and the disadvantaged.[15]

DEVELOPMENTAL READING PROGRAM GOALS

Contemporary reading programs such as the Houghton Mifflin Readers are designed to present a developmental reading program that strives to achieve two basic goals. (1) The development of an ever-increasing control of those specific skills that will enable the pupil to read well independently, and (2) the development of an enthusiastic and ever-broadening interest in reading.[16]

Four major behavioral objectives form the basis of the Houghton Mifflin instructional program. These four objectives are concerned with the mastery of these skills.

Decoding skills—Behavioral Objective 1.   In order to demonstrate his ability, when reading silently, to convert printed language into the oral language it represents, the pupil reads aloud material of an appropriate difficulty level with acceptable pronunciations and expression and with a reasonable fluency.

Comprehension skills—Behavioral Objective 2.   The pupil correctly answers questions concerning material that he has read at an appropriate difficulty level—questions that test not only his literal comprehension but also his ability to go beyond what has actually been stated in the text.

Reference and study skills—Behavioral Objective 3.   The pupil demonstrates good study procedures by (1) making efficient use of reference aids such as indexes, dictionaries, encyclopedias, card catalogs, maps, tables, and graphs in locating needed information; (2) appraising the reliability of such information; (3) organizing such information in outline form.

Literary skills—Behavioral Objective 4.   The pupil discusses, at an appropriate maturity level, the literary nature and merit of material he has read.[17]

Since the ultimate goal of the reading program is the development of an enthusiastic and ever-broadening interest in reading, then all of the youngsters' reading activities should be directly or indirectly employed to encourage the acquiring of lifetime reading interests and habits. The basal reader serves not only to develop reading competence but to create interest in independent reading for both pleasure and information. Each unit in the basal reader is built around a theme chosen because of its strong pupil appeal; for example: Dream of Freedom; Dreamers and Doers; Legends, Myths, and Other Tales; You Can't Help Laughing. The unit theme is an interest-building, motivational device that serves as a springboard to independent reading. The classroom teacher who is alert to the motivational power of the reading theme will capitalize on this interest by planning with the library media specialist for scheduled class or group associational reading experiences in the library media center. The library media specialist welcomes this opportunity to acquaint the children with the unsuspected wealth of reading, viewing, and listening experiences appropriate to the further exploration of the reading unit theme. Here is a perfect opportunity to acquaint the children with all the wonderful informational and recreational reading resources that might never be discovered if the children were denied this associative reading experience.

Self-directed knowledge building does not imply total student competence to work without informed guidance, nor innate student ability to sense from title or format or indeed the card catalog the very book one will enjoy reading. In the field of reading, the best is not always known to children and, through ignorance of delightful alternatives or possibilities, they can well limit themselves to less than the best or most enjoyable. The library media specialist's greatest joy lies in personalizing the child's introduction to the world of books and in fostering delight in reading.

In answer to the laissez-faire advocates who believe that any form of reading guidance infringes on the rights of the student as a free individual, Cleary offers the following rebuttal:

A study conducted in 1967–1968 for a period of thirty-six weeks in an elementary school in Florida focused on the relationship which should exist between the effective teaching of reading, reading achievement, and librarian-centered reading guidance programs.

Seventy-five fifth-grade pupils were placed in three matched groups, two experimental and one control, with contaminating variables controlled. Group A was provided a scheduled librarian-centered reading guidance program. Group B was provided the more traditional scheduled type of library experience. Control Group C had no scheduled period in the library, but all three groups had free access to the library one day a week for circulation privileges.

A battery of pre- and post-reading achievement tests revealed significant findings. The mean improvement for Group A was mathematically greater than Groups B and C in the following subtest areas: speed, accuracy, word recognition, and the use of indexes and the dictionary. Reading inventories and study forms showed marked positive gains for Group A in attitudes toward reading and toward the library. When the study began, 52 percent of the pupils in Group A ranked reading last among five leisure-time preferences, 16 percent ranked it either as a first or second choice. At the close of the study, 42 percent ranked reading first or second choice and only 4 percent ranked reading last.

As the close of the study, participants in Group B who experienced the "traditional" library period common to a majority of elementary schools showed no statistically significant gains in reading skills and reading habits. In some of the sub-areas studied, negative reactions to the library and to reading were revealed. In both evaluated areas—reading habits and skills—findings disclosed that Group B's library experience was the least effective of the three groups.

The present trend, however, is toward the library experiences offered Group B, namely the opportunity for pupils to discover, to browse, to choose books and learning materials, to watch films, to learn how to use all types of materials. This type of library experience does not produce satisfactory results. More *direct* guidance needs to be provided by the librarian, with experiences that build lasting skills and interest in books.

The experiences offered Group A are easy to provide when the librarian knows and loves the great literature of childhood, understands curriculum and child development theory, and carries forward a planned, developmental guidance program in the library. This is equally true of teachers who recognize that skill without interest does not start the child on his way to a sustained love for reading.[18]

Knowledge of the student as an individual is a prerequisite for effective reading guidance. Before a library media specialist can attempt to recommend books to be read, films to be viewed, or recordings to be heard, to any student whether on the elementary or secondary level, he or she must be aware of the student's reading level. Unfortunately, students do not master the skill of reading at equal rates as they move from grade to grade. By eighth grade the range of reading ability may well reach from four years below grade level to four years above. "By the time students are in the eleventh grade there will be a ten-year differential between the best and the poorest readers."[19] What is possible for the able reader is overwhelmingly impossible for the disabled reader. When the teacher and the library media specialist preplan a class or group to work in the library, part of the planning time should be spent identifying special student needs and interests: for example, Jack is anxious to read about the bombing of Pearl Harbor but he is reading on the third-grade level—can you give him something that he can manage? Library media specialists build their knowledge of individual students through observation and day-to-day contact; stored away in their memory banks, ready for immediate retrieval, are the vital statistics of individual student interests, goals, concerns, special needs, abilities, and disabilities.

CRITERIA FOR SELECTING MEDIA TO SUPPORT THE READING PROGRAM

The reading teacher and the library media specialist share jointly the responsibility for selecting library resources to support the teaching of reading. In evaluating these resources the following criteria can serve to relate media evaluation to the needs of the reading program:

Is this material relevant to the theme of the reading unit?

Is this material worthy of the pupil's time and attention?

Is this material appropriate in vocabulary, concept, and format for this age, grade, and maturity level?

Is this material a means of integrating reading with other curricular subjects?

Is this material motivational with strong pupil appeal?

Is this material educationally significant?

Is this material justifiable in cost?

The effectiveness of these criteria can be enhanced if they are placed in a reading media evaluation format such as Checklist 2.

As library media specialists search for reading materials, they are mindful of the special needs of those who are disadvantaged socially, culturally, emotionally, or intellectually. It is recommended by the U.S. Office of Education that schools in disadvantaged areas provide the special services of a library media specialist and the facilities and resources of a building library media center.[20]

> The school organization and administration, teaching staff, curriculum content and activities, and special services must be focused patiently and effectively on developing the social and intellectual backgrounds and skills which are essential to success in school, and on enabling each student *to progress at his own rate* with dignity and integrity to the end that he will wish to make the most of his educational opportunities.[21]

The complex aspect of the task facing the teacher and the library media specialist is to provide instructional media that are uniquely suited to the personal, social, cultural, and educational needs of each disadvantaged child. They must search for materials that will speak directly to children on their own perception levels. In large measure the hope of enabling disadvantaged children to overcome their inadequacies lies in providing instructional materials that will capture, sustain, and reward the children's interest in learning to learn. In selecting books for disadvantaged children certain criteria need to be considered.

CHECKLIST 2 FORM FOR SELECTING RESOURCES TO SUPPORT A READING UNIT

READING MEDIA EVALUATION FORM

Date _____

Previewed by _____ School _____

Basic reader _____ Unit # _____ Title _____

Type of material (Indicate by checking):

Art print	_____	Graph	_____	Realia	_____
Book	_____	Map	_____	Recording	_____
Cassette	_____	Motion picture	_____	Resource kit	_____
Chart	_____	Poster	_____	Study print	_____
Filmstrip	_____	Programmed		Transparency	_____
Flannel graph	_____	medium	_____		
				(Other medium)	

Title _____ Author _____ Copyright date _____

Publisher/manufacturer _____ Cost _____

Pilot use by:

Class _____ Group _____ Individual Pupil _____

Your evaluation: Yes   No

1. Is this material relevant to the theme of the reading unit?   _____   _____

2. Is this material worthy of the pupil's time and attention?   _____   _____

3. Is this material appropriate for this age and grade level?   _____   _____
   Specify grade _____

4. Is this material appropriate in concept for this age and grade level?   _____   _____

5. Is this material appropriate in format for this age and grade level?   _____   _____

6. Is this material a means of integrating reading with the other language arts?   _____   _____

7. Is this material a means of integrating reading with other curricular areas?   _____   _____
   Specify _____

8. Is this material motivational with strong pupil appeal?   _____   _____

9. Is this material educationally significant?   _____   _____

10. Is this material worthy of inclusion in the library collection?   _____   _____

CRITERIA FOR SELECTING BOOKS FOR DISADVANTAGED CHILDREN

SPECIFIC INTEREST FACTORS IN CONTENT

1. Stories about teen-agers like themselves with whom they can identify: characters from different socioeconomic backgrounds and from other racial and national groups.
2. Realistic experiences related to pupils' own lives.
3. Suspense.
4. Action and adventure; exciting episodes of courage and skill.

5. Genuine emotion, giving insight into how people feel when they behave in certain ways and into what motivates them.
6. Humor.
7. Significance—content that helps young people to understand their world and their life today.
8. Information about something they can do or can become.
9. Character and personality building qualities.

INTEREST FACTORS IN STYLE

1. A quick, dramatic beginning.
2. Much conversation; few long descriptive passages, but sufficient description to make the scene and characters real.
3. Logical organization, not complex and confusing.
4. Simple, straightforward, clear sentences.
5. Few difficult, unfamiliar words—words often explained by the context.
6. Style natural and somewhat colloquial, not stilted and artificial.
7. Illustrations that clarify the text; pictures, diagrams, maps, and charts inserted close to the text and helping to interpret it.
8. Literary merit—unity, coherence, and emphasis; colorful and vigorous style.

PHYSICAL MAKEUP DESIRED

1. Size—adult in appearance, but short enough to prevent pupils' being discouraged by length.
2. Print—deep black, clear letters, easy to read.[22]

Programming the Reading Support Program

Nowhere in the instructional program is the science of instructional technology of greater significance than in the implementation of the school's reading program. Just as the placement of steel girders within the framework of a building cannot be hit or miss, so the placement of library media support resources and guidance within the framework of the reading program cannot be left to whim or chance.

Central to the success of the reading support program are these three basic assumptions:

1. The reading teacher and the library media specialist will work together throughout the school year to bring greater depth, breadth, and relevance to the reading program.
2. The reading teacher will plan with the library media specialist in face-to-face, prescheduled planning sessions to spell out not only the developmental support needs of the reading program, but also the cross-discipline integration possibilities with other curricular areas.
3. The reading teacher and the library media specialist will work together to build into the reading support program such a high degree of diversity and flexibility that each individual student will not only be encouraged but will be nurtured in self-actualizing reading pursuits.

In order to build unity, continuity, balance, and harmony in the "seamless"* reading curriculum, procedural guidelines should be spelled out and followed in planning reading support activities. The following guides enable

---

*In *Curriculum Change Toward the 21st Century* (Washington, D.C.: National Education Association, 1977, p. 60), Harold G. Shane proposes that education be seen as a seamless continuum of experiences rather than merely recurrent or periodic.

the library media specialist when structuring a media support activity to insure uniform excellence within the reading support program.

1. Provide print and nonprint resources that will bring depth, breadth, and relevance to the basal reading textbook unit and will match the spectrum of student ability, interest, and preference.

2. Provide the complete literary work—novel, short story, biography, autobiography, play, poem, pun, essay, journal, diary, legend, myth, fairy tale, tall tale, fable—if that work is abridged or condensed in the basal reader.

   EXAMPLE. When the students read in the fourth-grade Houghton Mifflin Basic Reader *Keystone* excerpts from *Jennifer, Hecate, Macbeth, William McKinley, and Me, Elizabeth* by Elaine Konisburg; from *The Cat Who Went to Heaven* by Elizabeth Coatsworth; from *Call It Courage* by Armstrong Sperry; from *Ben and Me* by Robert Lawson; from *A Day in the Life of Henry Reed* by Keith Robertson; and from *Wind in the Willows* by Kenneth Grahame, the students should have available to them each of the books from which the excerpt in the reader has been taken.

3. Provide information that will enable the students to visualize the writer as a human being.

   EXAMPLE. When the students read in the fifth-grade Houghton Mifflin Basic Reader *Medley* the selection "The Wolf Pack" from *The Little House on the Prairie* by Laura Ingalls Wilder, the students should have available the following: *Yesterday's Authors of Books for Children*, vol. 2; the sound filmstrip *Meet the Newbery Author: Laura Ingalls Wilder*, available from Miller-Brody Productions, Inc.; and "Never Too Late— Little House in the Big Woods" in *The Story behind Modern Books* by Elizabeth Rider Montgomery.

4. Provide sequels to the basic reader's selection, if sequels exist; if the selection is part of a series, acquaint the students with the remaining titles in the series.

   EXAMPLE. When the students read in the fourth-grade Houghton Mifflin Basic Reader *Keystone* the excerpt from *A Day in the Life of Henry Reed* by Keith Robertson, they should have the opportunity to read the sequels: *Henry Reed, Inc.; Henry Reed's Baby-Sitting Service; Henry Reed's Big Show;* and *Henry Reed's Journal.*

5. Provide various illustrated editions of the literary work excerpted in the basic reader.

   EXAMPLE. When the students read in the fourth-grade Houghton Mifflin Basic Reader *Keystone* the excerpt from *Wind in the Willows* by Kenneth Grahame, the students should have available to them the editions of that work illustrated by: Adrienne Adams (The River Bank, Scribner, 1978); Arthur Rackham (Heritage Press, 1940); Ernest Shepard (Scribner, 1933); and Tasha Tudor (World, 1966).

6. Provide other works by the author of the selection in the basal reader.

   EXAMPLE. When the students read in the fifth-grade Houghton Mifflin Basic Reader *Medley* "Paul Revere's Big Ride," by Jean Fritz, taken from her book *And Then What Happened, Paul Revere*, the students should have the opportunity to explore other books written by Jean Fritz such as: *The Animals of Doctor Schweitzer; Brady; The Cabin Faced West; Can't You Make Them Behave, King George; Early Thunder; George Washington's Breakfast; What's the Big Idea, Ben Franklin; Where Was Patrick Henry on the 29th of May; Who's That Stepping on Plymouth Rock; Why Don't You Get a Horse, Sam Adams;* and *Will You Sign Here, John Hancock.*

7. Provide viewing and listening experiences that will heighten the students' enjoyment and appreciation of the selection from the basal reader. EXAMPLE. When the students read in the sixth-grade Houghton Mifflin Basic Reader *Galaxies* the informational article "Volcanoes: Windows in the Earth" by William H. Matthews they should have the opportunity to extend their knowledge of volcanoes not only by reading but also by using nonprint media such as: the filmstrip *Physiographic Changes: Volcanoes and Earthquakes* (SVE); the motion picture *The Earth: Volcanoes* (Coronet); the slide set "Earth Science: Volcanism & Diastrophism" (SVE); and the study-print set "Volcanoes" (Instructional Aids).

8. Provide the students with other literary works that parallel the theme, the plot, the setting, or the characterization of the selection in the basal reader. EXAMPLE. When the students read in the sixth-grade Houghton Mifflin Basic Reader *Galaxies* the excerpt from *Island of the Blue Dolphins* by Scott O'Dell, they should have the opportunity to explore via print and nonprint media the classic theme of fight to survive against incredible odds. Typical of the wealth of reading, viewing, and listening materials supporting this theme are the following: Books: *Akavak. An Eskimo Journey* by James Houston (Harcourt); *Firestorm* by Maurine Gee (Morrow); *Jon the Unlucky* by Elizabeth Coatsworth (Holt); *Julie of the Wolves* by Jean George (Harper); *The Loner* by Ester Wier (McKay); *My Journals and Sketchbooks* by Robinson Crusoe (Harcourt); *Swiss Family Robinson* by Johann Wyss (Grosset); *The Village That Slept* by Monique De Ladebat (Coward); *Zeb* by Lonzo Anderson (Knopf); and *Zia* by Scott O'Dell (Knopf). Sound Filmstrips: *Julie of the Wolves* (Miller-Brody); *The Loner* (Miller-Brody); *Meet the Newbery Author: Scott O'Dell* (Miller-Brody). Motion Pictures: *Island of the Blue Dolphins* (Teaching Film Custodians); *Swiss Family Robinson* (Disney).

9. Provide the students with other examples of the literary type or genre as that of the reading selection in the basal reader: If the selection in the reader is from a historical novel, the students should have the opportunity to explore other historical novels; if the selection in the reader is from a biography or autobiography, the students should have the opportunity to explore other biographies and autobiographies; if the selection in the reader is from a narrative poem, the students should have the opportunity to explore other narrative poems; if the selection in the reader is a myth, a legend, or a folktale, the students should have the opportunity to explore other myths, legends, and folktales, etc.

THE LITERATURE PROGRAM

Students need not only to learn to read but to learn to read literature. The library media program is involved directly in each program designed to promote the study and the enjoyment of literature—library media are indeed the content of the literature program.* The teaching of literature on the elementary level is usually an integral part of the formal reading program with the reading textbook providing myriad literary examples for the students to use as they build and practice their skills of reading. On the secondary level the literary anthology is the most common tool employed in the teaching of literature; yet, as the examples included in the preceding section on the reading program illustrate, class reading from a basal reader or from a literature anthology cannot suffice if students are to learn to read, to interpret, and to enjoy literature. In any serious attempt to introduce students to our literary heritage, the basal reader or the literature anthology can serve merely as an introduction or as a point of departure that leads out of the classroom and into the book-lined shelves of the library media center.

Today's school library media specialist should have an adequate reference collection of basic tools available for guidance when designing reading and/or literature enrichment and/or acceleration experiences. The following are basic tools of proven value that each media specialist should have readily at hand:

BIOGRAPHICAL TOOLS

ELEMENTARY LEVEL

Authors and Illustrators of Children's Books: Writings on Their Lives and Works, ed. by Miriam S. Hoffman and Eva A. Samuels. New York: R. R. Bowker, 1972.

Junior Book of Authors, by S. J. Kunitz and H. Haycraft, 2nd ed. New York: H. W. Wilson, 1951.

More Junior Authors, by Muriel Fuller. New York: H. W. Wilson, 1963.

Something about the Author: Facts and Pictures about Contemporary Authors and Illustrators of Books for Young People, by Anne Commire. Detroit: Gale, 1971- .

Third Book of Junior Authors, by Doris de Montreville and Donna Hill. New York: H. W. Wilson, 1972.

Yesterday's Authors of Books for Children. Detroit: Gale, 1978- .

SECONDARY LEVEL

American Writers, ed. by Leonard Unger, 6 vols. and Supplement 1. New York: Scribner, 1974–1979.

Author Biographies Master Index, 2 vols. Detroit: Gale, 1978.

British Writers, ed. by Ian Scott-Kilvert, 7 vols. New York: Scribner, 1979–1981.

Contemporary Authors. Detroit: Gale, 1962- .

Dictionary of Literary Biography. Detroit: Gale, 1978- .

European Authors, 1000–1900: A Biographical Dictionary of European Literature, ed. by Stanley Kunitz and Vineta Colby. New York: H. W. Wilson, 1967.

*For information concerning literature program design and implementation contact Jack Luskay, Assistant Professor, Clarion State College, Clarion, Pa. 16214, tel. 814-226-2272.

Living Black American Authors: A Biographical Directory, ed. by Ann A. Shockley and Sue P. Chandler. New York: R. R. Bowker, 1973.

Something about the Author: Facts and Pictures about Contemporary Authors and Illustrators of Books for Young People, by Anne Commire. Detroit: Gale, 1971- .

Twayne's English Authors Series. Boston: G. K. Hall, 1964- .

Twayne's United States Authors Series. Boston: G. K. Hall, 1964- .

Twayne's World Authors Series. Boston: G. K. Hall, 1966- .

Twentieth Century Authors: A Biographical Dictionary of Modern Literature. New York: H. W. Wilson, 1942; Supplement, 1955.

University of Minnesota Pamphlets on American Writers. Minneapolis, Minn.: University of Minnesota Press, 1959- .

World Authors, ed. by John Wakeman. New York: H. W. Wilson, 1975.

BIBLIOGRAPHIES, GUIDES, HANDBOOKS, AND INDEXES

ELEMENTARY LEVEL

Adventuring with Books: A Booklist for Pre-K–Grade 8, ed. by Patricia Cianciolo. Urbana, Ill.: National Council of Teachers of English, 1977.

Best Books for Children: Preschool Through the Middle Grades, ed. by John T. Gillespie and Christine Gilbert. New York: R. R. Bowker, 1978.

Books for the Gifted Child, by Barbara Baskin and Karen Harris. New York: R. R. Bowker, 1980.

Books to Help Children Cope with Separation and Loss, comp. by Joanne E. Bernstein. New York: R. R. Bowker, 1977.

Core Media Collection for Elementary Schools, by Lucy G. Brown and Betty McDavid, 2nd ed. New York: R. R. Bowker, 1978.

Feature Films on 8mm, 16mm, and Videotape, ed. by James L. Limbacher, 6th ed. New York: R. R. Bowker, 1979.

Index to Collective Biographies for Young Readers, by Judith Silverman, 3rd ed. New York: R. R. Bowker, 1979.

Index to Educational Audio Tapes. Los Angeles, Calif.: National Information Center for Educational Media, published on a 2½ year cycle.

Index to Educational Records. Los Angeles, Calif.: National Information Center for Educational Media, published on a 2½ year cycle.

Index to Educational Video Tapes. Los Angeles, Calif.: National Information Center for Educational Media, published on a 2½ year cycle.

Index to 8mm Motion Cartridges. Los Angeles, Calif.: National Information Center for Educational Media, published on a 2½ year cycle.

Index to 16mm Educational Films, 4 vols. Los Angeles, Calif.: National Information Center for Educational Media, published on a 2½ year cycle.

Index to 35mm Filmstrips, 3 vols. Los Angeles, Calif.: National Information Center for Educational Media, published on a 2½ year cycle.

Introducing Books: A Guide for the Middle Grades, by John T. Gillespie and Diana L. Lembo. New York: R. R. Bowker, 1970.

Introducing More Books: A Guide for the Middle Grades, by Diana L. Spirt. New York: R. R. Bowker, 1978.

Juniorplots: A Book Talk Manual for Teachers and Librarians, by John T. Gillespie and Diana L. Lembo. New York: R. R. Bowker, 1967.

Literature and Young Children, ed. by Bernice E. Cullinan and Carolyn W. Carmichael. Urbana, Ill.: National Council of Teachers of English, 1977.

More Juniorplots: A Guide for Teachers and Librarians, by John T. Gillespie. New York: R. R. Bowker, 1977.

A Multimedia Approach to Children's Literature: A Selective List of Films, Filmstrips, and Recordings Based on Children's Books. Chicago: American Library Association, 1977.

Notes from a Different Drummer: A Guide to Juvenile Fiction Portraying the Handicapped, by Barbara H. Baskin and Karen H. Harris. New York: R. R. Bowker, 1977.

Paperbound Books for Young People: Preschool Through Grade 12. New York: R. R. Bowker, 1979.

Storytelling: Art and Techniques, by Augusta Baker and Ellin Greene. New York: R. R. Bowker, 1977.

Subject Guide to Children's Books in Print. New York: R. R. Bowker, 1970- .

Using Literature in the Elementary Classroom, ed. by John W. Stewig and Sam L. Sebesta. Urbana, Ill.: National Council of Teachers of English, 1978.

World of Storytelling, The, by Anne Pellowski. New York: R. R. Bowker, 1977.

SECONDARY LEVEL

Adolescent Literature, Adolescent Reading, and the English Class, ed. by Kenneth Donelson. Urbana, Ill.: National Council of Teachers of English, 1972.

Anatomy of Wonder: Science Fiction, ed. by Neil Barron. New York: R. R. Bowker, 1976.

Biography Index: A Cumulative Index to Biographical Materials in Books and Magazines. New York: H. W. Wilson, 1947- .

Black Literature for High School Students, by Barbara D. Stanford and Karima Amin. Urbana, Ill.: National Council of Teachers of English, 1978.

Black Playwrights 1823-1977: An Annotated Bibliography of Plays, by James V. Hatch and OMANii Abdullah. New York: R. R. Bowker, 1977.

Books for Secondary School Libraries, comp. by a Committee of Librarians from Member Schools of the National Association of Independent Schools, 5th ed. New York: R. R. Bowker, 1976.

Books for the Gifted Child, by Barbara Baskin and Karen Harris. New York: R. R. Bowker, 1980.

Books for You: A Booklist for Senior High Students, ed. by Kenneth Donelson. Urbana, Ill.: National Council of Teachers of English, 1976.

Books to Help Children Cope with Separation and Loss, comp. by Joanne E. Bernstein. New York: R. R. Bowker, 1977.

Cassell's Encyclopedia of World Literature, ed. by J. Buchanan-Brown, rev. ed., 3 vols. New York: Morrow, 1973.

Core Media Collection for Secondary Schools, by Lucy G. Brown, 2nd ed. New York: R. R. Bowker, 1979.

Essay and General Literature Index. New York: H. W. Wilson, 1900- .

The Fair Garden and the Swarm of Beasts: The Library and the Young Adult, rev. ed. New York: Hawthorn Books, 1974.

Fantasy Literature: A Core Collection and Reference Guide, by Marshall B. Tymn, Kenneth J. Zahorski, and Robert H. Boyer. New York: R. R. Bowker, 1979.

Feature Films on 8mm, 16mm, and Videotape, ed. by James L. Limbacher, 6th ed. New York: R. R. Bowker, 1979.

Fiction Catalog, ed. by Estelle A. Fidell, 10th ed. New York: H. W. Wilson, 1980.

Fiction for Adolescents: Theory and Practice, ed. by James E. Davis. Urbana, Ill.: National Council of Teachers of English, 1977.

Good Reading, ed. by J. Sherwood Weber, 21st ed. New York: R. R. Bowker, 1978.

Granger's Index to Poetry, ed. by William J. Smith, 6th ed. New York: Columbia University Press, 1973.

Great Books of the Western World, ed. by Robert M. Hutchins and Mortimer J. Adler, 54 vols. Chicago: Encyclopaedia Britannica, 1952.

Guide to Play Selection, ed. by Joseph Mersand, 3rd ed. New York: NCTE and R. R. Bowker, 1975.

High Interest—Easy Reading for Junior and Senior High School Students, ed. by Marian E. White, rev. ed. Urbana, Ill.: National Council of Teachers of English, 1972.

Hooked on Books: Program and Proof, by Daniel Fader and Elton B. McNeil, rev. ed. New York: Berkeley Publishers, 1977.

Index to Collective Biographies for Young Readers, by Judith Silverman, 3rd ed. New York: R. R. Bowker, 1979.

Index to Educational Audio Tapes. Los Angeles, Calif.: National Information Center for Educational Media, published on a 2½ year cycle.

Index to Educational Records. Los Angeles, Calif.: National Information Center for Educational Media, published on a 2½ year cycle.

Index to Educational Video Tapes. Los Angeles, Calif.: National Information Center for Educational Media, published on a 2½ year cycle.

Index to 8mm Motion Cartridges. Los Angeles, Calif.: National Information Center for Educational Media, published on a 2½ year cycle.

Index to 16mm Educational Films, 4 vols. Los Angeles, Calif.: National Information Center for Educational Media, published on a 2½ year cycle.

Index to 35mm Filmstrips, 3 vols. Los Angeles, Calif.: National Information Center for Educational Media, published on a 2½ year cycle.

Juniorplots: A Book Talk Manual for Teachers and Librarians, by John T. Gillespie and Diana L. Lembo. New York: R. R. Bowker, 1967.

Literature as Exploration, by Louise M. Rosenblatt, 3rd ed. Urbana, Ill.: National Council of Teachers of English, 1976.

Literature by and about the American Indian: An Annotated Bibliography for Junior and Senior High School Students, by Anna Lee Stensland. Urbana, Ill.: National Council of Teachers of English, 1973.

Literature of Women's Studies, by Maryann Turner. New York: R. R. Bowker, 1979.

McGraw-Hill Encyclopedia of World Drama, 4 vols. New York: McGraw-Hill, 1972.

Mexican American Literature, ed. by Philip D. Ortigo. Urbana, Ill.: National Council of Teachers of English, 1978.

More Juniorplots: A Guide for Teachers and Librarians, by John T. Gillespie. New York: R. R. Bowker, 1977.

On Teaching Literature: Essays for Secondary School Teachers, ed. by Edward B. Jenkinson and Jane S. Hawley, English Curriculum Study Series. Bloomington, Ind.: Indiana University Press, 1967.

Paperbound Books for Young People: Preschool Through Grade 12. New York: R. R. Bowker, 1979.

Reader's Adviser, The: A Layman's Guide to Literature, ed. by Sarah L. Prakken, F. J. Sypher, and Jack A. Clarke, 12th ed., 3 vols. New York: R. R. Bowker, 1974–1977.

Readings and Feelings: An Introduction to Subjective Criticism, by David Bleich. Urbana, Ill.: National Council of Teachers of English, 1975.

Short Story Index. New York: H. W. Wilson, 1953– .

Subject Guide to Books in Print. New York: R. R. Bowker, 1957– .

Teachers' Guide to World Literature for the High School, ed. by Robert O'Neal. Urbana, Ill.: National Council of Teachers of English, 1966.

Teaching Fiction: Short Stories and Novels, ed. by Kenneth Donelson. Urbana, Ill.: National Council of Teachers of English, 1974.

Teaching Literature in Grades Seven Through Nine, ed. by Edward B. Jenkinson and S. Hawley, English Curriculum Study Series. Bloomington, Ind.: Indiana University Press, 1967.

Teaching the Epic, ed. by Margaret Fleming. Urbana, Ill.: National Council of Teachers of English, 1974.

Thematic Units in Teaching English and the Humanities, ed. by Sylvia Spann and Mary Beth Culp. Urbana, Ill.: National Council of Teachers of English, 1975; Supplement 1977.

Your Reading: A Booklist for Junior High Students, by Jerry L. Walker. Urbana, Ill.: National Council of Teachers of English, 1975.

Models of literature unit support experiences that have been designed and field-tested by library media specialists working with teachers and students are provided in the following examples: Example 10, Literature Enrichment

Unit, "Call It Courage"; Example 11, Literature Enrichment Unit, "The Rain Forest"; Example 12, Literature Enrichment Unit, "The Old Man and the Sea"; and Example 13, Pittman Literature Learning Guide, "No Man Is an Island."

EXAMPLE 10 LITERATURE ENRICHMENT UNIT, "CALL IT COURAGE"

Grade: 4
Gifted and Talented Program

1. Introduce the entire book from which the reading selection has been taken.
   Call It Courage by Armstrong Sperry. Macmillan paperback.
2. Introduce biographical material about the author, Armstrong Sperry.
   Something about the Author. Gale Research. Vol. 1, pp. 204–205
3. Introduce material explaining how the book came to be written.
   The Story behind Modern Books by Elizabeth Montgomery. pp. 136–141.
4. Introduce the story in the following formats:
   FILMSTRIPS
      Adventure. Sound filmstrip. Pied Piper Productions.
      Call It Courage. Sound filmstrip. Miller-Brody Productions.
   RECORDING
      Call It Courage. Record or cassette. Miller-Brody Productions.
5. Introduce other books written by Armstrong Sperry.

FICTION	NONFICTION
Black Falcon	*All about the Jungle*
Danger to Windward	*Amazon: River Sea of Brazil*
Hull-Down for Action	
Lost Lagoon	
Rain Forest	
Storm Canvas	

6. Introduce media paralleling the theme "Courage to Survive."
   PRINT
      Adventure in Survival by Maurice Bean
      Escape by Sigurd Senje
      Firestorm by Maurine Gee
      Island of the Blue Dolphins by Scott O'Dell
      Jon the Unlucky by Elizabeth Coatsworth
      Julie of the Wolves by Jean George
      Landslide by Veronique Day
      A Long Vacation by Jules Verne
      Strange Intruder by Arthur Catherall
      Three without Fear by Robert DuSoe
      Two on an Island by Bianca Bradbury
      The Village That Slept by Monique De Ladebat
      White Water, Still Water by J. Allan Bosworth
      Wild Venture by James Johnson
      Zeb by Lonzo Anderson
   NONPRINT
      River Boy. 2 filmstrips with recording. Educational Enrichment Materials.
7. Introduce media that further develop topics mentioned in *Call It Courage.*
   Newbery Medal
   Bookmarks—Children's Book Council
   Posters
   The John Newbery Medal. Treasure Trove Library Binders, Distributed by Weise-Winkler Bindery.
   Your Newbery Friends. Miller-Brody Productions.

EXAMPLE 11 LITERATURE ENRICHMENT UNIT, "THE RAIN FOREST"*

Grade: 6
Great Books: Past and Present
Goal: To lead the students to discover, within a novel, background information on manners and customs, social and economic problems, and values of primitive societies.
Teaching objectives:

To encourage each student to discover new dimensions in his ability to read with perception, challenge, and delight.

To introduce the students to the concept of cultural differences.

To acquaint the students with the role of the anthropologist, the sociologist, and the ornithologist.

To provide opportunities for the students to explore the writings of Armstrong Sperry and Jim Kjelgaard.

To provide opportunity for the students to answer the question "Would I be able to survive in a rain forest culture?"

Partial teaching procedure:

1. Introduce Armstrong Sperry as a writer using:
   Junior Book of Authors. Wilson
   Something about the Author. Gale Research
   Story behind Modern Books by Elizabeth Montgomery
2. Have students check the card catalog to discover all the books written by Sperry available in their library.
3. Have students volunteer to read and to share with the class their appraisal of the following Sperry writings
   FICTION   NONFICTION
     Black Falcon   *All about the Jungle*
     Call It Courage   *Amazon: River Sea of Brazil*
     Danger to Windward
     Frozen Fire
     Hull-Down for Action
     Lost Lagoon
     Storm Canvas
4. Build knowledge of the novel as a literary form.
   Develop a working definition: A story with characters and a plot, long enough to fill one or more volumes. Novels are usually about people, scenes, and happenings such as might be met in real life.
   Categorize as to type:
     Adventure   Mystery
     Jungle   Travel
   Discuss the following:
     Style of writing   Building of suspense
     Reader involvement
5. Determine the authenticity of information about New Guinea as given in the novel *The Rain Forest* with information presented in a nonfiction account such as *New Guinea: A Journey into Yesterday* by Eleanor Baker by checking the following topics:
     Animal life   Homes
     Cannibals   Jungles
     Ceremonies   Plants
     Clothing   Pygmies
     Communication   Superstition
     Food   Weapons
6. Have the students compare *The Rain Forest* with *Boomerang Hunter* by Jim Kjelgaard.

*Note: This unit is a multidisciplinary unit integrating concepts from anthropology, sociology, geography, and natural sciences while using an adventure novel as the teaching-learning vehicle.

EXAMPLE 11 (cont.)

Compare and contrast Kjelgaard's style with that of Armstrong Sperry.
Check the information given by Kjelgaard in *Boomerang Hunter* about the Australian aborigines with the information given by Sperry in *The Rain Forest* about the aborigines of New Guinea.

7. Have students check the card catalog to discover all the books written by Kjelgaard available in their library.

EXAMPLE 12 LITERATURE ENRICHMENT UNIT, "THE OLD MAN AND THE SEA"

Grade: 11 or 12
Literary Work: *The Old Man and the Sea* by Ernest Hemingway
Based on: "The Old Man and the Sea," twelfth-grade unit in *12,000 Students and Their English Teachers: Tested Units in Teaching Literature, Language Composition,* by the Commission on English,* pp. 17–24.
Procedure to be followed in selecting media:

1. The Scribner Library paperback edition of *The Old Man and the Sea* by Ernest Hemingway is recommended by the Commission on English and all references made in the unit are page references to the Scribner paperback edition.

2. Introduce library resources that will provide critical analysis of and commentary on the literary value of *The Old Man and the Sea*. For example:
   Twentieth Century Interpretations of The Old Man and the Sea: A Collection of Critical Essays, ed. by Katharine T. Jobes.
   The Old Man and the Sea, by Ernest Hemingway. Teacher's Guide. Living Literature Series.

3. Introduce library resources that will explain how and why *The Old Man and the Sea* came to be written. For example:
   "Old Man and the Sea." *Life Magazine*, September 1, 1952, vol. 33, pp. 34–54.

4. Introduce library resources that introduce Hemingway as a human being as well as a writer. For example:
   PRINT
   Ernest Hemingway: An Introduction and Interpretation by Sheridan Baker. American Authors and Critics Series.
   My Brother, Ernest Hemingway by Leicester Hemingway.
   Hemingway: The Writer as Artist by Carlos Baker.
   Hemingway and His Critics: An International Anthology ed. by Carlos Baker.
   "Hemingway: A World View." A Symposium. *Saturday Review of Literature,* July 29, 1961, pp. 10–30.
   NONPRINT
   Ernest Hemingway: The Man. 2 sound filmstrips with record or cassette. Guidance Associates.
   Ernest Hemingway: The Writer. 2 sound filmstrips with record or cassette. Guidance Associates.

5. Introduce *The Old Man and the Sea* in format other than print. For example:
   The Old Man and the Sea. Sound filmstrip with record or cassette. Miller-Brody Productions.

6. Introduce other works written by Ernest Hemingway. For example:
   Farewell to Arms
   A Hemingway Reader, ed. with an introduction by Charles Poore.
   The Snows of Kilimanjaro
   For Whom the Bell Tolls

*Copies of this book may be ordered from the College Entrance Board, Publications Order Office, Box 592, Princeton, N.J. 08540.

EXAMPLE 12 (cont.)

7. Introduce other works that parallel the theme, plot, setting, or character portrayal of *The Old Man and the Sea.* For example:
   PRINT
   "The Great Fish of Como" in *Fragments of My Fleece* by Dean Acheson. pp. 47–53.
   Moby Dick by Herman Melville.
   NONPRINT
   Winslow Homer seascapes. Art prints and slides.

8. Introduce library resources that extend the understanding of persons, places, things, events, problems, or concepts highlighted in *The Old Man and the Sea.* For example:
   PRINT
   Deep Sea Fishing by John Wright. Dufour.
   Fishes and Their Ways by Clarence Hylander. Macmillan.
   The Pulitzer Prize Novels by W. J. Stucky. University of Oklahoma Press.
   Ways of Fishes by Leonard Schultz. Van Nostrand.
   "Winslow Homer: Painter of the Seas." *Oceans Magazine*, vol. 6, no. 3, May 1973, pp. 60–67.
   Wonderous World of Fishes by Leonard Schultz et al. National Geographic Society.
   Young Sportsman's Guide to Salt Water Fishing by Ray Ovington. Nelson.
   NONPRINT
   "La Mer" by Debussy. Toscanini conducting the NBC Orchestra. Program notes by Rachael Carson. RCA Victor.

EXAMPLE 13 PITTMAN LITERATURE LEARNING GUIDE, "NO MAN IS AN ISLAND"

Subject:	English
Grade:	12
Unit:	Seventeenth-Century English Literature
Topic:	"No Man Is an Island" by John Donne

Introduction: John Donne set forth a philosophy which has been unending in its influence on human thought since it was first stated in seventeenth-century England. Donne wrote: "No man is an island, intire of itselfe; every man is a peece of the Continent, a part of the Maine . . . any man's death diminishes me, because I am involved in Mankinde; and therefore never send to know for whom the bell tolls; It tolls for thee."

The purpose of this learning guide is twofold:
1. To acquaint you with John Donne as a human being as well as a poet, philosopher, and minister.
2. To provide opportunities for you to explore further the philosophy that no man is an island.

You are free to read any or all of the sources listed below.

Source A   *Grace to a Witty Sinner: A Life of Donne* by Edward Le Comte.

Source B   *Take Heed of Loving Me* by Elizabeth Vining. A fictionalized biography of Donne.

Source C   "There Are No Islands Anymore" by Edna St. Vincent Millay. A poem written at the beginning of World War II pleading that the United States lay aside neutrality and keep England and France from being defeated by Germany.

Source D   *The Growing Human Family* by Minoo Masani. Chapter 12, "No Man Is an Island," sets forth the plea for one world.

EXAMPLE 13 (cont.)

Source E | *For Whom the Bell Tolls* by Ernest Hemingway. A novel of the Spanish Civil War.

Source F | "No Man Is an Island," a song by Joan Whitney and Alex Kramer, recorded by Fred Waring and his Pennsylvanians on the record "Songs of Inspiration."

Check the following to discover information:

Source A | *Indexicon.* Harvard Classics.
   Topic: John Donne

Source B | *Essay and General Literature Index.*
   Topics: Alienation
        Brotherhood of Man
        John Donne

Source C | *Readers' Guide to Periodical Literature.*
   Topics: Alienation
        Brotherhood of Man
        John Donne

Source D | *No Man Is an Island: An Inquiry into Alienation* by The Center for Humanities. A sound-slide learning program including: 160 slides in two Kodak Carousel cartridges; two cassette tapes or recordings; and a learning guide.

SAFEGUARDING STUDENT READING INTEREST

When selecting books, the teacher and the library media specialist should keep in the foreground of their thinking the fact that the books that are popular with today's children and youth are characterized by action, conflict, suspense, and clear language.[23] Likewise, they must heed the warning that "a book does not have to be dull to be good."[24]

Traditionally, English classes have been less than enjoyable. Even though interest has long been recognized as the strongest factor predicting success in any teaching-learning situation, student interest in English is frighteningly lacking. Experts have long agreed that the formal book report and the restrictive required reading list have successfully and persistently beaten student interest in reading and literature to death. In 1945, the Harvard Committee on General Education in a Free Society, in its report, identified required book reports as a trend to be discouraged.[25] Fourteen years later, in 1959, Robert C. Pooley writing in the *English Journal* deplored the same practices decried by the Harvard Committee:

> In literature we have forced unready youth through selections unsuited to their abilities and experiences and in the name of literary appreciation have created attitudes of dislike and contempt for good literature. By a combination of misplaced zeal and unhappy procedures we have succeeded in making English for the great mass of students the most disliked subject in the curriculum.[26]

And more than a decade later many leaders in the field lamented the persistence of the destructive practices of required reading and book reports. To cite but a few comments:

The book report has probably done more to destroy the love of reading and the joy of books than any other single educational practice.[27]

Everyone seems to agree that the primary purpose for teaching literature is to instill the pupils with the love and appreciation for good reading. To judge from the results, much of literature teaching has just the opposite effect. After years of English courses tremendous numbers of American boys and girls— and men and women—*hate literature.* Why? *Because literature has been taught in such a manner so as to make it hateful.*[28]

"Book-report days" are still among the most detested in those schools where students make written or oral reports according to old, creaking formulas.[29]

Surveys of the school subject preferences of children usually reveal that language class is rated the favorite by one in ten, but is the least liked by about three in ten. Within the specifics of the language course the item most frequently listed as the least preferred is book reporting.[30]

If the aim of English teaching is to increase the students' ability and desire to understand and to appreciate literature, then the evidence cited above should discourage the persistence of restrictive reading lists and required oral and written book reports.

Teachers in the past have defended employing book lists and required book reports as essential practices that enable the teacher to discover whether or not the student is reading. Paul Anderson suggests that teachers employ a variety of checklists or reaction sheets that will help the teacher discover what the students are reading as well as their reaction to what they have read (see Examples 14, 15, and 16). Educational Reading Services* offers for sale a most attractive reading summary report form that third and fourth graders enjoy using. These forms lend themselves well to the compilation of a class looseleaf notebook of suggested books to be enjoyed by classmates—a most effective improvement over the required book list of the saber-toothed-tiger days.

EXAMPLE 14 BOOK SUMMARY FORM: GRADES 3–4†

BOOK REPORT

Name of book _____

Author _____

Illustrator (if any) _____

Name some of the characters _____

_____

Tell which character you liked best _____

_____

The part of the book I liked best was _____

_____

_____

Do *one* of these things:
1. Tell your class part of the story.
2. Make a picture.
3. Make something suggested by book.

My name is _____ Room No. _____

*Educational Reading Services, 320 Rte. 17, Mahwah, N.J. 07430; prices on request.
†From Paul S. Anderson, *Language Skills in Elementary Education,* 2nd ed. (New York: Macmillan, 1972), p. 160.

EXAMPLE 15 PERSONAL READING NOTEBOOK*

Here are some ways in which information about the things in my book have helped people

_____

_____

Below are some unsolved problems or questions (about things in my book) which scientists
are still working on _____

_____

I recommend this book because _____

_____

Name_____ Date_____

EXAMPLE 16 BIOGRAPHY REPORT FORM*

Title_____
Author_____ Number of pages _____
Illustrator_____

The biographer (one who writes about a real person) tells the following childhood incident
in the life of his subject _____

_____

_____

The subject of the biography is _____

_____

The following people were important in helping this real person to grow into a famous adult

_____

_____

A problem which this person had to overcome was _____

_____

This person overcame his problem in this way _____

_____

_____

This person had the following characteristics which I admire _____

_____

_____

I think the most exciting adventure which this person had was _____

_____

_____

Chambers offers the following suggestions, which should trigger teacher
awareness of a variety of techniques for encouraging children to share their
reaction to reading and books:

1. Make a listening post. On a tape recorder have children comment on a recent
   book they have read. Change the tape every two weeks.

*From Paul S. Anderson, *Language Skills in Elementary Education*, 2nd ed. (New York: Macmillan, 1972), p. 162.

2. Choose a favorite author or illustrator and give a brief account of his life. List his books.
3. Locate the settings of regional stories or legends on a map. The map can be a library corner display. Children can discuss their favorite regional story using the map as a visual aid.
4. Feature special kinds of books for a once-a-week discussion. Such categories as "Family Books," "Mystery Books," "Humorous Books," "Animal Stories," etc. can be featured in successive weeks. Children can share their favorite categories with each other during that time.
5. Have children discuss what they think a certain author is like as he reveals himself in several books.
6. Prepare an advertisement for a book and write a brief review of the book for the school or classroom newspaper.
7. Write a television or radio script based upon a book or part of a book.
8. Create and tell riddles about a book, its plot, or characters.
9. Match titles of books with authors.
10. Have an imaginary interview with an author.
11. Prepare a series of clues to be used in identifying a book.
12. Construct a diorama or paint a mural representing a favorite book.
13. Make a series of illustrations for a favorite book. Discuss these illustrations with the class.
14. Create book jackets for favorite books.
15. Prepare oral reports to emphasize the relationship between the illustrations and the content of a book.
16. Illustrate a story through the use of puppets.
17. Make a crossword puzzle about a favorite book.
18. Make a pictured time line showing important points in a book. This technique is best for historical fiction or biography.
19. On a tape recorder present a dramatization of an incident in a favorite book. Use music, special effects, and dramatic expression. Play it to the class. Offer it to other classes.
20. Prepare and present a monologue from a favorite book.
21. Pantomime part of a story.
22. Make mobiles of important people and animals in a story.
23. When possible, compare the original form of a story with other versions of it as comics, rewritten versions, commercial film versions. Contrast the two forms.
24. Make a bulletin board of a favorite author and his books.
25. Make a bulletin board of favorite books.
26. Prepare a "This Is Your Life" program concerning a favorite character. Record it on tape.
27. Make a book list where children list five books that "everyone should read."[31]

Hook lists the following devices to replace the "dull routine pattern for reports":

1. A small group of students reads the same book. The chairman and teacher prepare a list of thought questions to be answered independently before the class. Differences of opinion may lead to discussion, and create class interest in the book.
2. ". . . a bright-eyed bookworm with wide reading experiences might be asked for a careful statement of theme, a high-level analysis of some character's motivation, a discussion of some structural aspect of the author's craftsmanship, or a comparison with another piece of literature. Most important, reporting must not be a case of either this or that for an entire class."
3. Students who have read books on similar topics (occupations, animals, history, etc.) exchange information about their books before the class.
4. A student tries to "sell" a book to another student, who believes that he would not like it.

5. "Conversation circles" with student chairmen discuss books on similar topics.
6. The class prepares a "newspaper" with stories based upon books read.
7. On a spindle, each student places the name of a book he has read. By the next day, the teacher has added a pertinent specific question concerning the book. In class, the student answers the question.
8. Students may work out dialogs, monologs, pantomimes, short plays, or television dramatizations, pertaining to the book read.
9. Students prepare appropriate book jackets including "blurbs." Advanced students write reviews, criticisms, and evaluations.
10. "Tell the story again from the viewpoint of another character in the story." "Show how color or key words or ideas run through the story. Discuss their purpose and effectiveness." "Place yourself in the protagonist's position and relate how plot would have been affected with you as the hero." "Imagine the character in the book in a different setting. . . . Change mood, time, or setting and show how it affects characters and plot." "Imagine an eighteenth century schoolboy, accustomed to reading Shakespeare, Milton, Addison, etc., reading your book. What would be his reactions?" "Write a letter in the style, with the feeling, in the character of the subject of the biography, e.g., Thoreau writes to President Nixon." "What characteristics of the main character are present in all successful men and women? What are his or her unique characteristics?"
11. One of the simplest and best methods of providing a motivated check on reading is to have the students record whatever reading they do, together with a brief comment. The Cumulative Reading Record (NCTE) is ideal for this purpose. The teacher encourages the students to bring into class discussions references to their reading, just as adults do. Since the teacher notes carefully what each student has been reading, he may frequently address to a student a question upon which his recent reading should throw some light. The class soon learns to expect and welcome such casual questions, and reads more carefully because of them. At the same time, students are learning that their outside reading may be related to many topics of discussion. They thus gradually acquire a more adult view of reading than they may gain from some other devices.[32]

Both Anderson and Chambers recommend encouraging the youngsters to keep a personal reading notebook. The author of this book has had marked success on both the elementary and secondary level in getting students interested in keeping such a record through the use of attractive reading records such as those available from the following commercial sources:

Bardeen Press, Syracuse, New York. *Reading Guidance Book.*

Bradford Printing Service, Winston-Salem, North Carolina. *Rainbow Reading Record.*

Gaylord Brothers, Inc., Syracuse, New York. *Books I Have Read.*

National Council of Teachers of English, Urbana, Illinois. *Cumulative Reading Record.*

Sturgis Library Products, Sturgis, Michigan.* 21 separate reading·record booklets.

A word of caution is in order—keeping a personal reading record should not be a required activity (see Example 15); the reading records should not be graded and, indeed, should not be checked by teacher or librarian. If this device is to

---

*Sturgis Library Products, Box 130, Sturgis, Mich. 49091, is the largest producer and distributor of library promotional materials such as: bookmarks, enlarged catalog cards, posters, displays, memorial book plates, and reading club materials. A free catalog is available on request.

be motivational, the record of what the student has read for pleasure should not become a matter for teacher supervision.

Cleary, in assessing the role of the library media specialist as an active participant in the school's reading and literature development program, states:

> A reading guidance program will succeed in direct proportion to the care with which the librarian plans for developing close relationships with the pupils in the school; the skill with which he formulates specific instructional objectives for reading guidance in the library and devises creative means for reaching these objectives; the consideration he gives to both individual and group guidance; and the pains he takes to identify and use certain general guidance devices in meeting the needs of the reluctant, the retarded, and the gifted reader.[33]

One very effective device for the library media specialist to consider using to discover individual student reading interests is a reading interest inventory (see Appendix J). There is no substitute for knowledge of what an individual student enjoys as a firm basis for effective reading guidance.

The inclusion of science fiction as a respectable literary genre worthy of being included in the English curriculum is evidence that the traditional classics approach to the teaching of literature is losing its stranglehold. Calkins and McGhan in *Teaching Tomorrow: A Handbook of Science Fiction for Teachers* attribute the willingness to include science fiction in the English curriculum to the following emerging concepts:

1. Survey courses (such as a year's work in American or English Literature) no longer seem so valid. In their place, new courses are being developed to give students an opportunity to study some special fields in depth.
2. Reading materials are being selected in relation to the experience and interests of the student rather than to some arbitrary concept of what constitutes a "classic" which will improve his mind.
3. All students need a series of successful reading experiences to develop the basic skills and attitudes needed so that they will continue to read and explore independently.
4. Changes in public attitudes about what constitutes good taste make it possible to include contemporary selections with more freedom of vocabulary. Also other countries and cultures have produced writing that students need to discover.
5. Learning will be enhanced if the student gains an increased sense of involvement by participating in decision-making about the class. He needs a voice in the reading choices and systems of evaluation.
6. The high school English teacher is no longer the dispenser of wisdom. The teacher's role should be that of organizing the group for discovery, of providing the materials, and of assisting in identifying valid goals for group achievement.[34]

Fortunately, a wealth of quality science fiction abounds. Calkins and McGhan's book is a gold mine for teachers and library media specialists searching for the best in science fiction. Here they will find, in addition to suggestions for using science fiction in the classroom, the following lists: Book Dealers, Book Publishers, Professional Magazines, Amateur Publications, Science Fiction Conventions, Science Fiction Organizations, Science Fiction Motion Pictures, Science Fiction for Girls, Critical Works, Science Fiction Indexes, Recommended Novels, and Supplementary Books. Another excellent source of suggested science fiction titles is *Anatomy of Wonder* by Neil Barron, which indexes more than 1,100 science fiction titles.[35]

THE PROBLEM OF CENSORSHIP

NCTE has provided definite guidelines to be followed in dealing with the problem of censorship in its publication *The Students' Right to Read,* which is included in Appendix B of this book. The NCTE report form "Citizen's Request for Reconsideration of a Work" is included in Chapter 5 of this book. See Example 17 for a sample "permission to read" form, which is one approach to short-circuiting community protestation.

EXAMPLE 17 MODEL PARENT PERMISSION TO READ FORM*

Date _____

To the Parents of _____ Students:
(Name of school)

One of the objectives of the _____ library is to provide a collection of materials to
(Name of school)
serve a school population characterized by widely developed levels of student maturity. Our students want and need to read about many realities of life. This type of vicarious experience may be a positive factor in preparing students to deal eventually with real experiences in their own lives.

It has become increasingly clear that many books dealing with contemporary social issues often contain strong language or incidents of sex or violence because it is necessary to the realistic portrayal of character development or plot. All books selected for the _____ library must meet established criteria. If a book contains elements such as those mentioned above, it may be included in the _____ library collection provided that it meets the established criteria and that the elements contained are not purposefully or sensationally exploited.

We recognize, however, there should be guidance in student selection of some books dealing with social issues. These books have been placed on a shelf in the library designated for the more mature readers. If a student wishes to borrow a book from this shelf he must first secure a book summary sheet for his parents' review and approval.

Your son or daughter wishes to borrow the book summarized below. Please indicate whether or not you approve. Sign and return this sheet.

The Inner City Mother Goose by Eve Merriam is an adaptation of the classical nursery rhymes to present a striking view of ghetto life as seen by those who live it.

This book is reserved for those mature enough to recognize the thought and problem behind it and not dissect it for its strong word usage and visual aspects. It is necessary to take this book as a whole and to accept the attitude and tone as that of the people it illustrates. If it were to be adapted to agree with the background and attitude of its readers it would have no social value.

_____
(Signature of principal)

_____
(Signature of librarian)

_____ I grant approval for this book to be borrowed.
_____ I do not grant approval for this book to be borrowed.

Parent's signature _____ Date _____

COMMUNICATION COMPETENCIES

NCTE encourages the viewing of language arts skills not as separate and isolated teaching and learning experiences but as integrated parts of the whole communication process. In summarizing the research on the teaching of the

*Used with permission of the Hampton Middle School, Allison Park, Pa. 15101.

separate elements such as grammar, usage, vocabulary, spelling, the NCTE highlights the following:

> There is little transfer value in isolated oral drill on usage for promoting changes in speech.
>
> It has not worked to teach formal grammar in isolation as a means of improving writing.
>
> Most students learn to write and read by performing real tasks: writing stories, notices, letters, and reports for classroom "audiences"; reading factual articles, advertisements, stories, and other real messages.
>
> Spelling and vocabulary are best learned in context; sentence building is more productive than either sentence analysis or labeling.
>
> For some capable students, school loses credibility when work is mainly busy-work drill; many "average" students need help *during* the process of reading and writing far more than they need isolated drill on parts; and some less able students are turned off from reading and writing (and sometimes from school) when exercises on parts of reading and writing don't lead to skill as readers and writers.[36]

The real basics in English teaching are language processes that involve three basic levels in ascending order (see Table 3):

1. Imitative processes related to basic literacy at the recognition and recall level
2. Organizing processes related to fluency in the use of basic language tools
3. Critical, creative, and evaluative processes involving originality and conscious choice of language alternatives

The language arts curriculum contributes to the attainment of the following basic educational goals:

1. *Thinking ability*—language is the medium of thought
2. *Self-realization*—expressive use of language extends beyond social or utilitarian exchanges to various modes of creative expression
3. *Human relationships*—knowledge of one's own culture and respect for other cultures are acquired in large measure through language
4. *Economic competency*—standard English is basic to the development of economic competency
5. *Civic responsibility*—required skill in language as one listens to campaign speeches, reads about government, and learns to analyze the techniques of propaganda

TABLE 3 LANGUAGE PROCESSES AND SKILLS*

LEVELS OF PROCESSES	LANGUAGE SKILLS		
	READING	ORAL LANGUAGE	WRITING
Imitative	Recognition and recall of ideas	Basic auditory perception, discriminatory reproduction (in any dialect)	Basic literacy in manipulating symbols
Organizing	Organizing and interpreting ideas	Ease and fluency of oral communication	Organizing and producing messages in sentences, paragraphs, etc.
Critical/creative evaluation	Reading critically and selectively	Conscious choice of language alternatives	Conscious choice of patterns to suit purpose (originality, style)

*From "What Are the 'Basics' in English," SLATE 1, no. 2 (Aug. 1976): 2.

6. *Learning how to learn*—innumerable lifelong learning skills permeate the language arts program [see Appendix L, "Thinking-Learning-Communicating Skills Continuum, K–12"][37]

The language arts curriculum also provides listening, speaking, reading, and writing experiences that integrate cognitive and affective behaviors (see Table 4).

NCTE is the world's largest subject-matter association numbering more than 100,000 members. The council focuses on the major concerns of teachers of English and the language arts, and publishes many professional tools for the guidance of its members. Recent NCTE publications devoted to the language arts processes are: *Composition: A Media Approach*, by Frederick B. Tuttle (1978); *Interpersonal Communication: Innovations in Instruction*, by Paul G. Friedman (1978); and *Writing about Ourselves and Others*, by Richard Beach (1977). NCTE distributes Educational Resources Information Center (ERIC) publications produced jointly with the NCTE as well as those ERIC publications produced jointly with the Speech Communication Association (5205 Leesburg Pike, Falls Church, Va. 22041). Several of the ERIC documents in the Theory and Research into Practice Series (TRIP) of special concern to the library media specialist as well as to English and speech teachers are: *Development of Functional Communication Competencies: Pre-K–Grade 6*, edited by Barbara S. Wood (1977); *Development of Functional Communication Competencies: Grade 7–12*, edited by Barbara S. Wood (1977); and *Selected Print and Nonprint Resources in Speech Communication: An Annotated Bibliography K–12*, compiled by Jerry D. Feezel, Kent R. Brown, and Carol A. Valentine (1976). The two TRIP publications on the development of functional communication competencies provide numerous practical suggestions for classroom teaching strategies.

In addition to the foregoing, NCTE publishes a number of journals, handbooks, monographs, resource units, and reading lists, and acts as a sales agent not only for professional publications but for a large number of commercially prepared books, pamphlets, filmstrips, recordings, art and study prints, maps, and charts vital to the teaching of English. A library media specialist concerned with building a professional library collection in general, or a professional library collection for the English resource center in particular, should consult the NCTE catalog for first-purchase suggestions regularly. This invaluable resource guide, which also indexes all NCTE/ERIC publications, is revised annually and distributed free on request.*

PROGRAMS FOR THE GIFTED

As of 1979, 27 states had made statutory provision for the education of children who are exceptional "by virtue of giftedness."[38] The NCTE survey of teaching conditions in English conducted in 1977 reported that 45 percent of the schools responding to the survey had special classes for the gifted students.[39] One of the qualifications for a program designed for the gifted student is that it be distinctive and different and embrace enrichment or acceleration of content, independent study, individualization of instruction, curricular modification, and instructional methods designed to develop reasoning processes such

---

Professional Publications for the Teacher of English and Language Arts is distributed free of charge by the National Council of Teachers of English, 1111 Kenyon Rd., Urbana, Ill. 61801.

TABLE 4 TABLE OF SPECIFICATIONS FOR THE LANGUAGE ARTS*

Content Skills Units	COGNITIVE BEHAVIOR						AFFECTIVE BEHAVIOR			
	Knowledge	Comprehension	Application	Analysis	Synthesis	Evaluation	Receiving	Responding	Valuing	Attitudes
	Terminology Information Concepts	Defining Interpreting Generalizing	Inferring Predicting	Elements Relationships	Creating	Objective Subjective Criteria	Awareness Willingness Attentiveness	Compliance Willingness Satisfaction	Acceptance Preference Commitment	Positive Neutral Negative
Listening a. b. . . .										
Speaking a. b. . . .										
Reading a. b. . . .										
Writing a. b. . . .										

*From John U. Michaelis, Ruth H. Grossman, and Lloyd F. Scott, *New Designs for Elementary Curriculum and Instruction* (New York: McGraw-Hill, 1975), p. 159.

as creativity, critical thinking, and evaluative thinking. Likewise, it is recommended that the elementary and secondary programs for the gifted in reality be a single, seamless, ongoing program that has been carefully designed ever to broaden, ever to deepen, ever to reinforce and extend learning through a logical progression of interlocking, cohesive, and mutually supportive learning experiences. Linguistics is an example of an area of the English curriculum ideally suited for inclusion in a program designed for gifted students. Linguistics, which includes the study of the historical development of language, the study of the major aspects of language, and the study of dialects, is a relatively neglected area of the standard English curriculum. Example 18, Linguistics Study Unit, "Fun with Words"; Example 19, Linguistics Study Unit, "The Wizardry of Words"; and Example 20, Linguistics Study Unit, "American English: Inherited, Manufactured, and Fractured" are examples of an interlocking pattern of linguistics study for third-grade students, sixth-grade students, and twelfth-grade students respectively in a gifted curriculum program. These examples of units for the gifted students are excerpted from *Creating Programs for the Gifted: A Guide for Teachers, Librarians, and Students.*[40]

EXAMPLE 18 LINGUISTICS STUDY UNIT, "FUN WITH WORDS"

Grade: 3
Gifted and Talented Program
Project Goal: To provide learning experiences which will introduce the students to words—
their meaning, their power, their beauty
Teaching Objectives:
This project has been designed to provide these basic understandings:

Skill is the ability to do something well

Skill with words is the ability to use words well

The dictionary and the thesaurus are two important tools to be used in acquiring skill with words

The fictional character Amelia Bedelia uses the *literal* meaning of words

Some words have relatives called: synonyms, antonyms, homonyms, and homographs

Building one's vocabulary is a lifelong process

Working crossword puzzles is an effective way to build knowledge of words

This project has been designed to foster these attitudes and appreciations:

Appreciation of the multiple meaning of words

Appreciation of the many opportunities to use words creatively

Appreciation of the beauty of word usage in poetry and song

Delight in discovering new words

Delight in experimenting with words

Delight in playing word games

Delight in reading about Amelia Bedelia and her many mixed-up word adventures

Delight in reading other books written by Peggy Parish

Teaching Strategies:

No time limits are imposed on this project. Number of students in the group coupled, with student interest are the factors determining the duration of the project whether it be two weeks, two months, or longer.

A basic part of group orientation to the project is to provide opportunities for the students to explore the synergistic effect of sharing knowledge gained and then to determine appropriate methods and procedures for pooling information.

EXAMPLE 18 (cont.)

Partial Procedural Outline:
I. Group orientation to the project
  A. The adventures of the literal-minded maid Amelia Bedelia are enjoyed by the group
    1. The *Amelia Bedelia* series of books written by Peggy Parish (Harper) are read and discussed by the group

      Amelia Bedelia

      Come Back, Amelia Bedelia

      Good Work, Amelia Bedelia

      Play Ball, Amelia Bedelia

      Teach Us, Amelia Bedelia

      Thank You, Amelia Bedelia

    2. The *Amelia Bedelia* series of filmstrips (New York Times) are enjoyed by the group

      Amelia Bedelia

      Come Back, Amelia Bedelia

      Play Ball, Amelia Bedelia

      Thank You, Amelia Bedelia

  B. *The First Book of Language and How to Use It* by Mauree Applegate (Watts) serves as an introduction to the study of words
    1. You have a built-in motion picture projector in your mind

      This projector takes up no room, runs silently, and is very easy to operate

      This projector shows on the screen of your mind what you see, what you hear, and what you imagine

    2. Words can make pictures in the mind of the listener and the reader
    3. In order to help people understand what you mean, you must know how words work
  C. The dictionary and the thesaurus are two "word banks"
    1. The dictionary gives the following information about words:

      Meaning

      Correct spelling

      Pronunciation

      Synonyms

      Antonyms

      Part of speech

      Sometimes a picture or an illustration

    2. Locating a word in the dictionary and studying it does *not* mean it is yours

      A word becomes part of your vocabulary when you use it easily

      Most adults have a vocabulary of at least 10,000 words

      President Wilson had about 60,000 words in his vocabulary

    3. During this school year, each student is going to keep a list of new words he has discovered
    4. Using the Scott, Foresman *Beginning Dictionary*, discover how a dictionary can help you

      Read the section entitled, "Using this dictionary"

      Can you teach yourself:

        How to find a word

        How to find a meaning

        How to use the pronunciations

EXAMPLE 18 (cont.)

How to use this dictionary for spelling and writing

The parts of a dictionary entry

5. A thesaurus is a treasury or storehouse of words arranged in categories

Using a variety of words increases your word power

Using the Scott, Foresman thesaurus *In Other Words: A Beginning Thesaurus* discover how a thesaurus can help you replace "tired" words

Read the "Self-Help Introduction"

Using *In Other Words . . . A Thesaurus Exercise Book*, test your ability to use this reference tool

D. A pun is a play on words
1. Using *Pun Fun* by Ennis Rees (Hale), select several puns you enjoy
2. Using other books of puns which you will find in your school library, select those you particularly enjoy; perhaps you and your friends will compile a notebook of puns to share with your classmates

E. Many poems use words that rhyme
1. Why do you think that TV commercials use rhyming words to sell a product?
2. Rhymes, games, and chants are not only part of your childhood, but they were part of your parents', your grandparents', and your great-grandparents' childhood
3. The book *Did You Feed My Cow?* by Margaret Taylor (Harcourt) contains a number of rhymes and chants that have been popular for a number of years

Borrow *Did You Feed My Cow?* from the school library and take it home to share with your parents, grandparents, and other relatives; perhaps you will be surprised to discover the number of rhymes and chants they will know

Try your hand at making up a rhyme or a chant

4. Frequently when asked to write in a friend's autograph book, a person will write a poem

The following books contain a number of poems which have been written in autograph books:

Remember Me When This You See by Lillian Morrison (Scholastic)

Yours Till Niagara Falls by Lillian Morrison (Scholastic)

5. The following poetry books are fun to explore:

Animal Antics in Limerick Land selected by Leland Jacobs (Garrard)

Arithmetic in Verse and Rhyme selected by Allan and Leland Jacobs (Garrard)

Catch Your Breath: A Book of Shivery Poems selected by Lilian Moore (Garrard)

Funny Bone Ticklers in Verse and Rhyme selected by Leland Jacobs (Garrard)

Funny Folks in Limerick Land selected by Leland Jacobs (Garrard)

Poetry for Bird Watchers selected by Leland Jacobs (Garrard)

Poetry for Chuckles and Grins selected by Leland Jacobs (Garrard)

Poetry of Witches, Elves, and Goblins selected by Leland Jacobs (Garrard)

Poetry on Wheels selected by Lee Hopkins (Garrard)

Sports and Games in Verse and Rhyme selected by Allan and Leland Jacobs (Garrard)

F. Dr. Seuss, in his stories, makes up many nonsense words; see how many nonsense words you can discover in the following books:

Bartholomew and the Oobleck by Dr. Seuss (Random House)

Horton Hears a Who by Dr. Seuss (Random House)

How the Grinch Stole Christmas by Dr. Seuss (Random House)

EXAMPLE 18 (cont.)

I Had Trouble in Getting to Solla Sollew by Dr. Seuss (Random House)

The Lorax by Dr. Seuss (Random House)

McElligot's Pool by Dr. Seuss (Random House)

Sneetches and Other Stories by Dr. Seuss (Random House)

There's a Wocket in My Pocket! by Dr. Seuss (Random House)

Thidwick: The Big-Hearted Moose by Dr. Seuss (Random House)

II. Individual students will work at their own rate and proceed to explore the world of words in each subsequent learning project
  A. Each child will keep the form "New Words I Have Discovered" up to date throughout the school year
  B. Spelling bees and definition bees will be held periodically

EXAMPLE 19 LINGUISTICS STUDY UNIT, "THE WIZARDRY OF WORDS"*

Learning Project: The Wizardry of Words
Grade: 6

Project Goal: To provide learning experiences which will enable the gifted student to understand, appreciate, and value his/her language heritage—its history, symbol system, structure, power, diversity, and beauty

Teaching Objectives:
  This project has been designed and structured to provide these basic understandings:

  The history of language is an integral part of the history of civilization

  Language is a social tool or organism—the product of the society that employs it

  Language is not a fixed, immutable, circumscribed object but is an ever-growing, ever-changing body of facts and habits

  Many different languages have evolved from one parent language

  American English possesses qualities peculiar unto itself for while it has maintained much of the mother tongue it reflects unique facets of America's culture, literature, and social history

  American culture is not homogeneous; therefore, certain linguistic features are peculiar to certain regions and are not general to others

  This project has been designed and structured to foster and develop these attitudes and appreciations:

  Appreciation of man's linguistic heritage from the past

  Appreciation of the complex nature of language

  Appreciation of the value of utilizing dictionaries—general and special—as power tools for effective self-expression

  Respect for and interest in linguistic differences among diverse cultures

  Curiosity as to how certain words and expressions have originated

  Appreciation of the power and beauty of the written and the spoken word

  Delight in experimenting with language—its moods, colors, flavor, pattern, variety, and power

  Appreciation of the value to be accrued from successful group cooperative enterprises

  Appreciation of the high degree of satisfaction attained from successfully completing a challenging assignment

*From *Learning Unlimited: An Instructional Program for the Intellectually Gifted and Creatively Talented Student*, vol. I, 1977 (North Hills School District, 55 Rochester Rd., Pittsburgh, Pa. 15229).

EXAMPLE 19 (cont.)

Teaching Strategies and Methods:

No time limitations are imposed on this project. Number of students in the GATE group coupled with student interest are the factors determining the duration of the project whether it be two weeks, two months, or longer

A basic part of group orientation to the project is to provide opportunities for the students to explore the synergistic effect of sharing knowledge gained and then to determine appropriate methods and procedures for pooling information

Each student, after orientation to the purpose, scope, and dimension of the project will draw up and sign a contract specifying the particular area of knowledge-building he/she will be responsible for completing

Following the completion of the project, each student will assess his/her degree of accomplishment by checking the form ACHIEVEMENT-GROWTH EVALUATION

Procedural Outline:

I. Group orientation to and overview of this project
   A. Definition of basic terms serves as a unifying experience
      1. *Linguistics:* the science of language; comparative study of language structures and the study of the history and historical relationship of languages
      2. *Semantics:* the branch of linguistics that involves the scientific study of word meanings, especially their development and alteration
   B. Group shares understanding gained from reading *What's Behind the Word?* by Sam and Beryl Epstein (Scholastic paperback)
      1. The group uses the Table of Contents as an outline to be followed in building understanding (an excellent example of utilizing the Table of Contents as an orientation tool)
      2. The group begins its understanding of linguistics by analyzing information gained under three main headings:

Our language begins

If there were no words

Every word has a history

Families of languages

The beginnings of English

English grows

English keeps changing

English comes to the New World

From the Indians

From the French

From the Dutch

From the Spanish

The written word

How writing began

Picture writing

The alphabet is born

From written words to printed words

Words borrowed from all over the world

Modern English grows

New words from old

Words from names of famous people

Stuck-together words

Words that sound like what they mean

Tricks with words

EXAMPLE 19 (cont.)

A new twist to old words

Watch for brand names

Slang words and how they happen

Some words are twins

Words from all over the map

Where does your first name come from?

Last names came later

Did you know?

    C. The group reads *The Magic of Words* (Childcraft 1975 Annual) and adds additional subtopics to the list derived from *What's Behind the Word?*

    D. Individual students contract for the area or areas of in-depth knowledge-building for which they will be responsible

II. Individual students work at their own rate and proceed to develop their special areas of information

    A. Each student will search out his own materials

    B. Each student will determine which alternative learning road to travel

    C. Each student will determine when the assignment has been completed

    D. The GATE teacher will be available for consultation and guidance upon student request

III. The group will summarize this project by weaving in, where appropriate, insight and information each has gained

    A. The group will view the following motion pictures:

        1. *Discovering Language: The Alphabet Story* (Coronet)

        2. *Discovering Language: How English Borrowed Words* (Coronet)

        3. *Discovering Language: How English Changes in America* (Coronet)

        4. *Discovering Language: How Words Are Made* (Coronet)

        5. *Discovering Language: How Words Get New Meanings* (Coronet)

        6. *Discovering Language: Varieties of English* (Coronet)

    B. Following the viewing of each motion picture, the students will contribute what each has discovered through individualized study

    C. When all six motion pictures have been presented and discussed, then the group will identify significant topics which have not been adequately developed or have been omitted entirely

        1. Individual students will volunteer to search out the overlooked or incomplete topics

        2. These students will then share with the group the information needed to complete the project

EXAMPLE 20 LINGUISTICS STUDY UNIT, "AMERICAN ENGLISH:
INHERITED, MANUFACTURED, AND FRACTURED"*

Unit: American English: Inherited, Manufactured, and Fractured (Abridged)
Subject: English
Grade: 12

Goal: This unit will provide opportunities for the student to understand, appreciate, and value American English as the product of American society and as a réflection of the culture, folkways, and characteristic psychology of the American people

Teaching objectives:
    1. This unit has been designed to develop these basic understandings:

        Language is a social tool or social organism—the product of the society that employs it

---

*This unit has been developed and taught by Corinne P. Clendening, Coordinator of the Elementary Gifted and Talented Program, North Hills School District, Pittsburgh, Pa. 15229.

EXAMPLE 20 (cont.)

Language is not a fixed, immutable, circumscribed object but is an ever-changing body of facts and habits

The use of language depends in large part upon such factors as home environment, education, occupation, recreation, and political and social involvement

Speech is but one mode of communication; nonverbal language is also a basic communications skill

American English possesses certain qualities peculiar to itself for while it has maintained much of the mother tongue it reflects unique facets of American cultural and social history and development

American culture is pluralistic and far from homogeneous; therefore, certain linguistic features are peculiar to certain regions and are not general to others

Recognizing propaganda, shoddy advertising, and political double-talk is a basic competency essential for functional literacy*

2. This unit has been designed to develop these attitudes and appreciations:

Appreciation for the student's language heritage and the complex nature of language—its symbol system, structure, history, power, diversity, and beauty

Respect for and interest in linguistic differences among diverse cultures

Curiosity as to why linguistic differences exist

Satisfaction and challenge in word exploration and study

Appreciation that to be literate in a world rich in the symbols of language means to be able to communicate ideas clearly and to analyze and *enjoy* what is seen, heard, and read†

Teaching procedure:
1. This unit will be offered as a six-week elective course
2. This unit will employ the following teaching-learning strategies and methods:

Each student will share responsibility for building background knowledge in depth; leading class discussions; participating in dramatizations; and in designing and conducting opinion polls

After class orientation to the unit, each student will have unlimited time to work in the high school library to build his knowledge in an area of specialization

Procedural outline:
1. The class will be oriented to the study of American English by viewing and discussing the sound filmstrip series *Language and Its Mysteries* (Centron Educational Films)

The following concepts will be stressed:

Language is uniquely human

Language is a learned social tool

Languages come in families

The story of language is the story of human activity

2. The class will view the following motion pictures and then will synthesize understandings gained to date:‡

The English Language: How It Changes (Coronet)

The English Language: Patterns of Usage (Coronet)

---

*Harold G. Shane, *Curriculum Change Toward the 21st Century* (Washington, D.C.: National Education Association, 1977), Premise XXVIII, p. 68.

†Ibid.

‡These two Coronet motion pictures reinforce and extend the concepts presented in the Coronet series "Discovering Language" introduced previously in the sixth-grade unit "The Wizardry of Words" (see Example 19). This is an illustration of Harold G. Shane's concept of the "seamless curriculum."

EXAMPLE 20 (cont.)

3. Following class orientation experiences, each student will work in the library completing his independent linguistics research project and will, at the conclusion of his research, share with his class the knowledge he has gained. The research topics and activities offered for student consideration include the following:

Using these three dictionaries, the *Oxford English Dictionary*, *The Random House Dictionary of the English Language*, and *Webster's Third New International Dictionary of the English Language*, compare the definitions for the following linguistic terms:

American English	Nonverbal communication
Black English	Parole
Langue	Phatic language
Lexicon	Regional dialects
Linguistics	Social dialects
Nonstandard English	Standard English

Discover Professor Henry Higgins's theory concerning English dialects

SOURCES: *My Fair Lady* by Alan Lerner and Frederick Lowe (New American Library)

My Fair Lady, Columbia Masterworks Recording

Discover the six dialect areas in the United States

SOURCES: *American Speaking*, National Council of Teachers of English Recording

Dialects and Dialect Learning Kit, National Council of Teachers of English

Discover the meaning and the psychological use of "doublespeak." What is the significance of the National Council of Teachers of English Doublespeak Award?

SOURCES: *Double-Speak in America* by Mario Pei (Hawthorn)

Weasel Words: The Art of Saying What You Don't Mean by Mario Pei (Harper)

Words in Sheep's Clothing by Mario Pei (Hawthorn)

Discovering the stories behind people's names

SOURCES: *First Names First* by Leslie Alan Dunkling (Universe Books)

New Dictionary of American Family Names by Elsdon Smith (Harper)

What's in a Name by Favius Friedman (Scholastic)

Discover the stories behind place names

SOURCES: *Our Language: The Story of the Words We Use* by Eloise Lambert (Lippincott)

Place Words by Bill Severn (Washburn)

Words on the Map by Isaac Asimov (Houghton)

Word Origins and Their Romantic Stories by Wilfred Funk (Funk and Wagnalls)

Discover the word histories of scientific terms

SOURCES: *More Words of Science* by Isaac Asimov (Houghton)

Naming Living Things by Sarah Riedman (Rand McNally)

Word Origins and Their Romantic Stories by Wilfred Funk (Funk and Wagnalls)

Words of Science by Isaac Asimov (Houghton)

Discover stories of curious word origins

SOURCES: *A Hog on Ice and Other Curious Expressions* by Charles Funk (Harper)

Horsefeathers and Other Curious Words by Charles Funk (Harper)

Thereby Hangs a Tale: Stories of Curious Word Origins by Charles Funk (Harper)

EXAMPLE 20 (cont.)

What's Behind the Word? by Harold Longman (Coward)

What's in a Word by Harold Longman (Coward)

Discover word histories for your favorite sport

SOURCES: *Baseball Language: A Running Press Glossary* by Richard Scholl (Running Press)

Sports Lingo: A Dictionary of the Language of Sports by Harvey Frommer (Atheneum)

Discover the meaning of the word "slang," and why slang plays an important part in the American English scene; an excellent source of information is found in the Introduction, Foreword, and/or Preface of the following:

SOURCES: *Dictionary of Slang and Unconventional English* by Eric Partridge (Macmillan)

New Dictionary of Americanisms by Sylvia Clapin (Gale)

Our Language: The Story of the Words We Use by Eloise Lambert (Lothrop)

Slang Today and Yesterday by Eric Partridge (Routledge and Kegan)

Discover why Mario Pei refers to "pidgin English" as "the adult, international, and interracial version of hyporcorism"

SOURCES: *Book of Pidgin English* by John J. Murphy (Smith & Patterson)

The Many Hues of English by Mario Pei (Knopf)

Our Language: The Story of the Words We Use by Eloise Lambert (Lothrop)

Discover how Clarence L. Barnhart and his research staff select new words for inclusion in a dictionary of new English words; check the *World Book Year Book* for each year subsequent to the publication of *The Barnhart Dictionary of New English Since 1963* (published by Harper and Row in 1973) to discover the new words contained in the Year Books' "Dictionary Supplement"

SOURCES: *The Barnhart Dictionary of New English Since 1963*, edited by Clarence L. Barnhart (Harper)

World Book Year Book, 1974–to date (Field Enterprises)

Discover what is meant by "P. D. English" and why it has continued as a distinctive cultural dialect for over two hundred years

SOURCES: *Hex Marks the Spot in the Pennsylvania Dutch Country* by Ann Hark (Lippincott)

Pennsylvania Dutch by Fredric Klees (Macmillan)

Pennsylvania Dutch Cook Book by J. George Frederick (Peter Smith)

Traditionally Pennsylvania Dutch by Edward C. Smith and Virginia Thompson (Hastings House)

THE LIBRARY RESEARCH PAPER

The research paper is universally employed by the English teacher as a culminating learning experience for it provides, in one meaningful assignment, opportunity for students to read, to listen, to take notes, to organize their thoughts, to gain experience in the principle tools of research, and, finally, to write a paper of some length and significance on a subject with which each has become thoroughly conversant.* Corinne P. Clendening in her chapter "The High School Level: Examples of Planning, Preparing, and Imple-

*NCTE highlights in the NCTE *Catalog* the New York State English Council Monograph *Research Papers: A Guided Writing Experience for Senior High School Students* by Richard Corbin and Jonathan Corbin (Rochester, N.Y.: New York State English Council, 1978).

menting Library-User Instructional Programs" provides sound principles to be followed by the library media specialist and the classroom teacher in designing a library-based research project. Excerpts from Clendening's chapter follow:

> Although differences of professional opinion abound concerning the wisdom and necessity of having librarians teach the formal high school library research paper, the paper still continues to be the favorite vehicle of many English and social studies teachers for teaching and/or evaluating student proficiency in research study skills. The following questions should be considered in collaboration with the teacher before the high school librarian undertakes a research project:
>
> > *How should the research paper be taught?*   Should the unit be taught as a single, in-depth paper requiring a lengthy period of investigation? Or should the unit employ several developmental papers of limited scope? Should both research and writing take place in the library? Or should only the research take place in the library and the writing take place in the classroom?
> >
> > *When should the research paper be taught?*   Should the research paper be taught at the beginning of tenth grade as a diagnostic means of assessing the degree of student competence? Or should the paper be taught during the twelfth grade as a culminating activity in preparation for college-bound students and as a final evaluative assessment of student mastery?
> >
> > *Should the research paper be taught to all students?*   Should the research paper be required of all students? Or should the paper be required only of those students who are college bound? Can the research paper be justified as a worthwhile learning experience for the less than able learner?
> >
> > *Where within the school's curriculum can the research paper most effectively be taught?*   Should the research paper be considered a logical responsibility of the English program? Or should the teaching of the research paper be the shared responsibility of a teaching team representing several or more subject areas?[41]

Clendening recommends that "How To Do Research" (a section contained in the last volume of *World Book Encyclopedia, Research Guide/Index*) be used as a research outline plan by the student.

W. Keith Kraus suggests in his publication *Murder, Mischief, and Mayhem: A Process for Creative Research Papers*[42] an innovative approach to teaching the research paper. Kraus suggests specific exercises designed to familiarize students with the difficulties peculiar to newspaper research. He also explains how to motivate and help students organize their projects. In his book, Kraus presents ten unedited student research papers, including footnotes and working bibliography.

DEPENDENCE OF THE LANGUAGE ARTS PROGRAM ON THE LIBRARY MEDIA PROGRAM

Library resources are the raw materials required as basic content for the English program designed both to develop the basic communication skills—reading, writing, listening, and speaking—and to develop student interest in and appreciation of literature. The library media center is the learning laboratory where students come to work with these raw materials whether as members of a class or group or as individuals. The library media center is a most effective means of both humanizing and individualizing the English instructional program; here students can find resources that will fit their special learning needs, their special learning style, and their uniquely personal interests. Here students are sure to find audiovisual media to offset and compensate for a reading deficiency; here students are sure to find a wide variety of novels, poems, journals, biographies, plays, or musical comedies to fit their special reading style; here students are sure to find a wealth of resources uniquely reflective of their current consuming interests. And, above all, here students learn the skill of inquiry—how to search for ideas, how to evaluate and select ideas, how to organize and communicate ideas—the very basis of functional literacy.

Direct communication between English teacher and library media specialist both in the design and in the implementation of the program is imperative if the program is to succeed; for a program designed to develop accuracy and comprehension in reading, clarity and fluency in speaking, correctness and effectiveness in writing, and attentiveness and awareness in listening, and to activate and nurture creativity is but a nebulous hope without the essential support and guidance of the library media program to bring it to fruition.

NOTES

1. National Study of School Evaluation, *The Evaluative Criteria for the Evaluation of Secondary Schools*, 5th ed. Copyright © 1978, p. 101. Reprinted by permission of the National Study of School Evaluation, Washington, D.C.
2. John U. Michaelis, Ruth H. Grossman, and Lloyd F. Scott, *New Designs for Elementary Curriculum and Instruction* (New York: McGraw-Hill, 1975), p. 179.
3. National Council of Teachers of English, *Recommended English Language Arts Curriculum Guides K–12* . . . (Urbana, Ill.: National Council of Teachers of English, 1978).
4. The President's Commission on National Goals, *Goals for Americans* (Englewood Cliffs, N.J.: Prentice-Hall, 1960), p. 86.
5. Research and Policy Committee of the Committee for Economic Development, *Innovation in Education: New Directions for the American School* (New York: Committee for Economic Development, 1968), p. 34.
6. Florence D. Cleary, *Blueprints for Better Reading: School Programs for Promoting Skill and Interest in Reading* (New York: H. W. Wilson, 1972), pp. 18–20. Reprinted by permission of the H. W. Wilson Company. Copyright © 1972 by Florence D. Cleary.
7. Stanley M. Elam, ed., *A Decade of Gallup Polls of Attitudes toward Education 1969–1978* (Bloomington, Ind.: Phi Delta Kappa, 1978), p. 340.
8. Ibid., p. 231.
9. Rudolf Flesch, *Why Johnny Can't Read* . . . (New York: Harper, 1955).
10. James E. Allen, "The Right to Read—Target for the 70's," *Elementary English* 47: 488.
11. David Harman, "Illiteracy: An Overview," *Harvard Educational Review* 47, no. 2 (May 1970): 227.
12. Mary C. Austin et al., *The First R: The Harvard Report on Reading in Elementary Schools* (New York: Macmillan, 1963), p. 232.
13. James C. MacCampbell and Eleanor Peck, eds., *Focus on Reading* (Cambridge, Mass.: New England School Development Council, 1964), p. 29.
14. Margaret Early, ed., *First Splendor*, The Bookmark Reading Series (New York: Harcourt, 1968), pp. T14–T15.
15. Paul C. Burns, Betty Broman, and Alberta Lowe, *The Language Arts in Childhood Education*, 3rd ed. (Chicago: Rand McNally, 1975), pp. 386–388.
16. William K. Durr et al., eds., *Images* (Boston: Houghton, 1971), p. 8.
17. Ibid., pp. 8–10.
18. Florence D. Cleary, *Blueprints for Better Reading*, pp. 12–13.
19. Robert Carlsen, *Books and the Teen-Age Reader: A Guide for Teachers, Librarians and Parents*, rev. ed. (New York: Harper, 1971), p. 3.

20. Helen K. Macintosh et al., *Administration of Elementary School Programs for Disadvantaged Children*, Disadvantaged Children Series No. 4 (Washington, D.C.: U.S. Department of Health, Education, and Welfare, 1966), p. 15.
21. Ibid., p. 5.
22. Dorothy E. Withrow, Helen B. Carey, and Bertha M. Hirzel, *Gateways to Readable Books . . .* , 5th ed. (New York: H. W. Wilson, 1975), p. 20.
23. Harold G. Shane et al., *Interpreting Language Arts Research for the Teacher* (Washington, D.C.: Association for Supervision and Curriculum Development, 1971), p. 105.
24. Leonard H. Clark et al., *The American Secondary School Curriculum*, 2nd ed. (New York: Macmillan, 1972), p. 222.
25. *General Education in a Free Society: A Report of the Harvard Committee* (Cambridge: Harvard University Press, 1945), pp. 110–111.
26. Robert C. Pooley, "The Professional Status of the Teacher of English," *English Journal* 48 (Sept. 1959): 311.
27. Dewey W. Chambers, *Children's Literature in the Curriculum* (Chicago: Rand McNally, 1971), p. 186.
28. Clark et al., *The American Secondary School Curriculum*, pp. 220–221.
29. J. N. Hook, *The Teaching of High School English*, 4th ed. (New York: Ronald Press, 1972), p. 107.
30. Paul S. Anderson, *Language Skills in Elementary Education* (New York: Macmillan, 1972), p. 158.
31. Chambers, *Children's Literature in the Curriculum*, pp. 189–190.
32. Hook, *The Teaching of High School English*, pp. 107–108.
33. Cleary, *Blueprints for Better Reading*, p. 140.
34. Elizabeth Calkins and Barry McGhan, *Teaching Tomorrow: A Handbook of Science Fiction for Teachers* (Dayton, Ohio: Pflaum/Standard, 1972), pp. 2–3.
35. Neil Barron, *Anatomy of Wonder: Science Fiction* (New York: R. R. Bowker, 1976).
36. "What Are the 'Basics' in English," *SLATE* 1, no. 2 (Aug. 1967): 2.
37. Michaelis, Grossman, and Scott, *New Designs*, p. 177.
38. David Feldman, "Toward a Nonelitist Conception of Giftedness," *Phi Delta Kappan*, May 1979, p. 662.
39. Arthur N. Applebee, *A Survey of Teaching Conditions in English, 1977* (Urbana, Ill.: National Council of Teachers of English, 1978), p. 58.
40. Corinne P. Clendening and Ruth A. Davies, *Creating Programs for the Gifted: A Guide for Teachers, Librarians, and Students* (New York: R. R. Bowker, 1980).
41. Corinne P. Clendening, "The High School Level: Examples of Planning, Preparing, and Implementing Library-User Instructional Programs," in *Educating the Library User*, ed. by John Lubans, Jr. (New York: R. R. Bowker, 1974), pp. 163–174.
42. W. Keith Kraus, *Murder, Mischief, and Mayhem* (Urbana, Ill.: National Council of Teachers of English, 1978).

9 The Library Media Program Supports the Social Studies Program

. . . unravel the present into its constituent parts. For the present is the past rolled up for action, and the past is the present unrolled for our understanding.

Will and Ariel Durant*

Libraries are the keepers of our history and our culture. But they are not merely storehouses of the relics of the past, but meeting places for people and ideas, vital partners in our system of education.

Wilbur J. Cohen†

As knowledge without action is impotent, so action without knowledge is reprehensible.

The National Council for the Social Studies‡

"To prepare young people to be humane, rational, participating citizens in a world that is becoming increasingly interdependent" is the basic goal of the social studies program.[1] If we are to survive, any lesser goal is untenable. In consonance with world survival skills, the social studies program also carries the weight of the school's serious obligation to prepare future citizens purposefully in *enlightened* commitment to the American ideal of personal excellence. In actuating this goal of global concern, the social studies program shares with the other disciplines the concern for the "enhancement of human dignity through learning and commitment to rational processes."[2] Commitment to human dignity implies that all students will have the opportunity to attain their optimum potential as students, as citizens, and as human beings.

COMPONENTS OF THE SOCIAL STUDIES PROGRAM

The social studies program is a multidiscipline program. Basic concepts from history, geography, economics, political science and law, anthropology, sociology, psychology, and philosophy are interrelated and are mutually supportive of one another (see Figure 5). Yet the social studies program is far more than the content of these eight separate disciplines. The National

---

*Will Durant and Ariel Durant, *Will and Ariel Durant: A Dual Autobiography* (New York: Simon and Schuster, 1977), p. 319.

†Wilbur J. Cohen, Chairman, National Commission on Libraries, "Letter to the President," October 3, 1968.

‡The National Council for the Social Studies, "Position Statement: Revision of the NCSS Social Studies Curriculum Guidelines," *Social Education* 43, no. 4 (Apr. 1979): 262.

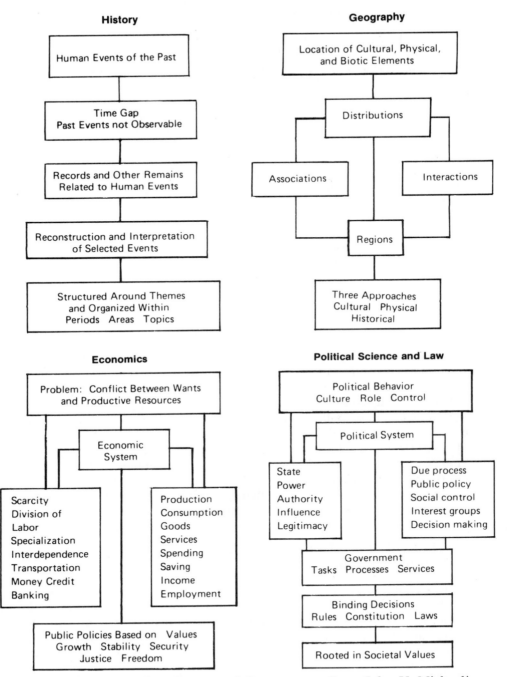

FIGURE 5. Social Studies: Conceptual Components. From John U. Michaelis, *Social Studies for Children in a Democracy: Recent Trends & Developments*, 6th ed. Copyright © 1976, pp. 148–149. Reprinted by permission of Prentice-Hall, Inc., Englewood Cliffs, N.J.

FIGURE 5 (cont.)

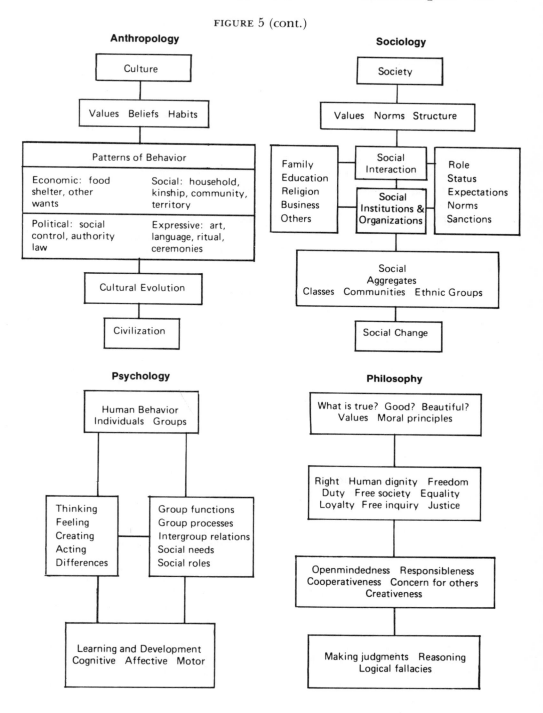

Council for the Social Studies (NCSS) has identified the following four components as being basic:

1. Knowledge about the real world and knowledge about the worthiness of personal and social judgments [see Chapter 6, under the heading "What Knowledge"]

    The broad function of knowledge is to provide the reservoir of data, ideas, concepts, generalizations, and theories which in combination with thinking, valuing, and social participation can be used by the student to function rationally and humanely

2. Abilities provide the means of achieving objectives, and ideally one who is able and skillful can reach objectives

    Included in the ability concept are intellectual, data processing, and human relations competencies

3. Valuing must be considered as an intellectual operation

    Students need systematic and supportive help in examining differences among other persons and groups and in clarifying the values conflicts within themselves

4. Social participation in a democracy calls for individual behavior guided by the values of human dignity and rationality and directed toward the resolution of problems confronting society

    Social participation means the application of knowledge, thinking, and commitment in the social arena—at the local, state, national, and international levels

It is essential that these four curriculum components be viewed as equally important; ignoring any of them weakens a social studies program. The relationship among knowledge, abilities, valuing, and social participation is tight and dynamic. Each interacts with the others. Each nourishes the others.[3]

GUIDING PRINCIPLES

In the *Evaluative Criteria*, the basic evaluation tool for secondary education, the following guiding principles are set forth:

Social studies is the study of human social relationships—past, present, and projected into the future. Subject matter for the social studies is drawn from three main sources: academic disciplines (anthropology, economics, geography, history, political science, psychology, social psychology, and sociology), enduring social issues, and perceived concerns of students. The physical environment, together with the psychological and biological components, is considered to the extent that it enhances understanding of social relationships.

The primary objective of the social studies program is to prepare thoughtful, active citizens who can function productively in a multicultural, rapidly changing, and increasingly interdependent world. The social studies program should provide a variety of affective and cognitive experiences which contribute to the dignity of each human being. These humanistic values should be realized through an open examination of controversial issues and diverse life-styles.

The social studies program should be founded upon the notion that a democratic society depends upon responsible citizens to make rational decisions consistent with basic democratic values. Active experiences and participation in the democratic process are essential.

The social studies classroom, the school, and the community provide settings where students can inquire into questions dealing with social values and behavior. The search for and the study of alternative solutions to important social problems can be achieved most effectively through the process of inquiry.[4]

John Michaelis, Ruth Grossman, and Lloyd Scott in their comprehensive text *New Designs for Elementary Curriculum and Instruction* provide the following guiding principles to unify and strengthen the teaching of social studies:

The breadth and scope of the program should adequately sample major areas of human activity; include ethnic, environmental, and other studies of critical importance; be balanced in terms of disciplinary emphasis, cultures, and areas selected for study; and be related to problems, events, and issues of importance in daily living.

The sequence of topics and units should be related to developmental stages and characteristics of children; provide for the progressive development of concepts, generalizations, skills, processes, and affective objectives; and permit adaptations and modifications at various levels so that individual differences can be met and important contemporary affairs can be given attention.[5]

NCSS CURRICULUM GUIDELINES

These guidelines represent a set of standards for social studies programs. They are not intended to prescribe a uniform program or even to propose an ideal program. In a pluralistic and changing society no one such program could be prescribed, even if more were known about the process of education than is presently available.[6]

THE SOCIAL STUDIES PROGRAM SHOULD BE DIRECTLY RELATED TO THE AGE, MATURITY, AND CONCERNS OF STUDENTS

1. Students should be involved in the formulation of goals, the selection of activities and instructional strategies, and the assessment of curricular outcomes.
2. The school and its teachers should make steady efforts, through regularized channels and practices, to identify areas of concern to students.
3. Students should have some choices, some options within programs fitted to their needs, their concerns, and their social world.
4. Students should have a special studies experience at all grade levels, K–12.
5. The program should take into account the aptitudes, developmental capabilities, and psychological needs of the students.

THE SOCIAL STUDIES PROGRAM SHOULD DEAL WITH THE REAL SOCIAL WORLD

1. The program should focus on the social world as it is, its flaws, its strengths, its dangers, and its promise.
2. The program should emphasize pervasive and enduring social issues.
3. The program should demonstrate the relationships between the local and global aspects of social issues.
4. The program should include analysis and attempts to formulate potential resolutions of present and controversial global problems such as racism, sexism, world resources, nuclear proliferation, and ecological imbalance.
5. The program should provide intensive and recurring cross-cultural study of groups to which students themselves belong and those to which they do not.
6. The program should offer opportunities for students to meet, discuss, study, and work with members of racial, ethnic, and national groups other than their own.
7. The program should build upon realities of the immediate school community.
8. Participation in the real social world, both in school and out, should be considered a part of the social studies program.

9. The program should provide the opportunity for students to examine potential future conditions and problems.

THE SOCIAL STUDIES PROGRAM SHOULD DRAW FROM CURRENTLY VALID KNOWLEDGE REPRESENTATIVE OF HUMAN EXPERIENCE, CULTURE, AND BELIEFS

1. The program should emphasize currently valid concepts, principles, and theories in the social sciences.
2. The program should develop proficiency in methods of inquiry in the social sciences and in techniques for processing social data.
3. The program should develop students' ability to distinguish among empirical, logical, definitional, and normative propositions and problems.
4. The program should draw upon all of the social sciences such as anthropology, economics, geography, political science, history, and the behavioral sciences.
5. The program should draw from other related fields such as law, the humanities, the natural and applied sciences, and religion.
6. The program should represent some balance between the immediate social environment of students and the larger social world; between small group and public issues; among local, national, and global affairs; among past, present, and future directions; among Western and non-Western cultures; and among economically developed and developing nations.
7. The program should include the study not only of human achievements, but also of human failures.

OBJECTIVES SHOULD BE THOUGHTFULLY SELECTED AND CLEARLY STATED IN SUCH FORM AS TO FURNISH DIRECTION TO THE PROGRAM

1. Objectives should be carefully selected and formulated in the light of what is known about the students, their community, the real social world, and the fields of knowledge.
2. Knowledge, abilities, valuing, and social participation should all be represented in the stated objectives of social studies programs.
3. General statements of basic and long-range goals should be translated into more specific objectives conceived in terms of behavior and content.
4. Classroom instruction should rely upon statements which identify clearly what students are to learn; learning activities and instructional materials should be appropriate for achieving the stated objectives.
5. Classroom instruction should enable students to see their goals clearly in what is to be learned, whether in brief instructional sequences or lengthy units of study.
6. Instructional objectives should develop all aspects of the affective, cognitive, and psychomotor domains.
7. Objectives should be reconsidered and revised periodically.

LEARNING ACTIVITIES SHOULD ENGAGE THE STUDENT DIRECTLY AND ACTIVELY IN THE LEARNING PROCESS

1. Students should have a wide and rich range of learning activities appropriate to the objectives of their social studies program.
2. Activities should include formulating hypotheses and testing them by gathering and analyzing data.
3. Activities should include using knowledge, examining values, communicating with others, and making decisions about social and civic affairs.
4. Students should be encouraged to become active participants in activities within their own communities.
5. Learning activities should be sufficiently varied and flexible to appeal to many kinds of students.
6. Activities should contribute to the students' perception of teachers as fellow inquirers.

7. Activities must be carried on in a climate which supports students' self-respect and opens opportunities to all.
8. Activities should stimulate students to investigate and to respond to the human condition in the contemporary world.
9. Activities which examine values, attitudes, and beliefs should be undertaken in an environment that respects each student's rights to privacy.

STRATEGIES OF INSTRUCTION AND LEARNING ACTIVITIES SHOULD RELY ON A BROAD RANGE OF LEARNING RESOURCES

1. A social studies program requires a great wealth of appropriate instructional resources; no one textbook can be sufficient.
2. Printed materials must accommodate a wide range of reading abilities and interests, meet the requirements of learning activities, and include many kinds of material from primary as well as secondary sources, from social science and history as well as the humanities and related fields, from other nations and cultures as well as our own, and from current as well as basic sources.
3. A variety of media should be available for learning through seeing, hearing, touching, and acting, and calling for thought and feeling.
4. Social studies classrooms should draw upon the potential contributions of many kinds of resource persons and organizations representing many points of view, a variety of abilities, and a mix of cultures and nationalities.
5. Classroom activities should use the school and community as a learning laboratory for gathering social data and for confronting knowledge and commitments in dealing with social problems.
6. The social studies program should have available many kinds of work space to facilitate variation in the size of groups, the use of several kinds of media, and a diversity of tasks.

THE SOCIAL STUDIES PROGRAM MUST FACILITATE THE ORGANIZATION OF EXPERIENCE

1. Structure in the social studies program must help students organize their experiences to promote growth.
2. Learning experiences should be organized in such manner that students will learn how to continue to learn.
3. The program must enable students to relate their experiences in social studies to other areas of experience.
4. The formal pattern of the program should offer choice and flexibility.

EVALUATION SHOULD BE USEFUL, SYSTEMATIC, COMPREHENSIVE, AND VALID FOR THE OBJECTIVES OF THE PROGRAMS

1. Evaluation should be based primarily on the school's own statements of objectives as the criteria for effectiveness.
2. Included in the evaluation process should be assessment of progress not only in knowledge, but in skills and abilities, including thinking, valuing, and social participation.
3. Evaluation data should come from many sources, not merely from paper-and-pencil tests, including observations of what students do outside as well as inside the classroom.
4. Regular, comprehensive, and continuous procedures should be developed for gathering evidence of significant growth in learning over time.
5. Evaluation data should be used for planning curricular improvements.
6. Evaluation data should offer students, teachers, and parents help in the course of learning and not merely at the conclusions of some marking period.
7. Both students and teachers should be involved in the process of evaluation.
8. Thoughtful and regular re-examination of the basic goals of the social studies curriculum should be an integral part of the evaluation program.

SOCIAL STUDIES EDUCATION SHOULD RECEIVE VIGOROUS SUPPORT AS A VITAL AND RESPONSIBLE PART OF THE SCHOOL PROGRAM

1. Appropriate instructional materials, time, and facilities must be provided for social studies education.
2. Teachers should not only be responsible but should be encouraged to try out and adapt for their own students promising innovations such as simulation, newer curricular plans, discovery, and actual social participation.
3. Decisions about the basic purposes of social studies education in any school should be as clearly related to the needs of its immediate community as to those of society at large.
4. Teachers should participate in active social studies curriculum committees with decision-making as well as advisory responsibilities.
5. Teachers should participate regularly in activities which foster their professional competence in social studies education: in workshops, or in-service classes, or community affairs, or in reading, studying, and travel.
6. Teachers and others concerned with social studies education in the schools should have competent consultants available.
7. Teachers and schools should have and be able to rely upon a district-wide policy statement on academic freedom and professional responsibility.
8. Social studies education should expect to receive active support from administrators, teachers, boards of education, and the community.
9. A specific minimal block of time should be allocated for social studies instruction each week.

The NCSS standards outlined in the preceding guidelines are directly supportive of the following premises from the National Education Association (NEA) Cardinal Principles for Educational Change (see Chapter 2):

1. The need to develop a spirit of "global community" in an increasingly interdependent world has reaffirmed an important task for education: to recognize and to respect the concepts of multiethnic, polycultural, and multilingual education in pluralistic societies both in the United States and abroad.
2. Education has assumed new significance as a positive force for peace in a world capable of destroying itself.
18. Present social trends, which are characterized by accelerating change and increasing complexity, have enhanced the need for basic communication skills such as the ability to handle the written and spoken word and to deal with number concepts.
20. Traditional instructional methods should be expanded to include problem-solving approaches, and their emphasis on cognition and on valuing should be renewed.
21. Interdisciplinary learning should be stressed and the art of comprehending and anticipating complex relationships should be fostered.
24. There is a need to teach the concept of alternative futures since, lacking a desirable image of tomorrow's possible worlds, one lacks purpose, goals, and the motivating spirit of community that are needed to serve as guides to action.
25. Instruction in subject matter fields should develop a deepening understanding of contemporary threats to the biosphere, include socially useful service in its maintenance, and communicate to youth the need for achieving balance or equilibrium between humans and their environment.
26. So that desirable alternative futures can be envisioned, work in the social studies should be redesigned so as to promote a grasp of human geography and of planetary cultures as they exist today.

THEORY VERSUS PRACTICE

The value of the NCSS guidelines lies not in their being formulated and published, but in their being studied, discussed, and understood by the educational profession and then implemented by the administrators, the classroom teachers, and the library media specialists as they plan and work together in the local school district and in the individual school buildings. Just as the record for innovation adoption and implementation has been disappointing (see Chapter 2, under the heading "Educational Resistance to Change"), so is a report of observations of social studies teaching practices made by Michael Elliott and Kerry Kennedy and reported in the April 1979 issue of *Social Education*.[7] This study indicates wide disparity between the theory of excellence and actual classroom practice.

Elliott and Kennedy summarized the social studies image of excellence as being "conceptually based, interdisciplinary (or multidisciplinary) in nature, concerned with valuing and valuing processes, emphasizing inquiry learning and inductive teaching, as well as being committed to student-centered learning [see Table 5]."[8] A summary of their findings follows:

Observation #1. We have not seen much teaching organized around concepts (e.g., power, conflict, change, cooperation, etc.). Most courses of study . . . emphasized a chronological approach. . . . *In almost all of the history classes . . . the textbook has played a dominant role. It seems to be the main guide to the organization of content which teachers employ* [emphasis supplied]. This textbook orientation is reinforced through frequent homework assignments which require the reading of a set number of pages in the text and the answering of . . . end-of-chapter questions.

Observation #2. The social studies is primarily seen as a collection of single disciplines, taught separately, with history and government predominating. . . . our expectations that social studies practice would be geared to an inter- or multidisciplinary focus have not, in the main, been confirmed.

Observation #3. Much, if not most, social studies teaching is expository in nature. The lecture appears to permeate practice at the secondary level.

Observation #4. In nearly all the schools we have visited, the curriculum has been determined long before it is presented to students in the classroom. Such practices seem to work against the chance that the needs and interests of students will be incorporated into what is taught. It seems to be difficult for many teachers to cater to individual differences within the classroom. In general, most of the teachers we observed directed their teaching to the so-called "average" ability students. They ignored those with significant reading and learning problems, or those who needed to be extended to achieve their potential.

Observation #5. No matter how content is organized and presented in a social studies classroom, there is always an element related to value issues but such issues are rarely explored.

Conclusion: By and large, social studies content and practice do not appear to follow the writings of social studies methods texts, and/or curriculum projects, or the arguments of leading social studies educators. It is not, in the main, interdisciplinary (or multidisciplinary) in nature, inquiry or inductive oriented, student centered, or focused on values.[9]

If the NCSS guidelines are to be implemented, then those who are responsible for developing instructional programs and strategies must scientifically relate practice to theory. John Michaelis advocates four interrelated sets of objectives when planning social studies instruction. The following have been adapted from Michaelis's book *Social Studies for Children in a Democracy:*[10]

CONCEPTUAL OBJECTIVES

To develop understanding of data, concepts, themes, and generalizations, including the ability to identify and describe:

TABLE 5 MAJOR EMPHASES AS CONCEPTUALIZED IN SELECTED SOCIAL STUDIES TEXTBOOKS PUBLISHED IN THE UNITED STATES, 1966-1976*

AUTHOR	TYPE OF INFORMATION TO BE EMPHASIZED	SOURCE OF DATA TO BE UTILIZED	INSTRUCTIONAL PROCEDURES	VIEW OF THE STUDENT	VALUES AND VALUING PROCESSES
Fenton (1966) [*Teaching the New Social Studies—An Inductive Approach*, Holt]	"Facts do not speak for themselves. They have meaning only when the minds of men order them into patterns." (pp. vi-vii)	"On the whole, the structure of the social sciences has served as the most important guide in the selection of the substantive body of knowledge to teach." (p. vi)	"What will be its (the social studies) nature? It will involve ... the use of a mode of inquiry involving the development and validation of hypotheses...." (p. v)	"... structure could be combined with the needs and interests of the child, and with contemporary social problems, to provide useful guides to content selection." (p. vi)	"Affective objectives emphasize a feeling, an emotion, or a degree of acceptance or rejection. Many of the traditional objectives of social studies teachers lie in the affective domain. For example, social studies teachers try to influence the attitudes of their students toward their work.... They want each student to examine his values, to organize them into a value system, and to develop a personal philosophy." (p. 40)
Jarolimek (1967) [*Social Studies in Elementary Education*, Macmillan]	"Better social studies programs ... make certain the child has the opportunity to extend his understanding of basic and elementary concepts of geography, history, government, economics, and sociology as they bear on the study of people and their struggle to solve the perennial problems of mankind." (p. 8)	"People's ways of living simply cannot be explained adequately or accurately in terms of a single discipline, such as history or geography. ... If programs are to be really effective they must be interdisciplinary to some extent." (p. 3)	"Inductive procedures have been recommended for elementary school teaching for at least two generations under the title *problem-solving*...." (p. 377)	"... teachers today must make more careful studies of individual children, take a broader view of their teaching task, and concern themselves with more than the intellectual development of children, important as this is." (p. 18)	"One of the great challenges of social studies teaching today is not to *give* values to pupils but to help them understand the value-system; learn the sources of some of our values; recognize and deal with the value-components of civic and social issues; and form their own value-system on a rational basis." (p. 10)
Hunt and Metcalf (1968) [*Teaching United States Social Studies...*, Harper]	"Concepts ... are the basis of all thinking and knowing.... (Teachers sometimes say that thinking is impossible without facts. It is more to the point to say that thinking is impossible without concepts)." (p. 83)	"Teaching materials should be drawn from a selection of conflicting propositions in such controversial areas as race and minority group relations, social class, economics, sex, courtship and marriage, religion and morality, and national and pa-	"Viewing the content of learning as the data of reflection, rather than as predetermined collections of facts, poses difficult problems for teachers and textbook writers; it seems to exclude the possibility of selecting subject matter in advance of the reflective acts in which it is to be used. A way around this dilemma would appear to be an authentic problem-centered approach, in which teaching materials are selected and textbooks written so as to incorporate data which are relevant to existing or potential problems of students. Such content		"Progress toward solution of moral problems would occur more rapidly if public education included a reflective study of value alternatives." (p. 121) "We want students to be consistent in their values, but we also want them to justify values by recourse to criteria derived from a philosophy to which they subscribe. Whether they choose to subscribe to a democratic philosophy is their decision to make—probably the most important decision in their lives." (p. 142)

(cont. on next page)

	"triotic beliefs, plus a wide range of relevant data to be used in testing them.... The content of any act of thought is likely to cut across subject matter boundaries." (p. 288)	"may be regarded as truly problem centered; *it has the general characteristic of presenting contrasting or conflicting ideas and the factual data pertinent to them.*" (pp. 283–284)			"While knowledge is an essential component of the decision-making process, it is not sufficient. To make a rational decision, the social actor must also identify and clarify his values, and relate them to the knowledge that he has derived. The valuing component is a very important part of the decision-making process, because values frequently determine what knowledge an individual will accept or reject. Value confusion often results in social action that is contradictory and bizarre." (p. 445)
Banks and Clegg (1973) [*Teaching Strategies for the Social Studies*, Addison-Wesley]	"The organizing concepts, generalizations, and theories of the various (social science) disciplines are emphasized in this section because of the author's belief that each of the disciplines provides students with a unique way to view human behavior, one that is essential for sound decision making." (p. viii)	"Children must view social issues from an interdisciplinary perspective in order to understand the immense complexity of contemporary social problems." (p. viii)	"Helping children to identify and formulate precise, explicit, and researchable questions is one of the most challenging tasks faced by the teacher in the inquiry-oriented elementary classroom." (p. 47)		
Fraenkel (1973) [*Helping Students Think and Value . . .*, Prentice-Hall]	"If teachers wish to help students understand themselves and their world more completely, they must do more than merely help students to learn facts. They must help them acquire more theoretical knowledge such as concepts and generalizations." (p. 94)	"The most abundant sources of fundamental ideas for social studies teachers at present are the disciplines of social science." (p. 131)	"A major contention is that an emphasis upon helping students to formulate their own concepts and ideas rather than only to learn the concepts and ideas of others has a number of advantages, the most important being that such an emphasis helps students learn to think for themselves." (p. 174)	"Social studies content should be relevant to the students' concerns." (p. 134)	"Value education, however, is unavoidable. All of us engage in valuing. A teacher's actions, sayings, discussion topics, choice of reading assignments and materials, class activities, and examinations suggest that he believes certain ideas, events, individuals, or other phenomena are more important than others for students to consider. . . . The issue, therefore, is not whether values should be taught, for teachers cannot avoid teaching values. More relevant concerns involve helping students to identify their own and others' values, helping them to deal with value conflicts, justifying certain values to teach, and deciding how to teach them." (pp. 230, 231)

TABLE 5 (cont.)

AUTHOR	TYPE OF INFORMATION TO BE EMPHASIZED	SOURCE OF DATA TO BE UTILIZED	INSTRUCTIONAL PROCEDURES	VIEW OF THE STUDENT	VALUES AND VALUING PROCESSES
Michaelis (1976) [*Social Studies for Children in a Democracy . . .*, Prentice-Hall]	"As in other areas of the curriculum, the trend in social studies is to clarify the conceptual structure of the instructional program. Key concepts and generalizations from the social sciences are used to structure content within units and to plan sequences of instruction." (p. 18)	"The trend is clearly toward interdisciplinary approaches with appropriate use of other approaches depending on the focus of study." (p. 38)	"Some programs, using what is called a conceptual approach, are organized around concepts and main ideas; others, via what is called an inquiry approach, are organized to emphasize inquiry modes and processes of inquiry; still others, via what is called a topical approach, are traditionally organized around themes and topics. A promising new development is to link all three together in an inquiry-conceptual approach to the study of significant settings or topics. . . ." (p. 20)	"Probably no factor is more important in meeting individual differences than the teacher's point of view. Teachers who truly value differences and recognize the uniqueness of each child are the ones who plan most effectively to meet individual differences. They care deeply about all children . . . and they recognize the individualized instruction is a right as well as a need of all children. . . ." (p. 121)	"Increased attention to values and valuing processes is bringing a better balance between the cognitive and affective dimensions of instruction. New programs include attention to the values, attitudes, and valuing processes needed to handle value-laden issues. Strategies for clarifying values and feelings in events under study and in situations vital to students have been developed, and attention is now being given to the development of an understanding and appreciation of religion in the lives of people in our country and in other lands. The impact of religious values on lifestyles, the use of values in decision making, and the influence of social, economic, and political values on human behavior are brought to higher levels of understanding as students progress through the program. The historical, cultural, and social conditions that have contributed to the diversity of religious and other values are included in units for middle and high schools." (pp. 14–15)

*From Michael J. Elliott and Kerry J. Kennedy, "Australian Impressions of Social Studies Theory and Practice in Secondary Schools in the United States," in *Social Education* 43, no. 4 (April 1979), pp. 292 and 293. Reprinted with permission of the National Council for the Social Studies.

Roles, interaction, and interdependence of individuals at home, in the neighborhood and community, in our state and nation, and in other lands.

Functions of the family, government, education, and other institutions in our country and in other lands.

Basic human activities common to all societies, including transportation, government, communication, education, production and consumption of goods and services, conservation, and esthetic and religious expression.

Contributions of individuals and groups to man's changing cultural heritage.

Aspirations and problems of minority groups, their cultural heritage, and steps that are needed to assure them full participation in the rights and responsibilities of a democratic society.

Environmental problems and concerns, causes and effects of pollution, and steps necessary to insure a high quality of life in our environment.

Influences of values, traditions, technological developments, education, and other aspects of culture on individual and group behavior.

Purposes, processes, and problems of decision making in the community, state, nation, and other lands, and how individuals and groups influence the decision-making process.

Geographical, historical, social, economic, and political factors related to topics and settings selected for study.

Democratic beliefs essential to our way of life, including:

Respect for the human dignity and worth of each individual.

Responsibility for maintaining rights and freedoms under law.

Freedom of speech, religion, press, assembly, and inquiry.

Equality of justice, security, and opportunity for all.

Faith in the ability of men to govern themselves.

Use of intelligence to solve human problems.

Government by consent of the governed.

Majority rule with minority respect and protection.

Cooperative action for the common good.

Separation of church and state.

Cooperation with others to secure world peace.

INQUIRY OBJECTIVES

To develop competence in using modes, methods, and processes of inquiry, including the ability to:

Use such inquiry processes as recalling, observing, comparing/contrasting, classifying, interpreting, defining, generalizing, analyzing, synthesizing, inferring, predicting, hypothesizing, and evaluating.

Make plans for investigating topics and problems, collecting data, organizing and processing data, deriving conclusions, and assessing outcomes and procedures of inquiry.

Use problem-solving procedures flexibly with attention to the analytic mode in which generalizations are derived, the integrative mode in which particular events and conditions are reconstructed, and the policy or decision-making mode in which alternatives are appraised.

State questions that include role, division of labor, and other key concepts that are helpful in observing, interpreting, classifying, and using other inquiry processes.

State generalizations based on adequate evidence that join two or more concepts in a meaningful relationship, such as: Families around the world use resources to meet their needs for food, shelter, and clothing.

Distinguish warranted from unwarranted conclusions, factual statements from statements of opinion, generalizations from supporting evidence, statements of what ought to be from statements of what is, and time-bound or space-bound generalizations from those of broad applicability.

Demonstrate in discussion the importance of suspending judgment when evidence is inadequate, testing hypotheses, assessing the basis for predictions, and other attitudes of effective inquiry.

SKILL OBJECTIVES

To develop competence in using basic skills in the social studies including the ability to:

Use a variety of data sources including primary and secondary materials, textbooks, *library materials*, current periodicals, community resources, and audiovisual materials [emphasis supplied].

Locate, gather, appraise, summarize, and report information.

Read social studies material critically, listen critically, and study independently.

Interpret and make maps, graphs, tables, time lines, and other graphic materials.

Interpret sequences of events, time periods, chronology, and trends.

Organize materials from several sources and present it in pictorial, oral, written, and graphic form.

Work as a member of groups, participating in decision making, carrying out plans, adhering to group standards, and evaluating individual and group efforts.

AFFECTIVE OBJECTIVES

To identify, describe, and demonstrate in individual behavior and group activities the attitudes, values, and feelings of individuals who:

Place high premiums on objectivity, thoughtful skepticism, longing to know, respect for logical thinking, consideration of premises and consequences, search for data and their meaning, and other values of rational inquiry.

Recognize personal feelings and opinions as possible sources of error and bias that influence interpretations and points of view.

Consider multiple causes of events, evidence that is contrary to personal views, and the limitations of generalizations.

Search for new perspectives, creative ideas, divergent views, and new ways of dealing with issues and problems.

Are sensitive to the influences of moral, ethical, and spiritual values in human affairs.

Value democratic beliefs, human freedom, civic responsibilities, enlightened loyalty, and other aspects of our American heritage.

Value the contributions of individuals and groups to our cultural heritage, including contributions to knowledge made by historians and social scientists.

Respect duly constituted authority, due process of law, and procedures for making changes.

Have self-respect and show respect for others regardless of race, creed, social and economic status, and national origin.

Examine critically the actions of those entrusted with the general welfare of individuals and groups.

Evaluate their own actions and the efforts of others to implement democratic beliefs.

Are open-minded, responsible, cooperative, and creative, and show concern for others in group endeavors.

INSTRUCTIONAL TECHNOLOGY
AND PROGRAM DESIGN

When designing or implementing any phase of the social studies program, kindergarten through grade twelve, the administrator, the curriculum committee member, the classroom teacher, and the library media specialist must use the guidelines and objectives as basic criteria against which to measure adequacy of program content, process, and product. When developing instructional programs in the field of social studies, curriculum guides and checklists are an invaluable means of building uniform adequacy in each unit as well as in the total program itself (see Chapter 7, Checklist 1, Media Programming Components; Example 21, Social Studies Unit Planning; Example 22, Teacher-Library Media Specialist Unit Planning Guide; Checklist 3, Checklist of Instructional Media; Checklist 4, Checklist of Variations and Adjustments to Meet Individual Differences; Checklist 5, Planning for Less Able or Slower Learning Students; and Checklist 6, Variations and Adjustments for Gifted Students. Examples 21 and 22 and Checklists 3–6 follow).

EXAMPLE 21   SOCIAL STUDIES UNIT PLANNING*

Unit Title _____   Date _____

Main Idea to Be Developed: Key Concepts and Terms:	Related Skills:	Related Attitudes and Values:	Questions to Stimulate Reflective Thinking:
Text References: Supplementary References: Audiovisual Resources: Community Resources:	Oral and Written Language Activities:	Dramatic Activities:	Construction Activities
	Related Curriculum Activities (Science, Math, Art, Music):		

This form can be used in developing unit plans. Notice that it consists of three components: (1) the learnings to be achieved; (2) the references and resources to be used; and (3) the activities to be performed. A plan such as this should be developed for each Main Idea included in the unit.

*From John Jarolimek, *Social Studies in Elementary Education*, 5th ed. (New York: Macmillan, 1977), p. 38. Reprinted by permission of Macmillan, Inc. Copyright © 1977.

EXAMPLE 22 TEACHER-LIBRARY MEDIA SPECIALIST UNIT PLANNING GUIDE:

TOPIC AND FUNDAMENTAL ANALYSIS FORM

Subject _____

Grade _____

Unit _____

Teacher _____

School _____

PLEASE INDICATE UNDER THE APPROPRIATE HEADING EACH SPECIFIC
TOPIC OR FUNDAMENTAL REQUIRING LIBRARY MEDIA SUPPORT

PERSONS	PLACES	THINGS	EVENTS	IDEAS AND CONCEPTS	SKILLS

CHECKLIST 3 CHECKLIST OF INSTRUCTIONAL MEDIA*

READING MATERIALS

— Textbooks that focus on geography, history, or civics, or those that contain all the social sciences

— Unit booklets on a variety of topics ranging from family life and neighborhood workers to other lands and famous people

— Reference materials, including almanacs, anthologies, atlases, dictionaries, directories, encyclopedias, gazetteers, government bulletins, scrapbooks, yearbooks, and data banks

— Fugitive materials, including bulletins, clippings, folders, leaflets, simulation games, pamphlets, and free or inexpensive materials

— Current materials, including children's weekly news publications, children's magazines, daily newspapers, and adult magazines

— Literary materials, including biography, fiction, folklore, short stories, and travel books

— Source materials, including ballots, diaries, directions, logs, maps, minutes of meetings, recipes, and timetables

— Programed materials, including geographic, historical, and other content arranged in a step-by-step sequence

— Self-help materials, including charts, checklists, directions, outlines, study guides, teacher-prepared practice materials, and workbooks

— Display materials, including titles, captions, signs, and labels

— Teacher-prepared materials, including charts, rewritten material, scrapbooks

AUDIOVISUAL MATERIALS

Realia and Representations of Realia:

— models	— collections	— museums
— objects	— products	— dioramas
— samples	— miniatures	— panoramas
— exhibits	— ornaments	— mockups
— textiles	— utensils	— marionettes
— costumes	— tools	— puppets
— instruments	— facsimiles	— dolls
— other _____		

Sound and Film Resources:

— films	— cassettes	— recordings
— radio and television	— film loops	— sound filmstrips
— videotapes		

Pictures and Pictorial Representations:

— photographs	— postcards	— montages
— pictures	— prints	— murals
— drawings	— etchings	— filmstrips
— sketches	— albums	— silent films
— slides	— scrapbooks	— opaque projections
— transparencies	— microfilms	— storyboards
— other _____		

Symbolic and Graphic Representations:

— maps	— cartoons	— chalkboard
— globes	— posters	— bulletin board
— atlases	— diagrams	— flannel board
— charts	— graphs	— time lines
— other _____		

CHECKLIST 3 (cont.)

Projectors and Viewers:

__ slide	__ film	__ opaque
__ stereoscope	__ overhead	__ film loop

Players and Recorders:

__ record	__ tape	__ cassette

Supplies and Materials for Production:

__ lettering devices	__ slide making	__ bookbinding
__ map outlines	__ chart making	__ map making
__ transparencies	__ picture mounting	__ model making
__ other _____		

COMMUNITY RESOURCES

__ Study (or field) trips (industries, museums, etc.) _____

__ Resource visitors (panel or individuals) _____

__ Television (travel programs, historical plays) _____

__ Published materials (newspapers, libraries, chamber of commerce bulletins) _____

__ Persons to interview (travelers, police) _____

__ Welfare and service organizations (Red Cross, service clubs) _____

__ Service projects (safety programs, cleanup) _____

__ Possible field studies (housing, pollution) _____

__ Visual resources (pictures, realia) _____

__ Local current events (campaigns, drives) _____

__ Resources within the school (collections of materials, teachers who have traveled) __

__ Community recreational resources (parks, marinas) _____

__ Other _____

CHECKLIST 4　CHECKLIST OF VARIATIONS AND ADJUSTMENTS
TO MEET INDIVIDUAL DIFFERENCES*

DIAGNOSIS

Has information been collected on individual differences?

__ interests	__ capabilities	__ language skills
__ problems	__ reading level	__ achievement
__ other _____		

*From John U. Michaelis, *Social Studies for Children in a Democracy: Recent Trends & Developments*, 6th ed. Copyright © 1976, pp. 129–130. Reprinted by permission of Prentice-Hall, Inc., Englewood Cliffs, N.J.

CHECKLIST 4 (cont.)

INDIVIDUAL STUDY

What variations and adjustments can be made in individual research activities?

__ topics to investigate   __ depth and breadth   __ type of report
__ sources of data   __ people to interview   __ *use of library**
__ assistance from others   __ use of free time   __ form of presentation
__ other _____

INDIVIDUAL TUTORIAL

__ by the teacher   __ by another pupil   __ by programed material
__ by a parent   __ by a teacher aide   __ by computer
__ other. _____

SUBGROUPS

What subgroups might be formed within the class?

__ interest groups   __ groups needing special instruction
__ reading groups   __ groups to make maps, murals, and the like
__ committees   __ groups of two or three for team learning
__ work centers   __ groups for interviewing, finding materials, and the like
__ other _____

METHODS AND ACTIVITIES

__ individual   __ small group   __ whole group
__ discovery lessons   __ expository lessons   __ home study
__ different questions for subgroups   __ different explanations for subgroups   __ varied directions for subgroups
__ different standards for individuals   __ varied assignments for individuals or groups   __ varied assessment of outcomes
__ other _____

MATERIALS

What variations or adjustments can be made in instructional materials?

__ reading materials on various levels   __ audiovisual materials for group and individual use   __ community resources for group and individual use
__ rewritten material   __ library resources   __ work centers
__ study guides   __ practice materials   __ taped material
__ reading lists   __ use of material in kits   __ picture sets
__ other _____ __

TIME

What variations in time should be made for individuals and groups?

__ building readiness for use of materials   __ introducing a topic or problem   __ carrying out basic activities
__ assimilation of new ideas   __ accommodation of new ideas   __ expressing one's own ideas
__ making maps and other items   __ preparing oral and written reports   __ home study and use of community resources
__ other _____

*Emphasis supplied.

CHECKLIST 4 (cont.)

STANDARDS AND EVALUATION

What variations and adjustments should be made in expectations and assessment of outcomes?

__ quantitative	__ qualitative	__ vocabulary
__ concepts	__ information	__ main ideas
__ use of inquiry processes	__ use of map reading and other skills	__ expression of feelings
__ self-evaluation	__ evaluative charts	__ testing
__ other _____		

CHECKLIST 5   PLANNING FOR LESS ABLE OR SLOWER
LEARNING STUDENTS*

_____ Variations and adjustments in reading materials made as noted in Checklist 4

_____ Additional explanations to clarify purposes, questions, or directions for activities

_____ Provision for review and extra practice to clinch key learnings and build a base for extended learning

_____ Emphasis on concrete and specific rather than on abstract and verbal presentations and discussions of ideas related to topics under study

_____ Extended time to complete basic map work, preparation of oral reports, and other core activities

_____ Provision of simplified study guides based on pictures, diagrams, and charts

_____ Number of concepts and level of concept development adjusted to challenge but not frustrate each student

_____ Provision of opportunities for creative expression through art, music, dramatic activities, construction, and other activities so that the thrill of expressing oneself becomes a part of the less able child's learning in the social studies

_____ Provision to utilize special talents in drawing, painting, making models, constructing objects, making maps, and the like

_____ Identification of special contributions less able students can make in discussion and other activities such as reporting findings gleaned from pictures, maps, charts, diagrams, and easy-level reading materials

_____ Identification of students with whom they can work effectively in team learning, committee work, making murals, arranging displays, preparing group reports, planning contributions to discussion, and other group activities

_____ Appropriate reading, visual, and auditory materials arranged in learning centers

_____ Provision for making summaries of achievement at frequent intervals to provide knowledge of progress and encouragement

_____ Attention to regular feedback on progress, commendation for effort, and constructive assistance in self-evaluation in order to provide motivation

_____ Provision for home study with guided home cooperation in finding and using reading materials, pictures, clippings, current events, and other items related to topics under study

CHECKLIST 6   VARIATIONS AND ADJUSTMENTS FOR GIFTED STUDENTS†

_____ Provision of a variety of challenging reading materials, maps, and other sources to optimize development of inquiry skills

---

*From John U. Michaelis, *Social Studies for Children in a Democracy: Recent Trends & Developments*, 6th ed. Copyright © 1976, p. 140. Reprinted by permission of Prentice-Hall, Inc., Englewood Cliffs, N.J.

†From John U. Michaelis, *Social Studies for Children in a Democracy: Recent Trends & Developments*, 6th ed. Copyright © 1976, pp. 141–142. Reprinted by permission of Prentice-Hall, Inc., Englewood Cliffs, N.J.

CHECKLIST 6 (cont.)

_____ Provision of a balanced program of activities to promote well-rounded development of intellectual, social, physical, and emotional growth
_____ Extension of learning by means of additional opportunities to formulate hypotheses,
draw inferences, state generalizations, synthesize main ideas, and contrast points
of view
_____ Provision of many opportunities for independent inquiry, use of library and community resources, and synthesis of data from several sources
_____ Emphasis on self-direction and self-evaluation and individual growth and achievement through practice activities and group work that meet individual needs
_____ Encouragement of individual initiative and planning, leadership, concern for others,
sharing, teamwork, and regard for different types of contributions
_____ Provision of direct instruction and guidance to develop basic skills, concepts, inquiry processes, and emotional stability and to avoid gaps or deficiencies in essential learning
_____ Extension of learning through wide reading of materials that take students far
beyond basic and supplementary texts
_____ Emphasis on positive traits and attitudes such as individualism without being
overbearing, self-criticism without being overly critical of others, and respect for
intellectual attainment without lack of regard for other accomplishments
_____ Provision of opportunities for creative expression in individual and group work,
oral and written reports, map making, construction, and other activities
_____ Avoidance of activities that may be needed by other students but are boring or
irrelevant to the needs and pace of learning of students, such as reteaching of
selected material, reviews of concepts taught earlier in the week, drill on terms that
may be useful for less able students, and other items already mastered by students
_____ Provision of home study with planned home cooperation to extend and enrich reading, construct models and other objects, use library resources, visit places, and
interview experts to gather data on topics under study

CONTEMPORARY CURRICULAR AREAS
OF EMPHASIS

LAW-RELATED EDUCATION

Crime and antisocial behavior, especially on the part of youth, represent a
continuing crisis in American society (see Chapter 1). In an effort to reverse
this trend, the U.S. Law Enforcement Assistance Administration (LEAA), the
American Bar Association (ABA), NEA, and NCSS have cooperated in developing law-related education programs.

> The need for law-related education is clear. Polls tell us that our citizens are grow-
> ing more cynical and dispirited, and scholars tell us that we cannot look to tra-
> ditional civic education courses for this remedy. To an increasing number of
> Americans, law-related education is one way to revitalize American civic educa-
> tion. Donald Santarelli, former LEAA Administrator, said he viewed law-related
> education as a means of tempering the attitudes "that can lead the nation toward
> anarchy and vigilantism. . . . Law-related education . . . is a vital response to a
> growing crisis in our society."[11]

In *Law-Related Education in America: Guidelines for the Future*, the recommendation is made that courses in law and legal processes be integrated
within the regular courses of study.[12] The following examples illustrate the
manner in which law-related learning experiences can be appropriately integrated within the framework of the regular instructional program: Case Study
7, The Scopes Trial (see Chapter 3), is integrated in the tenth-grade biology

unit "Evolution"; Example 1, Law and Justice Pilot Project (see Chapter 6), provides a case study showing how a citizen can become directly involved in the state and the federal lawmaking process—this learning experience is part of the regular fifth-grade social studies unit "California and the West"; Example 2, Mexico—Its History, Its Land, and Its People (see Chapter 6), includes law and justice as two topics to be researched in this sixth-grade social studies unit; Example 23, Westward Ho! The Wagons, or, If I Had Been a Pioneer Trailblazer, provides an in-depth study of pioneer law and order as part of the fifth-grade Gifted and Talented Enrichment (GATE) Program; Example 24, If I Had Lived During the Middle Ages, provides an in-depth study of crime and punishment as well as law and justice during the Middle Ages as part of the sixth-grade Gifted and Talented Program.

EXAMPLE 23 WESTWARD HO! THE WAGONS, OR, IF I HAD BEEN A PIONEER TRAILBLAZER

Gifted and Talented Enrichment (GATE) Program
Learning Project Westward Ho! The Wagons, or, If I Had Been a Pioneer Trailblazer
Grade: 5
Project Goals:

> To provide learning experiences which will enable the GATE student to perceive and value American history in general, and the Westward Movement in particular, as an ongoing heroic drama with the happenings of the past setting the stage for the happenings of the present and the future

> To introduce the GATE student to the inquiry method and to the mysteries of adventurous, creative thinking

Teaching Objectives:
> This project has been designed and structured to provide these basic understandings:

>> The Westward Movement in American History is more than recorded events: it is men and women and young people doing things—making choices; deciding what is important and what is not; taking a stand for what they believe; venturing into the unknown; being courageous despite overwhelming odds; facing trouble and uncertainty; often succeeding but sometimes failing

>> Life, liberty, and the pursuit of happiness—and all other basic human rights—have been painfully and slowly won at the cost of great human suffering and sacrifice

>> Reading biographies is an exciting way to relive the historic happenings of the past for people are the shapers of history

>> All societies and all human beings are interdependent; no society and no human being can long survive as an island unto itself

> This project has been designed and structured to foster and develop these attitudes and appreciations:

>> Appreciation of the rich heritage each American inherits from the past; the perception that contemporary man stands on the shoulders of those who have gone before

>> Appreciation of the fact that America has been shaped by many kinds of people from many walks of life; perception that destiny is no respecter of race, color, or creed

>> Appreciation of the fact that, while many great and famous people helped build America, countless others—pioneer men, women, and young people whose names go unrecorded, unnoted, and unsung—were the means and the force that carried civilization from the Atlantic to the Pacific

>> Appreciation of the continuity and interrelatedness of history; the perception that history is an unrolling tapestry of human events

EXAMPLE 23 (cont.)

Appreciation of the human attributes of greatness; perception of the necessity of critically and objectively evaluating the personal quality of those seeking leadership positions in the school, the community, the state, and the nation

Appreciation of biography as a rich source of insight into the past; perception of the human dimension of history as expressed by Thomas Carlyle, "The history of the world is but the biography of great men"

Appreciation that "legend" makes history larger than life; perception that in legend the line between fact and fiction is all too often obliterated

Appreciation of historical novels as an effective means of vicariously experiencing the happenings of the past

Appreciation of the necessity and the value of reading between and beyond the lines

Appreciation of the value to be accrued from successful group endeavors

Appreciation of the high degree of satisfaction to be attained by completing a challenging assignment

Teaching Strategies and Methods:

No time limitations are imposed on this project. Number of students involved coupled with student interest are the factors that determine the duration of each GATE project whether it be two weeks, two months, or longer

A basic part of group orientation to this project is to provide opportunities for the students to explore the synergistic effect to be derived from sharing knowledge

Each student, after orientation to the purpose, scope, and dimension of this project, will draw up and sign a performance contract specifying the special area of knowledge-building for which he/she will be responsible

Procedural Outline:
  I. Group orientation to and overview of this project
    A. Definition of basic terms
      1. *Adventurous thinking:* Daring to think bold, new thoughts; projecting beyond the facts to fashion creative, yet plausible, answers to tantalizing questions such as: "What if . . .?" "What would happen if . . .?" "Do you suppose . . .?" "Is there a possibility . . .?"
      2. *Creativity:* The power to develop to the fullest all abilities, those that are known and those that are hidden; to be all that one can be. The magic of creativity is to form new ideas, to invent, to discover
      3. *Frontier:* The farthest part of a settled country; where the wilds begin
      4. *Pioneer:* A person who settles in a part of the country that has not been occupied before except by primitive tribes
    B. Discussion of the value of learning about America's past
      1. William Jay Jacobs, American historian, in his book *Search for Freedom: America and Its People* [New York: Benziger, Bruce, & Glencoe, 1973, p. ix], explains the value of the past in the light of the present and the future as follows:

        "What is the past?

          The past is what happened yesterday. And it is what happened all the yesterdays before that . . .

          The past is things that men have built . . .

          The past is the different tools and machines that men have used to make all those buildings . . .

          The past is art . . .

          The past is music . . .

          The past is everything that has ever interested human beings . . .

          The past is feelings . . .

          The past is ideas . . .

EXAMPLE 23 (cont.)

The past is events . . .

The past is all these things, and many more. But most of all, the past is people

Who built America? Certainly, great men built the American nation. . . . But they were not alone. They are only part of the story.

Many men and women whose name nobody remembers also built the American nation: the pioneer woman tending her fire in a wilderness cabin; the storm-tossed New England fisherman; the Negro slave, his back bent with work in a Southern cotton field.

Who built America? The Pony Express riders—most of them teenagers. . . ; the farmer harvesting his crop alone in a Kansas wheat field; the Mississippi River steamboat pilot guiding his sternwheeler through treacherous currents.

Who built America? The steelworker feeding coal to a fiery furnace in Pittsburgh for pennies a day; . . . the country doctor faithfully making calls . . . ; the immigrant peddler wandering through the West. . . .

America was built by many people. Most of them were ordinary people—carpenters and mechanics and lawyers and truckdrivers and housewives and students and railroad workers. Ordinary people.

And you? What about you?

Someday America will be yours. You will inherit it. And the decisions about what kind of country it will be—those choices will be yours.

America is forever new. It is always being built. And you are its future builders."

2. The purpose of this project is to help you answer the question, "Who built America in the past, and what will I be able to contribute to America's present and America's future?"
3. People make the difference
   During this project, each student will compile a list of people who have influenced American history in either a positive or a negative way

C. Exploration of the process of adventurous, creative thinking
   1. What is creativity?

      Latin root word, *creare* meaning to make

      Greek root word, *krainen* meaning to fulfill—a promise, a prophecy, or oneself

      The magic of creativity is to form new ideas, to invent, to discover

      Creativity includes the ability to wonder, to be surprised and puzzled, to see what others have seen and to respond differently

   2. Four steps in creative thought

      Preparation—gathering facts and seeking answers

         Facts are the raw materials from which creative thought is fashioned

      Incubation—the mind works with the facts and ideas

      Inspiration—a sudden solution or a unique idea

      Verification—testing the solution or idea

   3. Imagination is the mind's eye

      Imagination is the ability to form in the mind a picture or idea of something that is not present

      Such pictures are like the images in a kaleidoscope

EXAMPLE 23 (cont.)

We use imagination to recreate the past; to wonder about unfamiliar people or places; and to toy with ideas about the future

4. Creative power is a hidden treasure

Margaret Mead, the anthropologist, estimated that man uses but 6% of his creative potential

Can you develop creativity? Psychologists say "yes"

Practice improves creativity

Highly creative people invent new responses when solving problems—they experiment with what might have been

Creative thinking looks for a number of ideas, for variety and originality

D. At the conclusion of this project, the student will be given the challenge of creatively imagining what his/her life could have been, if he/she had been a pioneer trailblazer

II. The group begins to build its knowledge of westward migration in American history
  A. The students read the *World Book* reprint "Pioneer Life"
    1. Attention is called to the fact that the article was critically reviewed by Robert G. Athearn, Professor of History at the University of Colorado
      The significance of a "signed article" is discussed
    2. The necessity of following through on the two cross references—"Western Frontier Life" and "Westward Movement"—is stressed
    3. The trans-vision map reprint from the *World Book* is used throughout the reading of the reprint "Pioneer Life in America" and of the reprints "Western Frontier Life" and "Westward Migration"
      Maps are invaluable in visualizing both time and place
    4. Using the main and subheadings of the reprint "Pioneer Life," the following outline is developed:
      a. Pioneer life in America
        (1) Conquering the wilderness
        (2) Establishing the frontier
      b. Moving westward
        (1) Crossing the Appalachians
        (2) How people traveled
        (3) Trails of the pioneers
      c. A pioneer settlement
        (1) A pioneer home
        (2) Education and religion
        (3) Law and order
        (4) Social activities
        (5) Indian attacks
      d. Crossing the Plains
        (1) The wagon train
        (2) Life on the trail
  B. The group views and then discusses the motion picture *Daniel Boone* (Coronet)
    1. The value of using a motion picture is explored
    2. The significance of the term "film literacy" is introduced and discussed
    3. Professor John Michaelis, University of California, believes that motion pictures are very important when studying history because:

      "Processes, people, the world of nature, various types of activities, and significant events can be seen in action in a realistic setting

      "Contemporary affairs, past events, and faraway places can be brought into the classroom

      "Processes that cannot be visualized in any other way can be seen in action on the screen

EXAMPLE 23 (cont.)

"A broad sweep of events may be seen with various relationships high-lighted, as in films showing the development of inventions, the growth of institutions, or the contributions of great men and women"*

    4. The group reacts to Michaelis's appraisal of the value of motion pictures

  C. The group views, discusses, and then evaluates the educational effectiveness of the following motion pictures:
    1. *Folksongs of the Western Movement, 1787-1853*
    2. *Pioneer Journey Across the Appalachians*
    3. *Pioneer Living: Education and Recreation*
    4. *Pioneer Living: The Home*
    5. *Pioneer Living: Preparing Foods*
    6. *Travel in America in the 1840s*

  D. Each student reads the historical novel *Young Pioneers* by Rose Wilder Lane
    1. The students discover that the author of this novel is the daughter of Laura Ingalls Wilder
    2. The students read other novels portraying the westward movement
    3. The students discuss the value of historical novels as an effective means of vicariously reliving the past (see Example 27)

  E. The students read the article "Western Frontier Life" and develop the following outline:
    1. Life on the frontier
      a. The people
      b. Food
      c. Clothing
      d. Amusements
      e. Religion
      f. Frontier towns
      g. Life in the country
    2. Transportation and communication
    3. Law and order
      a. Crime
      b. Law enforcement
      c. Indian fighting
    4. An American tradition
      a. Literature
      b. Music
      c. Art
      d. Entertainment

III. Each student selects a topic or topics from the above outline to research
  A. The concept of "film literacy" is reintroduced and the students select appropriate sound filmstrips from the following bibliography:
    1. *The Cowboy: Tough Man on a Mustang* (American Pageant)
    2. *Gold and Dreams of Gold*

      Gold Towns of the Old West

      Ghost Towns—What Happened

      How Gold Is Mined

      A Modern-Day Prospector Named George

    3. *The Gunslingers* (American Pageant)
    4. *Pathfinders Westward* (SVE)

      Daniel Boone's Wilderness

      Rivers and Roads to the Mississippi

      Lewis and Clark Expedition, parts I and II

*John U. Michaelis, *Social Studies for Children in a Democracy: Recent Trends and Developments*, 5th ed. (Englewood Cliffs, N.J.: Prentice-Hall, 1972), p. 481.

EXAMPLE 23 (cont.)

First Trails into the West

The Mountain Men

5. *Pioneer Women and Belles of the Wild West* (Teaching Resources)
6. *Settling the West* (SVE)

The Trail Blazers

The Miners

Wagon Trains to Railroads

The Cattlemen

The Farmers

Growth of Towns and Cities

7. *Stories from the Old West* (SVE)

El Camino Real

Vaquero! Vaquero!

The Comanches: Greatest Horsemen of the West

The Pony Express Rider

Iron Horse, Golden Spike

Pawnee: The Buffalo Pony

8. *The West: The Way It Was* (American Pageant)
9. *Westward Migration* (SVE)

Into the Southwest

The Oregon Country

The Gold Rush

Three Routes to Eldorado

B. The students check the U.S. Landmark series to discover titles appropriate for their topic
   1. Attention is directed to the Landmark colophon
      An emblematic or ornamental device used to identify a publishing house or a series of books
   2. Recommendation is made that the students check the biographical note about the author that is found in the back of the book
      Is the author qualified by training and experience to be recognized as an authority?
   3. Attention is directed to the list of series titles found at the back of each book in the series

IV. As a culminating activity the students as a group nominate candidates for a Hall of Fame of American Frontiersmen
   A. A "Who's Who in the Westward Movement" serves as a summary of names highlighted in American historical annals
   B. Students nominate their candidates and defend each candidate's claim to fame
   C. The students, based on their observations of the westward movement and their appraisal of the human drama of the period, discuss the validity of the statement "truth is stranger than fiction."

V. The group views and then discusses the motion picture *Westward Ho! The Wagons* (Disney Studios)
   A. Does this motion picture give a valid picture of the times?
   B. Was this motion picture biased in its portrayal of either the white man or the Indians?
   C. Who was your favorite character in this motion picture?
   D. If you had been the director of *Westward Ho! The Wagons* what changes, if any, would you have made?

EXAMPLE 23 (cont.)

E. What insight into human nature did you gain from viewing this motion picture?

F. If you had been a pioneer trailblazer, what adventures might you have had?

WHO'S WHO IN THE WESTWARD MOVEMENT

Teacher's Answer Key

Please place in the parentheses (   ) before each name the number of the phrase which best describes that person.

Persons	*Descriptive Phrases*
(17) Grizzly Adams	1. Adventurer and explorer; a mountain named for him
(10) Stephen Austin	2. Apache warrior
(34) Sam Bass	3. Author of *Ox-Team Days on the Oregon Trail;* lived to be 98
(9) Charles Bent	4. Blazed the Wilderness Trail
(4) Daniel Boone	5. California mission priest
(19) Jemima Boone	6. Designed hunting knife; killed at the Battle of the Alamo
(6) Jim Bowie	7. Discovered the Great Salt Lake
(7) Jim Bridger	8. Discovered Yellowstone
(38) Kit Carson	9. Established a fort and trading post on the Santa Fe Trail
(29) George Catlin	10. Father of Texas
(22) John Chapman	11. Father of the Wild West Show
(11) Bill Cody	12. Founder of the Church of the Latter-Day Saints
(21) Sam Colt	13. Frontier doctor
(8) John Colter	14. Frontier peace officer; nicknamed "Wild Bill"
(15) Davy Crockett	15. Frontier legendary hero; killed defending the Alamo
(32) Abigail Scott Duniway	16. Gold discovered at his mill in California
(39) Wyatt Earp	17. Hermit in the Sierras; tamed and trained bears
(33) Escalante	18. Historian of the Santa Fe Trail
(23) Mike Fink	19. Indian captive
(31) John Charles Fremont	20. Indian guide for the Lewis and Clark Expedition
(2) Geronimo	21. Inventor of the six-shooter
(18) Josiah Gregg	22. Johnny Appleseed
(14) Bill Hickok	23. Keelboatman, marksman, fighter, teller of "tall tales"
(37) Sam Houston	24. Led first wagon train over Oregon Trail
(27) Andrew Jackson	25. Led Mormons over Oregon Trail to Great Salt Lake
(35) Mary Layola	26. Missionary to Oregon Indians
(13) Ephraim McDowell	27. "Old Hickory"
(3) Ezra Meeker	28. One-armed explorer of the Colorado River
(40) Annie Oakley	29. Painted Indian portraits now in the Smithsonian Institution
(1) Zebulon Pike	30. Painted western frontier scenes
(28) John Wesley Powell	31. "The Pathfinder"
(30) Frederic Remington	32. Pioneer suffragette
(20) Sacajawea	33. Priest explorer of Colorado, Utah, and Arizona

EXAMPLE 23 (cont.)

(5) Junipero Serra
(36) Sitting Bull

(12) Joseph Smith
(24) Jedediah Smith

(16) John Sutter

(26) Narcissa Whitman
(25) Brigham Young

34. Robin Hood of Texas
35. Roman Catholic nun, missionary to the Oregon Indians
36. Sioux warrior
37. Tallest Texan; hero of the Battle of San Jacinto
38. Trapper and scout; explored Death Valley
39. U.S. marshall; "Lion of Tombstone"
40. Woman sharpshooter

EXAMPLE 24 IF I HAD LIVED DURING THE MIDDLE AGES*

The Gifted and Talented Enrichment (GATE) Program
Learning Project: If I Had Lived During the Middle Ages: An Experiment in Adventurous Thinking
Grade: 6
Project Goals:

To provide learning experiences which will enable the gifted student to perceive and enjoy history as an ongoing heroic drama with the happenings of the past setting the stage for the happenings of the present and the future

To introduce the gifted student to the inquiry method and to the mysteries of adventurous, creative thinking

Teaching Objectives:

This project has been designed and structured to provide these basic understandings:

History is the recorded memory of the past, the source to be consulted when searching for the answers to the eternal questions:

"Who is man?"

"What has he achieved?"

"Why has he sometimes failed?"

"What might he become?"

"What could my role be in the drama of history yet to be written?"

Positive human characteristics such as courage, bravery, idealism, honesty, integrity, patriotism, empathy, and selflessness and each of their negative counterparts have had dynamic impact on historical events

All societies and all human beings are interdependent; no society and no human being can survive as an island unto itself

Life, liberty, and the pursuit of happiness—and all other basic human rights—have been painfully and slowly won at the cost of great human suffering and sacrifice

Biography is a rich source of insight into the human dimension of history

The acronym TARGET (the major goal of the GATE program) stands for:
Thinking

Applying

Reacting

Growing

Exploring

Total learning

*From *Learning Unlimited: An Instructional Program for the Intellectually Gifted and Creatively Talented Student*, vol. 1, 1977 (North Hills School District, 55 Rochester Rd., Pittsburgh, Pa. 15229).

EXAMPLE 24 (cont.)

This project has been designed and structured to foster and develop these attitudes and appreciations:

Appreciation of man's historical heritage from the past; the perception that contemporary man stands on the shoulders of those who have gone before

Appreciation of the continuity and interrelatedness of history; the perception of history as an ongoing, unrolling tapestry of human events

Appreciation of the fact that the basic human rights which are taken for granted in the United States were undreamed of during the Middle Ages and are still unobtained in many contemporary societies

Perception of the human attributes of greatness and of the necessity of critically evaluating the personal quality of those seeking leadership positions in the schools, community, the state, and the nation

Perception of the ideas behind the statement, "A thing of beauty is a joy forever"

Perception of the value of biography as stated by Thomas Carlyle, "The history of the world is but the biography of great men"

Appreciation of the necessity and value of reading between and beyond the lines and of questing beyond the obvious

Appreciation of the value to be accrued from successful group endeavors

Appreciation of the high degree of satisfaction to be attained by completing a challenging assignment

Teaching Strategies and Methods:

No time limitations are imposed on this project. Number of students involved coupled with student interest are the factors that determine the duration of each GATE project whether it be two weeks, two months, or longer

A basic part of group orientation to this project is to provide opportunities for the students to explore the synergistic effect to be derived from sharing knowledge

Each student, after orientation to the purpose, scope, and dimension of this project, will draw up and sign a performance contract specifying the special area of knowledge-building for which he/she will be responsible

Procedural Outline:
    I. Group orientation to and overview of this project
       A. Definition of basic terms
          1. *Adventurous thinking:* Daring to think bold, new thoughts; projecting beyond the facts to fashion creative, yet plausible, answers to tantalizing questions such as: "What if . . .?" "What would have happened if . . .?" "Do you suppose . . .?" "Is there a possibility that . . .?"
          2. *Middle Ages:* The period of European History between ancient and modern times, c. 500 A.D. and 1500 A.D. This period is also referred to as the Medieval period
       B. Discussion of the project subtitle: An Experiment in Adventurous Thinking
          1. The group views the motion picture *Leonardo da Vinci* (Walt Disney Educational Media Company)
            Discusses the fact that this motion picture is one of a series entitled, "They Made the Difference" and observes:

                "The history of the world is but the biography of great men"—Thomas Carlyle

                "What is the past?

                    The past is what happened yesterday. And it is what happened all the yesterdays before that . . .

                    The past is things that men have built . . .

                    The past is the different tools and machines that men have used to make all those buildings . . .

EXAMPLE 24 (cont.)

The past is art . . .

The past is music . . .

The past is everything that has ever interested human beings . . .

The past is feelings . . .

The past is ideas . . .

The past is events . . .

The past is all these things, and many more. But most of all, the past is people."—William Jay Jacobs, *Search for Freedom: America and Its People* (Benziger, 1973), pp. 9-10.

During this project, each student will compile a list of people who have influenced history in either a positive or negative manner

2. The group extends its knowledge of Leonardo da Vinci
Explores his contribution as an adventurous thinker, citing as examples his work as:

Anatomist	Mathematician
Architect	Musician
Author	Naturalist
Caricaturist	Painter
Engineer	Philosopher
Inventor	Sculptor

3. The group explores the process of adventurous thinking

Thinking requires ideas with which to work

Leonardo da Vinci kept notebooks on his ideas, observations, and conclusions

Adventurous thinking takes the information acquired through the inquiry process and shapes that information into unique patterns of thought

Roget's *International Thesaurus* lists the following synonyms for the word *inquiry*

Search	Check
Test	Analysis
Survey	Diagnosis
Review	Question
Contemplation	Query
Investigation	Problem
Probe	Issue
Exploration	

The basic steps in problem solving are:

Recognizing that a problem exists

Defining and delimiting the problem

Formulating hypotheses concerning the problem

Gathering data and drawing conclusions

Testing the conclusions and noting the consequences of the conclusions

After building background knowledge of life during the Middle Ages, each student will adventurously answer the question, "What would my life have been like, if I had lived during the Middle Ages?"

II. The group begins to build its knowledge of life during the Middle Ages by reading and then discussing each of the following basic sources:
A. *Living in a Castle* by R. J. Unstead (Addison-Wesley, 1971)

EXAMPLE 24 (cont.)

Use of the Table of Contents as an overview of a subject; for example, this book's Table of Contents lists the following topics:

Living in a castle	Morning at Wentworth Castle
Wentworth Castle	At the castle
The Great Hall	The daily round
The hall and the solar	Everyday tasks
The people of the household	Manners and clothes
Food and drink	The lady of the household
Meat, fish and vegetables	Dinner at the castle
Spice and herbs	Table manners: two courses
Sugar, wine and ale	Work and play

B. *Living in a Medieval City* by R. J. Unstead (Addison-Wesley, 1971)
Use of the Table of Contents as an overview of a subject; for example, this book's Table of Contents lists the following topics:

Fifteenth-century Florence	Shops and banks
The people	About the city
Clothes	Crime
The poor	Schooling
Craftsmen and artists	Girls
Houses	Amusements
Work	

C. *Living in a Medieval Village* by R. J. Unstead (Addison-Wesley, 1971)
Use of the Table of Contents as an overview of a subject; for example, this book's Table of Contents lists the following topics:

Benfield	Village craftsmen
The villagers	The cottars
The land	Two poor widows
Cultivating the land	Hay-making
John Middleditch—villein	Hay-making customs
John's cottage	Summer tasks
A villein's duties	Harvest time
The reeve	Poaching
Officials of the manor	The Manor Court
The priest	Festivals

D. *Living in a Crusader Land* by R. J. Unstead (Addison-Wesley, 1971)
Use of the Table of Contents as an overview of a subject; for example, this book's Table of Contents lists the following topics:

Crusading	Fighting the infidel
Why men went on crusades	Founding the Crusader States
Preaching the crusade	How the Crusaders ruled Outremer
The People's Crusade	Christians and Moslems
Preparing for the crusade	Life in Outremer
The way to the East	The military orders
To Jerusalem!	Crusader castles
The mailed knight	The Italian merchants
The infantry	The end of Outremer
New methods of war	

EXAMPLE 24 (cont.)

III. Individual students take the responsibility for searching the Table of Contents of one or more of the following sources to discover additional topics not mentioned above
A. *The Age of Chivalry* by the editors of the *National Geographic* (National Geographic Society, 1969)
B. *Cathedral: The Story of Its Construction* by David Macaulay (Houghton Mifflin, 1973)
C. *Chivalry and the Mailed Knight* by Walter Buehr (Putnam, 1963)
D. *The Crusaders* by Walter Buehr (Putnam, 1959)
E. *Everyday Life in Medieval Times* by Marjorie Rowling (Putnam, 1968)
F. *Knights, Castles and Feudal Life* by Walter Buehr (Putnam, 1957)
G. *Knights in Armor* by Shirley Glubok (Harper and Row, 1969)
H. *Knights of the Crusades* by the editors of *Horizon* Magazine (Harper and Row, 1962)
I. *Life in the Middle Ages* by Jay Williams (Random House, 1966)
J. *Life on a Medieval Barony* by William Davis (Harper and Row, 1928)
K. *Made in the Middle Ages* by Christine Price (Dutton, 1961)
L. *Master Builders of the Middle Ages* by the editors of *Horizon* Magazine (Harper and Row, 1969)
M. *Medieval Days and Ways* by Gertrude Hartman (Macmillan, 1937)
N. *The Medieval Establishment* by Geoffrey Hindley (Putnam, 1970)
O. *Warrior Knights* by the editors of Time-Life Books (Little, 1969)
P. *The West in the Middle Ages* by Anne Bailey and Seymour Reit (Golden Press, 1966)
Q. *When Knights Were Bold* by Eva Tappan (Houghton Mifflin, 1911)
IV. Individual students will contract for researching a topic or topics selected from the list compiled above
A. A typical list of research topics follows:

Alchemy	How goods were sold
Astrology	Illuminated manuscripts
Bestiaries	Jewels and enamels
Caravans and cargoes	Jousts and tournaments
Castles	Knights—training and weapons
Cathedrals	Law and justice
Chivalry	Medicine, disease, pestilence
Cloth and clothing	Merchant guilds
Craftsmen and their guilds	Monks and monasteries
Crusades	Music
Crime and punishment	Peasants' Revolt
Daily life in a castle	Plays
Daily life in a town	Religion
Daily life on a manor	Religious art
Fairs	Science and technology
Falconry	Schools
Farms and farming	Scribes and books
Feudal society	Stained glass
Food and feasting	Standards of living and social classes
Furniture	
Games, sport, and recreation	Tapestries
Heraldry	Troubadours and minstrels
Holy Grail	Women's role

EXAMPLE 24 (cont.)

Famous People:

King Alfred	John Gutenberg
King Arthur	Saint Joan of Arc
Roger Bacon	Marco Polo
Saint Bernard	Mohammed
Charlemagne	Peter the Hermit
Chaucer	King Richard the Lionhearted
Eleanor of Aquitaine	William of Normandy
Saint Francis	

B. In addition to researching histories and biographies, the students will be encouraged to read the literature of the Middle Ages and contemporary historical novels to gain insight into the manners and customs of the period. For example:

Adam of the Road by Elizabeth Gray (Viking Press, 1942)

The Book of Hugh Flower by Lorna Beers (Harper, 1952)

The Boy's King Arthur by Sidney Lanier (Scribner, 1973)

Chanticleer and the Fox retold by Barbara Cooney (Crowell, 1958)

Connecticut Yankee in King Arthur's Court by Samuel Clemens (Dodd, 1960)

The Door in the Wall by Marguerite DeAngeli (Doubleday, 1969)

Heroic Deeds of Beowulf by Gladys Schmitt (Random House, 1962)

Hidden Treasure of Glaston by Eleanore Jewett (Viking Press, 1946)

Men of Sherwood by D. E. Cooke (Holt, 1961)

Merry Adventures of Robin Hood by Howard Pyle (Scribner, 1903)

The Sleepers by Jane Curry (Harcourt Brace, 1968)

V. Individual students work at their own rate and proceed to develop their special areas of information
  A. Each student will search out his own materials
  B. Each student will determine which alternative learning route to travel
  C. Each student will determine when he has completed his assignment adequately
  D. The GATE teacher will be available for consultation and guidance upon student request
VI. The group will weave together the information they have gained from their individual research
  A. Following the group discussion of individual research, each student will summarize his understanding of the socioeconomic problems of the Middle Ages by comparing the standard of living of the various social classes during the Middle Ages
     The following definition will serve as a springboard:
     Standard of living: A level of subsistence of a social class with reference to the adequacy of necessities and comforts in daily life
  B. The group will then contrast the standard of living during the Middle Ages with the standard of living in the United States today
     The concept of life expectancy will be introduced and discussed
VII. As a culminating activity the group will view the motion picture *A Connecticut Yankee in King Arthur's Court* and then write their reaction
  A. Following the viewing of the motion picture, each student will summarize the insight and understanding he has gained by writing his own imaginative projection into the Middle Ages using the project title "If I Had Lived During the Middle Ages" as the launching pad
  B. The group will, upon hearing the imaginative essay of each student, vote to select the best one
     The essay judged best will be submitted as an entry in the North Hills School District GATE creative writing contest

ABA publishes a number of books and booklets on law-related education.* The library media specialist should find the following of particular value:

Bibliography of Law-Related Materials: Annotated, 2nd ed.

Law-Related Education in America: Guidelines for the Future

Media: An Annotated Catalogue of Law-Related Audio-Visual Materials

Teaching Teachers About Law

Update on Law-Related Education, a periodical published fall, winter, and spring

NEA has prepared in-service training materials for law-related education that include the following:†

Future Rights Enforcement (Cassette tape)

Law Enforcement Education in the Middle Grades

Values, Law-Related Education, and the Elementary School Teacher

Youth and the Law (Cassette tape)

CURRENT HISTORY AND THE ALTERNATIVE FUTURES APPROACH

The social studies program has an obligation to prepare students to anticipate and to cope with future changes. Draper Kauffman, Jr., in his book *Futurism and Future Studies* proposes four basic ways that students can be prepared to cope with the future:

1. We can provide students with better, more sophisticated ways of thinking about the future.
2. Since the sheer complexity of our social and physical environment is a major part of the problem, we can provide students with the skills and concepts needed to understand complex systems.
3. Although we cannot predict the future, we *can* identify and help students to understand many of the major issues which will—one way or another—shape the future.
4. And since continued rapid change is one of the few certainties, we can help students to understand change and to cope with it.[13]

Kauffman identifies key topics that should be incorporated into the curriculum.[14] Many of those listed are appropriate for the social studies, for example: war and peace, population and food, resources and development, the environment, economic shortsightedness, economic cycles, job obsolescence, unemployment and welfare, growth, politics and government, centralization, values and diversity, equity and social justice, and corruption. In summarizing the importance of these key issues, Kauffman stated, "The more students know about these critical issues, and the choices, values, preconditions, and possible consequences which they entail, the better prepared they

---

*American Bar Association, 1155 E. 60 St., Chicago, Ill. 60637, tel. 312-947-3960.
†NEA Distribution Center, Academic Building, Saw Mill Rd., West Haven, Conn. 06516, tel. 203-934-2669.

will be to understand the future and to act responsibly as citizens of the future."[15]

The alternative futures approach views the present as current history and stresses the cause-and-effect relationship between current and future happenings. An invaluable tool, *News In Print: Key Issues* (R. R. Bowker) provides insight into many of the key issues highlighted by Kauffman. News summaries are selected from the world's largest current affairs data base with over 1,400,000 article summaries from the *New York Times* and 60 other authoritative newspapers and periodicals. The result is a new way of combining abstracts, index information, and full *New York Times* articles in a time-saving format easily used and understood.

Relevance

The real challenge to the social studies teacher is to infuse teaching with relevance—to relate what is being taught to the needs, interests, and aspirations of the individual student. Building career awareness is a basic ingredient of a relevant social studies program, kindergarten through grade twelve. No aspect of the program can have greater personal import for students than to consider future career alternatives as they explore the world, past and present. Building such understanding is usually not part of the function of the social studies textbook, but is the special contribution of the teacher, who painstakingly plans to highlight career exploration where and when possible. Example 6, The Tasaday: A Study of a Primitive Culture Frozen in Time (see Chapter 7) includes specific career information about the ethnologist, the archeologist, the historian, and the paleontologist; it also suggests that the student consult the career resource center at the senior high school.

Polycultural Education

Polycultural education is defined as those educational experiences which "enable students to better appreciate and value their own ethnocultural dimensions and the ethnocultural dimensions of others."[16] Cross-cultural and multicultural education are synonyms for polycultural education; in philosophy, goals, and purpose they are identical. The American Association of Colleges for Teacher Education, in its "Statement to Serve as a Guide for Multicultural Education," explains the meaning of multicultural education as follows:

> Multicultural education is education which values cultural pluralism. Multicultural education rejects the view that schools should seek to melt away cultural differences or the view that schools should merely tolerate cultural pluralism . . . cultural pluralism rejects both assimilation and separatism as ultimate goals. Instead, multicultural education affirms that schools should be oriented toward the cultural enrichment of all children and youth through programs pointed to the preservation and extension of cultural alternatives.[17]

Basic to polycultural education is the ideal that every person will respect and value his own ethnocultural identity and will extend the same respect and value to the cultures of all others.[18] The social studies program shares with all other disciplines the responsibility for integrating within the framework of the instructional program opportunities for achieving both self and planetary perspective.

SOCIAL STUDIES SKILLS

June Chapin and Richard Gross in their basic handbook *Teaching Social Studies Skills* provide the following reasons why skills must be emphasized in the social studies K–12 curriculum:

1. For effective learning in the social studies, three components are necessary: interest, content (data), and use of skills to uncover, process, and interpret data. Too frequently in the past the focus has been only on content.
2. Subject matter cannot be taught as an end in itself. Studies show that even college students forget about three-fourths of the content of their courses; younger students probably forget more. Thus, merely social studies content has limited value. . . . The needed skills and the motivation to use them must be given more consideration in planning the social studies curriculum.
3. Skills are growing in importance in a world where scientific knowledge is doubling every decade. The social sciences and history have so much content that even specialists can barely keep up with the data in their own areas. Since it is impossible to teach all social science content . . . there is a need to emphasize the processes of how to come to know and how to apply knowledge, rather than to emphasize content as in the past.
4. Many social studies educators have not thought out the relationships of the so-called traditional social studies skills (reading, listening, etc.) either to the "new social studies" or to the needs of students to master certain competencies to live in a changing society. Some traditional skills such as locating information, appear in the emerging new social studies in a different format and with a different emphasis. The new materials place more demands on skill development than ever before, yet assume that students have already mastered such basic skills as reading and effective group discussion. The need for teaching such skills as interpreting primary sources,* using statistical evidence,† or analyzing case studies‡ has increased, but this has not been recognized by many teachers.
5. Further research in such fields as cognitive processes, self-concepts, and teaching/learning interactions is forcing a reevaluation of what type of learning is possible in a classroom. . . . Indeed, there has almost been a revolution, changing a basic philosophy from what schools should do *to* students, to what schools should do *for* students. More emphasis is placed on learning experiences to give children the appropriate background, as in Head Start, rather than waiting for students to "become ready" to learn.
6. The very complexity of, and rapid changes in our urban industrial society also means that students will have to choose relevant data from a constantly changing stream of knowledge. Because students are bombarded by the communications media, more attention must be devoted to teaching them how to sort out the growing data. Each student must "make the facts his own" and assimilate the information, and increasingly students must learn to revise and reevaluate what they have already learned. To do this, students must distinguish between different skills, such as forming a hypothesis and making a generalization. Failure to realize these distinctions results in confused thinking.[19]

---

*For a prototype of a learning experience employing primary sources see Chapter 7, Example 7, Learning Guide in U.S. History.

†For a prototype of a learning experience employing statistical evidence see Chapter 10, Example 34, Test Your City's Quotient.

‡For a prototype of a learning experience employing the case study approach see Chapter 7, Example 6, The Tasaday: A Study of a Primitive Culture Frozen in Time.

Social studies skills encompass thinking skills, learning skills, communicating skills. Each basic thinking-learning-communicating skill has been identified and placed in a continuum to facilitate skill integration within the framework of the social studies program, kindergarten through grade twelve (see Appendix L). An in-depth coverage of a developmental skills program is presented in Chapter 12.

INTEGRATION OF LITERATURE WITH THE SOCIAL STUDIES PROGRAM

Literature is a vital component of the social studies program. In the words of Michaelis:

> Literature makes a rich contribution to social learning. . . . Literary selections are used in the social studies to heighten interest, deepen understanding, create moods and atmosphere, portray the diversity of ways of living and thinking among people in various cultures, stimulate imagination, give colorful backgrounds, promote more complete identification with others, give a warm feeling for the problems of others, improve attitudes toward others, build appreciation for the contributions of others, provoke creativity, and give vivid impressions of ways of living being studied in various units.[20]

Michaelis warns the teacher that reading literature should be an experience of delight and enjoyment. To safeguard the positive aspects of reading literature, the following points should be kept in mind when incorporating literature into the social studies program:

1. Enjoy it, do not dissect it; analyze it only if analysis increases enjoyment.
2. Share it, do not ask questions; do not give tests on it or evaluate it, as is done with factual materials.
3. Approach it to have fun, not to study, as is done in work-type materials.
4. Be aware of fiction and fantasy; do not teach them as facts.
5. Let the children discover values, moods, and meanings; do not moralize or struggle to develop certain points of real interest to yourself.
6. Let children memorize their favorites.
7. Use varied techniques and activities to share and enjoy literary selections in social studies—book reports, card files of favorite poems and stories, choral reading, creative writing, dramatization, filmstrips, independent reading, films, oral reading by children, oral reading by the teacher, programs and pageants, puppets and marionettes, radio and TV programs, recordings, and storytelling.[21]

The integration of literature with the social studies program can best be achieved by the cooperative planning and team efforts of the social studies teacher, the English teacher, and the library media specialist. For example, the unit *The Crucible* by Arthur Miller (see Example 25) is the result of the joint efforts of such a teaching team.

EXAMPLE 25   INTEGRATED ENGLISH-SOCIAL STUDIES UNIT

Unit: *The Crucible* by Arthur Miller
Subjects: Social Studies and English
Grade: 11

Goal: To provide opportunity for the students who have just completed an in-depth study of the McCarthy Era to compare the witch hunt of the 1950s with the Salem Witch Trials of 1692.

EXAMPLE 25 (cont.)

Teaching objectives:
1. The students will build their knowledge of the Salem Witch Trials by reading primary source materials.
2. The students will build their knowledge of the McCarthy hearings trials by reading primary source materials and by viewing videotapes of actual Senate hearings.
3. The students after reading *The Crucible* will analyze the main characters of the play and try to discover why intolerance and superstition travel in tandem.
4. The students will compare the mob hysteria of the Colonial Period with that of the United States during the McCarthy hearings.

Teaching procedure:
1. The play, *The Crucible*, is read in paperback format (Bantam).
2. The students, following the reading of the play, are given two weeks to build their understanding of both the McCarthy hearings and the Salem Witch Trials by working in the library media center where material such as the following is available:

PRINTED RESOURCES: Salem Witchcraft

Annals of Witchcraft in New England and Elsewhere in the United States from Their First Settlement: Drawn Up from Unpublished and Other Well Authenticated Records of the Alleged Operations of Witches and Their Instigator, the Devil. Somerset Publishing, 1869.

The Devil in Massachusetts: A Modern Inquiry into the Salem Witch Trials by Marion Starkey. Doubleday.

The Devil's Shadow: The Story of Witchcraft in Massachusetts by Clifford Alderman. Messner.

Mirror for Witches by Esther Forbes. Houghton Mifflin.

New England's Place in the History of Witchcraft by George Burr. Facsimile edition. Books for Libraries.

Records of Salem Witchcraft. Copies from the original documents. 2 volumes. American History, Politics and Law series. Da Capo.

Tituba of Salem Village by Ann Petry. Crowell.

Witchcraft at Salem by Chadwick Hanson. Braziller.

Witchcraft of Salem Village by Shirley Jackson. Random House.

NONPRINT RESOURCES: Salem Witchcraft

The Crucible. Recording. Spoken Arts.

The Witchcraft of Salem Village. Recording. Enrichment Records.

PRINTED RESOURCES: McCarthy hearings

Congressional Record, 1952–1953.

Day of Shame by Charles E. Potter. Coward.

Freedom in Jeopardy: The McCarthy Years by Burt Hirschfeld. Milestones in History series. Messner.

Joe McCarthy and McCarthyism: The Hate that Taunts America by Roberta Feuerlicht. McGraw-Hill.

See It Now, edited by Edward R. Murrow and Fred W. Friendly. Simon and Schuster.

Senator Joe McCarthy by Richard Rovere. Harcourt.

The Time of the Toad: A Study of Inquisition in America by Dalton Trumbo. Harper.

NONPRINTED RESOURCES: McCarthy hearings

McCarthy Senate Hearings. University Microfilm.

Biography and historical fiction are unique sources of background information about historical people, places, and times. Both have strong motivational appeal for they give the student opportunity to participate vicariously in the historical past rather than sitting passively as a reluctant mourner in the mausoleum of things long dead and gone. Both biography and historical fiction breathe fresh life into the social studies curriculum and give the student a sense of being personally involved in the living drama of man's past. Both can also serve as vehicles for individualizing instruction and for teaching and applying the inquiry method. The two learning guides "Biography Summary" and "Historical Novel Summary," which follow (Examples 26 and 27), have been devised to encourage the student to analyze and interpret information gained by reading biography and historical novels; they also provide opportunity for the student to draw inferences, conclusions, and impressions. Both of these learning guides are designed to minimize writing and to maximize thinking—a far cry from the traditional written book report.

EXAMPLE 26   BIOGRAPHY SUMMARY

Unit: Colonial America   Pupil _____

I read the following biography:

Title _____ Author _____

This is the story of _____ who lived in the colony or colonies

of _____ during the period:

```
├──┤├──┤├──┤├──┤├──┤├──┤├──┤├──┤├──┤├──┤├──┤├──┤├──┤├──┤├──┤├──┤
1620  '30   '40   '50   '60   '70   '80   '90  1700  '10   '20   '30   '40   '50   '60   '70
```

While reading this biography I learned these facts about colonial manners and customs:

Concerning food, I discovered
    The various kinds of food commonly eaten. For example:

    How foods were prepared. For example:

    How foods were stored. For example:

    Other facts such as:

Concerning homes, I discovered
    What colonial houses looked like. For example:

    The number and size of rooms. For example:

    The various pieces of furniture commonly used. For example:

Concerning household chores, I discovered
    The typical chores performed by the women of the family. For example:

    The typical chores performed by the men of the family. For example:

    The typical chores performed by the children of the family. For example:

    Other facts such as:

EXAMPLE 26 (cont.)

Concerning clothing, I discovered
  The kinds of garments worn and how they were made. For example:

Concerning schools, I discovered
  How colonial schools differed from our schools today. For example:

Concerning occupations, I discovered
  The following occupations which were new to me:

  Other facts such as:

Concerning animals, I discovered
  The following mentioned:

EXAMPLE 27   HISTORICAL NOVEL SUMMARY

Student _____Date_____

I read the following novel:

Title _____ Author _____

This story takes place in _____ and tells about people and events during

the _____ period of history.

From reading this novel I discovered:
  The following facts concerning family life:

  The following facts concerning manners and customs:

  The following facts concerning social problems:

  The following facts concerning occupations:

  The following facts concerning religion:

  The following facts concerning education:

  These additional significant facts: (If you wish, use the reverse side)

Each unit in the social studies program can offer bonus-rich opportunities for literature integration if the social studies teacher and the library media specialist will cooperatively plan *which* literary works could be introduced *where* within the teaching and learning program. For instance, Example 23, Westward Ho! The Wagons, or, If I Had Been a Pioneer Trailblazer, and Example 24, If I Had Lived During the Middle Ages, highlight, as a basic part of the learning project, a number of biographies and historical novels. Each biography and historical novel included in these two learning projects is not only a quality work of literature but has wide and lasting student appeal. Unfortunately, if the social studies program did not introduce these titles to the students, it is unlikely that the students would discover them on their own.

When it comes to motivating interest in biography and historical drama and historical fiction, the social studies teacher, the English teacher, and the library media specialist have a powerful ally in television. Consistently, interest reaches fever pitch after viewing televised programs such as "Gone with the Wind," "Holocaust," "Roots I" and "Roots II," "Backstairs at the White House," and, for the younger set, "The Little House on the Prairie" series. So powerful has the reaction been to "Roots" and "Holocaust"* that a number of schools have structured mini-units to probe the social and historical implications of these two works in depth.

Literature "should play an important part in social studies instruction" because it conveys "so well the affective dimension of human experience."[22] Students who are turned off by the textbook may well be turned on by a novel, a play, or a biography that delights as it informs. A preplanning session between the social studies teacher (or a teacher of any other discipline) and the library media specialist, in addition to implementing the teaching goals and objectives of a particular unit or learning project, is often the beginning of a continuing learning chain reaction. This is particularly true in the case of literary interests generated by a social studies unit or learning project that can last for a lifetime—a windfall profit paying lifelong dividends.

SOCIAL STUDIES DEPENDENCE ON LIBRARY MEDIA AND SERVICES

The NCSS in its guidelines for social studies programs devotes one major area out of a total of nine to the standard "Strategies of Instruction and Learning Activities Should Rely on a Broad Range of Learning Resources." The rationale given by NCSS for its standards for the employment of learning resources includes the following:

Learning in the social studies requires rich resources.

No single textbook will do.

Accomplishing objectives which represent all of the components of social studies education depends upon more information, more points of view, more appeals, and more suitability to individual students.

Printed materials must be available for differing abilities in reading and for differing needs in concreteness and abstraction.

Students must have books, periodicals, basic references, case studies, graphs, tables, maps, articles, and literary materials suitable for the subject at hand.

Multiple media offer many avenues to learning.

Films and sound-filmstrips; pictures; recordings of speeches; discussions and music; mock-ups; artifacts; models; audiotapes; dramatic scripts or scripts for role-playing; diagrams; simulation exercises; programs on television—these and others call upon the use of many senses, thought and feeling; thus, they enrich learning.

No one kind of material or resource will be satisfactory for all students, nor for any one student at all times and for all purposes.

Instructional resources must be suitable for the learning tasks and for the students who are learning.[23]

This rationale clearly indicates how important it is for the social studies teacher to plan with the library media specialist for the systematic integration

Study Guide to Books on the Holocaust is available to teachers at no charge from Avon Books, Education Dept., 959 Eighth Ave., New York, N.Y. 10019.

of library media resources and library media center services within the framework of the total instructional program.

Because media are vital to the success of the social studies program, the wise selection of media is imperative. The Secondary Curriculum Committee of the Indiana Council for the Social Studies devised the evaluation tool shown as Checklist 7 for use in evaluating social studies instructional support media.[24]

CHECKLIST 7　SELECTED CRITERIA FOR EVALUATING SOCIAL STUDIES MATERIALS

The attached evaluation is designed to aid social studies teachers in assessing materials for adoption in their classrooms and schools. The form was designed by the Secondary Curriculum Committee of the Indiana Council for the Social Studies and is reproduced with their permission.

The questions on the form were designed to give a staff common bases for evaluating all materials under consideration. Although designed initially for the secondary social studies, the form is appropriate for evaluating elementary materials as well.

It is suggested that a local group may wish to modify the criteria by determining which items are crucial, establishing a weight system according to their own objectives, or eliminating any items deemed inappropriate.

QUESTIONS TO CONSIDER IN EVALUATING SOCIAL STUDIES MATERIALS

Directions: Circle the one number indicating the degree or extent of the question stated. Add the total points circled in each category, and divide the total number by the number of items circled in each category.

    Key: 1—Great extent
         2—Some extent
         3—No extent
         4—Unable to judge

DESCRIPTIVE CHARACTERISTICS

1. If you are a supporter of a multiple materials concept, to what extent do the materials being considered adequately meet this idea?　　1　2　3　4
2. If there is a teacher's guide, to what extent do you believe it is generally useful?　　1　2　3　4
3. A. If you believe an instructional strategy should be primarily inductive, to what extent are the materials appropriate?　　1　2　3　4
　　B. If you believe an instructional strategy should be primarily deductive, to what extent are the materials appropriate?　　1　2　3　4
　　C. If you believe both deduction and induction are essential to the instructional strategy, to what extent are the materials appropriate?　　1　2　3　4
4. A. If you feel the recommended teacher behavior should be expository, to what extent are these materials applicable?　　1　2　3　4
　　B. If you feel the recommended teacher behavior should be a director of learning, to what extent are these materials applicable?　　1　2　3　4
　　C. If you feel the recommended teacher behavior to be something other than those mentioned above, to what extent are these materials applicable?　　1　2　3　4
5. If there are tests with the package, to what extent are they applicable for general use in your school? (Be sure to consider instructional techniques and approaches of your fellow faculty.)　　1　2　3　4
6. To what extent are the author(s) and publisher contributors to social studies education?　　1　2　3　4
7. To what extent have the materials been tested by the author(s) prior to publication?　　1　2　3　4
8. To what extent do the field tests show favorable results?　　1　2　3　4

                        Total points　　_____
                        Descriptive characteristics average　　_____

CHECKLIST 7 (cont.)

ANTECEDENT CONDITIONS

1. To what extent is the subject matter relevant to the level of the student for whom the materials are being considered?

    (1) Gifted   1   2   3   4
    (2) Average   1   2   3   4
    (3) Underachievers   1   2   3   4
    (4) Girls   1   2   3   4
    (5) Boys   1   2   3   4
    (6) Pupils who need highly structured experiences   1   2   3   4
    (7) Pupils who can work without supervision   1   2   3   4

2. To what extent would each kind of pupil (for whom this program is considered) be interested in this program?

    (8) Gifted   1   2   3   4
    (9) Average   1   2   3   4
    (10) Underachievers   1   2   3   4
    (11) Girls   1   2   3   4
    (12) Boys   1   2   3   4
    (13) Pupils who need highly structured experiences   1   2   3   4
    (14) Pupils who can work without supervision   1   2   3   4

3. To what extent would the experiences and background of most teachers who will be using these materials in this school enable them to handle these materials effectively?   1   2   3   4

4. To what extent could in-service programs be used to remedy any teacher deficiencies in knowledge or skills?   1   2   3   4

5. To what extent will the community permit these types of materials to be used?   1   2   3   4

6. To what extent does your school have equipment that is essential to the use of the materials? (Consider such items as A.V. equipment, space available for large-small group instruction, adequate resource center, etc.)   1   2   3   4

Total points _____

Antecedent conditions average _____

RATIONALE AND OBJECTIVES

1. To what extent does the program relate to the goals of your school system?   1   2   3   4

2. To what extent are the objectives stated in behavioral terms?   1   2   3   4

3. To what extent does the program develop its stated objectives relative to:

    Culture concepts   1   2   3   4
    Socialization   1   2   3   4
    Philosophical and religious influences   1   2   3   4
    Ethnocentrism   1   2   3   4
    Geographic concepts   1   2   3   4
    Economic concepts   1   2   3   4
    Interdependence   1   2   3   4
    Political behavior concepts   1   2   3   4
    Change   1   2   3   4

4. To what extent does the program develop its stated objectives relative to:

    Process of inquiry skills   1   2   3   4
    Psychomotor skills   1   2   3   4
    Developing attitudes and values   1   2   3   4

Total points _____

Rationale and objectives average _____

CONTENT

1. To what extent is the subject matter relevant to the level of the student for whom the materials are being considered?   1   2   3   4

CHECKLIST 7 (cont.)

2. To what extent are the concepts developed (in those disciplines being considered)?

Anthropology | 1 | 2 | 3 | 4
Sociology | 1 | 2 | 3 | 4
Political science | 1 | 2 | 3 | 4
Economics | 1 | 2 | 3 | 4
History | 1 | 2 | 3 | 4
Geography | 1 | 2 | 3 | 4
Social psychology | 1 | 2 | 3 | 4

3. To what extent does the program teach attitudes and values?   1   2   3   4

Total points _____

Content average _____

INSTRUCTIONAL THEORY AND TEACHING STRATEGIES

1. To what extent is the teaching strategy to be used explicitly stated?   1   2   3   4
2. To what extent does the program foster inquiry?   1   2   3   4
3. To what extent does the program design maintain proper teacher-pupil balance?   1   2   3   4
4. To what extent does the program develop concepts and generalizations?   1   2   3   4
5. To what extent does the program develop concepts and generalizations in a sequential and systematic way?   1   2   3   4
6. To what extent is there an acceptable variety and balance of teaching strategies?   1   2   3   4
7. To what extent does the program provide sufficient facts to support generalizations?   1   2   3   4
8. If the materials require one dominant teaching technique, to what extent is it desirable (in terms of your staff, students, and acceptable techniques)?   1   2   3   4

Total points _____

Instructional theory and teaching strategies average _____

MATERIALS

1. To what extent is each of the following available? (Rate only those that are needed to fully implement these materials.)

Background paper for the teachers | 1 | 2 | 3 | 4
Supplemental materials for the pupil | 1 | 2 | 3 | 4
Bibliography | 1 | 2 | 3 | 4
Films | 1 | 2 | 3 | 4
Filmstrips | 1 | 2 | 3 | 4
Books | 1 | 2 | 3 | 4
Slides | 1 | 2 | 3 | 4
Magazines or student handouts | 1 | 2 | 3 | 4
Transparencies | 1 | 2 | 3 | 4
Realia or artifacts | 1 | 2 | 3 | 4
Recordings | 1 | 2 | 3 | 4
TV programs | 1 | 2 | 3 | 4
Film loops | 1 | 2 | 3 | 4
Others (list) | 1 | 2 | 3 | 4

Total points _____

Materials average _____

OVERALL JUDGMENTS

1. To what extent do you believe these materials would be more effective than those you are currently using?   1   2   3   4
2. To what extent would you rate these materials?

Effective   1   2   3   4

CHECKLIST 7 (cont.)

Interesting	1	2	3	4
Stimulating	1	2	3	4
Meaningful	1	2	3	4
Challenging	1	2	3	4
Rewarding	1	2	3	4

3. If these materials are being considered for general adoption, to what extent would you recommend these materials for adoption for general use in the department, i.e., by all teachers?   1 2 3 4

4. If the materials being examined are considered for experimental use by a limited number of teachers, to what extent would you recommend these materials for adoption?   1 2 3 4

5. To what extent may these materials be used without additional community involvement?   1 2 3 4

Total points   ————————

Overall judgments average   ————————

Frequently the classroom teacher will ask the library media specialist for help in meeting special class needs; for example, Case Study 16 is illustrative of a typical request by a classroom teacher in motivating and sustaining class interest.

CASE STUDY 16

An eighth-grade social studies teacher faced with teaching a class of 30 exceptionally bright students who thought that they already knew more than they needed to know about American history came to the library media specialist for help. As each new unit was taught, the class refused to put forth any effort. The teacher asked the library media specialist to help structure a pretest to introduce the upcoming unit "Civil War and Reconstruction." Together, the teacher and the library media specialist identified 60 people whose biographies could well serve as content for the study of the Civil War (see Example 28).

EXAMPLE 28　UNIT PRETEST: THE CIVIL WAR AND RECONSTRUCTION*

Subject: Social Studies

Grade level: 8

Name _____   Number indicated YES _____

                                                 Number indicated NO _____

After you have studied this list of famous Americans, please write "yes" or "no" before each name to indicate whether or not the person was involved directly or indirectly with the events of the Civil War.

Louisa May Alcott	Matthew Brady
Clara Barton	John Brown
August Bondi	Bill Cody
John Wilkes Booth	George Cook
Belle Boyd	Stephen Crane

*This pretest was developed cooperatively by classroom teacher and school librarian to create and sustain student interest in discovering who these people were and why they were significant.

EXAMPLE 28 (cont.)

George Custer	Robert E. Lee
Jefferson Davis	Abraham Lincoln
Varina Howell Davis	Thaddeus Lowe
Dorothy Dix	James Russell Lowell
Abner Doubleday	George McClellan
Stephen A. Douglas	George Meade
Frederick Douglass	John Hunt Morgan
Daniel Emmett	John Mosby
John Ericsson	Samuel Mudd
Edward Everett	James Pettigru
David Farragut	Joseph Pulitzer
Nathan B. Forrest	Edmund Ross
Barbara Frietchie	Dred Scott
William Lloyd Garrison	William H. Seward
Ulysses S. Grant	Philip Sheridan
Horace Greeley	William T. Sherman
Rose O'Neil Greenhow	Edwin Stanton
William Gregg	Harriet Beecher Stowe
Cornelia Hancock	James E. B. Stuart
John Hay	Charles Sumner
Oliver Wendell Holmes, Jr.	Roger Taney
Sam Houston	Harriet Tubman
Julia Ward Howe	Molly Tynes
"Stonewall" Jackson	Lewis Wallace
Andrew Johnson	Walt Whitman

The teacher invited the library media specialist to come to the classroom to introduce the unit. The library media specialist distributed the pretest, gave the directions, conducted the discussion following the marking of the test, and alerted the students to the various primary source materials available for their use. The students were shocked to discover how many of these people they did not know—out of a possible 60 (all names on the list should have been marked *yes*) the highest number known to any student was 25; the majority could not identify 20. The pretest was more than a motivational device. It was a means of orienting the students to the unit and to the biographies essential for adequate understanding of the Civil War and Reconstruction. The students for the first time in that school year had a challenge in history class, for they discovered how much they did not know and yet needed to know. The history teacher, discovering that the pretest was an effective method of challenging the gifted, continued to employ a pretest as an introduction for subsequent units and asked for the library media specialist's help in structuring each pretest.

The library media specialist shares with the social studies faculty the responsibility for selecting resources not only for the district professional library but especially for inclusion in the building social studies laboratory. In searching for social studies laboratory materials, first consideration must be given to the publications of NCSS. The NCSS yearbooks are devoted to a scholarly review of research, experience, and trends. Bulletins are issued by the association with a frequency of from one to three times a year; each is devoted to practical guidance for the social studies practitioner. The official journal of NCSS, *Social Education*, is an invaluable source of information on research, trends, policy statements, contemporary concerns, curriculum development, and instructional strategies and resources; it also includes as a regular feature reference to current Educational Resources Information Center (ERIC) documents in the social studies and social science areas. (See Appendix K for information about ERIC services and the clearinghouse addresses.)

The social studies program that is reflective of the NCSS guidelines will be conceptually based and interdisciplinary in nature, will go beyond a single textbook, will be concerned with the valuing process, will emphasize inquiry learning, will humanize teaching and individualize learning, and will relate learning experiences to future alternatives. Such a program demands the continuing support of the library media center functioning as a learning laboratory and the guidance of the library media specialist serving as a team teacher directly involved in the planning and implementation of the program. Success of the social studies program requires the highest degree of library support and involvement.

NOTES

1. National Council for the Social Studies, "Position Statement: Revision of the NCSS Social Studies Curriculum Guidelines," *Social Education* 43, no. 4 (Apr. 1979): 262. Reprinted with permission of the National Council for the Social Studies.
2. Ibid.
3. Ibid., pp. 262–266.
4. National Study of School Evaluation, *The Evaluative Criteria for the Evaluation of Secondary Schools*, 5th ed. Copyright © 1978, p. 221. Reprinted by permission of the National Study of School Evaluation, Washington, D.C.
5. John U. Michaelis, Ruth H. Grossman, and Lloyd F. Scott, *New Designs for Elementary Curriculum and Instruction* (New York: McGraw-Hill, 1975), pp. 324–325.
6. National Council for the Social Studies, "Position Statement," pp. 261–278. Reprinted with permission of the National Council for the Social Studies.
7. Michael J. Elliott and Kerry J. Kennedy, "Australian Impressions of Social Studies Theory and Practice in Secondary Schools in the United States," *Social Education* 43, no. 4 (April 1979): 291–296. Reprinted with permission of the National Council for the Social Studies.
8. Ibid., pp. 293–294.
9. Ibid., pp. 294–295.
10. John U. Michaelis, *Social Studies for Children in a Democracy*, 6th ed. (Englewood Cliffs, N.J.: Prentice-Hall, 1976), pp. 8–10. Reprinted by permission of Prentice-Hall, Inc., Englewood Cliffs, N.J. Copyright © 1976.
11. Special Committee on Youth Education for Citizenship, *Law-Related Education in America: Guidelines for the Future* (Chicago: American Bar Association, 1975), p. 69.
12. Ibid., pp. 30–31.
13. Draper L. Kauffman, Jr., *Futurism and Future Studies* (Washington, D.C.: National Education Association, 1976), p. 10.
14. Ibid., pp. 29–42.
15. Ibid., p. 42.
16. Robert L. Williams, *Cross-Cultural Education: Teaching toward Planetary Perspective* (Washington, D.C.: National Education Association, 1977), p. 7.
17. Ibid., p. 10.
18. Ibid.
19. June R. Chapin and Richard E. Gross, *Teaching Social Studies Skills* (Boston: Little, Brown, 1973), pp. 1–3. Copyright © 1973 by Little, Brown and Company (Inc.). Reprinted by permission.
20. Michaelis, *Social Studies for Children in a Democracy*, p. 357.
21. Ibid., pp. 358–359.

22. John Jarolimek, *Social Studies in Elementary Education*, 5th ed. (New York: Macmillan, 1977), p. 87.
23. National Council for the Social Studies, "Positions Statement," pp. 270-271.
24. Indiana Council for the Social Studies, "Suggested Criteria for Evaluating Social Studies Materials," in *Social Studies Today: Guidelines for Curriculum Improvement* (Harrisburg, Pa.: Bureau of General and Academic Education, Department of Education, 1970), pp. 74-80.

10 The Library Media Program Supports the Science and Mathematics Programs

Science needs all kinds of people . . . just as art does, or philosophy, or politics, since each person can ask different questions and see different worlds.

Abraham H. Maslow*

Science is not technology; it is not gadgetry; it is not some mysterious cult; it is not a great mechanical monster. Science is an adventure of the human spirit. It is an essentially artistic enterprise stimulated largely by disciplined imagination, and based largely on faith in the reasonableness, order, and beauty of the universe of which man is a part.

Warren Weaver†

It is essential for teachers to know more than they are expected to teach and to be able to learn more than they already know, for without such knowledge progress is essentially impossible.
Commission on Pre-Service Education of Teachers of Mathematics‡

Mankind is constantly buffeted by change of future shock proportion. In large measure, the kind, the degree, and the velocity of change are influenced for better or for worse by man's scientific and technological acumen. Since science and technology are the forces that create, harness, and channel change, both are charged with the responsibility for safeguarding mankind from change of a cataclysmic nature. Change without order is chaos! It is the special function and responsibility of the school's science program to prepare future citizens to make value judgments when dealing with change of a scientific and technological nature. Today's youth must be prepared to deal with ideas not yet thought and discoveries unimagined.

SCIENCE EDUCATION: BASIC GOALS, PRINCIPLES, AND OBJECTIVES

The National Science Teachers Association (NSTA) published a working paper in December 1978 entitled *Science Education: Accomplishments and Needs.* The purpose of the working paper was to determine the goals, principles, and aims of science education as society moves into the 1980s. The goal, which had first been stated by the NSTA Committee on Curriculum Studies in 1971, was endorsed as still being the primary goal for the future, i.e., the de-

---

*Abraham H. Maslow, *Motivation and Personality*, 2nd ed. (New York: Harper, 1970), p. 5.

†Warren Weaver in The Report of the President's Commission on National Goals, *Goals for Americans*, The American Assembly, Columbia University, New York (Englewood Cliffs, N.J.: Prentice-Hall, 1960), p. 105.

‡Commission on Pre-Service Education of Teachers of Mathematics, *Guidelines for the Preparation of Teachers of Mathematics* (Reston, Va.: National Council of Teachers of Mathematics, 1973), p. 5.

velopment of "scientifically literate and personally concerned individuals with a high competency for rational thought and action."[1] A scientifically literate person is identified in the working paper as one who:

1. Uses science concepts, process skills, and values in making everyday decisions as he interacts with other people and with his environment.
2. Understands that the generation of scientific knowledge depends upon the inquiry process and upon conceptual theories.
3. Distinguishes between scientific evidence and personal opinion.
4. Identifies the relationship between facts and theory.
5. Recognizes the limitations as well as the usefulness of science and technology in advancing human welfare.
6. Understands the interrelationships between science, technology, and other facts of society, including social and economic development.
7. Recognizes the human origin of science and understands that scientific knowledge is tentative, subject to change as evidence accumulates.
8. Has sufficient knowledge and experience so that he can appreciate the scientific work being carried out by others.
9. Has a richer and more exciting view of the world as a result of his science education.
10. Has adopted values similar to those that underlie science so that he can use and enjoy science for its intellectual stimulation, its elegance of explanation, and its excitement of inquiry.
11. Continues to inquire and increase his scientific knowledge throughout his life.[2]

The following general principles were identified as basic:

Contemporary science programs must provide a broad education in science for all citizens and a more specialized scientific education for individuals who will become scientists and technicians.

A broad general education in science should provide every person—child or adult —basic knowledge about the natural world, an understanding of the methods of scientific investigation, especially of the relationships between theory and evidence, an appreciation of the limits of scientific inquiry, and some knowledge of the ways in which scientific research can be used to improve daily life.

It should also provide an awareness of social and moral problems which may arise in the practice of scientific research and in technological applications in the world.

More specialized education additionally would provide science-prone students with more sophisticated knowledge and experiences in traditional and emerging scientific fields.

Teachers, parents, students, and policy-makers should not view a curriculum for the talented students in science as elitist. . . . Too often, the talented student in science has been discriminated against through neglect.

Science curricula must provide opportunities for meaningful experiences for all students regardless of their interests and ability in science.

A variety of teaching materials and methods must be developed so that real differences in the interests and needs of the students can be accommodated and nurtured [emphasis supplied].

Failure to recognize and respond to student differences in cognitive development has resulted in frustration, fear, and failure for some students. For others, the result has been boredom and insufficiently challenging encounters with the phenomena of science.

Nearly all students can learn what is necessary to learn if schools approach instruction sensitively and sensibly.

Enough is now known to justify the development and existence of different approaches to the teaching and learning of science to accommodate the different skills and needs of individual students.

Curriculum development and revision is a continuous process. The quest of discovering the "best" teaching materials, the "best" teaching methods, and the "best" preservice and inservice teaching procedures must be continuous.

Changing social circumstances, different national priorities, and new information . . . influence the content of the science curriculum and methods of teaching.

As new knowledges changes current views of the nature of society, science, and learning, there must be a continual reassessment of the aims of science teaching. Some of the aims of today will endure into the future period. Others will be interpreted with different emphasis while still others will become obsolete and be discarded. Inasmuch as curricula should be based upon goals of instruction, changes in curricula should follow evolving goals.[3]

NSTA made the following recommendations for the 1980s:

There must be continued emphasis on the processes, concepts, principles, and generalizations of science as they are enduring, valuable, and necessary in an era of rapidly expanding knowledge.

> It is unwise to concentrate solely on discipline-oriented topics and courses.
>
> Science cannot be divorced from the critical realities of contemporary life and society [see Example 29, Pros and Cons of Space Colonization].
>
> Neither can science continue to be seen as value-free.
>
> Science must be studied in the context of the times and society.
>
> Knowledge is only one dimension; there are also philosophical, moral, ethical, and practical dimensions of science.
>
> When the many different dimensions of science are combined symbiotically in the curriculum, a larger number of students will gain greater benefits from science instruction.

On the elementary level there is a need for the development of more suitable support materials such as books, and film loops, audiotapes, games, and simulations.

The junior high school curriculum should not be a scaled-down version of the traditional senior high school programs. Neither will the junior high school curriculum be the textbook-oriented read-about science program that exists in many localities and schools. Student-centered courses which are flexible and offer opportunities for exploration, discovery, and student choice must be available.

The natural and social context of the emerging adolescent must be used as reference points in the selection of content and activities.

Materials and activities for small group and individual work must be developed [see Example 30, A Multidisciplinary Science Mini-Unit].

Because of the diversity of needs, interests, and abilities among senior high students, a wide range of instructional programs must be available in grades 10–12.

First-hand experiences with the phenomena and material of science are a necessary component of a student's study of science on the senior high school level.

The senior high school science curriculum should be enhanced by the development of new courses and the addition of new areas of studies . . . there has been a lack of emphasis and courses in scientific fields of general interest such as astronomy, oceanography, geology, and meteorology. Despite the emphasis in environmental science, there are few laboratory courses or units in this field [see Example 31, Lesson Plan: Alternate Sources of Energy].

The development of various alternatives to the present pattern of science curriculum should provide access to more areas of study, make it possible to meet the needs of more students, and create an overall curriculum that reflects the current nature of science and society.[4]

In *Evaluative Criteria for the Evaluation of Secondary Schools*, the basic evaluation tool for secondary education, the following guiding principles for the teaching of science are set forth:

The science curriculum consists of those courses and activities designed to allow the individual student to interact with science as a discipline and to experience empirical inquiry as a method of investigation. Emphasis is placed on the processes of science so that students can discover and interpret scientific knowledge, develop positive attitudes and interests related to science and scientists, and recognize that these behaviors can be applied in making decisions in an age influenced by science and technology.

Provisions should be made for using instructional strategies which reflect the nature of science and meet the needs of the learner. An understanding of the nature of science is stimulated through the use of the laboratory as a focal point for engaging in the processes of science. Opportunities should be provided for students to apply methods and knowledge of science to formulate possible solutions for the problems of society.[5]

TRENDS IN THE TEACHING OF SCIENCE

Paul Hounshell and Edwin West, Jr., in their article "Trends in the Teaching of Science," identify major trends in science teaching as follows:

1. Emphasis on the "why" of science.

    The trend today is to utilize man's capabilities as a thinker and to encourage him to seek the answers to the "why" behind the "what." In other words, science should be taught as an intellectual pursuit.

    The student learns how to think as a scientist, the ways and approaches of a scientist, and the attitudes of a scientist.

    Through the search for explanation of phenomena, learning becomes a process of self-directed self-discovery.

2. Greater student involvement in the teaching-learning act.

    Unless the student understands and engages in learning activities similar to those of a scientist, he will not, in all probability, come to "know" science, to think scientifically, and to acquire the attitudes, skills, and competencies which are to be desired in contemporary man.

3. Emphasis on problem solving rather than problem doing.

    True problem solving . . . involves an open-ended investigation, one in which the solution of one problem leads to the creation of additional ones. *The problem is approached in a variety of ways, utilizing numerous resources and many texts* [emphasis supplied].

4. Utilization of a multiplicity of learning materials.

    Funds made available through the Elementary and Secondary Education Acts for purchasing learning aids and materials have enabled educators to take steps toward making learning more lifelike [emphasis supplied].

    With the multiplicity of new materials, teachers have been able to make learning relevant as well as appealing to various senses and approaches [emphasis supplied].

    This utilization of a variety of aids facilitates the processes of true problem solving for it allows the learner to go to many sources in search for solutions to problems [emphasis supplied].

5. Emphasis on individualized instruction.

    The changes which have facilitated the individualization of instruction are not only instructional (independent study programs, nongraded or continuous progress programs, programmed learning, modular scheduling), but also electronic (tape recorders, copy machines, microfilm readers, computers, projectors, etc.) and architectural (flexible structures, changeable as needs dictate; better planned . . . laboratories and classrooms).

6. Emphasis on the structure of science.

. . . those fundamental, underlying concepts or principles which tie or hold the discipline together have had a profound effect on curriculum development in science.

. . . teaching the structure of a discipline (a) makes the discipline more understandable and comprehensible; (b) allows for greater comprehension of detail; (c) fosters transfer of learning; and (d) facilitates narrowing the gap between advanced and elementary knowledge.

7. Emphasis on open-ended evaluations.

An open-ended type of evaluation makes allowances for individual differences, backgrounds, perceptions, and at the same time includes questions which foster problem solving or application type evaluations.

8. Emphasis on self-concept development.

If a science classroom lends itself to student involvement . . . students will, in all probability, experience success in learning. This, in turn, will foster feelings of adequacy on the part of the learner.

9. Emphasis on development of values.

We must find ways of creating school and classroom atmosphere which facilitates the process of exploration and discovery of personal meaning—where there can be a freeing, expanding, and changing of perception.

Students need to have many choices; when they discover something of interest, they need to have plenty of time to work at it.

Self-selection in an environment rich in materials, where students sense that how they feel and what they think are important, can be extremely effective in helping students to become more fully functioning [emphasis supplied].[6]

John Michaelis, Ruth Grossman, and Lloyd Scott also stress the necessity of providing students with a multimedia approach for teaching and learning. "Obviously, the single textbook approach to science education is becoming obsolete. The demands of contemporary science teaching insure an increasing adoption of the systems or multimedia approach."[7] Inference demands the preplanned and integrated use of library media and services as a compatible partner in the science systems approach.

NEA CARDINAL PRINCIPLES
FOR EDUCATIONAL CHANGE

The following premises from the NEA Cardinal Principles for Educational Change (see Chapter 2) have direct bearing on contemporary science teaching:

5. There are standards that are essential to life on a planet sometimes imperiled by the less thoughtful of its human population. A consensus needs to be reached with respect to secular "commandments" that are an expression of values chosen to serve as referents while humankind works to restore, or to husband, its resources in an overexploited environment.

20. Traditional instructional methods should be expanded to include problem-solving approaches, and their emphasis on cognition and on valuing should be renewed.

21. Interdisciplinary learning should be stressed and the art of comprehending and anticipating complex relationships should be fostered [see Example 29, Pros and Cons of Space Colonization; Example 30, A Multidisciplinary Science Mini-Unit; Example 32, Our Wonderful World of Animals; and Example 33, Our Wonderful World of Plants].

24. There is need to teach the concept of alternative futures since, lacking a desirable image of tomorrow's possible worlds, one lacks purpose, goals, and the motivating spirit of community that are needed to serve as guides to action [see Example 29, Pros and Cons of Space Colonization].
25. Instruction in subject matter fields should develop a deepening understanding of contemporary threats to the biosphere, include socially useful services in its maintenance, and communicate to youth the need for achieving balance or equilibrium between humans and their environment [see Example 30, A Multidisciplinary Science Mini-Unit; Example 31, Lesson Plan: Alternate Sources of Energy; Example 32, Our Wonderful World of Animals; and Example 33, Our Wonderful World of Plants].
27. In studying possible futures the natural and physical sciences, both in content and in methodology, should serve as illustrations of truth-validating inquiry [see Example 29, Pros and Cons of Space Colonization].

CONTEMPORARY CURRICULAR AREAS OF EMPHASIS

ALTERNATIVE FUTURES APPROACH

The National Education Association has provided science teachers with a number of publications that will help the teacher translate the premises outlined above into supportive teaching-learning experiences. *Futurism and Future Studies* by Draper L. Kauffman, Jr., identifies the key issues for the teaching of science as follows:

1. *Pros and cons of science and technology* must be understood and evaluated [Example 29, Pros and Cons of Space Colonization, is a prototype learning project addressed to this key issue].

    Scientific progress has brought unquestionable benefits . . . with medicine and communication as outstanding examples, but it has also created an appalling capacity for species self-destruction and a continually increasing rate of social change.

    The current environmental-technological base for our civilization is inherently transitory, since it depends on consuming the environment and resources which make it possible in the first place.

    Many of the social problems created by proliferating technology will require further developments in technology for their solution.

    The continued development of science and technology is essential to our survival.

    The problem is to keep tight rein on harmful technologies without, at the same time, putting deadening restrictions on the scientific research so urgently needed.

2. *Energy* is a basic technical problem science needs to solve.

    We must find an acceptable substitute for our dependence on petroleum and natural gas, which will last three decades at the most, even with conservation.

    Coal is plentiful and cheap, but new technologies are needed to extract it and burn it without unacceptable damage to the environment.

    Hydroelectric, tidal, and geothermal power are limited to specific locations and cannot contribute much of the overall energy supply.

    Atomic fission is both dirty and dangerous.

    Hydrogen fusion would be a virtually inexhaustible and relatively nonpolluting power source, but it may take 30 years or more to develop a working technology.

Solar energy is an excellent source for space heating and cooling, but both it and wind power are intermittent . . . and still too expensive to use as primary sources of electricity [see Example 31, Lesson Plan: Alternate Sources of Energy].

3. *Environmental technology* is a necessary complement to solving the energy problem.

An environmentally sound technological system for solving the energy problem must meet four basic requirements:
1. To save energy and recycling costs, all durable goods should be designed for the maximum possible lifespan and ease of recycling.
2. All non-renewable resources and all human-made compounds which are not biodegradable must be restricted to use within tightly closed recycling loops.
3. Disposal of biodegradable wastes must be carefully limited to the long-term handling capacity of the environment.
4. All natural wastes must be returned to the soil along with whatever additional minerals are needed to maintain the soil in its most fertile condition.

4. *Biological engineering* poses grave problems.

The potential exists for manipulating the genetic code from which all living organisms are constructed and, thereby, creating organisms to order.

The danger of accidentally creating an entirely new disease organism to which human beings would have no resistance is great.[8]

EXAMPLE 29 PROS AND CONS OF SPACE COLONIZATION

Gifted and Talented Program
Grade: 7 and 8
Subject: Science, Language Arts, and Social Studies
Learning Project: *Pros and Cons of Space Colonization* (Abridged)

Project Goals:
To provide learning experiences which will enable the student to perceive and to make value judgments concerning the problems involved in space colonization.

To provide learning experiences which will enable the student to develop the ability to discern all the options in making choices in society.

Teaching Objectives: Content Framework
This project has been designed to provide these basic understandings:

Isaac Asimov, writing in the *National Geographic* (July 1976), stated that "we can build space colonies . . . in the near future [which] would fulfill functions that are now fulfilled by cities on the surface of the earth."

T. A. Heppenheimer, in his book *Colonies in Space* (Harrisburg, Pa.: Stackpole, 1977), states:

Colonies in space is the next giant step for mankind, evolutionary in its impact—thousands of people living and working in attractive, earthlike space communities and eventually solving the world's energy problems. This is not fantasy, not just a vague outline of future possibilities.

Thousands of prominent individuals—scientists, industrialists, writers and editors, members of Congress—are now aware of this all-but-inevitable exciting human reality that can start becoming fact before the end of the twentieth century.

Space is mankind's new frontier. Serious and careful studies have shown that large space colonies can be built soon.

Ray Bradbury, in the introduction to *Colonies in Space*, attempts to discredit the short-sightedness of those who question spending billions on space colonization so long as poverty and want torture and enslave millions here on earth.

EXAMPLE 29 (cont.)

The U.S. Congress is vested by the U.S. Constitution with the power "to lay and collect taxes, duties, imposts and excises, to pay the debts and provide for the common defense and general welfare. . . ." In establishing the hierarchy of need, Congress must make value judgments. The question must be asked in the light of the Constitution, which needs (defense, social, economic, etc.) are of the greatest import. On what bases should value judgments be made? The complexity of today's society precludes simplistic answers.

An informed citizen who is functionally literate must be competent to:

Relate the lessons of history to man's quest for understanding and solving contemporary problems.

For example:

Excessive taxation was a contributing factor to the decline and eventual fall of the Roman Empire.

Excessive taxation was a contributing factor in precipitating the American Revolution.

Excessive taxation—property tax collection per person increased 111% in the ten-year period 1966-1976—has led to a nationwide taxpayers' revolt with the first shot being fired in California on June 6, 1978, when the California voters, by a two-to-one margin, amended the state Constitution to slash property taxes by 57% and to erect high barriers against major increases in state and local levies for years to come.

Following the revolt of the California voter on June 6, 1978, President Carter (*U.S. News and World Report*, June 19, 1978) stated: "The people of California have reflected a strong national dissatisfaction with taxes that unfairly burden middle-income taxpayers and demonstrate their impatience with the steadily increasing cost of government."

In the light of the evidence from the past, namely, that governments have toppled when taxes became oppressive, and in light of contemporary evidence of taxpayer rebellion, is it logical to "buy" Heppenheimer's prediction that space colonization will be subsidized by tax dollars before the end of the 20th century?

An informed citizen who is functionally literate must be competent to:

Make value judgments based on the effective use of critical thinking skills including:

   1. Defining the problem

   2. Developing a tentative answer; hypothesizing

      Examining and classifying available data

      Seeking relationships, drawing logical inferences

      Stating the hypothesis

   3. Testing the tentative answer

      Arranging evidence

      Analyzing evidence

   4. Developing a conclusion

      Finding meaningful patterns or relationships

      Stating the conclusion

   5. Applying the conclusion

      Testing against new evidence

      Generalizing the results.

Apply critical thinking skills when participating in a debate and when listening to a debate.

Teaching Strategies:

The class will be introduced to the thinking of Asimov, Heppenheimer, and Bradbury as an orientation to this learning project.

EXAMPLE 29 (cont.)

The class will react to the possibility of space colonization in the near future.

At the conclusion of this initial discussion, the class will be led to make the observation that before a value judgment can be made research must be undertaken, the pros and cons debated, and an honest appraisal of the facts ascertained.

In cooperation with the English teacher the class explores the procedures, rules, and regulations for preparing and presenting a debate, in order that the members of the class can prepare and present a debate on space colonization and then make informed value judgments.

EXAMPLE 30 A MULTIDISCIPLINARY SCIENCE MINI-UNIT

Mini-unit: The Scientific Method in Theory and Application (revised)
Subject: Science, Social Studies, and Speech
Grade: 9

Goal: To enable the student to understand, to utilize, and to appreciate the scientific method of problem solving.

Teaching Objectives:

To provide learning experiences which will enable the student to discover how scientists by solving problems have changed man's way of living.

To provide opportunities for the student to question, observe, compare, formulate hypotheses, experiment, employ inductive and deductive reasoning, draw conclusions, and organize and communicate findings.

To provide opportunities for the student to work as an individual, as a member of a small group, and as a member of the total class.

Procedure: (The unit is reproduced here only in part.)

I. A committee of students, "the teaching committee," shares with the classroom teacher and the library media specialist the responsibility for planning and for teaching this unit.

A. One week prior to the introduction of this unit to the class the teaching committee, all of whom have volunteered for this job, work in the library media center under the guidance of the library media specialist making tentative plans for the introduction, the development, and the culmination of this unit.

1. The library media specialist explains the role of the teaching committee.
2. Committee members volunteer to be responsible for special assignments such as:

Introducing the unit to the class.

Identifying and explaining basic terminology.

Previewing, selecting, and presenting to the class both print and nonprint media.

Designing and producing transparencies.

Leading class discussions.

Coordinating the work of the separate committees as well as individual students.

II. Class is introduced to the unit in the library media center.

A. The library media specialist explains the purpose of the procedure for studying this unit.

B. Members of the teaching committee introduce basic terminology and concepts such as:

1. Science is a special way man investigates the natural world in which he lives.
2. Science is usable and classified information.

C. Chairman of the teaching committee asks for volunteers to be responsible for finding the answers to the following:

1. What is science?

EXAMPLE 30 (cont.)

2. When did man develop science?
3. Can science help man solve problems?
4. What is superstition?
5. What is scientific evidence?
6. What is fact? What is a concept?
7. What is inductive reasoning?
8. What is deductive reasoning?
9. What is a hypothesis? How does a scientist arrive at a hypothesis?
10. What is research?
11. What is the difference between science and technology?

III. The class works in the library media center building background knowledge.
  A. The science teacher and the library media specialist work with individuals and groups as requested.
  B. The teaching committee makes arrangements for students to preview motion pictures, filmstrips, etc.

IV. A member of the teaching committee presents the motion picture *The Nature of Science: Obtaining Facts* (Coronet) and leads the discussion following the presentation of the film.
  A. Class discusses the following:
    1. How scientific facts are proven.
    2. Is astrology a science?
    3. Why are people superstitious?
    4. Why do newspapers and magazines include horoscopes?
    5. Does advertising on TV and in newspapers and magazines capitalize on human gullibility?
    6. The Romans had a saying, "Let the buyer beware"; does this slogan apply today?
  B. The five steps basic to applying the scientific method are reviewed and examples of how each step is of equal importance are given.
    1. Observation—curiosity, imagination, perseverance, accuracy, and patience are essential.
      a. Luther Burbank, as a child, used his power of observation to begin his search for improving food-giving plants.
      b. Ephraim McDowell, pioneer surgeon, based his belief that abdominal surgery would not be fatal upon his observation that human tissue in the human extremities was capable of regeneration and healing.
    2. Hypothesis—making a guess about the unknown based on available facts.
      a. William Harvey, who discovered how blood is circulated, first observed that the valves in an animal heart and in a human heart were like little doors which were one-way openings. He asked himself why these doors would not permit blood to flow back and forth in the veins; searching for the answer to this question caused him to discover how blood is pumped from one side of the heart, through the lungs, through the arteries, to all parts of the body, and finally back to the heart again.
      b. Thomas Edison, one of the greatest inventors the world has ever known, made countless scientific breakthroughs because of his uncanny ability to make educated guesses based on observable facts.
    3. Experiment—testing the hypothesis.
      a. Pierre and Marie Curie, discoverers of radium, laboriously isolated one gram of radium salts from eight tons of pitchblende and determined the atomic weights and properties of radium and polonium. They refused to patent their processes or otherwise to profit commercially from their discovery.
      b. George Washington Carver, agricultural chemist, experimented with agricultural products trying to discover new uses for common crops such as peanuts, sweet potatoes, soybeans, and cotton. Through his efforts hundreds of new uses were discovered for food crops and new revenue sources were opened to the farmer; chemurgy, the branch of chemistry

EXAMPLE 30 (cont.)

dealing with the use of farm and forest products for purposes other than food and clothing, came into being. Carver refused to patent any discovery and made all of his discoveries free for the taking.

4. Theory—the hypothesis is proven to be correct by experimentation.
   a. Charles Darwin, English naturalist, through the scientific method proved the theory of evolution in both plants and animals.
   b. Thomas Malthus, an English minister, advanced the theory that living beings multiply at such a rate that the world cannot possibly supply enough food for them all and that it is, therefore, necessary for large numbers of animals to die—and people, too, through disease and wars—to keep the world population in balance.
5. Proof—the ability of the theory to stand up under any test which anyone at all can think up.
   a. Statistical proof of the effectiveness of miracle drugs validates the claim that penicillin can destroy or sharply check the growth of various harmful bacteria such as staphylococci, gonococci, and pneumococci.
   b. The population explosion, which now has reached the alarming proportion of doubling each 35 years, gives credence to the theory of Thomas Malthus, advanced in 1798 in "An Essay on the Principle of Population."
C. The following devices are employed to test student power of observation.
   1. A student is sent from the room and the class attempts to describe in detail what he or she is wearing.
   2. After viewing the photograph "Animal Camouflage," which is projected via the opaque projector, the class lists all of the animals they are able to recall; they are also asked to describe the environmental details of the picture.
   3. A tray containing 20 common articles is passed from student to student; each student tries to list the 20 articles five minutes after viewing the tray.
V. The class views the motion picture *Galileo* (Coronet), and a member of the teaching committee generates discussion by asking the following questions:
   A. What were the causes which forced Galileo to retract his statement that the earth moves around the sun? Should he or should he not have retracted his statement?
   B. Jonathan Swift, a seventeenth-century satirist, once made the statement, "When a true genius appears in the world, you may know him by this sign, that the dunces are all in confederacy against him." Is this human failing evidenced in the trial of Galileo?
   C. Michael Servetus, a Spaniard, was condemned as a heretic and burned at the stake in 1553 because he presented arguments against Aristotle's ideas that only heavenly matter could move in a circle and that everything else had a beginning and an end. What is a heretic? Why were heretics accused of being in league with the devil? What was the Spanish Inquisition? Is this not a good example of the contrast between supposition and scientific evidence?
VI. The class views the motion picture *Health Heroes* (Coronet), and a member of the teaching committee introduces each of the five students responsible for further elaboration on contributions of the five scientists—Pasteur, Lister, Jenner, Leeuwenhoek, Koch—depicted in the motion picture.
VII. Under the leadership of a member of the teaching committee the class discusses the concept of the scientist as a human being. The following topics are developed and explored:
   A. What are the characteristics of a scientist?
   B. What is the concept of open-mindedness?
   C. What competencies must a scientist have?
   D. Can a scientist ever stop learning?
   E. A scientist can suggest better ways of doing things but he or she cannot force people to accept his or her recommendations.
   F. What are the career possibilities in the field of science and technology?
   G. True scientists rate their efforts in terms of bettering society rather than achieving financial gain for themselves.

EXAMPLE 30 (cont.)

VIII. The class discusses evidence in today's world that human beings still refuse to think scientifically. A member of the teaching committee introduces the theme of human indifference to scientific truth by providing a demonstration:
   A. Members of the class vote whether or not filter-tipped cigarettes trap all of the nicotine in a cigarette.
   B. Using the mechanical smoker, a student demonstrates that a large amount of nicotine is still trapped in the lungs when a filter-tipped cigarette is smoked.
   C. The January 1979 Report of the U.S. Surgeon General on the Harmful Effects of Tobacco Smoking is studied.
      1. Smokers are at least 20 times as likely to succumb to lung cancer as non-smokers.
      2. Cigarette smokers are from 6 to 10 times as likely to die of cancer of the larynx as nonsmokers.
   D. The 1979 statistical analysis of heart attack death ratios released by the American Cancer Society is studied.
      1. Mortality rate from coronary heart disease among men 40–49 years old was 5.51 times as great from heavy smokers as for nonsmokers.
      2. Mortality rate from coronary heart disease among women 40–49 years old was 3.31 times as great for heavy smokers as for nonsmokers.
IX. As a culminating activity students each write a paragraph explaining why they believe the scientist of their choice has made the most significant contribution to man's scientific knowledge.
   A. Each student shares with the class his or her reasons for selecting the scientist he or she considers to have made the most significant contribution to man's advancing civilization.
   B. On a time line, the class records each scientist nominated as worthy of a Nobel Prize for science.

EXAMPLE 31 LESSON PLAN: ALTERNATE SOURCES OF ENERGY*

Lesson No. 4 (abridged)
Subject: Alternate Sources of Energy
Assignment: Report on at least five alternate energy sources.
Objective: To enable the student, with the aid of lecture and references, to write a short (one-half to one page) report on at least five alternate sources of energy (including history, present use, operation, and future use) which will be evaluated by the instructor.
   I. Review of previous lesson
      A. Questions
      B. Reminder of assignment on pollution due tomorrow
      C. Analyze fuel-burning exercise
   II. Alternate energies
      A. Developed from fuel shortage
      B. Developing technology
      C. Future importance
         1. Careers
   III. Basic alternate sources
      A. Solar
      B. Wind
      C. Geothermal
      D. Gravitational
      E. Methanol
      F. Hydrogen and alcohol (fuel cells)

*From Frederick E. Posthuma, *Energy and Education: Teaching Alternatives* (Washington, D.C.: NEA, 1978), pp. 132–135.

EXAMPLE 31 (cont.)

IV. Solar
   A. The sun the source of all energy
   B. Two days' production equals energy of all remaining oil, gas, and coal
   C. Historic use
      1. 1878 World's Fair in Paris
      2. Farmers drying crops
   D. Categories
      1. Photovoltaic cells
         a. Works on chemical reaction to produce electricity
         b. Utilized in space
         c. Expensive
         d. Inefficient (10–25%)
      2. Collector panels
         a. Liquid
            (1) Sun's rays heat liquid inside panels
            (2) "Greenhouse effect"
         b. Air (overhead)
            (1) Sun heats air flowing through panel
            (2) No problems with freeze-up in the winter
         c. Basic cost
            (1) $4 to $7 per square foot
            (2) Whole panels—$144 to $600
            (3) Controls—$700 to $900 (including storage)
            (4) Total system costs two and one-half to three times as much as con-ventional heating system
            (5) Cost beginning to decrease as panels go into mass production and oil and gas prices continue to rise
            (6) Danger of fraud
   E. Materials
      1. Aluminum
         a. Corrodes easily unless coated
      2. Steel
         a. Corrodes easily and is heavy
      3. Copper
         a. Costly but conducts heat well
V. Wind
   A. Development of ancient technology
      1. Used for pumping water and grinding grain
   B. Varies from place to place; speeds irregular
   C. Small-scale generation tested throughout country
      1. Feasible in remote areas
      2. Feasible in areas with average winds of seven miles per hour or more
      3. Units still costly and require substantial capital layouts
      4. More experimentation needed
   D. Large-scale generation being studied and done
      1. Problems
         a. Cost
         b. Blade angles or pitch
         c. Height of construction necessary to fully utilize winds
         d. Nonconstant production of electricity
            (1) Storage a big problem
            (2) Uses low discharge batteries
VI. Geothermal
   A. Tapping earth's energy
      1. Reservoirs inside earth of hot brine or steam
      2. Utilized to run turbines

EXAMPLE 31 (cont.)

B. Natural steam field in California
   1. Could satisfy more than 40% of electrical needs of city the size of San Francisco
C. Problems
   1. Inefficient conversion
   2. Few natural steam fields in the United States
   3. Cost
   4. Turbines tend to deteriorate more quickly because of brine solution composition

VII. Gravitational
   A. Utilizes rotation of earth to produce energy
   B. Basically uses tides
      1. Incoming tides stored in container (e.g., dam)
      2. Water flows out through turbines that run generators as energy is needed
   C. Mechanical device at sea converts bobbing of waves into usable energy
   D. Problems
      1. Costly and still very experimental
      2. Geographical locations

VIII. Methanol
   A. Gas made from municipal wastes through process of anaerobic digestion
      1. As wastes decay bacterial actions produce gas that can be burned
   B. Advantages
      1. Easily stored
      2. Does not cause dieseling or backfiring in automobiles
      3. Nonpolluting
      4. Wastes obtained almost anywhere
      5. Byproduct usable as manure
   C. Disadvantages
      1. Extremely high octane
         a. Octane rating of 120 or more
         b. Highly flammable when mixed in proper proportions of air
      2. Can supply only limited amount of energy

IX. Hydrogen and alcohol
   A. Hydrogen
      1. Produced from water
         a. Clean burning
      2. Expensive to produce
      3. Storage and transportation problems
      4. Can be converted into methanol
   B. Alcohol
      1. Clean burning
      2. Expensive to produce
      3. Nonpolluting

X. Other sources
   A. Temperature gradient of sea
   B. Fuel cells
   C. Magnetohydrodynamic
      1. Pulverizing coal under tremendous temperature and passing it through magnetic field to cause an electromotive force to result

XI. Summary
   A. Reminder of assignment

Energy and Education: Teaching Alternatives, another NEA publication edited by Frederick E. Posthuma, contains informative articles on all aspects of the teaching of the energy question. The degree and comprehensiveness of information contained in this book are indicated by the following list, which has been reproduced from the Contents of the book:*

Energy, by Ernest L. Boyer

Teaching About the Nuclear Power Controversy by Simulation, by Thomas Tanner

Our School-Made Solar Project, by Jerry Silver and Kurt Johnson

Investigating the Aerosol Issue, by William C. Ritz

Six Ways to Reduce Energy Consumption, Office of Consumer Affairs and U.S. Department of Commerce, National Bureau of Standards

Solid Waste—Individual Citizen Action Check List for the Home and Community, Citizens Advisory Council on Environmental Quality

Leisure and the Energy Crisis, by Max Kaplan

Net Energy: Figuring the True Yield, by John W. Moore and Elizabeth A. Moore

Some Guidelines for Energy Programs, by King C. Kryger

Energy Teaching Centers, by Lois E. Kenick

Where Does America Get Its Energy?—Energy Conservation Activities for Young Learners, Office of Conservation Education, Federal Energy Administration

Mini-Unit 3: Which Source of Energy Is Best for Heating My Community?, Energy-Environment Mini-Unit Guide

Mini-Unit 4: Energy and Its Natural Sources, Energy-Environment Mini-Unit Guide

Energy Curriculum Lesson Plans, by Fredrick E. Posthuma

Energy Resource List, by Fredrick E. Posthuma

Science, technology, and society are one and inseparable; therefore, an interdisciplinary approach is requisite to dealing with the key issues delineated above. A life survival skill, shared in responsibility by all those who teach, is being able to recognize that the future is predetermined by the present (see Fig. 6). Today's society is so complex that there are not, and never will be, simplistic answers to problems posed by science, technology, and society itself. The National Council for the Social Studies has endorsed the following concept in its publication *Science and Society: Knowing, Teaching, Learning,* edited by Cheryl Charles and Bob Samples:

> Nature and culture, science and society, are intertwined. They are part of a larger whole. We as social studies/social science educators have countless opportunities in a given year's instructional program to choose skills and topics that strengthen student awareness of this interrelatedness. Such emphasis can be placed without detriment to the goals of social studies curricula and without neglect of essential concepts in the social sciences and social studies.
>
> Jonas Salk tells us, with power and conviction, that a shift toward pluralism, toward a cultural transformation in values, and towards survival is probably encoded within our genes. He argues that nature has sculptured survival and honored existence into our genetic fiber.
>
> However, Salk believes we have choices to make, choices that will affect the quality of life. . . .
>
> We are, with each thought we have and with each action we take, helping to create our personal future and the future of those who follow. The gifts and burdens of science and technology are ours—and will multiply.

---

*From Frederick E. Posthuma, *Energy and Education: Teaching Alternatives* (Washington, D.C.: National Education Association, 1978), p. 5.

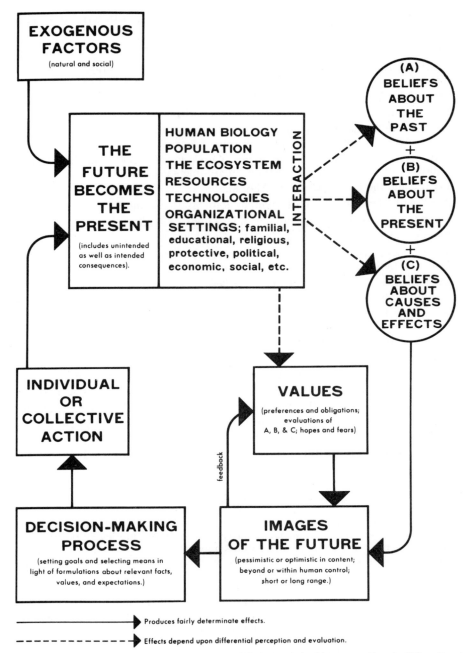

FIGURE 6. Cybernetic-Decisional Model of Social Change. From *The Sociology of the Future* by Wendell Bell and James A. Mau, editors. © 1971 by Russell Sage Foundation, New York. Reprinted by permission.

Social studies teachers can make a profound contribution to the present—and future—by leading the way in bringing science to life for young people. Science is life. Society is life. Social studies teachers are uniquely prepared to bring the two together in instructional settings, and to do so for the future and quality of all life on this planet [see Example 29, Pros and Cons of Space Colonization, and Example 31, Lesson Plan: Alternate Sources of Energy].[9]

RELEVANCE AND REALITY

Special importance must be assigned to the teaching of science on the elementary level. If students are ever to become committed to meeting the scientific, technological, and social problems of the future and not be overwhelmed by the task, they must have a thorough grounding in the mysteries and mystique of science. Students must at a tender and impressionable age be introduced to the enchantments, the beauty, and the marvels of the natural world in which they live. In their hands lies the hope of bringing science and society, culture and nature, into balance and harmony. In a very real sense the elementary-school child of the present *is* the future.

The library media specialist has a significant instructional role in bringing depth, breadth, and relevance to the science curriculum. Limiting science education to a single textbook is obsolete.[10] NSTA recommends the multimedia approach as a means of making science learning more lifelike. Without logistical assistance from the library media specialist, the classroom teacher does not have the time to search out the large number and variety of media needed in the modern science program. For example, the *NICEM Index to Environmental Studies* (Los Angeles, Calif.: National Information Center for Educational Media, 1977), brings together a comprehensive bibliographical listing of 26,000 nonbook media titles! Even the purchase of a commercially prepared multimedia kit is not always the answer. Instructional programs of excellence reflect teacher-originated and customized teaching and learning experiences which in turn require instructional media over, above, and beyond even the most excellent of kits. Example 32, Our Wonderful World of Animals, and Example 33, Our Wonderful World of Plants, are prototypes of learning projects that require a wealth of print and nonprint materials in addition to the contents of the two Bowmar Nature Series multimedia kits, excellent though these may be. These two learning projects are also prototypes of science instruction that provide "an environment rich with resources that excite children and assure their curiosity" and "offer opportunities for learners to wonder, to explore, to raise questions, to find answers to questions, to form generalizations, to create."[11]

EXAMPLE 32   OUR WONDERFUL WORLD OF ANIMALS*

Gifted and Talented Program (GATE)
Learning Project: The Wonderful World of Animals
Grade: 2
Goal: To quicken within the student an insatiable curiosity about the mysteries of animal behavior and to foster an enduring compassionate concern for the welfare of all animals.

---

*While this learning project is designed primarily for the Gifted and Talented Enrichment Program, many of the learning activities could be successfully shared with students in the regular classroom.

EXAMPLE 32 (cont.)

Teaching Objectives:

This project has been designed and structured to provide opportunities for the students:

To explore animal behavior—adaptations, life cycles and styles, and habitats—with scientific accuracy, wonder, challenge, and delight.

To share with fellow GATE students and with classmates what he/she has learned about animal behavior.

To explore career opportunities in the fields of animal study and care.

To become acquainted with Aileen Fisher as a naturalist and as an author.

To perceive the difference between fact and fantasy.

To discover the variety and kinds of books shelved in school library in the 500s and 600s dealing with animals.

To read, to view, to listen, to think, and to communicate thought accurately and effectively with wonder and delight.

Teaching Strategies and Methods:

No time limitations are imposed on this project. Number of students in the GATE group coupled with student interest are the factors determining the duration of the project, whether it be two weeks, two months, or longer.

A basic part of the orientation to this project is to explore with the students the advantage to be gained by sharing not only with fellow GATE students but with their classmates what they have learned about the wonderful world of animals.

After group orientation to the project, each student is encouraged to explore as widely as he/she wishes.

Procedural Outline:

I. Group orientation to the project
  A. The students explore the meaning of the project title "The Wonderful World of Animals."
    1. *Wonderful:* causing wonder; marvelous; remarkable
    2. *World:* all of certain parts, people, or things of the earth
  B. The students apply the two definitions and make a list of examples such as:
    1. *Wonderful*
      Using the card catalog, discover the titles of books beginning with the word WONDERFUL. For example:

      The Wonderful Egg by Dahlov Ipcar

      Wonderful Flight to the Mushroom Planet by Eleanor Cameron

      Wonderful Wizard of Oz by Frank Baum

      Wonderful World of Cats by Beth Brown

      Wonderful World of Dogs by Beth Brown

      Wonderful World of Horses by Ned Hoopes

    2. *World*
      Using the card catalog, discover the titles of books beginning with the word WORLD. For example:

      World of Christopher Robin by A. A. Milne

      World of Pooh by A. A. Milne

      World of the Ant by David Costello

      World of the Opossum by James Keefe

      World of the Prairie by David Costello

  C. The students pool their impressions of the television program "The Wild, Wild World of Animals."
    1. What kinds of animal programs have they seen?

EXAMPLE 32 (cont.)

2. What kinds of information about an animal does "The Wild, Wild World of Animals" provide?
  D. The students compile a list of kinds of information they would like to discover about animals ("The Ways of Animals" list).
    1. This list will be used as a guide throughout this project.
    2. The list will be expanded by the students to reflect new kinds of insight gained during this project.
II. Exploring the multimedia kit "The Ways of Animals" (Bowmar Nature Series)
  A. Before the kit is opened, the students speculate as to the meaning of the title "The Ways of Animals."
  B. Upon opening the kit, the students discover 10 books, 10 filmstrips, and 10 cassettes.
  C. The students discover that Aileen Fisher is the author of each of the following 10 books:
    1. *Animal Disguises*
    2. *Animal Houses*
    3. *Animal Jackets*
    4. *Filling the Bill*
    5. *Going Places*
    6. *No Accounting for Tastes*
    7. *Now That Days Are Colder*
    8. *Sleepy Heads*
    9. *Tail Twisters*
    10. *"You Don't Look Like Your Mother," Said the Robin to the Fawn*
  D. The students discover that a sound filmstrip matches each of the books in the kit.
III. The students as a group read the book *Animal Disguises*, and then see the matching filmstrip.
  A. The students share their ideas gained from the book and filmstrip.
    1. An animal can blend into his surroundings so well that it "may cause you to blink or trick you to think he isn't there at all."
    2. An animal's color and shape can help protect it from its enemies.
    3. When an animal's color or shape blends with its surroundings, we say the animal is camouflaged.
    4. Some animals have colorings that mimic the appearance of animals its enemies avoid. This kind of protection is called mimicry.
  B. The students begin a science word list.
    1. The words *camouflage* and *mimicry* are listed and the students define the meaning of each of the terms.
    2. The students will each take responsibility for discovering important new science words in each of the remaining nine books by Aileen Fisher and in each of the accompanying filmstrips.
  C. Each student selects one or more of the books to read and then shares with the GATE group.
    1. In preparation, the group reviews the list of "The Ways of Animals" previously compiled.

      Each student is responsible for identifying the specific "ways" found in the Aileen Fisher book he or she has read.

      Each student is responsible for adding to the list new "ways" he or she has discovered.

    2. Each student, upon completion of the book, previews and studies the matching filmstrip.

      Important concepts are identified.

      New words are listed and defined.

      In preparation for sharing the filmstrip with the GATE group each student is encouraged to search out other media: books, pictures, filmstrips, and/or slides.

EXAMPLE 32 (cont.)

IV. If the classroom teacher wishes, the GATE students will share their understanding of "The Ways of Animals" with the class.
  A. When scheduled to do so by the classroom teacher, each student will show a filmstrip and provide the explanation.
    1. Prior to projecting the filmstrip, the student will introduce new terms.
    2. Following the presentation, the student will answer questions, mention other sources of information, and offer to help the class members locate materials.
  B. If the classroom teacher wishes, the GATE students will organize and maintain a learning center, "The Ways of Animals," in the classroom.
V. The GATE students as individuals pursue their exploration of animal behavior.
  A. Using a life science concept learning guide, the students will categorize the information under the following headings:

1. Food	7. Growth
2. Shelter	8. Change
3. Coverings	9. Dependency
4. Rest	10. Interdependency
5. Protection	11. Adaptations
6. Movement	12. Does this animal live in or near our community?

  B. If the classroom teacher wishes, the GATE students will continue to share with their classmates new information gained.
VI. The GATE students search out other books written by Aileen Fisher.
  A. By checking the card catalog in the school library, they discover the following:
    1. *Cricket in a Thicket*
    2. *Going Barefoot*
    3. *In the Woods, in the Meadow, in the Sky*
    4. *Listen, Rabbit*
    5. *Where Does Everyone Go?*
  B. As part of the Reading Club (Bookworms) activities, the students read and discuss Aileen Fisher
    1. As a naturalist
    2. As a poet
    3. As an author
    NOTE: If the students have not been introduced to the sound filmstrip set "How to Grow Bookworms" (Eye Gate House), several of the filmstrips can be introduced here. For example:
      Why We Read
      How to Share Our Reading
    The Bookworm bookmarks, book title summary chart, reading record booklet, and membership pins (Library Products)* can also be introduced at this time.
  C. If the classroom teacher wishes, the GATE students can share with their classmates, either in the library or the classroom, the Wonderful World of Aileen Fisher.
VII. As a culminating activity, the students explore a number of avenues under the heading "What more do we need to know?"
  A. Does the *Childcraft* reference set have additional information?
    1. Volume 5 is entitled *About Animals*—the contents lists the following:

	Page
The Animal Kingdom	4
It's a Mammal	28
It's a Bird	50
It's a Fish	68
It's a Reptile	82
It's an Amphibian	98
Many-Legged Creatures	110
The World of the Sea	130

*Library Products, Box 130, Sturgis, Mich. 49091, tel. 616-651-5076.

EXAMPLE 32 (cont.)

The Hidden World	148
Staying Alive	158
Animal Ways	172
The Animals' World	190
Living Together	214
Animals of Long Ago	214
People and Animals	232
Domestic Animals	256
Vanishing Animals	294
Favorite Animals	304
Hard Words	322

   2. *Childcraft Annuals*
      About Animals—1971
      Animals in Danger—1974

B. Does the Compton's *Precyclopedia* reference set have additional information?
   1. Volume 1 contains the following:

Animals—Can You See It?	74–79
The Special Long Sleep	80–83
A Tale About Tails	84–87
How to Catch a Giraffe	88–91
Animal Partners	92–97
Insect Castle Builders	98–103

   2. Volume 12 contains the following:

Choosing a Pet	74–81
The Pets in the Dream	82–83
Which Dog?	84–85

C. Does *Disney's Wonderful World of Knowledge* reference set have additional information? (Attention is called to the joining of the two words, *Wonderful* and *World*, in the title of this set.)
   1. Volume 1 contains the following:

Animals—In Jungles and Forests	9–33
Animals—Beasts of the Open Country	34–53
With Water, Ice, and Snow	55–69
A Mountain Peak Is Home	71–79
Life at the Poles	81–91
They Live in Water but Need Air	93–99
They Who See Best in the Dark	101–105
The Animals Who Live with Us	107–122

   2. Volume 6 contains the following:

Birds in Flight	9–59
Amphibians and Reptiles	61–77
Fish: A World of Blue Light	79–99
Insects	101–123

   3. Volume 12 contains the following:

Man's Best Friends	39–59

D. What career opportunities are there in the field of working with and/or taking care of animals?
   1. The filmstrip series "Working with Animals" (Troll) introduces a number of

EXAMPLE 32 (cont.)

careers in the care and training of animals. The following sound filmstrips explain the skills, duties, and environment of each career:

Animal Careers for You

Canine Control Officer

Pet Shop Worker

Veterinarian and Aides

Park Naturalist

Humane Educator

2. The following books introduce a variety of careers working with animals:

Animal Doctors by Carla Greene

At the Pet Hospital by Jane Hefflefinger

Careers in Animal Care by Christopher Benson

Careers in Conservation by Christopher Benson

I Know an Animal Doctor by Ckika Iritani

I Want to Be a Zoo Keeper by Carla Greene

I Want to Be an Animal Doctor by Carla Greene

What Can She Be? A Veterinarian by Gloria Goldreich

3. Interviewing community friends who work with animals is a good way to find out about careers working with animals.

How do you prepare for an interview?

How do you schedule an interview?

What questions do you ask?

How do you thank a person for his/her time?

How can you share the information with your fellow GATE group or with your classmates?

E. What agencies protect animals from neglect and/or cruelty?
1. If you want to locate information on animal care in the yellow pages of the telephone book, under what headings would you look?

Using the yellow pages index, see if you can discover people and agencies that care for and protect animals.

Two headings give information: "Animal Hospitals" and "Animal Shelters."

2. Check the animal hospitals and see how many you can find that are located near where you live.
3. Check the animal shelters list; carefully write the name of the shelter, the address, and the telephone number on an index card.
4. Make a list of questions to ask the person in charge of each shelter.

Be sure to ask how the agency gets money to support its work.

Be sure to ask if the agency has booklets which will explain its work.

Be sure to ask if the agency will send someone from the agency to talk to the GATE group, and/or your class, and/or your school.

5. How can you help protect animals from neglect and cruelty?

Could you sponsor a "Be Kind to Animals" week?

What could you do to teach and to demonstrate kindness?

How could you get your parents, friends, and neighbors to take part in your special "Be Kind to Animals" week?

VIII. Field experiences for the GATE students to participate in and, if the classroom teacher wishes, to share with their classmates.

EXAMPLE 32 (cont.)

A visit to:

The aviary

An animal hospital

A pet shop

The zoo

IX. Discovering the wonderful world of animals in:
  A. Books of fiction and fantasy such as:
    1. Walter Brooks, *Freddy the Detective*
    2. Marcia Brown, *Once a Mouse* and *Puss in Boots*
    3. Thornton Burgess, *Old Mother West Wind*
    4. Ruth and Latrobe Carroll, *Tough Enough*
    5. Louise Fatio, *Happy Lion*
    6. Marjorie Flack, *Walter the Lazy Mouse*
    7. Jean Fritz, *How to Read a Rabbit*
    8. Hugh Lofting, *Dr. Dolittle*
    9. A. A. Milne, *Winnie-the-Pooh*
    10. Lilian Moore, *Little Raccoon and the Thing in the Pool*
    11. Clare Newberry, *Marshmallow*
    12. Beatrix Potter, *The Tale of Peter Rabbit*
    13. Hans Rey, *Curious George*
    14. George Selden, *Cricket in Times Square*
    15. Tomi Ungerer, *Emilie*
    16. E. B. White, *Charlotte's Web*
  B. Poetry such as:
    1. William Cole, *I Went to the Animal Fair*
    2. Aileen Fisher, *Listen, Rabbit*
    3. Leland Jacobs, *Animal Antics in Limerick Land* and *Poetry for Bird Watchers*
    4. Lilian Moore, *Little Raccoon and Poems from the Woods*
  C. Songs such as:
    1. "Frog Went A-Courtin'"
    2. "Here Comes Peter Cottontail"
    3. "Old Dog Tray"
    4. "Rudolph the Red-Nosed Reindeer"
    5. "Talk to the Animals"
    6. "Who's Afraid of the Big Bad Wolf?"
  D. Story prints such as:
    1. "The Baby Show" by Margaret Ross
    2. "Bedtime" by Margaret Ross
    3. "Benjamin Bunny" by Beatrix Potter
    4. "Goodnight Time" by Molly Brett
    5. "Jemima Puddle-Duck" by Beatrix Potter
    6. "Mickey Mouse" by Walt Disney
       NOTE: Many of the Disney animal characters are to be found in the 12-volume
       reference set, *Disney's Wonderful World of Knowledge.*
    7. "Peter Rabbit" by Beatrix Potter
    8. "The Village Shop" by Margaret Ross
  E. Study prints such as:
    1. "Farm and Ranch Animals" (SVE)
    2. "Pets" (SVE)
    3. "Zoo Animals" (SVE)
X. Special reinforcing activities for the GATE students and, if the classroom teacher wishes, for their classmates.
  A. Study the book *Which Is Which?* by Solveig Russell and learn how to tell the difference between:
    1. Butterflies and moths
    2. Arabian and Bactrian camels

EXAMPLE 32 (cont.)

3. Bees and wasps
4. Land snails and slugs
5. African and Indian elephants
6. Monkeys and apes
7. Toads and frogs
8. Beavers and muskrats
9. Alligators and crocodiles
10. Seals and sea lions

B. Make a list of the strange things that animals, birds, fish, insects, and reptiles do. Have a contest to see who in the GATE group or in the class can identify the animal, bird, fish, insect, or reptile you are describing. The following books by Leonora Hornblow will help you start your list of strange things:
1. *Animals Do the Strangest Things*
2. *Birds Do the Strangest Things*
3. *Fish Do the Strangest Things*
4. *Insects Do the Strangest Things*
5. *Reptiles Do the Strangest Things*

C. Make bird feeders and bird shelters to help your feathered friends over the winter. The following book has a number of suggestions: *Bird Feeders and Shelters You Can Make* by Ted Pettit.

D. Form a committee to discover animal programs to be presented on television. This committee will be responsible for alerting the GATE group and, if the classroom teaches wishes, the class each Monday as to the scheduled animal program during that week.

THE WAYS OF ANIMALS

Student _____   Date _____

The Name of the Animal I Learned About Is _____
This Is What I Learned About the Behavior of This Animal:

Food _____
_____
_____

Shelter _____
_____
_____

Coverings _____
_____
_____

Rest _____
_____
_____

Protection _____
_____
_____

Movement _____
_____
_____

Growth _____
_____
_____

Change _____
_____
_____

EXAMPLE 32 (cont.)

Dependency _____

_____

_____

Interdependency _____

_____

_____

Adaptation _____

_____

_____

Does this animal live in our community? _____

EXAMPLE 33   OUR WONDERFUL WORLD OF PLANTS*

Gifted and Talented Program (GATE)
Learning Project: Our Wonderful World of Plants
Grade: 2–3
Goal: To quicken within the student an insatiable curiosity about the mysteries of the world of plants and an abiding appreciation of the beauty and order of the world of plants.

Teaching Objectives:
This project has been designed and structured to provide opportunities for the students:

To explore the world of plants—varieties, characteristics, life cycles, adaptations and habitats—with scientific accuracy, wonder, challenge, and delight.

To share with fellow GATE students and with classmates what has been learned about the ways of plants.

To explore career opportunities in the fields of plant study, propagation, and care.

To become acquainted with Millicent Selsam as a naturalist and as an author of science books for children.

To discover the variety and kinds of books dealing with plants that are available in the school library media center.

To summarize what has been learned in the previous unit, Our Wonderful World of Animals, together with what has been learned in this unit, Our Wonderful World of Plants, by organizing a student nature guide.

To read, to view, to listen, to think, and to communicate thought accurately, effectively, and creatively.

Teaching Strategies and Methods:
No time limitations are imposed on this project. Number of students in the GATE group coupled with student interest are the factors determining the duration of the project, whether it be two weeks, two months, or longer.

A basic part of the orientation to this project is to explore with the students the advantage to be gained by sharing not only with fellow GATE students but with their classmates what they have learned about the wonderful world of plants.

After group orientation to the project, each student is encouraged to explore as widely as he or she wishes.

Procedural Outline:
    I. Group orientation to the project.
        A. The students view the sound filmstrip *The Bears' Nature Guide: Almost Everything Small Bears and Kids Need to Know about . . . the Animals, the Plants, the Earth Itself* (Random House).

*While this learning project is designed primarily for the Gifted and Talented Enrichment Program, many of the learning activities could be successfully shared with students in the regular classroom.

EXAMPLE 33 (cont.)

1. This serves as a review of the learnings gained from the unit Our Wonderful World of Animals.
2. It serves, also, as an introduction to the world of plants.

  B. The students read the book *The Bears' Nature Guide,* and explore the possibility of each student's making a nature guide to record his or her own observations and thoughts about the world of nature.

II. As an introduction to the unit, the students read *A First Look at the World of Plants* by Millicent E. Selsam and Joyce Hunt (New York: Walker, 1978).

  A. The students become acquainted with the joint authors.

  B. Checking the card catalog in the school library, the students discover the following books by Selsam and/or Hunt:

1. *A First Look at Flowers*
2. *A First Look at Leaves*
3. *Mimosa, the Sensitive Plant*
4. *Popcorn*
5. *The Tomato and Other Fruit Vegetables*
6. *Vegetables from Stems and Leaves*

  C. Reading any one of the above books introduces the students to the following concepts:

1. Any living thing that is not an animal is a plant.
2. Some plants have roots, stems, and leaves; some do not.
3. Some plants have flowers; some do not.
4. Some plants are green; some are not.
5. Some plants are so small that they can only be seen under a microscope.
6. Bacteria are the tiniest plants in the world; each plant is a single cell.
7. Bacteria get their food from other plants and animals.
8. Algae are almost as small as bacteria; chlorophyll makes algae and other plants green.
9. Liverworts and mosses are called bryophytes; they have no real roots, stems, or leaves.
10. Fungi are not green like algae, liverworts, and mosses; they have no roots, stems, or leaves.
11. Mushrooms are a common type of fungus.
12. Puffballs are fungi that are round like balls.
13. Molds are the fungi you see growing on bread, fruit, cheese, and sometimes leather.
14. Ferns have real roots, stems, and leaves; they form new plants from spores just as mosses and fungi do.
15. Gymnosperms have roots, stems, and leaves like ferns; they produce seeds instead of spores.
16. Angiosperms are flowering plants; their seeds have a covering called a fruit.
17. To tell angiosperms apart you have to look at the leaves, the flowers, and the fruits.
18. Any part of a plant that has seeds in it is called a fruit.

  D. The students summarize what they have learned in their *Nature Guide.*

III. The students explore the multimedia kit "The Ways of Plants" (Bowmar Nature Series).

  A. Upon opening the kit, the students discover 10 books, 10 filmstrips, and 10 cassettes.

  B. The students discover that Aileen Fisher is the author of each of the 10 books in the kit, just as she had been the author of the 10 books in the kit "The Ways of Animals."

  C. The titles of the 10 books in the kit are:

1. *Now That Spring Is Here*	6. *Petals Yellow and Petals Red*
2. *Mysteries in the Garden*	7. *Swords and Daggers*
3. *And a Sunflower Grew*	8. *Prize Performance*
4. *Seeds on the Go*	9. *A Tree with a Thousand Uses*
5. *Plant Magic*	10. *As the Leaves Fall Down*

EXAMPLE 33 (cont.)

D. In preparation for exploring the contents of the kit "The Ways of Plants," the students discuss what the "ways" of plants might include.

   1. They define the following terms:

      Biology: the study of living things

      Zoology: the study of animals and animal life

      Botany: the study of plants and plant life

      Biologist: a person who is an expert in the field of biology

      Botanist: a person who is an expert in the field of botany

      Zoologist: a person who is an expert in the field of zoology

   2. Each student in this learning project will have the opportunity to discover how botanists think and act.

   3. In searching out information on the "ways" of plants, the students, in order to write plant *biographies*, will use the following as guides:

      The name of the plant

      Where the plant lives

      Description of the plant; roots, stems, flowers, leaves, seeds

      Conditions favorable to the plant's growth

      Interesting facts about the plant

      Whether or not this plant grows in the community

      Whether or not this plant is beneficial to mankind

      Whether or not this plant is beneficial to animals

IV. Each student selects one or more of the books from the kit to read and then prepares to introduce the book to the group.

  A. Upon completion of the book and the viewing of the matching filmstrip, the student, in conference with the school library media specialist, will identify and then select additional materials—books, filmstrips, study prints, charts, and slides—to share with the group.

  B. He or she will lead group discussion following his or her presentation.

  C. The group will add to their *Nature Guide* new and interesting information they have gained.

  D. If the classroom teacher wishes, the student will share this information with the class.

V. Following the presentation and discussion of the concepts obtained from reading the books and viewing the filmstrips contained in the Bowmar kit, "The Ways of Plants," the following culminating activities will follow:

  A. The group will write a letter to Aileen Fisher sharing with her their thoughts and feelings about her nature study books.

  B. The group will view the 8mm motion picture *Basic Needs of Plants* (Encyclopaedia Britannica), which reemphasizes many of the concepts encountered in this learning project, including:

    1. Experiments showing why plants must have minerals, water, light, and air to thrive.

    2. The scientific method of observing, testing and retesting, and drawing conclusions.

  C. The group will add to their *Nature Guide* additional information of significance to them.

  D. The students will work in the library media center exploring topics either of their own invention or ones they have chosen from the following list:

    1. Amazing plant facts

    2. Balance in nature

    3. Banyan trees

    4. Bees, flowers, and pollination

    5. Contributions of Johnny "Appleseed" Chapman

EXAMPLE 33 (cont.)

6. Contributions of Luther Burbank
7. Contributions of George Washington Carver
8. Flowerpot gardens
9. Food from plants
10. Giants of the plant world
11. House plants
12. How plants move
13. Insect-eating plants
14. The origin and importance of Arbor Day
15. Plant experiments
16. Plants as pets
17. Plants that cure
18. Plants that give off light
19. Plants that give us beverages, candy, and chewing gum
20. State flowers, trees, birds, mammals, insects, and fish
21. Strangler fig
22. Textiles from plants
23. Trees in our community
24. Tropical flowers
25. Tropical fruits
26. Unusual seeds
27. What does a conservationist do?
28. What does a farmer do?
29. What does a florist do?
30. What does a forester do?
31. What does a naturalist do?
32. What does a plant experimenter do?
33. What is a terrarium and how do you make one?
34. The wonderful world of flowers
35. The wonderful world of trees

PRIVATE QUESTS: THE HIDDEN CURRICULUM

The school library media specialist has a unique opportunity to personalize the teaching of science, kindergarten through grade 12. The "hidden curriculum" is in reality the sum total of all the quests for understanding initiated by all the individual students, which transcend the formal instructional program. The library media center is the learning laboratory for the "hidden curriculum," the "open sesame" for student exploration into the zone of potentiality.

MATHEMATICS EDUCATION: BASIC SKILLS AND COMPETENCIES

During the period from the launching of Sputnik I in October 1957 until the close of the sixties, extensive innovation, renovation, and redesign characterized the mathematics program, K through 12. So extensive and far-reaching were the changes in the mathematics program that the National Council of Teachers of Mathematics (NCTM) referred to this turbulent time as the "Revolution in School Mathematics."[12]

In order to keep the "new" mathematics program from becoming "old,"

NCTM appointed in 1972 a Committee on Basic Mathematical Competencies and Skills to provide guidelines for meeting the mathematical needs of all citizens. The committee report, "Mathematical Competencies and Skills Essential for Enlightened Citizens," was published in the November 1972 issue of the *Mathematics Teacher*.[13] Among the skills and competencies outlined as basic are many which require library media support. For example:

1. Convert to Roman numerals from decimal numerals and conversely; e.g., date translation [see Example 37, Pittman Learning Guide: Roman Numerals].
2. Recognize and use properties of operations such as grouping, order, etc.
3. Solve problems involving percent.
4. Estimate results.
5. Construct a mathematical sentence from a given verbal sentence.
6. Translate mathematical sentences into verbal problems.
7. Apply measures of length, area, volume, weight, time, money, and temperature.
8. Read maps and estimate distances between locations.
9. Interpret information from a graphical representation.
10. Apply the concepts of ratio and proportion to construct scale drawings and to determine percent and other relations.
11. Determine mean, median, and mode for given numerical data.
12. Analyze and solve simple probability problems.
13. Recognize the techniques used in making predictions and estimates from samples.
14. Construct graphs indicating relationships of two variables from given sets of data.
15. Interpret information from graphs and tables.
16. Detect and describe flaws and fallacies in advertising and propaganda where statistical data and inferences are employed.
17. Gather and present data to support an inference or argument.
18. Maintain personal bank records.
19. Plan a budget including record-keeping of personal expenses.
20. Apply simple interest formulas to installment buying.
21. Estimate the real cost of an article.
22. Compute taxes and investment returns.
23. Use the necessary mathematical skills to appraise insurance retirement benefits.

The NCTM Committee on Basic Mathematical Competencies and Skills reflects in its guidelines the same high degree of concern for having the student perceive the role of mathematics in society that the NSTA Committee on Curriculum Studies evidenced in its guidelines pertaining to the societal role of science. The six desired outcomes of math instruction that are identified by the Committee on Basic Mathematical Competencies and Skills as pertaining to the role of mathematics in society require the direct support of the library media program. These outcomes are:

1. Knowing the ways in which computers are used in science, technology, business, and government.
2. Recognizing the evolutionary development of mathematics by noting the historical milestones in the development of mathematical ideas.
3. Being aware of the great frequency with which mathematical skills are used by individuals in their daily lives.
4. Recognizing that there are problems that, by their nature, do not lend themselves to solution by mathematical methods.
5. Recognizing that some professions require knowledge of the most sophisticated and complex mathematical techniques.
6. Being aware that mathematics finds direct applications not only in the natural sciences but in the behavioral and social sciences and arts as well.[14]

The National Council of Supervisors of Mathematics issued in October 1977 a "Position Paper on Basic Skills."[15] In this position paper, the council identified 10 components of basic skills that could serve as guidelines for state and local school systems. These are:

1. Proficiency in mathematics cannot be acquired without individual practice. We, therefore, endorse the common practice of making regular assignments to be completed outside of class. We recommend that parents encourage their children to set aside sufficient time each day to complete these assignments and that parents actively support the request of teachers that homework be turned in. Students should be encouraged to develop good study habits in mathematics courses at all levels and should develop the ability to read mathematics.

2. Homework and drill are very important pedagogical tools used to help the student gain understanding as well as proficiency in the skills of arithmetic and algebra; but students should not be burdened with excessive or meaningless drill. We, therefore, recommend that teachers and authors of textbooks step up their search for interesting problems that provide opportunity to apply these skills. We realize that this is a difficult task, but we believe that providing problems that reinforce manipulative skills as a by-product should have high priority, *especially those that show that mathematics helps solve problems in the real world* [emphasis supplied].

3. We are aware that teachers must struggle to maintain standards of performance in courses at all levels from kindergarten through college and that serious grade inflation has been observed. An apparent growing trend to reward effort or attendance rather than achievement has been making it increasingly difficult for mathematics teachers to maintain standards. We recommend that mathematics departments review evaluation procedures to insure that grades reflect student achievement. Further, we urge administrators to support teachers in this endeavor.

4. In light of 3 above, we also recognize that advancement of students without appropriate achievement has a detrimental effect on the individual student and on the entire class. We, therefore, recommend that school districts make special provisions to assist students when deficiencies are first noted.

5. We recommend that cumulative evaluations be given throughout each course, as well as at its completion, to all students. We believe that the absence of cumulative evaluation promotes short-term learning. We strongly oppose the practice of exempting students from evaluations.

6. We recommend that computers and hand calculators be used in imaginative ways to reinforce learning and to motivate the student as proficiency in mathematics is gained. Calculators should be used to supplement rather than to supplant the study of necessary computational skills.

7. We recommend that colleges and universities administer placement examinations in mathematics prior to final registration to aid students in selecting appropriate college courses.

8. We encourage the continuation or initiation of joint meetings of college and secondary school mathematics instructors and counselors in order to improve communication concerning mathematics prerequisites for careers, preparation of students for collegiate mathematics courses, joint curriculum coordination, remedial programs in schools and colleges, an exchange of successful instructional strategies, planning of in-service programs, and other related topics.

9. Schools should frequently review their mathematics curricula to see that they meet the needs of their students in preparing them for college mathematics. School districts that have not conducted a curriculum analysis recently should do so now, primarily to identify topics in the curriculum which could be either omitted or de-emphasized, if necessary, in order to provide sufficient time for the topics included in the above statement. We suggest that, for example, the following could be de-emphasized or omitted if now in the curriculum:

(A) logarithmic calculations that can better be handled by calculators or computers,

(B) extensive solving of triangles in trigonometry,

(C) proofs of superfluous or trivial theorems in geometry.

10. We recommend that algebraic concepts and skills be incorporated wherever possible into geometry and other courses beyond algebra to help students retain these concepts and skills.

GUIDING PRINCIPLES

In *Evaluative Criteria for the Evaluation of Secondary Schools*, the basic evaluation tool for secondary education, the following guiding principles for the teaching of mathematics are set forth:

> The secondary school mathematics curriculum consists of those courses, units of instruction, and activities designed to contribute to both the common and special mathematical needs of secondary school students. The curriculum places the proper amount of stress on developing (1) accuracy and facility in performing fundamental mathematical operations, (2) ability to analyze and solve problems of a variety of types and varying degrees of difficulty, (3) an understanding of the nature and structure of mathematics so that students will be able to apply the basic principles to new areas, and (4) competency in responding as an efficient consumer. The curriculum includes concepts and processes of mathematics upon which technical and scientific progress depends, and to which societal changes respond. Provisions are made for students to develop competence in such aspects as proof, organization of data and other information, and the drawing of conclusions, both specific and general.[16]

NEA CARDINAL PREMISES FOR EDUCATIONAL CHANGE

The following premises from the NEA Cardinal Principles for Educational Change (see Chapter 2) have direct bearing on contemporary mathematics teaching:

3. Learning is a lifelong process, and education, therefore, should be seen as a seamless continuum of experiences from early childhood to old age.

6. The aspirations and abilities of the student are best served when the student's learning experiences are at least partly self-directed rather than selected entirely by teachers.

9. Good instruction is personalized rather than individualized.

18. Present social trends, which are characterized by accelerating change and increasing complexity, have enhanced the need for *basic communication skills* such as the ability to handle the written and spoken word and to *deal with number concepts* [emphasis supplied].

20. Traditional instructional methods should be expanded to include problem-solving approaches, and their emphasis on cognition and on valuing should be renewed.

21. Interdisciplinary learning should be stressed and the art of comprehending and anticipating complex relationships should be fostered.

27. In studying possible futures the natural and physical sciences, both in content and methodology, should serve as illustrations of truth-validating inquiry.

28. In the symbolic sciences—language arts, foreign language, mathematics, linguistics, and the like—more heed should be given both to basic communication skills as well as to the ability to recognize propaganda, shoddy advertising, and political double-talk.

CONTEMPORARY CURRICULAR AREAS OF EMPHASIS

CLASSROOM LEARNING CENTERS

Classroom learning centers have proven to be an effective means of motivating interest and of individualizing instruction. Edwina Deans, in her article "The Laboratory Approach to Elementary Mathematics," recommends that the mathematics teacher include at least three general types of material in the learning center.

> The first type is largely motivational and encourages children to learn mathematics. The second type provides horizontal enrichment of the basic program for each child at his level. The third type offers vertical enrichment of the kind that enables the child to work on extensions of topics included in the program and on selected topics outside the program.
>
> Games, mathematical puzzles, and tricks are examples of the motivational type of material. . . .
>
> Shortcuts for adding and multiplying, schemes for finding a person's age and the month in which he was born or for telling the number a person is thinking of, and the arrangement of numbers in magic squares may look like tricks to the observer. However, with the use of cue cards which take children through a sequence of activities, a student may discover the rules and principles on which puzzles and tricks of this sort are based.[17]

Deans makes the recommendation that the math laboratory learning center "be operated with the full cooperation of the school's library resource center, thus ensuring that films, filmstrips, tapes, and supplementary books and reference materials will be readily available."[18] The library media specialist is the key to alerting the mathematics teacher to print and nonprint media worthy of consideration for inclusion in a classroom learning center. Fortunately, there is a wealth of mathematics enrichment and acceleration materials that both inform and delight the student. For example, the following materials are typical of the new informational-motivational math materials:

> The Young Math Books Series published by Thomas Y. Crowell Company is designed for primary grades; available in paperback as well as hardback
>
> Algebra
>> *666 Jellybeans! All That?: An Introduction to Algebra* by Malcolm E. Weiss
>
> Geometry and Topology
>> *Angles Are as Easy as Pie* by Robert Froman
>> *Circles* by Mindel and Harry Sitomer
>> *The Ellipse* by Mannis Charosh
>> *Exploring Triangles: Paper Folding Geometry* by Jo Phillips
>> *Lines, Segments, Polygons* by Mindel and Harry Sitomer
>> *Maps, Tracks, and the Bridges of Konigsberg* by Michael Holt
>> *Right-Angles: Paper-Folding Geometry* by Jo Phillips
>> *Rubber Bands, Baseballs, and Doughnuts: A Book about Topology* by Robert Froman
>> *Shadow Geometry* by Daphne Harwood Trivett

Spirals by Mindel and Harry Sitomer

Straight Lines, Parallel Lines, Perpendicular Lines by Mannis Charosh

3D, 2D, 1D by David Adler

What Is Symmetry? by Mindel and Harry Sitomer

Young Math Activity Cards: Geometry

Measurement and Metric

Area by Jane Jonas Srivastava

Bigger and Smaller by Robert Froman

How Little and How Much: A Book about Scales by Franklyn M. Branley

Long, Short, High, Low, Thin, Wide by James T. Fey

Measure with Metric by Franklyn M. Branley

Volume by Jane Jonas Srivastava

Weighing and Balancing by Jane Jonas Srivastava

Young Math Activity Cards: Measurement

Numbers

Averages by Jane Jonas Srivastava

Base 5 by David Adler

Binary Numbers by Clyde Watson

Building Tables on Tables: A Book about Multiplication by John Trivett

Fractions Are Parts of Things by J. Richard Dennis

How Did Numbers Begin? by Mindel and Harry Sitomer

Less Than Nothing Is Really Something by Robert Froman

Number Ideas through Pictures by Mannis Charosh

Odds and Evens by Thomas C. O'Brien

Roman Numerals by David Adler

Solomon Grundy, Born on Oneday: A Finite Arithmetic Puzzle by Malcolm E. Weiss

Wholes, Halves, Thirds, and Quarters by Michael Holt

Zero Is Not Nothing by Harry Sitomer

Young Math Activity Cards: Numbers

Applied Mathematics

Computers by Jane Jonas Srivastava

Estimation by Charles F. Linn

Perspective by Charles F. Linn

Probability by Charles F. Linn

Statistics by Jane Jonas Srivastava

Logic

Fibonacci Numbers by Judith Gersting and Joseph K. Kuczkowski

A Game of Functions by Robert Froman

Graph Games by Frederique and Georges Papy

Mathematical Games for One or Two by Mannis Charosh

Venn Diagrams by Robert Froman

Yes-No: Stop-Go: Some Patterns in Logic by Judith Gersting and Joseph K. Kuczkowski

Just as the Crowell Young Math Books Series provides for primary children mathematical experiences previously limited to the secondary level, so are there innumerable titles of print and nonprint media that will widen and deepen mathematical understanding on the middle grade levels. Typical of the many fascinating, readable, and highly informative modern enrichment-accelerated math books are: *The I Hate Mathematics Book* by Marilyn Burns (Little, Brown, 1975), *This Book Is About Time* by Marilyn Burns (Little, Brown, 1978), and *Mathemagic: The 1978 Childcraft Annual* (World Book, 1978). A mathematics teacher who is innovative enough to see the value of providing a learning center in the classroom will welcome the cooperative help of the library media specialist in identifying those special learning center resources that might well be known only to the library media specialist.

THE INTERDISCIPLINARY APPROACH

In *Curriculum Change Toward the 21st Century*, Harold Shane stressed the necessity for mathematics communication skills to be used in providing interdisciplinary solutions to problems. The complexity of contemporary social, political, and economic problems cuts across academic discipline boundaries. In enlightened instructional programs the social studies teacher and the math teacher will plan and work together, pooling and sharing their specialized competencies, to provide learning experiences that integrate mathematics communication skills with the social studies. For example, in the twelfth-grade political science unit "Propaganda, Polls, and Public Opinion," the social studies teacher will enlist the aid of the math teacher in preparing the students to construct opinion polls, administer them, collect the data, and communicate the results. Example 34, Test Your City's Quotient, provides an illustration of a typical questionnaire type of poll that students in the political science class could employ and interpret with the help of the senior high school math teacher.

EXAMPLE 34   TEST YOUR CITY'S QUOTIENT*

To find out how well our city satisfies your needs, rate each factor by circling the appropriate number. The idea is to rate Pittsburgh according to your own perspective (see box below for your score).

	Worst	Below Average	Average	Above Average	Best
Climate					
Temperature, humidity	1	2	3	4	5
Days of sunshine	1	2	3	4	5
Lack of wind, dust	1	2	3	4	5
Change of season	1	2	3	4	5
Pollution					
Air quality	1	2	3	4	5
Drinking water	1	2	3	4	5
Recreational water	1	2	3	4	5
Quiet (lack of noise)	1	2	3	4	5
Beauty (lack of unsightly eyesores)	1	2	3	4	5
Terrain (proximity of)					
Mountains, hills	1	2	3	4	5
Lakes, rivers, oceans	1	2	3	4	5

*Copyright © 1978 James Gregory Lord; first published in *Cleveland* magazine.

EXAMPLE 34 (cont.)

	Worst	Below Average	Average	Above Average	Best
Trees, wildlife	1	2	3	4	5
Diversity of terrain	1	2	3	4	5
Housing					
Choices available	1	2	3	4	5
Quality	1	2	3	4	5
Cost (value)	1	2	3	4	5
Esthetic appeal	1	2	3	4	5
Local Travel					
Public transportation	1	2	3	4	5
Roads	1	2	3	4	5
Parking	1	2	3	4	5
Auto expense	1	2	3	4	5
Education					
Public schools	1	2	3	4	5
Private schools	1	2	3	4	5
Colleges, universities	1	2	3	4	5
Graduate, professional schools	1	2	3	4	5
Adult education	1	2	3	4	5
Vocational training	1	2	3	4	5
Public libraries	1	2	3	4	5
Health, Social Service					
(quality, proximity, availability)					
Medical care	1	2	3	4	5
Counseling and crisis centers	1	2	3	4	5
Welfare services	1	2	3	4	5
Social Conditions					
Absence of poverty	1	2	3	4	5
Integration (religious, ethnic, racial					
and economic)	1	2	3	4	5
My comfort with races here	1	2	3	4	5
Public services (fire, police)	1	2	3	4	5
Worklife					
Demand for my specialty	1	2	3	4	5
Availability of jobs	1	2	3	4	5
Pay standards	1	2	3	4	5
Low cost of living	1	2	3	4	5
Media					
Newspapers, magazines	1	2	3	4	5
Radio, local TV	1	2	3	4	5
Sophistication					
Latest fashions available	1	2	3	4	5
Retail diversity	1	2	3	4	5
International foods	1	2	3	4	5
Ethnic communities	1	2	3	4	5
Ease of air travel	1	2	3	4	5
Public awareness of foreign cultures	1	2	3	4	5
Local Politics					
Public interest in politics	1	2	3	4	5
Open to newcomers	1	2	3	4	5
Competency of officials	1	2	3	4	5
Responsiveness to my needs	1	2	3	4	5
Sense of Community					
Proximity of relatives	1	2	3	4	5
Proximity of old friends	1	2	3	4	5
Ease in making friends	1	2	3	4	5
Like-minded people	1	2	3	4	5

EXAMPLE 34 (cont.)

	Worst	Below Average	Average	Above Average	Best
Helpfulness	1	2	3	4	5
My sense of belonging	1	2	3	4	5
Public attitude toward civic responsibility	1	2	3	4	5
Crime					
Feeling of safety:					
In home neighborhood	1	2	3	4	5
In other areas of city	1	2	3	4	5
In downtown	1	2	3	4	5
Culture and Entertainment					
Classical music	1	2	3	4	5
Ballet, dance	1	2	3	4	5
Popular music	1	2	3	4	5
Films	1	2	3	4	5
Theater	1	2	3	4	5
Zoological attractions	1	2	3	4	5
Art museums	1	2	3	4	5
Other museums	1	2	3	4	5
Nightlife					
Nightclubs	1	2	3	4	5
Bars, discos	1	2	3	4	5
Cafes, coffeehouses	1	2	3	4	5
Restaurants	1	2	3	4	5
Sports, Fitness					
Spectator sports	1	2	3	4	5
Participatory sports, activities	1	2	3	4	5
Recreational facilities, parks	1	2	3	4	5
Pittsburgh's Image					
Local	1	2	3	4	5
National	1	2	3	4	5
Pittsburgh's Overall Ability to Satisfy My Needs	1	2	3	4	5

TOTALS

GRAND TOTAL

WHAT'S YOUR SCORE?

	Now that you've rated our city here's how your rating rates:
395	Perfect! Look no further—you're already living in a state of geographic bliss.
350–394	Pittsburgh is as special a place as you need. Do not heed critics.
275–349	You're here for perfectly good reasons and it's nobody's business that you hold some nagging doubts.
200–274	You may well be suffering from terminal inertia. Go take a trip somewhere, anywhere.
100–199	You are becoming a bit of a bore in your appraisal of the negatives. Perhaps you might consider going west, or east, or south . . .
80–99	Try Cleveland.
79	Perfect low score! Philadelphia?

In like fashion in an enlightened instructional program the science teacher and the math teacher will plan and work together to provide learning experiences that integrate mathematics communication skills with the science program. For example, in bringing relevance to the tenth-grade biology unit "The Environmental Revolution," the biology teacher will enlist the aid of the math teacher in updating the Environmental Quality Index, 1969-1979 (National Wildlife Federation*). This index provides a statistical analysis of environmental quality trends for the decade 1969-1979 under the headings wildlife, air, soil, minerals, forests, living space, and water.

When in the eleventh and twelfth grades biography is being studied in English class, the mathematics teacher should encourage students to consider reading about mathematicians from the past who have made significant breakthroughs in humanity's mathematical knowledge. John Holt, in his thought-provoking work *Instead of Education: Ways to Do Things Better* (Dutton, 1976), advocates incorporating biography within the regular instructional program.

> A part of Mathematics, Physics, or Philosophy is the account of what other *mathematicians* or *physicists* or *philosophers* have done. But our "knowledge" of these things is a record of what these people *did;* what questions they asked, how they went about getting the answers, what answers they got, what conclusions they drew from their answers. *Whatever we do in these fields is added to, and therefore, part of, what others did before.*[19]

Example 35, Great Mathematicians Prior to the Twentieth Century, typifies the kind of list the mathematics teacher could provide for students to consider when preparing biographies for their unit in English class.

EXAMPLE 35   GREAT MATHEMATICIANS PRIOR TO THE TWENTIETH CENTURY

Abel, Niels Henrik	1802–1829	Clausius, Rudolph	
Adams, John Couch	1819–1892	Julius	1822–1888
Ahmes (A'h-mose')	?–1650 B.C.	Copernicus, Nicholas	1473–1543
Airy, Sir George Biddell	1801–1892	D'Alembert, Jean	
Al-Kh(o)warizmi	c.780–850	leRond	1717–1783
Anaxagoras	?500–428 B.C.	Dedekind, Richard	1831–1916
Apollonius of Perga	?262–200 B.C.	Desargues, Gerard	1593–1662
Archimedes	?287–212 B.C.	Descartes, Rene	1596–1650
Argand, J. R.	1768–1822	Diophantus	c.275
Bernoulli, Jean	1667–1748	Dirichlet, Peter Gustav	1805–1859
Bessel, Friedrich W.	1784–1846	Eddin, Nasir	1201–1274
Bolyai, Janos (Johann)	1802–1860	Euclid of Alexandria	c.300 B.C.
Boole, George	1815–1864	Eudoxus of Cnidus	c.408–355 B.C.
Burgi, Jobst (Joost)	c.1552–1632	Euler, Leonhard	1707–1783
Cantor, Georg	1845–1918	Fermat, Pierre de	1601–1665
Cardano, Girlamo	1501–1576	Ferro, Scipio	1465–1526
Carnot, Lazare	1753–1823	Fibonacci, Leonardo	
Cauchy, Augustin		(Leonardo of Pisa)	1180–1250
Louis	1789–1857	Fourier, Jean Baptiste	1768–1830
Cayley, Arthur	1821–1895	Galilei, Galileo	1564–1642
Clairaut, Alexis Claude	1713–1765	Galois, Evariste	1812–1832

*National Wildlife Federation EQ Index may be obtained free by writing Educational Services, National Wildlife Federation, 1412 16th Street, N.W., Washington, D.C. 20036. Bulk quantities cost 25¢ for 2-100 copies; 15¢ each for orders totaling more than 100.

EXAMPLE 35 (cont.)

Gauss, Karl Friedrich	1777–1855	Lobachevsky(i), Nikilai	
Gibbs, Josiah Williard	1839–1903	Ivanovish	1793–1856
Gregory, David	1638–1675	Maclaurin, Colin	1698–1746
Grossman, Hermann		Moivre, Abraham de	1667–1754
Gunther	1809–1877	Monge, Gaspard	1746–1818
Gudermann, Christof	1798–1852	Napier, John	1550–1617
Hamilton, Sir William R.	1805–1865	Navier, Claude Louis	
Harriot, Thomas	1560–1621	Henri	1785–1836
Hermite, Charles	1822–1901	Newton, Sir Isaac	1642–1727
Hero of Alexandria	?250	Oughtred, William	1574–1660
Hilbert, David	1862–1943	Pappus	c.400
Hipparchus	?130 B.C.	Pascal, Blaise	1623–1662
Huygens, Christian		Plucher, Julius	1801–1868
(M. Zulichem)	1621–1695	Poincare, Jules Henri	1854–1912
Jacobi, Carl Gustav	1804–1851	Poisson, Simeon Denis	1781–1840
Kepler, Johannes	1571–1630	Poncelot, Jean V.	1788–1867
Khayyam, Omar	c.1044–1123	Ptolemy, Claudius	c.150
Kowalewski, Sonja		Pythagoras of Samos	c.580–500
(Sophie)	1850–1891	Reinhold, Erasmus	1511–1553
Kronecker, Leopold	1823–1891	Riemann, Georg	
Kummer, Ernst Eduard	1810–1893	Friedrich	1826–1866
Lagrange, Joseph		Russell, Bertrand	1872–1970
Louis	1736–1813	Stevinus, Simon	1548–1620
Laplace, Pierre Simon	1749–1827	Stifel, Michael	1487–1567
Lauchen, Georg		Stokes, Sir George	
Joachim von		Gabriel	1819–1903
(Rheticus, Rhaeticus)	1514–1576	Sylvester, James	
Legendre, Adrien		Joseph	1814–1897
Marie	1752–1833	Tartaglia, Nic(c)olo	c.1500–1557
Leibniz, Gottfried,		Taylor, Brook	1685–1731
Wilhelm von	1646–1718	Thales of Miletus	c.640–546 B.C.
Leverrier, Urbain Jean	1811–1877	Torricelli, Valngelista	1608–1647

In an innovative math program, the vision of the math teacher transcends the limitations of the textbook and the confines of the classroom. Not infrequently, this teacher, in cooperation with the library media specialist, will design an instructional unit based entirely upon the resources and services of the school's library media center. Depth, breadth, and relevance in the mathematics program will never come to fruition if the teacher and the students are restricted to textbook and classroom. Example 36, Mathematics as a Communication Tool, is a prototype of the degree and kind of concept development and coverage possible when the library media center becomes the learning laboratory for mathematics teaching.

EXAMPLE 36   MATHEMATICS AS A COMMUNICATION TOOL

Subjects: Mathematics, Social Studies, and Science
Grade: 10
Unit: Mathematics as a Communication Tool

Goal: To provide opportunity for the students to learn to use mathematical skills as a means of communication.

Objectives:

To provide opportunity for the students to discover the impact value of statistical information presented in graph, chart, and table form.

EXAMPLE 36 (cont.)

To provide opportunity for the students to bring a high degree of relevance to their study of science and social studies.

To provide opportunity for the students to become conversant with sources of current statistical information.

To provide opportunity for the students to become conversant with opinion polls as an effective means of judging opinions and attitudes.

Topics:

1. Ecology
   Air pollution
   Energy consumption
   Sources of energy consumed in the U.S.
   Noise pollution
   Solid wastes generated in the U.S.
   Sources of solid wastes generated in the U.S.
   Water pollution
   Sources of water pollution in the U.S.
2. Education
   Attainment by age, race, and sex
   Attainment by ethnic groups
   Enrollment in schools by age and sex
   Income by years of schooling
3. Labor
   Employed persons by major occupational groups and sex
   Employment and unemployment in the U.S.
   U.S. labor force earnings
4. Law enforcement
   Business losses due to crime by type of crime
   Full-time police department employees
   Index of crime
   Riot and civil disorder losses, U.S.
   Salary scales of police patrolmen and patrolwomen
   Total arrests by age, by sex, by crime
   World crime statistics
5. Narcotics
   Active narcotics addicts in selected cities
   Addiction in the U.S.
6. Population*
   Birth rate in U.S., 1900–to date
   Death rates in the U.S., 1900–to date
   Growth U.S., 1610–to date
   Immigration to and emigration from the U.S.
   Life expectancy rates by race, age, and sex, U.S.
   Life expectancy rates by race, age, and sex in foreign countries
   Marriage and divorce in U.S., 1900–to date
   World population doubling times
7. Public opinion
   American way of life: politics, patriotism, isolation
   The climate of the high school
   Counseling and educational needs of adolescents
   Drugs and narcotics
   Evaluation of educational attitudes
   People problems: population, prejudice, poverty, peace
   Vocational plans and prejudices of adolescents
   What is wrong and right with today's youth

*For latest census data contact Henry Smith, chief of the Bureau of Public Information, Washington, D.C. 20233, tel. 301-763-7273.

CHALLENGING THE GIFTED

The mathematically talented student is entitled to a mathematics program compatible with his or her special capabilities. The library media specialist and the classroom teacher must not confuse creative thinking ability in mathematics with measured intelligence or IQ. In mathematics as in science or in any other subject area, creative thinking ability is closely related to subject matter achievement and interest. There is no set pattern of subject interest common to students with high measured intelligence; neither talent nor creativity is indicated by an IQ! When planning enrichment experiences the teacher and the library media specialist should relate difficulty of performance with demonstrated mathematics ability and interest, not with an IQ.

Programmed instruction is an innovative way to challenge the mathematically gifted learner. When commercially prepared programs commensurate with individual student ability and interest are not available, the library media specialist and/or the mathematics teacher can design and structure learning programs to meet these special student needs. The Pittman guide illustrated in Example 37 (see Chapter 7 for an explanation of the Pittman method of media programming) was developed to enable a talented sixth grader to delve more deeply into the realm of Roman numerals.

EXAMPLE 37   PITTMAN LEARNING GUIDE: ROMAN NUMERALS

Subject:	Mathematics
Grade:	6
Topic:	Learning to Use Roman Numerals
Subtopic 1:	How did the Romans write their numbers 1 through 1,000?
	Source A Lauber, Patricia. *The Story of Numbers*. Random House, pp. 46–53.
or	
	Source B *The New Book of Knowledge;* vol. 16. Grolier.
or	
	Source C *The Reader's Digest Almanac*. Reader's Digest. Check the Index for Roman Numerals.
or	
	Source D *The World Almanac*. Doubleday. Check the Index for Roman Numerals.
Subtopic 2:	How did the Romans add numbers?
	Source Simon, Leonard. *The Day the Numbers Disappeared*. McGraw-Hill, p. 37.
Subtopic 3:	How did the Romans subtract numbers?
	Source Simon, Leonard. *The Day the Numbers Disappeared*. McGraw-Hill, p. 37.

EXAMPLE 37 (cont.)

Subtopic 4:	How did the Romans multiply numbers?

Source
Highland, Esther. *The How and Why Wonder Book of Mathematics.* Grosset & Dunlap, p. 31.

Optional activity 1: Review what you have learned about Roman numerals by using the Cyclo-teacher* with the following:
Cycle M46—sides 1 and 2
Cycle M47—sides 1 and 2
Cycle M48—sides 1 and 2

Optional activity 2: Prepare a transparency or a poster showing Roman numerals for:

1	100	4,000	25,000	1,000,000
10	1,000	5,000	50,000	5,000,000
50	2,000	10,000	100,000	10,000,000

Source
The World Book, vol. 16. Field Enterprises.

Optional activity 3: Make a series of flash cards to be used in testing your class's ability to interpret Roman numerals.

Optional activity 4: Place on transparencies problems in addition, subtraction and multiplication using Roman numerals you wish to present to your class.

Optional activity 5: The Statue of Liberty holds in her left hand a tablet on which the date July IV, MDCCLXXVI, is written. Can you translate that date into arabic numerals? Do you know why this date is significant?

LIBRARY MEDIA PROGRAM: FACILITATOR OF SCIENCE AND MATHEMATICS INNOVATION

NSTA and NCTM have called for bold, new, innovative programs for the teaching of science and mathematics. These educators have specified a rigorous program for the future. They advocate an interdisciplinary approach to provide depth, breadth, and relevance; a problem-solving approach emphasizing cognition and valuing; individualization of instruction matching both aspirations and abilities of students in providing for self-directed learning experiences; and life preparation for anticipating futuristic developments. Such an ambitious and commendable quest for excellence mandates that teaching and learning in both the science and mathematics disciplines go beyond the restrictions of textbook and classroom, and can come to fruition only when science teachers, mathematics teachers, and library media specialists directly involve the library media program in planning for, implementing, and facilitating those lofty hallmarks of interdisciplinary excellence.

*The Cyclo-teacher is a self-instructional teaching machine with programmed cycles for each of the disciplines on the elementary and junior high school level. This machine and its accompanying cycles are only sold by Field Educational Publications, Inc., 609 Mission St., San Francisco, Calif. 94105.

NOTES

1. National Science Teachers Association, *Working Paper: Science Education: Accomplishments and Needs* (Washington, D.C.: National Science Teachers Association, 1978), p. 3.
2. Ibid., pp. 3–4.
3. Ibid., pp. 4–6.
4. Ibid., pp. 16–21.
5. National Study of School Evaluation, *The Evaluative Criteria for the Evaluation of Secondary Schools*, 5th ed. Copyright © 1978, p. 209. Reprinted by permission of National Study of School Evaluation, Washington, D.C.
6. Paul B. Hounshell and Edwin L. West, Jr., "Trends in the Teaching of Science," in *The High School Journal* 53, no. 4 (January 1970), pp. 207–216. Copyright © 1970, by the University of North Carolina Press.
7. John U. Michaelis, Ruth H. Grossman, and Lloyd F. Scott, *New Designs for Elementary Curriculum and Instruction* (New York: McGraw-Hill, 1975), pp. 301–303.
8. Draper L. Kauffman, Jr., *Futurism and Future Studies* (Washington, D.C.: National Education Association, 1976), pp. 38–42.
9. Cheryl Charles and Bob Samples, eds., *Science and Society: Knowing, Teaching, Learning* (Washington, D.C.: National Council for the Social Studies, 1978), p. 75.
10. Michaelis, Grossman, and Scott, *New Designs*, p. 303.
11. Calhoun C. Collier et al., *Modern Elementary Education: Teaching and Learning* (New York: Macmillan, 1976), p. 219.
12. National Council of Teachers of Mathematics, "Mathematical Competencies and Skills Essential for Enlightened Citizens," *Mathematics Teacher*, Nov. 1972, p. 672.
13. Ibid., pp. 673–674.
14. Ibid., pp. 675–676.
15. National Council of Supervisors of Mathematics, "Position Paper on Basic Skills," in *The Arithmetic Teacher*, vol. 25, Oct. 1977, pp. 19–22.
16. National Study of School Evaluation, *Evaluative Criteria*, p. 161.
17. Edwina Deans, "The Laboratory Approach to Elementary Mathematics," in Glen Hass, Joseph Bondi, and Jon Wiles, *Curriculum Planning: A New Approach* (Boston: Allyn and Bacon, 1974), p. 310.
18. Ibid., 309.
19. John Holt, *Instead of Education: Ways to Do Things Better* (New York: Dutton, 1976), pp. 16–17.

11 The Library Media Program Supports the Humanities Program

To be educated . . . means also to know something of the experience of beauty—if not in the sense of creating it or discoursing about it, then at the very least, in the sense of being able to respond to it, to respond both to the beauty of nature and to the art made by our fellow men.

Charles E. Silberman*

All of the arts, poetry, music, ritual, the visible arts, the theatre, must singly and together create the most comprehensive art of all, a humanized society and its masterpiece, free man.

Bernard Berenson†

The establishment in 1965 of the National Foundation on the Arts and Humanities by the 89th Congress provided an impetus which has resulted in a new high level of educational concern for the humanities, the interdisciplinary approach to the study of man. Today's educators are taking to heart Petrarch's dictum that "the proper study of man is man," and are building into the curriculum opportunities for the student, on both the elementary and the secondary levels, to study man as a creator and as a perceptor of beauty.

There are countless definitions of the term "humanities," each providing a frame of reference somewhat different from the others. The following definition provided by Marguerite Hood, Professor of Music Education at the University of Michigan, undergirds the discussion of the humanities in this book:

> The humanities . . . are the subject areas which deal with man as a human being, with the development of his ideas through the successive periods in the history of the world, with the influences which have been brought to bear on those ideas, and with the culture creations, intellectual or artistic, which have grown out of those ideas.[1]

The goal of the humanities program is to enable the students to view culture as "a continuous texture, rolling endlessly off a loom, with colors and patterns growing sometimes richer and more vivid, sometimes fading to drabness, sometimes recalling older patterns, sometimes developing new. What is expected of

Note: For information concerning the design, development, and implementation of humanities programs, consult Associate Professor William Waack, University of Northern Iowa, Cedar Falls, Iowa 50613, tel. 319-266-5116.

*Charles E. Silberman, *Crisis in the Classroom: The Remaking of American Education* (New York: Random House, 1970), p. 115.

†Sidney G. Tickton, ed, *To Improve Learning*, vol. 2 (New York: R. R. Bowker, 1971), pp. 228–229.

study of the humanities is that they familiarize us with antecedent stretches of the work, so that we have a basis for evaluating and perhaps shaping new patterns."[2] This goal is a worthy one for traditionally students have been denied a look at the complete tapestry of their cultural heritage; at best they have been given a strand here and there, a bit, a piece, a fragment.

Just as there are numerous definitions of the term humanities, so there are widely divergent views as to how the teaching of the humanities should be organized and managed—whether they should be taught as separate courses or whether they should be integrated within the framework of existing courses of study. In 1965 Fred Stocking, recognized authority in the field of humanities course design, made the following observations concerning humanities courses:

1. There is no such thing as an *ideal* course in the humanities for high school students: an excellent course might be designed in any of a dozen different ways, and the best course for any school exploits the particular talents which are available.
2. The better courses are usually taught by two or more teachers—one from music or art, one from literature, one from history, for instance. But unless there happen to be two or more teachers who share an exuberant desire to work together in such a course, a single energetic and enthusiastic teacher, with diverse interests and mastery of several disciplines, might well be preferable.
3. The best courses awaken that kind of interest in the humanities which is based on depth of understanding rather than on a glib familiarity with names and titles, or on the social fun of field trips. That is, good courses never make any attempt at coverage. One novel, one painting, and one opera out of the middle of the 19th century might well provide more than enough material for a semester.
4. The goal of such a course should be: first, to arouse interest in the arts as providing experiences valuable for their own sake; second, to show that an art work acquired deeper meaning when placed in its historical context; and third, to make clear that a full understanding of—and delight in—any one of the arts requires the eventual mastery of difficult, complicated, and highly rewarding intellectual disciplines.[3]

The simplest humanities courses unify literature, art, and music; the more comprehensive courses embrace history and philosophy, as well as literature, art, and music; the most comprehensive include social science, religion, science, literature, philosophy, music, and art. Most humanities courses are organized around major themes such as:

The Great Event Theme—for example: The Impact of the Crusades on Man's Search for a Better Life; The Moon Walk, *Star Wars*, and the Future

The Great Man Theme—for example: Pope John XXIII, Apostle of Humility and Love; Albert Schweitzer, Apostle of Reverence for Life; Norman Rockwell, Mirror of America

The Great Philosophies Theme—for example: Man's Search for Utopia; What Does It Mean to Be Human?; An Inquiry Into the Nature of Man: His Inhumanity and His Humanity

The Contemporary Social Problems Theme—for example: Nuclear Energy, Curse or Blessing; Technology, Master or Slave; Social Justice, Myth or Reality

The Integration of Several Themes—for example: Children's Rights, Women's Rights, and the Bill of Rights; The Declaration of Independence and Will Durant's Declaration of Interdependence*

*Will and Ariel Durant, *A Dual Autobiography* (New York: Simon and Schuster, 1977), pp. 236–238.

CONTEMPORARY AREAS OF EMPHASIS

The following premises from the NEA Cardinal Principles for Educational Change have wide applicability in the area of the humanities (see Chapter 6):

1. The need to develop a spirit of "global community" in an increasingly interdependent world has reaffirmed an important task for education: to recognize and to respect the concepts of multiethnic, polycultural, and multilingual education in pluralistic societies both in the United States and abroad.
2. Education has assumed new significance as a positive force for peace in a world capable of destroying itself.
21. Interdisciplinary learning should be stressed and the art of comprehending and anticipating complex relationships should be fostered.
26. So that desirable alternative futures can be envisioned, work in the social studies should be redesigned so as to promote a grasp of human geography and of planetary cultures as they exist today.

MULTIETHNIC AND POLYCULTURAL CONCEPTS

As previously stated in Chapter 9, the school has been assigned a major responsibility for developing intergroup understanding based on respect for the worth and dignity of every individual, regardless of race, color, creed, or socioeconomic status. The need for multicultural education was officially recognized by the U.S. Congress in 1974 when it passed the Ethnic Heritage Studies Program Act. This legislation declared that "all persons in the educational institutions of the Nation should have an opportunity to learn about the differing and unique contributions to the national heritage made by each ethnic group" and authorized Elementary and Secondary Education Act funds for the development of ethnic studies.

NEA, because it believes that humanization of American education is perhaps the most pressing challenge facing today's schools, has developed a multimedia program on multiethnic education. Included in this program is *Roots of America: A Multiethnic Curriculum Resource Guide for 7th, 8th, and 9th Grade Social Studies Teachers.* This guide employs a true humanities approach as evidenced in the following policy statement:

> This is reality: Ours is a multicultural society. Our population includes U.S. citizens of European, Asian, African, Central and South American, Caribbean and Native American descent. All of these groups have contributed to the total cultural fabric of our society. Our laws, music, art, language, and literature reflect the values of this diversity. Our public educative process is obligated to reflect this reality. All people have the right of access to materials that express the rich multilingual, multicultural nature of our society. Our heritage of freedom of speech and freedom of inquiry demands this. The goals of a democratic society require it.[4]

The eight units included in *Roots of America* are:

1. The Native American Experience
2. The Mexican American Experience
3. The Black American Experience
4. The Jewish American Experience
5. The Italian American Experience
6. The Polish American Experience
7. The Japanese American Experience
8. The Puerto Rican Experience

Each of the eight units contains a wealth of print and nonprint media—a wealth so vast as to be found *only* in a well-stocked school library media center!

The National Council for the Social Studies (NCSS) appointed in 1976 a Task Force on Ethnic Studies. This task force prepared *Curriculum Guidelines for Multiethnic Education: A Position Statement* (Washington, D.C.: National Council for the Social Studies, 1976). These guidelines are of historical significance for they are the first to be stated and endorsed by American educators. So important are these guidelines that NCSS prepared "The Multiethnic Education Program Evaluation Checklist" (see Checklist 8) to facilitate each school's initiation of a multiethnic program.

CHECKLIST 8   THE MULTIETHNIC EDUCATION PROGRAM
EVALUATION CHECKLIST*

RATING	GUIDELINES
Strongly ⟷ Hardly at all	
— — — —	1.0 Does ethnic pluralism permeate the total school environment?
— — — —	1.1 Is ethnic content incorporated into all aspects of the curriculum, preschool through grade 12 and beyond?
— — — —	1.2 Do instructional materials treat ethnic differences and groups honestly, realistically, and sensitively?
— — — —	1.3 Do school libraries and resource centers have a variety of materials on the histories, experiences, and cultures of many different ethnic groups?
— — — —	1.4 Do school assemblies, decorations, speakers, holidays, and heroes reflect ethnic group differences?
— — — —	1.5 Are extracurricular activities multiracial and multiethnic?
— — — —	2.0 Do school policies and procedures foster positive interactions among the different ethnic group members of the school?
— — — —	2.1 Do school policies accommodate the behavioral patterns, learning styles, and orientations of those ethnic group members actually in the school?
— — — —	2.2 Does the school provide a diversity of instruments and techniques in teaching and counseling students of different ethnic groups?
— — — —	2.3 Do school policies recognize the holidays and festivities of different ethnic groups?
— — — —	2.4 Do school policies avoid instructional and guidance practices based on stereotyped and ethnocentric perceptions?
— — — —	2.5 Do school policies respect the dignity and worth of students as individuals *and* as members of ethnic groups?
— — — —	3.0 Are the school staffs (administrative, instructional, counseling, and supportive) multiethnic and multiracial?
— — — —	3.1 Has the school established and enforced policies for recruiting and maintaining multiethnic, multiracial staffs?
— — — —	4.0 Does the school have systematic, comprehensive, mandatory, and continuing multiethnic staff development programs?

Curriculum Guidelines for Multiethnic Education: A Position Statement (Washington, D.C.: National Council for the Social Studies, 1976), pp. 42–48. Reprinted with permission of the National Council for the Social Studies.

CHECKLIST 8 (cont.)

RATING	GUIDELINES
Strongly ←——→ Hardly at all	

RATING	GUIDELINES
— — — —	4.1 Are teachers, librarians, counselors, administrators, and the supportive staff included in the staff development programs?
— — — —	4.2 Do the staff development programs include a variety of experiences (such as lectures, field experiences, curriculum projects, etc.)?
— — — —	4.3 Do the staff development programs provide opportunities to gain knowledge and understanding about different ethnic groups?
— — — —	4.4 Do the staff development programs provide opportunities for participants to explore their attitudes and feelings about their own ethnicity and others'?
— — — —	4.5 Do the staff development programs examine the verbal and nonverbal patterns of interethnic group interactions?
— — — —	4.6 Do the staff development programs provide opportunities for learning how to create and select multiethnic instructional materials and how to incorporate ethnic content into curriculum materials?
— — — —	5.0 Does the curriculum reflect the ethnic learning styles of students within the school?
— — — —	5.1 Is the curriculum designed to help students learn how to function effectively in different cultural environments and master more than one cognitive style?
— — — —	5.2 Do the objectives, instructional strategies, and learning materials reflect the cultures and cognitive styles of the different ethnic groups within the school?
— — — —	6.0 Does the curriculum provide continuous opportunities for students to develop a better sense of self?
— — — —	6.1 Does the curriculum help students strengthen their self-identities?
— — — —	6.2 Is the curriculum designed to help students develop greater self-understanding?
— — — —	6.3 Does the curriculum help students improve their self-concepts?
— — — —	6.4 Does the curriculum help students better understand themselves in the light of their ethnic heritages?
— — — —	7.0 Does the curriculum help students to understand the wholeness of the experiences of ethnic groups?
— — — —	7.1 Does the curriculum include the study of societal problems some ethnic group members experience, such as racism, prejudice, discrimination, and exploitation?
— — — —	7.2 Does the curriculum include the study of historical experiences, cultural patterns, *and* social problems of different ethnic groups?
— — — —	7.3 Does the curriculum include both positive and negative aspects of ethnic group experiences?
— — — —	7.4 Does the curriculum present ethnics as active participants in society *and* as subjects of oppression and exploitation?
— — — —	7.5 Does the curriculum examine the diversity within each ethnic group's experience?

CHECKLIST 8 (cont.)

RATING	GUIDELINES

Strongly ⟷ Hardly at all

— — — —   7.6 Does the curriculum present ethnic group experience as dynamic and continuously changing?

— — — —   7.7 Does the curriculum examine the experiences of ethnic group people instead of focusing exclusively on the "heroes"?

— — — —   8.0 Does the curriculum help students identify and understand the ever-present conflict between ideals and realities in human societies?

— — — —   8.1 Does the curriculum help students identify and understand the value conflicts in problematic situations?

— — — —   8.2 Does the curriculum examine differing views of ideals and realities among ethnic groups?

— — — —   9.0 Does the curriculum explore and clarify ethnic alternatives and options within American society?

— — — —   9.1 Does the teacher create a classroom atmosphere reflecting an acceptance of and respect for ethnic differences?

— — — —   9.2 Does the teacher create a classroom atmosphere allowing realistic consideration of ethnic alternatives and options?

— — — —   10.0 Does the curriculum promote values, attitudes, and behaviors which support ethnic pluralism?

— — — —   10.1 Does the curriculum help students examine differences within and among ethnic groups?

— — — —   10.2 Does the curriculum foster attitudes supportive of cultural democracy and other democratic ideals and values?

— — — —   10.3 Does the curriculum reflect ethnic pluralism?

— — — —   10.4 Does the curriculum present ethnic pluralism as a vital societal force that encompasses both potential strength and potential conflict?

— — — —   11.0 Does the curriculum help students develop decision-making abilities, social participation skills, and a sense of political efficacy needed for effective citizenship?

— — — —   11.1 Does the curriculum help students develop the ability to distinguish facts from interpretations and opinions?

— — — —   11.2 Does the curriculum help students develop skills in finding and processing information?

— — — —   11.3 Does the curriculum help students develop sound knowledge, concepts, generalizations, and theories about issues related to ethnicity?

— — — —   11.4 Does the curriculum help students develop sound methods of thinking about ethnic issues?

— — — —   11.5 Does the curriculum help students develop skills in clarifying and justifying their values and relating them to their understanding of ethnicity?

— — — —   11.6 Does the curriculum include opportunities to use knowledge, valuing, and thinking in decision-making on ethnic matters?

— — — —   11.7 Does the curriculum provide opportunities for students to take action on social problems affecting ethnic groups?

— — — —   11.8 Does the curriculum help students develop a sense of efficacy?

CHECKLIST 8 (cont.)

RATING	GUIDELINES
Strongly ←→ Hardly at all	

— — — — 12.0 Does the curriculum help students develop skills necessary for effective interpersonal and interethnic group interactions?

— — — — 12.1 Does the curriculum help students understand ethnic reference points which influence communication?

— — — — 12.2 Does the curriculum help students try out cross-ethnic experiences and reflect upon them?

— — — — 13.0 Is the multiethnic curriculum comprehensive in scope and sequence, presenting holistic views of ethnic groups, and an integral part of the total school curriculum?

— — — — 13.1 Does the curriculum introduce students to the experiences of persons of widely varying backgrounds in the study of each ethnic group?

— — — — 13.2 Does the curriculum discuss the successes and contributions of members of some group in terms of that group's values?

— — — — 13.3 Does the curriculum include the role of ethnicity in the local community as well as in the nation?

— — — — 13.4 Does content related to ethnic groups extend beyond special units, courses, occasions, and holidays?

— — — — 13.5 Are materials written by and about ethnic groups used in teaching fundamental skills?

— — — — 13.6 Does the curriculum provide for the development of progressively more complex concepts, abilities, and values?

— — — — 13.7 Is the study of ethnicity incorporated in instructional plans rather than being supplementary or additive?

— — — — 14.0 Does the curriculum include the continuous study of the cultures, historical experiences, social realities, and existential conditions of ethnic groups with a variety of racial compositions?

— — — — 14.1 Does the curriculum include study of several ethnic groups?

— — — — 14.2 Does the curriculum include studies of both white and non-white groups?

— — — — 14.3 Does the curriculum provide for continuity in the examination of aspects of experience affected by race?

— — — — 15.0 Are interdisciplinary and multidisciplinary approaches used in designing and implementing the multiethnic curriculum?

— — — — 15.1 Are interdisciplinary and multidisciplinary perspectives used in the study of ethnic groups and related issues?

— — ←→ — 15.2 Are approaches used authentic and comprehensive explanations of ethnic issues, events, and problems?

— — — — 16.0 Does the curriculum use comparative approaches in the study of ethnic groups and ethnicity?

— — — — 16.1 Does the curriculum focus on the similarities and differences among ethnic groups?

— — — — 16.2 Are matters examined from comparative perspectives with fairness to all?

— — — — 17.0 Does the curriculum help students to view and interpret events, situations, and conflict from diverse ethnic perspectives and points of view?

CHECKLIST 8 (cont.)

RATING	GUIDELINES
Strongly ⟷ Hardly at all	

	17.1 Are the perspectives of different ethnic groups represented in the instructional program?
— — — —	
	17.2 Are students taught why different ethnic groups often perceive the same historical event or contemporary situation differently?
— — — —	
— — — —	17.3 Are the perspectives of each ethnic group presented as valid ways to perceive the past and the present?
— — — —	18.0 Does the curriculum conceptualize and describe the development of the United States as a multidirectional society?
— — — —	18.1 Does the curriculum view the territorial and cultural growth of the United States as flowing from several directions?
— — — —	18.2 Does the curriculum include a parallel study of the various societies which developed in the geo-cultural United States?
— — — —	19.0 Does the school provide opportunities for students to participate in the aesthetic experiences of various ethnic groups?
— — — —	19.1 Are multiethnic literature and art used to promote empathy for people of different ethnic groups?
— — — —	19.2 Are multiethnic literature and art used to promote self-examination and self-understanding?
— — — —	19.3 Do students read and hear the poetry, short stories, novels, folklore, plays, essays, and autobiographies of a variety of ethnic groups?
— — — —	19.4 Do students examine the music, art, architecture, and dance of a variety of ethnic groups?
— — — —	19.5 Do students have available the artistic, musical, and literary expression of the local ethnic communities?
— — — —	19.6 Are opportunities provided for students to develop their own artistic, literary, and musical expression?
— — — —	20.0 Does the school foster the view of ethnic group languages as legitimate communication systems?
— — — —	20.1 Are students taught about the nature of languages and dialects?
— — — —	20.2 Is the student taught in his or her dominant language or dialect when needed?
— — — —	20.3 Does the curriculum explore the role of languages and dialects in self-understanding and within and among ethnic groups?
— — — —	20.4 Are the language policies and laws within the United States studied from political perspectives?
— — — —	21.0 Does the curriculum make maximum use of local community resources?
— — — —	21.1 Are students carefully involved in the continuous study of the local community?
— — — —	21.2 Are members of the local ethnic communities continually used as classroom resources?
— — — —	21.3 Are field trips to the various local ethnic communities provided for students?
— — — —	22.0 Do the assessment procedures used with students reflect their ethnic cultures?

CHECKLIST 8 (cont.)

RATING	GUIDELINES
Strongly ⟷ Hardly at all	

— — — —	22.1 Do teachers use a variety of assessment procedures which reflect the ethnic diversity of the students?
— — — —	22.2 Do teachers' day-to-day assessment techniques take into account the ethnic diversity of the students?
— — — —	23.0 Does the school conduct ongoing, systematic evaluations of the goals, methods, and instructional materials used in teaching about ethnicity?
— — — —	23.1 Do assessment procedures draw on many sources of evidence from many sorts of people?
— — — —	23.2 Does the evaluation program examine school policies and procedures?
— — — —	23.3 Does the evaluation program examine the everyday climate of the school?
— — — —	23.4 Does the evaluation program examine the effectiveness of curricular programs, academic and non-academic?
— — — —	23.5 Are the results of evaluation used to improve the school program?

On the elementary as well as on the secondary level there are myriad opportunities to integrate multiethnic understandings and appreciations within the framework of the ongoing instructional program. For example, the elementary reading program offers rich opportunities for integrating the humanities in general and multiethnic understandings and appreciations in particular within its course content. As an illustration, a sixth-grade reader has a unit entitled "Dream of Freedom." This unit contains several poems, a quotation, several excerpts from novels, and several short articles on the theme that the dream of freedom has motivated most immigrants to come to the United States. The perceptive teacher will view this unit as an opportunity to lead the students to discover that each immigrant brings something of value with him or her and that many immigrants have made outstanding contributions to the American way of life. Each selection can lead to a number of appropriate enrichment learning experiences, just as the selection "Miss Liberty," which covers but six pages in the reading text, can logically lead to the following:

A biography of Auguste Bartholdi, the French sculptor who designed the Statue of Liberty.

A biography of Emma Lazarus, who wrote the poem "The New Colossus," which is inscribed on the bronze tablet affixed to the entrance of the Statue of Liberty.

A biography of Irving Berlin, an immigrant, who wrote the musical setting for the song "Give Me Your Tired, Your Poor," which is based on the poem "The New Colossus," and who wrote the song "God Bless America" to express his deep love for and devotion to his adopted country.

A biography of Joseph Pulitzer, an immigrant, who raised money to complete the pedestal for the Statue of Liberty, and who left money, at his death, for annual awards for those who have made unique contributions in the fields of journalism, literature, and music.

Descriptions of the Statue of Liberty, including the American Automobile Association *Tour Book*, which not only describes the Statue of Liberty but gives directions as to how to reach it, when it is open to the public, and the cost of the boat trip.

Ethnic American Minorities: A Guide to Media and Materials, edited and compiled by Harry A. Johnson (New York: R. R. Bowker, 1976), is an invaluable bibliographic tool. The teacher and the library media specialist will find this bibliography a veritable gold mine, for it contains—in addition to background informational articles on the history, the social and psychological needs, the occupational and educational status, and curriculum alternatives— annotated entries for hundreds of films, filmstrips, slides, transparencies, audio recordings and audio cassettes, video cassettes, study prints, pictures, posters, and graphics.

INTERDISCIPLINARY LEARNING

The National Council of Teachers of English (NCTE) published in 1975 *Thematic Units in Teaching English and the Humanities*, edited by Sylvia Spann and Mary Beth Culp, in a loose-leaf binder with tabs. NCTE describes this resource guide as follows:

> These 15 unit plans focus on getting students involved in English the way they are involved in life—questioning, reflecting, probing, wondering, and sometimes rebelling. The plans are designed so that students use all their language skills as they explore problems and questions inherent in the human condition. Includes units of family life, the occult, death, the literature of sports, rural culture and folklore, an introduction to filmmaking, media and the representation of life, utopias, conscience vs. established authority, and growing old. . . . Each unit includes general objectives, notes on evaluation, list of materials needed, daily lesson plans, suggested related activities, and bibliography.[5]

In 1977, NCTE published *Thematic Units in Teaching English and the Humanities: First Supplement*,[6] which presented five additional units dealing with issues of vital interest to today's youth. As in the original guide, these units are flexible and can be expanded or shortened to accommodate student interest and time available. No theme is structured as a rigid framework; the purpose of every unit is to provide stimulation and guidelines from which a teacher may branch out with individual creativity.

Another interdisciplinary teaching guide, *Teaching the Decades: A Humanities Approach to American Civilization* by Brooke Workman, was published by NCTE in 1975. In the Foreword, the purpose and scope of this humanities approach to teaching English are set forth as follows:

> *Teaching the Decades* . . . is a guide to an interdisciplinary course that can be taught by one teacher—any teacher who has a little sense of adventure and a pinch of confidence. Central to the course are two very American values: it is flexible; it works.
>
> Here is enough flexibility to tempt the professional who knows that a humanities course cannot be packaged, and at the same time enough specifics to tempt the novice who hopes that it can be. Essentially what both will find is a method rather than a course, a methodology that is illustrated with a humanities approach to American civilization. It describes a way of learning that is applicable to survey courses but is illustrated here with postholing in one of three decades. In postholing, students will dig deep into a short span of American life in its totality—

oral as well as written history,* radio, movies, best sellers, architecture, painting, poetry, drama, dance, music—but all essentially as a way of learning, a way of examining American values, a way of coming to a better understanding of themselves and their friends.[7]

Example 38, American Humanities: Tentative Schedule for the 1920s Unit, and Example 39, American Humanities: Names and Terms of the 1920s, indicate course design and areas of emphasis as well as the 100 topics that are highlighted in *Teaching the Decades.*

Teaching the Decades is a prime example of the value to be accrued from the classroom teacher's using the school library media center as an instructional support partner. These teaching units will generate interest that should carry the students into rewarding areas of exploration far beyond the 100 topics listed in the guide for each of the three separate units on the decades. Each topic in Example 39 could well lead into a number of significant related topics; for example:

The Monkey Trial and Clarence Darrow are included in the basic topic list. In addition to the foregoing, other exciting possibilities include—

Darwin's Theory of Evolution

William Jennings Bryan

John T. Scopes

The Monkey Trial and the Sacco-Vanzetti Trial are included in the basic topic list. In addition to these two trials, the Loeb-Leopold Trial of 1924 deserves attention.

In addition to the Volstead Act, which is listed as basic, the 19th Amendment giving nationwide suffrage to women, which was signed into law in 1920, is of equal significance and should be highlighted.

In addition to the novelists, playwrights, and poets listed, the following literary giants should be acknowledged:

Stephen Vincent Benet, *John Brown's Body*

Louis Bromfield, *Early Autumn*

Willa Cather, *Death Comes for the Archbishop* and *One of Ours*

Edna Ferber, *So Big*

Booth Tarkington, *Alice Adams*

Edith Wharton, *The Age of Innocence*

Thornton Wilder, *Bridge of San Luis Rey*

In addition to the several musicians listed, the following composers, lyricists, and performers deserve to be noted:

Irving Berlin

Duke Ellington

George and Ira Gershwin

Jerome Kern

Jelly Roll Morton

Cole Porter

Vincent Youmans

*An excellent guide to oral history as a teaching tool is *Oral History as a Teaching Approach* by John A. Neuenschwander (Washington, D.C.: National Education Association, 1976).

Only an innovative and creative teacher would attempt to teach such a comprehensively demanding program as *Teaching the Decades*. Such an innovative and creative teacher will "latch onto" the library media center as the means of achieving his or her teaching goals.

EXAMPLE 38   AMERICAN HUMANITIES: TENTATIVE SCHEDULE
FOR THE 1920s UNIT*

THE IDEA OF CULTURE

1. Orientation
2. Meeting Each Other
3. Culture and Values in Children's Literature
4. Dominant Values and the Top Ten of TV
5. Heroes, Heroines, and Consensus Seeking
6. Other Cultures and Culture Shock
7. Film: *The Humanities Approach*
8. Theories of American Civilization
9. Artifact Day
10. Artifact Day

HISTORY: THE DECADE, 1920s

11. Orientation: Terms and Tentative Schedule
12. Read *Only Yesterday:* Chapters 1, 5, 6, 8, 10, and pages 266–70, 284–89.
13. Film: *The Golden Twenties*
14. Filmstrip-Record or Documentary Records
15. Formation of History Small Groups and Activity Committees (e.g., Handbook, Artifacts, Bulletin Board, Radio)
16. Reading, Research, Small Group Procedures
17. History Small Group 1
18. History Small Group 2
19. History Small Group 3
20. History Small Group 4
21. Class Consensus on History; Orientation to Oral History, Genealogy
22. Open Day
23. Oral History Presentations
24. Oral History Presentations
25. Oral History and Genealogy Presentations
26. Orientation: Term Projects

POPULAR CULTURE—RADIO, FILMS, BEST SELLERS

27. Radio Recordings
28. Radio Recordings
29. Decade Films
30. Decade Films
31. Decade Films
32. Orientation: Best Sellers
33. Reading; Proposals Due; First Conferences
34. Reading; First Conferences
35. Reading; First Conferences
36. *Ragged Dick*
37. *The Great Gatsby*
38. *The Man Nobody Knows*
39. *Babbitt* or *Main Street*
40. Self-Evaluation Day

ARCHITECTURE AND PAINTING AS ARTIFACTS

41. Architecture
42. Frank Lloyd Wright and American Architecture
43. Film: *Frank Lloyd Wright*
44. Orientation: Painting As Art and Artifact
45. The Armory Show
46. Study of Decade Paintings
47. Study of Decade Paintings
48. Study of Decade Paintings
49. Student Teaching of Paintings
50. Student Teaching of Paintings
51. Film on Decade Artist
52. Student Teaching
53. Field Trip: Art Gallery
54. Student Teaching
55. Student Teaching

POETRY AND PLAYS AS ARTIFACTS

56. Orientation: Poetry As Artifact
57. Preparation for Small Groups
58. Small Group 1: Poetry
59. Small Group 2: Poetry
60. Small Group 3: Poetry
61. Orientation: Plays As Artifacts
62. Reading and Rehearsal; Resource Person
63. Reading and Rehearsal
64. *The Hairy Ape*
65. *They Knew What They Wanted*
66. *Porgy*
67. Small Group One-Act Presentation
68. Project Final Outline Due; Discussion of Final Project

*From *Teaching the Decades: A Humanities Approach to American Civilization* by Brooke Workman (Urbana, Ill.: National Council of Teachers of English, 1975), pp. 5–6.

EXAMPLE 38 (cont.)

69. Second Conferences
70. Second Conferences

DANCING AND MUSIC AS CULTURAL EXEMPLARS

71. Dancing
72. Dancing
73. Orientation: Music As Cultural Expression
74. Formation of Music Committees
75. Committee Planning Day
76. Music Committee Presentation
77. Music Committee Presentation
78. Music Committee Presentation
79. Music Committee Presentation

CONCLUSION

80. Term Papers Due
81. Student Project Presentations
82. Student Project Presentations
83. Student Project Presentations
84. Student Project Presentations
85. Student Project Presentations
86. Discussion and Selection of Final Test Artifacts
87. Writing the Final Test
88. Writing the Final Test
89. Return of Term Papers; Discussion
90. Self-Evaluation; Course Evaluation

FINAL TEST

During the last week of American Humanities, you will select a large envelope containing artifacts. You are to imagine that you are living in the distant future—say 3000 A.D.—and on another planet. You have discovered a new planet on your travels, a barren planet on which you find a time capsule containing this envelope. After you return to your home planet, your anthropology society asks that you present a paper in which you describe the artifacts, theorize as to their meaning, and expand upon your analysis by suggesting what you think this barren planet once had for a culture. You are able to translate language, though you will only know what the artifacts say in themselves. Your report will be from three to five pages.

EXAMPLE 39 AMERICAN HUMANITIES: NAMES AND TERMS OF THE 1920s*

Gertrude Ederle
Douglas Fairbanks
The Galloping Ghost
KDKA
The Jazz Singer
flapper
Volstead Act
F. Scott Fitzgerald
Monkey Trial
Man O' War
Aimee Semple McPherson
H. L. Mencken
Sinclair Lewis
Will Rogers
flivver
George Herman Ruth
The Sheik
Spirit of St. Louis
Teapot Dome
Sacco and Vanzetti
Eugene O'Neill
Florenz Ziegfeld
Rudolph Valentino
St. Valentine's Day Massacre
Rudy Vallee
Gene Tunney

Al Smith
Al Capone
bootleggers
Black Six Scandal
Black Thursday
Clara Bow
Jack Dempsey
Four Horsemen
Emile Coué
Floyd Collins
Enrico Caruso
Peaches and Daddy
Eugene Debs
The Red Scare
normalcy
Calvin Coolidge
Rhapsody in Blue
Charles Lindbergh
Jazz Age
speakeasies
Billy Sunday
Clarence Darrow
Paul Whiteman
Main Street
Bruce Barton
The Waste Land

*From *Teaching the Decades: A Humanities Approach to American Civilization* by Brooke Workman (Urbana, Ill.: National Council of Teachers of English, 1975), p. 34.

EXAMPLE 39 (cont.)

"Avalon"	Bix Beiderbecke
This Side of Paradise	Fats Waller
Hal Roach	Blind Lemon Jefferson
Harry Houdini	Frank Lloyd Wright
Dorothy Dix	Bobby Franks
Carl Sandburg	Laurel and Hardy
Babbitt	Gertrude Stein
KKK	Ernest Hemingway
Jimmy Walker	Charleston
Warren Harding	Harlem Renaissance
Louis Armstrong	George Bellows
Mah Jongg	*The Smart Set*
Tin Lizzie	*What Price Glory?*
Al Jolson	Edna St. Vincent Millay
Buster Keaton	Bobby Jones
W. C. Fields	Henry Ford
Tom Mix	Knute Rockne
Erich von Stroheim	bathtub gin
The Great Gatsby	marathon dancing
The Saturday Evening Post	Herbert Hoover
bobbed hair	Miss America
Charlie Chaplin	skyscrapers
John Marin	knickers
Bing Crosby	Freud

To demonstrate the rich opportunities possible through teacher and librarian planning together for humanities integration see Example 40, Book Illustrators and Their Art. This unit was designed cooperatively by the teachers of reading, English, and art together with the library media specialist as a sixth-grade culminating activity. Realizing that many of the "great" illustrators have special appeal for the elementary level, this unit served a unique purpose, namely, to provide an opportunity for the students to revisit their favorite stories and to delight once again to the storytelling art of illustrators.

EXAMPLE 40 BOOK ILLUSTRATORS AND THEIR ART

Unit: Book Illustrators and Their Art (revised and expanded)
Subject: Humanities Interdisciplinary Unit
Grade: 6
Goal: To provide a culminating experience which will quicken student awareness of and interest in book illustrators and their art.
Objectives:
    1. To provide opportunity for the students to explore book illustration as an art form.
    2. To provide opportunity for the students to become reacquainted with illustrated books they have previously enjoyed.
    3. To provide opportunity for the students to experiment with book illustrations.
Teaching Procedure:
    I. Students are introduced to the unit.
      A. The filmstrip *Enjoying Illustrations* (Pied Piper) is viewed by the class.
        1. Students learn some of the ways illustrations contribute to the enjoyment of books.
        2. Students are asked to list at least three different ways illustrators can treat the same subject.
        3. Students are encouraged to make illustrations expressing emotion, mood, and character.

EXAMPLE 40 (cont.)

    B. The motion picture *Robert McCloskey* (Weston Woods) is shown.
       1. Students meet Robert McCloskey and visit his studio.
       2. Students discover that craftsmanship must go hand-in-hand with inspiration.
  II. Students are introduced to Randolph Caldecott.
    A. Students learn that he was an English artist and illustrator who lived 1846-1886.
    B. Students learn that he is best known for his series of 16 children's picture books, which includes:
       1. *Frog He Would A'Wooing Go* (Warne)
       2. *House that Jack Built* (Warne)
       3. *Sing a Song of Sixpence* (Warne)
       4. *Three Jovial Huntsmen* (Warne)
      FILMSTRIPS (sound)
       1. *Hey Diddle Diddle* (Weston Woods)
       2. *Sing a Song of Sixpence* (Weston Woods)
    C. Students learn that the Caldecott Medal is awarded each year to the illustrator voted as being the best. They examine:
       1. Caldecott Medal filmstrips (Weston Woods)
       2. Caldecott Medal posters (Horn Book)
 III. Students are introduced to Leslie Brooke.
    A. Students learn that he was an English artist and illustrator, a contemporary of Randolph Caldecott.
    B. Students discover that he created a series of books called the *Johnny Crow* books, which includes:
       1. *Johnny Crow's Garden* (Warne)
       2. *Johnny Crow's New Garden* (Warne)
       3. *Johnny Crow's Party* (Warne)
      FILMSTRIPS (sound)
       1. *Johnny Crow's Garden* (Spoken Arts)
       2. *Johnny Crow's New Garden* (Spoken Arts)
       3. *Johnny Crow's Party* (Spoken Arts)
       4. *The Tailor and the Crow* (Spoken Arts)
    C. Students learn that he had illustrated some of the traditional English nursery stories.
       1. *Story of the Three Bears* (Warne)
       2. *Story of the Three Little Pigs* (Warne)
       3. *This Little Pig Went to Market* (Warne)
 IV. Students are introduced to Kate Greenaway.
    A. Students learn that she was a poet and illustrator and was a contemporary of both Caldecott and Brooke.
    B. Students learn that she is best known for her books decorated with flowers, fruits, merry children, and landscapes, such as:
       1. *A—Apple Pie* (Warne)
       2. *The Kate Greenaway Treasury* (Collins-World)
       3. *The Language of Flowers* (Warne)
       4. *Marigold Garden* (Warne)
       5. *Mother Goose* (Warne)
       6. *Under the Window* (Warne)
      FILMSTRIPS (sound)
       1. *Marigold Garden* (Spoken Arts)
       2. *Under the Window* (Spoken Arts)
       3. *Kate Greenaway's Games* (Spoken Arts)
       4. *The Pied Piper of Hamelin* (from Robert Browning's poem) (Spoken Arts)
  V. Students are introduced to E. H. Shepard as the illustrator who created the World of Pooh
    A. The motion picture *Mr. Shepard and Mr. Milne* (Weston Woods) is viewed.
    B. The following books illustrated by Shepard are examined and discussed:
       1. *Christopher Robin Book of Verse* (Dutton)
       2. *Christopher Robin Story Book* (Dutton)

EXAMPLE 40 (cont.)

    3. *Hans Andersen's Fairy Tales* (Walck)
    4. *House at Pooh Corner* (Dutton)
    5. *Now We Are Six* (Dutton)
    6. *Pooh Cook Book* (Dutton)
    7. *The Pooh Get-Well Book: Recipes and Activities to Help You Recover from Wheezles and Sneezles* (Dutton)
    8. *Pooh Party Book* (Dutton)
    9. *Pooh's Song Book* (Dutton)
    10. *Pooh's Story Book* (Dutton)
    11. *Reluctant Dragon* (Holiday)
    12. *When We Were Very Young* (Dutton)
    13. *Wind in the Willows* (Scribner)
    14. *Winnie the Pooh* (Dutton)
  C. The following audiovisual materials are available for student examination:
  ART PRINTS
    1. *Pooh: His Art Gallery* (Dutton)
    2. *Pooh Posters* (Weston Woods)
  REALIA—Stuffed animals
    1. Eeyore (Sears Roebuck)
    2. Kanga (Sears Roebuck)
    3. Owl (Sears Roebuck)
    4. Piglet (Sears Roebuck)
    5. Pooh (Sears Roebuck)
    6. Rabbit (Sears Roebuck)
    7. Tigger (Sears Roebuck)
  REALIA—Figurines
    1. Christopher Robin (Beswick)
    2. Eeyore (Beswick)
    3. Kanga (Beswick)
    4. Owl (Beswick)
    5. Piglet (Beswick)
    6. Pooh (Beswick)
    7. Rabbit (Beswick)
    8. Tigger (Beswick)
VI. Students are introduced to the following illustrators and the books they have illustrated; they are encouraged to analyze, compare, and contrast the various styles of illustration:
  A. Joan Anglund, illustrator of:
    1. *A Child's Book of Old Nursery Rhymes* (Atheneum)
    2. *Christmas Is a Time of Giving* (Harcourt)
    3. *Cup of Sun: A Book of Poems* (Harcourt)
    4. *Do You Love Someone?* (Harcourt)
    5. *A Friend Is Someone Who Likes You* (Harcourt)
    6. *Goodbye, Yesterday* (Atheneum)
    7. *In a Pumpkin Shell: A Mother Goose ABC* (Harcourt)
    8. *Look Out the Window* (Harcourt)
    9. *Nibble Nibble Mousekin: A Tale of Hansel and Gretel* (Harcourt)
    10. *Pocketful of Proverbs* (Harcourt)
    11. *Spring Is a New Beginning* (Harcourt)
    12. *What Color Is Love?* (Harcourt)
    13. *A Year Is Round* (Harcourt)
  ART PRINTS
    1. *Packet of Pictures* (Harcourt)
  REALIA
    1. Anglund Plates—Months of the Year (Dekor Shop, Walter, West Germany)
  B. James Daugherty, illustrator of:
    1. *Abe Lincoln Grows Up* (Harcourt)
    2. *Andy and the Lion* (Viking Press)

EXAMPLE 40 (cont.)

   3. *Daniel Boone* (Viking Press)
   4. *Landing of the Pilgrims* (Random)
   5. *Of Courage Unlimited* (Viking Press)
   6. *Poor Richard* (Viking Press)
   7. *Rainbow Book of American History* (World)
FILMSTRIPS (sound)
   1. *Andy and the Lion* (Weston Woods)
   2. *The Loudest Noise in the World* (Weston Woods)
MOTION PICTURE
   1. *James Daugherty* (Weston Woods)

C. Disney Studios, illustrators of:
   1. *Alice in Wonderland* (Golden Press)
   2. *Bambi* (Golden Press)
   3. *Ben and Me* (Golden Press)
   4. *Brementown Musicians* (Golden Press)
   5. *Cinderella* (Golden Press)
   6. *The Little Red Hen* (Golden Press)
   7. *Mary Poppins* (Golden Press)
   8. *Peter Pan* (Golden Press)
   9. *Pinocchio* (Golden Press)
  10. *Snow White* (Golden Press)
  11. *Three Little Pigs* (Golden Press)
  12. *Uncle Remus Stories* (Golden Press)
  13. *Winnie the Pooh and His Friends* (Golden Press)
  14. *Winnie the Pooh and the Blustery Day* (Golden Press)
  15. *Winnie the Pooh and the Honey Tree* (Golden Press)
FILMSTRIPS (sound)
   1. *Alice in Wonderland* (Walt Disney Educational Media)
   2. *Bambi* (Walt Disney Educational Media)
   3. *Ben and Me* (Walt Disney Educational Media)
   4. *Cinderella* (Walt Disney Educational Media)
   5. *Mary Poppins* (Walt Disney Educational Media)
   6. *Peter Pan* (Walt Disney Educational Media)
   7. *Pinocchio* (Walt Disney Educational Media)
   8. *Snow White* (Walt Disney Educational Media)
   9. *Three Little Pigs* (Walt Disney Educational Media)
  10. *Winnie the Pooh and the Blustery Day* (Walt Disney Educational Media)
  11. *Winnie the Pooh and the Honey Tree* (Walt Disney Educational Media)
  12. *Winnie the Pooh and Tigger* (Walt Disney Educational Media)
MOTION PICTURES
   1. *Ben and Me* (Walt Disney Educational Media)
   2. *The Many Adventures of Winnie the Pooh* (Walt Disney Educational Media)

D. Katherine Evans, illustrator of:
   1. *The Boy Who Cried Wolf* (Albert Whitman)
   2. *A Bundle of Sticks* (Albert Whitman)
   3. *A Camel in the Tent* (Albert Whitman)
   4. *The Maid and Her Pail of Milk* (Albert Whitman)
   5. *The Man, the Boy, and the Donkey* (Albert Whitman)
FILMSTRIPS (sound)
   1. *A Bundle of Sticks* (Educational Enrichment Materials)
   2. *A Camel in the Tent* (Educational Enrichment Materials)
   3. *The Maid and Her Pail of Milk* (Educational Enrichment Materials)
   4. *The Man, the Boy, and the Donkey* (Educational Enrichment Materials)

E. Gyo Fujikawa, illustrator of:
   1. *Child's Book of Poems* (Grosset)
   2. *A Child's Garden of Verses* (Grosset)
   3. *Fairy Tales and Fables* (Grosset)
   4. *Mother Goose* (Grosset)

EXAMPLE 40 (cont.)

ART PRINTS
1. *Portfolio of Fujikawa Reproductions* (Grosset)

F. Paul Galdone, illustrator of:
1. *Androcles and the Lion* (McGraw)
2. *Barbara Frietchie* (Crowell)
3. *Blind Men and the Elephant* (McGraw)
4. *Cinderella* (McGraw)
5. *First Seven Days* (Crowell)
6. *The Frog Prince* (McGraw)
7. *Gingerbread Boy* (Seabury)
8. *The Hare and the Tortoise* (McGraw)
9. *Henny Penny* (Seabury)
10. *Hereafterthis* (McGraw)
11. *The History of Little Tom Tucker* (McGraw)
12. *The Horse, the Fox, and the Lion* (Seabury)
13. *The House That Jack Built* (McGraw)
14. *The Life of Jack Sprat, His Wife and His Cat* (McGraw)
15. *The Little Red Hen* (Seabury)
16. *Little Tuppen* (Seabury)
17. *The Magic Porridge Pot* (Seabury)
18. *The Monkey and the Crocodile* (Seabury)
19. *The Moving Adventures of Old Dame Trot and Her Comical Cat* (McGraw)
20. *Obedient Jack* (Watts)
21. *Old Mother Hubbard and Her Dog* (McGraw)
22. *The Old Woman and Her Pig* (McGraw)
23. *Puss in Boots* (Seabury)
24. *Three Aesop Fox Fables* (Seabury)
25. *The Three Bears* (Seabury)
26. *The Three Billy Goats Gruff* (Seabury)
27. *The Three Little Pigs* (Seabury)
28. *The Three Wishes* (McGraw)
29. *Tom, Tom the Piper's Son* (McGraw)
30. *The Town Mouse and the Country Mouse* (McGraw)
31. *The Wise Fool* (Pantheon)
FILMSTRIPS (sound)
1. *The House That Jack Built* (Weston Woods)
2. *Old Mother Hubbard and Her Dog* (Weston Woods)
3. *Old Woman and Her Pig* (Weston Woods)
MOTION PICTURES
1. *Old Mother Hubbard and Her Dog* (McGraw)
2. *The Old Woman and Her Pig* (McGraw)

G. Janusz Grabianski, illustrator of:
1. *Andersen's Fairy Tales* (Hawthorn)
2. *Androcles and the Lion* (Watts)
3. *Big Book of Animal Fables* (Watts)
4. *Big Book of Animal Stories* (Watts)
5. *Big Book of Pets* (Watts)
6. *Big Book of Wild Animals* (Watts)
7. *Grabianski's Birds* (Watts)
8. *Grabianski's Cats* (Watts)
9. *Grabianski's Dogs* (Watts)
10. *Grabianski's Horses* (Watts)
11. *Grabianski's Wild Animals* (Watts)
12. *Grimm's Fairy Tales* (Hawthorn)
13. *Ten Tales from Shakespeare* (Watts)
ART PRINTS
1. *Grabianski's Portfolio* (Watts)

EXAMPLE 40 (cont.)

H. Ezra Keats, illustrator of:
1. *Brave Riders* (Crowell)
2. *Danny Dunn and the Anti-Gravity Paint* (McGraw)
3. *Danny Dunn and the Homework Machine* (McGraw)
4. *Danny Dunn and the Weather Machine* (McGraw)
5. *Danny Dunn on a Desert Island* (McGraw)
6. *The Egyptians Knew* (McGraw)
7. *The Eskimos Knew* (McGraw)
8. *Grasses* (Walck)
9. *Hi, Cat* (Macmillan)
10. *The Indians Knew* (McGraw)
11. *John Henry: An American Legend* (Pantheon)
12. *The Pilgrims Knew* (McGraw)
13. *The Snowy Day* (Viking Press)
14. *Wonder Tales of Dogs and Cats* (Doubleday)
FILMSTRIPS (sound)
1. *John Henry: An American Legend* (Guidance Associates)
2. *The Snowy Day* (Weston Woods)
MOTION PICTURES
1. *Ezra Jack Keats* (Weston Woods)
2. *John Henry* (Holt)
3. *The Snowy Day* (Weston Woods)
POSTERS
1. *At Home* (Macmillan)
2. *At School* (Macmillan)
3. *In the Community* (Macmillan)
4. *The Snowy Day* (Horn Book)
I. Edna Miller, illustrator of:
1. *Mousekin Finds a Friend* (Prentice-Hall)
2. *Mousekin's Christmas Eve* (Prentice-Hall)
3. *Mousekin's Family* (Prentice-Hall)
4. *Mousekin's Golden House* (Prentice-Hall)
5. *Mousekin Takes a Trip* (Prentice-Hall)
6. *Mousekin's Woodland Birthday* (Prentice-Hall)
7. *Mousekin's Woodland Sleepers* (Prentice-Hall)
FILMSTRIPS (sound)
1. *Mousekin Finds a Friend* (Educational Enrichment Materials)
2. *Mousekin's Christmas Eve* (Educational Enrichment Materials)
3. *Mousekin's Family* (Educational Enrichment Materials)
4. *Mousekin's Golden House* (Educational Enrichment Materials)
J. Beatrix Potter, illustrator of:
1. *Appley Dapply's Nursery Rhymes* (Warne)
2. *Letters to Children* (Walker)
3. *Roly Poly Pudding* (Warne)
4. *The Sly Old Cat* (Warne)
5. *The Story of a Fierce Bad Rabbit* (Warne)
6. *The Tailor of Gloucester* (Warne)
7. *The Tale of Benjamin Bunny* (Warne)
8. *The Tale of Jemima Puddle-Duck* (Warne)
9. *The Tale of Johnny Townmouse* (Warne)
10. *The Tale of Little Pig Robinson* (Warne)
11. *The Tale of Mister Jeremy Fisher* (Warne)
12. *The Tale of Mister Todd* (Warne)
13. *The Tale of Mrs. Tiggy-Winkle* (Warne)
14. *The Tale of Mrs. Tittlemouse* (Warne)
15. *The Tale of Peter Rabbit* (Warne)
16. *The Tale of Pigling Bland* (Warne)

EXAMPLE 40 (cont.)

17. *The Tale of Squirrel Nutkin* (Warne)
18. *The Tale of the Flopsy Bunnies* (Warne)
19. *The Tale of Timmy Tiptoes* (Warne)
20. *The Tale of Tom Kitten* (Warne)
21. *The Tale of Two Bad Mice* (Warne)

BIOGRAPHY OF BEATRIX POTTER
1. *The Art of Beatrix Potter* with an Appreciation by Anne Carroll Moore (Warne)
2. *Nothing Is Impossible: The Story of Beatrix Potter* by Dorothy Aldis (Atheneum)

CRAFT BOOKS
1. *Needlepoint Designs after Illustrations by Beatrix Potter* by Rita Weiss (Dover)
2. *Toys from the Tales of Beatrix Potter* by Margaret Hutchings (Warne)

CRAFT PROJECTS
1. *Plaster Molds* supplied by Activa Products, Inc. (582 Market St., San Francisco, Calif. 94104)
   Benjamin Bunny
   Hunca Munca
   Jemima Puddle-Duck
   Jeremy Fisher
   Mrs. Tiggy-Winkle
   Peter Rabbit
   Tom Kitten
   Tom Thumb

ART PRINTS
1. *Benjamin Bunny* (Warne)
2. *Peter Rabbit* (Warne)
3. *Squirrel Nutkin* (Warne)
4. *A Mural: The Tale of Peter Rabbit* (Warne)

FILMSTRIPS (sound)
1. *The Tailor of Gloucester* (Spoken Arts)
2. *The Tale of Benjamin Bunny* (Spoken Arts)
3. *The Tale of Benjamin Bunny* (Weston Woods)
4. *The Tale of Mr. Jeremy Fisher* (Spoken Arts)
5. *The Tale of Mrs. Tiggy-Winkle* (Spoken Arts)
6. *The Tale of Peter Rabbit* (Spoken Arts)
7. *The Tale of Peter Rabbit* (Weston Woods)
8. *The Tale of Squirrel Nutkin* (Spoken Arts)
9. *The Tale of Two Bad Mice* (Spoken Arts)

REALIA—Figurines
1. Benjamin Bunny (Beswick)
2. Benjamin Bunny's Father (Beswick)
3. Flopsy, Mopsy, and Cotton-Tail (Beswick)
4. Hunca Munca (Beswick)
5. Jemima Puddle-Duck (Beswick)
6. Lady Mouse (Beswick)
7. Peter Rabbit (Beswick)
8. Poorly Peter Rabbit (Beswick)
9. Squirrel Nutkin (Beswick)
10. Tailor of Gloucester (Beswick)

K. Norman Rockwell, illustrator of:
1. *Norman Rockwell: A Sixty Year Retrospective* edited by Thomas S. Buechner (Abrams)
2. *Norman Rockwell Illustrator* by Arthur L. Guptill (Watson-Guptill)
3. *The Norman Rockwell Storybook* (Simon and Schuster)
4. *Norman Rockwell's Americana ABC* (Abrams)
5. *Tom Sawyer* (Heritage Press)

ART PRINTS
1. *Boys and Dog on a Raft* (Becky Thatcher Gift Shop, Hannibal, Mo. 63857)
2. *Boys Smoking a Pipe* (Becky Thatcher Gift Shop)

EXAMPLE 40 (cont.)

3. *Boys Walking Girl Home from School* (Becky Thatcher Gift Shop)
4. *The Four Seasons* (New York Graphics)
5. *Rockwell's Americans* (Scholastic)

L. Arthur Rackham, illustrator of:
1. *Cinderella* (Lippincott)
2. *Once Upon a Time: The Fairy-Tale World of Arthur Rackham* (Viking Press)
3. *Sleeping Beauty* (Lippincott)

M. Tasha Tudor, illustrator of:
1. *Around the Year* (Walck)
2. *Child's Garden of Verses* (Walck)
3. *Fairy Tales from Hans Christian Andersen* (Walck)
4. *First Delights: A Book about the Five Senses* (Platt)
5. *Little Princess* (Lippincott)
6. *Little Women* (World)
7. *Secret Garden* (Lippincott)
8. *Wind in the Willows* (World)
9. *Wings from the Wind: An Anthology of Poetry* (Lippincott)

ART PRINTS
1. Various illustrations available upon request (Walck)
2. Original illustrations and reproductions (The Dutch Inn Gift Shop, 211 N. Water St., Mill Hall, Pa. 17751)

GREETING CARDS
1. Christmas Scenes (The Dutch Inn Gift Shop)
2. Family Gatherings (The Dutch Inn Gift Shop)
3. Flowers and Garlands (The Dutch Inn Gift Shop)

N. Edwin Tunis, illustrator of:
1. *Colonial Craftsmen and the Beginnings of American Industry* (World)
2. *Colonial Living* (World)
3. *Frontier Living* (World)
4. *Indians* (World)
5. *Oars, Sails and Steam* (World)
6. *Shaw's Fortune: The Picture Story of a Colonial Plantation* (World)
7. *Weapons* (World)
8. *Wheels* (World)

O. Brian Wildsmith, illustrator of:
1. *Brian Wildsmith's Birds* (Watts)
2. *Brian Wildsmith's Circus* (Watts)
3. *Brian Wildsmith's Fishes* (Watts)
4. *Brian Wildsmith's the Twelve Days of Christmas* (Watts)
5. *Brian Wildsmith's Wild Animals* (Watts)
6. *Child's Garden of Verses* (Watts)
7. *The Hare and the Tortoise* (Watts)
8. *The Lion and the Rat* (Watts)
9. *The Miller, the Boy and the Donkey* (Watts)
10. *The Owl and the Woodpecker* (Watts)
11. *Oxford Book of Poetry for Children* (Watts)
12. *The Rich Man and the Shoe-maker* (Watts)

FILMSTRIPS
1. *Brian Wildsmith's Birds* (Weston Woods)
2. *Brian Wildsmith's Wild Animals* (Weston Woods)
3. *The North Wind and the Sun* (Weston Woods)
4. *The Rich Man and the Shoe-maker* (Weston Woods)

ART PRINTS
1. *A Brian Wildsmith Portfolio* (Watts)
2. *Brian Wildsmith's Animal Portfolio* (Watts)

P. Newell C. Wyeth, illustrator of:
1. *Boy's King Arthur* (Scribner)
2. *The Deerslayer* (Scribner)

EXAMPLE 40 (cont.)

    3. *Drums* (Scribner)

    4. *Mysterious Island* (Scribner)

    5. *Robin Hood* (Scribner)

    6. *Robinson Crusoe* (Scribner)

    7. *Treasure Island* (Scribner)

    8. *Westward Ho* (Scribner)

VII. Students are given the opportunity to examine and compare various illustrated editions of the same title, for example:

  A. *Child's Garden of Verses* as illustrated by:

    1. Gyo Fujikawa (Grosset)

    2. Tasha Tudor (Walck)

    3. Brian Wildsmith (Watts)

  B. *Little Women* as illustrated by:

    1. Barbara Cooney (Crowell)

    2. Betty Fraser (Macmillan)

    3. Tasha Tudor (World)

  C. *The Man, the Boy and the Donkey* or *The Miller, His Son and Their Donkey* as illustrated by:

    1. Roger Duvoisin (McGraw-Hill)

    2. Katherine Evans (Albert Whitman)

    3. Brian Wildsmith (Watts)

  D. *Mother Goose* as illustrated by:

    1. Gyo Fujikawa (Grosset)

    2. Kate Greenaway (World)

    3. Tasha Tudor (Walck)

    4. Brian Wildsmith (Watts)

  E. *Robinson Crusoe* as illustrated by:

    1. Roger Duvoisin (World)

    2. Lynd Ward (Grosset)

    3. Newell C. Wyeth (Scribner)

  F. *Story of the Three Pigs* as illustrated by:

    1. Leslie Brooke (Warne)

    2. William Pene DuBois (Viking Press)

    3. Disney Studios (Walt Disney Productions)

    4. Paul Galdone (Seabury)

    5. William Stobbs (McGraw-Hill)

  G. *Winnie-the-Pooh* as illustrated by:

    1. Disney Studios (Walt Disney Productions)

    2. E. H. Shepard (Dutton)

VIII. Students are given the opportunity to become acquainted with illustrated books from foreign countries; for example, these illustrated children's books from Japan:

  A. *Hansel and Gretel*, illustrated by Yoshitaro Isaka (Gakken Publishing, imported by Japan Publications Trading Co., 1255 Howard St., San Francisco, Calif. 94103)

  B. *How the Withered Trees Blossomed*, illustrated by Yasuo Segawa (Kodansha, Ltd., imported by Lippincott). Note: This book is printed in Japanese style—it is to be read from back to front; the text is in Japanese calligraphy as well as in English.

  C. *The Nutcracker*, illustrated by Fumiko Hori (Gakken Publishing, imported by Japan Publications Trading Co.)

  D. *The Sorcerer's Apprentice*, illustrated by Ryo Hei Yauagihara (Gakken Publishing, imported by Japan Publications Trading Co.)

  E. *William Tell*, illustrated by Hiroshi Mizusawa (Gakken Publishing, imported by Japan Publications Trading Co.)

IX. Students are encouraged to try their hand at story illustration, or one or more of the following activities:

  A. Designing book jackets.

EXAMPLE 40 (cont.)

B. Designing bookplates and/or bookmarks.
C. Designing greeting cards with a storybook motif.
D. Designing needlework patterns of storybook characters.

Unlimited opportunities to integrate humanities offerings within the framework of existing courses of study abound on both the elementary and secondary levels. Scores of possibilities will suggest themselves as the classroom teacher plans with the library media specialist. As an example, the Sample Resource Unit: The Civil War and Reconstruction, which is included in Appendix D, lists under Recommended Teaching Procedures numerous humanities integration experiences. The following example is illustrative of how cooperative planning can enliven and enrich an instructional unit.

Desiring to breathe new life into a study of the Bill of Rights, the political science teacher consults the school library media specialist. The library media specialist offers for the teacher's consideration numerous avenues for approaching humanities enrichment and integration. Several interest-laden possibilities are offered, including:

Norman Rockwell's painting of the *Four Freedoms* together with their accompanying essays beautifully written by Booth Tarkington, Will Durant, Stephen Vincent Benet, and Carlos Bulosan;

William Randolph Hearst's abuse of the freedom of the press in contrast with the Code of Ethics or Canons of Journalism prepared by the American Society of Newspaper Editors; and

The famous "Opinions" of Justice Oliver Wendell Holmes, the "Great Dissenter," who defended the right of an American citizen to hold beliefs contrary to the official position of the government.

In addition to working with classroom teachers to integrate the humanities within the framework of *existing* courses of study, the library media specialist is frequently called upon to serve as the resource consultant for curriculum committees and individual classroom teachers searching for professionally and commercially prepared humanities units and/or learning projects. After having been briefed by the committee or teacher, the library media specialist provides assistance and guidance to the curriculum planners by:

Alerting them to the various resource units available from the professional organizations, such as *Teaching the Decades: A Humanities Approach to American Civilization, Thematic Units in Teaching English and the Humanities: First Supplement*, published by NCTE; and *Roots of America: A Multiethnic Resource Guide for 7th, 8th, and 9th Grade Social Studies Teachers*; and *Women's Studies*, published by NEA.

Alerting them to model teaching units available from publishers, such as "A Study Guide to Studs Terkel's *Working: People Talk about What They Do All Day and How They Feel about What They Do*," "A Study Guide to the *Holocaust*," and "A Study Guide for a Mini-Unit on Death," all distributed free of charge by the Avon Books Education Department;* and

*Avon Books Education Department, 959 Eighth Ave., New York, N.Y. 10019.

the "Sample Interdisciplinary Unit" prepared by the Encyclopaedia Britannica Educational Corporation (see Appendix C).

Alerting them to the programs of proven excellence available from a number of commercial producers of humanities materials such as those produced and distributed by The Center for Humanities, Inc., which produces Sound-Slide programs on the following humanities themes:

Deciding Right from Wrong: The Dilemma of Morality Today

Freedom and Responsibility: A Question of Values

The Humanities: An Approach to Living in the Modern World

An Inquiry into the Nature of Man: His Inhumanity and His Humanity

Man Alone and Loneliness: The Dilemma of Modern Society

Man and His Values: An Inquiry into Good and Evil

Man as Hero: Tragic and Comic

Man's Search for Identity

Man's Search for the Meaning of Life

The Many Masks We Wear

No Man Is an Island: An Inquiry into Alienation

The Pursuit of Happiness: Man's Search for the Good Life

The Reality of Imagination: An Inquiry into Human Creativity

What Does It Mean to Be Human?

Who Am I? Where Did I Come From? Where Am I Going? The Eternal Questions

The Guidance Associates, producers of excellent instructional audiovisual programs, have initiated a series of humanities programs including:

The Age of Leonardo and Michelangelo

The Dawn of the Twentieth Century

The Literature of Protest

Man in the Nuclear Age

Prejudice

A World Between Wars

Alerting them to the National Association for Humanities Education, which serves as a clearinghouse for humanities programs, bibliographies, and consultants*

Alerting them to the various humanities resource materials, including commercially prepared kits available either in the school library media center or the district instructional materials center.

In addition to working with fellow teachers to integrate the humanities within the teaching-learning program, the library media specialist has unlimited opportunities to quicken and nurture student interest in things of an esthetic nature. Just as the sounds and images that abound in the environment go unheard, unseen, unsuspected, and unenjoyed until the television receiver

*National Association for Humanities Education, Box 628, Kirksville, Mo. 63501.

is plugged in, turned on, and fine-tuned, so the sound and sight of man's creations both past and present go unheard, unseen, unsuspected, and unenjoyed if men and women are not "plugged in, turned on, and fine-tuned" to their cultural heritage. By alerting individual students and groups of students to cultural learning experiences in the fields of literature, art, music, history, science, religion, philosophy, and psychology, the library media specialist functions as a teacher of the humanities.

NOTES

1. Marguerite Hood, "The Contribution of Fine Arts and Music to the Humanities," in *The Humanities and the Curriculum*, ed. by Louise M. Berman (Washington, D.C.: Association for Supervision and Curriculum Development, 1967), p. 16.
2. Moses Hadas, *Old Wine, New Bottles: A Humanist Teacher at Work* (New York: Simon and Schuster, 1962), p. 16.
3. Fred H. Stocking, "High School Humanities Courses: Some Revelations and Warnings," in *The English Leaflet*, vol. 53, no. 5, Fall 1965, pp. 37–38.
4. *Roots of America: A Multiethnic Curriculum Resource Guide for 7th, 8th, and 9th Grade Social Studies Teachers*, developed by the New Jersey Education Association and the National Education Association (Washington, D.C.: National Education Association, 1975), p. 9.
5. Sylvia Spann and Mary Beth Culp, eds., *Thematic Units in Teaching English and the Humanities* (Urbana, Ill.: National Council of Teachers of English, 1975), note inside back cover.
6. National Council of Teachers of English, *Thematic Units in Teaching English and the Humanities: First Supplement* (Urbana, Ill.: NCTE, 1977).
7. Brooke Workman, *Teaching the Decades: A Humanities Approach to American Civilization* (Urbana, Ill.: National Council of Teachers of English, 1975), p. vi.

12 The Library Media Program Implements the Developmental Skills Program

It has been said that the mark of an educated man is not his ability to recall answers to specific questions but his ability to recall and utilize sources that will provide answers to questions or give clues to answers.

Ella C. Leppert*

Many thoughtful observers believe that the thinking capacities of most students are rarely used and that distressingly low levels of thinking are manifested in most classrooms.

June R. Chapin and Richard E. Gross†

It is more important to generate intellectual curiosity and a passion for knowledge, and to cultivate good habits of thought and inquiry, than to concentrate on learning countless detailed facts which may soon be forgotten or abandoned. . . . Knowledge and reason and their related skills must always lie at the center of the goals of instruction.

The Research and Policy Committee of the Committee for Economic Development‡

"Perhaps much of what the pupil learns . . . will wear thin or become obsolete but skills learned in school continue to be functional indefinitely, or for as long as they are needed. Skills are the most permanent of learnings."[1] Since developing citizens who are functionally literate is the goal of education in our free society, "the purpose which runs through and strengthens all other educational purposes—the common thread of education—is the development of the ability to think."[2] Knowing how to think, knowing how to learn, and knowing how to communicate are requisite to effective citizenship; therefore, no skills are more worthwhile building than those thinking-learning-communicating tools basic for an informed electorate.

Because skills are basic for informed citizenship, the National Council for the Social Studies (NCSS) devoted its thirty-third Yearbook to an in-depth study of the philosophy, the content, and the process of constructing a developmental skills program, K–12. Throughout this yearbook the point is made that pupils develop skills most effectively when there is systematic instruction and continuing application of the skills. The following principles of learning and teaching have been emphasized as a basis for a developmental skills program:

*Ella C. Leppert, "Locating and Gathering Information," in *Skill Development in the Social Studies*, ed. by Helen McCracken Carpenter, Thirty-Third Yearbook (Washington, D.C.: National Council for the Social Studies, 1963), p. 53.

†June R. Chapin and Richard E. Gross, *Teaching Social Studies Skills* (Boston: Little, Brown, 1973), p. 125.

‡The Research and Policy Committee, *Innovation in Education: New Directions for the American School* (New York: Committee for Economic Development, 1968), p. 33.

1. The skill should be taught functionally, in the context of a topic of study, rather than as a separate exercise.
2. The learner must understand the meaning and purpose of the skill, and have motivation for developing it.
3. The learner should be carefully supervised in his first attempts to apply the skill, so that he will form correct habits from the beginning.
4. The learner needs repeated opportunities to practice the skill, with immediate evaluation so that he knows where he has succeeded or failed in his performance.
5. The learner needs individual help, through diagnostic measures and follow-up exercises, since not all members of any group learn at exactly the same rate or retain equal amounts of what they have learned.
6. Skill instruction should be presented at increasing levels of difficulty, moving from the simple to the more complex; the resulting growth in skills should be cumulative as the learner moves through school, with each level of instruction building on and reinforcing what has been taught previously.
7. Students should be helped, at each stage, to generalize the skills, by applying them in many and varied situations; in this way, maximum transfer of learning can be achieved.
8. The program of instruction should be sufficiently flexible to allow skills to be taught as they are needed by the learner; many skills should be developed concurrently.[3]

In applying these principles, teachers should keep in mind that, although it is possible to make a general plan for continuity in skill development, it is impossible to set a particular place in the school program where it is always best to introduce a specific skill. Many factors enter into the final decision of the teacher, as he or she works with a specific class, and the general plan can serve only as a guide to what seems to be good practice. True continuity in skill development is that which is developed within the learner, not that which can be blocked out in a general plan. Furthermore, it can never be assumed that children have gained command of a particular skill merely because they have been exposed to it. Review and reteaching of skills that have been stressed at an earlier grade level are often necessary, even with the most capable students.

THINKING-LEARNING-COMMUNICATING SKILLS CONTINUUM

NCSS recommends that a chart be prepared to outline a planned, sequential program for skill development that cuts across subject lines and bridges the gap between the elementary and the secondary school.[4] This skills development chart would serve as a reminder to every teacher that effective teaching of skills should be part of a cumulative program running from the early school years through high school. It would help the teacher plan so as to reinforce whatever command of skills the pupils have already attained at the same time that he or she leads them to a higher level of performance.

In compliance with the recommendation made by NCSS, the author of this work has prepared a Thinking-Learning-Communicating Skills Continuum, K–12. Given below is a broad outline of the main headings of the continuum, which indicates the organizational pattern of some four hundred integrated thinking-learning-communicating skills; the continuum in its entirety is found in Appendix L.

PART ONE: THINKING SKILLS
    I. Thinking processes:

   A. Make effective use of perceptive thinking.
   B. Make effective use of associative thinking.
   C. Make effective use of conceptual thinking.
   D. Make effective use of problem solving.
   E. Make effective use of critical thinking.
   F. Make effective use of creative thinking.
   G. Make effective use of adventurous thinking.

II. Thinking in the cognitive area:
   A. Make effective use of knowledge-building skills.
   B. Make effective use of comprehension skills.
   C. Make effective use of application skills.
   D. Make effective use of analysis skills.
   E. Make effective use of synthesis skills.
   F. Make effective use of evaluation skills.

III. Thinking in the affective area:
   A. Make effective use of receiving (attending) skills.
   B. Make effective use of responding skills.
   C. Make effective use of valuing skills.
   D. Make effective use of organizing skills.
   E. Make effective use of characterizing/valuing skills.

PART TWO: LEARNING SKILLS

I. Locating information:
   A. Make effective use of libraries.
   B. Make effective use of books.
   C. Make effective use of dictionaries.
   D. Make effective use of encyclopedias.
   E. Make effective use of other basic reference tools.
   F. Make effective use of periodicals and periodical indexes.
   G. Make effective use of newspapers and newspaper indexes.
   H. Make effective use of U.S. government documents, publications, and indexes.
   I. Make effective use of pamphlets.
   J. Make effective use of primary source materials.
   K. Make effective use of audiovisual media.

II. Acquiring information through purposeful and appreciative reading:
   A. Develop reading competence.
   B. Adjust reading rate to purpose.
   C. Read to form relationships.
   D. Read literature with perception and appreciation.

III. Acquiring information through purposeful and appreciative listening:
   A. Develop listening competence.
   B. Make effective use of critical listening.
   C. Make effective use of appreciative listening.

IV. Acquiring information through purposeful viewing and observing:
   A. Recognize that viewing is visual inspection.
   B. Recognize that observing goes beyond viewing and stresses adherence to criteria or following a scientific model.
   C. Recognize that viewing is purposeful looking and that observing is carefully and scientifically studying and interpreting what is seen.

    D. Apply critical thinking skills when "reading" visual media.

    E. "Read" visual media and employ the inquiry processes.

    F. Study teacher-constructed and commercially prepared learning guides.

    G. Organize and consolidate the ideas gained from viewing with ideas gained from other print and nonprint sources as well as from own past experience.

    H. Explore the artistic, technical, psychological, biographical, and historical components of the fine arts.

    I. Become acquainted with the great artists, past and present, and their works.

    J. "Read" the record of man's historical past.

    K. Recognize abilities essential for effective observation.

V. Constructing and interpreting surveys and opinion polls:

    A. Recognize that a survey is an investigation of things as existing or of events past.

    B. Recognize that a poll is a sampling or collection of opinions.

    C. Recognize that an opinion is an answer that is given to a question in a given situation.

    D. Recognize the basic steps employed in conducting an opinion poll.

    E. Recognize various data-collecting techniques.

    F. Analyze nationally recognized surveys.

    G. Design and field test surveys.

VI. Learning through group and social interaction:

    A. Recognize that excellence in interpersonal relationships is based on psychological maturity.

    B. Recognize the characteristics of a psychologically mature person.

    C. Perceive the characteristics of an effective group member.

    D. Recognize the purpose and function of a committee.

    E. Recognize the purpose and function of a panel.

    F. Recognize the purpose and function of a buzz group.

    G. Appreciate the value of parliamentary procedure.

VII. Organizing information:

    A. Make effective use of outlining techniques.

    B. Recognize the distinguishing characteristics and mechanics of the two basic outlining systems.

    C. Make effective use of note-taking techniques.

PART THREE: COMMUNICATION SKILLS

I. Writing as a communication tool:

    A. Perceive the significance of writing.

    B. Perceive the significance of functional literacy.

    C. Perceive the hallmarks of excellence in written communication.

II. Writing the essay:

    A. Perceive the distinguishing characteristics of the essay form.

    B. Become aware of the techniques employed in designing and structuring the essay.

III. Writing the research paper:

    A. Recognize the purpose and value of the research paper.

    B. Study the procedure to follow as outlined in basic style manuals or research guides.

IV. Speaking as a communication tool:
  A. Perceive that speech is a vehicle for conveying thought and emotion.
  B. Perceive that effective speaking is a learned process.
  C. Perceive the requirements for a speech of quality and effectiveness.
  D. Perceive the distinguishing characteristics of the speech designed to entertain or amuse.
  E. Perceive the distinguishing characteristics of the speech designed to inform or instruct.
  F. Perceive the distinguishing characteristics of the speech designed to stimulate or actuate through emotion.
  G. Perceive the distinguishing characteristics of the speech designed to convince or move to action.
  H. Perceive the distinguishing characteristics of debate.

The Thinking-Learning-Communicating Skills Continuum may well serve as a point of departure for teachers and administrators to use in formulating their own continuum for the skills program in their own school or school system. "When teachers thus clarify their own purposes for teaching skills, become sensitized to their pupils' need for skill development, and identify ways for meeting those needs, major benefits to the instructional program will result that could never come from uncritical acceptance of an already formulated program."[5] Florence Cleary, in her extremely practical guidebook, *Blueprints for Better Reading: School Programs for Promoting Skill and Interest in Reading*, stresses the necessity of the school library media specialist being directly involved in each phase—designing, implementing, and evaluating—of the school's skill development program. She recommends that, when teachers and the library media specialist are developing plans for the teaching and practice of skills, they ask themselves, *"What* are the specific skills to be taught and mastered? *When, where,* and *how* are they to be taught? *Who* will teach them?"[6] The library media specialist must also take the major responsibility for answering the question, With *what* will it be taught? Example 41, The Introduction, Reinforcement, and Extension of Chronology and Time Line Skills, is a prototype of a spiral approach to integrating skills within the framework of an ongoing instructional program.

EXAMPLE 41 THE INTRODUCTION, REINFORCEMENT, AND EXTENSION
OF CHRONOLOGY AND TIME LINE SKILLS

The introduction, reinforcement, and extension of each basic skill outlined in the Thinking-Learning-Communicating Continuum [see Appendix L] is carefully integrated within the framework of the teaching-learning program. The goal is to enable every student to progress steadily to an ever higher level of skill competence as he or she moves from one learning experience to the next.

The following is but a limited sampling of the opportunities afforded the student to achieve mastery of chronology and time line skills.

GRADE THREE
  Unit: Transportation
    Skill Integration Activities:
      The time line is reintroduced stressing the general sequence of transportation developments rather than a sequence of specific dates.
    Resources:

Going Places by Land: A Time Line Story (Child's World), 16 picture-story cards

EXAMPLE 41 (cont.)

Going Places by Water: A Time Line Story (Child's World), 16 picture-story cards

Going Places by Air: A Time Line Story (Child's World), 16 picture-story cards

GRADE FOUR
Unit: Japan
Skill Integration Activities:
The concept of the time line is extended to—
1. Link and sequentialize events
2. Highlight the interplay of people and events
Resource:
Adventures with World Heroes by Henry Bamman et al. (Benefic Press), Natsume Kinnosuke, pp. 234–235

GRADE FIVE
Unit: The Civil War
Skill Integration Activities:
The concept of chronologies is introduced—
1. Perceiving the distinguishing characteristics of chronologies and their informational value
2. Using chronologies to identify significant events and people
The concept of using encyclopedias and almanacs to discover chronologies and time lines is introduced—
1. Making effective use of encyclopedias
2. Recognizing distinguishing characteristics and informational value of almanacs
Resources:
Arrow Book Club Time Line (Scholastic). Drawings along a time line highlight persons and events in American history beginning with the year 1420 and ending with the year 2000. This time line serves as a model to be followed when converting chronologies into time line entries.

Abraham Lincoln Life Line (Scholastic). Drawings along a time line highlight important events in the life of Abraham Lincoln. This time line serves as a model to follow when highlighting important events in a person's life.

Highlights of American History (*World Book*, vol. 20). Drawings along a multilevel zigzag time line highlight persons and events in American history beginning with the year 1600 and ending with the year 1885. This time line serves as a model to follow when developing a zigzag or spiral time line to portray an extensive period of time.

A Chronology from 2300 B.C. to 1976 A.D.: Information Please Almanac. This chronology provides a checklist of important persons and events in American history beginning with the year 1600, to be used in expanding the time line *Highlights of American History* (*World Book*, vol. 20).

GRADE SIX
Unit: The Aztecs, the Mayas, and the Incas
Skill Integration Activities:
The concept of synthesizing chronology listings into time lines is introduced—
1. Making use of synthesizing skills.
2. Recombining parts of previous experience with new material; reconstructing a new order or pattern.
Resources:
Chronology Chart of the Aztec World and World Events: The Aztecs . . . by Victor von Hagen (Collins-World)

Chronology Chart of the Inca World and World Events: The Incas . . . by Victor von Hagen (Collins-World)

Chronology Chart of the Mayan World and World Events: The Maya . . . by Victor von Hagen (Collins-World)

These three chronologies are combined to form a three-level time line representing

EXAMPLE 41 (cont.)

the important events and people in the history of the Aztecs, the Incas, and the Mayas.

GRADE SEVEN

Unit: The Prehistoric World

Skill Integration Activities:

The concept of synthesizing chronology listings into time lines is reinforced by—

1. Making use of synthesizing skills.
2. Recombining parts of previous experience with new material; reconstructing a new order or pattern.

Resources:

An Encyclopedia of World History—Ancient, Medieval, and Modern, Chronologically Arranged, ed. by William L. Langer (Houghton), pp. 3–6. Introduces the student to the prehistoric periods of history—

1. Paleolithic
2. Mesolithic
3. Neolithic
4. Chalcolithic
5. Bronze Age
6. Iron Age

Introduces the student to the concept of how centuries and years before and after Christ are reckoned.

The Road of Civilization (Richtext Press). Presents the chronological view of history beginning with the date 1,000,000 B.C. and ending with the year 1965 A.D. Introduces the use of a chronology to identify man's advancing civilization under the six headings—

1. Food
2. Shelter
3. Communication
4. Science
5. Transportation
6. Manufacturing and trade

The Geological Time Scale: Periods and Systems and Derivation of Names (Science Dictionary of the Animal World by Michael Chinery, Watts), pp. 122–123.

Time Chart of Fossil Man (Our Human Ancestors, ed. by Frances M. Clapham, Watts). Presents in a detailed time line the history of animals and humans beginning with the date 10,000,000 B.C. and ending with the year 10,000 B.C.

GRADE EIGHT

Units: Each American History Unit

Skill Integration Activities:

The concept of chronologies is reintroduced and extended—

1. Perceiving the distinguishing characteristics of chronologies and their informational value.
2. Using chronologies to identify significant events and people.

The concept of informational retrieval as a learning tool:

1. Making effective use of basic reference tools.
2. Valuing books as carriers of knowledge—rich data banks for informational retrieval.
3. Grasping, translating, inferring the intent; selecting, organizing, and expressing ideas.

Resources:

The Annals of America (Encyclopaedia Britannica Corp., 20 vols.). This 20-volume set is a chronological record of American life, action, and thought from 1492 to 1968. This comprehensive reference set is a collection of source materials of American history including laws, speeches, transcriptions of dialogues, on-the-scene reports, reminiscences and other primary sources; this is an excellent tool for identifying significant people, events, and developments to be placed on a time line begun in the first unit in eighth-grade American History and continued throughout the year.

American History Atlas by Martin Gilbert (New York: Macmillan). This atlas presents

EXAMPLE 41 (cont.)

the history of America in 112 maps beginning with 50,000 B.C. and ending with 1968; this is an excellent reference tool for identifying significant people and events to be highlighted on a time line begun in the first unit in eighth-grade American History and continued throughout the year.

GRADES ELEVEN AND TWELVE
  Units: Each Advanced Placement World History and/or U.S. History Unit
    Skill Integration Activities:
      The concept of the time line is reinforced and extended—
        1. Linking and sequentializing events.
        2. Highlighting the interplay of people and events.
      The concept of informational retrieval as a learning tool is reinforced:
        1. Making effective use of basic reference tools.
        2. Valuing books as carriers of knowledge—rich data banks for informational retrieval.

  Resources:

  The Timetables of History by Bernard Grun (New York: Simon & Schuster). An encyclopedic reference tool presents a horizontal linkage of people and events: the range covers recorded history from its first exact date, 4241 B.C., through 1974; each double page has seven columns and the reader can scan any given year horizontally and discover what was taking place under the categories: history and politics; literature and the theater; religion, philosophy, and learning; visual arts; music; science, technology, and growth; and daily life.

LEARNING TO LEARN IN THE SCHOOL LIBRARY MEDIA CENTER

Frances Henne, coeditor of the 1960 Standards for School Library Programs, and Professor Emeritus of the School of Library Science, Columbia University, succinctly sets forth the role of the library media specialist in teaching the use of the library and its resources. Her article, "Learning to Learn in School Libraries," is a classic, deserving thoughtful and appreciative reading. This article is included in its entirety in Appendix N. In discussing the nature of the library's involvement in teaching students the skills of learning, Henne offers the following:

Recommendations about the nature of library instruction will affect, and also be affected by, philosophy concerning the scope of library services. Current thought about the distinction to be made between independent use of the library by students and desirable library services provides an example. *In the viewpoint of many school librarians the mere process of locating and finding materials in the library holds little intellectual benefit for students, and time thus spent is generally wasted time.* The many processes involved in what students do with materials—evaluation, synthesis, reflection, thinking, appreciation, or whatever—are the important factors, not the searching, locating, and assembling of materials.

At points like these, it is essential for new thinking and new decisions in order to determine how much students should know about the use of the library and its resources, how consistently and persistently they must apply their skills and knowledge independently and without assistance from librarians, when this independent pursuit of materials results in a waste of time, and what variations should be recommended for different groups of students. Deploring the spoon-feeding of students, as librarians so frequently do, may actually mean deploring a more intelligent use of a student's time and efforts; and self-directed study or learning is not necessarily synonymous with self-directed finding of materials.

No matter how the school may allocate the responsibilities for teaching the various study skills, whether to teachers alone, or librarians alone, or a combination of both—the librarians' responsibilities and opportunities for observing and helping students in the use of material . . . are clearly indicated. This principle applies to all schools. In those schools where independent study and self-directed learning are carefully planned for the students, these activities of the librarians represent key factors in a successful program. The librarian is the one who has the opportunity to observe, among other matters, the student's ability to use materials, to take notes, to outline, and to evaluate and synthesize materials. The school librarian's role in the program of study skills and methods of inquiry is that of a teacher and guidance specialist. The librarian's follow-up services in seeing how effectively students are using the library materials they have selected for their immediate needs are strategic and valuable ones.[7]

Today's school library media center should function as a learning laboratory where, in the words of Dr. Henne, the student comes to learn how to learn—to sharpen and refine his or her ability to read, to write, to listen, to view, to think, and then to communicate with competence. Thinking skills are the means of preparing future citizens for intelligent participation in political, economic, social, and personal decision making; therefore, skill teaching is as crucial as the teaching of subject matter or content. The school library media specialist has a vital teaching role to play in designing and implementing learning experiences for the integration of skill mastery within the framework of the ongoing teaching and learning program.

NOTES

1. John Jarolimek, "The Psychology of Skill Development," in *Skill Development in Social Studies*, ed. by Helen McCracken Carpenter, Thirty-Third Yearbook (Washington, D.C.: National Council for the Social Studies, 1963), p. 33. Reprinted with permission of the National Council for the Social Studies.
2. Education Policies Commission, *The Central Purpose of American Education* (Washington, D.C.: National Education Association, 1961), p. 12.
3. Eunice Johns and Dorothy McClure Fraser in *Skill Development in Social Studies*, pp. 311–312. Reprinted with permission of the National Council for the Social Studies.
4. Ibid., p. 311.
5. Ibid.
6. Florence Damon Cleary, *Blueprints for Better Reading: School Programs for Promoting Skill and Interest in Reading*, 2nd ed. (New York: H. W. Wilson, 1972), p. 191. Reprinted by permission of the H. W. Wilson Company. Copyright © 1972 by Florence D. Cleary.
7. Frances Henne, "Learning to Learn in School Libraries," in *School Libraries*, American Association of School Librarians, vol. 15, no. 4, May 1966, pp. 15–23.

13 Evaluating the Effectiveness of the School Library Media Program

Man cannot live by incompetence alone.

Laurence J. Peter*

Educational quality is neither permanent nor absolute. Quality, because it is directly related to the school's ability to meet adequately the emergent needs of contemporary society, is both relative and transitory. An educational program judged as excellent five years ago may be only mediocre today, and might be inferior next year if it lacks the capability of keeping pace with the changing and emerging needs of society and of the individual in society. Excellence in any educational endeavor is never static, never permanent, never won! Therefore, continuous reappraisal, renovation, and innovation must become an educator's way of life.

PURPOSE OF EVALUATION

Evaluation is employed by educators to determine the degree of excellence being achieved by an educational program, method, innovation, or any combination of these. Just as the quantity and quality of gold are determined both by its being weighed and by its being tested by acid, so is the quantity and the quality of an educational endeavor assayed by its being objectively "weighed" on the scales of established standards and/or criteria and by its being appraised critically by the acid test of functional excellence in practice. In any professional evaluation there must be truthfulness and seriousness of purpose that precludes ignoring or minimizing the educational dross and highlighting or maximizing the educational gold. The professional educator must keep faith with the purpose of education—the improvement of instruction.

*Laurence J. Peter, *The Peter Prescription: How to Be Creative, Confident, and Competent* (New York: Morrow, 1972), p. 221.

DEFINITION OF TERMS

Precise definition of terms brings objectivity to a discussion of evaluative techniques and procedures. Each of the following terms, basic to building a working knowledge of evaluation, has been abstracted from the *Dictionary of Education:*

> *Checklist.* A prepared list of items that may relate to a person, procedure, institution, building, etc., used for purposes of observation and/or evaluation, and on which one may show by a check mark or other simple method the presence, absence, or frequency of occurrence of each item on the list.
>
> *Criterion, criteria,* pl. A standard, norm, or judgment selected as a basis for quantitative and qualitative comparison.
>
> *Evaluative criteria.* (1) The standards against which a person or group or a procedure may be checked; (2) the factors considered by an accrediting agency in analyzing the status of an educational institution to determine whether it shall be accredited.
>
> *Evaluative method.* The procedure in a study that has evaluation as its chief purpose and that in most cases includes some definite fact finding, through observation, and that involves the careful description of aspects to be evaluated, a statement of purpose, frame of reference, and criteria for the evaluation, and the degrees or terms that are to be employed in recording judgments.
>
> *Inventory.* In the field of evaluation, a test or checklist used to determine the subject's or examiner's ability, achievement, aptitude, interest, or likes, generally in a limited area.
>
> *Rating scale.* A device used in evaluating products, attitudes, or other characteristics of instructors or learners.
>
> *School survey.* A study or evaluation of a school, a school system, or any part thereof; may be fact finding, or may indicate the strong and weak features as judged by definite criteria; *commonly concluded with suggestions for needed changes and/or recommendations for more desirable practices.*
>
> *Standard.* (1) A goal or objective or criterion of education expressed either numerically as a statistical average or philosophically as an ideal of excellence; (2) any criterion by which things are judged.[1]

EVALUATING THE EDUCATIONAL PROGRAM

Evaluation of the educational program originated on the high school level, was extended to the junior high school during the sixties and, during the seventies, was extended to the elementary school. The most commonly used evaluative instruments for school evaluation are those prepared by the National Study of School Evaluation. This organization, originally known as the Cooperative Study of Secondary School Standards, has taken the responsibility since 1933 for preparing evaluative criteria.

The work of the National Study of School Evaluation is carried on by a General Committee composed of appointed representatives from the six governing regional associations:

Middle States Association of Colleges and Schools, Commission on Secondary Schools, Science Center, 3624 Market St., Philadelphia, Pa. 19104

New England Association of Schools and Colleges, Inc., 131 Middlesex Tpke., Burlington, Mass. 01803

North Central Association of Colleges and Schools, Commission on Schools, 1221 University Ave., Boulder, Colo. 80302

Northwest Association of Schools and Colleges, Commission on Schools, Blue Mountain Community College, Box 100, Pendleton, Oreg. 97801

Southern Association of Colleges and Schools, Commission on Secondary Schools, 795 Peachtree St., N.E., Atlanta, Ga. 30308

Western Association of Schools and Colleges, Accrediting Commission for Secondary Schools, 1614 Rollins Rod., Burlingame, Calif. 94010

Publications of the National Study of School Evaluation

The National Study currently publishes:

Evaluative Criteria, 5th ed., 1978

Junior High School/Middle School Evaluative Criteria, 1970

Elementary School Evaluative Criteria, 1973

Evaluative Guidelines for Multicultural/Multiracial Education, 1973

Secondary School Evaluative Criteria: Narrative Edition, 1975

Student Opinion Inventory, 1974

Teacher Opinion Inventory, 1975

Parent Opinion Inventory, 1976

Elementary School Evaluative Criteria Audio Filmstrip, 1977

A given school district wishing to initiate a secondary or an elementary school evaluation under the auspices of the National Study of School Evaluation, must contact the appropriate regional association for direction and guidance as to the procedure to be followed in scheduling and carrying out the evaluative process.

Evaluative Criteria, Criteria for Evaluating Junior High Schools, and *Elementary School Evaluative Criteria* are instruments designed for internal-external evaluation. The general procedure is for the school to conduct a self-evaluation preparatory to an external evaluation by a guest committee of educators. Frequently, as long as a year is spent by the faculty in self-study and self-appraisal. School library media specialists by the nature of their faculty status are required to serve on various evaluative teams and to take an active part in all phases of the school's evaluation of the overall educational program.

During faculty analysis and evaluation of the educational program four questions are kept constantly in the foreground of each teacher's thinking as he or she quests for truth:

What are our directional goals and basic philosophy?

What experiences should we provide in the light of our directional goals and basic philosophy?

What evidence of progress or retrogression do we find?

What remedial, renovative, and innovative action should we undertake to strengthen noted weaknesses and to increase the educational effectiveness and efficiency of the total program?

EVALUATING THE SCHOOL LIBRARY MEDIA PROGRAM

Evaluative Criteria in section 6, "Learning Media Services," includes the following guiding principles:

GUIDING PRINCIPLES

These principles are offered for your acceptance, rejection, or modification. Please feel free to make changes.

One of the important purposes of the educational program is to provide the student with a variety of self-enriching ideas and experiences which lead to intellectual curiosity, achievement, and the establishment of a life-long pattern of learning. Utilization of human resources and the full range of media which includes printed and audiovisual forms of communication and their accompanying technology are required to implement the purposes and program of the school or district.

Trends which began to receive national attention in the 1940's have influenced the development of the single administrative unit known as the media center which furnishes those services traditionally associated with the library and provides a wide variety of audiovisual and electronic services. This single administrative unit requires the skills of media professionals and nonprofessional supportive staff, e.g., paraprofessionals, technicians, production personnel, clerical staff, and student assistants. The media center serves not only a leadership function in improving the educational environment but also a supportive function by providing the resources for learning. The criteria that follow are intended for the evaluation of the entire range of learning media services, even though their administration may not yet be unified.[2]

Guiding principles from *Evaluative Criteria*, pertaining to the separate disciplines, are included in Chapter 8 (English), Chapter 9 (Social Studies), and Chapter 10 (Science and Mathematics).

Checklists are used in *Evaluative Criteria* as the faculty self-evaluation instrument. Checklist 9, "Media Program," is typical of the evaluative instrument. The checklist items are judged on the following scale:

   5   Excellent
   4   Good
   3   Fair
   2   Poor
   1   Missing but Needed
   na   Not applicable

Evaluation and self-study on an annual and continuing basis are recommended for building and maintaining school library media programs of functional excellence. Frances Henne, crusader for library media programs of educational excellence, has prepared a unique overview of the history, purpose, procedures, and tools of school library media program evaluation. Dr. Henne's observations provide school library media specialists with a philosophic approach to practical, objective, professional self-study—rewarding reading for all who would gain insight into constructive, effective school library media program evaluation. This professional mentor recommends that:

Evaluations, whether self-survey or conducted by outside specialists, involve not only the school librarians but also the administration, faculty, and, not infrequently, students and parents. The pattern of having some person or persons "blow in, blow off, and blow out," although not unknown in the annals of school library evaluation, has little, if anything, to commend it. Under any circumstances evaluations should be constructive in design and intent, with the primary purpose of working with and assisting the school and the librarians to effect improvements in the library benefiting students and teachers.[3]

CHECKLIST 9   MEDIA PROGRAM*

The media program:

1. Is an integral component of the total educational program	na	1	2	3	4	5
2. Provides a humanistic environment for learning	na	1	2	3	4	5
3. Includes an active public relations program which emphasizes on-going mutual communication between the media staff and the total school community	na	1	2	3	4	5
4. Provides for the coordination of the procurement, availability and utilization of materials and equipment by individual departments	na	1	2	3	4	5
5. Reflects an active awareness of current developments in education	na	1	2	3	4	5
6. Provides assistance in planning for effective use of media	na	1	2	3	4	5
7. Provides open access through flexibility in scheduling and extended hours	na	1	2	3	4	5

Services to students:

8. Include orientation sessions to the media center and its services	na	1	2	3	4	5
9. Provide for a comprehensive program of guidance in the development of skills in reading, viewing and listening	na	1	2	3	4	5
10. Provide for the development of research and reference skills to achieve independence in learning	na	1	2	3	4	5
11. Assist students in the use of available networks of libraries and information centers	na	1	2	3	4	5
12. Provide instruction and encouragement in the use of computer-assisted instruction, dial access systems, and data storage and retrieval systems as necessary	na	1	2	3	4	5
13. Aid in creatively reporting the results of research efforts, e.g., slide/tape presentations, video programs, illustrated reports, etc.	na	1	2	3	4	5
14. Provide guidance in the selection and use of the most effective medium to achieve the objectives and accommodate individual needs and abilities	na	1	2	3	4	5

Services to faculty and staff:

15. Include cooperation in the development of in-service training and/or orientation programs	na	1	2	3	4	5
16. Provide indices to and bibliographies of media to aid in selecting materials for instructional planning and use	na	1	2	3	4	5
17. Include information on new materials and equipment which have been acquired	na	1	2	3	4	5
18. Include the development of resource lists on selected subjects	na	1	2	3	4	5
19. Provide professional assistance in the production of media	na	1	2	3	4	5
20. Include ordering and scheduling the use of rented or borrowed material	na	1	2	3	4	5
21. Provide media for reserve, classroom, and satellite collections	na	1	2	3	4	5
22. Incorporate assistance in the improvement of teaching through instructional development projects	na	1	2	3	4	5

*From National Study of School Evaluation, *Evaluative Criteria*, 5th ed. Copyright © 1978, p. 290. Reprinted with permission of the National Study of School Evaluation, Washington, D.C.

Tools for Media Program Evaluation

Among the evaluative instruments available for assessing the strength and weakness of a school library media program on the building level, the following are recommended because each represents a unique approach to evaluation: Example 42, Find Your Media Center Service Profile; Example 43, Criteria of Excellence Checklist; Example 44, Self-Study Guide: School Library; Example 45, Illinois Standards for School Media Programs and the School Evaluation Form; Example 46, Self-Evaluation Form: School Media Programs; and Appendix G: A Faculty Self-Study of the Elementary School Library Media Center.

EXAMPLE 42   FIND YOUR MEDIA CENTER SERVICE PROFILE*

The following checklist has been designed to facilitate evaluation of your library media center program using the latest state and/or national standards for the profile points.

SEE HOW YOUR LIBRARY RATES

1. Find the item (1, 2, 3, 4) in each of the seven sections (A, B, C, D, E, F, G) which most nearly applies to your library media program.
2. Center a dot in the appropriate box corresponding to the item number and the section letter on the summary grid, "Your Media Center."

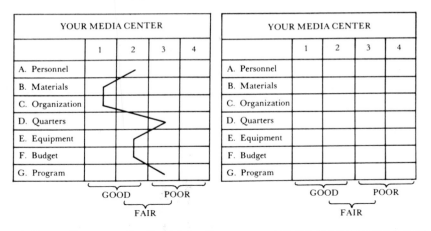

3. Draw a line connecting the dots on the summary grid; this line is your library media center service profile.
4. If your profile is *good*, keep moving ahead toward superior service;
   If your profile is *fair*, you need to concentrate on bringing your program up to standard;
   If your profile is *poor*, plan with your principal the procedure to be followed in improving your library media center program.

PROFILE POINTS

A. Personnel

1. One full-time media specialist plus one full-time technician and one full-time media aide per 250 students.
2. One full-time media specialist plus one full-time media aide per 250 students.
3. One full-time media specialist per 250 students.
4. Less than one full-time media specialist per 250 students.

*Adapted by Joyce B. Scholl from "Mr. Administrator: What Is Your Library Service Profile?" prepared by the Michigan State Library, Lansing, Mich.

EXAMPLE 42 (cont.)

B. MATERIALS

1. Twenty or more books per pupil plus 36 or more pieces of nonbook media per pupil.
2. Ten books per pupil plus 18 pieces of nonbook media per pupil.
3. Five books per pupil plus 9 pieces of nonbook media per pupil.
4. Fewer than 5 books per pupil.

C. ORGANIZATION

1. All print media classified and cataloged and all nonprint media cataloged, with charging procedure systematized for all media and facilitating equipment.
2. Only books classified and cataloged with charging system.
3. Media not classified but organized in some orderly manner with simple charging system.
4. Media not organized, no charging system.

D. QUARTERS

1. Space to seat 15 percent of student enrollment at 40 square feet per student plus reception, large group instruction, conference, office, work, storage, production, and professional materials areas.
2. Space to seat largest class plus reception, conference, office, work, and storage areas.
3. Space to seat largest class, plus work and storage areas.
4. Space insufficient to seat largest class.

E. EQUIPMENT

1. Shelving and cabinet storage to accommodate with growth allowance entire media collection; furniture to implement all media center activities, plus hardware to activate all media.
2. Shelving and cabinet storage to accommodate media collection, furniture to implement some media center activities, plus hardware to activate some media.
3. Some shelving and cabinet storage, some implementing furniture.
4. Shelving, seating.

F. BUDGET

1. Six percent of the district average per pupil operational cost (for average daily attendance) for media center purposes other than original installation, salaries, plant maintenance.
2. Four percent of the district average per pupil operational cost (for average daily attendance) for media center purposes other than original installation, salaries, plant maintenance.
3. Two percent of the district average per pupil operational cost (for average daily attendance) for media center purposes other than original installation, salaries, plant maintenance.
4. One percent of the district average per pupil operational cost (for average daily attendance) for media center purposes other than original installation, salaries, plant maintenance.

G. PROGRAM

1. The media center program functioning as an integral supporting component of the total educational program: voluntary recreational reading plus *planned* informational curriculum support actively presented for all students and faculty on an open schedule.
2. Recreational reading and curriculum support programs available to students and faculty on an open schedule.
3. Recreational reading and reference use available to students and faculty.
4. Study halls scheduled into media centers.

EXAMPLE 43   CRITERIA OF EXCELLENCE CHECKLIST*

Directions: Read the statements carefully. In the spaces provided under each of the broad categories, Program, Research, Implementation, check the columns which best identify the school library.

The school library program, as an integral part of any school's instructional program contributing to the development and implementation of the total curriculum and achievement of the educational objectives of the school, shows evidence of the following:

	PROGRAM			RESEARCH			IMPLEMENTATION		
	Fully Operational	Partially Operational	Non-Operational	Presently Under Study	Planned for Study	No Study Planned	Expect Achievement 1-2 Years	Expect Achievement 3-5 Years	Do Not Expect to Achieve
	A	B	C	A	B	C	A	B	C
1. At the district level, a school supervisor who gives direction and leadership in the development of a total district-wide school library program.									
2. At the building level, at least two trained librarians (and/or audiovisual personnel), with additional paid supporting staff.									
3. A unified program which reflects a depth and variety in the selection of all types of media, with the necessary equipment available for use in the support of the instructional program.									
4. Effective design in physical arrangement of facilities to accommodate use by teachers and students, individually and in small or large groups.									

5. Efficient organization and easy accessibility to all services, materials, and equipment for teachers' and students' use before, during, and after the school day.

6. Provision for, and assistance to, teachers and students in the production of new materials for instructional use.

7. Participation of library personnel with teachers in the planning and implementation of the curriculum as a means of integrating library services with the instructional program of the school.

8. Planned and coordinated inservice for teachers to provide training in the production and use of instructional media.

9. Purposeful instruction for students, as individuals or in small or large groups, in library and research skills evolving from the needs of the instructional program.

10. Consultative and special services to teachers to provide support in the performance of their educational roles.

11. Availability of a wide variety of learning opportunities for the individual which offer the challenge and motivation necessary to aid a student in his intellectual, social, and emotional development.

12. Continuous evaluation of the library program in support of the educational philosophy and purposes of the school and the needs and interests of the teachers and students served.

*Robert N. Case, "Criteria of Excellence Checklist" in *School Libraries*, Spring 1969, pp. 43–46. Reprints available from: School Library Manpower Project, American Association of School Librarians, 50 E. Huron St., Chicago, Ill. 60611.

EXAMPLE 44   NEW YORK STATE EDUCATION DEPARTMENT COOPERATIVE
REVIEW SERVICE SELF-STUDY GUIDE: SCHOOL LIBRARY*

Instructions

This guide should be completed by each librarian and by the department chairman, if there is
one.

Note that items consist of standards and practices that generally characterize good school
programs.

Base your conclusions on the total program in the subject or service area, rather than on a
single subject or grade level of the program.

If you wish to qualify an item, enter an explanatory note in the space after it, or at the end of the
section. If more space is needed, additional sheets may be attached. Identify by number
and part all items which you have added as qualifying statements.

If any important program features are not listed, insert a statement concerning these in the
space headed "Comments" at the end of each section.

At the end of this Guide there is a Summary for indicating strong aspects of the total program,
and areas in which improvement is needed. *Care in filling out this Summary is especially important in future planning for program improvement.*

Definition of Terms Used

Strong Aspect: Consistently above average. A practice, condition, or item that is recognized
as an outstanding feature of the program.

Needs Improvement: Below average. Obvious weaknesses should be checked in this column.

PROGRAM OBJECTIVES

Check the column most applicable to each item.
    Column SA: Strong aspect
    Column NI: Needs improvement
(If the item *does not exist*, or *does not apply* in your school system, please
explain this under *Comments*, referring to the item by number.)

	SA	NI
1. The librarian and other members of the faculty, working under the direction of the principal, have prepared a clear statement of the objectives that should be achieved by the school	___	___
2. The librarian, working under the direction of the principal and with other members of the faculty, has prepared a clear statement which indicates how:		
The library program is directed and developed in relation to the school's objectives and program	___	___
The library supports and reinforces the curriculum	___	___
The library's unique functions and objectives are achieved for all personnel	___	___
3. The plans for school administration enable pupils to use the library freely	___	___
4. The library serves the total school community in all subject fields with provision made for frequent individual and group use	___	___
5. The appearance and atmosphere of the library and the helpfulness of the library staff invite browsing, reading, listening and viewing, and study	___	___
6. The librarian stimulates the optimum utilization of library resources	___	___
7. The library contributes to the improvement of reading skills and appreciation	___	___

*This form is currently in revision. Contact Dr. Albert F. Merz, Bureau Chief, New York State Edu-
cation Department, Education Building Annex, Albany, N.Y. 12224, tel. 518-474-5925.

SA   NI

8. The teachers encourage pupils to use library resources in relation to school assignments, school activities, and their individual interests

9. The library is:

A teaching center

A service center

A guidance agency

An integrating agency

10. The librarian, working under the direction of the administration and with the faculty, has established a positive, effective working relationship with the public library

Information Requested

1. What percentage of the pupils use the library regularly and frequently for reference? _____

2. What was the average daily library attendance during the last school year? _____

3. Approximately what percentage of the pupils read regularly for pleasure? _____

4. What was the average book circulation per pupil during the last school year? _____

5. How many classes were scheduled for supervised reference and reading last year? _____

6. Have any federally-aided or state-aided programs contributed directly or indirectly to the library program? If so describe briefly the extent of this involvement (indicate which program, acquisitions, changes in staff, equipment, facilities).

Comments

THE LIBRARY STAFF

Check the column most applicable to each item.

Column SA: Strong aspect

Column NI: Needs improvement

(If the item *does not exist*, or *does not apply* in your school system, please explain this under *Comments*, referring to the item by number.)

SA   NI

1. The preparation of the librarian is appropriate and adequate for school library teaching and service

2. The librarian studies at frequent intervals and takes advanced professional, technical, or cultural courses

3. The librarian participates in professional activities (school and library, and in local and community activities)

4. The librarian cooperates with other libraries—school, public, college, and special—of the community, region, or state

5. The librarian keeps abreast of current development through professional reading

6. The librarian and/or the library staff has a reasonable amount of time for:

Working with individuals, pupils, and teachers

Recommending books and other media, stimulating reading, assisting with reference, and teaching individual groups and classes to use the library

Selecting and ordering books and media

	SA	NI
Planning and/or supervising the cataloging	___	___
Administering the library, supervising the clerical staff, teaching student assistants, and interpreting the library	___	___

7. The library *staff* is sufficient in size for the school's enrollment and program. (One *librarian* for each 500 pupils or major fraction thereof)   ___ ___

8. When classes are scheduled to the library for supervised reading and reference, their teachers remain with them and work with the librarian   ___ ___

9. Provision is made for sufficient clerical, secretarial, or technical assistance   ___ ___

10. Pupil assistants help with library routines and perform other library activities   ___ ___

11. School librarians are classified as teachers with specialization in library science, attend faculty meetings, and work for the attainment of the school's objectives   ___ ___

12. The chief or senior school librarian is considered as a department head and works with the principal on plans for the library program, supervision of the professional, clerical, and student library staff, and participates in meetings of department chairmen   ___ ___

13. The librarian is not assigned nonlibrary duties   ___ ___

Information Requested

School enrollment: _____   No. of librarians: _____

Qualification of librarians

Name _____

College Degree and Date _____

Library School Degree and Date _____

Other Degrees _____

Credits in Library Science _____

Credits audiovisual materials _____

Clerical Staff: No. full time _____   No. part time _____

Student Assistants: No. _____

Total periods a week of student service _____

Comments

LIBRARY RESOURCES

Check the column most applicable to each item.
    Column SA: Strong aspect
    Column NI: Needs improvement
(If the item *does not exist*, or *does not apply* in your school system, please explain this under *Comments*, referring to the item by number.)

1. The collection is appropriate and adequate for the school's pupils and program for:

	SA	NI
Reference work	___	___
Implementing the curriculum	___	___
General and recreational reading	___	___

2. The collection is satisfactory in size for the school enrollment (15–20 books for pupil for enrollment 500–1000; more per pupil in smaller schools)   ___ ___

3. The collection is satisfactory for:　　　　　　　　　　　　　　　SA　　NI

Pupils of average ability

The slow and retarded ____ ____

Those of superior ability ____ ____

____ ____

4. The collection includes:

Books and other media of all types recognized as important for and interesting to pupils

____ ____

Significant, reliable, accurate, up-to-date books and other media in the fields of:

History ____ ____

Economics ____ ____

Government ____ ____

Public affairs ____ ____

Guidance ____ ____

Science ____ ____

Practical arts ____ ____

Modern languages ____ ____

Literature ____ ____

Fiction ____ ____

5. Out-of-date, inappropriate and worn books are withdrawn from the collection

____ ____

6. Adequate funds are available for purchasing printed materials and other media

____ ____

7. Books and other school library resources are bought at frequent intervals throughout the school year

____ ____

8. After an adequate, basic book collection has been acquired, a minimum of one important book per pupil per year is added to the library in schools having 500 or more pupils (more in smaller schools)

____ ____

9. Periodicals are provided and include:

Magazines (a minimum of 25 titles for elementary schools, 75 titles for junior high schools, 75 titles for high schools)

____ ____

Newspapers (a minimum of 3 titles for elementary schools, 6 titles for junior high schools, 6 titles for high schools—with one local, one state, and one national newspaper included)

____ ____

Indexes ____ ____

10. A minimum expenditure of 1% of the national average for per pupil operational costs is allotted for maintaining an up-to-date collection of print and nonprint materials

____ ____

11. The librarian, together with the faculty and under the direction of the administrator, has developed a written selection policy governing all library resources

____ ____

12. Pamphlet and picture files are well developed and organized ____ ____

13. Recordings are supplied and circulated ____ ____

14. Filmstrips, collections of films, slides, transparencies, reproductions, realia, etc., are maintained and circulated

____ ____

15. Information as to sources of audiovisual materials is supplied ____ ____

16. An up-to-date collection of professional books and periodicals for the use of faculty and parent groups is provided (minimum of 200 book titles and 15 periodicals)

____ ____

17. The library has special, well-developed collections

Particular subjects (i.e.) ____ ____

Special purposes (i.e.) ____ ____

SA   NI

Commemorating particular persons
The contributions of minority groups

Information Requested

1. Number of volumes in book collection _____
2. Number of volumes added during last school year _____
3. Number of volumes added so far this year _____
4. Number of volumes per pupil _____
5. Number of periodicals _____ periodical titles on microfilm _____
6. Amount spent for books last year _____
7. Amount allotted for books this year _____
8. Amount allotted for periodicals this year _____
9. Number of filmstrips _____
10. Number of 8mm films _____
11. Number of disc recordings _____
12. Number of other audiovisual resources _____
13. Amount allotted to audiovisual resources: last year _____; this year _____
14. Total school per pupil expenditure _____
15. Per pupil expenditure for school library resources _____

Comments

LIBRARY QUARTERS

Check the column most applicable to each item.
    Column SA: Strong aspect
    Column NI: Needs improvement
(If the item *does not exist*, or *does not apply* in your school system, please explain this under *Comments*, referring to the item by number.)

SA   NI

1. The library is centrally located and accessible, yet remote from activities which hamper library use (gym, playground, music rooms)
2. The library space is arranged, lighted, furnished, and equipped for effective library functioning
3. Ten to 15 percent of the enrollment can be seated in the reading room
4. Shelving in a reading room is sufficient for the principal part of the collection
5. Shelving in the stackroom, conference room, or library classroom is sufficient for duplicate copies, special-purchase books, and magazine files
6. The library workroom has space, shelving, and equipment needed for organizing and processing materials, arranging exhibits, and record keeping
7. Additional space for listening, viewing, and storage is provided as audiovisual (communications) collections expand
8. The decorative features of the library (draperies, plants, flowers, pictures) are attractive and appropriate
9. In the secondary school the librarian is provided with or has easy access to a telephone

Information Requested

1. Number of pupils' seats:
   In reading room(s) _____
   In conference rooms _____
   In study carrels wired _____   unwired _____

Comments

LIBRARY ORGANIZATION AND ADMINISTRATION

Check the column most applicable to each item.
    Column SA: Strong aspect
    Column NI: Needs improvement
(If the item *does not exist*, or *does not apply* in your school system, please explain this under *Comments*, referring to the item by number.)

	SA	NI
1. All school library resources including nonbook materials are classified, cataloged, and processed for retrieval and circulation according to school library standards	____	____
2. Essential library records are complete, accurate, and up-to-date	____	____
3. Provision has been made for centralized or commercial cataloging and processing	____	____
4. Printed catalog cards are used for items not commercially or centrally processed	____	____
5. Processing kits are used when available	____	____
6. School library resources are preprocessed when possible	____	____
7. New books are processed and made available for use as promptly as possible	____	____
8. Case labels, shelf labels, signs, and posters are used to explain the library arrangement and to guide library users	____	____
9. Exhibits and displays arranged by librarians, teachers, and pupils call attention to books on particular subjects or themes, materials on questions of current interest, and recent acquisitions	____	____
10. The library reading room is available for use before, during, and after school hours	____	____
11. The library classroom and/or part of the reading room are available for:		
Large group or class instruction	____	____
Small group activities (reference, viewing, listening)	____	____
Individual study and reference	____	____
Browsing or directed reading	____	____
12. Teachers are urged to use the library and to encourage pupils to use it	____	____
13. Books and materials are loaned to classrooms, laboratories, shops, or reserved in the library, according to school needs	____	____
14. Adequate interlibrary loan procedures are established	____	____
15. Periodically efforts are made to determine whether present plans for admitting pupils to the library are encouraging the use of the reading room and use of library resources	____	____
16. The library functions fully because nonlibrary activities are excluded	____	____

Information Requested

1. Is the library open at all during evening hours?   Yes ( )   No ( )
Saturdays?   Yes ( )   No ( )

Comments

LIBRARY UTILIZATION

Check the column most applicable to each item.
    Column SA: Strong aspect
    Column NI: Needs improvement
(If the item *does not exist*, or *does not apply* in your school system, please explain this under *Comments*, referring to the item by number.)

SA   NI

1. The library is purposeful, busy, and orderly—quiet, but not silent   ___ ___

2. The librarian is an able teacher who helps pupils understand the purpose of the library, and shows them how to use its resources with good direction but without strain, tension, or rigid discipline   ___ ___

3. The librarian has an attitude which encourages pupils and teachers to request help, guidance, and advice   ___ ___

4. The librarian introduces reference tools and methods to classes and to individuals, and supervises pupils at work in the library   ___ ___

5. The librarian and the teachers cooperate in planning and providing library instruction which is relevant to the instructional process   ___ ___

6. Teachers make assignments and arrange for special reports which require the use of reference materials   ___ ___

7. Arrangements are made for classes to participate in library activities at the request of the librarian and/or teachers   ___ ___

8. The librarian and teachers introduce print and nonprint materials by:

Storytelling periods   ___ ___

Book talks   ___ ___

Reading clubs   ___ ___

Dramatizations   ___ ___

Bulletins   ___ ___

Exhibits   ___ ___

Book lists   ___ ___

Items in the school paper   ___ ___

Magazine displays   ___ ___

9. The librarian and teachers cooperate in periodically sponsoring a book fair to encourage leisure reading and to promote home libraries   ___ ___

10. Pupils have opportunities to:

Participate in book discussions   ___ ___

Review books   ___ ___

Recommend books for purchase   ___ ___

11. Pupils use the library, its tools, its materials:

Actively   ___ ___

Independently   ___ ___

Effectively   ___ ___

With apparent satisfaction   ___ ___

12. Many pupils read extensively according to their abilities   ___ ___

Comments

LIBRARY SERVICES

Check the column most applicable to each item.
    Column SA: Strong aspect
    Column NI: Needs improvement

(If the item *does not exist*, or *does not apply* in your school system, please explain this under *Comments*, referring to the item by number.)   SA   NI

1. The librarian assists individual pupils, teachers, and classes by finding and/or assembling needed facts, reference works, or reading, listening, and visual materials

2. The librarian provides timely materials for general school activities (safety campaigns, hobbies, conservation programs, etc.)   ____ ____

3. The librarian maintains a file of community resources (field trips, speakers, exhibits, etc.) useful for school purposes   ____ ____

4. The librarian develops pamphlet files for the guidance program, and for other school programs   ____ ____

5. The librarian helps teachers obtain and evaluate new materials for their classes or their own professional information   ____ ____

6. The librarian makes, or helps teachers and pupils make, reading lists and bibliographies of all resources   ____ ____

7. The librarian introduces teachers to selection aids, subject biographies, and new reference works   ____ ____

8. The librarian serves as a member of curriculum committees.   ____ ____

Comments

SUMMARY

Use as many pages as needed to indicate:

A. Outstanding aspects, practices, and features of the library program.

B. The area(s) of the library program in which most improvement is needed.

C. What is being done to strengthen or improve the aspects of the library program most in need of improvement? Describe any plans designed to establish the library as a materials center.

EXAMPLE 45   ILLINOIS STANDARDS FOR SCHOOL MEDIA PROGRAMS AND THE
SCHOOL EVALUATION FORM*

STANDARDS FOR SCHOOL MEDIA PROGRAMS

The development of the media standards is indicated in three phases. The phasing was set up to encourage schools to put to use human and physical resources already available or to provide financial support for an initial media program. Therefore Phase I suggests very modest goals while Phase III is a summary of the current national standards; no limits are set for what progressive schools and modern technology may accomplish in providing a media program for quality education.

Much of the statement of standards is the quantitative measure of staffing, space, materials, and equipment of the media center facility, but the qualitative aspect suggested under program and services is the most important. It is suggested that the media staff review the material in *Standards for School Media Programs* and analyze their own program to identify strengths, weaknesses, and progress toward specific goals. In reviewing this aspect media specialists must be aware that they are evaluating the results of their own educational and media competencies, the quality of their leadership and team-work role, and their accomplishments in planning and implementing an effective media program.

The following general statements will describe various aspects of the school media program.

STAFF

Media specialists, assisted by technicians and aides, make unique and vital contributions to the total educational program of the school. The professional staff work directly with teachers and students providing a wide variety of services. Supportive staff with specific skills and special abilities make it possible for the media specialists to concentrate on professional services and activities. Thus it is economically sound to provide sufficient supportive staff to perform all nonprofessional duties.

SPACE RECOMMENDATIONS

Space must be provided and functional areas must be created to accommodate the resources and services of the media program. Every center should provide for at least the basic areas in Phase I and for some of the additional and special areas as the media program develops and expands. The media facility should be fairly central to the instructional areas of the building but apart from the traffic normal to the student flow.

PROGRAM AND SERVICES

The media center's program, collections, and environment provide a broad spectrum of learning opportunities for large and small groups of students as well as for individual students. The focus of the media program is on facilitating and improving the learning process in its new directions—with emphasis on the learner, on ideas and concepts rather than on isolated facts, and on inquiry rather than on rote memorization. The media staff, teachers, and administrative personnel work together to provide every possible opportunity for the social, cultural, and educational growth of the student.

BOOKS

The number of titles, as well as the number of volumes which a media center holds, must be recorded to indicate the amount of duplication, the need for which will vary with the requirements of individual schools. Standard selection aids will provide a basis for the initial collection. Trained media personnel, working with the faculty, will be best qualified to select from these lists to meet the particular needs of each individual school and to provide balance in the collection.

*"Standards for Educational Media (Library and Audiovisual) Programs in Illinois" developed by the Office of the Superintendent of Public Instruction, the Illinois Audiovisual Association, and the Illinois Association of School Librarians. *Illinois Libraries*, vol. 54, no. 7, September 1972, pp. 523-552. Contact Valerie J. Downes, Director, Media and Library Services, Department of Public Instruction, 316 South Second St., Springfield, Ill. 62706, for copies of the Standards and Evaluation Form.

MAGAZINES

Annotated lists of recommended titles may be found in the various selection aids. The collection should include titles for recreational interests as well as curricular needs, and *Readers' Guide to Periodical Literature* should be provided as an index to the magazine material. For small collections, media personnel and teachers are advised to give preference to those periodicals which are indexed in *Abridged Readers' Guide to Periodical Literature* and in *Subject Index to Children's Magazines*. Larger collections may include language publications to match the schools' foreign language program.

NEWSPAPERS

The newspapers in the collection should provide local, state, and national coverage and represent differing editorial and reporting policies. Additional titles should be chosen for their special features appropriate to the school curriculum and local interests. Small libraries may wish to supplement their local and state daily papers with a Sunday edition of a national coverage newspaper. Large schools may find it advisable to include a foreign newspaper and the *New York Times Index*.

FILMSTRIPS, CARTRIDGES, LOOPS, SLIDES, CASSETTES, RECORDINGS

An abundance of viewing and listening materials should be made readily available providing resources for the academic needs and general interests of students and teachers. To insure a quality collection of nonbook materials, the media staff should be alert to locating other authoritative selection aids in this comparatively new field of resource materials.

16MM FILMS

Many variables affect the size of film collections owned by individual schools so quantitative standards cannot cover every situation. In most instances, when rental charges for a film during the year equal from one-fifth to one-seventh of the purchase price of the film, it becomes feasible to purchase. The number actually owned by a school is minimal when the school has access to cooperative holdings and/or good rental sources.

GRAPHIC MATERIALS

The catalogs of The Art Institute of Chicago and other art centers are useful for the selection of art prints. Other graphics suitable to the needs of the instructional program should be acquired through commercial agencies; however, where graphics are produced locally, it is essential that the media center should have ample equipment and supplies to meet production needs.

GLOBES, MAPS

Maps and globes must be provided in sufficient numbers to serve the instructional needs of the classrooms and must be kept up-to-date. Special types of globes may be desirable for the media center.

PAMPHLETS, CLIPPINGS AND MISCELLANEOUS MATERIAL

Specialized and ephemeral materials are frequently invaluable reference aids because the information they provide is more unique, pertinent, or up-to-date than any other print material. These materials have the further advantage of being free or relatively inexpensive. However, the collection loses its value unless it is well organized for ready use and continuously weeded to keep the holdings up-to-date and relevant.

EXPENDITURES

Funds for the initial collections of all materials in newly established media centers should come from capital outlay and not from the amount recommended for annual expenditures for materials. In providing annual funds for materials, it is important that no schools fall below 1 percent per student per year of the current state average per pupil instructional costs. Schools spending less than this amount for operational costs would still need to appropriate funds for resources on the basis of the national average in order to have sufficient resources for teaching and learning.

STANDARDS FOR SCHOOL MEDIA PROGRAMS IN THREE PHASES

CATEGORY	PHASE I	PHASE II	PHASE III
PROFESSIONAL STAFF K-8	1 full-time certified teacher with library science and audiovisual education for each 500 students. Below 400—one half-time teacher. (Training for each should total 18 semester hours of library and/or audiovisual course work within 3 years.)	1 full-time media specialist with certificate in instructional materials, library science or audiovisual for each 500 students.	1 full-time media specialist for each 250 students or major fraction thereof.
9-12	Provide assigned certified personnel with appropriate training to service both library and audiovisual functions at the rate of 1 full-time equivalent per 600 students. Training for each should total 18 semester hours of library and/or audiovisual course work within 3 years.	Provide certified media specialists to service both functions (library and/or audiovisual) at the rate of 1 full-time equivalent per 400 students.	1 full-time media specialist for each 250 students or major fraction thereof.
	As the number of specialists increases, provision should be made for balance in staff competencies for audiovisual and library services.		
SUPPORTIVE STAFF K-12	1 half-time media aide for each professional.	1 full-time media aide (clerical and/or technical) for each professional.	1 full-time media aide and 1 full-time media technician for each 250 students or major fraction thereof.
EXPENDITURES K-12	A total from all sources of 1.0% of the state average per pupil instructional costs.	A total from all sources of 3% of the state average per pupil instructional costs.	A total from all sources of 6% of the state average per pupil instructional costs.

QUARTERS: SPACE AND SEATING

K-12

Seating for 10% of the student enrollment at 40 sq. ft. per student, plus 2,500 sq. ft. for the basic functions.

30% of that seating in independent study carrels.

Seating for 10% of the student enrollment at 40 sq. ft. per student, plus 2,500 sq. ft. for the basic functions.

At least 1,000 sq. ft. for additional functions of the media program.

Seating for 15% of the student enrollment at 40 sq. ft. per student, plus 2,500 sq. ft. for the basic functions.

At least 2,000 sq. ft. for additional functions of the media program.

Space for special functions as determined by school program.

SPACE RECOMMENDATIONS (based on an enrollment of 1,000 or fewer; must be adjusted for larger enrollment)

BASIC	Space in Sq. ft.
Entrance, circulation, distribution	800–1,000
Reading and browsing; individual viewing and listening	2,000–6,000
(Space based on 15% of a student enrollment at 40 sq. ft. per student; minimum provision for 50 students)	
Administrative offices	600– 800
Workroom	300– 400
Stacks	400– 800
Magazine storage	250– 400
AV equipment distribution and storage	400– 600
Faculty center and professional materials	600– 800

ADDITIONAL	
Conference rooms (3–6) @ 150 sq. ft.	450– 900
Small group viewing and listening	200– 200
Classroom for media instruction and class projects	900–1,000
Maintenance and repair service	120– 300
Media production lab	800–1,000
Darkroom	150– 200
Materials and equipment storage for production	120– 120

SPECIAL ASPECTS	Space in Sq. ft.
Television	
Studio	–1,600
Storage	800–1,000
Office with work space	–1,200
Radio	– 500
Computerized learning laboratory	900–1,000
Storage and control center for remote access	900–1,000

STANDARDS FOR SCHOOL MEDIA PROGRAMS IN THREE PHASES, Continued

CATEGORY: PROGRAMS & SERVICES	PHASE I	PHASE II	PHASE III
SELECTION OF MATERIALS	Jointly by professional media staff with assistance from teachers and students.		
SELECTION OF MATERIALS	Slides, Tapes, Transparencies, Charts, Filmstrips, 8mm films, etc. Posters, etc.		
INSTRUCTION IN USE OF MATERIALS AND EQUIPMENT	To students: a continuous and sequential program on both an individual and group basis. To faculty: individual and group assistance, the latter by means of workshops. To media staff (technical, clerical, and student assistants): by individual, on-the-job training.		
COORDINATION OF MATERIALS WITH THE INSTRUCTIONAL PROGRAM	As number of professional staff allows the following activities should be considered: Assistance to teachers in planning and presenting instructional units. Assistance to teachers and department heads in selection of materials for departmental resource rooms. Participation in curriculum committee activities. Individual and group guidance to students in listening, viewing, reading, and evaluating. Assistance in research projects with special emphasis on helping the student develop independent study skills. Clearinghouse of information on in-service workshops and courses, professional meetings, and the educational resources of the community.		

SCHOOL EVALUATION FORM—STANDARDS FOR SCHOOL MEDIA PROGRAMS

CATEGORY: MATERIALS/LEVEL	PHASE I	PHASE II	PHASE III
BOOKS K-12	Basic collection chosen from standard book selection aids.		6,000 to 10,000 titles representing 10,000 volumes or 20 volumes per-pupil, whichever is greater.
	3,000 titles or 6 volumes per pupil, whichever is greater.	5,000 titles or 10 volumes per pupil, whichever is greater.	
	Books which are worn, out-of-date, or otherwise unacceptable should be discarded. This weeding process should be continuous.		
	Satellite libraries or resource rooms supplied by media funds will require additional volumes—including many duplicates.		
Professional	3 current professional titles per teacher district-wide. Collection may be decentralized.	6 current professional titles per teacher district-wide. Collection may be decentralized.	200-1000 titles.
Reference	Current and expanding reference collection selected from standard lists and to include at least 2 encyclopedias.	Current and expanding reference collection selected from standard lists and to include from 3 to 5 encyclopedias.	
MAGAZINES (See also MICROFORMS) K-6	10-24 titles (includes some adult non-professional periodicals).	25-39 titles (includes some adult non-professional periodicals).	40-50 titles (includes some adult non-professional periodicals).
7-9	10-24 titles.	25-49 titles.	100-125 titles.
9-12	60-99 titles.	100-124 titles.	125-175 titles.

SCHOOL EVALUATION FORM—STANDARDS FOR SCHOOL MEDIA PROGRAMS, Continued

CATEGORY: MATERIALS/LEVEL	PHASE I	PHASE II	PHASE III
MAGAZINES Cont.			
K–12	Necessary magazine indexes and duplication of titles and indexes as required.		
Professional	10–14 professional titles with access to Education Index.	15–39 professional titles plus subscription to Education Index.	40–50 professional titles with duplicates as needed; also Education Index.
NEWSPAPERS (See also MICROFORMS)			
K–8	1–2 titles	3–4 titles.	6–10 titles.
9–12	3–4 titles	5–6 titles with duplication as necessary.	6–10 titles.
	At least one local, one state, and one national newspaper eventually to be represented in the collection.		
PAMPHLETS, CLIPPINGS AND MISCELLANEOUS MATERIAL K–12	An organized collection of appropriate materials to implement curriculum, updated by an annual budget appropriation.	An organized collection of pamphlets, clippings, vocational information and other appropriate curriculum material, updated by an annual appropriation of approximately 5% of the budget. In secondary schools catalogs of colleges, universities and technical schools should be included.	Pamphlets, government documents, catalogs of colleges and technical schools, vocational information, clippings, and other materials appropriate to the curriculum and for other interests of students.

FILMSTRIPS

Purchase dependent upon teacher request and willingness to preview. However, the basic collection should include:

K-8	200 titles or ½ print per pupil or whichever is greater.	400 titles or 1 print per pupil, whichever is greater.	500–1,000 titles, representing 1,500 prints or 3 prints per pupil, whichever is greater.
9-12	200 titles.	400 titles.	

SUPER 8 OR 8MM FILMS

Purchase of the following dependent on amount of individualized instruction done in the school. However, the basic collection should include:

K-8	1 title per 10 pupils.	1 film per pupil with at least 100 titles.	1 ½ films per student with at least 500 titles supplemented by duplicates.
9-12	½ film per pupil with at least 100 titles.	1 film per pupil with at least 100 titles.	

16MM FILMS

K-12	Unrestricted access to a minimum of 1,000 titles (include cooperative film libraries and rental sources).	Unrestricted access to a minimum of 2,000 titles (include cooperative film libraries and rental sources).	Access to a minimum of 3,000 titles supplemented by duplicates and rentals (include cooperative film libraries and rental sources).

All quantitative statements exclusive of sponsored films.

TAPE AND DISC RECORDINGS

K-12	500 titles representing 500 records or tapes or 1 per pupil, whichever is greater.	750 titles representing 750 records or tapes or 3 per pupil, whichever is greater.	1,000–2,000 titles representing 3,000 records or tapes or 6 per pupil, whichever is greater (the number of titles to be increased in larger collections).

SCHOOL EVALUATION FORM—STANDARDS FOR SCHOOL MEDIA PROGRAMS, Continued

CATEGORY: MATERIALS/LEVEL	PHASE I	PHASE II	PHASE III
SLIDES K–12		A collection representing basic curriculum needs with additions for special interest or subject areas.	A collection representing basic curriculum needs. 2,000 (including all sizes).
GRAPHIC MATERIALS K–12		Art prints pictures, study prints, posters, photographs, charts, diagrams, graphs and other types as needed for the implementation of curriculum. Budget allowance for local production where applicable.	
GLOBES K–12		1 globe in media center, additional as needed. 2 globes in media center, additional as needed.	
K–8			1 globe in each teaching station and 2 in media center.
9–12			1 globe per 5 teaching stations and 2 in media center.
MAPS K–12		1 map for each region studied and special maps (economic, weather, political, historical, and others) for each area studied. Duplicate maps available for each class section requiring maps at the same time, the number of duplicates to be determined by sections of students and the availability of maps on transparencies and filmstrips.	

MICROFORM

9–12

5–10 news magazines on microfilm.

11–19 magazines and one national daily newspaper on microfilm.

To be purchased as available on topics in the curriculum. All periodical subscriptions indexed in Reader's Guide and newspaper files should be obtained as needed for reference.

TRANSPARENCIES

K–12

A collection of transparencies and subject matter masters representing teaching needs.

OTHER MATERIALS:

K–12

To be introduced as desirable or necessary for the development of the individual school program.

Programmed instructional materials

Realia

Kits

Prerecorded Video tapes

Remote access programs

Resource files

SCHOOL EVALUATION FORM—STANDARDS FOR SCHOOL MEDIA PROGRAMS, Continued

CATEGORY: EQUIPMENT/LEVEL	PHASE I	PHASE II	PHASE III
16MM SOUND PROJECTOR			
K–12	1 per 10 teaching stations plus 1 per media center.	1 per 5 teaching stations plus 2 per media center.	1 per 2 teaching stations plus 5 per resource center.
SUPER 8 OR 8MM PROJECTOR REMOTELY CONTROLLED			
K–8	1 per media center.	1 per 10 teaching stations plus 3 per media center.	1 per teaching station plus 25 per resource center.
9–12	6 per media center.	1 per 5 teaching stations plus 6 per media center.	
2×2 SLIDE PROJECTOR REMOTELY CONTROLLED			
K–8	1 per media center.	1 per 10 teaching stations plus 2 per media center.	1 per 3 teaching stations plus 5 per resource center.
9–12	2 per media center.	1 per 10 teaching stations plus 2 per media center.	

Equipment	Grade			
FILMSTRIP OR COMBINATION FILMSTRIP/SLIDE PROJECTOR	K–12	1 per 10 teaching stations plus 1 per media center.	1 per 5 teaching stations plus 1 per media center.	1 per teaching station plus 4 per resource center.
SOUND FILMSTRIP PROJECTOR	K–12	1 per media center.	1 per 10 teaching stations plus 1 per media center.	
10×10 OVERHEAD PROJECTOR	K–12	1 per 5 teaching stations plus 1 per media center.	1 per 3 teaching stations plus 2 per media center.	1 per teaching station plus 4 per media center.
OPAQUE PROJECTOR	K–12	1 per floor level.	1 per floor level plus 1 per media center.	1 per 15 teaching stations plus 2 per media center.
FILMSTRIP VIEWER	K–8	1 per 5 teaching stations plus 5 per media center.	1 per 3 teaching stations plus 5 per media center.	3 per teaching station plus the equivalent of 1 per teaching station in media center.
	9–12	5 per media center.	1 per 3 individual study stations.	

SCHOOL EVALUATION FORM—STANDARDS FOR SCHOOL MEDIA PROGRAMS, Continued

CATEGORY: EQUIPMENT/LEVEL	PHASE I	PHASE II	PHASE III
2×2 SLIDE VIEWER			
K-8	1 per media center.	2 per media center.	1 per teaching station plus 1 per media center.
9-12	1 per 20 teaching stations plus 1 per 20 individual study stations in media center.	1 per 20 teaching stations plus 1 per 20 individual study stations in media center.	
TV RECEIVER (MINIMUM 23 in. SCREEN)			
K-12	1 per school for classroom use plus 1 per media center where programs are available.	1 per floor level for classroom use plus 1 per media center where programs are available.	1 per teaching station and 1 per media center where programs are available.
MICROPROJECTOR			
K-12	1 per building or access.	2 per building or access.	1 per 2 grade levels in K-8. 1 per department where applicable in 9-12 plus 1 per media center.
RECORD PLAYER			
K-6	1 per 5 teaching stations plus 1 per media center.	1 per 2 teaching stations plus 5 per media center.	1 per teaching station plus 5 per media center.
7-12	1 per 10 teaching stations plus 1 per media center.	1 per 5 teaching stations plus 3 per media center.	1 per teaching station plus 5 per media center.
All Schools	1 set of earphones per player.	1 set of earphones per player.	

Equipment			
AUDIO TAPE RECORDER/PLAYER, INCLUDING REEL-TO-REEL CARTRIDGE AND CASSETTE			
K-8	1 per 5 teaching stations plus 1 per media center.	1 per 2 teaching stations plus 2 per media center.	1 per teaching station plus 10 per media center.
9-12	1 per 10 teaching stations plus 5 per media center.	1 per 5 teaching stations plus 5 per media center.	1 per 5 teaching stations plus 10 per media center.
All Schools	1 set of earphones for each recorder.	1 set of earphones for each recorder.	
LISTENING STATION			
K-12	2 portable listening stations with multiple student positions.	portable listening stations with multiple student positions at the rate of 1 per 10 teaching stations.	portable listening stations with multiple student positions at the rate of 1 per teaching station plus 1 per media center.
PROJECTION CART			
K-12	1 of appropriate height per major piece of projection equipment at time equipment is obtained.	Additional as needed.	1 per portable piece of equipment purchased at the time equipment is obtained.
PROJECTION SCREEN			
K-12	1 screen of appropriate size for every major piece of projection equipment.	1 screen per teaching plus 1 per media center.	1 permanently mounted screen per classroom plus additional screens of suitable size as needed for individual and small group use. The permanent screen should be no smaller than 70×70 with keystone eliminator.

SCHOOL EVALUATION FORM—STANDARDS FOR SCHOOL MEDIA PROGRAMS, Continued

CATEGORY: EQUIPMENT/LEVEL	PHASE I	PHASE II	PHASE III
TELEVISION DISTRIBUTION K-12		All new construction should include a central antenna system with internal video,tape distribution at each teaching and media center. Older buildings should be wired for television distribution with initiation of such programs.	
RADIO RECEIVER (AM-FM) K-12	1 per media center and additional as needed where appropriate programming is available.	1 per media center and additional as needed where appropriate programming is available.	1 per media center plus central distribution system (AM-FM).
PHOTOCOPYING MACHINE 7-12	1 per school.	1 per 30 teaching stations plus 1 per media center.	1 per 30 teaching stations plus 1 per media center.
THERMAL OR INFRARED-COPYING MACHINE K-12	1 per school.	1 per school.	

Item			
MICROREADER (SOME WITH MICROFICHE ATTACHMENT) 7–12	1 per media center.	1 per 40 student positions in main reading room.	Equivalent of 1 per 10 teaching stations to be located in the media center.
MICROREADER PRINTER 7–12		1 per media center.	1 per media center.
PORTABLE VIDEO TAPE RECORDER SYSTEM (INCLUDING CAMERAS) K–12		1 per building.	1 per 15 teaching stations with a minimum of 2 recorders per building.
LAMINATING MACHINE K–12	1 per district.	1 per district.	
LIGHT CONTROL K–12		Adequate variable light level control in every classroom and media center to the extent that all types of projected media can be utilized effectively together with devices that filter or restrict outside light.	

SCHOOL EVALUATION FORM—STANDARDS FOR SCHOOL MEDIA PROGRAMS, Continued

CATEGORY: EQUIPMENT/LEVEL	PHASE I	PHASE II	PHASE III
LOCAL PRODUCTION EQUIPMENT PER BUILDING K–12	Minimum: Paper cutters Thermo transparency maker Film splicer (16mm) Primer typewriter Tape splicer Mechanical lettering devices Dry mount press and tacking iron	Additional: Copy camera and stand Diazo transparency equipment Slide sorting equipment Audio-reproduction equipment Light box	Additional: Film rewind 35mm still camera 16mm camera 8mm camera Rapid process camera Equipment for darkroom Slide reproducer

This document does not list any items that will be considered standard for some districts. In the main these items would be considered "special" and appropriate acquisitions only when the instructional program would be compromised by their omission. This list includes, but is not restricted to:

- Auditorium type overhead projectors
- Auditorium or large group 16mm equipment
- 16mm magnetic sound equipment
- Broadcast T.V. (2,500 Mhz, etc.)
- Telelecture
- Large format and/or random access slide equipment
- Slide duplication equipment
- Tape (Reel or Cassette) duplication equipment

EXAMPLE 46   ILLINOIS SELF-EVALUATION FORM: SCHOOL MEDIA PROGRAMS

"Standards for Educational Media (Library and Audiovisual) Programs in Illinois" developed by the Office of the Superintendent of Public Instruction, the Illinois Audiovisual Association, and the Illinois Association of School Librarians. *Illinois Libraries.* vol. 54, no. 7, September 1972. pp. 523–552. Contact Valerie J. Downes, Director, Media and Library Services, Department of Public Instruction, 316 South Second Street, Springfield, Illinois 62706, for copies of the Standards and Evaluation Form.

The form has been developed in some detail in order to serve as the basis for a valid evaluation of a media program in the context of the preceding statement of standards. The construction of the form provides for the recording of data for measurement purposes and a statement of short-range goals as evidence of planning for progress.

This form may be duplicated to be used by the staff to determine the strengths and weaknesses of the media program in relation to state and national standards. Careful comparison of the data recorded and the phases of the Illinois plan will provide guidelines for setting up goals for continuous growth and development.

School _____

Date _____

CATEGORY:	EVALUATIVE DATA	PHASES				PROGRESS RATING Meeting last year's objectives	SHORT-RANGE GOALS Objectives for ensuing year
		-1	1	2	3		
STAFF:	No. of Student Staff Enrollment						
PROFESSIONAL							
SUPPORTIVE							

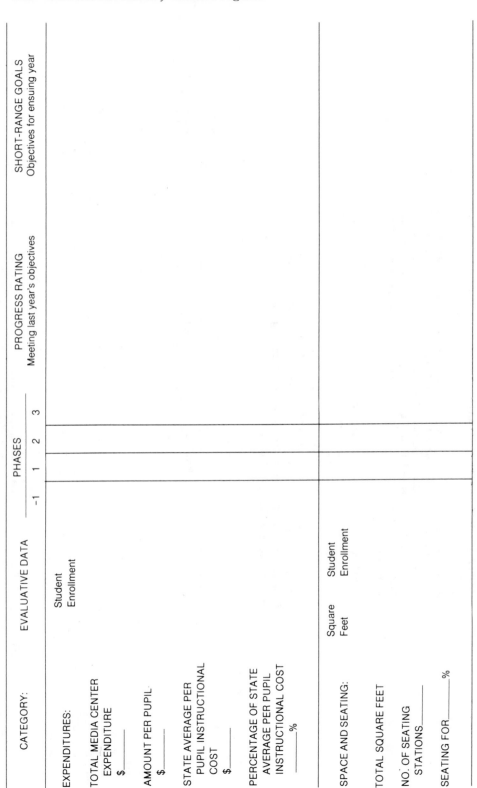

CATEGORY: PROGRAMS AND SERVICES	EVALUATIVE DATA	PHASES				PROGRESS RATING Meeting last year's objectives	SHORT-RANGE GOALS Objectives for ensuing year
		-1	1	2	3		
	List the details of the implementation of goals of programs and services						
SELECTION OF MATERIALS							
PRODUCTION OF MATERIALS							
INSTRUCTION IN USE OF MATERIALS AND EQUIPMENT (Students, faculty and media staff)							
COORDINATION OF MATERIALS WITH THE INSTRUCTIONAL PROGRAM							

CATEGORY: MATERIALS	EVALUATIVE DATA		PHASES				PROGRESS RATING Meeting last year's objectives	SHORT-RANGE GOALS Objectives for ensuing year
			-1	1	2	3		
BOOKS	No. of Titles	No. of Volumes						
Professional								
Reference								
Total collection								
No. of books per pupil								
MAGAZINES	No. of Titles	No. of Subscriptions						
General								
Professional								
No. of indexes								
NEWSPAPERS (Encircle types represented: local, state, national)	No. of Titles	No. of Subscriptions						

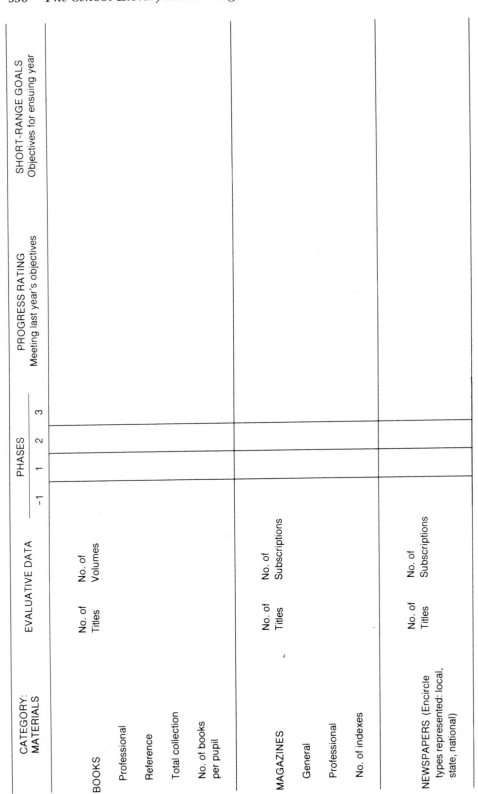

PAMPHLETS, CLIPPINGS, AND MISCELLANEOUS MATERIALS	No. of Items	
FILMSTRIPS	No. of Titles	No. of Prints
SUPER 8 OR 8MM FILMS	No. of Titles	No. of Films
16MM FILMS	No. of Titles	No. of Films
TAPE AND DISC RECORDINGS	No. of Titles	No. of Recordings
SLIDES	No. of Items	
GRAPHIC MATERIALS	No. of Items	

CATEGORY: MATERIALS	EVALUATIVE DATA	PHASES				PROGRESS RATING Meeting last year's objectives	SHORT-RANGE GOALS Objectives for ensuing year
		-1	1	2	3		
GLOBES	No. of Items No. of Teaching Stations						
MAPS	No. of Items						
MICROFORM	No. of Titles No. of Items						
TRANSPARENCIES	No. of Items						
OTHER MATERIALS	No. of Items						
Programmed instructional materials							
Realia							
Kits							
Prerecorded video tapes							
Remote access programs							
Resource files							

CATEGORY: EQUIPMENT	EVALUATIVE DATA No. of Carrels:		PHASES				PROGRESS RATING Meeting last year's objectives	SHORT-RANGE GOALS Objectives for ensuing year
	No. of Items	No. of Teaching Stations	-1	1	2	3		
16MM SOUND PROJECTOR								
SUPER 8 OR 8MM PROJECTOR REMOTELY CONTROLLED								
2×2 SLIDE PROJECTOR REMOTELY CONTROLLED								
FILMSTRIP OR COMBINATION FILMSTRIP/SLIDE PROJECTOR								
SOUND FILMSTRIP PROJECTOR								
10×10 OVERHEAD PROJECTOR								
OPAQUE PROJECTOR								
FILMSTRIP VIEWER								

CATEGORY: EQUIPMENT	EVALUATIVE DATA			PHASES				PROGRESS RATING	SHORT-RANGE GOALS
	No. of Items	No. of Carrels:	No. of Teaching Stations	-1	1	2	3	Meeting last year's objectives	Objectives for ensuing year
2×2 SLIDE VIEWER									
TV RECEIVER (MINIMUM 23" SCREEN)									
MICROPROJECTOR									
RECORD PLAYER Earphones									
AUDIO TAPE RECORDER PLAYER, INCLUDING REEL-TO-REEL CARTRIDGE AND CASSETTE Earphones									
LISTENING STATION									
PROJECTION CART									
PROJECTION SCREEN									

TELEVISION DISTRIBUTION	RADIO RECEIVER (AM-FM)	PHOTOCOPYING MACHINE	THERMAL OR INFRARED-COPYING MACHINE	MICROREADER (SOME WITH MICROFICHE ATTACHMENT)	MICROREADER Printer	PORTABLE VIDEO TAPE RECORDER SYSTEM (WITH CAMERAS)	LAMINATING MACHINE	LIGHT CONTROL

CATEGORY: EQUIPMENT	EVALUATIVE DATA No. of Carrels:		PHASES				PROGRESS RATING Meeting last year's objectives	SHORT-RANGE GOALS Objectives for ensuing year
	No. of Items	No. of Teaching Stations	-1	1	2	3		
LOCAL PRODUCTION EQUIPMENT PER BUILDING								
Paper Cutters								
Thermo transp. maker								
16mm film splicer								
Primer typewriter								
Tape Splicer								
Mechanical lettering devices								
Dry mount press								
Copy camera								
Diazo transp. equip.								
Slide sorting equipment								
Audio-reproduction equipment								
Light box								
Film rewind								
35mm still camera								
16mm camera								
8mm camera								
Rapid process								
Equipment for camera								
Slide reproducer darkroom								

LIST OTHER ITEMS
UNIQUE TO YOUR
MEDIA CENTER:

The Criteria of Excellence Checklist (Example 43) was first used by the School Library Manpower Project, funded by the Knapp Foundation of North Carolina Inc., as a means of identifying performance of service activities by all types of school library personnel at the building level. This tool measures the effectiveness of a school library program as an integral part of the school's instructional program, and includes both *research* and *implementation* in its assessment. It requires a minimum of time to complete but gives a detailed analysis of the adequacy of the school library's function as a supportive educational agent.

Example 44 is a comprehensive self-study guide designed as part of a district K–12 program evaluation. In format it resembles the *Evaluative Criteria of the National Study of School Evaluation*, providing not only checklists for the evaluation of existing programs but also opportunities for comments, recommendations, and projected improvements. The section of the guide entitled "Program Objectives" is an excellent device for focusing the attention of both faculty and administration on the function of the library as a teaching center, a service center, a guidance agency, and a curricular support agency.

Example 45 is a three-phase program for the implementation of the Illinois Standards for School Media Programs. Phase I suggests very modest goals, Phase II suggests more exacting standards, and Phase III reflects current national standards. Example 46 is the Self-Evaluation Form provided by the Illinois Department of Public Instruction to serve as the basis for a valid evaluation of a media program in the context of the preceding statement of standards as set forth in Example 45.

STAFF EVALUATION

Just as the quality of the teacher is the key to good education, so the quality of the library media specialist is the key to the degree of educational excellence achievable by the library media program. Inasmuch as the evaluation of the library media center staff is a major responsibility of the supervisor of the district library media program, discussion of staff evaluation will be found in Chapter 14, "The Supervisor of the Library Media Program."

A PLAN FOR ACTION

The real value to be derived from any evaluation lies in the corrective action resulting from the findings. Having completed an evaluation of the educational program or of the library media program, the library media specialist should take immediate action to study the findings and to put the recommendations for improvement into an operational master plan. This master plan should outline objectively the step-by-step procedure to be followed in upgrading the educational or library media program by strengthening noted weaknesses and by putting into operation recommended changes. This master plan should provide target dates and priorities for both immediate and long-range action such as is specified in the Illinois Self-Evaluation Form: School Media Program (Example 46). It is reasonable to develop the master plan on a three-, four-, and five-year basis, designating for the first year those concerns of the greatest significance, for the second year those concerns of the next greatest significance, and so on. Such an ongoing developmental plan for the consistent upgrading of a district school library media program should provide for all phases of the program: district school library media program coordinator and supportive staff, district instructional materials center, district centralized ordering and processing service, and district professional library, as well as providing library media programs in each district school that meets state or national standards for personnel, budget, media collections, facilities, and program.

The success of any educational evaluative endeavor is determined by the ability of the educational staff—teachers, library media specialists, supervisors, administrators—to relate specific program developmental needs to specific program modifications, renovations, and innovations. Such a task demands the cooperative efforts of an educational team of professionals who share the vision of educational excellence and who are competent to translate the vision into concrete operational designs. Such a team requires the efforts of a visionary library media specialist who can dream constructively and strive consistently to translate the dream into reality.

NOTES

1. Carter V. Good, ed., *Dictionary of Education*, 3rd ed. (New York: McGraw-Hill, 1973).
2. National Study of School Evaluation, *Evaluative Criteria*, 5th ed. Copyright © 1978, p. 277. Reprinted with permission of the National Study of School Evaluation, Washington, D.C.
3. Frances Henne, "School Libraries," in *Library Surveys*, ed. by Maurice F. Tauber and Irene R. Stephens (New York: Columbia University Press, 1967), p. 194.

14 The Supervisor of the Library Media Program

Judgment without justice is an inhumane activity that degrades the dignity and worth of the individual.

Russell and Judith Shelton Dobson*

Creative teachers . . . need creative supervision.

E. Paul Torrance†

The terms "supervision" and "supervisor" have a historical connotation which has caused them to be anathema to teachers in the past. To many these words automatically call to the foreground of memory a picture of authoritarian dictatorship. Unfortunately the misconception of the purpose and function of supervision inherited from the past continues to persist in the minds of teachers today.

When teachers needed only a high school diploma to be certified to teach, the supervisor was appointed to show teachers how to teach. Supervision began as a source of on-the-job training. There was not too much concern over the teacher's lack of subject knowledge—the textbook was expected to provide course content. It was only in the field of methodology that the teacher was judged in need of training. In order to provide professional know-how district and county supervisors made their rounds, evaluating the effectiveness of the teacher and making recommendations for improvement.

Unfortunately the constructive contribution of the countless many fine supervisors has been forgotten. The overwhelming flood of anecdotal accounts told and retold about the blatantly incompetent supervisor has obliterated the contribution of the competent supervisor from the teacher's historical memory. There are innumerable stories told about supervisors who had little concern for things of the mind; their major concern was for things of a housekeeping nature. They judged a teacher's competency on whether or not the window shades were even; whether or not the blackboard was washed and the erasers dusted; whether or not lights were burned unnecessarily; whether or

*Russell and Judith Shelton Dobson, *Humaneness in Schools: A Neglected Force* (Dubuque, Iowa: Kendall/Hunt, 1976), p. 28.

†E. Paul Torrance, *Education and the Creative Potential* (Minneapolis, Minn.: University of Minnesota Press, 1963), p. 11.

not the classroom was maintained at a proper temperature (no mean trick when the room was heated by a pot-bellied stove or by a furnace lacking a thermostatic control); whether or not every nubbin of chalk and every smidgin of paper were used; whether or not the teacher remembered to remove the bucket from under the leak in the roof the minute the rain had stopped. This type of vindictive, negative supervision led to the coining of the term "snoopervision." It was the kind of destructive supervision that caused teacher frustration and fear.

In the past the power of the supervisor was absolute—he held the teacher's professional life in his hands. It was upon the recommendation of the supervisor that a teacher's hope for reappointment and salary increase depended. For in the saber-toothed-tiger days a salary scale and tenure were not the rule. A teaching contract was for but one year—renewal was by board action. Each year the board decided who would be fired, who would be rehired, and what salary each would be paid. In large measure the recommendation of the supervisor determined the decision of the board. Because the supervisor held the job and salary future of the teacher in his hands he came to be feared as a collector of professional scalps.

CONTEMPORARY CONCEPT OF SUPERVISION

The traditional need for the supervisor to teach the teacher how to teach is long since past. Certification requirements have been upgraded to preclude the necessity of supervision based on methodology. The contemporary concept of supervision is a far cry from "snoopervision." The term as used in contemporary education means:

> All efforts of designated school officials directed toward providing *leadership* to teachers and other educational workers in the *improvement of instruction;* involves the stimulation of professional growth and development of teachers, the selection and revision of objectives, materials of instruction, and methods of teaching, and the evaluation of instruction.[1]

The function of supervision in today's educational endeavor has nothing in common with authoritarian dictatorship. The constant operational goal of modern supervision is improvement of instruction. Therefore, the major responsibility of the supervisor is to provide competent, constructive *leadership* and *guidance* to the educational staff. Today's supervisor does *not* dictate change, does *not* berate teachers, does *not* hire or fire teachers; his function is to inspire, to guide, to lead, to coordinate the efforts of the entire staff as they all work toward a common goal that is mutually understood and mutually respected.

SUPERVISOR AS A CHANGE AGENT

The focus of emphasis in constructive supervision is on the team approach to improving instruction. Therefore, the supervisor is an agent for constructive, timely, and creative change. It is the special province of the supervisor to foresee and anticipate needed change and then to facilitate and expedite group interaction in accomplishing the change. It is the responsibility of the supervisor to create a climate that will encourage and accommodate change.

A leader must give top priority to change since it is crucial for survival. Both his personal attitude and that of key people within the organization are important to the leader if he wishes to effect change. He must not be dogmatic about a pet idea, nor must he insist upon change for its own sake. A detailed plan of action, and possibly a long-range plan, must be carefully constructed. His timing must be right in order to solicit the support of subordinates and to avoid possible confusion which would have a negative effect on staff morale. A climate must be created which will encourage and accommodate change. When these conditions prevail, the particular strategies, tactics, or approaches utilized will probably determine the ultimate success of the desired change.[2]

The recommendations made by Kauss—that the supervisor should serve as a catalyst for change by preparing a detailed action plan and by utilizing strategies, tactics, and approaches conducive to promoting a climate that encourages as well as accommodates change—are echoed by Robert Alfonso, Gerald Firth, and Richard Neville in *Instructional Supervision: A Behavior System*. In this work they identify 37 propositions concerning the planning and strategy of change (see Checklist 10).

CHECKLIST 10 PLANNING AND STRATEGY OF CHANGE

Based on contemporary research and writings, the following propositions have been formulated concerning instructional supervisory behavior:

Proposition 1:   Planning and initiating change will be more effective when the objectives and policies of the organization are clear, realistic, and understood.

Proposition 2:   Change efforts will be more effective when they are carefully planned, have definite goals, and incorporate some functional method of problem-solving to attain the desired ends.

Proposition 3:   The effectiveness of change efforts will be enhanced when the people who are to be affected are involved in the planning and decision-making.

Proposition 4:   Change efforts will be more effective if they are supported by an appropriate, systematic, and comprehensive strategy.

Proposition 5:   Change will be more effective when the choice of a strategy is consistent with the focus of the change effort.

Proposition 6:   Change will be more effective when, at the appropriate point in the change process, the change agent's efforts shift from "selling" to "diffusion."

Proposition 7:   Change will be more effective within groups that do not see themselves in competition with each other.

Proposition 8:   A change effort will be more effective if it takes into account the demands of time, money, and energy that the change requires.

Proposition 9:   Changes that are primarily technological will be more effective if they are buttressed by direct experience and support in their implementation.

Proposition 10:   A change effort will be more effective if it is perceived as building on existing practice rather than threatening it.

Proposition 11:   The effectiveness of a change effort will be increased when one sees the nature of the change as enhancing his own personal relationships and status in the organization.

Proposition 12:   Change will be more effective when it is recognized that change efforts will be perceived differently by different people, as a result of the many forces at work within each individual.

Proposition 13:   The effectiveness of change efforts will be improved when those restraining factors which inhibit an individual's normal desire for change are recognized and dealt with deliberately.

CHECKLIST 10 (cont.)

Proposition 14:   Change efforts will be more effective if the change is not perceived as causing a loss of prestige or group esteem.

Proposition 15:   A change will be more readily accepted if it is not perceived as requiring a shift in one's attitude or belief system.

Proposition 16:   Change will be more effective if it recognizes differences in acceptance according to the personality fluctuations that occur with age.

Proposition 17:   Change will be more effective if it is not perceived as giving advantage to some other group or area within the organization.

Proposition 18:   Change will be more effective if it does not threaten the vested interests of powerful groups or individuals.

Proposition 19:   Change will be more effective if it does not appear to disturb the existing organizational structure of status, relationship, and recognition.

Proposition 20:   Change will be more readily accepted if it can be demonstrated to be practicable in the target system or a close approximation of it.

Proposition 21:   Change will be more effective when the conditions that exist within the target system are those which encourage change processes.

Proposition 22:   The effectiveness of a change effort will be increased when it is recognized that the characteristics of some changes make them easier to accept than others.

Proposition 23:   A change effort will be more successful if recognition is given to the different roles that individuals within a system play in accepting change.

Proposition 24:   A change effort will be more effective if recognition is given to the presence and influence of group norms.

Proposition 25:   Change will be more effective when leadership and acceptance from within the group to be influenced come from an individual with group membership and esteem.

Proposition 26:   The success of change efforts will be affected by the cohesiveness and the longevity of the group to be influenced.

Proposition 27:   A change effort will be more effective when it recognizes and utilizes the strength of group norms.

Proposition 28:   The effectiveness and stability of a change will be enhanced when a cohesive group commits itself to it, thereby setting up a new force field.

Proposition 29:   Change efforts will be more effective when the change agent, as perceived by other group members, has prestige and acceptance within the group.

Proposition 30:   Change is more likely to occur if there is a recognized role-responsibility for initiating and directing change in the system.

Proposition 31:   Change will be more effective when external contact and influence are components of the change process.

Proposition 32:   Change will be effective and is more likely to occur when it is brought about not by chance, but deliberately, and when it is initiated and guided by some active person or group.

Proposition 33:   A change agent will be more effective if he remains free from intimate involvement with the client system.

Proposition 34:   The change agent will be more effective if he has prestige and acceptance in the eyes of those in the client system.

Proposition 35:   Change will be more effective if linkage occurs between external and internal agents of change.

Proposition 36:   A change is more likely to be lasting if it receives continued evaluation after initial adoption.

Proposition 37:   Change efforts will be more effective and durable when they are buttressed by supportive forces.[3]

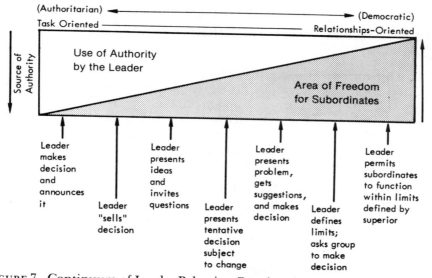

FIGURE 7. Continuum of Leader Behavior. Reprinted by permission of the Harvard Business Review. Adapted from the exhibit, "Continuum of Leadership Behavior" from "How to Choose a Leadership Pattern" by Robert Tannenbaum and Warren H. Schmidt (May–June 1973). Copyright © 1973 by the President and Fellows of Harvard College; all rights reserved.

In the authoritarian style of supervision all policies are determined by the leader; in the democratic style of supervision policies are open for group discussion, interaction, and decision. Paul Hersey and Kenneth Blanchard, in *Management of Organizational Behavior: Utilizing Human Resources*, second edition (Englewood Cliffs, N.J.: Prentice-Hall, 1972), contrast the authoritarian type of leadership with the democratic style by means of a graphic continuum of leader behavior (see Fig. 7).[4]

LEADERSHIP OF THE MERIT OF IDEAS

Harold Shane stressed the necessity of the "group process" approach to leadership in bringing about the curricular changes he recommended in *Curriculum Change Toward the 21st Century*. In his opinion:

As the schools encounter new opportunities for service and undertake new tasks suggested by the 28 cardinal premises, it seems inevitable that different concepts of leadership will appear and that these concepts will be based on greater participation by more people thus enabling persons affected by alternative choices and decisions to have a greater share in making them. . . .

As teachers, parents, students or others work together to bring about curriculum change, a leader is one who successfully contributes to group thinking and planning so that in the end everyone, or virtually everyone, is pleased or at least reasonably satisfied with the outcome. This is the *leadership of the merit of ideas* in attaining shared goals *rather than the leadership of status*. When group processes are functioning, suggestions or proposals that pass currency in the free market of ideas have a full and fair chance to determine what decisions shall be made and what actions shall be taken. Defensible *values* and persuasive, sound *ideas* rather than position or rank are what matter.[5]

ROLE OF THE SUPERVISOR OF THE DISTRICT SCHOOL LIBRARY MEDIA PROGRAM

The most comprehensive analysis of the services, responsibilities, knowledges, and abilities required of a district school library media program director, supervisor, or coordinator is found in the School Library Manpower Project publication, *Occupational Definitions for School Library Media Personnel.* Insight into the unique role and function of the supervisor of school library media programs demands careful study of the Manpower document from which the following excerpts have been taken:[6]

> *Position Title:* District School Library Media Director.
>
> *Reports To:* Designated administrative authority (may be the District Superintendent).
>
> *Supervises (may include):* Heads of the school library media centers; district school library media center supportive personnel.

The effective organization and implementation of district-wide school library media programs can provide students and teachers at the building level with a wider range of services and resources than would otherwise be possible. The responsibilities for planning, coordinating, and directing the district-wide school library media program are included in the occupational definition for the district school library media director.

The occupational definition requires a wide range of knowledges and abilities to enable the district school library media director effectively to meet the responsibilities of the position. In addition to administering a district school library media center the director must also coordinate school library media programs at a variety of levels. A broad understanding of other disciplines and the ability to relate and communicate the media field to others within and without the educational system are essential elements in the occupational definition of the district school library media director. The leadership and administrative qualities of the position are reflected in the policy- and decision-making responsibilities identified in the occupational definition.

The recommendations adopted by the Advisory Committee of the School Library Manpower Project state that a sixth-year or doctoral program is desirable to provide specialization and additional competencies beyond those of a school library media specialist. The nature of the services and responsibilities of the district school library media director's position makes it necessary to have special competencies beyond those of the head of the school library media center.

NATURE AND SCOPE OF POSITION

The primary role of the district school library media director is to provide leadership in all aspects of the district school library media program. The district school library media director serves on the school district administrative staff and is responsible for planning and coordinating district-wide programs to provide media services, which may include educational radio and television, programmed and computer-based teaching systems, information storage and retrieval, and display facilities. These programs may be at a single school, district, or multidistrict level. The incumbent provides leadership for the education of the individual by guiding school library media center personnel and school administrators in the planning, development, evaluation, and analysis of programs and services of the school library media center and the district school library media center personnel. The incumbent selects, supervises, and evaluates district school library media center personnel. The district school library media director is a member of the curriculum staff and relates the school library media program to the educational objectives of the district. The incumbent administers the district school library media center, which may embody such services as a professional library, a curriculum library, a materials examination center, a district school library media and equipment center, production of materials, and computer services. He makes recommendations for the recruitment and qualifications of school and district school library media center personnel and supportive staff, and is responsible for representing and communicating the objectives and scope of the school library media program to the community.

MAJOR DUTIES

The district school library media director plans and develops the direction for the school library media program of the district and makes recommendations to the district administration for the improvement of instruction through the school library media program. The incumbent contributes to curriculum planning and reevaluates the educational goals of the district with district curriculum personnel.

The district school library media director participates in district curriculum staff meetings and serves in a consultative capacity to subject and grade level specialists, heads of school library media centers and supportive staff, and building and district level administration.

The district school library media director systematically explores current developments and innovations in the field of instructional media. He relates these to trends in education and communicates pertinent information to district administration, building level administrators, faculty, and school library media center personnel. The incumbent plans, initiates, and develops the district school library media program to meet the educational goals and to permit flexibility for differences unique to individual schools. He provides the leadership for the implementation of the adopted program.

The district school library media director coordinates all school library media programs within the district and makes provisions for the use of inter-district and community library resources. Provision for free access by all schools to district and external media resources; optimum staffing of school library media centers; district-wide scheduling of presentations and exhibits; review of individual school library media programs for the prescribed educational functions; the centralized processes essential to the selection, acquisition, cataloging, preparation, and supply of materials and equipment; and the exercise of budget controls within the framework of the system are examples of some of the coordinating activities.

The district school library media director plans and develops policy recommendations, and implements and interprets established policy in such areas as: evaluation, selection, and use of media and equipment performance standards; budget expenditures; and personnel practices. The incumbent consults with heads of school library media centers and school administrators for the purposes of reviewing, analyzing, and making recommendations for school library media center budget proposals. After such consultation he plans, develops, proposes, justifies, and defends immediate and long-range budget requests for the district school library media program.

The district school library media director plans, schedules, and conducts media-related in-service and continuing education programs for faculty, administrators, school library media center staffs, and community groups.

The district school library media director interviews and makes recommendations for staff appointments to building and district school library media center positions based on personnel needs. He may serve as a consultant in the evaluation of school library media center personnel. He supervises and evaluates supporting staff in the district school library media center. The incumbent administers the services of: centralized media processing center, repair and maintenance facility, media collection, equipment testing and production of instructional materials, and other facilities provided for district-wide use.

The district school library media director uses his knowledge of construction design to plan for new and remodeled school district library media centers. He consults with school architects and makes recommendations to assure the inclusion of optimum facilities for media services in a variety of settings.

A district liaison function is performed by the district school library media director to interpret and carry out within his division all directions and policies formulated by the superintendent and/or school board. A liaison function is also performed with county, state, regional, and national education agencies. The incumbent provides appropriate reports to these agencies and to the district administration. He maintains lines of communication with the community, professional organizations, broadcasting and telecasting companies and stations, and producers and distributors of media and equipment and their agents. The district school library media director is aware of new developments in the field of media and related technology through his participation in various organizations, seminars, workshops, and conferences.

The district school library media director constantly examines and appraises existing school library media programs to determine their continuing feasibility and effectiveness, incorporating new features when required, and changing objectives, methods, and estimates of resources as circumstances demand. The district school library media director is alert to changing community resources, evolving community problems, and their effect upon the objectives of the school library media program. He develops immediate and long-range plans for school library media program development based on this knowledge.

Every district school library media director has the expertise as stated above. Through attainment of additional knowledge and/or experience, he may elect to concentrate further in a particular area such as: curriculum, administration, personnel management, organization and control of materials, media production and design, or media technology.

KNOWLEDGES AND ABILITIES

The nature of the services and responsibilities of the district school library media director's position makes it necessary to have special competencies beyond those of the head of the school library media center. The knowledges and abilities listed for the district school library media director are in addition to those identified for the head of the school library media center.

KNOWLEDGES

The district school library media director must have knowledge of:

School and community characteristics.

Government educational agencies including their organization, programs, requirements, and services.

Educational specifications for facility design and construction.

Organization and operation of centralized services, such as: cataloging and processing, information networks, warehousing, and traffic management.

School law.

School finance.

School administration.

Principles of supervision and personnel management.

Principles of service for special programs in the school community, such as: special education, exceptional children, programs for minority groups, vocational education, and the disadvantaged.

Publishing, producing, and manufacturing markets.

ABILITIES

The district school library media director must have the ability to:

Conceive, synthesize, promote, and direct broader gauged, geographically dispersed media programs as they relate to the many variables and complexities of the total school community, organization, and objectives.

Coordinate staff and operational activities to achieve harmony in the functions and services of the school library media program.

Determine personnel needs and assignments.

Supervise and evaluate personnel.

Justify budget requests and resolve fiscal problems.

Develop, interpret, and implement policy.

Contribute to the planning and design for new and remodeled school library media centers and other facilities related to the school library media service.

Project the enthusiasm, commitment, and self-confidence necessary for working with district, county, regional, state, and national level organizations, officials, academic authorities, mass media executives, contractors, and other allied individuals and groups.

Evaluate needs and demands from particular community sources and school authorities in the interest of achieving balanced district-wide programs.

TEAMING AT THE ADMINISTRATIVE LEVEL

The supervisor of the library media program shares with the school principal the responsibility for implementing the library media program in his school. This is a joint administrative concern. It is the principal who sets the educational priorities for his faculty; it is the principal who, by his attitude, encourages the teachers to plan with the library media specialist for class, group, and individual student use of the library media center.

Instructional changes which call for significant new ways of using professional talent, drawing upon instructional resources, allocating physical facilities, scheduling instructional time or altering physical space—rearrangements of the structural elements of the institution—depend almost exclusively upon administrative initiative.

Authority is a critical element in the shaping of institutional decisions. Schools depend heavily upon administrative authority in decision-making. Consequently, the control center of the institution, as schools are managed today, is the administrator. He may not be—and frequently is not—the original source of interest in a new type of program, but unless he gives it his attention and actively promotes its use, it will not come into being.[7]

The following advice is given to the principal concerning his responsibility for developing a dynamic library program for his school by Dr. George B. Brain, Dean of the College of Education at Washington State University:

The library program in your school will be a creative, dynamic one only if you (the principal) understand and discharge your obligations to it. You must:

1. Interpret the library program to teachers so that they see it in relation to the rest of the instructional program and also appreciate its interrelationship with each of the areas in the instructional program. Use inservice training to help your staff develop skills for diagnosis and to show them how diagnosis can serve as an aid to teaching. Correctly planned and executed by a principal whose educational philosophy recognizes the importance of the school library, this type of activity can lead to high staff morale, which in turn leads to a cohesiveness among the different departments in the instructional program, and, therefore, to a contribution to the individual student.

2. Select, or aid in selecting, the librarian with the same careful attention that you give to selecting a teacher.

3. Work with the librarian, applying the same principles of supervision that you use with the teaching staff. Include her in all curriculum planning activities

within the school. Assume the responsibility to make her and the teaching staff aware of their interdependence.

4. Provide for the best possible library program. This involves planning so that the librarian (a) works with children in small groups and entire classes, both in the library and in classrooms, and (b) gives individual attention to pupils.

5. Involve the librarian in the school program by requiring that she attend all meetings at which the content of courses is discussed and by expecting her to assume committee assignments and extra-curricular duties. (But do not assign duties at the lunch hour or before or after school, because this will curtail the library service.)

6. Make the program feasible administratively (a) by providing time for teachers and the librarian to plan together, (b) by scheduling so that children have time to use the library, and (c) by seeing that rules and regulations encourage maximum use of the library by children and their teachers.

7. Provide for evaluation of the library and its services. One of the best ways to provide for constant evaluation is to have a library evaluation committee (composed of staff members and the librarian) study the library and make recommendations concerning its improvement and use. Though much of the work can be done by others, you should serve as the core of this committee, for, without your support, improvements will not be made. More important, if you are a key person on this committee, you will be more aware of the needs of the library and more interested and sympathetic when funds are requested for improvements.[8]

Edward D. Kruse, then Superintendent of the North Hills School District, in his speech, "Manpower and Media for the Use of the Minority and the Majority," delivered before the American Association of School Administrators at the 1971 National Convention of the Association, echoed Dr. George Brain's belief that developing and supporting a quality school library media program is an imperative administrative responsibility. Kruse stated, "In my opinion, your school's or district's instructional media program will be a creative and dynamic one only if you, the administrator, will bring to your school library media program your administrative understanding, your administrative concern, and your administrative backing. Such understanding, such concern, such backing comes under the heading of 'administrative accountability.'"[9]

THE TEAM APPROACH TO LIBRARY MEDIA STAFF ORGANIZATION

The job of educational leadership is so demanding that it cannot be accomplished by the supervisor working in isolation from the rest of the staff. The only hope of achieving a district library media program of uniform excellence is to draw upon the expertise of the entire staff. Planning and working together as a cooperative professional team will not only develop a more efficient and effective district library media program, but will also assure a much more responsive and creative one. Teaming has a synergistic effect on educational planning and development; the pooled energies, efforts, competencies, background knowledge, and particular talents of the team members will carry the district library program to a much higher level of proficiency and instructional excellence than ever could be attained by library media specialists working in isolation one from the other. The coordinator or supervisor of library media services should serve as the team leader and share with the rest of the team decision making, policy formulation, program implementation, and evaluation. If the size of the library media staff warrants it, organization of the staff into two separate teams—one on the elementary level and one on the secondary level—will afford greater manageability. If the staff is to be organized as two separate teams, a team leader or head should be appointed to assist the coordinator or supervisor in planning and carrying out the team's activities. Examples 47 and 48 show typical job descriptions of an elementary and a secondary team leader.

EXAMPLE 47 JOB DESCRIPTION: HEAD, ELEMENTARY LIBRARY TEAM

The head of the elementary library team assists the Coordinator of Library Service in:

Evaluating, redesigning, and restructuring the elementary library program to reflect the emerging needs of the elementary educational program.

Making recommendations concerning procedures for and methods of strengthening library service on the elementary level.

Searching out, appraising, and selecting new resources for elementary building libraries and for elementary teaching laboratory libraries.

Serving on elementary curriculum study and revision committees and alerting the elementary librarians to anticipated curricular changes.

Designing innovative media usage patterns to support curricular changes.

Devising an on-the-job training program for elementary librarians new to the school district.

Serving as resource consultant to elementary teachers and elementary librarians searching for media to meet special teaching and learning support needs.

Serving in the special capacity of media program designer to develop individualized media programs and to test these programs.

Developing a study skills integration program to expedite and facilitate students learning how to learn effectively and efficiently.

Serving as a liaison contact with the staff of the public library, to plan for and implement a program of community and school library cooperation.

EXAMPLE 48 JOB DESCRIPTION: HEAD, SECONDARY LIBRARY TEAM

The head of the secondary library team assists the Coordinator of Library Service in:

Evaluating, redesigning, and restructuring the secondary library program to reflect the emerging needs of the educational program.

Making recommendations concerning procedures for and methods of strengthening library service on the secondary level.

Searching out, appraising, and selecting new resources for building libraries and for subject laboratory libraries.

Serving on secondary curriculum study and revision committees, alerting the secondary librarians to anticipated curricular changes.

Designing innovative media usage patterns to support curricular changes.

Devising an on-the-job training program for secondary librarians new to the school district.

Serving as resource consultant to teachers and to secondary librarians searching for media to meet special teaching or learning support needs.

Developing a study skills integration program to expedite and facilitate students learning how to learn effectively and efficiently.

Supervising a district centralized ordering and processing service.

Supervising the maintenance of a union catalog of district media holdings.

Planning and working with the secondary library staff to achieve the most effective and the most efficient use of library resources, facilities, and staff.

Serving as a liaison contact with the staff of the public library, to plan for and implement a program of community and school library cooperation.

Regularly scheduled staff meetings are essential for an effective library media in-service study and growth program. The chief school administrator should build into the school calendar opportunities for the library media staff to meet and to work together. It is the special responsibility of the coordinator or supervisor of the library media program to plan, or to delegate to the elementary and/or secondary team leader the responsibility for planning the agenda for staff meetings. Staff meetings should provide opportunities for the library media specialists to get to know each other, to work and to plan together as a team, and to:

1. Identify problems and set priorities for solving them.
2. Share successful library support activities, programs, and achievements.
3. Discuss anticipated curricular changes.
4. Examine new courses of study and determine the part the library media program can play in support of them.
5. Examine and evaluate new reference tools, new instructional media, and new equipment.
6. Evaluate the district or building library media programs and develop strategies for bringing these programs up to standard.
7. Update the district library policy and routine manual (see Appendix F).
8. Plan for the design and furnishing of new library media center facilities.
9. Plan for the staff in-service study and growth program.

The job description of the coordinator or supervisor of library media service should be included in the District Policy and Routine Manual for the Library Media Program so that each staff member will clearly perceive the function of the supervisor (see Example 49).

EXAMPLE 49 JOB DESCRIPTION: SUPERVISOR OF LIBRARY MEDIA SERVICE

The supervisor of library media service:

1. Orients library media specialists to the:

   District educational philosophy, standards, and program.

   District library media program philosophy and standards.

   Specialized function of the library media center as a learning laboratory.

   Team approach to the organization and function of the library media staff.

   Recommended procedure for the integration of the services of the library media center with the instructional program.

2. Orients new faculty members to the:

   Philosophy of the workshop-laboratory library media program.

   Function of the library media specialist as a team teacher.

   Necessity of teacher and student involvement in selecting instructional media.

   Procedure for scheduling class, group, and individual student working sessions in the library media center.

3. Plans with the library staff to:

   Coordinate building library media center service with the services of the district instructional materials center.

   Expedite centralized ordering and processing services.

EXAMPLE 49 (cont.)

Expedite interlibrary loans.

Evaluate and update existing media collections.

Field test media in curricular pilot programs.

Develop curricular support programs.

Determine effectiveness of building and district library media programs.

4. Plans with directors of elementary and secondary education, heads of departments, and/or curriculum study groups to:

Integrate media center services and resources with the instructional program.

Identify areas of curriculum support needing to be studied and upgraded.

Appraise the effectiveness of current library media programs.

Structure media support programs to match the developmental needs of new courses of study.

Study achievement test scores to identify areas needing improvement.

Evaluate and select textbooks and materials for the professional library and subject resource centers.

5. Plans with the administrative staff to:

Establish new library media centers.

Explain current needs and concerns of the district library media program.

Participate in policy-making and policy implementation.

Implement the integration of the district library media program with the K through 12 instructional program.

6. Administers the library media program by:

Alerting the library media staff to anticipated educational program changes.

Interviewing and recommending candidates for professional and clerical positions on the library media staff.

Recommending library media staff assignments to the chief school administrator.

Recommending media budget allocations to the chief school administrator.

Scheduling staff meeting for the library media staff personnel.

Planning and implementing an in-service study and growth program.

Apprising the library media staff of developments, studies, research, standards, and meetings in the professional fields of teaching and library science.

Developing, in cooperation with the library media staff, a short-range and long-range program for media service development and improvement.

Arranging with participating colleges and universities for the training of future library media specialists in district library media centers.

Initiating a public relations program to inform the community of the activities taking place in the library media centers.

STAFF EVALUATION

In many districts the coordinator or supervisor of library media programs is delegated the responsibility for evaluating the professional competence and performance of the library media staff. Montgomery County Public Schools' "Evaluation of Media Specialist Services" is provided as an example that can well serve as a model for a school district developing an evaluation form for its school library media specialists (see Example 50).

EXAMPLE 50 EVALUATION OF MEDIA SPECIALIST SERVICES

PERFORMANCE CRITERIA

1. Appraises student learning levels, interests, and needs.
   Indicators:
   a. Consults with teachers, counselors, or specialists.
   b. Maintains communication with media specialists who have worked, or will be working, with the same student(s) in MCPS.
   c. Observes students as a group and consults with them individually.
   d. Establishes and maintains procedures whereby students are able to communicate concerns and utilizes resultant data.
   e. Gathers information from student records, when necessary.
   f. Utilizes appropriate diagnostic tools to determine student media skill competencies.
   g. Analyzes circulation records and other pertinent data to determine needs and interests of the student and faculty.
2. Directs, organizes, and supervises the personnel and services essential to a unified media program.
   Indicators:
   a. Provides leadership for the involvement of students and staff in the development of written guidelines and procedures for governing the services and uses of the media center and school media program.
   b. Provides in-service opportunities for students and staff.
   c. Defines, assigns, and supervises the duties of media center staff and volunteers.
   d. Assesses competencies of media center staff and provides opportunities for growth.
   e. Participates in the evaluation of instructional materials aides and equipment aides.
   f. Works with principal and staff to establish and administer local school procedures regarding acquisition, processing, distribution, circulation, and inventory of media materials and equipment.
   g. Involves principal and staff in devising an effective loan system and implements MCPS circulation policies which provide maximum availability of all materials and equipment.
   h. Communicates with students, teachers, and parents about the media program's guidelines and procedures, services, and new materials.
   i. Consults with area and central office personnel on items such as policies and procedures, summer assignments, or renovations.
3. Directs, organizes, and supervises resources and facilities essential to a unified media program.
   Indicators:
   a. Plans a tentative media budget after consulting with the faculty, students, and administration about the instructional materials and equipment needs of the school.
   b. Manages expenditures from the media center account and coordinates uses of this account with other accounts within the school (such as textbooks, instructional materials, equipment, reading, and special education) and follows the MCPS ordering cycles for materials and supplies.
   c. Participates in the design, development, and writing of proposals for acquisition of local, state, or federal funds to support and extend the media program.
   d. Coordinates maintenance and repair of media materials and equipment to insure maximum utilization by and safety of students and staff.
   e. Takes initiative to see that educational media (materials and equipment) are inventoried, classified, or catalogued regardless of where they are housed or how acquired.
   f. Directs and is responsible for maintenance of media center records regarding inventory of holdings, budget, circulation, use of media center, and equipment repair.
   g. Coordinates the use of the media center facilities and provides accessibility to materials and equipment.
   h. Prepares and submits monthly activities reports and annual local, state, and federal reports, as well as special reports when required.
4. Assumes responsibility for evaluating, selecting, and acquiring materials and equipment to support the instructional program and to meet the varied interests, abilities, and maturity levels of the students served.

EXAMPLE 50 (cont.)

Indicators:

a. Follows MCPS policies and procedures (MCPS Regulation 365-3) for evaluating, selecting, and ordering materials and equipment and regularly communicates these policies and procedures to both students and staff and to the community as needed.

b. Utilizes professional reviewing media and visits the Division of Evaluation and Selection (DEMAT) a minimum of one-half day monthly to examine new materials.

c. Utilizes media selection tools, courses of study, curriculum guides, and subject bibliographies to select instructional materials.

d. Develops cooperatively with students and staff a procedure for the evaluation and selection of materials and equipment in the local school.

e. Assesses the collection with the assistance of the students and faculty to identify areas that need development and items which need to be replaced, duplicated, or withdrawn.

5. Participates in the planning, development, and implementation of the school program of instruction.

Indicators:

a. Assists in identifying the interests and needs of both students and staff for the purpose of continuous program planning.

b. Participates in planning for curriculum implementation and/or innovation.

c. Coordinates the implementation of the MCPS media research and communication skills program in the school.

d. Consults with students and staff in the selection and utilization of materials and equipment.

e. Communicates to students and staff, through orientation and relevant instruction, information regarding materials, equipment, and services available in the media center.

f. Utilizes instructional methods designed to motivate and enable students to achieve learning objectives.

g. Cooperates in the implementation of learning activities within the media center designed to meet a variety of needs, interests, and abilities.

h. Provides instruction for students and staff in production techniques and operation of equipment.

i. Assists students and staff in designing and producing materials to achieve instructional objectives.

j. Provides access to MCPS materials housed outside the local school; i.e., film library, EML, area-based resources.

k. Directs students and staff to available community resources.

l. Notifies the public library staff of student information needs.

m. Notifies students and staff of cultural, educational, and recreational opportunities.

6. Plans for and utilizes evaluation techniques that measure the effectiveness of the media program to determine which practices or objectives to maintain or modify.

Indicators:

a. Plans and conducts periodic evaluations of specific aspects of the media program with the assistance of students, staff, and community.

b. Evaluates new services to determine their effectiveness.

c. Uses available evaluative criteria in assessing the program.

d. Solicits cooperation of the faculty in evaluating progress of students in media skills development.

7. Establishes and maintains a media center environment which motivates and enables students and teachers to use the facilities and resources to attain instructional and personal objectives.

Indicators:

a. Organizes media center facilities to provide appropriate work areas for a variety of activities.

b. Organizes materials and equipment through a system of cataloging, classifying, and indexing which will facilitate accessibility for the user.

c. Adjusts physical arrangements and/or modifies noise levels in order to provide for a variety of learning styles and activities.

EXAMPLE 50 (cont.)

    d. Follows and expects students to use democratic procedures which show consideration for the rights of others.

    e. Plans and provides for a pleasing, attractive environment.

    f. Deals promptly with behavior which may be detrimental to the health or physical safety of others.

8. Appraises the effectiveness of his/her teaching practices, managerial practices, and instructional program not only in terms of achieving personal objectives but also in terms of the total school instructional program.

    Indicators:

    a. Assesses each lesson and/or unit in terms of student response to the techniques, activities, and materials, and also in terms of student attainment of the objectives.

    b. Uses results of lesson and/or unit assessments to continue to modify his/her instructional program and to plan further teaching-learning activities.

    c. Evaluates short-range achievement of objectives and long-range progress toward goals of the instructional program.

    d. Works with colleagues and students to evaluate the total program's effectiveness.

9. Participates in school management activities related to policies, regulations, and general school atmosphere.

    Indicators:

    a. Participates in the development and review of school guidelines and regulations.

    b. Observes school system policies and legal regulations.

    c. Cooperates with colleagues and students to maintain good atmosphere.

    d. Shares ideas, materials, and methods with other teachers.

    e. Encourages special interest activities for students and staff.

    f. Cooperates in relating school activities to community needs.

    g. Shares responsibility for care of equipment and facilities.

10. Establishes relationships with colleagues, students, parents, and community which reflect recognition of and respect for every individual.

    Indicators:

    a. Utilizes such human relations techniques as acceptance, praise, and humor, when appropriate.

    b. Maintains objectivity in relations with others.

    c. Maintains a positive attitude in working situations.

    d. Fosters an open atmosphere in which others feel free to express themselves.

    e. Listens and responds to the concerns of others.

    f. Cooperates in making the community feel a part of the school.

    g. Communicates effectively with the community about the school and the Montgomery County Public Schools.

11. Identifies areas for growth necessary to maintain or improve effectiveness, acquires appropriate training or information, and demonstrates successful application.

    Indicators:

    a. Applies knowledge and skills gained from course work, conferences, workshops, in-service activities, travel, or other enrichment activities.

    b. Reads professional and other published materials pertinent to the profession or specific subject areas to improve instruction.

    c. Participates in organizations or conferences supportive of professional responsibilities.

    d. Demonstrates awareness of current events and cultural trends.

    e. Seeks MCPS or area services available to help increase personal effectiveness.

    f. Appraises own professional growth using data related to professional course work, in-service activities, and professional reading.

    g. Takes advantage of opportunities to learn from colleagues, students, parents, and community.

The supervisor of library media services is usually evaluated by means of an administrative/supervisory personnel evaluation form. See Examples 51 and 52, which follow.

EXAMPLE 51 ADMINISTRATIVE AND SUPERVISORY PERSONNEL EVALUATION FORM*

Name: Date	___ 1st Year of Initial Assignment
Position Location	___ 2nd Year Or ___ Every 3rd Year in Same Assignment
Position Title Social Security No.	___ Evaluation Requested By _____
Grade Step Cert. Issue Date	___ Appointment to Another A&S Assign-
Expiration Date	ment—1st Year

I. PERSONAL QUALITIES A. Strengths:	II. PROF. QUALITIES AND GROWTH A. Strengths:
B. Goals for Improvement:	B. Goals for Improvement:
III. INSTRUCTIONAL LEADERSHIP A. Strengths:	IV. PERFORMANCE A. Strengths:
B. Goals for Improvement:	B. Goals for Improvement:
V. GENERAL COMMENTS A. Overall Evaluation:	VI. *SIGNATURES: Person Evaluated Date
B. Recommendation for Continuing Assign- ment or Reassignment:	Evaluator Date Conference requested with evaluator's imme- diate superior: Yes_____ No_____
C. Special Salary Consideration (defer or accelerate increment):	

*Signatures indicate completion of the evaluation process. If the person being evaluated does not agree with the contents of the evaluation, he may request a conference with the immediate superior of the evaluator.

Reviewer's Comments:

Reviewed by: _____ Date: _____

Received in Department of Professional Personnel _____ Date _____

*Department of Professional Personnel, Montgomery County Public Schools, Rockville, Maryland. *Evaluating Administrative/Supervisory Performance*, ERS Circular No. 6, 1971 (Washington, D.C.: Educational Research Service, American Association of School Administrators and NEA Research Division, 1971), p. 13.

EXAMPLE 52 ADMINISTRATIVE PERSONNEL EVALUATION FORM, PUEBLO, COLORADO*

	Unsatis-factory 0	Fair 1	Good 2	Excellent 3	
I. PERSONAL CHARACTERISTICS A. Appearance	—	—	—	—	× 1.0
Comments:					
B. Health and Vitality	—	—	—	—	× 1.0
Comments:					
C. Disposition	—	—	—	—	× 1.0
Comments:					
II. LEADERSHIP CHARACTERISTICS (Willingness to make decisions and accept responsibility; forcefulness; ability to effect desirable change; enthusiasm and initiative shown in work)	—	—	—	—	× 10.0
Comments:					
III. SUCCESS IN PROBLEM SOLVING (Judgment, logical thinking, creativity, imagination)	—	—	—	—	× 7.0
Comments:					
IV. PROFESSIONAL KNOWLEDGE AND UNDERSTANDING (Keeps current on educational trends)	—	—	—	—	× 6.0
Comments:					
V. SUCCESS IN SUPERVISION (Evaluating and improving teaching; developing a strong instructional program)	—	—	—	—	× 10.0
Comments:					
VI. ABILITY TO BUILD MORALE (Democratic in interpersonal relations; delegates; listens to other points of view)	—	—	—	—	× 5.0
Comments:					
VII. RELATIONS WITH COLLEAGUES (Professional ethics)	—	—	—	—	× 7.0
Comments:					
VIII. RELATIONS WITH COMMUNITY	—	—	—	—	× 8.0
Comments:					
IX. RELATIONS WITH STUDENTS	—	—	—	—	× 10.0
Comments:					
X. ATTENTION TO DETAIL AND ROUTINE (Aware of use of district facilities, services, reports, orders)	—	—	—	—	× 4.0
Comments:					

*Evaluating Administrative/Supervisory Performance, pp. 18–19.

EXAMPLE 52 (cont.)

Rating Scale:	Excellent	157–210	Fair	52–104
	Good	105–156	Unsatisfactory	0– 51

EVALUATION SUMMARY

Areas of Strength:

Areas in Need of Improvement:

Summary Comments:

The professionally competent supervisor or coordinator of the district library media program will provide innovative, creative leadership in devising increasingly more effective and more efficient ways to strengthen all aspects of the program. Proof of the leadership impact of the school library media supervisor or coordinator was uncovered by Alice Lohrer in her national survey of instructional centers. Miss Lohrer reported:

> In all types of schools where the materials program was functioning smoothly, staff members had know-how in administering the service. They knew children, materials, sources of selection, how to organize resources for use, and were more interested in providing services than in techniques. In such programs the invisible wall that is evident in other schools between the library and the audiovisual programs was nonexistent or had broken down. The needs of boys and girls rather than concern over media and devices took precedence in schools where librarians were developing effective programs of service. Working with teachers and experimenting with them in the use of mass media and in newer methods of teaching were also parts of such library programs. Openmindedness, cooperation, willingness to experiment and to learn were attitudes held by these school librarians. They had professional concern relating to the teaching functions of the school library program. *Programs that were under the direction and planning of city, town, or country school library supervisors or instructional materials coordinators seemed to function more smoothly and were developing more rapidly than was true in other school systems.*
>
> *Where there were supervisors or directors, another trend was noted which is not clearly represented in library literature. This is in the field of centralized processing for school libraries.*[10]

The supervisor or coordinator of the district library media program who has at heart a sincere concern for the educational program and for the library media program as an integral component of the educational program will inspire his staff to share his concern and to take an active part in devising ways to better both the educational program and the library media program. In order to inspire confidence in his staff, the supervisor or coordinator must possess: a sense of commitment, a sense of values, a sense of priorities, a sense of justice, a sense of loyalty, a sense of emotional balance, a sense of humor, and common sense in abundance!

NOTES

1. Carter V. Good, ed., *Dictionary of Education*, 3rd ed. (New York: McGraw-Hill, 1973).

2. Theodore Kauss, *Leaders Live with Crises* (Bloomington, Ind.: Phi Delta Kappa, 1974), p. 21.

3. Robert J. Alfonso, Gerald R. Firth, and Richard F. Neville, *Instructional Supervision: A Behavior System* (Boston: Allyn & Bacon, 1975), pp. 185–196. Copyright © 1975 by Allyn & Bacon, Inc. Reprinted with permission.

4. Paul Hersey and Kenneth Blanchard, *Management of Organizational Behavior: Utilizing Human Resources*, 2nd ed. (Englewood Cliffs, N.J.: Prentice-Hall, 1972), p. 71.

5. Harold G. Shane, *Curriculum Change Toward the 21st Century* (Washington, D.C.: National Education Association, 1977), pp. 72–73.

6. School Library Manpower Project, *Occupational Definitions for School Library Media Personnel* (Chicago: American Library Association, 1971), pp. 17–19.

7. Donald Ely, "Facts and Fallacies about New Media in Education," in *Revolution in Teaching: New Theory, Technology, and Curricula*, ed. by Alfred de Grazia and David A. Sohn (New York: Bantam Books, 1964), p. 47.

8. George B. Brain, *Increasing Your Administrative Skill in Dealing with the Instructional Program* (Englewood Cliffs, N.J.: Prentice-Hall, 1966), pp. 52–53.

9. Edward D. Kruse, "Manpower and Media for the Use of the Minority and the Majority," speech given at the American Association of School Administrators Convention, Atlantic City, N.J., on February 24, 1971.

10. Alice Lohrer, "School Libraries as Instructional Materials Centers with Implications for Training: A Progress Report of This Study under Title VII, National Defense Education Act," in *The School Library as a Materials Center: Educational Needs of Librarians and Teachers in Its Administration and Use*, ed. by Mary Helen Mahar (Washington, D.C.: U.S. Department of Health, Education, and Welfare, 1963), p. 14.

Epilogue:
What of the Future?

History repeats itself because no one was listening the first time.

Anonymous

This book began by examining the crisis in confidence in education existing in American society today. Schools have lost favor with the public during recent years. Spokespersons for the profession agree that heroic efforts will have to be made if lost confidence and trust in education are to be restored. To survive this crisis the education profession must put its own house in order. Today's educators must take to heart Jacques Barzun's urgent warning that the profession "lift the critique from a set of complaints to a set of purposes."[1]

The education profession must strengthen the educational enterprise in its entirety; this requires honesty, vision, leadership, and commitment. Jonas Salk has warned that the outcome in any crisis is gloomy only if the people fail to act with vigor and imagination.[2] Rather than being on the defensive, educators must boldly take the initiative—not just to survive but to achieve new heights in accomplishment. Salk has recommended turning crisis into advantage by reminding the profession that the first half of the Chinese ideograph for the word *crisis* really means *challenge.*[3]

In times of crisis, a profession, if it is to meet the challenge and the threat of change with vigor and imagination, must begin by re-examining its standards, for standards enunciate the aspirations of a profession. Standards are the hallmarks of professional excellence that define professional goals, that specify professional qualitative and quantitative requirements, and that direct professional planning and action. A vibrantly alive profession constantly strives not only to improve but to excel—standards are action guides for achieving professional excellence.

Standards for school library media programs have been officially issued in the United States by national library, media, or educational organizations six times in this century.[4] However, the 1960 *Standards for School Library Programs* alone have had dynamic impact on school library media program development—an impact so great that America's school libraries were thrust from the peripheral fringes of instructional noninvolvement right into the mainstream of the teaching-learning process itself. The 1960 *Standards* generated a momentum for school library development that reached its highest acceleration point during the sixties. Even though the 1960 *Standards* were revised in 1969 and 1975, the momentum for school library development drastically diminished during the seventies. Therefore, the time for the school library profession to re-examine its standards is at hand.

The phenomenal success of the 1960 *Standards* was not just a fortuitous accident but rather the direct result of the vision, vigor, imagination, and commitment of the School Library Standards Committee appointed by the American Association of School Librarians (AASL) and the AASL membership in general. Milbrey Jones, Chief of the School Media Resources Branch of the U.S. Office of Education, in attesting to the uniqueness of the 1960 *Standards* observed:

> No other statement of school library standards has had such influence on the educational community and the development of school library programs. Publication of the standards was accompanied by an extensive campaign to acquaint school personnel with the importance of school library programs and the role standards play in improving them. The School Library Development Project of the American Association of School Librarians was a well-administered, carefully planned, and successful effort to interpret *Standards for School Library Programs* to school administrators and other decision-makers with power to effect changes in standards and programs.
>
> Another characteristic which distinguishes the 1960 standards and sets them apart from others was the research used to formulate quantitative provisions. Questionnaires were sent to established school libraries characterized as having very good facilities and resources. In addition to facts about budget, staff, resources, and facilities, respondents estimated needs if they considered present conditions inadequate. This research, combined with the judgments of experts, supplied an authoritative base for setting standards which is not common to most standards.[5]

Inasmuch as the 1960 *Standards* have been by far the most effective in the hundred-year history of American school libraries, the master plan used or followed in designing and implementing those standards should well serve as the model for designing and implementing standards for school library media program development for the eighties. The Preface to the 1960 *Standards* clearly outlines in detail the basic procedure followed in formulating these standards. One particularly noteworthy principle should be emulated in structuring and implementing future standards; that is, the School Library Standards Committee must represent from the very beginning many groups interested in and responsible for library media programs in schools. The executive boards of 20 professional organizations—including the American Association of School Administrators, the Association for Supervision and Curriculum Development, the Department of Elementary School Principals, the National Association of Secondary School Principals, and the National School Boards Association—appointed their representatives to the committee in response to the invitation of AASL. These representatives were directly involved in all phases of the standards' design and implementation program. The policy that was followed was one of utilizing the judgments and experience of a large number of administrators, supervisors, classroom teachers, and librarians working in the schools as well as the official representatives of the 20 education associations. In a very real sense the group process approach to professional leadership advocated by Harold Shane in *Curriculum Change Toward the 21st Century*[6] was employed in formulating and implementing the 1960 *Standards for School Library Programs*. This instrument, indeed, was ahead of its time! Likewise, *Planning School Library Development: A Report of the School Library Development Project*[7] can well serve as the blueprint to be followed in implementing the school library media program standards for the eighties.

The greatest threat to education lies not from without but rather from within the profession itself. If educators, when under siege, allow frustration to turn to fear, and fear to turn to despair, then despair inevitably will lead to defeat. Loss of self-confidence by the profession is the greatest threat of all, for it leads surely to a fatal anemia of the spirit.

The library media specialist is a teacher and therefore is directly involved in meeting the challenge of the contemporary crisis in education. AASL is the voice of America's school library media specialists. This professional organization is the most effective means of meeting any professional crisis—present or future. Vision, leadership, imagination, and commitment are centered in, channeled through, and articulated by this professional association. History is the past rolled up for action;[8] and whether or not the school library media profession will survive the present and flourish in the future depends in large measure on the wisdom, creativity, vigor, and determination of the school library media specialists working in and through their national organization. AASL led the profession to new heights during the decade 1960-1970. *AASL can and must do it again!*

NOTES

1. Jacques Barzun, "The Professions Under Siege," in *Harpers*, October 1978, p. 68.
2. Jonas Salk as quoted by Albert Rosenfeld, "Good News on Population," in *Saturday Review*, March 3, 1979, p. 19.
3. Ibid.
4. Milbrey L. Jones, *Survey of School Media Standards* (Washington, D.C.: U.S. Office of Education, 1977), p. 1.
5. Ibid., p. 2.
6. Harold G. Shane, *Curriculum Change Toward the 21st Century* (Washington, D.C.: National Education Association, 1979), pp. 72-73.
7. Mary Frances Kennon and Lelia Ann Doyle, *Planning School Library Development: A Report of the School Library Development Project, American Association of School Librarians, February 1, 1971-July 31, 1962* (Chicago: American Library Association, 1962).
8. Will and Ariel Durant, *Will and Ariel Durant: A Dual Autobiography* (New York: Simon and Schuster, 1977), p. 319.

Basic Background Readings

FROM *GENERAL EDUCATION IN A FREE SOCIETY: A REPORT OF THE HARVARD COMMITTEE**

... The primary concern of American education today is not the development of the "good life" in young gentlemen born to the purple. It is the infusion of the liberal and humane tradition into our entire educational system. Our purpose is to cultivate in the largest possible number of our future citizens an appreciation of both the responsibilities and the benefits which come to them because they are Americans and are free. . . .

Such a concept of general education is the imperative need of the American educational system. It alone can give cohesion to our efforts and guide the contribution of our youth to the nation's future. (pp. xiii–xv)

General education, as education for an informed responsible life in our society, has chiefly to do with . . . the question of common standards and common purposes. Taken as a whole, education seeks to do two things: help young persons fulfill the unique, particular functions in life which it is in them to fulfill, and fit them so far as it can for those common spheres which, as citizens and heirs of a joint culture, they will share with others. (p. 4)

. . . The hope of the American school system, indeed of our society, is precisely that it can pursue two goals simultaneously: give scope to ability and raise the average. . . . (p. 35)

. . . The school is a civilizing place in the fundamental sense of giving young people the tools on which any civilization depends. . . . (p. 36)

. . . To the belief in man's dignity must be added the recognition of his duty to his fellow men. Dignity does not rest on any man as being separate from all other beings, which he in any case cannot be, but springs from his common humanity and exists positively as he makes the common good his own. . . . It is impossible to escape the realization that our society, like any society, rests on common beliefs and that a major task of education is to perpetuate them. (pp. 46–47)

* *General Education in a Free Society: A Report of the Harvard Committee.* Cambridge, Mass.: Harvard University Press, 1945.

This conclusion raises one of the most fundamental problems of education, indeed of society itself: how to reconcile this necessity for common belief with the equally obvious necessity for new and independent insights leading to change.... The true task of education is ... so to reconcile the sense of pattern and direction deriving from heritage with the sense of experiment and innovation deriving from science that they may exist fruitfully together.... (p. 47)

Democracy is the view that not only the few but that all are free, in that everyone governs his own life and shares in the responsibility for the management of the community. This being the case, it follows that all human beings stand in need of an ampler and rounder education. The task of modern democracy is to preserve the ancient ideal of liberal education and to extend it as far as possible to all the members of the community.... To believe in the equality of human beings is to believe that the good life, and the education which trains the citizen for the good life, are equally the privilege of all. And these are the touchstones of the liberated man: first, is he free; that is to say, is he able to judge and plan for himself, so that he can truly govern himself? In order to do this, his must be a mind capable of self-criticism; he must lead that self-examined life which according to Socrates is alone worthy of a free man. Thus he will possess inner freedom as well as social freedom. Second, is he universal in his motives and sympathies? For the civilized man is a citizen of the entire universe; he has overcome provincialism, he is objective, and is a "spectator of all time and all existence." Surely these two are the very aims of democracy itself. (pp. 52–53)

... The problem of general education is one of combining fixity of aim with diversity in application. It is not a question of providing a general education which will be uniform through the same classes of all schools and colleges all over the country, even were such a thing possible in our decentralized system. It is rather to adapt general education to the needs and intentions of different groups and, so far as possible, to carry its spirit into special education. The effectiveness of teaching has always largely depended on this willingness to adapt a central unvarying purpose to varying outlooks. Such adaptation is as much in the interest of the quick as of the slow, of the bookish as of the unbookish, and is the necessary protection of each. What is wanted, then, is a general education capable at once of taking on many different forms and yet of representing in all its forms the common knowledge and the common values on which a free society depends. (pp. 57–58)

... education looks both to the nature of knowledge and to the good of man in society. It is the latter aspect that we shall now turn our attention—more particularly to the traits and characteristics of mind fostered by education.

By characteristics we mean aims so important as to prescribe how general education should be carried out and which abilities should be sought above all others in every part of it. These abilities, in our opinion, are: *to think effectively, to communicate thought, to make relevant judgments, to discriminate among values.* They are not in practice separable and are not to be developed in isolation. Each is an indispensable coexistent function of a sanely growing mind.... (pp. 64–65)

Human personality cannot ... be broken up into distinct parts or traits. Education must look to the whole man. It has been wisely said that education aims at the good man, the good citizen, and the useful man.... the fruit of education is intelligence in action. The aim is mastery of life; and since living is an art, wisdom is the indispensable means to this end. (pp. 74–75)

. . . It is important to realize that the ideal of a free society involves a twofold value, the value of freedom and that of society. Democracy is a community of free men. We are apt sometimes to stress freedom—the power of individual choice and the right to think for oneself—without taking sufficient account of the obligations to cooperate with our fellow men; democracy must represent an adjustment between the values of freedom and social living. (p. 76)

. . . Democracy is the attempt to combine liberty with loyalty, each limiting the other, and also each reinforcing the other. (p. 77)

. . . The main upshot of all that has been said until now is so simple that any statement of it sounds almost absurdly flat. It is that, as Americans, we are necessarily both one and many, both a people following the same road to a joint future and a set of individuals following scattered roads as gifts and circumstances dictate. But though flat and truistic this double fact is the foundation of this report. Simple in itself, it is far from simple in its consequences. It means that, though common aims must bind together the whole educational system, there exists no one body of knowledge, no single system of instruction equally valid for every part of it. (p. 79)

. . . within a generation the problem of how best to meet this immense range of talent and need has grown up, like the fabled beanstalk, to overshadow virtually every other education problem. It is in truth at the heart of any attempt to achieve education for democracy. (p. 81)

. . . equal opportunity does not mean identical provisions for all. Rather, it means access for all to those avenues of education which match their gifts and interests. . . . Here we are back at what was called earlier the main task of our educational system: to nurture ability while raising the average. (p. 86)

. . . *How can general education be so adapted to different ages and, above all, differing abilities and outlooks, so that it can appeal deeply to each, yet remain in goal and essential teaching the same for all?* The answer to this question, it seems not too much to say, is the key to anything like complete democracy. (p. 93)

FROM *THE PURSUIT OF EXCELLENCE: EDUCATION AND THE FUTURE OF AMERICA**

There is no more searching or difficult problem for a free people than to identify, nurture and wisely use its own talents. Indeed, on its ability to solve this problem rests, at least in part, its fate as a free people. For a free society cannot commandeer talent: it must be true to its own vision of individual liberty. And yet at a time when we face problems of desperate gravity and complexity an undiscovered talent, a wasted skill, a misplaced ability is a threat to the capacity of a free people to survive.

But there is another and deeper reason why a free nation must cultivate its own human potential: such a task reflects the very purposes for which a free society exists. If our nation seeks to strengthen the opportunities for free men to develop their individual capacities and to inspire creative effort, our aim is as importantly that of widening and deepening the life purposes of our citizens as it is to add to the success of our national effort. A free society nurtures the individual not alone for the contribution he may make to the social effort, but also and primarily for the sake of the contribution he may make to his own realization and development.

* *The Pursuit of Excellence: Education and the Future of America.* ("America at Mid-Century Series," Special Studies Project Report V, Rockefeller Brothers Fund.) Garden City, N.Y.: Doubleday, 1958.

Hence a free nation's search for talent is always a critical aspect of its national existence. (p. v)

The greatness of a nation may be manifested in many ways—in its purposes, its courage, its moral responsibility, its cultural and scientific eminence, the tenor of its daily life. But ultimately the source of its greatness is in the individuals who constitute the living substance of the nation.

A concern for the realization of individual potentialities is deeply rooted in our moral heritage, our political philosophy, and the texture of our daily customs. . . . We believe that man—by virtue of his humanity—should live in the light of reason, exercise moral responsibility, and be free to develop to the full the talents that are in him. (p. 1)

. . . in its deepest sense our concern for human excellence is a reflection of our ideal of the overriding importance of human dignity. It is not a means but an end. It expresses our notion of what constitutes a good life and our ultimate values. (pp. 1–2)

Every democracy *must* encourage high individual performance. If it does not, it closes itself off from the main springs of its dynamism and talent and imagination, and the traditional democratic invitation to the individual to realize his full potentialities becomes meaningless.

. . . men are unequal in their native capacities and their motivations, and therefore in their attainments. In elaborating our national views of equality, the most widely accepted means of dealing with this problem has been to emphasize *equality of opportunity.* The great advantage of the conception of equality of opportunity is that it candidly recognizes differences in endowment and motivation and accepts the certainty of differences in achievement. By allowing free play to these differences, it preserves the freedom to excel which counts for so much in terms of individual aspiration, and has produced so much of man's greatness.

Having committed ourselves to equality of opportunity we must strive incessantly to make it a reality in our society. . . .

With respect to the pursuit of excellence there are several considerations that we must keep firmly in mind. First, we must not make the mistake of adopting a narrow or constricting view of excellence. *Our conception of excellence must embrace many kinds of achievement at many levels.* . . .

Second, we must not assume that native capacity is the sole ingredient in superior performance. Excellence . . . is a product of ability and motivation and character. And the more one observes high performance in the dust and heat of daily life, the more one is likely to be impressed with the contribution made by the latter two ingredients.

Finally, we must recognize that judgments of differences in talent are not judgments of differences in human worth.

To sum up, it is possible for us to cultivate the ideal of excellence while retaining the moral values of equality. Whether we shall succeed in doing so is perhaps the fundamental issue in the development of our human resources. A challenge must be recognized before it can be met. Our society will have passed an important milestone of maturity when those who are the most enthusiastic proponents of a democratic way of life are also the most vigorous proponents of excellence. (pp. 16–17)

. . . We must recognize that in many areas our educational facilities are poor and our educational effort slovenly. (p. 19)

. . . The fateful question is not whether we have done well, or whether we are doing better than we have done in the past, but whether we are meeting the stern demands and unparalleled opportunities of the times. And the answer is that we are *not*.

Not only must our educators handle a huge increase in the number of students, they must offer higher quality of education. From time to time one still hears arguments over *quantity* versus *quality* education. Behind such arguments is the assumption that a society can choose to educate a few people exceedingly well, but that it cannot do both. But a modern society such as ours cannot choose to do one or the other. It has no choice but to do both. Our kind of society calls for the maximum development of individual potentialities *at all levels*.

Fortunately the demand to educate everyone up to the level of his ability and the demand for excellence in education are not incompatible. We must honor both goals. We must seek excellence in a context of concern for all. (p. 22)

. . . By insisting that *equality* means an exactly similar exposure to education, regardless of the variations in interest and capacity of the student, we are in fact inflicting a subtle but serious form of inequality upon our young people. We are limiting the development of individual excellence in exchange for a uniformity of external treatment. . . . Because many educators reject the idea of grouping by ability, the ablest students are often exposed to educational programs whose content is too thin and whose pace is too slow to challenge their abilities.

No educational system can be better than its teachers. Yet we face severe problems both in the supply of teachers at all levels and in their quality. (pp. 22–23)

. . . We can be certain that there will never be enough teachers with the extraordinary human gifts which make for inspiring teaching. We must therefore utilize our superior teachers more effectively. (p. 25)

. . . It is important to accept the desirability of a rigorous reappraisal of present patterns and courageous experimentation with new patterns. This must include a candid weighing of essentials and non-essentials in the curriculum; more flexible and imaginative approaches to the problem of class size; and—at the level of higher education—the trying out of approaches which place more responsibility on the student for his own education. (p. 31)

. . . we must modernize and improve the quality of the courses themselves. Virtually every subject in the curriculum would profit by a lively reform movement. (p. 27)

Any educational system is, among other things, a great sorting out process. One of the most important goals is to identify and guide able students and to challenge each student to develop his capacities to the utmost. (pp. 28–29)

If we are really serious about equality of opportunity, we shall be serious about individual differences, because what constitutes opportunity for one man is a stone wall for the next. If we are to do justice to the individual we must seek for him the level and kind of education which will open *his* eyes, stimulate *his* mind and unlock *his* potentialities. We should seek to develop many educational patterns—each geared to the particular capacities of the student for whom it is designed.

But though the educational pattern may differ, the goals remain the same for all: enabling each young person to go as far as his aptitude will permit in fundamental knowledge and skills, and motivating him to continue his own self-development to the full along similar lines. (p. 32)

Unused talents lead to personal frustration but they also deprive a society of the mainspring of its vitality. To realize our ideal of maximum personal development, it is not only essential that we inspire our people to the best that is in them but it is also essential to give them an opportunity to exercise that best. A society must learn to regard every instance of a misuse of talent as an injustice to the individual and injury to itself. And it must cultivate the ideal and the exercise of excellence by every means at its disposal. (p. 35)

Excellent performance is a blend of talent and motive, of ability fused with zeal. Aptitude without aspiration is lifeless and inert.

And that is only part of the story. When ability is brought to life by aspiration, there is no further question of the ends to which these gifts are applied. We do not wish to nurture the man of great talent and evil purpose. Not only does high performance take place in a context of values and purpose but if it is to be worth fostering, the values and purposes must be worthy of our allegiance. (p. 45)

. . . there should be a general recognition that development of the individual's potentialities occurs in a context of values. Education is not just a mechanical process for communication to the young of certain skills and information. It springs from our most deeply rooted convictions. And if it is to have vitality both teachers and students must be infused with the values which have shaped the system.

No inspired and inspiring education can go forward without powerful undergirding by the deepest values of our society. The students are there in the first place because generations of Americans have been profoundly committed to a republican form of government and to equality of opportunity. They benefit by a tradition of intellectual freedom because generations of ardent and stubborn men and women nourished that tradition in Western Civilization. Their education is based upon the notion of the dignity and the worth of the individual because those values are rooted in religious and philosophical heritage. They are preparing themselves for a world in which, as Thornton Wilder said, "every good and excellent thing . . . stands moment by moment on the razor edge of danger and must be fought for." They are preparing themselves for a world which has always been shaped and always will be shaped by societies which have placed at the service of their most cherished values a firmness of purpose, discipline, energy, and devotion.

We do not wish to impose upon students a rigidly defined set of values. Each student is free to vary the nature of his commitment. But this freedom must be understood in its true light. We believe that the individual should be free and morally responsible; the two are inseparable. The fact that we tolerate differing values must not be confused with moral neutrality. Such tolerance must be built upon a base of moral commitment; otherwise it degenerates into a flaccid indifference, purged of all belief and devotion.

In short, we will wish to allow wide latitude in the choice of values, but we must assume that education is a process that should be infused with meaning and purpose; that everyone will have deeply held beliefs; that every young American will wish to serve the values which have nurtured him and made possible his education and his freedom as an individual. (pp. 48–49)

FROM *GOALS FOR AMERICANS**

The paramount goal of the United States was set long ago. It is to guard the rights of the individual, to ensure his development, and to enlarge his opportunity. . . .

The way to preserve freedom is to live it. Our enduring aim is to build a nation and help build a world in which every human being shall be free to develop his capacities to the fullest. (p. 1)

This Report . . . . is directed to the citizens of this country, each of whom sets his own goals and seeks to realize them in his life, through private groups, and through various levels of government. Choices are hard, and costs heavy. They demand subordination of lesser goals to the greater. But the rewards are beyond calculation, for the future of our nation depends on the result. (p. 2)

The status of the individual must remain our primary concern. All our institutions—political, social, and economic—must further enhance the dignity of the citizen, promote the maximum development of his capabilities, stimulate their responsible exercise, and widen the range and effectiveness of opportunities for individual choice.

From this concern springs our purpose to achieve equal treatment of men and women, to enlarge their incentives and to expand their opportunities for self-development and self-expression. (p. 3)

Democracy gives reality to our striving for equality. It is the expression of individual self-respect; it clears the way for individual initiative, exercise of responsibility, and use of varied talents. It is basic to the peaceful adjustment of differences of opinion. It must not be curtailed out of impatience to find quick solutions. (p. 5)

The development of the individual and the nation demand that education at every level and in every discipline be strengthened and its effectiveness enhanced. New teaching techniques must continue to be developed. The increase in population and the growing complexity of the world add urgency.

Greater resources—private, corporate, municipal, state, and federal—must be mobilized. A higher proportion of the gross national product must be devoted to educational purposes. This is at once an investment in the individual, in the democratic process, in the growth of the economy, and in the stature of the United States. (p. 6)

There must be more and better teachers, enlarged facilities, and changes in curricula and methods. . . . Above all, schooling should fit the varying capacities of individuals; every student should be stimulated to work to his utmost; authentic concern for excellence is imperative. (p. 7)

The very deepest goals for Americans relate to the spiritual health of our people. The right of every individual to seek God and the wellsprings of truth, each in his own way, is infinitely precious. We must continue to guarantee it, and we must ex-

*The Report of the President's Commission on National Goals, from *Goals for Americans* © 1960 by the American Assembly, Columbia University, New York. Reprinted by permission of Prentice-Hall, Inc., Englewood Cliffs, N. J.

ercise it, for ours is a spiritually-based society. Our material achievements in fact represent a triumph of the spirit of man in the mastery of his material environment.

The major domestic goals of equality and education depend overwhelmingly on individual attitudes and actions.

It is the responsibility of men and women in every walk of life to maintain the highest standards of integrity. (p. 22)

. . . Our goals will be attained and our account of life preserved if enough Americans take the national interest sufficiently into account in day-by-day decisions.

Above all, Americans must demonstrate in every aspect of their lives the fallacy of a purely selfish attitude—the materialistic ethic. Indifference to poverty and disease is inexcusable in a society dedicated to the dignity of the individual; so also is indifference to values other than material comfort and national power. Our faith is that man lives, not by bread alone, but by self-respect, by regard for other men, by convictions of right and wrong, by strong religious faith.

Man has never been an island unto himself. The shores of his concern have expanded from his neighborhood to his nation, and from his nation to his world. Free men have always known the necessity for responsibility. A basic goal for each American is to achieve a sense of responsibility as broad as his world-wide concerns and as compelling as the dangers and opportunities he confronts. (p. 23)

. . . Nothing can impair the influence of the United States with the uncommitted peoples as denials of equality before the law and equality of opportunity. (p. 39)

The basic natural resource of the United States is its people. It follows inescapably that the first national goal to be pursued—at all levels, federal, state, local, and private—should be the development of each individual to his fullest potential. No limits are known to the degree to which, by the expenditure of adequate time, energy, skill, and money, the human mind can be developed at various levels of ability.

This goal touches the foundations of democracy. From the first it was realized that popular government required an educated citizenry. The declaration in the Northwest Ordinance of 1787 is classic: "Religion, morality, and knowledge being necessary to good government and the happiness of mankind, schools and the means of education shall forever be encouraged." What was necessary then is doubly essential today.

The political necessity for the fullest, most competent, and most continuous education should be obvious. When any citizen, for whatever reason, is deprived of this development, it is a denial of one of his unalienable rights. It is a threat to the rights and wellbeing of the rest of us. It is a subtraction from the viability of our democracy. Every incompetent citizen is a menace to the freedom of all. (p. 53)

Political strength, economic growth, security of the nation unite in demanding personal development. Social considerations make the same demand. An underdeveloped citizen—physically, mentally, morally—is not an energizer but a burden upon society.

The effectiveness of democracy—the most rewarding and most difficult form of government—rests not alone upon knowledge and judgment but upon character. Only the morally mature individual will be determined to do away with slums, end corruption, and help lift the load from the poverty-stricken at home and abroad. Only through moral sensitiveness can there be escape from the smugness that wealth and comfort breed. Moral sense resists avarice and self-seeking. It stimulates that concern for his fellowmen by which society escapes disintegration, while giving the individual maximum play for his talents, tastes, and interests. (p. 55)

There is no such thing as "mass education." Every use of the phrase is a denial of a vital reality; education is a wholly individual process. The life of the mind—despite all pressures to invade it—remains a private life. It occurs in each person uniquely. We do democracy no service in seeking to inhibit thought—free, wide-ranging, hazardous.

. . . there must be vastly more concern to develop schools devoted to growth. It is not enough to pass child labor laws and compulsory attendance laws to keep young people off the labor market and immure them in buildings. The need is for challenge and stimulation.

If we make effective self-discipline in freedom the chief educational goal of the sixties, we shall bring a fresh perspective to all our tasks. It would be a clean break with the materialistic of determinism of the Soviets. It would establish the moral stance of the United States before the world. It would give us a vastly more efficient society. (p. 56)

. . . a society such as ours, dedicated to the worth of the individual, committed to the nurture of free, rational and responsible men and women, has special reasons for valuing education. Our deepest convictions impel us to foster individual fulfillment. We wish each one to achieve the promise that is in him. We wish each one to be worthy of a free society, and capable of strengthening a free society.

Education is essential not only to individual fulfillment but to the vitality of our national life. The vigor of our free institutions depends upon educated men and women at every level of the society. And at this moment in history, free institutions are on trial.

Ultimately, education serves all of our purposes—liberty, justice and all our other aims—but the one it serves most directly is equality of opportunity. We promise such equality, and education is the instrument by which we hope to make good the promise. It is the high road of individual opportunity, the great avenue that all may travel. That is why we must renew our efforts to remove barriers to education that still exist for disadvantaged individuals—barriers of poverty, of prejudice and of ignorance. The fulfillment of the individual must not be dependent on his color, religion, economic status or place of residence.

Our devotion to equality does not ignore the fact that individuals differ greatly in their talents and motivations. It simply asserts that each should be enabled to develop to the full, in his own style and to his own limit. Each is worthy of respect as a human being. This means that there must be diverse programs within the educational system to take care of the diversity of individuals; and that each of these programs should be accorded respect and stature. (p. 81)

Love of learning, curiosity, self-discipline, intellectual honesty, the capacity to think clearly—these and all other consequences of a good education cannot be insured by skillful administrative devices. The quality of the teacher is the key to good education. (p. 82)

In dealing with students, the first goal is equality of opportunity. (p. 83)

. . . each child should be dealt with in terms of his own abilities. Every child should have the benefit of an educational program designed to suit his capacities and to develop him to the limit of his potentialities—whatever that limit may be. None should be required to fit a pace and pattern of education designed for children of other capacities.

In dealing with children of differing potentialities, we must remember that all are worthy of respect as human beings. . . .

To urge an adequate program for the gifted youngsters is not to recommend favoritism. They do not need more attention than other children—in some situations they may even need less. They need a different *kind* of attention.

Attempts to identify children of unusual potentialities should begin when schooling begins. When a child's family and neighborhood background are culturally impoverished, the school may be the only channel through which his gifts can be nourished: the sooner they are discovered the better.

Children of high academic talent, most of whom will have to devote more years to education than the average youngster, should be given the opportunity to move more rapidly. There should be various forms of grouping by ability from the earliest years of school; and every effort should be made in and out of schoool to provide enrichment for the gifted student. (pp. 84–85)

All the organizational arrangements, all the methods and procedures that characterize American education today were originally devised to help us accomplish our purposes. If they no longer help us, we must revise them. The arrangements and methods must serve us and not control us. (p. 88)

If we really believe in individual fulfillment, our concern for education will reach far beyond the formal system. We shall expect people to continue to learn and grow in and out of school, in every possible circumstance, and at every stage of their lives. (p. 94)

. . . We must develop a philosophy and a technique of continuous reappraisal and innovation. (p. 99)

This report deals with concrete, practical measures. But all the arrangements will fail unless they are in the service of an authentic concern for excellence. We must raise standards in every phase of our national life. Education is no exception. We must do a better job. And good concern for educational quality must be widely shared. . . .

American education can be as good as the American people want it to be. And no better.

And in striving for excellence, we must never forget that American education has a clear mission to accomplish with every single child who walks into the school. Modern life has pressed some urgent and sharply defined tasks on education, tasks of producing certain specially needed kinds of educated talent. For the sake of our future we had better succeed in these tasks—but they cannot and should not crowd out the great basic goals of our educational system: to foster individual fulfillment and to nurture free, rational and responsible men and women without whom our kind of society cannot endure. Our schools must prepare *all* young people, whatever their talents, for the serious business of being free men and women. (p. 100)

FROM *STANDARD LIBRARY ORGANIZATION AND EQUIPMENT FOR SECONDARY SCHOOLS OF DIFFERENT SIZES**

FOREWORD, BY C. C. CERTAIN, *CHAIRMAN*

The Library Committee of the Department of Secondary Education of the National Education Association was organized in 1915 at the annual meeting in Oakland, Calif. The members of the Committee at that time decided that two purposes should be carried out during the year: first, to investigate actual conditions in high-school libraries throughout the United States; and second, to make these conditions known to school administrators and to secure their aid in bettering existing conditions. The first purpose was accomplisht thru a series of surveys. . . . A report based upon these surveys was presented to the Secondary Department at the New York City meeting in 1916 and publisht in the *Proceedings* of that year. Gathered together at that meeting were high-school principals, teachers, librarians, and state and city superintendents, who, in discussing the problems relating to high-school libraries, gave a new conception of the status of the library in the high school. It was thru this program that the Committee accomplisht its second purpose. . . . A full account of the meeting, with papers contributed by the speakers, is publisht in the *National Education Association Proceedings* for 1916.

It was the sense of the department at that time that the Library Committee should be continued and that it should work out a constructive program of library development acceptable to the Secondary Department. Professor Johnston consented to take the leadership in this movement. He was also chairman of the Commission on Unit Courses and Curricula of the North Central Association of Colleges and Secondary Schools. As chairman of this Commission he organized a library committee with the purpose of preparing, under the guidance of the members of the Commission, a much more detailed report than seemed possible in the National Education Association. It was my great pleasure to act as chairman of this Library Committee of the Commission to work under the leadership of Professor Johnston. He planned to secure the adoption of the projected report by the North Central Association and then to present it to the Secondary Department of the National Education Association for similar action.

Professor Johnston's untimely death in the early stages of these plans brought irreparable loss to the teaching profession. . . . I was askt to accept the chairmanship of the Library Committee of the Secondary Department and hence have had the privilege of carrying out the program planned by Professor Johnston. According to his plans I have presented the report of the Library Committee both to the North Central Association and to the Secondary Department of the National Education Association. The report has been adopted by both organizations. The action of these organizations has thus given school administrators a national standard for high-school library development. . . .

*Report of the Committee on Library Organization and Equipment of the National Education Association and of the North Central Association of Colleges and Secondary Schools, C. C. Certain, Chairman, Cass Technical High School, Detroit, Mich. (Chicago: American Library Association, 1920).

The Need of High-School Library Standardization, by Jesse Newlon, *Superintendent of Denver Schools*

In the building of high schools in the past twenty-five years it has been the custom to provide adequately, or approximately so, for science and a little less generously for household arts and manual arts. I do not wish to say anything whatever in disparagement of the provision made for science. We have not provided more than adequately; we have invested no more money in science than we should. In fact, the war has taught us that we must spend more money in every line than we have ever spent before. But in planning our high schools we have overlookt, with very few exceptions, the high-school library.

What is true of high schools in general is true of junior high schools in particular. The library in the junior high school is just as important as the library in the senior high school; indeed, far more so in many respects. Most boys and girls leave school before they reach the senior high school, in fact before they reach the tenth grade of the public schools. If we are really to teach them to use the library, if we are really to create in them an interest in good books, an interest in study, it must be done in the junior high school. In my mind the need of library development applies in particular to the junior high school.

There are few well-planned high-school libraries in the United States. Sometimes there is a large study-hall for the library—generally just one room with no workroom or conveniences of any kind for the library staff. The reason for this has been that in the science department we have had definite standards by which to design. These standards have been workt out during many years in the colleges and in the secondary schools. We have appreciated the importance of science in the high-school curriculum. We have had standards in the university laboratories. In the laboratories in the high schools we have laboratory equipment. It has been easy, therefore, to convince boards of education that it is necessary to provide these—and so for the chemistry department, the physics department, or for science of whatever kind common to the curriculum. We have been able to take boards of education to neighboring cities and show them what has been done, but we have been unable to do that in the library field.

Herein lies the importance of the report on *Standard Library Organization and Equipment for Secondary Schools of Different Sizes.* For the first time administrators see that *the library is the very heart of the high school* [emphasis supplied]. It will be possible now for those of us who believe in the importance of the library to talk in definite terms to boards of education when we are planning junior and senior high schools. I have had that pleasure within the last four months. In drawing up my plans I have been able to refer to this recent report setting forth library standards, and I am happy to say that in these two schools we are going to provide as adequately for the library as for the science and manual-arts departments.

Those of us who can deal with boards of education know that we are likely to get what we want if we know what we want. The person who approaches the board of education with a definite program in mind, knowing exactly what he wants, with recommendations and reasons for it, is likely to get what he wants, and that is true of the community. School superintendents and boards of education who have a constructive program to put before the community with good reasons for it will win, nine cases out of ten, and so this library report will make it possible to get good libraries—a thing we have not had in the past. Of course there are a few exceptions, but in general we do not have adequate arrangements in our high schools, either in room, in equipment, or in staff for libraries. . . . We can now offer boards of education a report that is official—really official. This report represents the best thought of those who have studied libraries thruout the country. Great good will come from that.

SUGGESTIONS FOR STATE HIGH-SCHOOL INSPECTORS

It is suggested that a committee be organized in each state to make a survey of library conditions in high schools. To begin the work of standardizing libraries, actual conditions should be studied in relation to the standards given in this report.

A complete survey should be made including such items as: (1) appropriate housing and equipment; (2) professionally trained librarians; (3) scientific service in the selection and care of books and other printed material, and in the proper classification and cataloging of this material; (4) instruction in the use of books and libraries; (5) adequate annual appropriations for salaries and for the maintenance of the library, for the purchase of books, for supplies, and for general upkeep; (6) a trained librarian as state supervisor of all the school libraries of the state.

Based upon this survey, a schedule of systematic library development should be outlined, with definite annual goals to be attained, until all standards have been achieved.

It is estimated that not more than five years should be required for the complete achievement of standards as given in this report.

Representatives of the state educational department and of the state library commission should be members of the surveying committee.

A statement of library conditions should be contained in the annual reports of state departments of education and in the reports of high-school inspectors. . . .

REQUISITES OF A STANDARD LIBRARY ORGANIZATION

The requisites of a standard library organization are: (I) appropriate housing and equipment of the high-school library; (II) professionally trained librarians; (III) scientific selection and care of books and other material, and the proper classification and cataloging of this material; (IV) instruction in the use of books and libraries as a unit course in high-school curricula; ( )de-quate annual appropriations for salaries and for the maintenance of the library, for the purchase of books and other printed matter, for the rebinding of books, for supplies, and for general upkeep; (VI) a trained librarian as state supervisor to be appointed as a member of the state education department, as in Minnesota, or under the library commission in co-operation with the state education department, as in New Jersey.

ATTAINABLE STANDARDS

The following standards are recommended as attainable in the high schools of the United States within the next five years. In general these standards apply to all high schools.

I. HOUSING AND EQUIPMENT

A. *Scientific Planning*

In establishing a new high school or a new library in a high school, the librarian should be secured in ample time to aid in planning the library room and in selecting the equipment and books. No school superintendent or high-school principal should undertake to plan a new library without the expert assistance of a trained librarian. Crudely designed libraries are wasteful of funds, of space, of time, and of educational force.

B. *Integral Part of High-School Organization*

The library must be an integral part of the high school [emphasis supplied], housed in the school building, and should not as a rule be open to the general public.

    1. *The room and its appointments.*—The library reading-room must be centrally located, well lighted and ventilated, and planned appropriately with reference to general reading, reference, and supplementary study. It must be emphatically a place of refinement, comfort, and inspiration. The room in all its appointments should be a place essentially attractive to high-school students and should be made as free of access to them as is possible.

    2. *Freedom of access.*—Freedom of access to the library must imply, not only freedom to consult books for reference and for supplementary and collateral study, but also freedom to read books for recreation and pleasure. The pupils should have direct access to the bookshelves.

C. *The Reading-Room*

    1. *Location.*—A central location on the second floor is usually found most satisfactory for the reading-room. It should have an exposure admitting plenty of light and sunshine. It should be separate from the study hall and should not be used for recitation purposes.

It should be near the study hall. The library if practicable should be connected with the study hall by a door or special passageway so that students may go from the study hall to the library without the necessity of securing passes to the library. Where this is not feasible the library should be as near as possible to the study hall.

    2. *Seating capacity and area.*—The reading-room should be provided with facilities to accommodate at one full period readers numbering from 5 percent to 10 percent of the total daily attendance of the school. In high schools enrolling 500 pupils the reading-room should have a seating capacity of from 40 to 50; and those enrolling 1000 should have a seating capacity of from 75 to 100. An area of at least 25 square feet per reader is required for complete accommodations and service. The minimum seating capacity in the small high school should be that of an average classroom.

Tables 3 by 5 feet and seating 6 persons are the standard size recommended. The width of the room should be ample to accommodate from 2 to 3 rows of tables placed with sides parallel to the short walls of the room if the room is rectangular in form. The rows of tables should be so placed that the fewest possible readers have to face the windows. A space of 5 feet should be allowed between the rows of tables and between the tables and the adjacent walls. Two rows of tables should be provided in small high schools and 3 rows in large schools.

3. *Use.*—The library reading room should be reserved exclusively for library use and not used for meetings that in any way interfere with the student visitors. The library should be essentially a *reading room* and *should not be converted into a study hall or a place for supervised study* [emphasis supplied].

4. *Lighting.*—The artificial lighting should be by means of electric ceiling fixtures of either the indirect or semi-indirect type.

5. *Finishes.*—White ceilings and light buff walls give the best lighting effects. Dark colors should be avoided in woodwork and trim.

6. *Wall space.*—All possible surface downward from a point 7 feet above the floor should be utilized for shelving. Chair railing, wainscoting, and baseboards should be omitted, and the walls plastered to the floor. Any necessary baseboards should be added after the shelving is in place.

7. *Floor covering.*—The floor should be covered with linoleum or cork carpet to deaden sound. . . .

II. THE LIBRARIAN

A. Qualifications

The librarian in the high school should combine the good qualities of both the librarian and the teacher and must be able to think clearly and sympathetically in terms of the needs and interests of high-school students [emphasis supplied].

A wide knowledge of books, ability to organize library material for efficient service, and successful experience in reference work should be demanded of every librarian. Most of all should the personality of the librarian be emphasized. Enthusiasm and power to teach and inspire are as essential in the high-school librarian as in the teacher. Successful library experience in work with boys and girls of high-school age, either in the reference room, in the children's department or school department of a public library, or in a high school should be required of candidates. Successful teaching experience in a high school is a valuable asset in the librarian.

B. Professional Requirements

The standard requirements for future appointments of librarians in high schools should be a college or university degree with major studies in literature, history, sociology, education, or other subjects appropriate to any special demands, as, for example, those of the technical high school, upon the library. In addition the librarian should have at least one year of postgraduate library training in an approved library school and one year's successful library experience in work with young people in a library of standing. . . .

C. Salaries

The salary of a high-school librarian should be adequate to obtain a person with the qualifications set forth in this report. It should not be lower than that of the English teacher. In departmentalized high schools the librarian should receive a salary equal to that of other department heads.

D. *Administrative Requirements*

1. *The library staff.*—The library staff should be sufficiently large to keep the library open continuously thru the day session, also before and after the session and evenings for night school, if local need demands this.

2. *Status of the librarian.*—In high schools having heads of departments the librarian should be made head of the library department, with status equal to that of the heads of other departments.

3. *Trained assistants.*—For every one thousand students in daily attendance a full-time trained assistant librarian is needed to help in the reference, technical, and clerical work and to allow the librarian time for conference with teachers and pupils, to give instruction, and to visit classes.

Professional requirements for assistant librarians: Standard requirements for assistant librarian should be the same as for the librarian. There should be no distinction between librarian and assistant librarian in the requirements for eligibility except in the matter of library experience.

4. *Judicious distinction in library service.*—In the administration of the library distinctions should be made as to clerical, administrative, technical, and educational work.

a. Clerical work: Clerical work of the high school of the nature of office work should not be demanded of the librarian. Under no circumstances should the librarian be expected to do clerical work properly required in the principal's office, such as keeping records of attendance and official records. To require such work of trained librarians is wasteful of educational resources and money.

Free textbooks should not be stored in the library, and they should be handled, not by the library staff, but by a special book clerk, whose duties should also include any selling where this is required.

b. Administrative work: The administrative work may be summarized as follows: Directing the policy of the library, selecting books, purchasing books, planning the room and its equipment, keeping records of expenses and planning the annual library budget, planning and directing the work of trained or student assistants, and building up a working collection of pamphlets, clippings, and of illustrative material.

The librarian should be present at all teachers' meetings and should have the ability to work for and with teachers so well that mistakes in adaptation of book collections to needs may not occur.

c. Technical work: The technical work may be summarized as follows: The classifying, cataloging, indexing, and filing of all printed matter so that it may be readily available for use; establishing a practical charging system to keep track of books and other materials borrowed from the library; attending to the proper binding and rebinding of books; and keeping necessary records and statistics of additions to library, use of library, etc.

d. Educational work: The educational work may be summarized as follows:

1. *Reference.*—Helping teachers and students to find suitable material on special topics, notifying teachers of new books and articles along professional lines, looking up answers to questions which have come up in classroom or laboratory, and preparing suggestive reference reading along the lines of the course of study.

2. *Instruction.*—Systematic instruction of students in the use of reference books and library tools, such as card-catalog indexes, etc., by the giving of

lectures, quizzes, and practical tests. In this instruction the relationship of the high-school library and the public library and the relation of the library to life outside of school should be emphasized.

3. *Educational and vocational guidance.*—Cultural and inspirational work in widening the interests of the students and in cultivating a taste for good reading. This is done thru posting interesting material on bulletin boards and compiling lists of interesting reading in books and magazines, thru reading clubs and personal guidance of the reading of individual students.

The librarian should also co-operate with vocational counselors in aiding students in the choice of vocations and should have on hand in the library pamphlets, catalogs, etc., on the occupations.

A card record for each student should be kept from year to year, showing the progress of the student's reading interests. Much attention should be given to individual and group conferences.

The work of the assistant librarian, altho under the direction of the librarian in charge, should be coordinated in many respects with that of the librarian and should be along inspirational and educational, as well as technical lines. The work of the assistant librarian should include, among other duties, keeping all statistical records, caring for magazines, newspapers, pictures, and clippings, helping with cataloging, assisting in enforcing discipline, helping in the supervision of clubs, and personally guiding the reading of students.

III. SCIENTIFIC SELECTION AND CARE
OF BOOKS AND OTHER MATERIAL
A. Selection and Care of Books and Printed Matter

The selection of books should be made with reference to:

1. Educational guidance and local industrial, commercial, and community interests.

2. Laboratory and classroom needs.

3. The general recreational and cultural needs of the students.

All books should be classified, shelf-listed, cataloged, and kept in good repair and in fit condition for ready use.

Book selections should be made by the librarian with the approval of the principal, and must be based upon (1) recommendations by heads of departments and teachers and (2) the general cultural needs of the students.

The library should be provided with the best reference books and with literature that has a natural human appeal to young people. There should be very few books of criticism, a few complete works of authors, a generous proportion of finely illustrated editions of standard books, popular scientific books, special reference books on methods of teaching, pictures appropriate for illustrative purposes, novels, short stories, books of travel, biography, modern drama, modern poetry, weekly and monthly magazines, and newspapers.

Subscription books should be avoided, with certain exceptions known to trained librarians. Information on this subject may be obtained from the state library commission.

Books that are out of date or seldom used should not be allowed to occupy valuable shelf space but should be stored where accessible, or should be otherwise disposed of.

Books greatly in demand should be supplied in duplicate to meet the demand not only adequately but generously.

B. *Centralization and Distribution of Visual Material*

The Library should serve as the center and co-ordinating agency for all material used in the school for visual instruction, such as stereopticons, portable motion picture machines, stereopticon slides, moving picture films, pictures, maps, globes, bulletin board material, museum loans, etc. Such material should be regularly accessioned and cataloged, and its movements recorded, and directed from the library. This will result in the greatest efficiency in the use of visual material, as the same material can often cover two or more courses; for example, a film of the "Tale of Two Cities" may be used in both literature and history classes, and material available for commercial geography may be helpful in project work of the English classes, as well as in industrial history or economics. By cooperation of the teachers the librarian may apply this material to each course at the most strategic times for the introduction of a new subject, for review, or whenever in the opinion of the teacher its use will be productive of the greatest inspiration and benefit.

The Library should also borrow and distribute to the teachers material available from public or even private agencies, such as museums, city, state or national bureaus or departments, business houses, collectors, etc. . . .

FROM *REPORT OF THE JOINT COMMITTEE ON ELEMENTARY SCHOOL LIBRARY STANDARDS**

FOREWORD

Modern demands upon the public school presuppose adequate library service. Significant changes in methods of teaching require that the school library supplement the single textbook course of instruction and provide for the enrichment of the school curriculum. Children in the school are actively engaged in interests which make it necessary for them to have the use of many books and a wide variety of materials, such as pictures and lantern slides. An essential consideration is that the books and materials be readily available when needed, and under the direction of a library staff which is part of the school organization.

In the traditional schoolroom, the library was more of a luxury than a necessity. Until recently there was no library in most public elementary schools. This was because the schoolroom procedure of the past was an impoverished procedure so far as social values were concerned. The teacher spent her time largely in urging the children from day to day to master, page by page or section by section, some instruction. It is a far cry from this traditional schoolroom with its textbook courses to the modern ideals of public school teaching. The modern school is being developed more and more in terms of activities bearing important relations to life outside of the school. The modern school is organized with the purpose of giving children an opportunity to live and develop normally in the home and later in other great social institutions to which they may belong. We no longer teach, or no longer should teach, in terms of deferred values. As some one has said, "The children themselves have a right to live," a right to do more than turn the pages of textbooks. There is need, therefore, of a new de-

---

*Report of the Committee on Elementary School Library Standards by C. C. Certain (Washington, D.C.: National Education Association, 1925).

partment in the school whose function it shall be to assemble and distribute the materials of instruction. This department, moreover, must serve in the specific capacity of giving instruction in the use of books and libraries. It has the dual purpose of library service and library instruction.

In its first purpose, that of school library service, it may be thought of as the one agency in the school that makes possible a definite systematic manipulation and control of the materials of instruction.

Certainly no other factor in school organization bears more directly upon educational environment than does the library [emphasis supplied]. When one considers how seriously a school may be cluttered up by the introduction of magazines and newspapers into classrooms, or how seriously work may be interrupted through a haphazard introduction into classrooms of moving pictures, stereopticons, or victrola records, he will appreciate the importance of having a centralized agency for storing these materials where they may be readily available exactly at the time when they are needed.

Aside from the fact that the school itself is liable to appear disordered without library facilities, there is another important consideration in the fact that good teaching methods depend upon the accessibility of appropriate materials of instruction.

Books, pamphlets, pictures, and maps through the school library are selected, classified, housed, and distributed when needed without loss of time. Then, too, the library has an important bearing upon the *esprit de corps* of the school.

When properly housed and designed, the library does much to contribute to institutional tone and atmosphere. Properly administered, the library makes subject-matter a normal influence in school life. The library is in a functional sense a coördinating agency controlling the use of subject-matter in curriculum activities.

STANDARD LIBRARY SERVICE FOR ELEMENTARY SCHOOLS, GRADES ONE TO SIX, INCLUSIVE

A. Definitions:
  1. Aim. The aim of the library shall be:
    a. To train children
      (1) To like to read that which is worth while
      (2) To supplement their school studies by the use of books other than textbooks
      (3) To use reference books and library tools easily and effectively
    b. To correlate the school library and the public library in order to make the proper connection
      (1) With leisure time
      (2) With practical needs
  2. Scope. The school library shall:
    a. *Serve an integral part of the daily life of the school* [emphasis supplied]
    b. Provide instruction leading directly to the use of books and the public library as a part of the required curriculum
    c. Be equipped with well-balanced collection of books selected by a competent school librarian . . . in coöperation with other competent school authorities . . .
    d. Not be open to the general public

3. Use. The use of the library shall include:
   a. Recreational reading

   It is of the utmost importance that full opportunity be given for recreational reading that is free from the constraint of assigned tasks and duty, the reading that springs from normal impulses and interests with consequent pleasure and enjoyment, the reading that is itself an experience worthwhile and life-giving

   b. Reference reading
   c. Story-telling of such merit that the finished rendering and effective presentation of the great stories will lead to reading
   d. Class discussion of books and magazines read by individual children to stimulate wider reading in the group and to give opportunity for natural practice of oral expression. This should not duplicate work done elsewhere in the school, but should spring naturally from the library reading interests of the children
   e. Both group and individual instruction in use of library organization and materials
   f. Class and pupil activity in searching for material on projects
   g. Circulation of books once a week
   h. Overnight circulation as necessary

B. Essentials:
   1. Book Collections
      a. Scope
         (1) Reference books
            (a) Any books which are consulted for definite points of information, such as dictionary, encyclopedia, and yearbook
            (b) General reference material, such as indexed texts to be used in all study of a fact-getting nature
            (c) All books for use of teachers and pupils, which must remain in the library for consultation purpose at all times
            (d) Material on all subjects of the curriculum
            (e) Examples of the best literature for all grades represented in the schools
            (f) Fugitive material of value in teaching
         (2) Books to be read for appreciation and enjoyment
         (3) Books for teachers

         Very few of these books should be bought from the school library budget
         (4) Duplicate copies of books in the circulating collection when more than three copies of each title are required
      b. Selection
         (1) Initial stock. The initial stock shall
            (a) Be based on curriculum subject needs and home reading lists
            (b) Be based on the approved standards for juvenile books included in authentic lists and publications of the National Education Association and the American Library Association
            (c) Include the reference books to be taught in accordance with the library course of study outlined
            (d) Include a selection of current magazines from an approved list
         (2) Added titles. The added title shall

(a) Keep collection up-to-date
(b) Supply omissions
  (3) Replacements
    (a) Only titles shall be replaced that have proved valuable
 c. Cataloging
  (1) A simple author, title, and subject catalog shall be provided
  (2) Analytics shall be provided
2. Other material
 a. Visual material
  –Cards and pamphlets
  –Clippings from newspapers and magazines
  –Moving picture films—loans from central office of Department of Visual Education
  –Pictures for illustrative purposes
  –Post cards
  –Stereopticon slides
  –Stereographs
 b. Victrola records
 c. This material shall be recorded by the librarian and distributed from the library
 d. Material available from public or even private agencies, such as museums, city, State, or National bureaus or departments, business houses, collectors, etc., shall be distributed by the library
 e. The library shall also be the distributing center for all materials from the department of visual education . . .
[C]. Administrative Requirements
 1. Distinction shall be made between library service and clerical service
  a. Clerical Work
   (1) Clerical work of the elementary school in the nature of office work shall not be demanded of the librarian
   (2) Under no circumstance shall the librarian be expected to do clerical work properly required in the principal's office, such as keeping records of attendance and official records. To require such work of trained librarians is wasteful of educational resources and money
   (3) Free textbooks shall not be handled by the library staff, but by the special book clerk. They shall not be stored in the library
  b. Administrative Work
  The administrative work may be summarized as follows:
   (1) Directing the policy of the library, selecting books, ordering, planning the room and its equipment, keeping records of pupils, and planning the annual budget, planning and directing the work of trained or student assistants, and building up a working collection of pamphlets, clippings, and of illustrative materials
   (2) The librarian shall be present at all teachers' meetings held with reference to courses and policy governing instruction, and be able to work for and with teachers in order to adapt the book collections to their needs
  c. Technical Work
  The technical work may be summarized as follows:

(1) Establishing a practical charging system to keep track of books and other materials borrowed; keeping records and statistics of additions to library, use of library, etc.; filing of all pamphlet material, that it may be readily available for use; keeping library in order, including simplest mending

(2) Collecting fines and tracing lost books

   (a) Lost and damaged books shall be paid for by the borrowers responsible

   (b) Overdue books shall be traced promptly by the library, so that fines may be unnecessary

   (c) It is desirable when penalties are necessary that they shall be adapted to the case in question, so as to have the greatest effect, such as deprivation of use of library, or a money fine

[D]. Library Instruction

The instruction is not to be formalized, but is to be in the nature of assistance to children in accordance with their needs. (See suggestions as to the nature of the needs of the various grades in list below of minimum essentials)

1. Aims

The aims of the course of study for library rooms in schools shall be:

a. To introduce children to many kinds of books on many subjects in order to foster and stimulate a love of reading

b. To develop an appreciative use of libraries through voluntary reading for information, recreation, or inspiration and to give skill in the use of reference materials and library tools in achieving those ends

c. In communities having a public library, to give every child in the school such direct contact with the public library service that as a citizen he will both continue to make use of that service and to contribute gladly to its support and extension

2. Methods

a. The methods of instruction shall be such that the children will acquire familiarity with library resources, arrangements, and manuals through the use of an organized library collection of attractive, interesting literature of the best types in each subject of the curriculum in a special library room suited to school purposes, under the direction of a school librarian. There should be allotted hours of library class work, and all grades of children should be brought under the influence of the library atmosphere and surroundings

b. The school librarian shall work in close coöperation with the teachers of the school and with the public library. He shall aim to assist in vitalizing the curriculum through making available in the library current material related to the topics being studied in the various classrooms and by aiding teachers in securing material needed for classroom work

c. The children are to be encouraged in their desire to read, and directed in their choice of books by the circulation of books in regular library ways at least once a week

3. Objectives

a. The children should acquire understanding of the organization, equipment, and reference material of the library, through explanations by the school librarian as need arises and skill in using the library through practice in finding materials needed in projects in other classes and subjects; voluntary reading for knowledge, pleasure, or inspiration and opportunity to borrow material for home reading

b. The children are to be introduced to many types of literature and their reading stimulated as need may arise.

The Students' Right to Read*

THE RIGHT TO READ AND THE TEACHER OF ENGLISH

For many years, there has been pressure on American schools to restrict or deny students access to books or periodicals deemed objectionable by some individual or group on moral, political, religious, ethnic, racial, or philosophical grounds. These pressures continue today, and English teachers have no reason to believe they will diminish. The fight against censorship is a continuing series of skirmishes, not a pitched battle leading to a final victory over censorship.

We can safely make two statements about censorship: first, any work is potentially open to attack by someone, somewhere, sometime, for some reason; second, censorship is often arbitrary and irrational. For example, classics traditionally used in English classrooms have been accused of containing obscene, heretical, or subversive elements. What English teacher could anticipate judgments such as the following—judgments characteristic of those made by many would-be censors:

> Plato's *Republic*: "This book is un-Christian."
>
> George Eliot's *Silas Marner*: "You can't prove what that dirty old man is doing with that child between chapters."
>
> Jules Verne's *Around the World in Eighty Days*: "Very unfavorable to Mormons."
>
> Nathaniel Hawthorne's *The Scarlet Letter*: "A filthy book."
>
> Shakespeare's *Macbeth*: "Too violent for children today."
>
> Fyodor Dostoevsky's *Crime and Punishment*: "Serves as a poor model for young people."
>
> Herman Melville's *Moby Dick*: "Contains homosexuality."

Modern works, even more than the classics, are criticized as "filthy," "un-American," "overly realistic," and "anti-war." Some books have been attacked merely for being "controversial," suggesting that for some people the purpose of education is not the investigation of ideas but rather the indoctrination of certain set beliefs and

*1972 Edition. Kenneth L. Donelson. National Council of Teachers of English, 1111 Kenyon Road, Urbana, Illinois 61801.

standards. The following statements represent complaints typical of those made against modern works of literature:

J. D. Salinger's *Catcher in the Rye*: "A dreadful dreary recital of sickness, sordidness, and sadism." (Without much question, Salinger's book has been for some time the most widely censored book in the United States.)

Kurt Vonnegut's *Slaughterhouse Five*: "Its repetitious obscenity and immorality merely degrade and defile, teaching nothing."

Edward Albee's *Zoo Story*: "Pure filth."

Harper Lee's *To Kill a Mockingbird*: "The word *rape* is used several times. Children should not see this in any literature book."

Some groups and individuals have also raised objections to literature written specifically for young people. As long as novels intended for young people stayed at the intellectual and emotional level of *A Date for Marcy* or *A Touchdown for Thunderbird High*, censors could forego criticism. But many contemporary novels for adolescents focus on the real world of young people—drugs, premarital sex, alcoholism, divorce, Vietnam, high school gangs, school dropouts, racism, protest movements, violence, and sensuality. English teachers willing to defend the classics and modern literature must be prepared to give equally spirited defense to serious and worthwhile adolescent books when allegations such as the following are made:

Susan Hinton's *The Outsiders*: "A glorification of violence and gangs."

Ann Head's *Mr. and Mrs. Bo Jo Jones*: "Teenagers are too young to learn about pregnancy."

Robert Lipsyte's *The Contender*: "Pro-black, and boxing is a foul racket to talk about with young people."

Nat Hantoff's *I'm Really Dragged But Nothing Gets Me Down*: "Vietnam is too controversial for any classroom, and the novel is anti-American."

Literature about ethnic or racial minorities is, and is likely to remain, "controversial" or "objectionable" to many adults. As long as groups such as blacks, Indians, orientals, Chicanos, and Puerto Ricans "kept their proper place" —awarded them by an Anglo society—censors rarely raised their voices. But attacks have increased in frequency as minority groups have refused to observe their assigned "place." Though nominally the criticisms of racial or ethnic literature have usually been directed at "bad language," "suggestive situations," "questionable literary merit," or "ungrammatical English" (usually oblique complaints about the *different* dialect or culture of a group), the underlying motive for some attacks has unquestionably been racial. Typical of censors' criticisms of ethnic works are the following comments:

Ralph Ellison's *Invisible Man*: "The book is biased on the black question."

Anne Frank's *Diary of a Young Girl*: "Obscene and blasphemous."

Eldridge Cleaver's *Soul on Ice*: "Totally objectionable and without any literary value."

Warren Miller's *The Cool World*: "Why do kids have to read dirty books like that?"

Books are not alone in being subject to censorship. Magazines or newspapers used, recommended, or referred to in English classes have increasingly drawn the censor's fire. Few librarians would regard their periodical collections as worthwhile or representative without some or all of the following publications, but all of them have been the target of censors on occasion:

Life: "Filth, offensive and obscene, racy, risque, leering matter."

Read Magazine: "Objectionable, un-American, filthy, subversive."

National Geographic: "Nudity and sensationalism, especially in stories on barbaric foreign people."

Scholastic Magazine: "Doctrines opposing the beliefs of the majority, socialistic programs; promotes racial unrest and contains very detailed geography of foreign countries, especially those inhabited by dark people."

National Observer: "Right-wing trash with badly reported news."

New York Times: "That thing should be outlawed after printing the Pentagon papers and helping our country's enemies."

The immediate results of demands to censor books or periodicals vary. At times, school boards and administrators have supported and defended their teachers, their use of materials under fire, and the student's right of access to the materials. At other times, however, special committees have been formed to cull out "objectionable works" or "modern trash" or "controversial literature." Some teachers have been summarily reprimanded for assigning certain works, even to mature students. Others have been able to retain their positions only after initiating court action.

Not as sensational, but perhaps more important, are the long range results. Schools have removed from libraries and classrooms and English teachers have avoided using or recommending works which might make members of the community angry. Many students are consequently "educated" in a school atmosphere hostile to free inquiry. Dedicated and able students considering teaching English as a career must find little encouragement in this restrictive educational climate.

The problem of censorship does not derive solely from the small anti-intellectual, ultra-moral, or ultra-patriotic groups which will always function in a society that guarantees freedom of speech and freedom of the press. The present concern is rather with the frequency and force of attacks by others, often people of good will and the best intentions, some from within the teaching profession. The National Council of Teachers of English, the National Education Association, the American Federation of Teachers, and the American Library Association, as well as the publishing industry and writers themselves, agree: pressures for censorship are great throughout our society.

The material that follows is divided into two sections. The first on "The Right to Read" is addressed to parents and the community at large. Separately printed by NCTE, it may be obtained in quantity for distribution. In the last section, "A Course for Action," are Council recommendations for establishing professional committees in every school to set up procedures for book selection, to work for community support, and to review complaints against any book or periodical.*

---

*Permission is granted to reproduce in whole or in part either or both sections, with proper credit to the National Council of Teachers of English. Because of specific local problems, some schools may wish to modify the statements and arrange separately for printing or duplication. In such cases, of course, it should be made clear that revised statements appear under the authorization and sponsorship of the local school or association, not NCTE. Separately printed statements on "The Right to Read" are available from NCTE, 1111 Kenyon Road, Urbana, Illinois 61801.

THE RIGHT TO READ

"The worthy fruit of an academic culture is an open mind. . . ." Charles W. Eliot, "First Inaugural Address," Harvard University, October 19, 1869.

". . . education should prepare people not just to earn a living but to live a life—a creative, humane, and sensitive life. This means that the schools must provide a liberal, humanizing education. And the purpose of liberal education must be, and indeed always has been, to educate educators—to turn out men and women who are capable of educating their families, their friends, their communities, and most importantly, themselves . . . . Of what does the capacity to educate oneself consist? It means that a person has both the desire and the capacity to learn for himself, to dig out what he needs to know, as well as the capacity to judge what is worth learning. It means, too, that one can think for himself, so that he is dependent on neither the opinions nor the facts of others, and that he uses that capacity to think about his own education, which means to think about his own nature and his place in the universe—about the meaning of life and of knowledge and of the relations between them." Charles E. Silberman, *Crisis in the Classroom: The Remaking of American Education*, 1970.

"The writer of fiction, if he is serious and conscientious, strives to re-create and illuminate experience. It is not his right to falsify. He has to be honest to his materials. He has to be honest to himself. He operates in the conviction that if anything is important it is truth as he has been led to see it." A. B. Guthrie, Jr., "The Peter Rabbit Library?" *Nieman Reports*, April 1958.

"Where suspicion fills the air and holds scholars in line for fear of their jobs, there can be no exercise of the free intellect. . . . A problem can no longer be pursued with impunity to its edges. Fear stalks the classroom. The teacher is no longer a stimulant to adventurous thinking; she becomes instead a pipe line for safe and sound information. A deadening dogma takes the place of free inquiry. Instruction tends to become sterile; pursuit of knowledge is discouraged; discussion often leaves off where it should begin." Justice William O. Douglas, United States Supreme Court: *Adler* v. *Board of Education*, 1952.

The right to read, like all rights guaranteed or implied within our constitutional tradition, can be used wisely or foolishly. In many ways, education is an effort to improve the quality of choices open to man. But to deny the freedom of choice in fear that it may be unwisely used is to destroy the freedom itself. For this reason, we respect the right of individuals to be selective in their own reading. But for the same reason, we oppose efforts of individuals or groups to limit the freedom of choice of others or to impose their own standards or tastes upon the community at large.

The right of any individual not just to read but to read whatever he wants to read is basic to a democratic society. This right is based on an assumption that the educated and reading man possesses judgment and understanding and can be trusted with the determination of his own actions. In effect, the reading man is freed from the bonds of discovering all things and all facts and all truths through his own direct experiences, for his reading allows him to meet people, debate philosophies, and experience events far beyond the narrow confines of his own existence.

In selecting books for reading by young people, English teachers consider the contribution which each work may make to the education of the reader, its aesthetic value, its honesty, its readability for a particular group of students, and its appeal to adolescents. English teachers, however, may use different works for different purposes. The criteria for choosing a work to be read by an entire class are somewhat different from the criteria for choosing works to be read by small groups. For example, a teacher might select John Knowles' *A Separate Peace* for reading by an entire class, partly because the book has received wide critical recognition, partly because it is relatively short and will keep the attention of many slow readers, and partly because it has proved popular with many students of widely differing abilities. The same teacher, faced with the responsibility of choosing or recommending books for several small groups of students, might select or recommend books as different as Nathaniel Hawthorne's *The Scarlet Letter*, Jack Schaefer's *Shane*, Alexander Solzhenitsyn's *One Day in the Life of Ivan Denisovitch*, Pierre Boulle's *The Bridge over the River Kwai*, Charles Dickens' *Great Expectations*, or Paul Zindel's *The Pigman*, depending upon the abilities and interests of the students in each group. And the criteria for suggesting books to individuals or for recommending something worth reading for a student who casually stops by after class are different from selecting material for a class or group. But the teacher selects books; he does not censor them. Selection implies that a teacher is free to choose this or that work, depending upon the purpose to be achieved and the student or class in question, but a book selected this year may be ignored next year, and the reverse. Censorship implies that certain works are not open to selection, this year or any year.

Many works contain isolated elements to which some individuals or groups may object. The literary artist seeks truth, as he is able to see and feel it. As a seeker of truth, he must necessarily challenge at times the common beliefs or values of a society; he must analyze and comment on people's actions and values and the frequent discrepancy between what they purport to live by and what they do live by. In seeking to discover meaning behind reality, the artist strives to achieve a work which is honest. Moreover, the value and impact of any literary work must be examined as a whole and not in part—the impact of the entire work being more important than the words, phrases, or incidents out of which it is made.

Wallace Stevens once wrote, "Literature is the better part of life. To this it seems inevitably necessary to add, provided life is the better part of literature." Students and parents have the right to demand that education today keep students in touch with the reality of the world outside the classroom. Much of classic literature asks questions as valid and significant today as when the literature first appeared, questions like "What is the nature of humanity?" "Why do people praise individuality and practice conformity?" "What do people need for a good life?" and "What is the nature of the good person?" But youth is the age of revolt, and the times today show much of the world in revolt. To pretend otherwise is to ignore a reality made clear to young people and adults alike on television and radio, in newspapers and magazines. English teachers must be free to employ books, classic or contemporary, which do not lie to the young about the perilous but wondrous times we live in, books which talk of the fears, hopes, joys, and frustrations people experience, books about people not only as they are but as they can be. English teachers forced through the pressures of censorship to use only safe or antiseptic works are placed in the morally and intellectually untenable position of lying to their students about the nature and condition of mankind.

The teacher must exercise care to select or recommend works for class reading and group discussion which will not embarrass students in discussions with their peers. One of the most important responsibilities of the English teacher is developing rapport and respect among students. Respect for the uniqueness and potential of the individual, an important facet of the study of literature, should be emphasized in the English class.

For students to develop a respect for each individual, no matter what his race or creed or values may be, multi-ethnic materials must become a part of the literature program in all schools, regardless of the ethnic composition of the school population. It is time that literature classes reflect the cultural contributions of many minority groups in the United States, just as they should acquaint students with contributions from the peoples of Asia, Africa, and Latin America.

What a young reader gets from any book depends both on the selection and on the reader himself. A teacher should choose books with an awareness of the student's interests, his reading ability, his mental and emotional maturity, and the values he may derive from the reading. A wide knowledge of many works, common sense, and professional dedication to students and to literature will guide the teacher in making his selections. The community that entrusts students to the care of an English teacher should also trust that teacher to exercise professional judgment in selecting or recommending books.

The Threat to Education

Censorship leaves students with an inadequate and distorted picture of the ideals, values, and problems of their culture. Writers may often be the spokesmen of their culture, or they may stand to the side attempting to describe and evaluate that culture. Yet, partly because of censorship or the fear of censorship, many writers are ignored or inadequately represented in the public schools, and many are represented in anthologies not by their best work but by their "safest" or "least offensive" work.

The censorship pressures receiving the greatest publicity are those of small groups who protest the use of a limited number of books with some "objectionable" realistic elements, such as *Brave New World, Lord of the Flies, Catcher in the Rye, The Stranger, Johnny Got His Gun, The Assistant, Catch-22, Soul on Ice,* or *Stranger in a Strange Land.* The most obvious and immediate victims are often found among our best and most creative English teachers, those who have ventured outside the narrow boundaries of conventional texts. Ultimately, however, the real victims are the students, denied the freedom to explore ideas and pursue truth wherever and however they wish.

Great damage may be done by book committees appointed by national or local organizations to pore over anthologies, texts, library books, and paperbacks to find sentences which advocate, or seem to advocate, causes or concepts or practices these organizations condemn. As a result, some publishers, sensitive to possible objections, carefully exclude sentences or selections that might conceivably offend some group, somehow, sometime, somewhere.

Many well-meaning people wish to restrict reading materials in schools to books that do not mention certain aspects of life they find offensive: drugs, profanity, Black Power, anti-war marches, smoking, sex, racial unrest, rock music, politics, pregnancy, school dropouts, peace rallies, drinking, Chicano protests, or divorce. Although he may personally abhor one or more of these facets of modern life, the English teacher has the responsibility to encourage students to read about and reflect on many aspects, good and bad, of their own society and of other cultures.

The English Teacher's Purposes and Responsibilities

The purpose of education remains what it has always been in a free society: to develop a free and reasoning human being who can think for himself, who understands his own and, to some extent, other cultures, who lives compassionately and cooperatively with his fellow man, who respects both himself and others, who has developed self-discipline and self-motivation and exercises both, who can laugh at a world which often seems mad, and who can successfully develop survival strategies for existence in that world.

The English teacher knows that literature is a significant part of the education of man, for literature raises problems and questions and dilemmas that have perplexed and intrigued and frustrated man since the dawn of time. Literature presents some solutions to complex problems and some answers to abiding questions, perhaps incomplete but the best we have found. Even more important, literature continues to raise questions man can never wholly answer: What is the relationship between power and moral responsibility? Why does the good man sometimes suffer and the evil man sometimes go untouched by adversity? How can man reconcile the conflict of duty between what he owes society and what he owes his own conscience? The continued search for answers, tentative as they must prove, is a necessary part of the educated man's life, and the search for answers may in part be found through reading.

Aware of the vital role of literature in the education of mankind, the English teacher has unique responsibilities to his students and to adults in the community. To his students, he is responsible for knowing many books from many cultures, for demonstrating a personal commitment to the search for truth through wide reading and continual critical questioning of his own values and beliefs, for respecting the unique qualities and potential of each student, for studying many cultures and societies and their values, and for exhibiting the qualities of the educated man. To adults, he is responsible for communicating information about his literature program; for explaining, not defending, what books he uses with what students, for what reasons, and with what results; and for communicating the necessity of free inquiry and the search for truth in a democratic society and the dangers of censorship and repression.

THE COMMUNITY'S RESPONSIBILITY

American citizens who care about the improvement of education are urged to join students, teachers, librarians, administrators, boards of education, and professional and scholarly organizations in support of the students' right to read. Only widespread and informed support in every community can assure that:

enough citizens are interested in the development and maintenance of a superior school system to guarantee its achievement;

malicious gossip, ignorant rumors, and deceptive letters to the editor will not be circulated without challenge and correction;

newspapers will be convinced that the public sincerely desires objective school news reporting, free from slanting or editorial comment which destroys confidence in and support for schools;

the community will not permit its resources and energies to be dissipated in conflicts created by special interest groups striving to advance their ideologies or biases; and

faith in democratic traditions and processes will be maintained.

APPENDIX C

A Sample Interdisciplinary Unit*

Interdisciplinary unit. This is the equivalent of from six to eight week's work in four subjects (English, Social Studies, Art, and Music) and requires a time block of 3 class periods per day. Activities are designed to cross subject lines while providing an abundance of work in basic skills (note the activities requiring writing). In a completely interdisciplinary program similar units in the sciences (Math and Science) and electives would be occurring concurrently with the attached unit.

A school year consists of from four to six units each in Humanities, Sciences, and Electives, or an equivalent of from twelve to eighteen units of learning.

UNIT I. CONTEMPORARY AMERICAN CULTURE

OVERALL UNIT OBJECTIVE

An understanding and comprehension of the character, direction, and concerns of Contemporary American cultures.

CONTRIBUTORY OBJECTIVE NO. 1

An understanding and working knowledge of the components of a culture.

Activities

1. Establish and post on a bulletin board a working definition of the word "culture."

2. Prepare and display a collage showing component parts or portions of a culture (consider S.A., C.A., U.S., and Can.).

3. Prepare and present a medley of songs showing components of a culture.

4. Read *The Outsiders*.

   (A) Choose one scene, write a script, and present a dramatization designed to show some components of American culture.

   (B) Write a thoughtful, well organized paper contrasting one particular aspect of Pony Boy's culture with a similar aspect of your culture.

5. Make up your own unique language, spoken by the members of a special "culture." Make rules for usage, and carry out some conversations in your invented language. Write a paper explaining some of the problems you en-

*The Humanities Horizon, A Britannica Newsletter published by Instructional Services Division, Encyclopaedia Britannica Educational Corp. vol. 5, no. 2, March 1972, pp. 5–10.

countered in developing a language, and point out some qualities necessary to an effective language.

6. Compose and post on the bulletin board one illustrated list showing the "free" things in life and another showing those things in life which require money. Show in your illustrations how important money is to a contented and happy life in America.

CONTRIBUTORY OBJECTIVE NO. 2

An understanding and appreciation of the role of the arts in contemporary American cultures.

Activities

1. Prepare and present a multi-media presentation showing your concept of contemporary American culture.

2. Collect examples of music, literature, art, film, and sculpture whose purpose is to convey social criticism. Display and comment on your examples to others.

3. Collect examples of music, literature, art, film and sculpture whose purpose is primarily commercial. Display and comment on your examples to the class.

4. Collect and bring to class examples of music, literature, art, film and sculpture that bear no recognizable relationship to contemporary American life and explain to the group your reasons for selecting these examples.

5. Create a work of music or literature or art that is a personal social comment on contemporary American culture. Display your commentary and have your audience evaluate its effectiveness.

6. Read and report on an American contemporary novel which deals with protest. Create a bulletin board or mobile to be a part of your report.

7. Using art as propaganda, try to create sympathy for or feeling against a particular subject. Explain in a carefully written paper, how you tried to accomplish this and what your results were.

8. View several TV commercials and determine what makes them works of art. Using your conclusions create 2 TV commercials, one which you regard as a work of art, and one which you do not regard as a work of art. Display these to the class.

9. Keep a log of TV shows you watch for one week and divide them into categories according to their purpose. Then tabulate the number of hours devoted to each category, and form some conclusions concerning the role of television in your life. Write a brief report on your findings.

10. Prepare an artistic presentation centered around the theme of drugs in contemporary American culture. Be sure your presentation makes a specific comment that others can understand. Have your audience state what they believe the comment to be.

11. Create and present a skit that reveals a personal opinion or interest or feeling.

12. Create a collage that exemplifies art as either a celebration of life, or an escape from reality, or as a purely aesthetic experience. Display the collage on a bulletin board.

13. Invite a number of artists, writers, composers, etc. to talk to the class regarding their concepts of how and why man creates. Then write a paper, make a film, or give a multi-media presentation concerning the results of these talks.

14. Take photographs of slides showing the role of art in industrial design. Present and explain these to the class.

15. Find and display one single-frame cartoon that makes a social or political statement. In a sentence or two indicate the significance of the statement made. Mount the cartoon and statement on colored paper ready for a bulletin board display.

16. Invite a resource person in to discuss and/or demonstrate the role of dance in contemporary American culture. Try to prepare your own dance to express a particular emotion or reaction.

17. See a contemporary American play and if possible, communicate with the professionals who are involved in the production of the play. Write a report to be shared with the class detailing some of their observations concerning the role of the theatre in contemporary American society.

18. Construct a photographic exhibit centered around a theme relevant to contemporary American culture. Display your exhibit in a prominent place.

19. Create or display examples of art that comment on or involve the role of technology in contemporary American society. Write a brief explanation to go with each exhibit.

20. Prepare a wall display showing contemporary use and treatment of the American flag. Consider the following areas: fashion, politics, advertising, art, etc. Draw some written conclusions about the significance of your display, and share these with your classmates.

21. Create a display showing and explaining official proper and/or legal ways of displaying the American flag. Put up this display in a conspicuous location.

22. Write a carefully constructed theme, after viewing the displays of activities 19 and 20, explaining your point of view about contemporary uses of the American flag.

23. Wear or bring something to school that indicates the influence of a culture other than that of the U.S. Explain this influence.

24. Demonstrate or display examples of contemporary American folk art. In a paper explain the role of the examples displayed in contemporary American culture.

25. Visit a local art show and select one particular work of art. Write a paper detailing your concept of the artist's purpose in creating the work.

26. Assume that you are a member of an ethnic group other than your own. Write a poem or short story (or any other short piece) expressing your identity.

27. Following a survey of contemporary American poetry, select and analyze one contemporary American poem which expresses a particular aspect of American culture.

28. Invite a city planner to discuss with the class the nature of city planning. Then draw up and display your own general plan for an effective city.

29. Collect and present to the class 2 examples of technological art. Give some personal reactions to these in your presentation. What do you feel the artist is trying to express in each case?

30. Write three letters to the editor representing three contrasting points of view regarding the role of rock music festivals as a social force. Display copies of your letters on the bulletin board.

31. Examine censorship of the arts in the U.S. today, and prepare both sides of a debate on this topic. You will be selected to represent one side only. Hold a classroom debate, and ask the audience to write short papers judging the effectiveness of the debate.

32. Collect, display, demonstrate or create examples of art used as propaganda. With each, provide an explanation of what it is to accomplish.

33. Bring in two reproductions of American art, one to represent idealism, the other, realism. Be able to defend your choice in a debate entitled, "Realism or Idealism in American art?"

CONTRIBUTORY OBJECTIVE NO. 3

An awareness of the nature of social organization within contemporary American cultures.

Activities

1. Watch five family situation TV programs. Compare and contrast the situations of American families.
   As an individual assignment, prepare a report indicating your findings.
   As a group assignment, present a panel discussion of your findings.

2. Prepare a TV tape or dramatic presentation showing your views of a contemporary family situation. List those characteristics you plan to emphasize. Show your tape or presentation to a group and have them determine how effectively you emphasized the intended characteristics.

3. Prepare a report on the changing role of the family in American culture.

4. Through a multi-media collage, indicate the fragmentation of American culture into various social organizations. (Use a variety of these organizations.) Determine how many organizations your viewers can list, and record your effectiveness.

5. Collect and perform pop music that reflects the aims and/or character of various·social organizations in United States culture. Have your audience list these aims or characteristics which they observe. Compare these lists with your purpose and determine your effectiveness.

CONTRIBUTORY OBJECTIVE NO. 4: COMMUNICATION

Insight into the role of media and communication in determining the values and nature (pattern-character) of American cultures.

Activities

1. Watch several family situation programs and several commercials. Compare and contrast the family situations presented in each. Consider each program and its commercial. Prepare a means of evaluating your findings and prepare a research paper presenting your results.

2. Watch 3 separate TV programs at varying times of the day. Consider the nature of the programs and the nature of the commercials. Prepare a chart, and illustrate your findings.

3. In a written paragraph, compare and contrast the reporting of a news article in a newspaper and TV news show.

4. Using your knowledge of the impact of media, start a fad; document the process you used, and the results of your project. Post your results on the bulletin board.

5. View the film "Communications Explosion." Prepare a visual display of your own interpretations of the effect of this explosion on your contemporary society.

6. Hold a bumper sticker contest to promote an idea, value or change within the school community. Record the results of your efforts and post them on a bulletin board.

7. Create a visual display illustrating different sides of the ecology problem. Show how corporations, citizens, groups, government, etc. use mass media to get across their side of the issue.

8. Examine the case of the Pentagon Papers. Show in a visual display how this case illustrates a problem of communication and the free press in a free society.

9. Use graphics to "sell something" to your classmates—a product of your own invention, or an idea or value. Record your effectiveness.

10. View carefully some commercials and make a chart showing what feelings or values are associated with each product or service being promoted.

11. Invite some persons to discuss with students the responsibilities and potential of different media in light of social problems. Record the results of this discussion in an essay.

CONTRIBUTORY OBJECTIVE NO. 5

An awareness and understanding of the American Dream, its dimensions, its realization, and its cultural significance.

Activities

1. Establish and post on a bulletin board a working definition of the "American Dream."

2. Extract from particular historical documents statements that you think reflect the American Dream. Describe 3 instances in which these ideals have and 3 instances in which these ideals have not been realized. Use an illustrated chart for displaying your descriptions.

3. Assume that you are a candidate for political office. Your platform is the American Dream. From the speeches and/or writings of one or more of the following persons extract what you believe to be their version of the American Dream and construct a political speech based on their ideas. Present this speech to the class:

Martin Luther King   Eldridge Cleaver
Ronald Reagan   Ogden Reid
Richard Ottinger   Shirley Chisholm
George Wallace   Lester Maddox

You may add to this list any political figure of similar stature.

4. Invite a legislator from the national or state level to discuss with students problems involved in the realization of the American Dream. Plan and display a course of action to remedy some of these problems.

5. Prepare and present a large group presentation showing how contemporary popular music reflects concern with the American Dream.

6. Compose a series of songs to be collected under the title, "The American Dream is Alive and Well and Living in Rye Town." Present this to your classmates as a series of ballads or in a hootenanny.

7. Collect and/or create a series of political cartoons depicting how various groups in American society feel about the American Dream and its reality. Share these with your classmates.

8. Prepare and present skits that reveal how various groups have either realized or not realized the American Dream. Examples of these groups might include the American Indian, Urban Blacks, suburban commuter, the successful industrialists, sports figures, movie stars, migrant workers, the elderly, the urban poor, Puerto Ricans, the rural poor, etc.

9. Collect or create cartoons showing types of individuals who are striving or not striving for the American Dream. Make a visual display that includes explanations of each individual's attitude.

10. Extract and perform excerpts from "Man of La Mancha" and "How To Succeed in Business Without Really Trying" which illustrate a particular interpretation of the American Dream. Explain in a short paper what aspects you were trying to depict.

11. Visit places involved in manufacturing or handling things commonly identified with the American Dream. Examples—Fisher Body Plant, Macy's, Con. Ed, IBM, Reader's Digest, General Foods, Kennedy Airport, Chase Manhattan Bank, NBC Studios, etc. Using a medium such as poetry, photography, painting, collage, etc. create your personal impression of this experience and display it in a prominent place.

12. Interview several immigrants regarding: what did they expect to find in America, who shared their expectations, what did they find, what regrets or appreciations do they now have, how do they now feel about the American Dream. Ask them to cite specific experiences. Write a creative paper or narration illuminating or featuring these experiences.

13. Invite some Senior Citizens to your class to discuss their observations and experiences regarding the "American Dream." Write an analysis of similarities and differences in their experiences.

14. View and report on several TV commercials that reflect the contemporary view of the American Dream. Write an analysis of the similarities and differences they present.

15. Bring in examples of board games that reflect aspects of the American Dream. Show this through a class demonstration. Design and make your own game that reflects this and have your classmates play your game.

16. Collect and bring to class examples of pop art that are reflections of the American Dream. Display them and discuss them with the class.

17. Invite community leaders to class to discuss local manifestations of the American Dream. Prepare a list of things that you can do to further your realization of the American Dream.

18. Make a collage that makes a personal comment on the role of the American Dream in your life. Display it in a prominent place.

19. Read a biography of a prominent person and write a report concerning the role of the American Dream in that person's life.

20. Compose and conduct a questionnaire to be given to local residents concerning the role of the American Dream in contemporary family life. Compile the results; create and display a chart and a collage illustrating your findings.

21. Read the concluding paragraphs of *The Great Gatsby* and George Babbitt's speech to the Rotary Club from the novel *Babbitt*. Write a report detailing the different visions of the American Dream described in each novel.

22. Read several statements of several leaders of the Women's Liberation Movement and present a speech or speeches designed to show their viewpoint on women's share in the American Dream.

23. View several TV soap operas and game shows and report to the class on the view of the American Dream presented by these programs.

24. Read *Death of a Salesman* and report on the differing views of the American Dream represented by the characters of Ben, Willie, Biff, and Dave Singleman.

25. Based on your observations of contemporary culture, write a paper giving your views on the status of the American Dream today.

26. Play the simulation game "Ghetto." Write a short paper describing and accounting for your character's success or lack of success in improving the quality of his or her life.

CONTRIBUTORY OBJECTIVE NO 6

An understanding of the role of environment in contemporary American culture.

Activities

1. Arrive at a working definition of "environment." Consider as many different kinds of environment as you can. Post your results in a prominent place.

2. Examine the following series of environments:

    A square inch of earth.
    A room in your house.
    Two minutes of riding in a car.
    One minute of attendance at a pop concert or school dance.
    Two minutes of silence.

    Write a report including the equipment you used for observations, the methods utilized, your observations, and a general statement based on your examination.

3. Theatrically create contrasting environments (physical, psychological, and philosophical). Share your creations with your classmates.

4. Create various physical environments and exhibit these to the class.

5. Describe in a talk or in writing man's relationship to nature as illustrated through a personal camping experience.

6. Write a paper or prepare a collage exploring the role of environment in man's ability to live comfortably. Possible environments to consider are the urban ghetto, suburban development, rural farm, etc.

7. Place yourself in an environment totally different from the one that you are now in. Write a paper answering the following: What things do you notice that are different? What effect do they have on you? How would you go about adjusting to them?

8. Make a visual display of an emotional environment here, in a large city, in a rural area, and so on. Then superimpose this emotional environment on a natural environment. Record your results in a well written narrative.

9. Find or create examples of art that reflects the environment in which it was created and examples of art that uses the natural environment. Display these examples.

10. Find and present to the class music that draws on the natural environment for inspiration or content. You may also use graphics.

11. Every man relates to his environment. Examine several works of literature and in a written report show how this is treated.

12. Collect pictures and writings that show how man has found beauty in different environments. Display them on a bulletin board.

13. Explore the tensions in schools today, and show how these combine to form an emotional environment. Express your findings in a creative work.

14. Create a discotheque that is organized around a particular theme. Invite the rest of the class to experience the environment you created and to comment on the effect of this environment on them.

15. Consider the human body as a physical environment, and through a graphic or written presentation show how modern America life affects this environment.

16. From a survey of newspaper and magazine ads, determine which environments Americans are most concerned with, and describe your conclusions in a written report.

17. Examine 2 characters from contemporary American literature. In a self-revealing monologue show how each character is affected by his own psychological environment.

18. In a presentation of your own design, show how the creation of a teenage environment is affecting the American culture today.

19. Invite a resource person from the field of psychology to discuss the interaction of environment and personality. Compile notes on this presentation and list significant points for public display.

CONTRIBUTORY OBJECTIVE NO. 7

An understanding and appreciation of contemporary American values, what they are, how they are expressed, and the role they play in determining contemporary life.

Activities

1. Establish a working definition of "values." Post this definition in a place where it can constantly be referred to by students and teachers working in this unit.

2. What values are expressed in contemporary art, music, dance, literature, history, architecture, philosophy? Devise a means for finding out and for sharing the results of your exploration of these media.

3. What classical works of art, music, dance, literature, history, architecture and philosophy are important in the contemporary American cultures? Devise a means of finding out. Share your findings with other students.

4. Read some contemporary novels and decide what values are important in them. Write a paper discussing the values of major characters in relation to contemporary American culture.

5. Look carefully at contemporary poetry and songs. Choose a particular work, and explain in a brief presentation what values are expressed and how you feel about these values.

6. Examine a variety of contemporary newspapers and magazines to learn what concerns are most important in contemporary American culture. Create and present a sharing experience using what you learn.

7. Identify one specific value you believe should be changed in some way, i.e., propagated, strengthened, lessened, etc. Devise and carry out a specific plan for changing or strengthening this value, and establish a means of evaluating your effectiveness.

8. Identify one value you feel very strongly about. Discover what you believe to be your most effective way of expressing this value. Solicit the views of six other people who will evaluate the effectiveness of your expression. Try to get some people who will agree with you and some who will disagree. Write a brief paper telling what you learned about effective expression. Consider whether the value you sought to express has changed any during this activity, or whether your attitude toward and interest in it have changed.

9. List categories (religious, social, economic, etc.) Do values in one category sometimes conflict with values in another? In what ways might they agree? Prepare a statement or chart on categories of values and polarization of values.

10. Make a careful study of the toy departments in one or more fairly large stores. Find out: What main categories of toys for children are represented? Which categories have the largest stock? Most variety? Largest displays? Highest prices? Which categories of toys sell the best? Which toys are poor sellers? Which are most popular with boys and girls of various ages? Combine all your information into an interesting and informative report that shows how American toys for children reflect the values of contemporary American cultures. Write a paper compiling your results.

11. Collect a variety of statements, both contemporary and traditional, which deal with "what an American should believe in." Identify them by source, author, and date of origin. Arrange and display these statements or excerpts to show how they are related to each other and to contemporary issues.

12. Invite to class some resource persons from the community to discuss with you how values are formed and how they play a role in people's everyday behavior. Consider a psychologist, clergyman, advertising person, lawyer, and others. Display on a bulletin board a list of the values and the roles they play.

13. Examine some popularly known magazine and TV advertisements to see what values are most often appealed to in an effort to sell particular products. List for each product or type of product what kind of person the ads are aimed at, for example, Ultra-Brite toothpaste, Marlboro cigarettes, Fab de-

tergent. Which ads seem to you to be most honest? Which are selling things which may prove harmful? What devices are employed in order to make the product seem very desirable? After you feel you understand something about advertising techniques, create some ads of your own in order to demonstrate how ads are related to people's values. Are these techniques ever employed in other fields? Prepare a demonstration for the class to convey your findings.

14. Watch and analyze carefully several popular TV programs, paying special attention to the following: Who or what, according to the program, is good, acceptable, or worthwhile? Specifically how does the program create a value-impression in you, the viewer? What kind of person would this program appeal to most? Least? What advertisers pay for this program? What is the relationship between types of programs and types of advertisers? Draw together some generalizations from your study and present them to the class.

15. Look carefully at a TV program schedule for a week and determine what kinds of programs are most often scheduled for prime time, what kinds of programs are most represented in the schedule, least represented, not represented. Take a poll of students and other groups to determine their favorite TV programs. What generalizations can you make about values represented and emphasized? Share these with the class graphically and verbally.

16. Design and make an appropriate flag for the New American Revolution. Explain the meaning of its colors, shape, symbols, etc.

17. Collect and perform or play several examples of modern popular songs that reflect a change in values from the 1950s through today. Extra possibility: Write and perform a pop song that you feel reflects the direction of American values in the future.

CONTRIBUTORY OBJECTIVE NO. 8

A comprehension of the forces that may polarize and/or unite various segments of American society today.

Activities

1. Bring to class examples of publications that are aimed at specific segments of society. Write a paper identifying the segment of society to which each publication appeals and the ways in which it appeals to that segment.

2. View six television programs, and prepare a chart showing which programs foster cultural interrelationships and which ignore them.

3. Compile a list of words that tend to polarize or unite segments of society. Explain what groups would react to which words in what way, and display your lists and explanations on a bulletin board.

4. Invite into your classroom theologians to discuss the qualities of, similarities etc. of various religions. Make and display a chart summarizing the main points of the discussion.

5. Read *The Outsiders* or other books with a similar theme and explore in a group discussion the types of socio-economic polarization that are described. Write a summary of your reactions to this discussion and submit it to your teacher.

6. You are a student of the Ridge Street School. Write a paragraph expressing your observations about what polarizing and uniting forces are at work in your school. Post your paragraph on a bulletin board.

7. You are a member of a family. Write a paragraph expressing your observations about what polarizing and uniting forces are at work in your family. Display a collection of these paragraphs on a bulletin board.

8. You are a member of a community. Write a paragraph expressing your observations about what polarizing and uniting forces are at work in your community. Display a collection of these paragraphs on a bulletin board.

9. Compose and conduct a questionnaire designed to display the differing points of view of American adolescents, young adults, parents and grandparents on the Viet Nam war, civil liberties, student dissent, drugs, or any other contemporary problem. Correlate and post the results of the questionnaire.

10. Using the results of the preceding questionnaire, and drawing upon your own personal experience, write and submit a paper expressing your views on the "generation gap."

11. A person from another country asks you, "What is an American?" In a paper, answer the question. Post your paper on a bulletin board.

12. In 10 short statements, answer the personal question "Who am I?" Prepare and exhibit a graphic display based upon your statements.

13. View a film or demonstrate a folk dance that reflects a particular culture. Write a paper describing what you observed.

14. View a film that illustrates the ethnic complexity of New York City and prepare a report reflecting this complexity.

15. Attempt to discern whether immigration regulations tend to polarize segments of American society. List any regulations which you feel do this, and discuss the ways in which they do this. Create a display which expresses your observations.

16. Take a field trip to specific areas which illustrate particular aspects or backgrounds of culture. Record your observations and write a general narrative showing what you learned.

CONTRIBUTORY OBJECTIVE NO. 9

An awareness of the many different life styles which exist within the American cultures.

Activities

1. Prepare and exhibit a collage of pictorial representations of life styles as depicted in the "slick" magazines.

2. Prepare a diary of a specific member of a social or cultural group quite different from your own. Consider groups in Canada and South America. Consider time cycles, clothes, fads, fashions, food. Share your diary with the class.

3. Trade ideas of foods, and dress through various cultures or groups. Then illustrate by a chart or demonstration the relation of geography to food and dress.

4. Consider and show through presentation, creation or performance examples of the relative role of the arts in various cultural groups.

5. Study and learn various forms of shelter and housing indigenous to various cultural groups. Prepare and display various examples of housing.

6. Establish a model housing contest. Each model or drawing made must reflect the particular life style of a particular cultural group. Be sure an explanation accompanies each entry.

7. Prepare a model community including housing. Through maps or diagrams, depict this community.

Sample Resource Unit:
The Civil War and Reconstruction*

OBJECTIVES

This unit should make progress toward the development of the following:

UNDERSTANDINGS

1. The Civil War was a result of complex economic, social, and political pressures, not of any single cause.
2. Political parties attempt to compromise differences among sections of the country.
3. The supremacy of the national government was established in a long, costly war.
4. Periods of crisis sharply test political leadership and a constitutional form of government.
5. The influence of cultural continuity makes it difficult to effect abrupt changes in men's institutions.
6. Severe treatment of defeated peoples tends to arouse bitter and lasting feelings.
7. There are no easy solutions to social problems.

SKILLS AND ABILITIES

1. Evaluating sources of information.
2. Taking notes on reading.
3. Adjusting the rate and method of reading to material and purpose.
4. Presenting ideas orally.
5. Relating different types of phenomena among map patterns.
6. Using pivotal dates to understand time relationships among events.

ATTITUDES AND HABITS

1. An interest in history and historical materials.
2. The habit of evaluating sources of information.

*Developed by Genevieve P. Zito, University of Minnesota High School. In Dorothy McClure Fraser and Edith West, *Social Studies in Secondary Schools: Curriculum and Methods* (New York: Ronald Press, 1961), pp. 431–446. *Note:* This sample Resource Unit continues to be the finest prototype available, despite the copyright date.

3. A desire to understand other people's points of view.

4. Skepticism of easy solutions.

OUTLINE OF CONTENT

I.   The Civil War and its aftermath resulted in repercussions which are still felt today.

    A. Many of today's civil rights problems date back to the Reconstruction period.

    B. The Civil War and Reconstuction had marked effects upon our political parties.

    C. The War and its aftermath left the South with serious economic problems, some of which have not yet been solved.

II. There was no single cause of the Civil War; it resulted from complex political, economic, and social pressures.

    A. The United States had not achieved national unity by 1860.

        1. The federal-state relationship remained unresolved.

            a. The authority of the federal government had been challenged repeatedly since 1789.

            b. Two divergent views of the constitutional relationship between the central government and the states developed.

        2. Economy and society varied in the North, the South, and the West.

            a. Many and significant changes marked the life of the Northwest section.

                (1) Economy was diversified.

                (2) Society was mobile, changing, and growing.

            b. Southern economy and society were relatively stable and static.

                (1) The economy was dominated by the plantation system.

                    (a) The South was chiefly an exporting area for staples and an importing area for manufactured goods.

                    (b) Four million slaves (1860) provided the labor to run the large and small plantations.

                    (c) The majority of Southerners were not large planters.

                    (d) Although the South was essentially agricultural, small industry was profitable in strategic areas.

                (2) The planter aristocracy controlled the social and political as well as the economic life of the South.

            c. Frontier settlement was a dominant concern in this era.

                (1) Extension into new lands was pushed by two conflicting groups: the small farmers and the larger planters.

                    (a) The plantation system expanded through Louisiana, Texas, and Missouri.

                    (b) Small farming expanded beyond the Northwest Territory into the plains area.

                    (c) Improved modes of transportation spurred on settlement.

                    (d) As settlement increased, the clash between the conflicting groups became increasingly serious.

                (2) The frontier gave men the chance to start anew and to build a new place in society.

                (3) Religious and social reformers had a profound influence in the frontier area.

    B. The struggle between the North and the South for control of the central government developed from 1820–1860.

1. Until 1850 a balance of power was maintained.
   a. Control of the West was determined by compromises.
      (1) The Missouri Compromise applied to territory acquired from France in 1803.
      (2) The desire for the annexation of Texas was matched by the acquisition of Oregon.
      (3) The Compromise of 1850 was an attempt to solve the struggle for land acquired from Mexico.
   b. Political parties attempted to compromise the sectional differences.
      (1) The Democrats tried to please supporters by arranging platforms and candidates to cater to all sections.
      (2) The Whigs, led by Clay, attempted to secure compromises which would satisfy both the Northern and Southern elements in the party.

2. After 1850 compromise gave way step by step to bitter controversies and war.
   a. The Compromise of 1850 proved unworkable. Agitation increased both in the North and in the South. Some Northern states refused to obey the fugitive slave law.
   b. The Kansas-Nebraska Act broke the Missouri Compromise and reopened the issue for the Louisiana purchase area.
      (1) Kansas became the site of armed clash between the slave-holders and the free-soilers.
      (2) The Republican Party united Western and Northern groups against the Southerners' desire for extension of slavery in the territory.
      (3) Propaganda by radicals on both sides increased.
   c. The Supreme Court in the Dred Scott decision declared the Missouri Compromise void, and made slavery legal in the territories.
   d. John Brown's raid encouraged more agitation on both sides.
   e. The election of 1860 created a crisis in politics.
   f. The Southern states seceded and established their own government.

C. The causes of the war continue to be a fertile field for historical interpretation.
   1. Some historians have believed that slavery was the fundamental cause of the war.
   2. Some historians have emphasized economic rivalry between sections as the cause of the war.
   3. Some historians have presented a psychological interpretation and have concluded that the war was the result of blunders on both sides.
   4. Some historians have emphasized the states' rights or constitutional issue.
   5. A number of historians have presented a broader political, economic, and social interpretation.

III. The supremacy of the national government was established in a long and costly war.
   A. The strategy employed by the Blue and Gray forces was simple and direct.
      1. The federal forces launched an offensive war with a threefold plan of attack: blockade of Southern ports, division of the Southern heartland, and capture of the Southern capital.

2. The South's strategy was mainly defensive, although the South did make attacks and raids into Union territory.

B. New kinds of warfare were introduced: ironclads, trenches, "total war," railroad raids, and so forth.

C. Problems behind the lines (such as finances, conscription, loyalty, diplomacy) increased as the war continued.

D. Superior Union resources and leadership led ultimately to the defeat of an exhausted South.

   1. The Union capitalized on its strengths.
      a. Federal armies were manned and supplied by a growing industry, an expanding population, and an improved transportation system.
      b. The Union used its official status to prevent European recognition of the Confederacy.
      c. Lincoln exerted forceful and effective leadership in centralizing the Union war effort.

   2. The Confederacy overestimated its advantages and failed to unify its defense efforts.
      a. European intervention was not forthcoming.
      b. The upper border states as well as the Ohio Valley states remained loyal to the Union despite activities of Southern sympathizers.
      c. Southern military forces, though ably led and trained, were poorly supplied, equipped, and coordinated.
      d. Davis failed to convince states'-righters of the need for a centralized war effort.

E. The war was very costly in lives, property, and money.

IV. Periods of crisis sharply test political leadership and a constitutional form of government.

A. From 1850 to 1860, as the political parties were realigning, many politicians attempted to assume leadership.

B. Lincoln, faced with the secession crisis, actively engaged in the struggle to preserve the Union.

   1. Lincoln exercised broad executive powers to organize and coordinate the war effort.
      a. He used his "war powers" to justify executive assumption of congressional powers.
      b. He made frequent use of executive decrees to facilitate mobilization of the Union's strength.
      c. He often changed military leaders to guarantee success of the Union's attack.
      d. He used strong measures to suppress anti-Union activity in the North.

   2. As president, Lincoln realized the importance of his political position.
      a. He used patronage to control and appease his party.
      b. He signed into laws the aims of the party platform of 1860.
      c. He evaluated the effects of the war on public opinion at home and abroad.
         (1) The issuance of the Emancipation Proclamation was carefully timed.
         (2) His bid for re-election in 1864 as a Union party candidate was successful despite many difficulties.

3. Lincoln kept a watchful eye on diplomacy to forestall European recognition of the Confederate government. He carefully weighed all diplomatic actions.

C. The need for security during the Civil War brought a challenge to civil liberties.

    1. Lincoln suspended the writ of habeas corpus and authorized military trials in non-war areas.

    2. A congressional investigating committee spurred on a government loyalty program.

    3. Loyalty oaths were required and widespread both in the North and in the South.

D. Although the supremacy of the national government was established by the war, effective national leadership was not present in the postwar era.

    1. Upon Lincoln's assassination, Johnson, a War Democrat from Tennessee, became president.

        a. Johnson, attempting to carry through Lincoln's plans for reconstruction, did not receive the support of the radical Republicans in control of Congress.

        b. Bitter political controversy over reconstruction led to the attempted impeachment of Johnson.

    2. The two-party system did not operate effectively in the Reconstruction period.

        a. The Democratic party, discredited by the war, was not able to compete successfully on a national level.

        b. The radical Republicans tried to prevent the resurgence of the Democratic party in the South through the Negro vote.

        c. The rise of political bosses increased and political corruption was rampant on all levels of government.

V. The federal government failed in its efforts to reconstruct the defeated South. In imposing abrupt changes in men's institutions, those in power did not consider the importance of cultural continuity.

A. Recreation of society and economy was the most pressing problem facing the nation after the war.

    1. Destruction of life and property was evident throughout the defeated South.

    2. The Negroes, newly freed by the Thirteenth Amendment, were handicapped socially and economically.

    3. The political status of the Confederate states and citizens was in doubt.

B. Congressional reconstruction sought to change drastically Southern society.

    1. The Congress refused to readmit the representatives of the Southern states reconstructed under the Lincoln-Johnson plan.

    2. Military occupation of the Southern states was prescribed until the states developed governments acceptable to Congress.

    3. New constitutions and governments were established, revolutionizing Southern political life.

        a. The traditional leaders were disenfranchised.

        b. The former slaves were made citizens, given the right to vote, and put into a position of leadership. Republicans campaigned actively for the Negro vote.

    c. To guarantee these reforms, the Fourteenth and Fifteenth Amendments had to be ratified.

    d. The Republican reconstruction governments were run by a coalition of carpetbaggers, scalawags, and freedmen under the protection of the federal army.

    e. Certain other reforms were made, such as tax supported schools, revised tax schedules, abolition of debtors' prisons.

C. White Southerners reacted with bitterness to military reconstruction. They strove to restore their former patterns of life.

    1. They developed various means to restore themselves to a position of dominance in society.

        a. At first, they struck back violently through secret organizations like the Ku Klux Klan.

        b. Devices such as the grandfather clauses, poll taxes, white primaries, and literacy tests were used to keep the Negro from voting.

        c. Segregation of the races in all areas of life became a dominant trend. The Negro was once again placed in an inferior social and economic position.

    2. They also tried to re-establish their economy.

        a. Production of staples continued to dominate the Southern economy, as sharecropping and tenant farming replaced the plantation system.

        b. Although transportation was improved and new industries such as cigarettes, textiles, and oil developed in the South, the economy remained essentially agrarian into the twentieth century.

VI. There are no easy solutions to social problems. Problems arising from the Civil War and Reconstruction era are still prevalent today.

    A. The nation is still sharply divided on the civil rights issue: The race problem is one of the most crucial problems facing the country today.

    B. Although sharecropping has been declining in recent years, it continues to be a serious social problem.

    C. Although inroads have been made in the Democratic stronghold, the South has a predominantly one party system with all of its limitations.

TEACHING PROCEDURES

INITIATORY ACTIVITIES

1. Prepare a bulletin board display entitled "The Civil War Is Felt Today." Use pictures and newspaper headlines to illustrate effects. Ask for volunteers to keep the display up to date during the unit.

2. Use a magazine or newspaper article on a recent civil rights issue or on a recent election to initiate a discussion showing how these issues and others can be traced back to the Civil War period. Point out the need for finding out more about a period which has had such lasting effects upon American society.

3. Give a pretest to determine the extent to which students have misconceptions about the causes of the war, conditions of slavery, and other aspects of the era.

4. To determine the extent to which students have been influenced by legend, have them discuss the reasons why Lincoln has become such an important symbol in American life. Tape this discussion and replay it later in the

unit. If a written activity is preferred, have each student write an essay on Lincoln as a symbol of American life. Have the students write reappraisals later.

5. Read aloud quotations from three or four historians, each representing a different interpretation of the Civil War. Have the class discuss these viewpoints. (Tape this discussion and replay it after the class has completed its study of causes of the war.) Point out the difficulties of historical interpretation, the role of bias, and so forth. Suggest that reading during the unit should help students decide which historian is most nearly right.

6. Give a pretest to discover the ability of students to evaluate sources of information. Discuss the results. Point out the need for evaluating sources in this unit by reading aloud passages from biased materials.

7. Since the Civil War period has been portrayed often in fictional materials, introduce several novels to the class for concurrent reading. Give students time to browse through the novels to create interest.

8. If biographies are preferred to fictional accounts, introduce the class to available books which cover this era. Put some of the book jackets on the bulletin board with excerpts from student reviews of past years under each. Have the students formulate questions to guide their reading. Describe the value of note-cards so that students can take proper notes as they read. Have the students serve as resource persons during class discussions which concern the personalities about whom they have read.

9. Have students read rapidly from different textbooks to gain an overview of the unit. For example, poor readers might use Gavian and Hamm, average readers Canfield and Wilder or Todd and Curti, and better readers Bailey, or Carmen and Syrette. Before students begin reading, remind them that their reading rate should be different from that which they use when reading for detail. Ask each student to list the four or five topics he finds most interesting. Use these lists to help prepare a sheet of suggested activities for the class.

10. Have class members select individual and group activities to investigate as they study the causes of the Civil War. A number are suggested below in the approximate order in which they might be presented in order to develop the suggested outline of content. Before beginning work on the topics, discuss with the class ways of improving oral and written work. For example, have them use the criteria which they developed at the beginning of the year to evaluate progress on oral reports in the last unit and to identify specific things on which they should work. If students have not presented panels or debates previously, or if their presentations need improvement, take time to discuss methods of making such presentations effective. Have students working in groups prepare brief written progress reports every day or every other day.

DEVELOPMENTAL ACTIVITIES

11. Have students review the federal–state relationship prior to 1850. Discuss the challenges to federal authority, the divergent interpretations of the Constitution, and the implications of this conflict. Have students build a chart tracing challenges to the supreme law of the land. Include in the chart a column on the cause of discontent, one on the section of the country most

involved and one on the action taken by the federal government. Have students continue this chart during the unit.

12. Have a group of students find out how their state felt about the approaching Civil War and the part it played prior to the war. Advise them to check local resources.

13. Have a group of students make maps locating the farming areas, mercantile areas, manufacturing sites, and routes of transportation in the North for 1820, 1840, and 1860. These maps can be made individually or as overlays. The class can use these maps as it discusses significant economic changes of this period.

14. Have a student use an historical atlas or *Historical Statistics* to compare maps of population or population data for the period 1800–1860. Let him write a report analyzing his findings in terms of their implications for the struggle between the North and the South.

15. Suggest that a student pretend he is a pre-Civil War planter who visits New York in 1858. He can write a series of letters to his wife describing features of Northern life which differ from those in the South and the factors which worry him about Northern strength.

16. If nothing has been done on the reform movements of 1830–1860 in a previous unit, consider these here, possibly by an informal lecture. Emphasize the climate of opinion and the impact of the reform movements on Northern and Western society.

17. If students have been reading novels (see activity seven), hold a class discussion in which they present their findings in terms of the biases of the authors and the conflicting descriptions of Southern life.

18. Have the students compare and evaluate eyewitness accounts of prewar Southern life. Either prepare a dittoed series of eyewitness reports or have students read in the many collections of such materials. Discuss the findings concerning conditions of Southern life and the validity of witnesses.

19. If activities 17-18 have not been used, have a group of students present a symposium on the conditions of plantation life in the antebellum South. Review with students the purposes of a symposium and aid them in selecting the information and in organizing the report.

20. Hold a panel discussion on the Southern defense of slavery.

21. Delegate a student to present an oral report on the movement against slavery in the South.

22. Have a group of students make a series of maps. On one they can locate the areas of large plantations, sites of Southern industry, and districts where cotton, tobacco, and rice were grown. Have them make a plastic overlay map of per capita slaves in Southern districts and superimpose this map over the other.

23. Have a student construct a graph showing cotton and tobacco exports for 1800, 1820, 1840, and 1860 and explain the implications of the graph to the class.

24. Assign several students or the entire class to prepare papers evaluating the reasoning behind the statement: "Cotton is King, sir; the North can not make war on cotton and win!"

25. Delegate a student to construct a graph showing wheat and corn production by states in the years 1800, 1840, and 1860. Have him explain to the class the reasons for the shift in leadership among the states.

26. Have the class compare and evaluate dittoed excerpts from eyewitness accounts of life on the Northwestern and Southwestern frontiers. Contrast frontier conditions with life on the seacoast, North and South.

27. Use an opaque projector to show a series of maps and various territories which were prominent in the prewar controversies. Discuss the significance of different features of the areas. Display pictures of these areas on the bulletin board. Attach them by string to the appropriate locations on large outline maps of each area. Ask students to compare patterns of different phenomena in these areas in an attempt to generalize about their usefulness for production of crops in which slave labor could be employed. Get volunteers to use a book on historical geography to find out whether or not these hypotheses can be verified.

28. Have a group of students present a "You Are There" program on the Senate debate over the admission of Missouri in 1820.

29. The Compromise of 1850 produced one of the most stirring debates in American history. Have a group of students analyze the roles played by Webster, Benton, Clay, Calhoun, and Houston in these debates and present their findings orally or in writing.

30. Have a student draw a series of cartoons, representing different viewpoints on some important event prior to the Civil War (for example, the Compromise of 1850 or the Dred Scott decision).

31. Assign students to present oral reports on the following questions: "How successful was the underground railroad?" "The fugitive slave law: did the North obey it?" "Who opposed the abolitionists in the North?"

32. Or, have a student write a paper on the ways in which Northern states obstructed efforts to enforce the fugitive slave law. Have him explain why this action was a threat to the federal union.

33. Have the class pretend that it is the Senate of 1854 which is considering the Kansas-Nebraska bill. Have each student choose a state to represent and determine what role a Senator from that state played in the original debate. The bill can be introduced, discussed, and voted upon.

34. Let a student imagine that he is a representative of the federal government and is investigating the clashes in Kansas. Have him prepare a written report of his findings.

35. Have students present oral reports on the following topics: "Founding of the Republican Party and Its Stand on Slavery," "Abolitionist Propaganda: Accounts of Slavery in the South," "Why Did the Supreme Court Decide That Dred Scott Was Still a Slave?"

36. Harriet Beecher Stowe's *Uncle Tom's Cabin* was one of the most effective pieces of propaganda produced in the Civil War era. Assign a student to read the novel and write a paper on its reception both at home and abroad.

37. Have a student write a series of letters concerning the Dred Scott decision to the editor of the *New York Times*. Include letters from a Republican, a Douglas Democrat, a Southern Democrat, and an abolitionist.

38. Have a student imagine that he is a reporter writing a series of articles on the Lincoln-Douglas debates.

39. Have a student find out what actually happened in the John Brown raid and why it caused such nationwide excitement and hysteria. Have him present his findings in a written report. Or have a group of students prepare an informal debate on the topic: "John Brown: Rabble-rouser or Martyr?"

40. Have groups of students prepare panels on the following topics: "Constitution: Provoker of the War?" "The West: Provoker of the War?" "Slavery: Provoker of the War?" and "Plantation Life *vs*. Industrialization: Provoker of the War?" Hold a culminating discussion on the causes of the war.

41. Or have a group of students debate the causes of the war under the following question: "Resolved, that slavery was the chief cause of the Civil War."

42. If activity five was used, replay the tape and ask students to examine their original viewpoints on causes of the war in the light of the knowledge they have acquired.

43. Have a group of students prepare a symposium on the fateful election of 1860. Or have the class discuss the election as an immediate cause of the war. In advance, have a student prepare charts analyzing the election results, popular and electoral. In addition, use a dittoed copy of the South Carolina Ordinance of Secession to show the Southern reaction to Lincoln's victory. Use this document in a reading exercise and as a review of the states' rights interpretation of the Constitution.

44. Have a group of students prepare a two page newspaper, complete with news items, editorials, background commentary, and fashion notes, for the day after Lincoln's election. Make the paper one for their local area. Have another group make a similar paper which might have appeared in a different section of the country.

45. Have a group of students dramatize events in Washington following South Carolina's Ordinance of Secession. They can use the pattern of "on-the-spot news broadcasts" used by radio and television reporters for modern political conventions.

46. Have a student make a map showing the areas in the Southern states which favored and opposed secession. Show this map along with the series prepared in activity 22 and have the class see what conclusions they can draw from the data.

47. Have a student prepare an oral report, trying to answer the following question: "Could Buchanan have arrested the approaching war?"

48. For a review, have the class choose the significant events, 1850–1860, and build a timeline to establish the pattern of these events. Have students evaluate the significance of these events and their relationships to one another. Also have the class build a chart comparing Northern and Southern strength in 1860, using the data already prepared in previous activities.

49. Introduce the section on the war by showing the Brady war photos which are available in book form, on slides, and on film. Other pictures are available in *Divided We Fought*.

50. Have students read textbook sections for the war years 1861–1865 to see the chronology of events. After the reading is completed, have them do an

exercise in which they arrange the following events in chronological order: Emancipation Proclamation, Gettysburg, Lincoln's Assassination, Vicksburg, Antietam, Appomattox, Trent Affair, Sherman's March.

51. Have a committee prepare a two page newspaper for their home town for the day after the attack on Fort Sumter. Use the pattern suggested in activity 44. Students might include imaginary interviews with Lincoln and with Jefferson Davis.

52. Have a student prepare an overlay map for the map made in activity number 46. It should show the chief features of Union's attack. Have the student explain the reasons for choosing these lines of assault.

53. Divide the class into five or six groups, each one to investigate one of the major battles of the war. Have students read authoritative accounts as well as accounts by participants in the battles. Also have each group prepare a large scale map of the battle area. Have each group leader present the findings of his group in an illustrated oral report.

54. Or have each of the five or six groups, investigate a significant war personality such as Lee, Grant, Jackson, Sherman, Farragut, or Morgan. Have students read primary accounts of these men as well as accounts in the *Dictionary of American Biography*. Have the group leaders report findings to the class.

55. Have a student read two or more viewpoints on some outstanding military figure of the period and write an analysis of his personality and of the competency and bias of the authors.

56. Assign a committee to add a chapter to a class booklet on "Our Town in American History." Suggest that they visit the local newspaper offices and county museums, and talk with people whose families have lived in the area since the Civil War. Suggest that they locate realia from the period. Have them prepare a display of materials, including replicas which they can make.

57. Have several students compare the reporting of key battles in Northern and Southern newspapers. They will find accounts in the *Confederate Reader* and in the *Union Reader*.

58. Have a student write a report based on firsthand accounts of life in the Northern and Southern armies.

59. Suggest that a student read and report on firsthand accounts of prison conditions in the North and in the South.

60. Ditto several pages of firsthand accounts of army life and discipline, draft riots, bounty-jumping, and prison conditions. Use the material in a discussion of the problem of manning the Union and the Confederate armies.

61. Have a student prepare a written report on the part played by the railroads in the war effort. Assign another student to prepare a report on advances in military and naval weapons and tactics.

62. Have a student give an oral report on: "Was the blockade the key to victory?" or "What were the effects of the blockade on Southern life?" Suggest that a student prepare charts on tonnage of items carried through the blockade.

63. Have a committee present a panel discussion: "Did England hold the balance of power in the War Between the States?"

64. Read aloud to the class Sherman's own account of his march through Georgia to motivate a discussion on the justification of his tactics.

65. Have a student use *Historical Statistics* and the *World Almanac* to prepare a chart comparing American casualties in the Revolution, the War of 1812, the Civil War, World War I, and World War II. Use this chart in a discussion of losses.

66. Have a panel or class discussion on the topic: "Why Did the North Win the War?" Use this discussion to: (1) bring together an appraisal of military leadership and strategy; (2) raise the question of the role political leadership played in the outcome of the war. Use the second point to lead into a discussion of the many problems facing the president in the Civil War.

67. If activity 66 is not used, discuss the problems facing the president in this crisis. Review the chief powers which the Constitution grants the president of the United States, as well as the precedents set by past presidents facing crises.

68. Use an opaque projector to show students some of the cartoons in *Lincoln in Caricature.*

69. Have students prepare oral reports and debates on the topics: "Government by Edict: Use of Executive Decrees by Lincoln," "The Emancipation Proclamation: Lincoln a Politician or Humanitarian?" "What Were Lincoln's Views About Slavery?"

70. Have a student prepare a written report on the topic: "Why Was the Thirteenth Amendment Necessary to Free the Slaves?"

71. Have several students analyze certain aspects of the Lincoln legends in oral or written reports. Possible topics: "The Slave Market Story," "The Anne Rutledge Story," "Mary Todd Lincoln."

72. Have a student pretend to be a news commentator who analyzes the significance of the election of 1864.

73. Have a student present an oral report on: "Why was Andrew Johnson chosen as Lincoln's running mate in 1864?"

74. Have a committee prepare a "Hear It Now" program in which they interview Charles Francis Adams in London during the Civil War.

75. Have a group of students present a symposium on Northern opposition to the War.

76. Suggest that another group debate the topic: "Resolved, that the security of the nation justifed Lincoln's restriction of civil liberties."

77. Have students write reports on such topics as: "How effective was the government loyalty program?" "An evaluation of the book, *Who Murdered Lincoln?*"

78. Have a class discussion in which students evaluate Lincoln's effectiveness in meeting the crisis which he faced. Discuss Lincoln's leadership in comparison with the Confederate leadership as a factor in the Union victory. If a tape was made as suggested in activity four, replay it and have students appraise their original ideas. If an essay was written, as suggested in activity four, have students do a written appraisal at this time. Compare the two sets of papers.

79. To introduce the section on reconstruction, use an opaque projector to show scenes of the South at the close of the war. In addition to the Brady photos, good illustrations are found in *The Desolate South*.

80. Following the pattern used in activity five, read aloud quotations from historians about the Reconstruction era. Discuss these viewpoints with the class, pointing out once again the problems of historical interpretation.

81. Have students read different accounts of the Reconstruction. Have some read the usual text treatments; have superior students read sections in the Amherst pamphlet, *Reconstruction in the South* or in standard works on the Reconstruction period. Have students take notes indicating which interpretation of the Reconstruction period is found in their reading. Have them prepare questions to aid in their notetaking.

82. Have a group of students consult the *Dictionary of American Biography* on the leading personalities of the Reconstruction era. See that they take careful notes on actions and attitudes toward reconstruction policies. Use these students as resource persons in class discussions of policies.

83. Have students read dittoed excerpts from Carl Schurz, John T. Trobridge, and Richard Taylor on conditions in the South after the war. Discuss the question of bias as well as the accuracy of the reports.

84. Or have a student read firsthand accounts of the destruction in the South after the war. Suggest he analyze three accounts and prepare a paper on his findings.

85. Have a group of students prepare a dramatic report of the opening session of Congress on December 4, 1865. Suggest they use "on-the-spot" interviews like those of present-day newscasters.

86. Have students make a chart comparing Johnson's plan for reconstruction with that of Congress. Discuss the ways in which the president and Congress tried to check one another in carrying out a reconstruction plan.

87. Have a symposium in which students consider the problems facing the newly freed slave as well as the attempts to adjust him to his new role in society.

88. Have a student read Booker T. Washington's *Up From Slavery* and in a written report, compare it with other firsthand accounts of the Negro in the South during Reconstruction.

89. Have a student give an oral report on the struggle over ratification of the Fourteenth Amendment. Suggest he include the 1866 congressional elections.

90. Discuss the motives of the Radicals in seeking Johnson's removal; then show the film of Johnson's impeachment. As a sequel to the movie, discuss the ways in which Congress attempted to control the Court in this era.

91. Have a student report on the role of the Ku Klux Klan during Reconstruction. Follow the report with a discussion of other means which the whites used to return to political control.

92. Have a student report on the disputed election of 1876 or on the South Carolina election of the same year.

93. Suggest that a student prepare a series of cartoons representing different viewpoints on the election of 1876.

94. Have a student prepare a graph on cotton exports in 1860, 1870, 1880, and 1890. Compare the chart with that made in activity 23.

CULMINATING ACTIVITIES

95. Have a summarizing discussion comparing conditions in 1880 with those in 1850 to see if the outcomes of the war had solved the problems giving rise to it. For example, compare economic and political balance between regions, status of the Negro in prewar and postwar days, and the effect of the war on acceptance of the Constitution as the supreme law of the land.

96. To review the time framework for this period, have a discussion based upon the student made charts, graphs, and maps. Use 1860 as an illustrative pivotal date. Demonstrate differences before and after the date for certain economic phenomena which helped shape political events (for example, railroad construction, settlement of the west, industrial development, cotton production, wheat production, immigration). Using the same date, point out the relationship of events occurring throughout the world (for example, unification movement in Italy and Germany as compared with nationalist movement in the United States; the freeing of the serfs in Russia as compared with the rising democratic thought in the United States).

97. Have students interview Southerners and report on their analysis of the present-day attitude toward Congressional reconstruction.

98. Have a student prepare a map showing patterns of farm ownership in the South today. Ask the student to explain his findings to the class.

99. Have a student analyze the last four presidential elections and give a report on: (1) the strength of the Democratic party in the Southern states, and (2) the areas of decided Republican power. Discuss the findings and relate them to the Civil War and Reconstruction period.

100. Discuss current news articles which show the problems of racial attitudes and segregation in the United States today. Have a student prepare a map showing the density of Negro population throughout the nation today. Have another student report on the percentage of Negroes voting in the South. Ask for volunteers to form a follow-up committee to bring current news related to this unit to the attention of the class during the remainder of the year.

101. Give a unit test. Readminister the pretest on evaluating sources, or give a similar test. Discuss the results.

APPENDIX E

A Guide for Constructing Mini-Courses*

The mini-course is an attempt to recognize the importance of individual study and personalized instructional emphasis. The high-school communication curriculum must be relevant and responsive to the changing needs and interests of students today. As one educator stated, "It provides the opportunity for students to 'open doors,' to explore and evaluate areas apart from the more prosaic demands of the classic curriculum."

The following general guidelines are based upon the authors' own personal involvement with the construction and application of mini-courses over the past three years and their exposure to effective mini-courses as developed in other educational institutions.[1] The one thematic point to stress in the construction of any mini-course is student involvement with pedagogical responsibility. Effective mini-courses are characterized by[2]:

1. Clearly stated objectives (usually behavioral objectives).
2. Objectives written by a professional (teacher, mini-course author, or instructional team) rather than by students.
3. Utilization of a variety of instructional strategies and learning tasks with 90% or more of the activities having been developed by a professional (teacher, course author, or instructional team), rather than by students.
4. Requirement of the completion of certain specified learning activities while allowing the student to select from the remaining activities those he wishes to use to fulfill the total number of activities to be completed for the course.
5. Clearly specified evaluation procedures.

The above characteristics reflect the COSEF instructional model approach to education as outlined by Brooks and Friedrich: Capabilities, Objectives, Strategy, Evaluation, and Feedback.[3]

INITIAL PROCEDURES

COURSE PARAMETERS

It is necessary for the course designer (or team) to give careful thought to what the course will be about, to what areas the course will and will *not* cover. It is a mini-

*William D. Brooks and Robert A. Vogel. Department of Communication, Purdue University. November 1972.

course, an abbreviated course *in scope*, but not an abbreviated course *in depth*. One is often used to thinking in terms of a semester or even a year course. Now one must think in terms of a shorter period of time. Consequently, *a* topic must be selected and careful attention given to boundaries beyond which this course is not planned to go.

LEVEL OF COURSE

There can be considerable differences between high school seniors and ninth graders in terms of their entering behaviors and capabilities. The same topic area can be used for both (or for third graders, first graders, or college students), but the objectives, learning strategies, and evaluative criteria would vary considerably in their complexity and sophistication. You should discuss your decisions relative to objectives, strategies, etc. with other teachers and, when there is time and opportunity, test the materials with the same level of students.

RESOURCE MATERIALS AND PERSONS

When one is trying to devise exciting and effective instructional strategies for an entire course (especially a mini-course), two heads or even three or four heads are better than one. It will be helpful to the team or individual course author to have located and made arrangements to have access occasionally to resource materials and persons.

THE STUDENT'S COPY OF THE COURSE

TITLE

The course should have an accurate, attractive, and compelling title. The key is "keep it simple."

INTRODUCTION

The course should begin with a clear, concise statement of why the student should take the course—a persuasive rationale. This rationale should be limited to two or three paragraphs and utilize the best psychological principles of persuasion (place yourself in the student's position).

COURSE OBJECTIVES

A list of instructional objectives should follow the rationale. They *may* be "informational" or "Magarian" as to type, but the *terminal behavior*(s) constituting the objective of the study must be clearly identified.[4]

COURSE OUTLINE

This need not be a detailed outline but rather a general over view, attractively presented, giving the student an idea of the major topics to be covered in the course. It should be limited to one page.

INSTRUCTIONS

This section should contain guidance for the student concerning the "mechanics" of the course, i.e., how he should take the course (Should he follow activities in order? Are there necessary books or other resources he should have *before* beginning the course? Where would he get them?) etc.

PRE-TEST

The pre-test should serve as a diagnostic measure assessing the entering behavior of the student. In addition it serves as a motivating and informative device for the student, i.e., it lets him know what he does or does not know and serves as a preview of the content to be covered in the course itself.

LEARNING ACTIVITIES

1. The projects used should be of a *wide variety, high interest,* and utilize the best strategies and principles of learning available.[5] Do not hesitate to vary the type of activities throughout the mini-course, i.e., games, role-playing, reading, writing solutions to problems, analyzing case studies, providing programmed pages, class discussion, real world application, viewing films, television, video-tapes, and listening to tapes and records. *Remember*, before the learner proceeds on to the "more enjoyable activities," he should have been first acquainted with those basic cognitive skills at the knowledge level pertaining to that particular topic.

2. Instructions in regard to *optional* and *required* activities as well as other general instructions to each section can be typed in caps. The activities (you may choose to use the word projects or assignments rather than activities) should be numbered sequentially. They should be *complete* so that the learner knows clearly and precisely what he or she is to do. A box ☐ should be drawn by each numbered project. Instructions should direct the learner to check-off each project when it is completed by placing an X in the appropriate box.

3. The procedure throughout any one section should be: first, the presentation of necessary cognitive information; second, the learning activity; third, verification or evaluation (depending upon the nature of the particular section, this may be optional). Typically, however, review questions, performance demonstrations, papers, and other products will be clearly called for in the sequence of activities.

4. *Not all* materials the learner will use must be in the mini-course packet. However, *all* directions and activities *must* be in the mini-course.

EVALUATION: MASTERY EXAM

Clear provisions for means of evaluating the learning must be included, but tests, etc. must be "torn-out" by the teacher before the student receives the mini-course, or prepared as materials that are not fastened in the mini-course. There are numerous evaluation techniques and sources of data (teacher, self, peer—oral, written, tests or other products) available.[6] *Do not hesitate to be innovative in your evaluative techniques*, but measurement procedures and criteria should be clearly identified to the learner. They should be valid, reliable, and functionally appropriate.

RESOURCES

This section consists of annotated bibliography directing the student to present required sources and future enrichment activities.

ADDITIONAL SUGGESTIONS

1. Depending upon the organization of the high school curriculum, the mini-course could be designed from 5 to 20 hours (one to four weeks). The concise course, however should be completed by the high school student in no more than *12 hours* of work, i.e., 3 weeks or 15 fifty-minute class periods. NOTE: No TIME schedule should be identified for the learner! Any individual learner, for example, may complete the course in 5 hours or less, or take 20 hours or more.

2. Although the mini-course as described here is an individualized learning strategy, it may *require* classroom activities, conferences with the teacher, or other situations involving interacting with other persons. In sum, the learning activities are designed to allow the instructor a latitude of involvement in the learning process.

3. Be realistic in the assignments, i.e., do not "bog" the learner down with heavy reading and paper assignments. Remember the time limit and place yourself in the learner's position.

4. Depending upon accessibility and other logistical factors, the mini-course designer may wish to paraphrase or include the necessary cognitive material; or may wish to cross-reference to other resources. In addition, all work (written assignments) could be completed within the booklet itself—with tear away sheets provided.

INSTRUCTOR'S COPY OF THE MINI-COURSE

The teacher is very much a part of mini-course instruction whether it is an individualized or a group approach that is used. Only the teacher is in a position to manage the learning system by monitoring the process and influencing the learning outcome by explaining, motivating, evaluating, supplying additional information, providing practice, etc.—in short, by responding to whatever factors or needs that require attention. It is essential that a separate instructor's copy of the mini-course be constructed. We advocate the use of the student's copy with the instructor aids, cues, lectures, materials, test keys, etc. added in the student's copy at the appropriate places throughout the course.

INSTRUCTIONS

This section should contain information describing how the course is implemented and other useful data. For example[7]:

1. The course is arranged so that one learning activity leads to another. The arrangement of the course might be viewed in the following format: cognitive information, activity, and evaluation.

2. The learning activities are designed to allow the instructor a latitude of involvement in the learning process. For example, in lieu of a written exercise the instructor might want to introduce a lecture and/or class discussion.

3. The course is designed to cover eight/fifty minute periods and one period for the mastery exam. The outside assignments break down as follows: Reading—3 hrs; TV viewing—3 hrs.

COURSE OBJECTIVES

Same as student's copy.

COURSE OUTLINE

Same as student's copy.

PRE-TEST

Same as student's copy, except that the correct answers are provided.

LEARNING ACTIVITIES

A rationale should be provided for each of the activities along with supplementary material where it may prove useful. It is important that all answers or guides to correct answers be included for each activity.

EVALUATION

This section should include the appropriate mastery test along with the correct answers. If performance skills (speeches, discussion, interviews, etc.) are included in final evaluation procedures, criteria should be identified.

RESOURCES

This section should consist of a complete annotated bibliography directing the teacher to the most useful sources, cross-referenced material, and future enrichment activities. This section should go beyond what is provided in the student's course copy.

FORM FOR EVALUATING MINI-COURSES

Author _____ Title of Course _____

	Low				High
1. How valuable and worthwhile is the topic of this course?	1	2	3	4	5
2. Are the objectives stated clearly?	1	2	3	4	5
3. How valuable and worthwhile are the objectives?	1	2	3	4	5
4. Is there a good variety and mix of instructional strategies?	1	2	3	4	5
5. Do the learning strategies require the student to be active?	1	2	3	4	5
6. Do the learning activities possess high interest for students?	1	2	3	4	5
7. How adequate is the pre-test?	1	2	3	4	5
8. How adequate are the post-tests?	1	2	3	4	5
9. Is provision made for evaluation and feedback throughout the course?	1	2	3	4	5
10. Is provision made for confirmation and reinforcement of learning?	1	2	3	4	5
11. Is the learning package attractive in its physical appearance?	1	2	3	4	5
12. Does the package include audio-tapes, slides, or film, and how good are these materials?	1	2	3	4	5
13. How valuable is the instructor's package?	1	2	3	4	5
14. Is the course of proper length? (5 to 15 hours)	1	2	3	4	5
15. Do the resources at the end of the course, provide for a wide sampling of materials available?	1	2	3	4	5
16. Overall, I rate this mini-course as:	1	2	3	4	5
	Total Points				

Remarks

Notes

1. See William D. Brooks, "Innovative Instructional Strategies For Speech Communication," *Today's Speech*, XX (Fall 1972), pp. 39–47.

2. *Ibid.*

3. William D. Brooks and Gustav Friedrich, *Teaching Speech Communication in the Secondary School* (Dubuque, Iowa: Wm. C. Brown Publishers, 1972), pp. 10–11.

4. See for example Brooks and Friedrich, *op. cit.*, Chapter 2; or Robert J. Kibler,

Larry L. Barker, and David T. Miles, *Behavioral Objectives and Instruction* (Boston, Allyn and Bacon, Inc., 1970).

5. For examples of strategies see Brooks and Friedrich, *op. cit.*, Chapter 4.

6. *Ibid*, Chapters 7 and 8.

7. Abstracted in part from Robert A. Vogel, "The Mass Media and Their Message" (mimeographed, Purdue University, Department of Communication, 1972).

Checklists for District and Building Library Policy and Routine Manual Inclusion

FOR THE DISTRICT LIBRARY MEDIA PROGRAM

If the school district does not endorse a K–12 unified library program, all items included in this checklist should be incorporated in the manual for the building library media center.

1. District educational program
   Philosophy
   Goals
   Objectives
   Aims
   Standards
2. District library program
   Philosophy
   Goals
   Objectives
   History of district library program
   Long-range library development plan
   District Instructional Materials Center
Address	Services
Staff	Holdings

   Building libraries
Addresses	Services
Staff	Holdings
3. State library recommendations
   Standards
   Mandates
4. Library curricular support program
   Teacher-librarian planning procedures
   Scheduling procedures
   Class, group, and individual student guidance program

Pilot studies
5. Media selection policies and procedures
    Rationale
    School Library Bill of Rights
    Criteria for media selection
    Question media
    Question media report form
6. Budgeting procedures
    Allocation formula
    Print media
    Nonprint media
    Equipment
    Supplies
7. Centralized technical services
    Ordering procedures
        Forms used
        On-approval routines
    Processing procedures
        Options
8. Library staff organization
    Coordinator of library service
        Job description
        Address and phone number
    Head of secondary library team
        Job description
        Address and phone number
    Head of elementary library team
        Job description
        Address and phone number
    Staff meetings
        Purpose
        Schedule
    Staff cooperation
        Team enterprise
        Pooled competencies
9. Inventory and weeding procedures

FOR THE BUILDING LIBRARY MEDIA CENTER

This manual is to be used in conjunction with the manual for the district library media program.

1. School calendar
2. Daily schedule
3. Bus schedule

4. Fire drill and emergency regulations
5. Faculty list
    Name
    Subjects taught
    Sections taught
    Homeroom number
    Free periods
6. Administrative staff
    Names
    Office location
7. Student list
    Name
    Homeroom number
    Library card number
    Achievement test scores
    Health and physical disabilities
8. Faculty committees
9. Student library assistants
    Training handbook
    How chosen?
    Contract form
    Probation regulations
    Grade average required
    Current student assistant list

Name	Special assignments
Homeroom	Appraisal of service
Free periods	

10. Library secretarial staff regulations
    Working hours
    Lunch period
    Free time
    Sick leave
    Vacation
    Personal days
    Emergency days
    Salary schedule
11. Fine procedures
    Policy statement

Lost media	Damaged media
Overdue media	Accumulated infractions

    Forms used
      Types
    Bookkeeping routines

Use of fines
12. Media ordering and processing routines
     Current budget allocation with running total
     Checklist of individual library practices
     Color coding index
     Forms used
     Inventory record
13. Student interest profiles
     Interest inventory
     When given?
     How administered?
     Individual student interest profiles

A Faculty Self-Study of the Elementary School Library Media Center*

This guide will help elementary school faculties begin a cycle of evaluation, revision, implementation and change which can coincide with other evaluation cycles, such as EQA testing or long-range planning, if desired. The processes described in the general procedures section are suggestions; each school or district should modify the procedures to accommodate its own unique situation.

This document is generally cognitive in nature because knowledge with understanding is still a primary reason for basic education. Attempts to "open" or humanize education as well as to involve the community in the schools, however, must also be considered in any self-study. This guide reflects attempts by including (1) a special section on the evaluation of experimental organizational, instructional and special subject programs, (2) items in all sections on affective education, individualizing instruction and using discovery, inquiry and exploration techniques with children and (3) comprehensive sections which examine the entire school program from different viewpoints. The open-ended commendations and recommendations summaries allow all participants to place proper emphasis on what each considers the most important findings of the study.

SUGGESTIONS FOR MARKING

The comprehensive study areas are divided into various categories, while the subject study areas are generally divided into three categories: content concepts, instruction and equipment and materials. The same marking system is used throughout the guide, though it is applied differently in some areas.

Possible markings have been placed in columns to the left of the items.

*The Pennsylvania Guide for School Library Media Specialists, ed. by Shirley A. Pittman (Pittsburgh, Pa.: Pennsylvania School Librarians Association, 1978), Appendix I-2. This guide is available from the editor at the cost of $5.50. Address: 186 McIntyre Rd., Pittsburgh, Pa. 15237, tel. 412-366-2071.

Each item should be marked with a check (√) or (x) in the column which appropriately indicates a faculty member's opinion.

Suggested criteria for the markings are:

O   In the opinion of the committee member the behaviors or circumstances described by this item are achieved in an *outstanding* manner in relation to the stated objectives of the school. O does not imply perfection but a consistently high level of effectiveness.

S   In the opinion of the committee member the behaviors or circumstances described by this item are achieved in a *satisfactory* manner in relation to the stated objectives of the school. S indicates an adequate level of effectiveness.

I   In the opinion of the committee member the behaviors or circumstances described by this item are achieved in an unsatisfactory manner in relation to the stated objectives of the school and are in *need of improvement.*

In addition to these qualitative markings, columns headed Y and N are not included so that those items which do not seem to lend themselves to qualitative marks can be checked "Yes" or "No." THESE COLUMNS SHOULD BE USED SPARINGLY; SINCERE ATTEMPTS SHOULD BE MADE TO EVALUATE AS MANY ITEMS QUALITATIVELY AS IS POSSIBLE. They can be used, however, when an item is *missing* from the school's curriculum or when an item is *not applicable* to the school's situation; in such instances the "No" column should be checked and then the *"Comments" column should be used* to record the member's justifications for inclusion in or continued exclusion from the curriculum. They can also be used for very obvious "yes" and "no" items and for equipment and other lists if desired. Again, the qualitative marks should be used as a rule.

LIBRARY/MEDIA SERVICES

The instructional program of the school is supported by a school library media center which is a vital, adaptable, constantly growing part of the school. To become educationally effective and significant it must be planned, developed and operated as an integral component of the overall educational philosophy of the school with full administrative support. It serves as a center for instructional materials (book, nonbook and related equipment) selected and organized by the staff and made readily accessible to aid faculty and students to achieve the objectives of the school. The constant aim of today's library media program is to stimulate each student to realize the optimum potential as a learner, as a citizen and as a human being. The library media center fulfills this purpose by providing resources for teaching and learning, supporting the curriculum and providing functional facilities and materials for students and staff.*

---

*This evaluation should be used in conjunction with *The Pennsylvania Guide for School Library Media Specialists* published by the Pennsylvania School Librarians Association, 1978.

O/S/I/Y/N	PHILOSOPHY	COMMENTS

1. There is a written philosophy of education in the school district.
2. The philosophy of the school district defines and supports the library media concepts.
3. The written philosophy of the library media center supports the district philosophy.

Evidence of Administrative Commitment
1. There is a planned continuous inservice program for staff growth in the use of media.
2. Library media personnel are included in planning and implementing the curriculum.
3. There is a library media budget which meets state standards for materials and proper staffing.
4. The school organization allows the free flow of students to the center throughout the school day.
5. There is a regularly scheduled planning and preparation time for the library media specialist (hereafter referred to as "the specialist").

Staff
1. Each library media center is staffed with a full-time certified professional for every 350 students.
2. If two or more professional specialists are employed in the same school, one is designated head with the responsibility for making final library media center decisions.
3. A qualified library media coordinator or supervisor with designated duties is employed

when there are two or more centers in the district.

4. At least one full-time adult clerk typist/library aid is employed to assist the specialist.
5. At least one additional trained professional or paraprofessional adult is employed to procure and maintain audiovisual equipment.
6. Adult volunteer help, when used, is thoroughly trained and carefully supervised.

Services and Activities

1. The library/media professional staff supports the teaching program in the classroom and in the library media center for every student in the school program.
2. The professional staff is conversant with all aspects of the educational program such as courses of study, textbooks, manuals, workbooks, resource units, teacher-made study guides and plans, pilot projects and culminating activities.
3. The professional staff is aware of individual student needs, interests, goals, abilities and progress rates.
4. The professional staff keeps abreast of current educational trends, methods, materials and research.
5. The professional staff is actively involved in curriculum planning, revision and implementation.
6. The professional staff participates in team and faculty meetings.
7. The professional staff provides relevant materials for

the professional growth of the faculty.

8. The staff establishes routines and procedures for selecting, ordering, processing, organizing, circulating and evaluating materials.

9. The staff maintains good cooperative relations with both academic and community libraries through conferences, visits and reports.

10. The staff correlates the building library media center program with the district library media center program.

11. The staff trains, schedules and supervises clerical, technical and student aides.

12. The staff prepares and administers the library media center materials budget.

13. The staff evaluates the building library media center program, services and materials in terms of adequacy in meeting curricular needs, state recommendations and national standards.

14. The staff works closely with school staff and students to promote the effective use of the library media center and its facilities.

15. The staff engages in purposeful instruction of students as individuals or in small groups in library and research skills (including the operation of necessary hardware) evolving from the needs of the instructional program as noted in the content areas section.

16. The staff provides service, guidance and resources which will individualize and per-

sonalize teaching and learning.

17. The staff participates actively in professional associations on the local, regional, state and national level.

18. The staff maintains a procedure manual which is user-oriented rather than institution-oriented.

19. The staff supervises clerical routines necessary for the effective use of the library media center.

20. The staff displays creative work of students (and others) in conjunction with ongoing educational programs.

21. The staff prepares collections and exhibits of materials for short or long term classroom loan.

22. The staff encourages student help to provide learning opportunities in numerous facets of the center's services.

Budget

1. The budget is planned cooperatively by the administrators and library media center staff on the basis of need priority.

2. Funds allotted for book and nonbook materials meet or surpass state recommendations.

3. Library media center materials may be purchased as needed at any time throughout the school year.

4. There is a separate allotment for professional materials for school staff.

5. Instructional materials are ordered through the library media center.

6. A specific allotment is made to purchase supplies, to repair and replace equipment and to rent films.

Materials

1. The materials collection meets or surpasses state recommendations.
2. Library media center acquisitions are made on the basis of prepurchase examination.
3. Faculty and students are involved in selection and evaluation of the educational media.
4. The materials collection includes a wide variety of media: book, nonbook and periodicals.
5. The materials collection is well chosen as to reading level, curriculum relevance and reader interest.
6. The materials collection is kept current and/or relevant.
7. The materials collection is maintained in usable, retrievable conditions.
8. All book and nonbook materials are cataloged and processed for easy assessibility to media center users.
9. The listening/viewing equipment is appropriate to the media collection.
10. Provision is made for the acquisition and circulation of a wide variety of professional materials, including periodicals, for the staff.
11. The collection includes materials which show members of all races and of both sexes in favorable, nonstereotypical roles.
12. The Pennsylvania Department of Education's Division of School Libraries is con-

sulted and use is made of the division's services and resources.

Facility

1. The library media center is in a central location convenient to students and teachers with accessible lavatories, drinking fountains and with easy access to independent outside exit.

2. The library media center meets state recommendations for space, lighting, ventilation and acoustics.

3. The library media suite is functionally adaptable to meet the needs simultaneously of large or small groups, individuals or full classes.

4. The library media center is carpeted.

5. The facility has a librarian's/ media specialist's office/ workroom with glass vision panels for supervision; supervision of entire facility is a priority.

6. Work areas, including a sink, for technical processing; previewing, preparation and repairing of materials are available in the library media center.

7. There is sufficient room in the facility for storytelling activity concurrent with classroom research and individual use of the center.

8. A special room convenient to the library media center is used to house the professional collection for the faculty.

9. There is provision for creative displays and/or exhibits.

10. There are numerous electrical outlets in suitable locations

O/S/I/Y/N	FACILITY	COMMENTS

for convenient and safe use of audio-visual equipment.

11. The furniture is suitable to the student population and the educational program.
12. A full service telephone is provided in the library media center.
13. There is provision for future expansion.
14. There is provision for the receipt of radio programs and ITV/ETV whether through a broadcasting council or a regional 2500MHz system.
15. Preparation has been made for the use of cable television.

Policies
1. A board-approved written materials selection policy for the district is in effect.
2. A manual for policies and procedures for the operation of the library media center is available which includes a detailed description of procedures concerning the acquisition, processing, circulation and maintenance of media and equipment.
3. Long-range plans for the improvement of the quality of the collection and of the facility and services have been developed.
4. Administrators, teachers and students assist the library media center staff in formulating policies.
5. Policies are evaluated annually.

Media Evaluation Guidelines

I. *BOOKLIST* CRITERIA FOR SELECTION OF MATERIAL*

Each item recommended for review in *The Booklist* should meet the following criteria which have been grouped below.

GENERAL CRITERIA

1. Is the item oriented to the curriculum? The item should be designed to provide sources of information and activities that relate to the objectives of the curriculum.

2. Does the item have appeal and interest? The interest level of the material should be geared to the age level of the curriculum experience.

3. Is the item worth the money? In relation to the total budget and the total collection the item should be worth the investment.

4. Is the item readily available? The item should be distributed on a nationwide basis and easily accessible in all areas of the country.

5. Is the packaging easily manipulated and durable? Packages should afford easy storage of materials and should be constructed of durable materials.

SUPER 8MM SINGLE CONCEPT FILMS

CONTENT

1. Does the film truly contain a single concept? The film should be limited to one idea, action or conceptual portion of a topic.

2. Is the information accurate and authoritative? The information should avoid unnecessary generalities; individual facts in visual and captioned form should be correct.

3. Is the information authentic?

4. Is the information up-to-date? The information should be current and include the latest developments.

ORGANIZATION AND FORMAT

1. Is the material filmed in a logical sequence? A continuity of information and concepts should be maintained to produce a completed message.

*The Booklist (Chicago: American Library Association). A semimonthly guide to book and nonbook media.

2. Are the frames well composed? The principles of artistic balance and design should have been observed in the photographing of the subject.

3. Are the captions easy to read? The style of lettering should be clean and the contrast of lettering and background distinct.

4. Is the time adequate for the concept?

USE

1. Is the single concept film an effective treatment for the curricular use? The medium should be appropriate to the message.

2. Does the film attract and hold the interest of students?

TECHNICAL QUALITIES

1. Are the visual qualities of exposure, focus and color adequate?

2. Are graphics used effectively? Graphic forms of illustration should not replace photographs when the real item would be more effective.

3. Is the cartridge and its parts of durable construction?

4. Does the cartridge contain a film lubricant for protection during repetitive showings? Since in the cartridge, film rides over film in a continuous loop, a lubricant helps to prevent scratching and aids smooth operation of the film and the cartridge.

OTHER

1. Are guides for students and teachers well written and useful?

2. Are the cartridge and its container clearly labeled for easy identification?

FILMSTRIPS

CONTENT

1. Is the scope of the material adequate? The topic should be covered in such a manner to convey a complete concept or understanding.

2. Is the information accurate and authoritative? The information should avoid unnecessary generalities; individual facts in visual and captioned form should be correct.

3. Is the information authentic? The material should avoid extreme bias or mis-leading emphasis. The quaint and unusual should be included only in relation to the total concept.

4. Is the information up-to-date? The information should be current and include the latest developments.

ORGANIZATION AND FORMAT

1. Are the frames arranged in a logical sequence? A continuity of information and concepts should be maintained to produce a completed message.

2. Are the frames well composed? The principles of artistic balance and design should have been observed in the photographing of the subject.

3. Are the captions easy to read? The style of lettering should be clean and the contrast of lettering and background distinct.

4. Is the number of concepts included appropriate to the grade level for which the material is intended?

USE

1. Is the filmstrip form an effective treatment for curricular use? The medium should be appropriate to the message.
2. Does the filmstrip attract and hold the interest of students?

TECHNICAL QUALITIES

1. Are the visual qualities of exposure, focus and color adequate?
2. Are graphics used effectively? Graphic forms of illustration should not replace photographs when the real item would be more effective.
3. Are the audio qualities of a sound filmstrip adequate? The sound reproduction should be clear and easily understood.
4. Does the narrator have a pleasing voice and well-timed delivery?
5. Are special effects used effectively? Background music and sound effects should not overwhelm the script and the editing of the narration should be clean.

OTHER

1. Are guides and other accompanying materials well done and useful?

GLOBES

CONTENT

1. Is the scope of the information adequate? The topic should be covered in such a manner to convey a complete concept or understanding.
2. Is the information up-to-date? The information should be current and include latest developments.
3. Is the information clearly portrayed on the globe?

ORGANIZATION AND FORMAT

1. Is a scale indicator included?
2. Are legends and indexes clearly indicated?
3. Are color contrasts used effectively to portray dimension and topography?
4. Is the surface finish suitable for marking and easy erasure?

USE

1. Is the print of a readable size and not crowded?

TECHNICAL QUALITIES

1. Is the mounting designed for flexible use?
2. Are the base and the globe made of durable materials?
3. Has the lamination of the gores been carefully done to achieve registration?
4. Are relief and contour construction durable?

STUDY PRINTS/ART PRINTS

CONTENT

1. Is the scope of the study print set adequate?
2. Is the information accurate and authoritative? The information should avoid unnecessary generalities; individual facts in visual and captioned form should be correct.

3. Is the information authentic? The material should avoid extreme bias or misleading emphasis. The quaint and unusual should be included only in relation to the total concept.

4. Is the information up-to-date? The information should be current and include the latest developments.

5. Is the integrity of the original item preserved? The reproduction of works of art should be as close to the original in color, texture, and size as technical possibilities will permit.

ORGANIZATION AND FORMAT

1. Are photographs or graphics well composed? The principles of artistic balance and design should have been observed in the photographing of the subject.

2. Is the subject of the print portrayed in some easily recognized ratio or scale of the original?

3. Is the subject of the print presented logically and clearly?

USE

1. Will the print have a broad use in the curriculum?

2. Is the set of prints easy to use and manipulate?

3. Does the print attract and hold the interest of students?

4. Is the print form an effective treatment for curricular use? The medium should be appropriate to the message.

5. Do the captions distract from the usefulness of the print?

6. Is the printed informational text accurate and does it extend the use of the print?

TECHNICAL QUALITIES

1. Are the visual qualities of exposure, focus and color adequate?

2. Are graphics used effectively? Graphic forms of illustration should not replace photographs when the real item would be more effective.

3. Is the print reproduced on a durable mounting?

4. Does the print have a durable surface finish?

5. Are there provisions for displaying the print easily and without damage to it?

RECORDINGS

CONTENT

1. Is the scope of the material adequate? The topic should be covered in such a manner to convey a complete concept or understanding.

2. Is the information accurate and authoritative? The information should avoid unnecessary generalities; individual facts in visual and captioned form should be correct.

3. Is the information authentic? The material should avoid extreme bias or misleading emphasis. The quaint and unusual should be included only in relation to the total concept.

4. Is the information up-to-date? The information should be current and include the latest developments.

5. Is the integrity of the original work preserved? The reading or dramatization of an original book, poetry, or play should portray the original intent of the author. Abridgements and adaptations should also preserve the original flavor of the work.

ORGANIZATION AND FORMAT

1. Is the material recorded in a logical sequence? A continuity of information and concepts should be maintained to produce a completed message.
2. Is the number of concepts included appropriate to the grade level for which the material is intended?

USE

1. Is the recording an effective treatment for curricular use? The medium should be appropriate to the message.
2. Does the recording attract and hold the interest of students?
3. Is the length of the recording appropriate to the attention span of the grade level for which it is intended?
4. Does the recording have an adequate introduction to identify the material?

TECHNICAL QUALITIES

1. Is the sound reproduction clear and intelligible?
2. Does the narrator have a pleasing voice and well-timed delivery?
3. Are special effects used effectively? Background music and sound effects should not overwhelm the script and editing of the narration should be clean.
4. Is the recording reproduced on durable material?

OTHER

1. Are accompanying guides, scripts, or texts adequate?
2. Is there adequate identification of item with packaging?

SLIDES—2 × 2

CONTENT

1. Is the scope of the material adequate? The topic should be covered in such a manner to convey a complete concept or understanding.
2. Is the information accurate and authoritative? The information should avoid unnecessary generalities; individual facts in visual and captioned form should be correct.
3. Is the information authentic? The material should avoid extreme bias or misleading emphasis. The quaint and unusual should be included only in relation to the total concept.
4. Is the information up-to-date? The information should be current and include the latest developments.

ORGANIZATION AND FORMAT

1. Are the slides arranged in a logical sequence? A continuity of information and concepts should be maintained to produce a completed message.
2. Are the slides well composed? The principles of artistic balance and design should have been observed in the photographing of the subject.
3. If captions are used, are they easy to read?

USE

1. Is the slide form an effective treatment for curricular use? The medium should be appropriate to the message.
2. Does the slide set attract and hold the interest of students?

TECHNICAL QUALITIES

1. Are the visual qualities of exposure, focus and color adequate?
2. Are graphics used effectively? Graphic forms of illustration should not replace photographs when the real item would be more effective.
3. Is the mount of a durable material?
4. Will the mount fit easily in the magazines of the common projectors?
5. Is the slide of a durable, easily maintained material? Glass and plastic slides are easier to clean of fingerprints and dust.

OTHER

1. Is the packaging protective to the slides and easy to manipulate?
2. Are guides and other accompanying materials well done and useful?

Transparencies

CONTENT

1. Is the scope of the material adequate? The topic should be covered in such a manner to convey a complete concept or understanding.
2. Is the information accurate and authoritative? The information should avoid unnecessary generalities; individual facts in visual and captioned form should be correct.
3. Is the information authentic? The material should avoid extreme bias or misleading emphasis. The quaint and unusual should be included only in relation to the total concept.
4. Is the information up-to-date? The information should be current and include latest developments.
5. Is clarity of presentation preserved? Layout should be uncluttered and concentrate on a single idea.

ORGANIZATION AND FORMAT

1. Are the transparencies easy to manipulate? The mounting device should be uncomplicated and durable.
2. Are multiple overlays clearly labeled for correct sequencing?
3. Are the cells arranged in a logical sequence? A continuity of information and concepts should be maintained to produce a completed message.
4. Are the cells well composed? The principles of artistic balance and design should have been observed in the arrangement of the subject information.
5. Is lettering readable and well spaced for maximum impact?
6. Are colors attractive?
7. Has color control been maintained from cell to cell? Density and brightness should be consistent throughout the set and its overlays.

USE

1. Is the transparency form an effective treatment for curricular use? The medium should be appropriate to the message.

2. Does the transparency attract and hold the interest of students?

3. Is there variety of design and color within the cells of a set of transparencies?

TECHNICAL QUALITIES

1. Are hinges and fastenings durable?

2. Are overlays in correct registration?

3. Are all materials of a durable quality?

4. Is the translucency of colors bright and clear?

OTHER

1. Is labeling and identification adequate?

2. Are guides and other accompanying materials well done and useful?

II. STUDENT BOOK EVALUATION GUIDE

Evaluator _____ Date of evaluation _____

Title _____ Author _____

Publisher _____ Copyright date _____

Type of book (please check) Fiction _____ Nonfiction _____

If fiction, what type of story is it?

_____ Adventure	_____ School
_____ Biographical	_____ Science
_____ Animal	_____ Sea
_____ Family	_____ Social problems
_____ Historical	_____ Sports
_____ Mystery	_____ Vocational
_____ Romance	_____ List other type

If nonfiction, what is the subject area?

_____ Art	_____ Plays
_____ Biography	_____ Poetry
_____ Geography	_____ Politics
_____ History	_____ Science
_____ Mathematics	_____ Social Problems
_____ Music	_____ Travel
_____ Myths, Folklore, Legends	_____ List other type

How would you rate this book in regard to the following:

	Excellent	Good	Fair	Poor
Readability	_____	_____	_____	_____
Appearance	_____	_____	_____	_____
Overall evaluation	_____	_____	_____	_____

Note: If you wish to make further comments, please write them on the reverse of this form.

III. EVALUATING TEXTBOOKS: TREATMENT OF MINORITIES*

Title of Book _____

_____
(Name of Evaluator)

Author _____

Publisher _____   Date _____

Key: S—superior; A—acceptable; U—unacceptable; NP—not pertinent

	S	A	U	NP	Page References
1. Includes materials on minorites where relevant	—	—	—	—	_____
2. Reflects respect for personal and cultural differences and the worth and importance of the individual	—	—	—	—	_____
3. Offers factual, realistic, mature treatment	—	—	—	—	_____
4. Gives balanced treatment of past and present	—	—	—	—	_____
5. Presents accurate, pertinent information	—	—	—	—	_____
6. Comes to grips with issues and problems	—	—	—	—	_____
8. Develops concepts of pluralistic society	—	—	—	—	_____
9. Shows cultural diversity in illustrative materials	—	—	—	—	_____
10. Includes cultural diversity in text material	—	—	—	—	_____
11. Emphasizes both positive and negative aspects	—	—	—	—	_____
12. Avoids distortion and bias	—	—	—	—	_____
13. Avoids use of name-calling or emotionally charged words	—	—	—	—	_____
14. Supports generalizations with the specific and the concrete	—	—	—	—	_____
15. Avoids stereotyping	—	—	—	—	_____
16. Aids in building positive attitudes and understandings	—	—	—	—	_____
17. Distinguishes between fact and opinion	—	—	—	—	_____
18. Gives attention to holidays, festivals, religious observances of various minority groups	—	—	—	—	_____
19.	—	—	—	—	_____
20.	—	—	—	—	_____

Summary or
General Estimate: —Superior   —Acceptable   —Unacceptable

Special Comments:

Guidelines for Textbook Selection: The Treatment of Minorities. Harrisburg: Pennsylvania Department of Public Instruction, 1969. p. 6

IV. CHECKLIST: BOOK SELECTION GUIDE*

Author _____ Title_____
Publisher _____ Copyright Date _____ Price _____
Fiction _____ Nonfiction _____ Reference _____ Grade Level ____
Evaluator _____ Recommendation _____
Key: E—excellent; G—good; F—fair; P—poor

PHYSICAL FEATURES	E	G	F	P	Comments
Size: Suitability	___	___	___	___	_____
Binding: Quality	___	___	___	___	_____
Attractiveness	___	___	___	___	_____
Paper: Quality	___	___	___	___	_____
Print: Readability	___	___	___	___	_____
Margins: Adequate	___	___	___	___	_____
Illustrations: Quality	___	___	___	___	_____

CONTENT					
Style	___	___	___	___	_____
Literary quality	___	___	___	___	_____
Organization	___	___	___	___	_____
Presentation	___	___	___	___	_____
Scope	___	___	___	___	_____
Pupil appeal	___	___	___	___	_____

SPECIAL FEATURES					
Table of Contents	___	___	___	___	_____
Index	___	___	___	___	_____
Glossary	___	___	___	___	_____
Maps, Diagrams, Charts	___	___	___	___	_____

POTENTIAL USE

Specific curriculum tie-in _____
Specific reader interest _____
Unique contribution _____

*North Hills School District, Pittsburgh, Pennsylvania 15229.

V. STUDENT GUIDE FOR SELECTING BOOKS TO ENRICH READING UNITS

Student _____ Homeroom _____ Date _____

Title of Reader _____ Title of Unit _____

Title of Selection _____

The title of the book I have read is _____

which was written by _____.

This book is: (Please check to indicate the appropriate type of book.)

_____ Fiction

_____ Nonfiction

I chose to read this particular book because: (Please check the appropriate reason.)

_____ The story in my reader was taken from this book.

_____ This book was similar to the story in my reader.

_____ This book was written by the same author who wrote the story in my reader.

I judge the reading level of this book to be: (Please check the appropriate answer.)

_____ This book is perfect for my reading group.

_____ This book is too difficult for my reading group.

_____ This book is too easy for my reading group.

In judging the reading appeal of this book, I rate it as follows: (Please check the appropriate percentage.)

_____ 100%

_____ 75%

_____ 50%

_____ 25%

_____ 0%

PLEASE USE THE REVERSE SIDE OF THIS FORM FOR ANY COMMENTS YOU WISH TO MAKE ABOUT THIS BOOK.

APPENDIX I

Model School Library Policy Statement

SCHOOL LIBRARY PHILOSOPHY AND POLICY STATEMENT AS ENDORSED BY THE EXLER SCHOOL BOARD*

The Exler School District believing that each American citizen is entitled to a quality, optimum education has designed an educational program which will encourage and enable each student to become intellectually and socially competent, to value moral integrity and personal decency, and to achieve self-understanding and self-realization.

The following objectives provide unity, direction, and guidance in both the design and implementation of the educational program:

1. To provide ample opportunity for each student to build his "house of intellect" commensurate with his mental potential.
2. To provide teaching experiences which will meet uniquely and adequately individual student needs, interests, goals, abilities, and creative potential.
3. To provide learning experiences and teaching guidance which will enable and encourage each student to build a positive set of values.
4. To provide teaching and learning experiences which will enable and encourage each student to understand, to appreciate, and to value his cultural, social, political, and economic heritage as an American, as a world citizen and as a human being.
5. To provide teaching and learning experiences which have been structured as a progressive continuum of related fundamentals from kindergarten through grade twelve.
6. To provide ample opportunity for each student to become conversant with the techniques of critical, analytical, reflective, logical, and creative thinking.

The Exler school libraries function as an integral part of the total educational program. The goal of the school library program is to facilitate and expedite the real-

*The Pennsylvania Guide for School Library Media Specialists, ed. by Shirley A. Pittman (Pittsburgh, Pa.: Pennsylvania School Librarians Association, 1978), Appendix B-1. This guide is available from the editor at the cost of $5.50. Address: 186 McIntyre Rd., Pittsburgh, Pa. 15237, tel. 412-366-2071.

467

ization and attainment of a quality, optimum education by each student. To reach this goal the following objectives give purpose and direction to the library program:

1. To provide an educationally functional and effective library program which will meet adequately the developmental needs of the curriculum and the personal needs, interests, goals, abilities, and creative potential of the students.

2. To provide informed and concerned guidance in the use of library services and resources which will personalize teaching and individualize learning.

3. To provide a planned, purposeful, and educationally significant program which will be integrated appropriately with the classroom teaching and learning program.

4. To provide library resources which will stimulate and promote interest in self-directed knowledge building.

LIBRARY INTEGRATION AND ENRICHMENT PROCEDURE

I. Programming for the purposeful and systematic use of library materials is the shared responsibility of teacher and librarian
    A. Teacher plans with librarian in a scheduled conference to
        1. Determine library contribution to unit development
        2. Determine library contribution to class and individual student achievement
    B. Teacher and librarian design cooperatively a media program to support the anticipated teaching program
        1. Exploring together the developmental needs of the unit
        2. Identifying specific topics, concepts, and skills to be introduced, reinforced, and extended
        3. Identifying specific teaching experiences and activities requiring supporting media
        4. Identifying specific learning experiences and activities requiring supporting media
        5. Identifying special student needs, interests, goals, and abilities requiring media accommodation
        6. Determining class, group, and individual student media usage patterns for knowledge building
        7. Designing a media usage sequence to match
          a. Specific topic, concept, and skill development patterns
          b. Specific teaching goals, experiences, and activities
          c. Specific learning needs, experiences, and activities
    C. Librarian searches for resources to support the teaching plan
        1. Matching materials to specific topic, concept, and skill development needs
        2. Matching materials to specific student needs, interests, goals, and abilities
        3. Relating materials in a usage pattern of logical sequential order
        4. Assembling, grouping, and relating materials
II. Implementing the media program is the shared responsibility of teacher and librarian
    A. Teacher orients his students to the specific contribution library resources are to make to the development of the teaching and/or learning plan

B. Teacher pre-plans with librarian for class, group, or individual student use of the library
C. Librarian serves as teacher
  1. Orienting students to materials of special or unique value
  2. Introducing students to new tools, techniques, or skills essential to building adequacy of understanding
  3. Guiding students in their use, interpretation, extension, association, integration, and evaluation of information
D. Librarian cooperates with classroom teacher
  1. Evaluating effectiveness of student, group, and class use of media
  2. Analyzing educational value of the media pattern and program
  3. Determining program adjustment and modification

POLICIES AND PROCEDURES FOR SELECTING LIBRARY MEDIA

While the legal responsibility for the purchase of all instructional materials is vested in the Exler School Board, the final responsibility for the selection of library materials has been delegated to the school librarians of the district.

The school librarians have been charged with the responsibility of identifying, ordering, and organizing materials which will implement, enrich, and support the educational program of the school and will meet the needs, interest, goals, concerns, and abilities of the individual students.

RATIONALE

The administrative staff of the Exler schools endorses the tenets set forth in the School Library Bill of Rights.

PROCEDURE

All library materials are to be ordered by the coordinator of library service or by librarians delegated this responsibility by the coordinator.

Administrators, supervisors, teachers, and students are to be encouraged to suggest materials to be added to the library collection and to share in evaluating materials being considered for purchase.

Whenever possible, both print and nonprint media are to be examined physically before purchase. If possible, materials should be bought "on approval" and, if judged unsuitable, returned to vendor for credit. Pilot testing of material in a classroom teaching situation is to be employed where class reaction and student use are to be determined.

Centralized ordering and processing of all school library materials are to be provided by the staff of the district instuctional materials center.

The reviewing of books and the evaluating of nonbook materials are to be a team enterprise; librarians and teachers are to share their knowledge in selecting instructional media.

CRITERIA FOR SELECTING MEDIA

1. Educational significance.
2. Need and value to the collection.
3. Reputation and significance of author or producer.
4. Clarity, adequacy, and scope of text or audiovisual presentation.

5. Validity, accuracy, objectivity, up-to-dateness, and appropriateness of text or audiovisual presentation.

6. Organization and presentation of contents.

7. High degree of readability and/or comprehensibility.

8. High degree of potential user appeal.

9. High artistic quality and/or literary style.

10. Quality format.

11. Value commensurate with cost and/or need.

QUESTIONED MEDIA

Review of questioned materials should be treated objectively, unemotionally, and as a routine matter. Criticisms of library books must be submitted in writing to the Superintendent, must be signed, and must include specific information as to author, title, publisher, and definite citation of objection.

A review committee will be appointed by the Superintendent to determine the validity of the objection. Appeals from the decision of the committee may be made through the Superintendent of the Board of Education for final decision.

District Sharing of Library Resources

Each of the Exler school libraries is an integral component of the total district library program and is not an entity in and of itself.

All librarians are guided by the educational philosophy and standards of the district; all are guided by the district library philosophy, objectives, and procedural plan.

Budget funds are allocated on the basis of a district program of uniform excellence and the individual library's role in that program.

Each library collection is considered a segment of the total district library collection. All materials are shared; all materials are made available upon request to any school library in the district.

Elementary Reading Interest Inventory*

Name _____ Grade _____ Date _____

Please help us discover the kind of reading you enjoy so we can buy books which will have special appeal just for you.

Step 1. Read the list carefully.

Step 2. Read the list again and put a line through each type of story you would *not* enjoy reading.

      Example: _____ Adventure

                 _____ American Revolutionary Period

                 _____ ~~Automobiles~~   (This indicates you would *not* enjoy reading a book about automobiles.)

Step 3. Read the list again and check the 5 types you would most enjoy reading.

      Example: _✔_ Baseball   (This indicates that you have selected baseball

                 _____ Basketball   stories to be one of your *five* most enjoyable

                 _____ Boating   types of reading.)

Types of fiction or story books

_____ Adventure	_____ Fairy Tales
_____ American Revolutionary Period	_____ Family Life
_____ Automobiles	_____ Fantasy
_____ Baseball	_____ Fishing
_____ Basketball	_____ Football
_____ Boating	_____ Frontier and Pioneer Life
_____ Camping	_____ Ghosts
_____ Cats	_____ Goblins
_____ Caves	_____ Historical
_____ Civil War Period	_____ Hockey
_____ Colonial Period	_____ Horses
_____ Courage	_____ Humorous
_____ Cowboys	_____ Hunting
_____ Dinosaurs	_____ Indians
_____ Dogs	_____ Interplanetary Travel

*North Hills School District, Pittsburgh, Pennsylvania 15229.

___ Middle Ages	___ Science
___ Minorities	___ Scuba and Skin Diving
___ Mystery and Detective	___ Sea
___ Nurses	___ Survival
___ Orphans	___ Tall Tales
___ Pets	___ Teen-Age
___ Pirates	___ War
___ Prehistoric Period	___ Wild Animals
___ Ranch Life	

Step 4. Please list any other types you would enjoy reading but have not found listed above.

Step 5. Please read the following list of non-fiction or factual books and put a line through any type you would *not* enjoy reading.

Step 6. Please read the list again and check the 5 types you would *most* enjoy reading.

Type of nonfiction or factual books

___ Animals	___ Fishing
___ Aquariums	___ Football
___ Archery	___ Gardening
___ Astronauts	___ Golf
___ Atomic Energy	___ History
___ Automobiles	___ Hockey
___ Aviation	___ Horseback Riding
___ Ballet	___ Horses
___ Baseball	___ Hunting
___ Basketball	___ Ice Skating
___ Biography	___ Indians
___ Biology	___ Jokes and Riddles
___ Boating	___ Knights
___ Bowling	___ Magic
___ Camping	___ Making a Motor
___ Care of Animals	___ Minorities
___ Cats	___ Nature Study
___ Chemistry	___ Nurses
___ Collecting Coins	___ Oceanography
___ Collecting Dolls	___ Painting
___ Collecting Rocks	___ Pets
___ Collecting Seashells	___ Plays
___ Collecting Stamps	___ Poetry
___ Computers	___ Science Experiments
___ Cooking	___ Scuba and Skin Diving
___ Crafts	___ Scouting
___ Dinosaurs	___ Sewing
___ Doctors	___ Skiing
___ Dogs	___ Space Exploration
___ Drawing	___ Submarines
___ Ecology	___ Swimming

_____ Television   _____ Veterinarians
_____ Tennis   _____ War
_____ Training a Dog   _____ Witchcraft

Step 7. Please list any other types you would enjoy reading but have not found listed above.

How to Use ERIC*

INTRODUCTION

Throughout the educational community, today's predominant themes are the acceleration of educational improvement and increased learning opportunities for students. Improved curriculums, new media, and more effective teaching methods are being designed and developed in laboratories, research programs, and classrooms throughout the country. These activities are going on at a rate unprecedented in the history of education.

All this recent and expanding activity has produced much valuable information. This information is contained in documents that have not always reached the people who need them. The purpose of the Educational Resources Information Center—ERIC—is to provide access to this literature.

ERIC is a national information system designed and developed by the U.S. Office of Education, and now supported and operated by the National Institute of Education (NIE), for providing ready access to descriptions of exemplary programs, research and development efforts, and related information that can be used in developing more effective educational programs.

WHAT IS ERIC?

A national information system

A source for obtaining documents on education

A network of decentralized information centers

WHAT DOES ERIC DO?

Collects, screens, organizes, and disseminates reports

Furnishes copies of educational documents at nominal cost

Acts as an archive of educational literature

Prepares interpretative summaries, research reviews, and bibliographies on critical topics in education

Services information centers throughout the country

Answers education information questions

*Educational Resources Information Center, National Institute of Education, Washington, D.C.

ERIC AS A RESOURCE

There are 16 Clearinghouses in the nationwide ERIC network. Each specializes in a different, multidiscipline, educational area. Each searches out pertinent documents—current research findings, project and technical reports, speeches and unpublished manuscripts, books, and professional journal articles. These materials are screened according to ERIC selection criteria, abstracted, and indexed. All of this information is put into the ERIC computer data base and announced in the ERIC reference publications. Through these sources any person interested in education has easy access to reports of innovative programs, conference proceedings, bibliographies, outstanding professional papers, curriculum-related materials, and reports of the most significant efforts in educational research and development, regardless of where they first appeared. It is through these channels that ERIC brings to the community of educators current information and also insures that valuable writings on the subject of education will be permanently stored and that documents which might otherwise be lost to the profession are safeguarded, and continually available.

ERIC CLEARINGHOUSES

The ERIC Clearinghouses have responsibility within the network for acquiring the significant educational literature within their particular areas, selecting the highest quality and most relevant material, processing (i.e., cataloging, indexing, abstracting) the selected items for input to the data base, and also for providing information analysis products and various user services based on the data base.

The exact number of Clearinghouses has fluctuated over time in response to the shifting needs of the educational community. There are currently 16 Clearinghouses. These are listed below, together with full addresses, telephone numbers, and brief scope notes describing the areas they cover.

ERIC CLEARINGHOUSE ON ADULT, CAREER, AND VOCATIONAL EDUCATION. Ohio State University, Center for Vocational Education, 1960 Kenny Rd., Columbus, Ohio 43210, tel. 614-486-3655. Career education, formal and informal at all levels, encompassing attitudes, self-knowledge, decision-making skills, general and occupational knowledge, and specific vocational and occupational skills; adult and continuing education, formal and informal, relating to occupational, family, leisure, citizen, organizational, and retirement roles; vocational and technical education, including new sub-professional fields, industrial arts, and vocational rehabilitation for the handicapped.

ERIC CLEARINGHOUSE ON COUNSELING AND PERSONNEL SERVICES. University of Michigan, School of Education Building, Rm. 2108, Ann Arbor, Mich. 48109, tel. 313-764-9492. Preparation, practice, and supervision of counselors at all educational levels and in all settings; theoretical development of counseling and guidance; use and results of personnel procedures such as testing, interviewing, disseminating, and analyzing such information; group work and case work; nature of pupil, student, and adult characteristics; personnel workers and their relation to career planning, family consultations, and student orientation activities.

ERIC CLEARINGHOUSE ON EARLY CHILDHOOD EDUCATION. University of Illinois, College of Education, 805 W. Pennsylvania Ave., Urbana, Ill. 61801, tel. 217-333-1386. Prenatal factors, parental behavior; the physical, psychological, social, educational, and cultural development of children from birth through the primary grades; educational theory, research, and practice related to the development of young children.

ERIC CLEARINGHOUSE ON EDUCATIONAL MANAGEMENT. University of Oregon, Eugene, Oreg. 97403, tel. 503-686-5043. Leadership, management, and structure of public and private educational organizations; practice and theory of administration; preservice and inservice preparation of administrators, tasks, and processes of administration; methods and varieties of organization, organizational change, and social context of the organization. Sites, buildings, and equipment for education; planning, financing, constructing, renovating, equipping, maintaining, operating, insuring, utilizing, and evaluating educational facilities.

ERIC CLEARINGHOUSE ON HANDICAPPED AND GIFTED CHILDREN. Council for Exceptional Children, 1920 Association Dr., Reston, Va. 22091, tel. 703-620-3660. Aurally handicapped, visually handicapped, mentally handicapped, physically handicapped, emotionally disturbed, speech handicapped, learning disabilities, and the gifted; behavioral, psychomotor, and communication disorders, administration of special education services; preparation and continuing education of professional and paraprofessional personnel; preschool learning and development of the exceptional; general studies on creativity.

ERIC CLEARINGHOUSE ON HIGHER EDUCATION. George Washington University, One Dupont Circle, Suite 630, Washington, D.C. 20036, tel. 202-296-2597. Various subjects relating to college and university students, college and university conditions and problems, college and university programs; curricular and instructional problems and programs, faculty, institutional research; federal programs, professional education (medical, law, etc.), graduate education, university extension programs, teaching-learning, planning, governance, finance, evaluation, interinstitutional arrangements, and management of higher educational institutions.

ERIC CLEARINGHOUSE ON INFORMATION RESOURCES. Syracuse University, School of Education, Syracuse, N.Y. 13210, tel. 315-423-3640. Management, operation, and use of libraries; the technology to improve their operation and the education, training, and professional activities of librarians and information specialists. Educational techniques involved in microteaching, systems analysis, and programmed instruction employing audiovisual teaching aids and technology, such as television, radio, computers, and cable television, communication satellites, microforms, and public television.

ERIC CLEARINGHOUSE FOR JUNIOR COLLEGES. University of California, Powell Library, Rm. 96, Los Angeles, Calif. 90024, tel. 213-825-3931. Development, administration, and evaluation of public and private community junior colleges. Junior college students, staff, curricula, programs, libraries, and community services.

ERIC CLEARINGHOUSE ON LANGUAGES AND LINGUISTICS. Center for Applied Linguistics, 1611 N. Kent St., Arlington, Va. 22209, tel. 703-528-4312. Languages and linguistics. Instructional methodology, psychology of language learning, cultural and intercultural content, application of linguistics, curricular problems and developments, teacher training and qualifications, language sciences, psycholinguistics, theoretical and applied linguistics, language pedagogy, bilingualism, and commonly taught languages including English for speakers of other languages.

ERIC CLEARINGHOUSE ON READING AND COMMUNICATION SKILLS. National Council of Teachers of English, 1111 Kenyon Rd., Urbana, Ill. 61801, tel. 217-328-3870. Reading, English, and communication skills, preschool through college. Educational research and development in reading, writing, speaking, and listening. Identification, diagnosis, and remediation of reading problems. Speech communication—forensics, mass communication, interpersonal and small group interaction, interpretation, rhetorical and communication theory, instruction development, speech sciences, and theater. Preparation of instructional staff and related personnel in these areas. All aspects of reading behavior with emphasis on physiology, psychology, sociology, and teaching. Instructional materials, curricula, tests and measurement, preparation of reading teachers and specialists, and methodology at all levels. Role of libraries and other agencies in fostering and guiding reading. Diagnostic and remedial services in school and clinical settings.

ERIC CLEARINGHOUSE ON RURAL EDUCATION AND SMALL SCHOOLS. New Mexico State University, Box 3AP, Las Cruces, N.Mex. 88003, tel. 505-646-2633. Education of Indian Americans, Mexican Americans, Spanish Americans, and migratory farm workers and their children; outdoor education; economic, cultural, social, or other factors related to educational programs in rural areas and small schools; disadvantaged of rural and small school populations.

ERIC CLEARINGHOUSE FOR SCIENCE, MATHEMATICS, AND ENVIRONMENTAL EDUCATION. Ohio State University, 1200 Chambers Rd., Third Fl., Columbus, Ohio 43212, tel. 614-422-6717. All levels of science, mathematics, and environmental education; development of curriculum and instructional materials; media applications; impact of interest, intelligence, values, and concept development upon learning; preservice and inservice teacher education and supervision.

ERIC CLEARINGHOUSE FOR SOCIAL STUDIES/SOCIAL SCIENCE EDUCATION. 855 Broadway, Boulder, Colo. 80302, tel. 303-492-8434. All levels of social studies and social science; all activities relating to teachers; content of disciplines; applications of learning theory, curriculum theory, child development theory, and instructional theory; research and development programs; special needs of student groups; education as a social science; social studies/social science and the community.

ERIC CLEARINGHOUSE ON TEACHER EDUCATION. American Association of Colleges for Teacher Education, One Dupont Circle, N.W., Suite 616, Washington, D.C. 20036, tel. 202-293-7280. School personnel at all levels; all issues from selection through preservice and inservice preparation and training to retirement; curricula; educational theory and philosophy; general education not specifically covered by Educational Management Clearinghouse; Title XI NDEA Institutes not covered by subject specialty in other ERIC Clearinghouses; all aspects of physical education.

ERIC CLEARINGHOUSE ON TESTS, MEASUREMENT, AND EVALUATION. Educational Testing Service, Princeton, N.J. 08540, tel. 609-921-9000 ext. 2176. Tests and other measurement devices; evaluation procedures and techniques; application of tests, measurement, or evaluation in educational projects or programs.

ERIC CLEARINGHOUSE ON URBAN EDUCATION. Teachers College, Box 40, Columbia University, 525 W. 120 St., New York, N.Y. 10027, tel. 212-678-3437. The relationship between urban life and schooling; the effect of urban experiences and environments from birth onward; the academic, intellectual, and social performance of urban children and youth from grade three through college entrance (including the effect of self concept, motivation, and other affective influences); education of urban, Puerto Rican and Asian American populations, and rural and urban black populations; programs and practices which provide learning experiences designed to meet the special needs of diverse populations served by urban schools and which build upon their unique as well as their common characteristics; structural changes in the classroom, school, school system, and community and innovative instructional practices which directly affect urban children and youth; programs, practices, and materials related to economic and ethnic discrimination, segregation, desegregation, and integration in education; issues, programs, practices, and materials related to redressing the curriculum imbalance in the treatment of ethnic minority groups.

EDUCATIONAL RESOURCES INFORMATION CENTER. Central ERIC, National Institute of Education, Washington, D.C. 20208, tel. 202-254-5555.

Thinking-Learning-Communicating Skills Continuum, K–12

This skill continuum is a basic multipurpose instructional planning and implementation tool. It provides an articulation framework for a school district's skill development program, K–12, pinpointing where within the program of studies each thinking-learning-communicating skill can be appropriately introduced, reinforced, and/or extended. This continuum is also an invaluable instructional planning guide for classroom teachers and school library media specialists to use when determining specific thinking-learning-communicating skills to be integrated within a teaching or learning program.

For each skill listed indicate the appropriate grade level for that skill to be introduced, reinforced, or extended.

PART ONE: THINKING SKILLS

	Introduce	Reinforce	Extend
I. THINKING PROCESSES			
A. Make effective use of perceptive thinking			
1. Visualizing mentally			
2. Discriminating properties of objects			
3. Discriminating among events			
4. Perceiving relationships			
5. Interpreting meanings			
B. Make effective use of associative thinking			
1. Linking and matching similar ideas, events, and problems			
2. Relating terms and meanings			
3. Translating signs and symbols			
4. Relating behavior traits and actions			
C. Make effective use of conceptual thinking			

PART ONE: THINKING SKILLS

Introduce   Reinforce   Extend

I. THINKING PROCESSES (cont.)

    1. Classifying data into groups
    2. Listing, grouping, and labeling data
    3. Generalizing common elements
    4. Comparing and contrasting categories of data
    5. Organizing data under specific headings such as: desirable, undesirable, feasible, infeasible

D. Make effective use of problem solving
    1. Defining the problem
        a. Encountering the problem
        b. Selecting the problem
        c. Stating the problem
        d. Framing tentative solutions
    2. Working on the problem
        a. Recalling known information and past experience
        b. Locating information
        c. Appraising, organizing, and interpreting information
    3. Drawing conclusions
        a. Stating possible conclusions
        b. Determining the most logical conclusion
        c. Reaching a conclusion
    4. Carrying out a conclusion
        a. Acting on a conclusion
        b. Reconsidering the conclusion

E. Make effective use of critical thinking
    1. Defining the problem
        a. Becoming aware of a problem
        b. Making it meaningful
        c. Making it manageable
    2. Developing a tentative answer: hypothesizing
        a. Examining and classifying available data
        b. Seeking relationships, drawing logical inferences
        c. Stating the hypothesis
    3. Testing the tentative answer

PART ONE: THINKING SKILLS

Introduce   Reinforce   Extend

I. THINKING PROCESSES (cont.)

    a. Assembling evidence
      –Identifying the needed evidence
      –Collecting the needed evidence
      –Evaluating the needed evidence

    b. Arranging evidence
      –Translating evidence
      –Interpreting evidence
      –Classifying evidence

    c. Analyzing evidence
      –Seeking relationships
      –Noting similarities and differences
      –Identifying trends, sequences, and regularities

4. Developing a conclusion
    a. Finding meaningful patterns or relationships
    b. Stating the conclusion

5. Applying the conclusion
    a. Testing against new evidence
    b. Generalizing the results

F. Make effective use of creative thinking
  1. Wondering why not, what if, just suppose
  2. Recalling past experiences*
  3. Gathering facts and seeking answers (**PREPARATION**)
  4. Observing the odd and the unusual
  5. Formulating new interpretations
  6. Grasping new relationships
  7. Incubating ideas (**INCUBATION**)
  8. Generating solutions spontaneously (**INSPIRATION**)
  9. Testing and proving validity of solutions (**VERIFICATION**)

*"Experience is one of the most important sources of raw material for creativity." From Jacolyn A. Mott, *Creativity and Imagination* (Mankato, Minn.: Creative Education, 1973), p. 26.

PART ONE: THINKING SKILLS

	Introduce	Reinforce	Extend

I. THINKING PROCESSES (cont.)

G. Make effective use of adventurous thinking
  1. Thinking bold, new thoughts
  2. Projecting beyond what is
  3. Risking defeat by attempting the impossible
  4. "Manipulating complexity, incompleteness, and imperfections to achieve break-throughs and genuine innovations"*

II. THINKING IN THE COGNITIVE AREA

A. Make effective use of knowledge building skills
  1. Building knowledge of specifics
  2. Building knowledge of ways and means of dealing with specifics; organizing
  3. Building knowledge of universals and abstractions
B. Make effective use of comprehension skills
  1. Relating knowledge to other material; seeing the full implication
  2. Translating, paraphrasing, or restructuring ideas
  3. Interpreting, summarizing, reorganizing
  4. Extrapolating; extending trends beyond given data
C. Make effective use of application skills
  1. Using abstractions in concrete situations
  2. Restructuring situations so the abstraction applies
D. Make effective use of analysis skills
  1. Analyzing elements; distinguishing facts from hypotheses
  2. Analyzing relationships; connections and interactions
  3. Analyzing organizational

---

*E. Paul Torrance, "What It Means to Become Human" in *To Nurture Humaneness*, ed. by Mary-Margaret Scobey and Grace Graham (Washington, D.C.: Association for Supervision and Curriculum Development, NEA, 1970), p. 7.

PART ONE: THINKING SKILLS

| | Introduce | Reinforce | Extend |

II. THINKING IN THE COGNITIVE AREA (cont.)

   principles; systematic arrangement

 E. Make effective use of synthesis skills
  1. Producing unique communication
  2. Producing a plan or proposed set of operations
  3. Formulating hypotheses or propositions
  4. Recombining of parts of previous experience with new material, reconstructing into a new order or pattern
  5. Producing a product that did not exist before

 F. Make effective use of evaluation skills
  1. Making judgments in terms of internal evidence
  2. Making judgments in terms of external criteria

III. THINKING IN THE AFFECTIVE AREA

 A. Make effective use of receiving (attending) skills
  1. Developing awareness; being conscious of a situation, object, or state of affairs
  2. Willing to receive; giving attention but remaining neutral
  3. Controlling or selecting focus of attention; selecting stimuli to attend to; attention controlled by learner

 B. Make effective use of responding skills
  1. Acquiescing in response; compliance or obedience
  2. Willing to respond; voluntary response; proceeding from one's own choice
  3. Deriving satisfaction in response; behavior accompanied by a feeling of pleasure, zest, or enjoyment

 C. Make effective use of valuing skills

PART ONE: THINKING SKILLS

	Introduce	Reinforce	Extend
III. THINKING IN THE AFFECTIVE AREA (cont.)			

      1. Accepting a value; showing consistency of response to the class of phenomena with which a belief or an attitude is identified

      2. Preferring a value; sufficient commitment to a value that the individual will pursue, seek out, or want it

      3. Committing one's self; belief involving a high degree of certainty bordering on faith; includes loyalty to a position, group, or cause

  D. Make effective use of organizing skills

      1. Conceptualizing a value; shown by attempts to identify characteristics of an object or position valued and by expression of judgments about a value

      2. Organizing a value system; bringing together a complex of values into an ordered relationship

  E. Make effective use of characterizing valuing skills

      1. Acting consistently in accordance with internalized values

      2. Developing a consistent philosophy of life or a code of behavior which becomes characteristic of the person

PART TWO: LEARNING SKILLS

I. LOCATING INFORMATION

  A. Make effective use of libraries

      1. Valuing a library as a learning laboratory

        a. A means of becoming a participant in all that mankind has ever thought, questioned, dreamed, created, and valued

PART TWO: LEARNING SKILLS

Introduce   Reinforce   Extend

I. LOCATING INFORMATION (cont.)

    b. A basic resource for build-
ing self-awareness and
achieving self-realization

    c. A source and a force for life-
long learning

2. Respecting information retrieval as a basic learning skill

3. Respecting the librarian as a
teacher whose subject is learning itself

    a. A source of concerned, in-
formed, and competent
guidance in how to locate,
organize, use, and evaluate
information

    b. A concerned counselor to be
consulted when searching
for answers to personal
problems or questing for
advice or reassurance

4. Respecting all media—print
and nonprint—as carriers of
knowledge worthy of exploration

5. Using the Dewey Decimal
Classification System as a guide
for locating books in the school
library

    000 General works
    100 Philosophy
    200 Religion
    300 Social science
    400 Language
    500 Pure science
    600 Technology
    700 The arts
    800 Literature
    900 History

6. Using the Library of Congress
Classification System as a guide
for locating books in public,
college, university, and special
libraries

    A General works—
polygraphy
    B Philosophy—religion

PART TWO: LEARNING SKILLS

	Introduce	Reinforce	Extend

I. LOCATING INFORMATION (cont.)

  C History—auxiliary
     sciences
  D History and topography
     (except America)
  E-F America
  G Geography—
     anthropology
  H Social sciences
  J Political science
  K Law
  L Education
  M Music
  N Fine arts
  P Language and literature
  Q Science
  R Medicine
  S Agriculture—plant and
     animal industry
  T Technology
  U Military service
  V Naval science
  Z Bibliography and library
     science

7. Using card catalog as the key
to the holdings of the library
 a. Books are indexed in card
   catalog by
   –Author
   –Title
   –Subject
 b. Author card contains most
   information
   –Author(s)
   –Editor(s)
   –Compiler(s)
   –Illustrator(s)
   –Full title and subtitle
   –Edition
   –Imprint—place of publi-
   cation, publisher, date of
   publication
   –Copyright date
   –Collation—number of
   pages, number of volumes,
   illustrations, size of book

B. Make effective use of books

PART TWO: LEARNING SKILLS

	Introduce	Reinforce	Extend

I. Locating Information (cont.)

1. Using title and subtitle of book as guide to contents
2. Using blurb on book jacket as indication of contents
3. Using title page to identify
   a. Author(s)
   b. Editor(s)
   c. Compiler(s)
   d. Illustrator(s)
   e. Edition
   f. Abridgement
   g. Translation
   h. Imprint information
      –Place of publication
      –Publisher
      –Imprint date
4. Using back (verso) of title page
   a. Date of first and subsequent copyright dates
   b. Owner(s) of copyright
   c. Place of copyright registration
5. Using table of contents to identify
   a. Titles of chapters
   b. Sequence of chapters
   c. Pages of chapters, appendices, lists of maps, lists of illustrations, glossary, bibliography, and index
6. Using preliminary information (front matter)
   a. End papers
   b. Frontispiece
   c. Dedication
   d. Preface
   e. Foreword
   f. Introduction
   g. Acknowledgments
   h. Contributors
   i. Usage notes
7. Using the index to discover
   a. Subjects or topics included in the book: persons, places, things, events, processes
   b. Main subjects and topics

PART TWO: LEARNING SKILLS

	Introduce	Reinforce	Extend
I. LOCATING INFORMATION (cont.)			

             listed in alphabetical order; subtopics listed after main topics

      c. Page numbers after main subjects, main topics, and subtopics

      d. Inclusive paging indicated by hyphen between the first and last page

      e. Poetry uses separate indexes for poet, title of poem, and first line of poem

      f. Cross references to key topics

  8. Using bibliography to identify

      a. Depth and breadth of information beyond content of book used

      b. Verification of sources cited; means of placing paraphrased information in context

  9. Using glossary and terminology list

      a. Discover special meaning of words

      b. Discover translation of foreign words

 10. Using illustrations—pictures, charts, graphs, maps—to heighten meaning of text

C. Make effective use of dictionaries

  1. Using dictionaries as data sources for

      a. Definitions of words

      b. Spelling of words

      c. Pronunciation of words

      d. History of words

      e. Synonyms

      f. Abbreviations

      g. Signs and symbols

      h. Foreign terms

      i. Diagrams

      j. Tables

  2. Recognizing the distinguishing characteristics of

PART TWO: LEARNING SKILLS

Introduce   Reinforce   Extend

I. LOCATING INFORMATION (cont.)

      a. Abridged language diction-
          aries
      b. Unabridged language dic-
          tionaries

  3. Recognizing the useful features
     of a dictionary
     a. Alphabetical arrangement
     b. Guide words
     c. Thumb index
     d. Hints on dictionary use
     e. Abbreviations
     f. Illustrations
     g. Diagrams
     h. Tables
     i. List of important people,
        places, and events
     j. Common given names

  4. Recognizing the distinguishing
     characteristics of
     a. Language dictionaries
     b. Specialized dictionaries

  5. Realizing the value of having a
     dictionary readily at hand when
     studying; developing the dic-
     tionary habit

D. Make effective use of encyclopedias
  1. Using encyclopedias as data
     sources for brief information
     about
     a. Persons
     b. Places
     c. Things
     d. Events
     e. Processes

  2. Recognizing the distinguishing
     characteristics of
     a. General encyclopedias
     b. Special encyclopedias

  3. Gaining facility in using
     a. Key words
     b. Guide words
     c. Cross references
     d. Indexes
     e. Reference outlines and study
        guides
     f. Illustrations

PART TWO: LEARNING SKILLS

I. LOCATING INFORMATION (cont.)

    4. Updating encyclopedias by checking annuals and yearbooks for
      a. Art
      b. Business
      c. Chronologies
      d. Drama
      e. Education
      f. Fashion
      g. International affairs
      h. Legislation
      i. Literature
      j. Medicine
      k. Motion pictures
      l. Necrologies
      m. Politics
      n. Radio and television
      o. Science
      p. Special reports on major issues
      q. Sports
      r. Transportation
      s. Urban problems and development
      t. Year in review
    5. Recognizing limitations of encyclopedic information
      a. Serves as an introduction; provides an overview of skeletal facts
      b. Serves as an outline identifying main topics to be researched further in other sources

E. Make effective use of other basic reference tools
    1. Recognizing distinguishing characteristics and informational value of abstracts
      a. List new literature in a specialized field
      b. Give brief abstracts of books and periodical articles listed
    2. Recognizing distinguishing characteristics and informational value of almanacs and fact books

PART TWO: LEARNING SKILLS

Introduce   Reinforce   Extend

I. LOCATING INFORMATION (cont.)

    a. Contain statistical information on all topics of universal interest

    b. Published each year

    c. Charts, tables, and graphs used for clarity and brevity

    d. General almanacs and fact books cover universal topics in limited detail

    e. Specialized almanacs and fact books provide in depth statistical analysis of a specific area

3. Recognizing distinguishing characteristics and informational value of atlases and gazetteers

    a. Atlases are books of maps

    b. Gazetteers are books of places: names, location, description

    c. Interpreting maps requires use of longitude, latitude, scale, key, legend, symbols

4. Recognizing distinguishing characteristics and informational value of bibliographies

    a. Bibliographies are lists of books and/or articles about a particular subject, a particular person, a particular author, a particular collection

    b. Bibliographies are used
      –To find out something about a given book: author's name, title, edition, publisher, date, cost
      –To find out what has been written on a given subject
      –To choose a book for a certain purpose

    c. Bibliographies of bibliographies are tools to be used in identifying special or general bibliographies

PART TWO: LEARNING SKILLS

Introduce   Reinforce   Extend

I. Locating Information (cont.)

    5. Recognizing distinguishing characteristics and informational value of handbooks and manuals

      a. The terms *handbook* and *manual* are used interchangeably

      b. Handbooks and/or manuals are reference books designed to help their readers to understand or use something

      c. Style manuals are basic guides to the mechanics of writing; an invaluable tool to be kept readily at hand and consulted when undertaking a writing assignment

    6. Recognizing distinguishing characteristics and informational value of indexes other than indexes to periodicals

      a. Indexes are location keys to anthologies of poetry, plays, essays, short stories, fairy tales, and general literature

      b. Concordances show in context each use of all important words used by an author of exceptional note or as found in the Bible

      c. Indexes to quotations may also include a concordance of key words

F. Make effective use of periodicals and and periodical indexes

  1. Realizing that magazines are called periodicals

    a. A periodical is a publication issued periodically, or at stated intervals

    b. Journals are periodicals issued by professional organizations and learned societies

  2. Valuing periodicals as rich

PART TWO: LEARNING SKILLS

Introduce   Reinforce   Extend

I. LOCATING INFORMATION (cont.)

    sources of information specially useful for

    a. Subjects requiring latest information available in print

    b. Subjects for which books are not available

    c. Contemporary opinion on a given subject, person, happening

    d. Current editorial comment

    e. Current bibliographies

3. Valuing periodical indexes as effective tools for locating information in periodicals

    a. Periodical indexes cover the period from 1802 to date

    b. *Readers' Guide to Periodical Literature* indexes articles within two weeks of publication date

4. Valuing microreproductions as ready reference sources for periodical information, past and present

    a. Microcard

    b. Microfiche

    c. Microfilm

5. Guarding against the threat of bias in periodical articles

6. Being aware of propaganda techniques

    a. Name calling

    b. Glittering generalities

    c. Transfer

    d. Testimonial

    e. Plain folks

    f. Card stacking

    g. Bandwagon

G. Make effective use of newspapers and newspaper indexes

1. Becoming acquainted with organization patterns of newspapers; the purposes of various sections

PART TWO: LEARNING SKILLS

	Introduce	Reinforce	Extend
I. LOCATING INFORMATION (cont.)			

2. Perceiving the reasons for article placement
3. Perceiving the dangers of news that is slanted, biased, sensationalized
4. Realizing the distinguishing features and significance of the front page
   a. Headline
   b. Banner
   c. Streamer
   d. Subhead
   e. Masthead
   f. Nameplate
   g. Flag
   h. Edition
   i. Motto
   j. Lead story
   k. News feature
   l. Index
   m. Byline
   n. Dateline
   o. Publisher
   p. Correspondent
   q. Weather ear
5. Realizing the distinguishing features and significance of news stories
   a. Lead paragraph
   b. Summary lead
   c. Copy editor
   d. Reporter
   e. News service
   f. Interpretive stories
   g. Investigative stories
   h. Editorializing
6. Realizing the distinguishing features and significance of the editorial page
   a. Syndicated column
   b. Syndication service
   c. Editorial
   d. Editorial cartoon
   e. Letters to the editor
   f. Opinion

PART TWO: LEARNING SKILLS

Introduce   Reinforce   Extend

I. LOCATING INFORMATION (cont.)

    g. Viewpoint
    h. Editorial board
    i. Editorial policy
  7. Judging reliability of a news report
    a. Comparing reports on the same event as found in several newspapers
    b. Comparing newspaper reports with news magazine reports
    c. Comparing reports in newspapers with those given by radio and television reporters
  8. Valuing the *New York Times Index* as an excellent reference tool
    a. Best quick source of information on events since 1851
    b. Indexing is thorough
    c. Use the index to find exact date of an event, to check proper names, and to discover cross references
  9. Valuing microreproductions of newspapers as research treasure troves

H. Make effective use of U.S. government documents, publications, and indexes
  1. Recognizing the distinguishing characteristics and informational value of federal documents
    a. Congressional documents
      –The *Congressional Record*
      –House and Senate Reports and Documents
      –Bills, resolutions, acts, statutes, laws
      –Hearings and Committee Prints
    b. Judicial documents
    c. Executive documents
      –Federal regulations

PART TWO: LEARNING SKILLS

	Introduce	Reinforce	Extend

I. LOCATING INFORMATION (cont.)

–Departmental documents

–Presidential documents

2. Recognizing the distinguishing characteristics and informational value of indexes to U.S. government publications

   a. *Monthly Catalog* is the only comprehensive, current listing

   b. *Selected U.S. Government Publications* is issued bi-weekly

   c. *Price Lists* are issued by 80 departments and agencies

3. Realizing that the Superintendent of Documents, U.S. Government Printing Office, Washington, D.C. 20402, is the information source and the sales agent for government publications

I. Make effective use of pamphlets

1. Recognizing the distinguishing characteristics and informational value of pamphlets

   a. Unbound publication

   b. Fewer than 100 pages

   c. Complete in itself

   d. Excellent sources on current topics not available in book form

2. Recognizing that unbound pamphlets are usually not filed with books

   a. Usually filed in filing cabinets (vertical files); arranged alphabetically by topic or subject

   b. Most important pamphlets are usually listed in the card catalog

3. Recognizing that the following are prolific sources of pamphlet material

   a. Local, state, and national governments

PART TWO: LEARNING SKILLS

Introduce   Reinforce   Extend

I. Locating Information (cont.)

b. The United Nations
c. Associations
d. Business and industry

J. Make effective use of primary source materials

1. Learning the essentials of historical method*
   a. Collection of objects and of printed, written, and oral materials that may be relevant
   b. Exclusion of materials (or parts thereof) that are unauthentic
   c. Extraction from the authentic material of testimony that is credible
   d. Organizing of that reliable testimony into a meaningful narrative or exposition

2. Determining the authenticity and significance of primary source materials†
   a. Who is the authority?
   b. What is his background?
   c. What is the purpose of the material?
   d. When and under what circumstances was the information recorded?
   e. Was the information written from memory or was it a direct account of what happened?
   f. Is there corroboration of the facts from other sources?
   g. Is the authority objective in the treatment of the material?
   h. Is the material pertinent?
   i. Is there mention in this

---

*Louis Gottschalk, *Understanding History: A Primer of Historical Method* (New York: Alfred A. Knopf, 1950), p. 28.

†Adapted from Alice Elkenberry and Ruth Ellsworth, "Organizing and Evaluating Information," in *Skill Development in Social Studies*, ed. by Helen McCracken Carpenter (Washington, D.C.: National Council for the Social Studies, NEA, 1963), p. 89.

PART TWO: LEARNING SKILLS

	Introduce	Reinforce	Extend
I. LOCATING INFORMATION (cont.)			

source of other documents,
people, or events that should
be researched?
3. Validating and utilizing information gained from
  a. Written or printed sources;
      reprints, facsimiles, and
      microreproductions
      –Account books
      –Bill of sales
      –Charters
      –Cookbooks
      –Court records
      –Deeds
      –Diaries
      –Eyewitness accounts
      –Handbills
      –Handbooks
      –Indenture papers
      –Journals
      –Legislative records
      –Letters
      –Memoirs
      –Military records
      –Newspapers
      –Pamphlets
      –Periodicals
      –Speeches
      –Tax records
  b. Disc and tape recorded
      materials
      –Debates
      –Hearings
      –Interviews
      –Newscasts
      –Plays
      –Poems
      –Songs
      –Speeches
  c. Artifacts; realia, museum
      replicas
      –Banners
      –Buildings
      –Buttons
      –Cemeteries
      –Ceramics

PART TWO: LEARNING SKILLS

Introduce   Reinforce   Extend

I. LOCATING INFORMATION (cont.)

          –Clothing
          –Currency
          –Flags
          –Furniture
          –Jewelry
          –Machines
          –Musical instruments
          –Paintings
          –Photographs
          –Religious articles
          –Sculptures
          –Stamps
          –Textiles
          –Tools
          –Vehicles
          –Weapons

K. Make effective use of audiovisual media

  1. Developing audiovisual literacy

    a. Preplan the purpose for using nonprint media

    b. Study carefully the guides and usage notes accompanying the various media

    c. Develop the habit of concentrated viewing, observing, and listening

    d. Link ideas gained from viewing, observing, and listening with previously gained understanding

    e. Take careful notes
      –Identify type of media, title, producer, series, and copyright or issuing date
      –For filmstrips, note specific frame or frames where information was found
      –For art prints and study prints, note specific print or prints where information was found
      –List those topics introduced in each filmstrip, tape, record, motion picture, etc., worthy of further research

PART TWO: LEARNING SKILLS

	Introduce	Reinforce	Extend

I. LOCATING INFORMATION (cont.)

    f. Following the first viewing, observing, and listening, review notes
       –Determine adequacy of notes; clear? complete?
       –Re-view, re-observe, or re-listen to check and/or re-vise notes

    g. Search for additional information in other print and/or audiovisual media

  2. Valuing nonprint media as authentic carriers of knowledge —rich data banks for information retrieval

II. ACQUIRING INFORMATION THROUGH PURPOSEFUL AND APPRECIATIVE READING

  A. Develop reading competence

    1. Decoding the meaning from the printed word

    2. Grasping, translating, inferring the intent, selecting, organizing, and expressing ideas

    3. Thinking, feeling, and imagining within the frame of reference being read

    4. Analyzing and appraising what is being read both critically and objectively

    5. Interacting intellectually and emotionally with what is being read

    6. Responding to the imagery, the beauty, and the power of words

    7. Synthesizing ideas gleaned from current reading with previous understandings

    8. Going beyond literal meaning to discover and savor hidden meaning

    9. Interpreting allusions and figures of speech

  10. Reading between, behind, and beyond the words

  11. Finding the facts, filtering the facts, facing the facts, and following the facts

PART TWO: LEARNING SKILLS

Introduce   Reinforce   Extend

II. Acquiring Information through
Purposeful and Appreciative Reading (cont.)

    12. Developing the habit of reading
with a dictionary readily at hand

    13. Linking ideas gained from read-
ing with those gained from
viewing, observing, and listening

    14. Valuing books as carriers of
knowledge—rich data banks
for informational retrieval

    15. Valuing reading as a basic tool
for life-long learning

    16. Valuing reading as an art as
well as a science

  B. Adjust reading rate to purpose

    1. Skimming

      a. Reading rapidly to discover
topic inclusion and arrangement of content

      b. Reading here and there,
looking for signal phrases

      c. Determining relevance and/
or significance of information

      d. Verifying statements, quota-
tions, dates, spellings,
statistics

      e. Locating tables, graphs,
charts, illustrations, maps

      f. Pinpointing where best to
begin to read for specific
information

    2. Cursory reading

      a. Reading rapidly

      b. Skipping unknown words
and puzzling ideas

      c. Reviewing previously read
material
        –Making a summary
        –Generalizing
        –Validating
        –Formulating questions
        –Identifying topics (persons,
places, things, events, processes, opinions) requiring
further study

PART TWO: LEARNING SKILLS

Introduce   Reinforce   Extend

II. ACQUIRING INFORMATION THROUGH
PURPOSEFUL AND APPRECIATIVE READING (cont.)

3. Study reading
   a. Reading deliberately with optimum concentration and understanding
   b. Using the SQ4R method*
      -Based on research on the college level: how to read college textbooks effectively
      -Study time can be reduced 25 percent without reducing comprehension
      -Comprised of six basic steps
      S—SURVEYING a chapter to determine author's outline
      Q—Developing QUESTIONS (developing topic headings into questions)
      R—READING; skimming for main ideas; scanning to discover signal or flag words
      R—RECITING; when an answer is found stop and recite answer in own words
      R—WRITING key words (permanent study notes) that serve as cues to answers
      R—REVIEWING by concentrating on key questions; review immediately following completion of the assignment; repeat at least once weekly to minimize forgetting
4. Critical reading
   a. Pausing to recall and associate what is being read with past experience
   b. Pausing to reflect, compare, and validate

*Kenneth H. Hoover, *The Professional Teacher's Handbook: A Guide for Improving Instruction in Today's Middle and Secondary Schools* (Boston: Allyn and Bacon, 1976), pp. II: 135–136.

PART TWO: LEARNING SKILLS

Introduce   Reinforce   Extend

II. ACQUIRING INFORMATION THROUGH
PURPOSEFUL AND APPRECIATIVE READING (cont.)

      c. Savoring what is said and
         how it is said
      d. Noting and evaluating the
         style of writing
      e. Delving deeply to uncover
         hidden meanings
      f. Comparing information
         from several sources noting
         similarities, differences, and
         omissions
      g. Noting relationships,
         images, allusions, implied
         meanings, emotional tones,
         biases, and prejudices
    5. Creative reading
      a. Reading with the heart, the
         imagination, and the soul as
         well as with the intellect
      b. Developing a mind-set for
         using information that is
         read
      c. Generating ideas uniquely
         different but supportive to
         what is being read
      d. Internalizing what is read;
         having a dialogue with the
         author
      e. Reacting creatively to what
         is read
          –Drawing a cartoon, poster,
           picture
          –Composing music, writing
           a song, matching music to
           mood, time period, or event
          –Writing a poem, play, short
           story, biography, scenario
      f. Weaving into the tapestry of
         thoughts and feelings the
         various attitudes, values,
         commitments, and insights
         gained from reading
  C. Read to form relationships
    1. Perceiving chronological and
      time relationships
      a. Developing an understand-
         ing of

PART TWO: LEARNING SKILLS

II. ACQUIRING INFORMATION THROUGH
PURPOSEFUL AND APPRECIATIVE READING (cont.)

> –How centuries are numbered
> –How historical periods are designated
> –How geological time is designated
> –How time lines sequentialize and link events
>
> b. Interpreting and comparing the Julian and Gregorian calendars
> c. Interpreting dates using the perpetual calendar
> d. Developing a vocabulary of definite and indefinite time expressions
> e. Interpreting charts, graphs, and tables
> f. Perceiving the distinguishing characteristics of chronologies and their informational value
>
> 2. Perceiving cause and effect relationships
>   a. Seeing the influence of human behavior on historical and contemporary events
>   b. Seeing the influence of attitudes, values, and commitments on behavior
>   c. Seeing the effect of geography on historical, social, cultural, industrial, economical, and political developments
>   d. Seeing the relationship between various forms of government and standards of living and levels of expectation
>   e. Seeing the relationship between adventurous thinking and human progress
>
> 3. Perceiving space and distance relationships

PART TWO: LEARNING SKILLS

| | Introduce | Reinforce | Extend |

    a. Recognizing the distinguishing characteristics and informational value of maps and globes

    b. Using cardinal and intermediate directions

    c. Using parallels and meridians when determining directions

    d. Using a highway map to locate places by using number-and-key

    e. Using distance, direction, and location when planning a trip

    f. Using tour guides and atlases to locate places and determine distances

    g. Comparing routes and distances for alternative means of travel

4. Perceiving the relative importance of ideas

    a. Identifying inherent properties of things

    b. Identifying, grouping, and interpreting ideas in order of significance

    c. Reading accounts from several sources and noting those events always, seldom, never mentioned

    d. Sequentializing ideas in priority order

    e. Using chronologies to identify significant events and people

    f. Using time lines to highlight the interplay of people and events

5. Perceiving analogous relationships

    a. Discerning similarities and likenesses

    b. Avoiding the mistaken idea that if two things are alike

PART TWO: LEARNING SKILLS

Introduce   Reinforce   Extend

II. ACQUIRING INFORMATION THROUGH
    PURPOSEFUL AND APPRECIATIVE READING (cont.)

in certain characteristics
they are alike in all characteristics

  c. Realizing that the strength
of an analogy depends on
whether or not similarities
are noteworthy or trivial

  d. Using analogies for clarifi-
cation; presenting the unfamiliar in terms of the
familiar as a means of explanation

 6. Applying what is read to personal experience

  a. Relating what is read to own
experience for validation,
assimilation, comparison,
and utilization

  b. Relating what is read to own
beliefs, attitudes, commitments, and values

D. Read literature with perception and
appreciation

 1. Recognizing and enjoying effective literary style

 2. Identifying the essential or basic
characteristics of effective literary expression

 3. Identifying the distinguishing
characteristics of the various
literary genre
–Autobiography
–Biography
–Drama
–Essay
–Fable
–Folklore
–History
–Legend
–Myth
–Novel
–Personal narrative
–Poem
–Short story

 4. Distinguishing between fact and
fiction, realism and fantasy

PART TWO: LEARNING SKILLS

Introduce   Reinforce   Extend

II. ACQUIRING INFORMATION THROUGH
PURPOSEFUL AND APPRECIATIVE READING (cont.)

5. Understanding the characteristics and purposes of figural and
idiomatic expression
6. Visualizing described settings
and actions
7. Responding to mood, tone, and
imagery of a literary work
8. Reading literature with the imagination; sharing vicariously
the action; interacting with the
ongoing drama of events
9. Responding creatively to what
has been read
10. Interpreting literary criticism
to mean endeavoring "to find, to
know, to love, to recommend
not only the best, but all the
good that has been known and
written in the world."*
11. Identifying the distinguishing
characteristics of the various
literary awards such as
–Caldecott Medal
–John Newbery Award
–Nobel Awards
–Pulitzer Awards
12. Using literary handbooks for
overview and insight
13. Developing an ever-widening
interest in and an ever-deepen-
ing appreciation of literature

III. ACQUIRING INFORMATION THROUGH
PURPOSEFUL AND APPRECIATIVE
LISTENING

A. Develop listening competence
1. Decoding the meaning from the
spoken word
2. Grasping, translating, inferring
the intent of the spoken word
3. Selecting, organizing, and
expressing ideas gained from
listening
4. Analyzing and appraising what

*William H. Burton et al., *Education for Effective Thinking* (New York: Appleton-Century-Crofts, 1960), p. 350.

PART TWO: LEARNING SKILLS

	Introduce	Reinforce	Extend

III. ACQUIRING INFORMATION THROUGH PURPOSEFUL AND APPRECIATIVE LISTENING (cont.)

is being said both critically and objectively

5. Interacting intellectually and emotionally with what is being said

6. Responding to the imagery, the beauty, and the power of the spoken word

7. Thinking, feeling, and imagining within the spoken frame of reference

8. Synthesizing ideas gained from listening with previous understandings

9. Going beyond the literal meaning of the spoken word; discovering and savoring implied meanings

10. Listening to find the facts, filter the facts, face the facts, and follow the facts

11. Linking ideas gained from listening with those gained from reading, viewing, and observing

12. Valuing recordings—disc and tape—as carriers of knowledge —rich data banks for informational retrieval

B. Make effective use of critical listening

1. Applying critical thinking skills when listening

2. Using the TA2R formula when listening for information
T—TUNE IN: preset your mind to listen attentively
A—ANALYZE what is being said: take notes in jot form: main ideas, supporting details, unfamiliar words, statistics, authorities cited
R—RESPOND: questioning; evaluating; forming associations; noting discrepancies and gaps in information;

PART TWO: LEARNING SKILLS

Introduce   Reinforce   Extend

III. ACQUIRING INFORMATION THROUGH
PURPOSEFUL AND APPRECIATIVE
LISTENING (cont.)

being sensitive to bias, prejudice, emotion ladened words,
unwarranted conclusions,
sweeping generalities, in-
tonation, facial expression
and gestures; making value
judgments about what is
being said
R—REVIEW notes; incubating
ideas gained and formulating
afterthoughts; validating
questioned statements and
statistics; linking what has
been learned with previous
knowledge

C. Make effective use of appreciative
listening
1. Being alive, open, and responsive to the beauty, power, and
imagery of sound
2. Listening with the heart, soul,
imagination, and spirit
3. Exploring the artistic, technical, biographical, psychological, and historical components
of music
4. Experiencing music; responding to melody, tone, harmony,
rhythm, and pattern
5. Coexisting with a composer in
"a moment of mutality"*
6. Responding to music in own
"inner time"†
7. Building an ever expanding
repertoire of treasured listening
experiences
8. Acquiring the habit of checking commercial catalogs to
identify new disc and tape recordings
9. Furnishing own "house of in-

*Gerard L. Knieter, "The Nature of Aesthetic Education" in *Toward an Aesthetic Education* (Washington, D.C.: Music Educators National Conference, 1971), p. 3–19.
†Maxine Greene, "Teaching for Aesthetic Experience" in *Toward an Aesthetic Education* (Washington, D.C.: Music Educators National Conference, 1971), pp. 21–24.

PART TWO: LEARNING SKILLS

	Introduce	Reinforce	Extend

III. ACQUIRING INFORMATION THROUGH
PURPOSEFUL AND APPRECIATIVE
LISTENING (cont.)

    tellect" with memories of listen-
ing experiences of limitless
delight

  10. Becoming acquainted with the
musical greats (composers and
performers), past and present,
who have left an imprint on the
development of music

  11. Experimenting with a variety
of musical forms and techniques

  12. Selecting and taping mood
music as background for a play,
poem, or dramatic reading

IV. ACQUIRING INFORMATION THROUGH
PURPOSEFUL VIEWING AND OBSERVING

  A. Recognize that viewing is visual
inspection; a critical assessment
with a definite purpose in mind

  B. Recognize that observing goes beyond viewing and stresses adherence
to criteria or following a scientific
model

  C. Recognize that viewing is purposeful looking and that observing is
carefully and scientifically studying and interpreting what is seen

  D. Apply critical thinking skills when
"reading" visual media such as

    1. Art prints and art objects

    2. Cartoons, drawings, and photo-
graphs

    3. Charts, graphs, and tables

    4. Diagrams

    5. Filmstrips, motion pictures,
and videotapes

    6. Maps

    7. Mock-ups and models

    8. Realia and museum objects

    9. Slides

    10. Specimens

    11. Study prints

    12. Television programs

    13. Transparencies for overhead
projection

  E. "Read" visual media and employ

PART TWO: LEARNING SKILLS

Introduce   Reinforce   Extend

IV. ACQUIRING INFORMATION THROUGH
PURPOSEFUL VIEWING AND OBSERVING (cont.)

the inquiry processes in communicating understanding
1. Analyzing data
2. Describing data
3. Explaining data
4. Classifying data
5. Categorizing data
6. Evaluating data
7. Predicting from data

F. Study teacher-constructed and commercially prepared learning guides
(which accompany many visual
media), before attempting to "read"
the visual medium
1. Identifying the purpose
2. Obtaining an introduction to
and an overview of the contents

G. Organize and consolidate the ideas
gained from viewing with ideas
gained from other print and nonprint sources as well as from own
past experience

H. Explore the artistic, technical, psychological, biographical, and historical components of the fine arts
1. Responding to the imagery, the
beauty, the form, and power of
the work of art
2. Viewing from the heart, soul,
imagination, and spirit

I. Become acquainted with the great
artists, past and present, and their
works
1. Visiting museums and becoming acquainted with the permanent art collection and special
loan collections
   a. Studying the catalog before
      the visit to become familiar
      with the holdings
   b. Using the catalog as a guide
      while touring the galleries
   c. Checking events calendars
      in the news media for notice
      of special exhibitions
2. Visiting art galleries

PART TWO: LEARNING SKILLS

	Introduce	Reinforce	Extend

IV. ACQUIRING INFORMATION THROUGH
PURPOSEFUL VIEWING AND OBSERVING (cont.)

    a. Studying the catalogs before
you visit

    b. Using the catalogs as guides
while touring the galleries

  J. "Read" the record of man's historical past

    1. Visiting museums of natural
history

    2. Searching for evidence of the
historical past in the community

  K. Recognize that essential to effective
observation are the abilities to

    1. Identify a focus, purpose, prob-
lem, or concern

    2. Establish criteria to guide ob-
servation

    3. Be objective; keep biases and
prejudices under control

    4. Identify appropriate data
sources

    5. Select relevant data

    6. Use all the senses

    7. Use appropriate instruments

    8. Control the variables

    9. Make necessary records

    10. Check observations for accuracy
and completeness

    11. Use scientific terminology
(classification nomenclature,
instruments, measurement, and
processes) when reporting findings

V. CONSTRUCTING AND INTERPRETING
SURVEYS AND OPINION POLLS

  A. Recognize that a survey is an investigation of things as existing or of
events past, to gain information or
to test hypotheses

  B. Recognize that a poll is a type of
survey

  C. Recognize that an opinion is an
answer that is given to a question
in a given situation

  D. Recognize that a poll is a sampling
or collection of opinions on a sub-

PART TWO: LEARNING SKILLS

Introduce   Reinforce   Extend

V. Constructing and Interpreting
   Surveys and Opinion Polls (cont.)

ject; the accuracy of the sample is
based on three different factors
  1. The size of the sample
     a. The bigger the sample, the
        more accurate the poll
     b. The bigger the sample, the
        smaller the difference be-
        tween the sample answer
        and the true population
        answer
  2. The answers people give
     a. How accurate a particular
        percentage is depends on the
        extent to which the respon-
        dents agree or disagree
     b. The more people disagree,
        the larger the sample has to
        be to represent all attitudes
  3. How the sample is picked
     a. All the different groups in
        the unit being surveyed must
        be represented
     b. For a nationwide survey, the
        sample must include people
        from different parts of na-
        tion, from cities and towns,
        from different ages, reli-
        gions, races, and incomes,
        both men and women
E. Recognize the basic steps employed
   when conducting an opinion poll
  1. Designing the overall plan
     a. Defining the issue or the
        question to be examined
     b. Deciding the procedure to
        follow
  2. Selecting the population sample
     a. Deciding type of people to
        interview
     b. Deciding how they are to be
        selected
  3. Designing the questionnaires
     a. Wording the questions
     b. Placing the questions in
        order
  4. Conducting the interviews

PART TWO: LEARNING SKILLS

	Introduce	Reinforce	Extend
V. CONSTRUCTING AND INTERPRETING SURVEYS AND OPINION POLLS (cont.)			

      a. Contacting the respondents

      b. Choosing one of three methods
        –By mail
        –By telephone
        –In person

    5. Processing the questionnaires

      a. Checking all questionnaires for accuracy

      b. Counting, cross-tabulating, and analyzing the answers

    6. Analyzing the findings

      a. Converting the figures into percentages

      b. Analyzing the data and drawing carefully reasoned conclusions

F. Recognize various data collecting techniques employed in conducting surveys

    1. Self-report techniques

      a. Using summary rating scales

      b. Inventorying attitudes

    2. Observational techniques

      a. Measuring specific behaviors requiring minimum inferences

      b. Inventorying social and emotional behavior

    3. Projective techniques

      a. Using sentence completion, essays, and ambiguous drawings for attitude measurement

      b. Inventorying social values, propaganda, and media content

G. Analyze nationally recognized surveys such as

    1. Gallup Polls

    2. Harris Polls

    3. Purdue University Polls

H. Design and field test a survey employing the six basic steps outlined in E above

PART TWO: LEARNING SKILLS

	Introduce	Reinforce	Extend

V. CONSTRUCTING AND INTERPRETING
SURVEYS AND OPINION POLLS (cont.)

    1. Summarizing the findings in
chart or graph form

    2. Interpreting the significance
of the findings in paragraph
form

VI. LEARNING THROUGH GROUP AND SOCIAL
INTERACTION

    A. Recognize that excellence in inter-
personal relationships is based on
psychological maturity

    B. Recognize that a psychologically
mature person is one who*

        1. Is secure within himself/herself

        2. Has the capacity to give as well
as receive genuine affection

        3. Has the ability to feel with
others and see things from their
point of view

        4. Is objective about himself/
herself, recognizing own limitations

        5. Is comparatively unselfish in
demands on others, willingly
shares ideas, responsibility,
time, and energy

        6. Is self-reliant and independent
in thinking and actions

        7. Has inner resources for living
and working alone without
shunning others

        8. Selects worthwhile long-term
goals and strives to attain them

        9. Has the capacity to size up a
situation

      10. Has a sense of justice; takes a
stand for what he/she believes
to be right

      11. Is respectful toward authority

      12. Recognizes that the real sub-
stance of a person is much more
than the outer, observable
dimension

      13. Recognizes that all human

*Adapted from Victor E. Pitkin, "Youth Development and Democratic Citizenship Education"
in *Citizenship and a Free Society: Education for the Future*, ed. by Franklin Patterson (Washington, D.C.: National Council for the Social Studies, NEA, 1960), pp. 37–38.

PART TWO: LEARNING SKILLS

VI. LEARNING THROUGH GROUP AND SOCIAL
INTERACTION (cont.)

        problems cannot be solved
        scientifically

  14. Takes the long view in solving
      human-relations problems;
      makes intelligent and sensitive
      choices

  15. Is sufficiently flexible to adjust
      to or cope with various types of
      situations

  16. Meets unexpected stresses and
      disappointments without going
      to pieces

  17. Has a basic set of values that
      guide his/her decisions

  18. Has self-confidence but knows
      the virtue of doubt

  19. Forms and defends opinions on
      the basis of reasoning

  20. Accepts such compromises as
      do not violate his/her funda-
      mental convictions

  21. Appreciates that it is meet and
      right to march to a different
      drumbeat just so long as one
      keeps in tune with his/her fel-
      low man and in step with his/
      her own best self

 C. Perceive that an effective group
    member is one who*

   1. Recognizes and utilizes the con-
     tributions of others, making
     them feel that their efforts are
     appreciated and needed

   2. Learns to preserve his/her in-
     dividuality, uniqueness, and
     personal creativity within a
     group setting

   3. Is both a good follower and a
     competent leader at appropriate
     times; learns how to comple-
     ment the efforts of another
     leader; how to organize, plan,
     draw out others, listen carefully;

*Raymond H. Muessig and Vincent R. Rogers, "Developing Competence in Group Participation
and Human Relations" in *Skill Development in Social Studies*, ed. by Helen McCracken
Carpenter (Washington, D.C.: National Council for the Social Studies, NEA, 1963), p. 246.

PART TWO: LEARNING SKILLS

Introduce   Reinforce   Extend

VI. LEARNING THROUGH GROUP AND SOCIAL
    INTERACTION (cont.)

move the group toward a course
of action

4. Enjoys sharing objects, ideas,
   and knowledge without always
   seeking credit, aggrandizement,
   or glory

5. Abides by the rules and regulations created and enforced by
   mutual consent and does not
   seek special privileges or feel
   that guidelines are only for
   others

6. Initiates changes in laws and
   standards that he/she feels are
   unfair to individuals or groups

D. Recognize the function of a committee as a small group endeavor
   requiring adherence to basic ground
   rules

   1. Establishing the purpose for
      forming the committee as the
      first step

   2. Selecting members to serve on
      the committee who are willing
      to work congenially and see that
      the job is done

   3. Selecting the chairperson on
      the basis of leadership qualifi-
      cations; one who will

      a. Focus the attention of the
         committee on the purpose
         for which it has been created

      b. Solicit ideas from the group;
         have the group reach a con-
         sensus on procedure

      c. Establish target dates and
         keep the group on schedule

      d. Be a facilitator, not a dictator

   4. Being an effective committee
      member requires

      a. Staying open to suggestions
         from other members

      b. Feeding in ideas for group
         consideration

      c. Fulfilling commitments
         accepted

      d. Sharing the responsibility of

PART TWO: LEARNING SKILLS

Introduce   Reinforce   Extend

VI. LEARNING THROUGH GROUP AND SOCIAL
   INTERACTION (cont.)

the chairperson and the
group to complete the committee's assignment

E. Perceive the function of a panel as
an information generating group

1. Discovering that a panel is
usually composed of five to
eight members seeking agreement on a problem

2. Discovering that the panel
group is usually selected because of interest

3. Discovering that in an initial
planning session a leader is
chosen; the problem is defined,
then subdivided into subtopics
for individual panelists to research

4. Discovering the responsibilities
of the panel leader to include

a. Guiding the panelists in
their research

b. Preparing a list of guide
questions to be answered by
the panelists in their presentation

c. Keeping the panel discussion moving

d. Inviting questions from the
audience; directing the questions to various members
of the panel

e. Summarizing the main
points of the discussion

F. Perceive the buzz group as an effective alternative to large group discussions

1. Recognizing that the buzz group
is commonly referred to as the
"six-six" procedure; groups of
six consult for six minutes

2. Realizing that there are serious
drawbacks to large group discussions

a. Some individuals hesitate to
speak before a large group

b. The problem often not

PART TWO: LEARNING SKILLS

Introduce   Reinforce   Extend

VI. LEARNING THROUGH GROUP AND SOCIAL INTERACTION (cont.)

         clearly defined; purpose of the discussion becomes submerged in extraneous comment

    c. All too frequently, discussion drags; extent of agreement or disagreement not easily assessed

  3. Realizing that buzz groups may be formed at random or by choice of topic being discussed

  4. Realizing that "buzzing" can be

    a. Informal, without even a chairperson or

    b. Carefully structured with an outline, chairperson, recorder, observer, and even a resource person

  5. Realizing that reporting to the large group can be oral or written

 G. Appreciate the value of parliamentary procedure being carefully followed in formal group meetings

  1. Using the standard handbook of parliamentary law, *Robert's Rules of Order*, to determine correct procedure for conducting business, making motions, and voting

  2. Perceiving the wisdom of having a parliamentarian settle questions of procedure

VII. ORGANIZING INFORMATION

 A. Make effective use of outlining techniques

  1. Realizing the value of the outline for organizing ideas

  2. Realizing the function of the outline as a blueprint to follow in writing a paper; a skeletal framework for organizing information

  3. Realizing that the framework of the outline is a hierarchy of logically related items

PART TWO: LEARNING SKILLS

VII. ORGANIZING INFORMATION (cont.)

    a. Broken into major divisions (headings), subdivisions, and sub-subdivisions

    b. Each division is subordinate to the item on the level immediately above

    c. All items within a division are of equal importance

    d. Minimum of two major divisions; maximum of six

    e. Balance within all divisions is the goal

    f. Main headings can stand alone or be subdivided

    g. May be in topic or sentence form; one or the other; cannot alternate or mix forms

B. Recognize the distinguishing characteristics and mechanics of the two basic outlining systems

  1. Understanding the notation system employed in the classic, standard, or Harvard form of outlining

    a. Use Roman numerals for main topics

    b. Use capital letters for subtopics

    c. Use Arabic numerals for points under each subtopic

    d. Use lower case letters for points under each sub-subtopic

    e. Put a period after each numeral and letter

    f. Indent topics under each division; indent subtopics under each topic; indent each point under subtopics

  2. Matching the following sample standard outline form to above explanation

    I. First main topic

      A. First subtopic

        1. First point

        2. Second point

PART TWO: LEARNING SKILLS

Introduce   Reinforce   Extend

VII. ORGANIZING INFORMATION (cont.)

   B. Second subtopic
    1. First point
    2. Second point
     a. First subpoint
     b. Second subpoint
   3. Understanding the decimal system of outlining
    a. Use Arabic numerals only
    b. Each main topic is numbered in sequence beginning with 1
    c. Each subtopic is numbered in sequence following a decimal point
   4. Matching the following sample decimal outline form to above explanation
    1. First main topic
     1.1 First subtopic
     1.2 Second subtopic
    2. Second main topic
     2.1 First subtopic
     2.2 Second subtopic
     2.3 Third subtopic
    3. Third main topic
     3.1 First subtopic
     3.2 Second subtopic
     3.3 Third subtopic
   5. Perceiving the value of using the decimal system of outlining for scientific and technical reports and for business and industrial reports
  C. Make effective use of note-taking techniques
   1. Establishing a definite procedure for note-taking
    a. Write notes in ink
    b. Use either 4 × 6 or 3 × 5 index cards for taking notes
    c. Place only one item of information on a card
    d. Each card should contain
     –The source and paging
     –The topic, heading, or "slug"
     –The note itself

PART TWO: LEARNING SKILLS

	Introduce	Reinforce	Extend

VII. ORGANIZING INFORMATION (cont.)

    e. Enclose quotations in quotation marks

    f. Reduce paragraphs to a few sentences

    g. Write only on one side of card; if additional cards are needed, staple them together

    h. Avoid copying verbatim information; write note in own words

  2. Establishing a definite procedure for writing bibliography cards or bibliography notebook entries

    a. Note on bibliography cards
  –Library call number for the source
  –Author's full name, last name first
  –Title of book, underlined
  –Imprint data: place of publication, publisher
  –Copyright date
  –Code designation to be used on note cards to indicate this book as the source of the note

    b. Encyclopedia notation on bibliography cards
  –Author of article, if signed
  –Title of article, in quotes
  –Name of encyclopedia, underlined
  –Copyright date
  –Volume number in Roman numerals
  –Page numbers of article

    c. Periodical notation on bibliography cards
  –Author of article, if signed
  –Title of article, in quotes
  –Name of periodical, underlined
  –Volume and number of issue, if given
  –Date of issue
  –Pages of the article, also

PART TWO: LEARNING SKILLS

Introduce　　Reinforce　　Extend

VII. ORGANIZING INFORMATION (cont.)

section for newspaper
article
-Code designation to be
used on note cards to indicate this source

d. Bibliography notebook entries
-Use 8½ × 11 inch, 3 ring
notebook paper
-Write, type, or photocopy
information
-Written or typed bibliography data follows exactly
the procedure outlined
above for bibliography
cards; only one source on
each page
-Photocopy technique saves
time, gives additional information
-Photocopy title page on
8½ × 11 inch paper
-Write copyright date
under imprint
-Write library call number
upper left-hand corner
-Write code designation on
upper right-hand corner
-Photocopy the table of contents
-Data bank for review of
book chapter coverage
-Quick source to consult
for information on new
topics in an expanded
search
-Notebook convenient to
carry to library when working on research
-Note-taking can still be on
cards using bibliography
code for reference to source
-Notebook permits photo-
copying of charts, graphs,
tables, lengthy quotations,
diagrams for information
retrieval

PART TWO: LEARNING SKILLS

<table>
<tr><td></td><td>Introduce</td><td>Reinforce</td><td>Extend</td></tr>
</table>

VII. ORGANIZING INFORMATION (cont.)

> 3. Sorting note cards preparatory
> to writing a paper
>> a. Sort note cards by topic or
>> "slug"
>> b. Arrange note cards for each
>> topic in sequence matching
>> topic placement in outline
>> for writing the paper
> 4. Matching the notes to each
> topic in the outline, read notes
> in sequence, decide
>> a. Adequacy of information
>> b. Need to delete, keep, or
>> search for additional infor-
>> mation

PART THREE:
COMMUNICATING SKILLS

I. WRITING AS A COMMUNICATION TOOL

> A. Perceive the significance of writing
>> 1. Realizing that writing is a tool
>> of thinking
>>> a. Clarity of written expression
>>> is evidence of clarity of
>>> thought
>>> b. Writing and reason are in-
>>> terdependent and insepar-
>>> able
>> 2. Realizing that writing is a
>> learned process
>>> a. Requires concentration
>>> b. Requires a disciplined will
>>> c. Requires craftsmanship
>> 3. Realizing that there are two
>> basic requirements for effective
>> writing
>>> a. Have something significant
>>> to say
>>> b. Say it skillfully with clarity,
>>> precision, and style
> B. Perceive the significance of func-
> tional literacy
>> 1. Realizing that functional liter-
>> acy means being able to read, to

PART THREE:
COMMUNICATING SKILLS

Introduce   Reinforce   Extend

I. WRITING AS A COMMUNICATION TOOL (cont.)

    write, to think, and to act with
    competence

  2. Realizing that functional literacy is a basic requirement for*
    a. Holding a decent job
    b. Supporting self and family
    c. Leading a life of dignity and pride

C. Perceive the hallmarks of excellence in written communication to be
  1. Honest, concise, and effective use of language
  2. Significant ideas organized in a clear, coherent, precise, and persuasive way

II. WRITING THE ESSAY

A. Perceive the distinguishing characteristics of the essay form
  1. Recognizing that the essay is a composition expressing a point of view
  2. Recognizing that the basic components of the essay are
    a. A significant thesis
    b. Accurate, adequate information
    c. Compelling writing style
  3. Recognizing that the basic types of the essay are
    a. Narrative
    b. Descriptive
    c. Expository
    d. Argumentative
  4. Realizing that ideas for the essay come from
    a. Reading
    b. Observing
    c. Remembering
    d. Reflective reasoning
    e. Creative thinking

B. Become aware of the techniques employed in designing and structuring the essay

*David Harmon, "Illiteracy: An Overview," in *Harvard Educational Review* 40, no. 2, May 1970, p. 227.

PART THREE:
COMMUNICATING SKILLS

	Introduce	Reinforce	Extend
II. WRITING THE ESSAY (cont.)			

1. Focusing on a subject of personal interest or concern
   a. Narrow the subject to a manageable thesis or theme
      -Avoid the trite, the commonplace, the "same old thing"
      -Search for a thought-provoking thesis; an attention grabber
   b. Be sure that sufficient information is available
2. Designing the essay
   a. Use the thesis as the internal organizer
   b. Organize ideas in jot outline form
   c. Gather information
      -Sift it, evaluate it
      -Relate it to jot outline
3. Prewriting the essay
   a. Use the jot outline as the blueprint
   b. Build the essay in three main parts
      -The beginning
      -The middle
      -The end
   c. State the thesis in the beginning paragraph
      -In opening sentence introduce the thesis in broad, general terms
      -State the thesis in the *last* sentence; set the stage for successive paragraphs
   d. Develop the thesis in the middle paragraphs
      -Arrange points in order of increasing interest
      -Save the most interesting or convincing until last
   e. Reword the thesis in the concluding paragraph

PART THREE:
COMMUNICATING SKILLS

Introduce   Reinforce   Extend

II. WRITING THE ESSAY (cont.)

   –Drive home the main point
   or points
   –Make final sentence the
   clincher
  4. Reading the essay critically
   a. Determine if
    –Sentences are sharp and
    clear
    –Paragraphs are related to
    thesis
    –Topic sentences are strong
    and precise
    –The thought is developed
    logically and smoothly
    –Unnecessary phrases need
    to be deleted
    –Punctuation and spelling
    are correct
   b. Answer the questions
    –Are you satisfied with the
    content and the organiza-
    tion?
    –Have you said what you
    wanted to say?
    –Is it the best you can do?
  5. Revising the essay
   a. Rewrite until the thought
   comes clear
   b. Read the final draft aloud
   once or twice
    –Does it read smoothly?
    –Does it still need to be pared
    or pruned?
    –Is it convincing?
   c. Make all corrections
  6. Typing the essay in final form
   a. Type finished essay on white
   paper 8½ × 11 inches
   b. Proofread carefully

III. WRITING THE RESEARCH PAPER

 A. Recognize the purpose and value of
 the research paper
  1. Perceiving research to mean
   –The careful, critical, disciplined process of inquiry

PART THREE:
COMMUNICATING SKILLS

	Introduce	Reinforce	Extend

III. WRITING THE RESEARCH PAPER (cont.)

      2. Perceiving the research paper to be
        –The organized, documented communication of information gained through research in support of the paper's thesis

      3. Perceiving the value of the research paper to be
        –Learning the basic techniques, procedures, and mechanics of research writing
        –Learning to identify, refine, and state a research problem or thesis
        –Learning to use library resources efficiently and effectively
        –Learning disciplined working habits; to follow the rules and procedures of standard research methodology
        –Learning to complete a time-consuming and demanding task in a craftsmanlike manner
        –Learning to think analytically and critically and to find challenge and satisfaction in doing so
        –Learning to communicate thought in a clear, concise, direct, and lively style

   B. Study the procedure to follow as outlined in a basic style manual or research guide*

      1. Discerning established procedure for preparing the research paper

      2. Following the established procedure from first to last step in
        a. Choosing a topic
        b. Preliminary reading
        c. Narrowing the topic

---

*James D. Lester, *Writing Research Papers: A Complete Guide*, 2nd ed. (Glenview, Ill.: Scott, Foresman, 1976) and Kate L. Turabian, *Student's Guide for Writing College Papers*, 3rd ed. (Chicago: University of Chicago Press, 1976).

PART THREE:
COMMUNICATING SKILLS

Introduce   Reinforce   Extend

III. WRITING THE RESEARCH PAPER (cont.)

    d. Stating the thesis
    e. Gathering information
    f. Preparing a working bibliography
    g. Preparing a preliminary outline
    h. Taking notes
    i. Preparing final outline
    j. Writing first draft
    k. Footnoting
    l. Reading first draft and revising it
    m. Writing the final draft
    n. Preparing the bibliography
    o. Proofreading

IV. SPEAKING AS A COMMUNICATION TOOL

A. Perceive that speech is a vehicle for conveying thought and emotion
    1. What is said and how it is said is evidence of mental and emotion processes
    2. Speech mirrors personality
B. Perceive that effective speaking is a learned process
    1. Requiring training and practice
    2. Requiring understanding and mastery of basic techniques, procedures, and mechanics of speaking
    3. Requiring the ability to communicate thought orally in a clear, concise, direct, and convincing style
C. Perceive the requirements for a speech of quality and effectiveness
    1. Seeing the similarity between the process of designing and structuring the essay and the process of designing and structuring the speech
    2. Viewing the speech as a spoken essay
    3. Recognizing that as the essay expresses a point of view, so does the speech

PART THREE:
COMMUNICATING SKILLS

IV. SPEAKING AS A COMMUNICATION TOOL (cont.)

    4. Recognizing that the basic components of a speech are
      a. A significant thesis
      b. Accurate, adequate, thought-provoking information logically presented
      c. Compelling speaking style
    5. Recognizing that the basic types of speeches are
      a. To entertain or amuse
      b. To inform or instruct
      c. To stimulate or actuate through emotion
      d. To convince or move to action

D. Perceive the distinguishing characteristics of the speech designed to entertain or amuse
    1. Recognizing the typical situations calling for this type of speech
      a. Parties
      b. Dinners
      c. Club meetings
    2. Recognizing the main purpose is to entertain or amuse plus
      a. Something of substance
      b. Something with appeal for the audience
    3. Recognizing the essentials of delivery and content
      a. Keep the speech moving
      b. Show that you are enjoying yourself
      c. Don't be sarcastic, rude, or degrading
      d. Don't use "tired" jokes
      e. Laugh at yourself
      f. Let one incident, story, or anecdote lead smoothly to the next
      g. Trigger humor by
        –Exaggeration
        –Puns
        –Poking fun at authority

PART THREE:
COMMUNICATING SKILLS

Introduce   Reinforce   Extend

IV. Speaking as a Communication Tool (cont.)

       –Irony

       –Absurdities

    h. Don't talk too long

  E. Perceive the distinguishing characteristics of the speech designed to inform or instruct

    1. Seeing the similarity between the process of designing and structuring the research paper and the process of designing and structuring an informational speech

    2. Recognizing the typical situations calling for this type of speech

      a. Reports of a scientific or scholarly nature

      b. Lectures by teacher, lawyer, traveler, writer, etc.

    3. Recognizing the main purpose to be

      a. Building understanding

      b. Helping audience grasp certain fundamental facts

      c. Creating interest in the subject

    4. Recognizing the essentials of delivery and content

      a. Speak distinctly with a well modulated voice

      b. Speak slowly enough for the audience to grasp the meaning; rapidly enough to hold the attention of the audience

      c. Establish rapport with the audience; let your delivery convince the audience of your sincerity

      d. Don't alienate the audience by talking over the heads of the listeners

      e. Limit the main points to no more than four

      f. Logically develop each point; don't digress

PART THREE:
COMMUNICATING SKILLS

IV. SPEAKING AS A COMMUNICATION TOOL (cont.)

        g. Use concrete data; avoid abstractions
        h. Use appropriate gestures
        i. Know your speech; convince the audience that you know what you are talking about and that you believe in what you are saying
        j. Don't exceed the time allotted for the speech

F. Perceive the distinguishing characteristics of the speech designed to stimulate or actuate through emotion

  1. Recognizing the typical situations calling for this type of speech
        a. Commencement exercises
        b. Dedications
        c. Eulogies
        d. Patriotic celebrations

  2. Recognizing the main purpose to be
        a. Stimulating listeners to greater devotion to a cause
        b. Inspiring listeners to greater effort coupled with lasting enthusiasm

  3. Recognizing the essentials of delivery and content
        a. Speak distinctly with a well modulated voice
        b. Speak slowly enough for the audience to grasp the meaning; rapidly enough to hold the attention of the audience
        c. Establish rapport with the audience; let your delivery convince the audience of your sincerity and depth of feeling
        d. Don't use notes; don't hesitate; keep your ideas moving
        e. Use a slogan or an apt phrase to stimulate interest

PART THREE: COMMUNICATING SKILLS

Introduce   Reinforce   Extend

IV. SPEAKING AS A COMMUNICATION TOOL (cont.)

    f. Be concrete and specific
    g. Use vivid examples, anec-
        dotes, or incidents
    h. Build upon fact and com-
        mon beliefs in fundamental
        human desires
    i. Use vivid imagery
    j. Use appropriate gestures
    k. Know your speech; convince
        the audience that you know
        what you are talking about
        and that you believe whole-
        heartedly in what you are
        saying
    l. Don't exceed the time al-
        lotted for the speech
G. Perceive the distinguishing char-
    acteristics of the speech designed to
    convince or move to action
    1. Recognizing the typical situa-
        tions calling for this type of
        speech
        a. Political meetings
        b. Civic mass meetings
        c. Corporate business meet-
            ings
        d. Legislative hearings
    2. Recognizing the main purpose
        to be
        a. Convincing the audience of
            the logic of your argument
        b. Committing the audience to
            action in support of your
            beliefs, proposals, or recom-
            mendations
    3. Recognizing the essentials of
        delivery and content
        a. Speak distinctly with a well
            modulated voice
        b. Speak slowly enough for the
            audience to grasp the mean-
            ing; rapidly enough to hold
            the attention of the audience
        c. Establish rapport with the
            audience; let your delivery

PART THREE:
COMMUNICATING SKILLS

IV. Speaking as a Communication Tool (cont.)

      convince the audience of
      your sincerity

   d. Appeal to the common sense
      of the audience

   e. Use concrete facts, sound,
      logical reasoning

   f. Define the criteria or stan-
      dards upon which your pro-
      posals or recommendations
      are made

   g. Stick to the point; don't in-
      troduce extraneous matter

   h. Make the conclusion a sum-
      mation of both the thesis
      and substantiating argu-
      ments, proposals, or recom-
      mendations

   i. Know your speech; convince
      the audience that you know
      what you are talking about
      and that you believe whole-
      heartedly in what you are
      saying

   j. Don't exceed the time al-
      lotted for the speech

  H. Perceive the distinguishing char-
    acteristics of debate

    1. Recognizing that debate is a type
      of argumentative speaking
      regulated by

      a. Time limitations

      b. Parliamentary or forensic
         rules

    2. Recognizing that the purpose
      of debate is for

      a. Arguing a proposition pro
         and con

      b. Arriving at and recording a
         decision

    3. Recognizing the rules and regu-
      lations of formal debate

      a. Time limits are imposed
         on debaters; typical distribu-
         tion of time for each of four
         speakers as follows

PART THREE:
COMMUNICATING SKILLS

Introduce   Reinforce   Extend

IV. SPEAKING AS A COMMUNICATION TOOL (cont.)

  Constructive speeches:
  –First affirmative—10
   minutes
  –First negative—10
   minutes
  –Second affirmative—10
   minutes
  –Second negative—10
   minutes
  Rebuttal speeches:
  –First negative—5
   minutes
  –First affirmative—5
   minutes
  –Second negative—5
   minutes
  –Second affirmative—5
   minutes

 b. The argument is conducted according to parliamentary rules

  Each side receives equal treatment

 c. The subject is phrased in resolution form

  The decision is based on the "merits of the question"

APPENDIX M

Facilities Planning*

Any administrator faced with the responsibility of designing a new school library facility or for renovating existing facilities should involve the librarian in all phases of this planning. Too often the librarian—most intimately concerned with the functional plant—is consulted after decisions are made and rectification of mistakes financially unfeasible.

Before one fact is placed on a worksheet or one line on a preliminary layout sketch, the librarian should review the basic principles of functional school library design. *Media Center Facility Design for Maryland Schools* (Baltimore, Md.: Division of School Library Development and Services, Maryland State Department of Education, 1975) is an excellent source of guidance.

With background from this or similar sources, plus knowledge of numbers of students and faculty to be served and of the kind of library program anticipated, the librarian will be prepared to preplan the school library physical plant intelligently. The function-facilities-space worksheet included here can serve as pattern for such preplanning.

A blueprint, North Hills Intermediate High School Library Complex, is included to assist the librarian in visualizing the relation of function to design and to space allocation.

Just as consultation with the librarian should precede facilities layout, so consultation with other members of the library staff should precede detailing plant facilities and furnishings. Therefore, included here also for librarian guidance is the In-Service Secondary Library Staff Meeting Agenda which directed the North Hills secondary library staff in determining details of plant facilities and furnishings.

*Mrs. Joyce B. Scholl, School Library Development Consultant, 122 Rose Ave., Pittsburgh, Pa. 15229.

FUNCTION–FACILITIES–SPACE WORKSHEET FOR
PREPLANNING THE SCHOOL LIBRARY PHYSICAL PLANT

I. RECEPTION OR CIRCULATION AREA

FOR _____ STUDENTS

FUNCTION	FACILITY CONSIDERATIONS	SPACE REQUIRED
A. Controlling library complex	1. Central location 2. Safety glass view panels 3. Uninterrupted view 4. Access to corridor 5. Access to suite components 6. Library complex intercom control 7. Library complex master light switch	
B. Admitting and dismissing library users	1. Unimpeded traffic flow 2. Ample entrance/exit	
C. Charging out and receiving back instructional materials	1. Book depository 2. Depressible book truck 3. Check out surface (two level for elementary) 4. Charging machine 5. Electrical outlet 6. Book truck passage 7. Storage shelves/bins	
D. Accommodating reserve instructional materials	1. Back counter shelving 2. Reserve stacks	
E. Maintaining circulation mechanics	1. Card files 2. Lockable drawers 3. Book trucks	
F. Scheduling, training, supervising clerical help	1. Clerical stations 2. Duty posting board	
G. Giving directions and announcements	1. Display spaces 2. Bulletin board	
H. Providing temporary storage for library users' personal effects	1. Storage lockers	
I. Providing for copying of print materials	1. Copying equipment 2. Coin changer 3. Supplies dispenser	

Number of students_____
Space required (sq. ft.)_____

II. GENERAL USE AREA

FUNCTION	FACILITY CONSIDERATIONS	FOR _____ STUDENTS SPACE REQUIRED

A. Providing for individual reading, writing, examining, analyzing, comparing, contrasting, thinking, enjoying, questing,	1. Location convenience
	2. Ease of control
	3. Unimpeded traffic flow
	4. Adjustable shelving
	  a. Perimeter and double faced
	  b. Full and counter height
	  c. Sized for
	    (1) Standard books
	    (2) Quarto books
	    (3) Picture books (for elementary)
	  d. Provided with
	    (1) Backs
	    (2) Section, shelf labels
	    (3) Book supports
	    (4) Step stools
	5. Work surfaces
	  a. Tables
	  b. Carrels
	  c. Picture book tables with wells (for elementary)
	  d. Index/reference tables (for secondary)
	6. Seating
	  a. Chairs
	  b. Picture book table stools (for elementary)
	  c. Storytelling cushions/hassocks (for elementary)
	  d. Rocking chairs (for elementary)
	  e. Shelf-side benches/stools
	7. Files
	  a. Card catalog
	  b. Pamphlets
	  c. Graphics	

8. Dictionary stands
9. Atlas stands
10. Globes
11. Portable, expandable display screens

B. Providing for directions, announcements, display

1. Intercom connection
2. Clock
3. Chalkboard/tackboard
4. Bulletin board
5. Display surface/rack

Number of students —————
Space required (sq. ft.)—————

III. SPECIAL USE AREAS

FOR _____ STUDENTS

FUNCTION	FACILITY CONSIDERATIONS	SPACE REQUIRED
A. Providing for librarian office	1. Library suite and corridor access 2. Safety glass control panels 3. Desk, posture chair 4. Files 5. Shelving/counter 6. Electrical outlets 7. Telephone 8. Conferee chair 9. Coat storage	
B. Providing for conference, seminar, small group instruction	1. Library suite access 2. Safety glass control panels 3. Electrical outlets 4. T-V viewing screen 5. Projection screen 6. Overhead projector and projection cart 7. Chalkboard/tackboard 8. Map/chart rack 9. Shelving 10. Table 11. Seating	
C. Providing for large group instruction	1. Library suite and corridor access 2. Electrical outlets 3. T-V viewing screen	

4. Projection screen
5. Overhead projector and projection cart
6. Chalkboard/tackboard
7. Shelving
8. Writing/work surfaces
9. Seating
10. Professional station
11. Podium/lectern

D. Providing for listening and viewing

1. General use area juxtaposition
2. Maximum privacy, light controlled carrels
   a. Free standing
   b. Wall hung
3. Electrical outlets
4. Individual projection surfaces
5. Seating
6. Dial access equipment
7. Equipment carts
8. Phonographs with earphones
9. Listening posts with earphones
10. Tape recorders with earphones
11. Projectors
    a. Film
    b. Filmstrip
    c. Rear screen
    d. Single concept
    e. Sound filmstrip
    f. Slide
12. Shelving/storage
13. Media aide station

E. Providing for AV media previewing

1. Viewers
   a. Filmstrip
   b. Slide
   c. Transparency

F. Providing for practicing, recording, seminar activities

1. General use area juxtaposition
2. Acoustical privacy
3. Safety glass control panels
4. Carrel/work surface
5. Seating
6. Storage/shelving

	7. Electrical outlets
	8. Typewriter(s)
	9. Tape recorder(s)
	10. Waste disposal
	11. "In use" light
G. Providing for periodical use	1. General use area juxta-position
	2. Shelving
	a. Periodical display
	b. Periodical stacks
	3. Microreader stations
	4. Electrical outlets
	5. Microreader
	6. Microreader-printer
	7. Newspaper display rack
	8. Files/file boxes
	9. Seating
	10. Media aide station
H. Providing professional library facilities	1. Library suite and corridor access
	2. Electrical outlets
	3. Shelving/stacks
	4. Files/storage cabinets
	5. Work surfaces
	6. Seating

Number of students _____

Space required (sq. ft.)_____

IV. WORK/STORAGE AREA

FUNCTION	FACILITY CONSIDERATIONS	FOR _____ STUDENTS SPACE REQUIRED
A. Providing for media the facilities to select, order, receive, examine, process, organize, schedule, evaluate, circulate, inventory, repair, store	1. Corridor access	
	2. Dollies	
	3. Book trucks	
	4. Waste disposal	
	5. Sink, running water	
	6. Counter, two level	
	7. Electrical outlets	
	8. Adjustable shelving	
	9. Bins	
	10. Drawers	
	11. Storage cabinets	
	12. Files	
	a. Movable card	
	b. Letter and legal vertical	

      c. Jumbo
      d. Map
      e. Portable card catalog
      f. Recordex visual
  13. Work stations
  14. Chairs/stools
  15. Library suite access
  16. Safety glass view panels
  17. Telephone
  18. Hat, coat racks
  19. Typewriter desk
  20. Posture chair
  21. Typewriter
  22. Adding machine
  23. Labeling machine
  24. Pencil sharpener
  25. Stapler

B. Providing for supplies the facilities to select, order, receive, house, distribute, inventory

  1. Storage cabinets
  2. Dispensers
      a. Adhesive
      b. Label
      c. Cord
      d. Plastic jacket
      e. Tape
      f. Paper
  3. Tote boxes

C. Providing for media accessibility

  1. Adjustable perimeter shelving
  2. Stacks
  3. Bins
      a. Equipment
      b. Realia
      c. Kit
      d. Object
  4. Counters
  5. Rolling equipment floor space
  6. Cabinets
      a. Disc
      b. Film
      c. Filmstrip
      d. Flat graphic
      e. Microform
      f. Programmed instruction
      g. Slide
      h. Stencil, master
      i. Tape
      j. Transparency

7. Book truck passage space
8. Files

Number of students_____
Space required (sq. ft.)_____

V. PRODUCTION AREA

		FOR _____ STUDENTS
FUNCTION	FACILITY CONSIDERATIONS	SPACE REQUIRED

A. Facilitating *all* production activities in each of the following areas	1. Library suite and delivery entrance access
	2. Job rated electrical wiring
	3. Light control
	4. Electrical outlets
	5. Sinks, running water
	6. Heat and stain resistant, sound deadening flooring
	7. Exhaust, ventilating fans/direct fume vents
	8. Humidity control
	9. Dollies, hand trucks
	10. Waste disposal
	11. Work surfaces/counters
	12. Cabinets/shelving/bins/drawers
	13. Files
	   a. Standard
	   b. Jumbo
	   c. Map
	   d. Special
	14. Packaging equipment
	   a. Wrapping paper dispenser
	   b. Tape dispenser and moistener
	   c. Cord dispenser
	15. Media specialist stations	

B. Providing for graphics production	1. Typewriter desk, chair
	2. Typewriters
	   a. Standard
	   b. Special keyboard
	   c. Primary
	3. Mimeograph
	4. Mimeograph stencil files
	5. Mimeograph light board	

6. Spirit duplicator
7. Three-hole punch
8. Paper cutter
9. Electric stapler
10. Collator
11. Spiral binding equipment
12. Dry mount press and tacking iron
13. Transparency production systems
14. Transparency viewer
15. Overhead projector/screen
16. Sink, running water
17. Drying racks
18. Laminator
19. Airbrush
20. Ventilating shield and hood
21. Drawing board
22. Mechanical lettering devices
23. Sign making equipment
24. Multilith

C. Providing for photographic production

1. Dark room
2. Dark room equipment
   a. Electric warning signal
   b. Acid resistant, multi basin sinks, running water
   c. Timer
   d. Paper cutter
   e. Drying rack
   f. Photo modifier and stand
   g. Photo copier and stand
   h. Slide reproducer
3. Cameras with accessories
   a. 35mm
   b. 16mm
   c. 8mm
   d. 35mm still
   e. Rapid process (Polaroid)

	4. Flood lighting equipment
	5. Light box
	6. Film rewind
	7. Film splicers
	8. Tape splicer
	9. Portable chalkboard
	10. Composing stick and print
D. Providing for three-dimensional construction (ETV stage sets, dioramas, mock-ups)	1. Sink, running water
	2. Work bench
	3. Carpentry tools
	a. Hand
	b. Power
	4. Paint spray equipment
	5. Heating equipment
E. Providing for electronic production and retrieval	1. Coaxial cable outlets
	2. Acoustical privacy
	a. Sound proof floor
	b. Sound proof walls
	c. Sound proof ceiling
	3. TV studios
	a. "On camera"
	(1) Camera and accessories
	(2) Monitor
	(3) Video taping equipment
	(4) Warning light
	(5) Storage
	(6) Trolley for drapes
	b. Rehearsal
	4. TV office
	5. TV properties storage
	6. Dial access
	a. Control console
	b. Storage center
	7. Computerized learning laboratory
	8. Language laboratory area

Number of students_____

Space required (sq. ft.)_____

Total space required (sq. ft.) _____

IN-SERVICE SECONDARY LIBRARY STAFF MEETING

North Hills School District

Chairman, Helen Rea

Agenda: Staff examination of the blueprint (see plan) to decide the following for the North Hills Intermediate High School Library Complex:

1. About student convenience lockers in the range inside the main library entrance:

    What size should each locker be?

    How many lockers should there be in this section?

    Should all lockers have doors or should some be merely convenience boxes for the placing of extra student books while the student is working in the library?

    How many lockers should have locks in anticipation of the student needing to protect his tape recorder or portable typewriter until he returns to work in the library?

    What other recommendations should be made pertaining to these lockers?

2. About the charging desk:

    What sections would you suggest being placed in the charging desk?

    Would you recommend two wells for charging machines?

    Where would you recommend placing the charging machine or machines?

3. About electricity controls:

    Would you recommend having switches (1) in each area of the main room? (2) in each conference room? (3) in each seminar room?

    Would you recommend having a master light switch for control of the lights in the total library complex?

    Would you recommend a master control at the charging desk to shut off the school intercom when tapes are being made?

4. About storage:

    How much and what width shelving would you recommend for each librarian's office?

    Should magazine shelving be placed in the main shelving area or in a special magazine floor rack?

    Where and how should newspapers be housed?

    What kind of record storage should be provided: cabinet or shelving, open or closed?

    Would it be feasible to house microfilm in the periodical-reserve storage room and have students request it at the desk?

    Would you recommend storage of anything else in the periodical room?

    What type of locker for coats, etc., do you recommend for the workroom and the librarian's office?

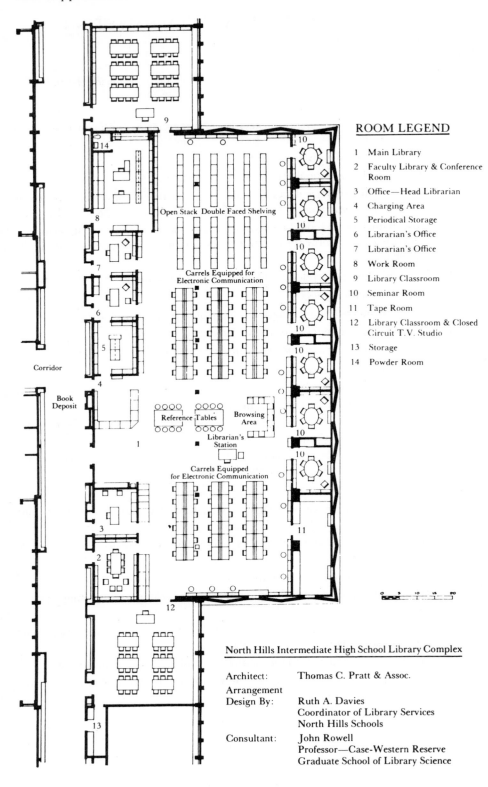

ROOM LEGEND

1 Main Library

2 Faculty Library & Conference Room

3 Office—Head Librarian

4 Charging Area

5 Periodical Storage

6 Librarian's Office

7 Librarian's Office

8 Work Room

9 Library Classroom

10 Seminar Room

11 Tape Room

12 Library Classroom & Closed Circuit T.V. Studio

13 Storage

14 Powder Room

Open Stack Double Faced Shelving

Carrels Equipped for Electronic Communication

Corridor

Book Deposit

Reference Tables

Browsing Area

Librarian's Station

Carrels Equipped for Electronic Communication

North Hills Intermediate High School Library Complex

Architect: Thomas C. Pratt & Assoc.

Arrangement
Design By: Ruth A. Davies
                  Coordinator of Library Services
                  North Hills Schools

Consultant: John Rowell
                  Professor—Case-Western Reserve
                  Graduate School of Library Science

5. About furniture:

   What type and what items of furniture would you recommend for the faculty library?

   What style and how many chairs do you recommend for (1) the main reading room? (2) the conference room? (3) the seminar rooms? (4) the workroom?

   Do you favor placing a Howe table with electronic listening well in each of the seminar rooms?

   Do you recommend one or more reference type tables?

   Would you recommend hassock type stools at reference tables?

   Would you favor putting the 120-drawer card catalog against the periodical room wall?

   Would you recommend a separate card catalog for the faculty library?

6. About equipment:

   What type typewriter should be specified for (1) librarian's office? (2) workroom? (3) seminar room? (4) other area needs?

   Would you recommend placing microfilm readers on carrels?

   For record players, what are your recommendations on (1) number needed for use in library? (2) make and model? (3) make and model of listening post? (4) make and model of earphones?

   For tape recorders, what are your recommendations on (1) number needed for use in library? (2) make and model?

7. About other furnishing for library complex:

   What do you recommend?

APPENDIX N

Learning to Learn in School Libraries*

Not surprisingly, discussions of changes being effected in school library programs by curricular and instructional developments, educational technology and facilities, automation, federal and state legislation, networks of library resources and services, computerized information services, and innovations too numerous to mention lead frequently to a consideration of teaching the use of the library and its resources. This venerable subject of library instruction is currently getting new nomenclature (*methods of inquiry*, for example), attracting critical examination and reappraisal, and generating some controversy.

PHILOSOPHY AND PRACTICE

Learning, with its many elements and variables of what is to be learned and how it is to be learned, what is to be taught and how it is to be taught, constitutes a complex discipline—the core of the educative process. Teaching study and research skills represents but a small segment, and teaching the use of the library and its resources falls within that segment.

Determining the objectives, content, and methodology of library instruction in contemporary elementary and secondary education is not the simple matter that it may appear to be, and our traditional approaches, shaped by long service and practice, may be affording librarians a specious form of security. The current emphasis in the schools on self-directed learning, inquiry, and independent study all too often contribute to an automatic solidifying of these established methods, with little or no critical evaluation of their current appropriateness.

With the widespread interest in and exploration of techniques for teaching learning, the art and methods of instruction, and the psychology of learning, it can reasonably be assumed that some agreements concerning the program of teaching study skills and methods of inquiry might eventually be reached in much the same way that decisions have been made in the last decade in planning programs in numerous substantive fields of the curriculum. (Analysis of these curricular programs for implications and suggestions for study, learning, and research skills holds great value.) It is true that designs for library instruction have been constructed on local and system levels, involving librarians, teachers, and curriculum specialists, but it seems timely that a

*Frances Henne, *School Libraries*, American Association of School Librarians, vol. 15. no. 4, May 1966. pp. 15–23.

systematic study on a national basis be implemented, utilizing techniques of discussion (symposia), study, and experimentation that the various commissions or other deliberative groups in the substantive fields have employed.

For the specifics of content (types of knowledge and skills) to be acquired by individual students and the decisions regarding the appropriate time, place, and methods for acquiring them can best and only be determined by the pooled judgments of experts in the academic subject fields, in curriculum construction, in instructional methods, in the psychology of learning, and in school librarianship. (This suggestion is a variation, and a significant variation, of one of the proposals made at the Conference within a Conference.) The expectations of college specialists would also be relevant. This recommendation in no sense rules out the importance of the school librarian's participation in the planning and implementing of programs thus evolved; but instruction relating to study skills and methods of inquiry, including the use of the library and its resources, is always a means to an end, and this end and the ways to reach it must involve the philosophy and experiences of curriculum specialists and specialists in the theory of learning.

Until we have the benefits of deliberations of the kinds suggested above, the nature of teaching library instruction will be shaped primarily on a local level. (It should be emphasized that the proposals noted here do not rule out the desirability of or the need for making adjustments necessary for the individual school. The integration with the school's curriculum would always be local in a very real sense.) Some current theories and developments that are occupying the attention of many school librarians in the area of library instruction are presented in the remainder of this paper. Many represent topics that have been with us a long, long time, but now seem to be pressing forward for action and decision on a wide scale.

THE NATURE OF LIBRARY SERVICE

Recommendations about the nature of library instruction will affect, and also be affected by, philosophy concerning the scope of library services. Current thought about the distinctions to be made between independent use of the library by students and desirable library services provides an example. *In the viewpoint of many school librarians the mere process of locating and finding materials in the library holds little intellectual benefit for students, and time thus spent is generally wasted time.* The many processes involved in what students do with materials—evaluation, synthesis, reflection, thinking, appreciation, or whatever—are the important factors, not the searching, locating, and assembling of materials.

At points like these, it is essential for new thinking and new decisions in order to determine how much students should know about the use of the library and its resources, how consistently and persistently they must apply their skills and knowledge independently and without assistance from librarians, when this independent pursuit of materials results in a waste of time, and what variations should be recommended for different groups of students. Deploring the spoon-feeding of students, as librarians so frequently do, may actually mean deploring a more intelligent use of a student's time and efforts; and self-directed study or learning is not necessarily synonymous with self-directed finding of materials.

Thus expanded location, information, and bibliographic services are being recommended, and in some cases in actual operation, on school building and system levels for both teachers and students. The centralized bibliographic and abstracting services developed by Leonard Freiser in Toronto are well known. The potential of system and regional centers, with their bibliographic apparatus, retrieval machinery, and specialized service is briefly described in the national standards for school libraries. All of these developments, on-going and projected, can make materials and the content of materials more accessible and facilitate and expand information and other library services. The philosophy of expanded library services for teachers and students pertains to the library program in the school, and is not restricted to centralized system operations.

HOW MUCH, FOR WHOM, WHEN, AND WHERE?

In the program of library instructions, the recognition of individual abilities (individualization) is stressed. Various designs in curriculum construction (ungraded schools, track curricula, advanced placement and accelerated programs, provisions for exceptional children, among others) are geared to the individual and varying abilities existing among students, and so must the library program of instruction. These adaptations will vary from school to school and within schools. For the most able students, regardless of whether they are economically able to go to college, the school's program of research skills is required in full. For others, the amount of instruction may range from practically nothing to other levels, depending upon the abilities and characteristics of the students. For some students, and in certain schools this may be many students, the only library skill that they should have to acquire is an awareness, imprinted indelibly and happily upon them, that the library is a friendly place where the librarians are eager to help. To these students, the delights of periodical indexes and other library tools must ever remain closed. When the program of library instruction is truly integrated with classroom instruction, the needs of the retarded, the slow, the underachieving, the average, and the academically talented are taken care of in a realistic and natural way.

When decisions about what students need to know are reached by the school, their implementation requires careful planning by the school's administrators, teachers, and librarians that is comparable to, but obviously not identical with, the planning required for the substantive areas of the curriculum. The principal assumes responsibility for this area as seriously as he does for other parts of the instructional program. The head school librarian can serve, and frequently does, as the chairman of the school's committee (or equivalent) that plans and implements the school's program of teaching study skills and methods of inquiry. This committee includes teachers representing the various subject areas and grade levels in the school. All faculty members, of course, are ultimately involved in the program.

Local circumstances may necessitate or commend variations on the principles enumerated above, but basic objectives and desired outcomes remain essentially the same. For example, a system curriculum coordinator may work with the school committee. In some school systems the school library supervisor or coordinator develops the study and research skills program with the cooperation of the system subject and area specialists or with librarians and teachers representing each of the schools. Whether plans are developed at building, system, or state levels, the program must be geared to meet the needs of the objectives and instructional methods of the individual schools, and the administration, librarians, and faculty of the school must become actively involved in these procedures.

ANALYSIS OF ASSIGNMENTS

Whether in conjunction with developing a research skills program or in some other context, analysis and evaluation of assignments are high priority pursuits in many schools. Since the program of library instruction is integrated with the curriculum and objectives and content of the component parts of the curriculum determine the kinds of library resources to be used and any skills needed for their use, an analysis of all assignments made in the school proves useful. Theoretically, analyses of curricular content should reveal the kinds of study and research skills to be taught, but this cannot be assumed to apply to every school. In any event, knowledge of the assignments provides information needed to indicate an appropriate integration of the program with curriculum content.

This analysis also enables the librarians to evaluate the adequacy of the library's resources to meet student needs. For the program of teaching study skills and the methods of inquiry involves not just teaching the types of knowledge and skills entailed, but also opportunities to put them into operation through the use of a wide variety of school library resources. Independent research and inquiry are important in themselves, whether the student locates the necessary materials or has them located for him, and the library's resources must therefore be comprehensive and adequate for his purpose. Analysis of assignments can be and frequently is delegated to the head school librarian when the major objective relates to determining the adequacy of the school library resources. This form of evaluation is kept up-to-date by the teacher's reporting assignments to the school librarian on a continuing basis, and by having the librarians serve on the school's curriculum committees. A long history in the school of such reporting and representation will obviate the need for innovating a systematic analysis of assignments in terms of available library resources.

Scrutiny of assignments is important, as experience has frequently shown, for reasons other than those already noted, including locating busywork, pointless duplication, antiquated exercises, and sheer foolishness—and then making the improvements in order.

TEACHING STUDY SKILLS

No matter how the school may allocate the responsibilities for teaching the various study skills, whether to teachers alone, or librarians alone, or a combination of both— the librarians' responsibilities and opportunities for observing and helping students in the use of materials (and, in the process, evaluating their competencies) are clearly indicated. This principle applies to all schools. In those schools where independent study and self-directed learning are carefully planned for the students, these activities of the librarians represent key factors in a successful program. The librarian is the one who has the opportunity to observe, among other matters, the student's ability to use materials, to take notes, to outline, and to evaluate and synthesize materials. The school librarian's role in the program of study skills and methods of inquiry is that of a teacher and guidance specialist. The librarian's follow-up services in seeing how effectively students are using the library materials they have selected for their immediate needs are strategic and valuable ones.

All of which means that school librarians must have a knowledge of recent developments and approved techniques concerning the skills and psychology of learning and related topics. More is implied here than the content covered in the educational or teaching requirements commonly required for the certification of school librarians. From part of the school librarian's double-pronged certification requirements, comes some understanding, enriched later through experience, of teaching methods and developments; but the content prescribed in the principle stated above goes beyond this rudimentary preparation. (Being taught how to construct lesson plans is not the point intended!)

THE LEARNING CENTER

The library forms a natural environment for the kind of guidance that has just been described, and the designation of the school library as a study or learning laboratory does not need to have the chill connotation that some attach to it. A library *is* a learning center, and learning embraces reading a book for fun or aesthetic enjoyment as much as it does examining materials to abstract information or ideas for a term paper. It is not unnatural that in many schools the library is called the Learning Center. The Learning Center evolves directly and purely from the recent emphasis in the educational programs of the schools on the processes of learning: learning skills and competencies to be acquired by students; the materials and apparatus to be used by them (including traditional library resources as well as newer media); and the careful planning of time for study in the students' schedules—now done in some schools by computers. Inquiry, independent or individual study, and self-directed learning occupy a strong position in the philosophy of modern education, and in this development the school library's resources and its program of teaching study and research skills form a key and integral part at all levels of elementary and secondary education.

Along with the new focus on the library as a learning center, we can note changes in the attitude toward the library as the place for study. The image of the old-fashioned library study hall rightly evokes chilling horror in the hearts of school librarians, and the comments that follow do not apply to this concept. Today, students should and must have the opportunity to study, to learn, in a library and not in the bleak and barren environment of a study hall. Now, with the developments in school library facilities—library areas, resource centers, and all the multi-dimensional forms they take—the goals have changed. The idea portrayed in the oft reiterated cliché that curricular and instructional changes have made modern high school libraries comparable to those in many liberal arts colleges of yesteryear and to junior college libraries of today is true, and it must be put into operation in all respects, not just in raising the maturity level of the resources collections. Making it possible for all students to study and work in a library environment requires certain conditions, since no one is asking for a return to the old-fashioned library study hall with its frequently attendant policing and disciplinary problems. The minimal conditions include: sufficient quarters and facilities for the library, sufficient staff, sufficient resources, and, if students have scheduled study periods, intelligently and carefully planned programs for study. Let it be stressed that current national standards for school libraries relating to facilities and to staff do not sufficiently provide for an automatic conversion of library areas into study halls or vice versa.

THE I.M.C. AND THE SKILLS OF LEARNING

With more and more school libraries becoming instructional materials centers with fully equipped facilities and with functional programs of service, the librarian's role has expanded. Students, in the pursuit of their studies, use a cross-media or multi-media or single medium approach, and receive appropriate guidance from the school librarians in the selection of these materials and in their effective use. This principle means more than showing a student how to use a filmstrip viewer, or machinery for teaching tapes, or an 8mm sound film projector, or the micro-reader, or the apparatus for listening to recordings, or the dial equipment for banks of resources now making their appearance, or the apparatus for making transparencies, or machines and devices for programmed instruction. The program of teaching the use of library resources includes guidance in teaching students viewing and listening skills. Opportunities to help students to acquire film literacy are rapidly increasing for school librarians.

Learning how to view and how to listen and acquiring the skills of perception that evaluation and appreciation of the media require represent abilities that young persons have to acquire through time, effort, and guided experiences, in much the same manner they master the mechanical skills and developmental aspects of reading. Such instruction includes guidance in helping students to turn naturally to media other than print as the best and possibly the only appropriate or artistic forms of communication, to realize when audiovisual media complement printed materials, and to know when they have no relevance or are inferior for the purposes at hand. School librarians also have exciting opportunities to present to students the realm of the cinema as an art form.

ACADEMIC CREDIT

Unfortunately, the imporance attached to the skills of learning and methods of research sometimes results in the revival of outmoded techniques of the implementation of undesirable practices. No academic credit at any grade level should be given for instruction in the use of the library and its resources. Logically, this principle is a superfluous one, since the well-planned program, fully integrated with the curriculum, would not make such an eventuality possible. Library skills are means to other educational ends, and not ends in themselves. Library skills do not represent a separate substantive discipline and hence should not be designated as course content carrying academic credit. Nonetheless, there seems to be a growing and alarming tendency to formalize this instruction. Even when no academic credit is given, no justification exists for having either courses in this area or a detached string of lessons. Ironically enough, the use of programmed aids and of audiovisual materials in conjunction with library instruction often contributes to the perpetuation of arbitrary, nonintegrated instruction.

ACCESSIBILITY

The materials of learning are made easily accessible to students, and the schools provide the necessary materials, time, facilities, and staff, that give students optimum benefits in the pursuit of their studies and for nonacademic purposes as well.

This principle covers many vital parts of the school library's program. For library facilities, the following developments can be noted: the expansion of library quarters (main library areas, resource centers, learning areas, and other space provisions) and new organizational patterns for library areas on a subject or grade level basis. Equipment has been expanded to include wet and dry carrels, language laboratories, teaching machines, micro-readers, audiovisual equipment of all types, machinery for the production and reproduction of materials, and other items. Experiments with electronic machines for dialing materials, or comparable devices, are under way.

In order to meet the needs of students, the resources of school libraries are constantly being improved and expanded. Particular emphasis is being given to developing reference resources (including those in the elementary schools, since the requests of teachers and children constantly require consultation and use by the librarians of resources that are far from being elementary), the periodical collections, the collections of audiovisual materials, and the professional materials for teachers. In secondary schools a major drive has been made to provide the resources needed for accelerated, advanced placement, honors, and enriched courses. In order to satisfy quantitative demands for particular materials school libraries are providing materials in sufficient duplication. The acquisition and use of paperbacks in school libraries have rightly assumed sizable proportions.

Making materials easily accessible can also be seen in the current circulation policies of school libraries that are elastic and flexible, making it possible for students to withdraw all kinds of materials easily, and some kinds of equipment. Further evidence can be noted in the extension of the hours and days that many school libraries are open for student use. Even recent movements toward printed book catalogs and new classification arrangements have a direct bearing on making materials accessible.

The need to meet, at the very least, existing national standards for size of library staff becomes critically imperative, since so much individual work with students in the school library and group work with them in the library areas and elsewhere form a basic part of the research and study skills program—and this but one part of the school library's services.

Quite probably, the notoriously substandard conditions relating to size of school library staff that have persistently plagued school libraries—and not the lack of carefully delineated philosophy of library instruction—have led to an over-emphasis on teaching and requiring students to work independently in libraries, rather than providing them with library services that would do much of this location and collection of materials.

STUDENT USE OF OTHER LIBRARIES

Amidst what must be millions of words written and spoken about students crowding into public libraries, the essential points are sometimes lost in the welter of verbiage. As far as elementary and secondary school students are concerned, the most immediate fact to recognize and concentrate upon is that school libraries must be developed and they must meet the standards for resources and programs. The important goal to reach and to be concentrated upon is that of bringing school libraries up to these standards as quickly as possible. Providing substitutes for these measures, no matter how noble the intents, simply means supporting the perpetuation of inferior conditions in the schools. When the schools fully meet their responsibilities in providing the resources of teaching and learning, in having library programs and services that meet recognized standards, and in making the school library resources and services truly accessible, lamented pressures on the public library might even fade away; and colleges would no longer have to give elementary and secondary school level courses in library instruction.

If endeavors to improve school library conditions fail or improvements come too slowly, and if the public libraries continue to assume responsibilities for providing services and resources to meet curricular needs of students, then what implications can be drawn? One would be that the principles outlined for teaching students about study skills and methods of inquiry must be recognized and followed by the public library in its own program of service. This is relatively simple in those numerous instances where students attend schools that have programs of library instruction but still flock to the public library because of inadequacies in the collections of the school libraries, the inaccessibility of the school libraries, or for other reasons. Otherwise it is not simple, and even quite unmanageable, because library instruction must be related to curricular content and assignments, must stress the multi-media approach in the process of learning, and must provide group and individual guidance of many kinds—clearly functions of the schools and the educational process. *(It is not as simple a matter as just knowing in advance what the assignments are.)*

In the current scene, a paradox emerges. On the one hand, we have the numerous references to the problems created by student use in libraries other than those in schools (most often public, but sometimes college, university, and special libraries), and on the other we have a proliferation of community, regional, and state plans setting forth various proposals for reference and research resource centers to serve all groups (including students) and also proposals for other types of cooperative library services. As we hear more and more about the latter (not infrequently, with the pleasant jingle of federal and state funds in the background), we hear less and less about the evils emanating from students swarming into libraries outside their schools.

There is no question that the future holds changes, even marked changes, in the forms of library services, the audiences served, the organizational and administrative patterns, and the kinds of cooperative planning. The philosophy behind some of these possible trends was introduced decades ago. A plea is made that proposals for cooperative resources and services be based on sound evidence and sound theories. The viewpoint is submitted that we have not yet assembled all the essential facts and that we will never have a true picture of conditions until school libraries reach recommended standards for resources, facilities, and services. Only then will we be in a position to collect the data needed for planning. We do not even know enough now about the nature of the materials that students use for their academic purposes in the school library or elsewhere, or about the number and characteristics of students using or not using library resources. As part of their responsibilites in planning the programs of study skills and methods of inquiry, school librarians might well find out about the specific materials used by students, the purposes for which they use them, where they get them, and the reasons for using resources other than the school library.

We tend to assume that students need materials for their curricular purposes that are too rare or too scholarly to roo expensive or too infrequently used to justify their inclusion in school library collections, and this assumption is probably fallacious. (We also tend to assume that all public library collections are superior to all school library collections, and this is definitely fallacious.) We tend to ignore existing and proposed school system and multi-school system plans for materials centers, for centralized processing, and for other cooperative library services among schools. Too often the creators of state and regional library plans have little real understanding of what a good school library program is or the reasons why modern schools must have the resources of teaching and learning. Under any circumstance, state, regional, and local planning for libraries should actively involve school administrators and other educators, and too often this has not been the case.

Plans and practices that perpetuate substandard conditions in school libraries or that recommend organizational patterns which violate the educational objectives and services that are uniquely characteristic of school libraries, do a disservice to students and teachers. There are innumerable reasons why this is true, but the one to conclude with here is that learning to learn in libraries forms a natural part of the education of youth, best achieved where a richness of materials is easily accessible and under the guidance of teachers and librarians expert in their knowledge of the students, the curriculum, the ways of teaching, and the ways of learning.

Terminology*

The aboriginal logical sin, from which flows most bad intellectual consequences, is failure to define.

John Dewey†

Ability. A generalized power to carry on an integrated complex of related activities. William H. Burton, p. 98.

Affective domain. Educational objectives which describe changes in interest, attitudes, and values, and the development of appreciations and adequate adjustment. Benjamin Bloom, p. 7.

Analysis. The breakdown of a communication into its constituent elements or parts such that the relative hierarchy of ideas is made clear and/or the relations between the ideas expressed are made explicit. Benjamin Bloom, p. 205.

Application. The use of abstractions in particular and concrete situations. The abstractions may be in the form of general ideas, rules or procedures, or generalized methods. The abstractions may also be technical principles, ideas, and theories which must be remembered and applied. Benjamin Bloom, p. 205.

Articulation. The organization of classroom instruction, cocurricular activities, and other interdependent and interrelated services of the school system so as to facilitate the continuous and efficient educational progress of students from grade to grade and from school to school. Carter Good, p. 42.

Breadth of understanding. Significantly related topics, concepts, experiences, and activities essential to adequate understanding but not in textbook are introduced for learner exploration.

Cognition. In general, the process of knowing; in particular, the process of knowing based upon perception, introspection, or memory. Carter Good, p. 113.

Cognitive domain. Educational objectives which deal with recall or recognition of knowledge and the development of intellectual abilities and skills. Benjamin Bloom, p. 7.

Comprehension. The lowest level of understanding. It refers to a type of understanding or apprehension such that the individual knows what is being communicated and can make use of the material or idea being communicated

---

*Sources of definitions other than the author's own are identified at the end of the terminology listing.

†Dewey, John. *How We Think.* rev. ed. Boston, Mass.: D.C. Heath, 1933. p. 160.

without necessarily relating it to other material or seeing its fullest implications. Benjamin Bloom, p. 204.

Content. The substance of a teaching or learning resource; a unit or course of study, a teaching or learning program or plan.

Continuity. The planned, ordered progression of learning experiences designed to build understanding in a cohesive, unified, interrelated sequence, K–12. Synonym: vertical articulation.

Creativity. The ability to or the quality of producing something new, unique, original, not-before-existent. A creative act finds a new unity in the variety of nature, sees a likeness among items not thought of before. William Burton, p. 394.

Depth of understanding. Developing more fully the topics, concepts, experiences, and activities which are treated inadequately in the textbook.

Educational technology. A way of thinking as much as it is a way of doing. It is a new way of organizing and analyzing education, a concern with the education process as a system, and a consideration of each element as part of the system. Richard Hooper, in Sidney Tickton, ed., vol. 2, p. 144.

Evaluation. The making of judgments about the value . . . of ideas, works, solutions, methods, material, etc. It involves the use of criteria as well as standards for appraising the extent to which particulars are accurate, effective, economical, or satisfying. The judgments may be either quantitative or qualitative. Benjamin Bloom, p. 185.

Exceptional child. One who deviates markedly either above or below the group norm in mental, emotional, physical, social, or sensory traits to a degree that special services are required to help the child profit from educational experience. Leo J. Kelly and Glenn A. Vergason.

Expedite. To speed on its way; to foresee and avoid obstacles or hindrances and thereby save time.

Facilitate. To provide the guidance and the resources requisite to expediting teaching or learning.

Fact. Any act, event, circumstance, or existence which comes to pass. It is determined by measuring, counting, identifying, or by describing through consistent use of agreed upon definitions of terms. William H. Burton, p. 99.

Fundamental. An idea that has wide as well as powerful applicability. Jerome Bruner, p. 18.

Goals. The statement of the long-range, directional purposes which will guide the school in its educational planning to meet the needs of the students.

Head librarian. The member of a library staff delegated the responsibility for administering and directing a building library program.

Implementation. To facilitate, expedite, or actualize the accomplishment of an educational plan, goal, or objective.

Implode. To burst inward causing a tidal wave in the learner's stream of consciousness.

Instructional technology. A systematic way of designing, carrying out, and evaluating the total process of learning and teaching in terms of specific objectives, based on research in human learning and communication, and employing a combination of human and nonhuman resources to bring about more effective instruction. Commission on Instructional Technology, in Sidney Tickton, ed., vol. 1, p. 7.

Interpretation. The explanation or summarization of a communication. Whereas translation involves an objective part-for-part rendering of a communication, interpretation involves a re-ordering, rearrangement, or a new view of the material. Benjamin Bloom, p. 205.

Knowledge. The recall of specifics and universals, the recall of methods and processes, or the recall of a pattern, structure, or setting. Benjamin Bloom, p. 201.

Knowledge imploding potential. The power to break through the constraints of previous understandings.

Library-based unit. A unit designed to be taught in its entirety through the utilization of library resources, facilities, and guidance; each phase of the designing, teaching, and evaluating of a library-based unit is a shared responsibility of classroom teacher and librarian.

Library coordinator or supervisor. The librarian delegated the administrative authority and responsibility for developing and implementing a district, county, regional, or state program of library service.

Listening. Hearing with discrimination and discernment.

Media management. Systematizing the organization and utilization of instructional media to assure easy accessibility and ready availability of all support media appropriate for each teaching or learning quest.

Media programming. Blueprinting a media usage sequence plan to build understanding in logical progression.

Mediating agent. A means of conveying, extending, or reinforcing knowledge; a teaching resource.

Medium, pl. media. A vehicle for conveying information; an agent for communicating ideas.

Objectives. Explicit formulations of the ways in which students are expected to be changed by the educational process. That is, the ways in which they will change in their thinking, their feelings, and their actions. Benjamin Bloom, p. 26.

Pilot study. A preliminary study conducted in an operational environment to test and determine the effectiveness and value of techniques, procedures, methods, and/or materials.

Profession. A calling requiring specialized knowledge and often long and intensive preparation including instruction in skills and methods as well as in the scientific, historical, or scholarly principles underlying such skills and methods, maintaining by force of organization or concerted opinion high standards of achievement and conduct, and committing its members to continued study and to a kind of work which has for its prime purpose the rendering of a public service. *Webster's*, p. 1811.

Relevance. Uniquely reflective of the individual student's needs, interests, goals, and abilities; reflective of the contemporary world.

Resource. An agent for communicating meaning; a rich deposit of information.

School librarian. A certified teacher possessing knowledge in depth of media content with specialized training in curriculum support techniques, in the selection, organization, and utilization of media, and in the design and development of customized teaching and learning strategies; vested with the professional responsibility of programming for the most efficient use of media to expedite teaching and to facilitate learning. The school librarian serves in the triple capacity of teacher, media programming engineer, and curriculum expediter.

School library. A learning laboratory providing all types and kinds of instructional media essential for the optimum support of the educational program, providing opportunity for each student to work with ideas intelligently, intensively, and extensively, while being competently guided in an environment conducive to maximal learning.

Strategy. An action plan calculated to expedite and facilitate learning from introduction to completion of a given task or topic.

Systems approach. The programmed use of media in a predetermined, structured pattern designed to build understanding of a given topic, concept, process, experiment, etc., in a logical, balanced progression or sequence.

Teaching laboratory. A teacher-study-work-planning center equipped with materials and machines essential for the development and implementation of effective, creative teaching programs.

Team teaching. The sharing by several or more teachers of the responsibility for teaching a given class. Each member of a teaching team has certain unique functions; all participate in planning, scheduling, and evaluating the team activities.

DEFINITION SOURCES

Bloom, Benjamin S., ed. *Taxonomy of Educational Objectives: The Classification of Educational Goals, Handbook I, Cognitive Domain.* New York: David McKay, 1956.

Bruner, Jerome S. *The Process of Education.* Cambridge, Mass.: Harvard University Press, 1960.

Burton, William H. *The Guidance of Learning Activities: A Summary of the Principles of Teaching Based on the Growth of the Learner.* 3rd ed. New York: Appleton, 1962.

Good, Carter V., ed. *Dictionary of Education.* 3rd ed. New York: McGraw-Hill, 1973.

Kelly, Leo J., and Vergason, Glenn A. *The Dictionary of Special Education and Rehabilitation.* Denver, Colo.: Love Publishing, 1978.

Tickton, Sidney G., ed. *To Improve Learning: An Evaluation of Instructional Technology.* 2 vols. New York: R. R. Bowker, 1971.

Webster's Third New International Dictionary. Springfield, Mass.: G. & C. Merriam Co., 1971.

Bibliography

Adult Services Division, Subcommittee on Indian Material. "Guidelines for the Evaluation of Indian Materials for Adults," *ASD Newsletter* VIII, no. 3 (Spring 1971).

Alfonso, Robert J., Firth, Gerald R., and Nevill, Richard F. *Instructional Supervision: A Behavior System.* Boston: Allyn and Bacon, 1975.

Allen, James E. "The Right to Read—Target for the 70's." *Elementary English* 47, p. 488.

American Association of School Librarians. "Policies and Procedures for Selection of Instructional Materials." *School Media Quarterly*, Winter 1977, pp. 109–116.

––––––. *Standards for School Library Programs.* Chicago: American Library Association, 1960.

–––––– and the Association for Educational Communications and Technology. *Media Programs: District and School.* Chicago: American Library Association, 1975.

American Association of School Librarians and the Department of Audiovisual Instruction of the National Education Association. *Standards for School Media Programs.* Chicago: American Library Association, 1969.

Anderson, Paul S. *Language Skills in Elementary Education.* New York: Macmillan, 1972.

Applebee, Arthur N. *A Survey of Teaching Conditions in English, 1977.* Urbana, Ill.: National Council of Teachers of English, 1978.

Austin, Mary C., et al. *The First R: The Harvard Report on Reading in Elementary Schools.* New York: Macmillan, 1963.

Barron, Neil. *Anatomy of Wonder: Science Fiction.* New York: R. R. Bowker, 1976.

Barzun, Jacques. *House of Intellect.* New York: Harper, 1959.

––––––. "The Professions Under Siege." *Harpers*, October 1978, pp. 61–68.

––––––. *Teacher in America.* Boston: Little, 1945.

Benjamin, Harold. *The Saber-Tooth Curriculum.* Memorial ed. New York: McGraw-Hill, 1972.

Bloom, Benjamin S., ed. *Taxonomy of Educational Objectives: The Classification of Educational Goals. Handbook I, Cognitive Domain.* New York: David McKay, 1956.

Boocock, Sarane Spence. "Today's Childhood—A Unique Condition." *Today's Education*, February/March 1979, pp. 50-53.

Brain, George B. *Increasing Your Administrative Skill in Dealing with the Instructional Program*. Englewood Cliffs, N.J.: Prentice-Hall, 1966.

Bruner, Jerome S. *The Process of Education*. Cambridge, Mass.: Harvard University Press, 1960.

_____. "The Process of Education Reconsidered." In *Curriculum Planning: A New Approach* by Glen Hass, Joseph Bondi, and Jon Wiles. Boston: Allyn and Bacon, 1974, pp. 172-181.

Burns, Paul C., Broman, Betty, and Lowe, Alberta. *The Language Arts in Childhood Education*. 3rd ed. Chicago: Rand McNally, 1975.

Burton, William H. *The Guidance of Learning Activities: A Summary of the Principles of Teaching Based on the Growth of the Learner*. 3rd ed. New York: Appleton, 1962.

_____, Kimball, Roland B., and Wing, Richard L. *Education for Effective Thinking*. New York: Appleton, 1960.

Calkins, Elizabeth, and McGhan, Barry. *Teaching Tomorrow: A Handbook of Science Fiction for Teachers*. Dayton, Ohio: Pflaum/Standard, 1972.

Carlsen, Robert. *Books and the Teen-Age Reader: A Guide for Teachers, Librarians and Parents*, rev. ed. New York: Harper, 1971.

Chambers, Dewey W. *Children's Literature in the Curriculum*. Chicago: Rand McNally, 1971.

Chapin, June R., and Gross, Richard E. *Teaching Social Studies Skills*. Boston: Little, 1973.

Charles, Cheryl, and Samples, Bob, eds. *Science and Society: Knowing, Teaching, Learning*. Washington, D.C.: National Council for the Social Studies, 1978.

Chisholm, Margaret E., and Ely, Donald P. *Media Personnel in Education: A Competency Approach*. Englewood Cliffs, N.J.: Prentice-Hall, 1976.

Clark, Leonard H., et al. *The American Secondary School Curriculum*. 2nd ed. New York: Macmillan, 1972.

Cleary, Florence Damon. *Blueprints for Better Reading: School Programs for Promoting Skills and Interest in Reading*. 2nd ed. New York: Wilson, 1972.

Clendening, Corinne P. "The High School Level: Examples of Planning, Preparing, and Implementing Library-User Instructional Programs." In *Educating the Library User*, ed. by John Lubans, Jr. New York: R. R. Bowker, 1974, pp. 163-174.

_____, and Davies, Ruth A. *Realizing Great Expectations: A Dynamic Program for the Gifted and Talented*. New York: R. R. Bowker, 1979.

Collier, Calhoun C., et al. *Modern Elementary Education: Teaching and Learning*. New York: Macmillan, 1976.

Committee on Library Organization and Equipment of the National Education Association and of the North Central Association of Colleges and Secondary Schools. *Standard Library Organization and Equipment for Secondary Schools of Different Sizes*. Chicago: American Library Association, 1920.

Cook, Maureen H., and Newman, Carol. *This Side Up: Making Decisions About Drugs*. Rockville, Md.: National Institute on Drug Abuse, 1978.

Corey, Stephen M. "The Poor Scholar's Soliloquy." *Childhood Education* 20, no. 5 (January 1944): 219-220.

Dale, Edgar. *Building a Learning Environment*. Bloomington, Ind.: Phi Delta Kappa, 1972.

Dobsen, Russell and Judith. *Humaneness in Schools: A Neglected Force.* Dubuque, Iowa: Kendall/Hunt, 1976.

Douglas, Paul H. *In the Fullness of Time.* New York: Harcourt, 1972.

Drews, Elizabeth M. *Learning Together: How to Foster Creativity, Self-Fulfillment, and Social Awareness in Today's Students and Teachers.* Englewood Cliffs, N.J.: Prentice-Hall, 1972.

Durant, Will and Ariel. *The Lessons of History.* New York: Simon and Schuster, 1968.

————. *Will and Ariel Durant: A Dual Autobiography.* New York: Simon and Schuster, 1977.

Edwards, Margaret A. *The Fair Garden and the Swarm of Beasts: The Library and the Young Adult.* New York: Hawthorn Books, 1974.

Elam, Stanley M., ed. *A Decade of Gallup Polls of Attitudes Toward Education, 1969–1978.* Bloomington, Ind.: Phi Delta Kappa, 1978.

Elliott, Michael J., and Kennedy, Kerry J. "Australian Impressions of Social Studies Theory and Practice in Secondary Schools in the United States." *Social Education* 43, no. 4 (April 1979): 291–296.

Fargo, Lucille F. "Training High School Students in the Use of the Library." *Addresses and Proceedings, 1913.* Vol. 51. Ann Arbor, Mich.: National Education Association, 1913.

Feldman, David K. "Toward a Nonelitist Conception of Giftedness." *Phi Delta Kappan*, May 1979, p. 662.

Flesch, Rudolf. *Why Johnny Can't Read . . .* New York: Harper, 1955.

General Education in a Free Society: A Report of the Harvard Committee. Cambridge, Mass.: Harvard University Press, 1945.

Getzels, Jacob W., and Jackson, Philip W. *Creativity and Intelligence.* New York: Wiley, 1962.

Gillespie, John T. *A Model School District Media Program.* Chicago: American Library Association, 1977.

Good, Carter V., ed. *Dictionary of Education.* 3rd ed. New York: McGraw-Hill, 1973.

Goodlad, John I. *The Dynamics of Educational Change: Toward Responsive Schools.* A Charles F. Kettering Foundation Program. New York: McGraw-Hill, 1975.

————. "The Schools vs. Education." *Saturday Review of Literature* 50 (April 19, 1969): 60.

Hadas, Moses. *Old Wine, New Bottles: A Humanist Teacher at Work.* New York: Simon and Schuster, 1962.

Hanna, Paul R., ed. *Education: An Instrument of National Goals.* New York: McGraw-Hill, 1962.

Harman, David. "Illiteracy: An Overview." *Harvard Educational Review* 47, no. 2 (May 1970).

Henne, Frances. "Learning to Learn in School Libraries." *School Libraries*, American Association of School Librarians 15, no. 4 (May 1966): 15–23.

————. "School Libraries." In *Library Surveys*, ed. by Maurice F. Tauber and Irene R. Stephens. New York: Columbia University Press, 1967.

Hersey, Paul, and Blanchard, Kenneth. *Management of Organizational Behavior: Utilizing Human Resources.* Englewood Cliffs, N.J.: Prentice-Hall, 1972.

Hicks, Warren B., and Tillin, Alma M. *Managing Multimedia Libraries.* New York: R. R. Bowker, 1977.

Holt, John. *Instead of Education: Ways to Do Things Better*. New York: Dutton, 1976.

Hook, J. N. *The Teaching of High School English*. 4th ed. New York: Ronald Press, 1972.

Hutchins, Robert M. "The Great Anti-School Campaign." *The Center Magazine*, January/February 1975.

Indiana Council for the Social Studies. "Suggested Criteria for Evaluating Social Studies Materials." In *Social Studies Today: Guidelines for Curriculum Improvement*. Harrisburg, Pa.: Bureau of General and Academic Education, Department of Education, 1970, pp. 74–80.

Innovations in the Elementary School. Report of a National Seminar. Dayton, Ohio: Institute for Development of Educational Activities, 1971.

James, William. "The Moral Philosopher and the Moral Life." In *Pragmatism and Other Essays*, ed. by J. L. Blau. New York: Washington Square Press, 1963.

Jarolimek, John. *Social Studies in Elementary Education*. 5th ed. New York: Macmillan, 1977.

————, and Foster, Clifford D. *Teaching and Learning in the Elementary School*. New York: Macmillan, 1976.

Jefferson, Thomas. *The Writings of Thomas Jefferson*, ed. by Albert Ellery Bergh, vol. 6. Washington, D.C.: Thomas Jefferson Memorial Association, 1970.

Joint Committee of the National Education Association and the American Library Association. *Elementary School Library Standards*. Chicago: American Library Association, 1925.

Kauffman, Draper L., Jr. *Futurism and Future Studies*. Washington, D.C.: National Education Association, 1976.

Kauss, Theodore. *Leaders Live with Crises*. Bloomington, Ind.: Phi Delta Kappa, 1974.

Kolesnik, Walter B. *Humanism and/or Behaviorism in Education*. Boston: Allyn and Bacon, 1975.

Krathwohl, David R., et al. *Taxonomy of Educational Objectives: The Classification of Educational Goals, Handbook II, Affective Domain*. New York: David McKay, 1964.

Kraus, W. Keith. *Murder, Mischief, and Mayhem*. Urbana, Ill.: National Council of Teachers of English, 1978.

Kruse, Edward D. "Manpower and Media for the Use of the Minority and the Majority." Speech given at the American Association of School Administrators Convention, Atlantic City, N.J., February 24, 1971.

Laszlo, Ervin. *The Inner Limits of Mankind: Heretical Reflections on Today's Values, Culture, and Politics*. New York: Pergamon, 1978.

Law-Related Educational Competencies. Pennsylvania Division of Interdisciplinary Programs, Bureau of Curriculum Services. Harrisburg, Pa.: Department of Education, 1974.

Leeper, Robert R., ed. *Curricular Concerns in a Revolutionary Era*. Washington, D.C.: Association for Supervision and Curriculum Development, National Education Association, 1971.

Lewy, Arieh, ed. *Handbook of Curriculum Evaluation*. Institute for Educational Planning. Paris: UNESCO and New York: Longman, 1977.

Lohrer, Alice. "School Libraries as Instructional Materials Centers with Implications for Training: A Progress Report of This Study Under Title VII,

National Defense Education Act." In *The School Library as a Materials Center: Educational Needs of Librarians and Teachers in Its Administration and Use*, ed. by Mary Helen Mahar. Washington, D.C.: U.S. Department of Health, Education, and Welfare, 1963, p. 14.

MacCampbell, James C., and Peck, Eleanor, eds. *Focus on Reading*. Cambridge, Mass.: New England School Development Council, 1964.

McGinnis, Dorothy. "Instructional Materials Centers—Something New?" *California School Libraries* 34, no. 1 (November 1962): 4-6.

Macintosh, Helen K., et al. *Administration of Elementary School Programs for Disadvantaged Children*, Disadvantaged Children Series No. 4. Washington, D.C.: U.S. Department of Health, Education, and Welfare, 1966.

MacKinnon, Donald W. "The Study of Creative Persons." In *Creativity and Learning*, ed. by Jerome Kagan. Boston: Houghton, 1967, p. 33.

McLuhan, Marshall. *Understanding Media: The Extensions of Man*. New York: New American Library, 1964.

Madison, James. *The Complete Madison: His Basic Writings*, ed. by Saul K. Podover. New York: Harper, 1953.

Mann, Horace. *Life and Works of Horace Mann*. 5 vols. Boston: Lee and Shepard, 1891. Vol. 3 "Annual Reports of the Secretary of the Board of Education of Massachusetts, 1839-1844."

Michaelis, John U. *Social Studies for Children in a Democracy*. 6th ed. Englewood Cliffs, N.J.: Prentice-Hall, 1976.

_____, Grossman, Ruth H., and Scott, Lloyd F. *New Designs for Elementary Curriculum and Instruction*. New York: McGraw-Hill, 1975.

Miller, Richard I. *Selecting New Aids to Teaching*. Washington, D.C.: Association for Supervision and Curriculum Development, 1971.

Morrow, Lance. "Wondering If Children Are Necessary." *Time* 113 (March 5, 1979): 42.

National Council for the Social Studies. "Position Statement: Revision of the NCSS Social Studies Curriculum Guidelines." *Social Education* 43, no. 4 (April 1979): 262.

National Council of Supervisors of Mathematics. "Position Paper on Basic Skills." *The Arithmetic Teacher* 25 (October 1977): 19-22.

National Council of Teachers of English. *Recommended English Language Arts Curriculum Guides K-12* ... Urbana, Ill.: National Council of Teachers of English, 1978.

National Council of Teachers of Mathematics. "Mathematical Competencies and Skills Essential for Enlightened Citizens." *Mathematics Teacher* (November 1972): 672.

National Education Association. "Teacher Opinion Poll." *Today's Education* 68 (February/March 1979): 20.

National Science Teachers Association. *Working Paper: Science Education—Accomplishments and Needs*. Washington, D.C.: National Science Teachers Association, 1978.

National Study of School Evaluation. *Evaluative Criteria for the Evaluation of Secondary Schools*. 5th ed. Washington, D.C.: National Study of School Evaluation, 1978.

Noble, Ernest P., ed. *Third Special Report to the U.S. Congress on Alcohol and Health*. From the Secretary of Health, Education, and Welfare, U.S. Department of Health, Education, and Welfare. Washington, D.C.: Government Printing Office, 1978.

Nystrand, Raphael O., and Cunningham, Luvern L. "Organizing Schools to Develop Humane Capabilities." In *To Nurture Humaneness: Commitment for the 70's*, ed. by Mary-Margaret Scobey and Grace Graham. Washington, D.C.: Association for Supervision and Curriculum Development, National Education Association, 1970, p. 120.

The Open Classroom: Informal Education in America. Dayton, Ohio: Institute for Development of Educational Activities, 1972.

Peter, Laurence J. *The Peter Prescription: How To Be Creative, Confident, and Competent*. New York: Morrow, 1972.

Pittman, Shirley A., ed. *Pennsylvania Guide for School Library Media Specialists*. Pittsburgh, Pa.: Pennsylvania School Librarians Association, 1978.

Pooley, Robert C. "The Professional Status of the Teacher of English." *English Journal* 48 (September 1959): 311.

Postman, Neil, and Weingartner, Charles. *Teaching as a Subversive Activity*. New York: Delacorte Press, 1969.

The Pursuit of Excellence: Education and the Future of America. America at Mid-Century Series, Special Studies Project Report V, Rockefeller Brothers Fund. Garden City, N.Y.: Doubleday, 1958.

Putnam, John F., and Chismore, W. Dale, eds. *Standard Terminology for Curriculum and Instruction in Local and State School Systems*. State Educational Records and Report Series: Handbook VI. Washington, D.C.: U.S. Department of Health, Education, and Welfare, 1970.

Ragan, William B., and Sheperd, Gene D. *Modern Elementary Curriculum*. 4th ed. New York: Holt, 1971.

Raths, Louis E., et al. *Values and Teaching*. Columbus, Ohio: Charles E. Merrill Books, 1966.

The Report of the President's Commission on National Goals. *Goals for Americans*. The American Assembly, Columbia University, New York. Englewood Cliffs, N.J.: Prentice-Hall, 1960.

Research and Policy Committee of the Committee for Economic Development. *Innovation in Education: New Directions for the American School*. New York: Committee for Economic Development, 1968.

"Revision of the NCSS Social Studies Curriculum Guidelines." *Social Education* 53, no. 4 (April 1979): 262.

Rokeach, Milton. *Beliefs, Attitudes and Values*. San Francisco: Jossey-Bass, 1969.

Roots of America: A Multiethnic Curriculum Resource Guide for 7th, 8th, and 9th Grade Social Studies Teachers. Developed by the New Jersey Education Association and the National Education Association. Washington, D.C.: National Education Association, 1975.

Rosenfeld, Albert. "Good News on Population." *Saturday Review* 6 (March 3, 1979): 19.

Saylor, J. Galen, and Smith, Joshua L., eds. *Removing Barriers to Humaneness in the High School*. Washington, D.C.: Association for Supervision and Curriculum Development, National Education Association, 1971.

School Library Manpower Project. *Occupational Definitions for School Library Personnel*. Chicago: American Library Association, 1971.

Schools for the 70's and Beyond: A Call to Action. A Staff Report from the Center for the Study of Instruction. Washington, D.C.: National Education Association, 1971.

Shane, Harold G. *Curriculum Change Toward the 21st Century.* Curriculum series. Washington, D.C.: National Education Association, 1977.

_____, et al., coordinator. *Interpreting Language Arts Research for the Teacher.* Washington, D.C.: Association for Supervision and Curriculum Development, 1971.

Silberman, Charles E. *Crisis in the Classroom: The Remaking of American Education.* New York: Random House, 1970.

Smith, Bessie. "Joint Administration of the High-School Library by the Board of Education and the Public Library." *Addresses and Proceedings,* 1916, vol. 54. Ann Arbor, Mich.: National Education Association, 1916.

Snider, Robert C. *Back to Basics.* Washington, D.C.: National Education Association, 1978.

Spann, Sylvia, and Culp, Mary Beth, eds. *Thematic Units in Teaching English and the Humanities.* Urbana, Ill.: National Council of Teachers of English, 1975.

Spears, Harold. "Kappans Ponder the Goals of Education." *Phi Delta Kappan* 55 (September 1973): 29–32.

Special Committee on Youth Education for Citizenship. *Law-Related Education in America: Guidelines for the Future.* Chicago: American Bar Association, 1975.

Spencer, Herbert. *Herbert Spencer on Education,* ed. by Andreas M. Kazamias. New York: Teachers College Press, Columbia University, 1966.

Squire, James R., and Applebee, Roger K. *High School English Instruction Today: The National Study of High School English Programs.* New York: Appleton, 1968.

Stocking, Fred H. "High School Humanities Courses: Some Revelations and Warnings." *The English Leaflet* 53, no. 5 (Fall 1965): 37–38.

Summary of Final Report: A National Study of Adolescent Drinking Behavior, Attitudes and Correlates. Rockville, Md.: National Clearinghouse for Alcoholic Information, 1975.

Taylor, Robert B. "Behind the Surge in Broken Marriages." *U.S. News and World Report* 86 (January 22, 1979): 53.

Terman, Lewis M. *The Measurement of Intelligence.* Boston: Houghton, 1916.

Tickton, Sidney G., ed. *To Improve Learning: An Evaluation of Instructional Technology.* 2 vols. New York: R. R. Bowker, 1971.

Torrance, E. Paul. *Education and the Creative Potential.* Minneapolis, Minn.: University of Minnesota Press, 1963.

Toynbee, Arnold J. *A Study of History,* abr. by D. C. Somervell. New York: Oxford University Press, 1946. 10 vols.

Twain, Mark. *Thirty Thousand Bequests and Other Stories.* New York: Gabriel Wells, 1923.

Williams, Robert L. *Cross-Cultural Education: Teaching Toward Planetary Perspective.* Washington, D.C.: National Education Association, 1977.

Workman, Brooke. *Teaching the Decades: A Humanities Approach to American Civilization.* Urbana, Ill.: National Council of Teachers of English, 1975.

Index

AASL. *See* American Association of
   School Librarians
Acquisitions process, flowchart, 122
Administrative and Supervisory Personnel
   Evaluation forms, 375-377
Affective domain, 44, 171, 198, 305
Alcohol abuse, 7-8
Alfonson, Robert, 361
Allen, James E., Jr., 143-144
Alternate Sources of Energy lesson plan,
   246-249
American Association of School
   Librarians, 9-10, 38, 39, 40
  and the challenge of the future, 379-381
  Policies and Procedures for Selection of
    Instructional Materials, 98-106
American Bar Association, 219
American Civil War unit, 119-121
American English: Inherited,
   Manufactured, and Fractured unit,
   177-180
Anatomy of Wonder, 167
Anderson, Paul S., 164n, 166
Appomattox and the End learning guide,
   119-121
Art. *See* Humanities
Art prints. *See* Study prints, selection
   criteria
Avon Books, 299n

Back to Basics, 95n
Barrett, Linda Anne, 135
Barron, Neil, 167
Barzun, Jacques, 1n, 8, 59, 379
Beach, Richard, 170
Benjamin, Harold, 26
Berenson, Bernard, 277n
Biography. *See* Literature program
Blanchard, Kenneth, 363
*Blueprints for Better Reading: School
   Programs for Promoting Skill and
   Interest in Reading*, 80, 142-143, 147,
   167, 307
Boocock, Sarane Spence, 5
Book Illustrators and Their Art unit, 30,
   290-299
Book production, statistics, 95
Book reports, 162-163
  forms for, 163-164
Books
  selection criteria, 106-107
  selection criteria for disadvantaged
    learners, 149-150
  student evaluation forms, 463, 466
Brain, George B., 367-368
Breadth of understanding, 41-42
Brooks, William D., 439n
Bruner, Jerome S., 31, 71-72
Budget, 125-126, 127

Building a Learning Environment, 71n, 73
Bureau of Public Information, 273n
Burns, Paul C., 146
Burton, William H., 65

Calkins, Elizabeth, 167
Call It Courage unit, 158
Carpenter, Helen McCracken, 303n
Case, Robert N., 321n
Case studies, 221
    Archaic Educational Practices, 27
    Compensating for Reading Disabilities,
        43
    Designing a Metal-Shop Project, 42
    Exploring the Library Media Center's
        Dictionary Collection, 42
    Individualized Learning Program, An,
        43
    Lack of an Overall Plan, 31
    Nixon Impeachment Proceedings, 43
    Preparing a Mini-Program for
        Independent Study, 40-41
    Preparing a Mock Trial for American
        History, 41
    Preparing a Science Debate, 43
    Reading Enrichment Experience, A, 42
    Researching the Scopes Trial, 41-42,
        205
    Selecting a Skit for Dramatic Club, 42
    Tasaday: A Study of a Primitive
        Culture Frozen in Time, 116-119
    Visiting the Parthenon in Nashville,
        Tennessee, 41
Cataloging process, 121
    flowchart, 123
Censorship. *See* Challenged materials
Center for the Humanities, The, 300
Centralized ordering and processing, 121,
    122, 123, 124
Certain, Charles C., 37, 38, 393n
Certain Standards. *See Standard Library
    Organization and Equipment for
    Secondary Schools of Different Sizes*
Challenged materials, 100, 101-105
    complaint forms for, 102-105
    permission to read form, 168
    Students' Right to Read, 406-412
Chambers, Dewey W., 164-165, 166
Change
    alternative futures, 219-220
    *Cardinal Principles for Educational
        Change,* 24-26
    Cybernetic-decisional model of social
        change, 250
    and the information explosion, 95-96
    planning and strategy checklist, 361-362
Chapin, June, 221, 303n
Charles, Cheryl, 249
Checklist, defined, 314
Chew Tow Yow, 71n

Child abuse, 5-6
Children's Defense Fund, 4n
Chisholm, Margaret E., 45
Civil War and Reconstruction pretest,
    230-231
Civil War and Reconstruction unit, 299,
    425-438
Cleary, Florence D., 80, 142, 147, 167,
    307
Clendening, Corinne P., 80n, 85n, 177n,
    180-181
Cognitive domain, 43-44, 171, 305
Cohen, Wilbur J., 185n
Commission on English, 160
Commission on Instructional
    Technology. *See To Improve
    Learning: An Evaluation of
    Instructional Technology*
Commission on Pre-Service Education
    of Teachers of Mathematics, 235n
Communicating skills, 135-136, 306-307,
    523-534
Communication, competencies, 168-169
Complaint procedures. *See* Challenged
    materials
Composition: A Media Approach, 170
Conant, James, 14
Contemporary American Culture unit,
    413-424
Controversial materials. *See* Challenged
    materials
Coordinator. *See* Supervision; Supervisor
Corbin, Jonathan, 181n
Corbin, Richard, 181n
Corey, Stephen, 50-51
Creating Programs for the Gifted, 80n,
    172-180
Creativity, 54-56
Crime, juvenile, 6-7
"Crisis in confidence," 1-11, 379
Crisis in the Classroom, 277n
*Criteria for Evaluating Junior High
    Schools,* 315
*Criteria for Modern School Media
    Programs,* 45
Criteria of Excellence checklist, 318,
    320-321, 357
Criterion (criteria), defined, 314
Crucible, The, unit, 222-223
Culp, Mary Beth, 286
Culture
    Contemporary American Culture unit,
        413-424
    learning guide, analysis of culture,
        117-119
    polycultural education, 220-221
    Tasaday: A Study of a Primitive
        Culture Frozen in Time, 116-119
Curriculum
    basic understandings, 73
    defined, 72

district curriculum study council, 75–77

guides for English program, 137–142, 171

guides for mathematics program, 265

guides for science program, 236–238

guides for social studies program, 189–192

knowledge priorities in, 73–75

library media program support for, 36, 40–44, 71–93

library media specialist support role for, 71–93

mini-course design, 439–443

packages, selection guides, 107–108

relevance in the, 56–59

Curriculum Change Toward the 21st Century, 10–11, 13n, 22–26, 52, 135n, 150n, 178n, 268, 363, 381

Curriculum Guidelines for Multiethnic Education, 280n

Curriculum packages, selection criteria, 107–108

Curriculum Study Council, District, 75–77

Cybernetic-Decisional Model of Social Change, 250

Cyclo-teacher, 275n

Dale, Edgar, 71n, 73–75

Darling, Richard L., 45n, 67n

Davies, Ruth A., 80n, 546

Deans, Edwina, 266

Decade of Gallup Polls of Attitudes toward Education, 1969–1978, 1, 7, 143

Depth of understanding, 40–41

Developing Multi-Media Libraries, 13n

Development of Functional Communication Competencies Pre-K–6, 170

Grade 7–12, 170

Dickens, Charles, 11

Discovery method. *See* Inquiry method

Discs. *See* Recordings, selection criteria

District library media director. *See* Supervisor

District library media program. *See* Library media program

Diversification, 53

Dobson, Judith Shelton, 359n

Dobson, Russell, 359n

Donelson, Kenneth L., 406n

Donne, John, 161–162

Drews, Elizabeth M., 51

Drug abuse, 7

Durant, Ariel, 9, 185n

Durant, Will, 8–9, 185n, 299

ERIC. *See* Educational Research Information Center

ESEA. *See* Elementary and Secondary Education Act

"Early Childhood Education: For What Goals?" 49n

"Educating for Flexibility," 71n

Education

archaic practices in, 27–32

central purpose of, 19

class approach in, 29

and equal opportunity, 14–15

in a free society, 13–15

historical perspective of, 13–14

innovations in, 29–30

resistance to change in, 26–32

and societal change, 2

strategies for survival, 9–11

under siege, 1–11, 379

Education and the Creative Potential, 359n

Educational goals, 14–26

basic directional goals, 15–16

Cardinal Principles for Educational Change, 24–26

Central Purpose of Education, 19

class approach as deterrent to, 29–30

Common Goals of Michigan Education, 21

deterrents to, case studies, 27, 31

Eighteen Goals of Education, 19–20

hierarchy of, 16

lack of overall plan as deterrent to, 31–32

language arts contribution to, 169–170

Pennsylvania's Goals of Quality Education, 21–22

for personal excellence, 58–59

Phi Delta Kappa, Eighteen Goals, 19–20

Purpose of Education, 17–19

rote recall as deterrent to, 30–31

Seven Cardinal Principles, 16–17

Seven Cardinal Principles Reinterpreted, 22–24

stressing values, 58–59

textbook veneration as deterrent to, 28

worship of print as deterrent to ?, 28–29

Educational Policies Commission, 17, 19

Educational program, evaluating, 314–316

Educational Reading Services, 163n

Educational Research Information Center, 170, 232, 474–477

Elementary and Secondary Education Act, 9

Elementary School Evaluation Criteria, 315

Elementary School Library Standards, 37–38, 400–405

Elliott, Michael, 193, 194

Ely, Donald P., 64n

Emerson, Ralph Waldo, 30, 31

Energy and Education: Teaching Alternatives, 246n, 248, 249n
English program
　affective behavior in, 171
　aims of, 136
　cognitive behavior in, 171
　communication competencies, 168–170
　composition, 140
　content specifications, 171
　curriculum guidelines, 137–142
　design of, 141–142
　evaluation of, 141
　and the gifted and talented student, 170–180
　goals of, 136, 169
　language processes and skills in, 169
　language study, 139–140
　library media program support for, 181–182
　linguistics units, 172–175, 175–177, 177–180
　media as message in, 140
　NCTE Curriculum Guidelines, 137–142
　objectives of, 138
　organization of, 138–139
　philosophy of, 137–138
　policies and procedures in, 138
　process as content, 139
　reading and literature experiences in, 140–141
　reading and literature programs, 142–168
　research paper, 180–181, 306
　safeguarding student interest, 162–163
　specifications for, 171
　trends in, 136
Environmental Quality Index, 271
Ersted, Ruth, 9, 38
Ethnic American Minorities: A Guide to Media and Materials, 286
Ethnic groups. *See* Multiethnic education
Ethnic Heritage Studies Program Act, 279
Eurich, Alvin, 59
Evaluating Administrative/Supervisory Performance, 375n
Evaluating textbooks, treatment of minorities, 464
Evaluation
　definition of terms used in, 314
　of educational program, 314–316
　faculty self-study of elementary library media center, 448–456
　of library media program, 310–358
　National Study of School Evaluation, 314–317
　performance criteria for media specialist services, 372–374
　personnel evaluation forms, 375–377
　purpose of, 313
　of staff, 371
"Evaluation at the Planning Stage," 71n

"Evaluation of Media Specialist Services," 371–374
Evaluative Criteria, 136, 188, 237–238, 265, 315–316, 316–317, 357
Evaluative criteria, defined, 314
Evaluative Criteria for Junior High Schools, 315
Evaluative method, defined, 314

Faculty Self-Study of the Elementary School Library Media Center, 448–456
Family, changes in, 4–6
Fargo, Lucille, 36
Films (single concept), selection criteria, 457–458
Filmstrips, selection criteria, 458–459
Find Your Media Center Service Profile, 318–319
First R: The Harvard Report on Reading in Elementary Schools, The, 145
Firth, Gerald, 361
Flexible scheduling. *See* Scheduling procedures
Focus on Reading, 145
Friedman, Paul C., 170
Fun with Words unit, 172–175
Future Shock, 1n
Futurism and Future Studies, 219, 240–241

GATE. *See* Gifted and Talented Education Program
Gallup Polls. *See Decade of Gallup Polls of Attitudes toward Education, 1969–1978, A*
General Education in a Free Society. See Harvard Report
Getzels, Jacob W., 56
Gibran, Kahlil, 63n
Gifted and Talented Education Program, 80–89, 170–180, 206–213, 213–219
　units, 85–88, 206–213, 213–219, 241–243, 251–259, 259–262, 274–275
　variations and adjustments checklist, 204–205
Gillespie, John T., 124
Globes, selection criteria, 459
Goals. *See* Educational goals
Goals for Americans. See National Goals Report
Goldman, Harvey, 57
Goodlad, John, 27, 28, 30, 58–59
Gould, Lawrence M., 59
"Great Anti-School Campaign," 1
Gross, Richard, 221, 303n
Guidance Associates, 300
Guidance of Learning Activities, The, 65
Guidelines for the Preparation of Teachers of Mathematics, 235n

Hall, Mary E., 36
Hamachek, Don, 65–66
Handbook of Curriculum Evaluation,
    71n, 72–73
"Handprints of necessity," 56n
Harman, David, 114, 524n
Harvard Report, 14–15, 28, 162, 383–385
Hemingway Ernest, 160–161
Henne, Frances, 9, 38, 310, 311, 316–317,
    548–555
Henry, Marguerite, 77, 78
Hersey, Paul, 363
Hicks, Warren B., 13n, 122n
Historical novel. *See* Literature program
Holland, Elmer J., 10
Holt, John, 271
Hood, Marguerite, 277
Hook, J. N., 165–166
Hounshell, Paul, 238
*Humaneness in Schools: A Neglected
    Force,* 359n
Humanities, 277–301
    areas of emphasis, 279–280
    and the Cardinal Principles for
        Educational Change, 279
    course design, 278
    curricular areas of emphasis in, 279–287
    definition of, 277
    goal of, 277–278
    and multiethnic education, 279–286
    National Foundation on the Arts and
        Humanities, 277
    tentative schedule for the 1920s unit,
        288–289
    units, 279–280, 285–300, 413–424
Humanities Horizon, The, 413n
Humanizing instruction, 49–53
Hutchins, Robert, 1

If I Had Lived During the Middle Ages
    unit, 213–219
Illinois Self-Evaluation Form: School
    Media Programs, 347–356
Illinois Standards for School Media
    Programs and the School Evaluation
    Form, 330–346, 347–356
"Image of Man, An: The Learner
    Himself," 63n
Index to Environmental Studies, 251
Individualizing instruction, 49–53
    checklist of variations for, 202–204
    planning for less able students checklist,
        204
    variations and adjustments for gifted
        students checklist, 204–205
Individualizing the Teaching Design, 53
Inflation, 2
Inner Limits of Mankind, The, 1n, 13n
*Innovation in Education: New Directions
    for the American School,* 303n

Inquiry method, 44, 53–54, 197–198, 306.
    See also Skills program
*Instead of Education: Ways to Do Things
    Better,* 271
Institute for Development of Educational
    Activities, 97
Instructional materials center. *See*
    Library media center
*Instructional Materials: Selection and
    Purchase,* 95n
Instructional media
    book selection criteria, 106–107, 463,
        465, 466
    Booklist Criteria for Selection of
        Material, 457–463
    challenged materials, 100, 101–105, 168,
        406–412
    checklist of, 201–202
    checklists for media advisory
    committee's reconsideration of, 103–
        104, 104–105
    curriculum packages selection guides,
        107–108
    essential carriers of information, 28–29
    morass, 96
    policies and procedures for selecting
        media, 99–101, 469–470
    request for reconsideration of materials
        forms, 101–105
    selection criteria, 99–100, 101, 106–110,
        457–463
    selection criteria for materials for
        disadvantaged, 149–150
    selection criteria for reading program
        materials, 148–149
    selection criteria for social studies
        materials, 227–230
*Instructional Supervision: A Behavior
    System,* 361
Instructional technology, 96–97
    defined, 97
    purpose of, 97, 133
Interest inventory, 471–473
International Institute for Educational
    Planning, 72
*Interpersonal Communication:
    Innovation in Instruction,* 170
Inventory, defined, 314

Jackson, Philip W., 56
James, William, 58
Jarolimek, John, 66, 199n
Jeffers, Robinson, 13
Jefferson, Thomas, 14
Job description
    district school library media director,
        364–367
    head of elementary library team, 369
    head of secondary library team, 369

Job description (cont.)
  supervisor of library media service,
    370–371
Johnson, Harry A., 286
Johnson, Henry, 36–37
Johnston, Annie, 78–80
Jones, Milbrey, 10n, 380

Kauffman, Draper, 219, 240
Kennedy, Kerry, 193, 194
Knapp Foundation, Inc., 9, 35n, 357
"Knapp Project Evaluated," 35n
Knight, Douglas M., 63n
Knowledge
  explosion, 96
  "What is worth knowing?" 73–74
Kolesnik, Walter, 8
Kraus, W. Keith, 181
Kruse, Edward D., 368

"Laboratory Approach to Elementary
    Mathematics, The," 266
Language arts. *See* English program
*Language Arts in Childhood Education,
    The,* 146
Language Skills in Elementary Education,
    164n
Laszlo, Ervin, 1n, 13n
Law and justice pilot project, 78–80
Law-related education, 77–80, 205–206,
    219
*Law-Related Education in America:
    Guidelines for the Future,* 205
Learning guides. *See* Pittman Learning
    Guides
Learning how to learn, 44, 548–555
Learning laboratory. *See* Library media
    center
Learning principles, 66–67
*Learning Resource Centers: Selected
    Readings,* 45
Learning skills, 305–306
Learning to learn, 310–311
"Learning to Learn in School Libraries,"
    548–555
Learning to Use Roman Numerals
    learning guide, 274–275
*Learning Together: How to Foster
    Creativity . . . ,* 51
*Learning Unlimited: An Instructional
    Program for the Intellectually Gifted
    and Creatively Talented Student,
    Vol. 1,* 175n, 213n
Leppert, Ella C., 303n
Lessons of History, 9
Librarian. *See* Library media specialist
Library. *See* Library media center; Library
    media program

Library-based unit, 91
Library Bill of Rights, 100, 105–106
Library media center
  budget for, 125–126, 127
  facilities planning and design, 124,
    535–547
  instructional activities, 128–133
  as learning laboratory, 32, 36–37, 47,
    124, 311
  scheduling of, 128–133
  staffing, 126, 128
  typical day in a secondary library media
    center, 130–133
  typical day in an elementary library
    media center, 129–130
Library media program
  breaks the textbook barrier, 35–36
  budget, 125–126, 127
  building level, 46, 124–125
  and curriculum support, 36, 38, 40–44
  design of, 44–47
  district, definition of, 46
  district instructional materials center,
    124
  district media services, 121–124
  educational role of, 1–2, 38, 39–40
  evaluating, 316–317
  evaluation forms, 317, 318–319, 320–321,
    322–329, 330–346, 347–356
  force for self-realization, 49–59
  goals expressed as functions, 124–125
  guides for reading program support
    activities, 150–152
  guiding principles, 316
  instructional force for excellence, 13, 32,
    35–37, 39–40, 47
  job description of district director for,
    364–367
  job description of elementary team
    leader for, 369
  job description of secondary team
    leader for, 369
  job description of supervisor for,
    370–371
  as keystone of quality educational
    program, 35
  and the multimedia approach, 36–37
  policy and routine manual for, 100–102,
    444–447, 467–470
  skills program support, 303–311
  staffing, 126, 128
  standards, 37–40
  supports the mathematics and science
    program, 235–275
  supports the reading program, 142–143
  supports the social studies program,
    226–232
  typical day in a secondary library media
    center, 130–133
  typical day in an elementary library
    media center, 129–130

Library media specialist
curriculum support role of, 71–93
definition of, 46
English program support role of, 146,
147–148, 150–152, 153, 157–158, 162,
167, 181–182
evaluation action plan for, 357–358
humanities program support role of,
300–301
humanizes instruction, 68–69
mathematics support role of, 266
performance criteria for, 372–374
performance requisites for, 64
plans with teachers, 67–68, 89–91
profile of, 64–69
reading program support role of, 142–
143, 145–146, 147–148, 150–152
role as instructional technologist,
95–133
teaching requisites for, 64–67
teaching role of, 32, 63–69
*Library Services for the Nation's Needs:
Toward Fulfillment of a National
Policy,* 63n
Linguistics, 139
units, 172–175, 175–177, 177–180
Listening skills, 305, 506–509
Literacy, functional, 143–144, 303, 306,
524n
Literacy, scientific, 235–236
Literature program
basic reference tools for, 153–157
biography, 164, 223–226
biography report forms, 164, 224–225
historical novel, 223–226
historical novel report form, 225
integration with social studies program,
222–226
library media program support of,
152–153
safeguarding student interest, 162–163
and science fiction, 167
techniques for sharing reading
reactions, 164–167
units, 158, 159–160, 160–161, 161–162,
222–223
"Locating and Gathering Information,"
303n
Lohrer, Alice, 377
Lord, James Gregory, 268n
Luskay, Jack, 97n, 153n

Macdonald, James B., 63n
McGhan, Barry, 167
MacKinnon, Donald W., 56
McLuhan, Marshall, 96
McMurray, John, 58
McMurrin, Sterling M., 96
McMurrin Report. *See To Improve*

*Learning: An Evaluation of Instruc-
tional Technology*
Madison, James, 14
Madison Conference, 35
Management of Organizational Behavior,
363
Managing Multimedia Libraries, 122n,
123n
Mann, Horace, 28, 35
"Manpower and Media for the Use of
the Minority and the Majority"
speech, 368
Manpower Project. *See* School Library
Manpower Project
Maryland State Department of Education,
45
Maslow, Abraham H., 235n
Mathematics program
basic competencies, 263
basic skills, 263–265
biography as part of, 271–272
and Cardinal Principles for Educational
Change, 265
challenging gifted students, 274–275
classroom learning centers for, 266–268
curricular areas of emphasis in, 266–273
guidelines for, 264
guiding principles, 265
interdisciplinary approach to, 268–273
role of mathematics in society, 263
unit, 272–273
Media, as message, 28–29, 96, 140
Media center. *See* Library media center
Media management, 97–133
defined, 97
district media services, 121–124
media match, 110–112
media mix, 112
media programming, 112–121
policies and procedures, 98–106
role of the library media specialist in,
133
selection criteria, 106–109
Media Personnel in Education, 45, 64n
Media programming, 112–114
components checklist, 112–113
Pittman Learning Guides, 114–116,
116–119, 119–121, 274–275
systems approach to, 113–114
Media Programs: District and School,
40, 45, 98n, 106, 128
Media staff. *See* Library media program;
Library media specialist
Mersand, Joseph, 135n
Merz, Albert F., 322n
Mexico: Its History, Its Lands, and Its
People unit, 80–82
Michaelis, John U., 171, 186–187, 189,
201, 204n, 209–210, 222–223, 239
Michigan, Common Goals of Education,
21

Miller, Arthur, 222
Mini-course
  construction guide for, 439–443
  evaluation form for, 441–443
Minority groups. *See* Multiethnic
  education
Model Parent Permission to Read Form,
  168
Model School District Media Program, A,
  124
Montgomery County (Maryland)
  personnel evaluation form, 371–374,
  375n
Motivation and Personality, 235n
Multiethnic education, 220–221
  curriculum guidelines for, 280–285
  Ethnic Heritage Studies Program Act,
  279
  evaluating textbook treatment of
  minorities, 464
  humanities program and, 279–280
  materials selection criteria, 108–109
  program evaluation checklist, 280–285
  reading program support of, 285–286
  Roots of America, 279–280
*Murder, Mischief, and Mayhem: A Process
  for Creative Research Papers,* 181
Murray, Marguerite, 35n
Mustang: Wild Spirit of the West, 77,
  78–80

NCSM. *See* National Council of
  Supervisors of Mathematics
NCSS. *See* National Council for the Social
  Studies
NCTE. *See* National Council of Teachers
  of English
NCTM. *See* National Council of Teachers
  of Mathematics
NDEA. *See* National Defense Education
  Act
NEA (National Education Association).
  See National Education Association,
  Teacher Opinion Poll
NICEM. *See* National Information Center
  for Educational Media
National Advisory Commission on
  Libraries, 63n, 185n
National Association for Humanities
  Education, 300n
National Center for Social Statistics, 4n
National Commission on Working
  Women, 4–5
National Committee for Prevention of
  Child Abuse, 5n
National Council for the Social Studies,
  185n, 189, 192, 193, 226, 231–232,
  249, 280, 303, 304
National Council of Supervisors of
  Mathematics, 264

National Council of Teachers of English,
  100, 137, 168–169, 170, 286
  curriculum guidelines, 137–142, 166, 170
  Students' Right to Read, 406–412
National Council of Teachers of
  Mathematics, 262–263, 275
National Defense Education Act, 10
National Education Association, Teacher
  Opinion Poll, 6–7
National Foundation on the Arts and
  Humanities, 277
National Goals Report, 14, 15–16, 235n,
  389–392
National Information Center for
  Educational Media, 156, 251
National Institute on Alcohol Abuse and
  Alcoholism, 7–8
National Institute on Drug Abuse, 7n
National Science Teachers Association,
  235, 237, 275
National Study of School Evaluation,
  314–317
National Wildlife Federation, 271n
Neuenschwander, John A., 287
Neville, Richard, 361
*New Designs for Elementary Curriculum
  and Instruction,* 171
New York State Education Department
  Cooperative Review Service Self-
  Study Guide, 322–329
"No Man Is an Island" learning guide,
  161–162

Observing skills, 305–306, 509–511
Occupational definitions. *See* Job
  description
*Occupational Definitions for School
  Library Media Personnel,* 45, 47, 64n,
  128, 364–367
Old Man and the Sea, The, unit, 160–161
Open classroom, 97
*Open Classroom: Informal Education in
  America,* 97–98
Opinion polls, 6–7, 268–270, 306, 511–514
Oral History as a Teaching Approach,
  287
Our Wonderful World of Animals unit,
  251–259
Our Wonderful World of Plants unit,
  259–262

Peccei, Aurelio, 1n
Pennsylvania Governor's Committee on
  Education, 35n
*Pennsylvania Guide for School Library
  Media Specialists, The,* 35, 45n, 448n,
  467

Pennsylvania's Goals of Quality
  Education, 21-22
Persinger, Nancy S., 119n
Peter, Laurence J., 313
*Peter Prescription: How to Be Creative,
  Confident, and Competent, The,* 313
Phi Delta Kappa, Survey of Educational
  Goals, 19-20
Pilot study, 77
  Law and Justice Pilot Project, 78-80
  Pilot Project Design and Analysis
    Guide, 83-84
  pilot projects, 82
Pittman, Shirley A., 35, 45n, 78n, 114n
  learning guides, 113-119, 161, 448n,
    467
  See also Pittman Learning Guides
Pittman Learning Guides, 113-119
  Appomattox and the End, 119-121
  Learning to Use Roman Numerals,
    274-275
  "No Man Is an Island," 161-162
  Tasaday: A Study of a Primitive Culture
    Frozen in Time, 116-119
  White Men Doom and Then Save the
    Buffalo, 114-116
Planning School Library Development,
  381
*Policies and Procedures for the Selection
  of Instructional Materials,* 98-106
Polycultural education. *See* Multiethnic
  education
Pooley, Robert C., 162
"Poor Scholar's Soliloquy, The," 50-51
"Position Paper on Basic Skills," 264-265
"Position Statement: Revision of the
  NCSS Social Studies Curriculum
  Guidelines," 185n, 189-192
Posthuma, Frederick E., 246n, 248, 249n
Postman Neil, 57
President's Commission on Law Enforce-
  ment and Administration of Justice, 6
President's Commission on Libraries. *See*
  National Advisory Commission on
  Libraries
Pretest method, 230-231
Primary source materials, 119-121, 221
Principal, media program support by,
  367-368
Problem solving. *See* Inquiry method
Process of Education, The, 31, 71-72
Profession, defined, 64
*Professional Publications for the Teacher
  of English and the Language Arts,*
  170n
Professional strategies, for survival, 9-11
"Professions under Siege," 1n
Programmed instruction. *See* Pittman
  Learning Guides
Prophet, The, 63n
Proposition 13, 3

Pros and Cons of Space Colonization
  learning project, 241-243
Pueblo (Colorado) Personnel Evaluation
  Form, 375-377
Purpose of Education, The, 17-19
*Purpose of Education in American
  Democracy,* 17-19
*Pursuit of Excellence: Education and the
  Future of America. See* Rockefeller
  Report

Rain Forest, The, unit, 42, 159-160
Rating scale, defined, 314
Reading program
  basic assumptions of, 142-143, 145-146,
    150
  behavioral objectives, 146
  Bill of Rights, 144-145
  criteria for selecting books for
    disadvantaged children, 149-150
  criteria for selecting media, 148
  developmental reading program goals,
    146
  functional literacy and, 143-144
  guides for structuring media support
    activities for, 150-152
  library media program support for,
    145-146
  library media specialist support for,
    150-152
  media evaluation form for, 149
  media selection criteria, 148-150
  personal reading notebook form, 164
  procedural guidelines for planning
    reading support activities, 150-152
  research concerning, 145, 147
  Right to Read, The, 143-145
  safeguarding student interest, 162-163
  Student Guide for Selecting Books to
    Enrich Reading unit, 466
  Students' Right to Read, 406-412
  techniques for sharing reaction to
    reading, 164-167
Recordings, selection criteria, 460-461
Relevance, 56-57, 220, 251
Request for reconsideration of materials
  forms, 102-103
Research and Policy Committee of the
  Committee for Economic
  Development, 303n
Research paper, 180-181, 306
*Research Papers: A Guided Writing
  Experience for Senior High School
  Students,* 180n
Resource units
  Civil War and Reconstruction, 299,
    425-438
  defined, 76-77
  Roots of America, 279, 299

Right to Read program, 143–145
  Bill of Rights, 144–145
  Students' Right to Read, 406–412
Rockefeller Brothers Fund. *See* Rockefeller
  Report
Rockefeller Report, 15, 385–389
Roots of America, 279, 299
Rowell, John, 10, 546

Saber-Tooth Curriculum, The, 26–27
Salk, Jonas, 10, 379
Samples, Bob, 249
Sandburg, Carl, 25
Scheduling procedures, 128
  typical elementary schedule, 129–130
  typical secondary schedule, 130–133
Schmidt, Warren H., 363
Scholl Joyce B., 318, 535n
*School Libraries for Today and
  Tomorrow*, 38
School Library Bill of Rights for School
  Library Media Programs, 46, 105–106
School Library Manpower Project, 64n,
  128, 357, 364
School library media program. *See* Library
  media program
School library standards
  Elementary School Library Standards
    (1925), 37–38, 400–405
  Media Programs: District and School
    (1975), 40, 45, 98n, 106, 128
  *School Libraries for Today and
    Tomorrow* (1945), 38
  *Standard Library Organization and
    Equipment for Secondary Schools of
    Different Sizes* (1918), 37, 393–400
  Standards for School Library Programs
    (1960), 9–10, 38–39, 310, 379–381
  Standards for School Media Programs
    (1969), 39–40
School media advisory committee, 102–105
School Media Resources Branch, U.S.
  Office of Education, 10n
School survey, defined, 314
*Schools for the 70's and Beyond: A Call
  to Action*, 51–52
*Science and Society: Knowing, Teaching,
  Learning*, 249
*Science Education: Accomplishments and
  Needs*, 235
Science fiction, 167
Science program
  alternative futures emphasis in, 240–241
  basic principles, 236–237, 237–238
  and Cardinal Principles for Educational
    Change, 239–240
  curricular areas of emphasis in, 240–241
  Evaluative Criteria, 237–238
  goals, 235–236

  a lesson plan, 246–248
  Pros and Cons of Space Colonization
    learning project, 241–243
  recommendations for the 1980s, 237
  scientific literacy, 236
  trends, 238–239
  units, 241–243, 243–246, 251–259,
    259–262
Scientific Method in Theory and
  Application unit, 243–246
*Selected Print and Nonprint Resources
  in Speech Communication*, 170
Selecting New Aids to Teaching, 107
Self-realization, 49–59, 74
Senn, Milton J. E., 49n
Seven Cardinal Principles, 16–18
Shane, Harold, 10–11, 13n, 22, 26, 52,
    135n, 150n, 178n, 268, 363, 381
Shrewsbury Ordinance, 35
Silberman, Charles E., 71, 277n
Skill Development in the Social Studies,
    303n
Skills program, 303–311
  chronology and time line skills, 307–310
  guiding principles, 303–304
  inquiry process, 44, 53–54
  social studies integration of, 197–198,
    221–222
  Thinking-Learning-Communicating
    Skills Continuum, 304–307, 478–534
Slides, selection criteria, 461–462
Smith, Bessie, 35–36
Snider, Robert C., 95n
Social Education, 231
Social interaction skills, 306, 514–518
*Social Studies for Children in a
  Democracy*, 201n, 202n, 204n
Social Studies in Elementary Education,
    199n
Social studies program
  American history learning guide,
    119–121
  and Cardinal Principles for Educational
    Change, 192
  components of, 185–188
  dependence on library media and
    services, 226–227
  evaluation of, 191
  guiding principles of, 188–189
  inquiry objectives, 197–198
  instructional media checklist, 201–202
  integration of literature with, 222–226
  interrelated with science program,
    249–251
  laboratory for, 231–232
  learning activities for, 190–191
  learning resources for, 191
  library media program support for,
    185–232
  and media selection criteria, 227–230

NCSS Curriculum Guidelines, 189–192
objectives of, 190, 193–198
planning for less able students checklist, 204
skill objectives for, 198, 221–222
textbook emphasis in, 194–196
theory versus practice in, 192–193
unit planning guides, 199–200
units, 78–80, 80–82, 119–121, 206–213, 213–219, 222–223, 425–438
variations for gifted students checklist, 204–205
variations to meet individual differences checklist, 202–204
Sociology of the Future, 250
Spann, Sylvia, 286
Speaking skills, 136, 307, 528–534
Speech Communication Association, 170
Spencer, Herbert, 31
Sperry, Armstrong, 42, 158, 159–160
Staff. *See* Library media program; Library media specialist
Standard, defined, 314
Standard Library Organization and Equipment for Secondary Schools of Different Sizes, 37, 393–400
Standards. *See* School library standards
Standards for School Library Programs, 9–10, 38–39, 310, 379–381
Standards for School Media Programs, 39–40
Stocking, Fred H., 278
Student book evaluation guide, 463
Students' Right to Read, 100, 406–412
Study Guide to Books on the Holocaust, 226
Study prints, selection criteria, 459–460
Sturgis Library Products, 166n
Supervision
authoritarian, 359–360, 363
contemporary concept of, 360
definition of, 360
democratic, 363
goal of, 360
historical perspective of, 359–360
job description of media program supervisor, 364–367, 370–371
leader behavior, 363
leadership of the merit of ideas, 363
Supervisor
as change agent, 360–361
designing library media program, 44–45
job description for, 364–367, 370–371
Swanson, Don, 96
Systems approach. *See* Media programming

Tale of Two Cities, A, 11
Tannenbaum, Robert, 363

Tapes. *See* Recordings, selection criteria
Tasaday: A Study of a Primitive Culture Frozen in Time learning guide, 116–119
Taxation, 2–3
Taxonomy of Educational Objectives: . . . Handbook I, Cognitive Domain, 43–44
Taxonomy of Educational Objectives: . . . Handbook II, Affective Domain, 44
Taylor, Robert B., 5
Teacher in America, The, 8
Teachers
physical violence against, 6–7
salaries, 3–4
Teaching of High School English, The, 135n
Teaching Social Studies Skills, 221, 303n
Teaching the Decades: A Humanities Approach to American Civilization, 286–287, 288n, 289n, 299
Teaching Tomorrow: A Handbook of Science Fiction for Teachers, 167
Teaching unit, defined, 63, 76–77
Team teaching, 30, 67–68
team approach to library media staff organization, 367–370
Teams for Better Education: The Teacher and the Librarian, 45n, 67n
Terman, Lewis, 49–50
Terminology, 557–567
building library program, 46
district library program, 46
library media specialist, 46
name changes in library media program, 39
Textbook, limitations, 28, 35–36, 38, 40, 138–139
Thematic Units in Teaching English and the Humanities, 286, 299
Thinking-Learning-Communicating Skills Continuum, 304–307, 478–534
Thinking skills, 304–305, 478–534
Tickton, Sidney G., 277n
Tillin, Alma M., 13n, 122n, 123n
To Improve Learning: An Evaluation of Instructional Technology, 29, 96–97, 277n
Toffler, Alvin, 1n
Torrance, E. Paul, 54–55, 359n
Toynbee, Arnold J., 72
Transparencies, selection criteria, 462–463
"Trends in the Teaching of Science," 238–239
Tuttle, Frederick B., 170
Twain, Mark, 133
12,000 Students and Their English Teachers, 160

Uniform Crime Reporting Section, U.S. Department of Justice, 6n
Unit
  multidisciplinary, 159n
  resource, 76–77
  selecting instructional unit or curriculum packages, 107–108
  social studies unit planning form, 199
  teacher-library media specialist unit planning guide, 200
  teaching, 77
Units
  American Civil War, 119–121
  American English: Inherited, Manufactured, and Fractured, 177–180
  American Humanities: Names and Terms of the 1920s, 289–290
  American Humanities: Tentative Schedule for the 1920s unit, 288–289
  Book Illustrators and Their Art, 290–299
  California and the West, 78–80
  Call It Courage, 158
  Civil War and Reconstruction, 299, 425–438
  Contemporary American Culture, 413–424
  Crucible, The, 222–223
  Fun with Words, 172–175
  If I Had Lived During the Middle Ages, 213–219
  Mathematics as a Communication Tool, 272–273
  Mexico: Its History, Its Land, and Its People, 80–82
  Old Man and the Sea, The, 160–161
  Our Wonderful World of Animals, 251–259
  Our Wonderful World of Plants, 259–262
  Pros and Cons of Space Colonization, 241–243
  Rain Forest, The, 159–160
  Scientific Method in Theory and Application, The, 243–246
  Westward Ho! the Wagons, or, If I Had Been a Pioneer Trailblazer, 206–213
  Wizardry of Words, The, 175–177
Urban Institute, 5n

Values, 57–59
  defined, 57
Viewing skills, 305–306, 509–511
Vogel, Robert A., 439n

Waack, William, 277n
Watergate, 2, 43
Weaver, Warren, 235n
Weingartner, Charles, 57
West, Edwin, 238
Westward Ho! the Wagons . . . unit, 206–213
"What is worth knowing?" 73–74
White Men Doom and Then Save the Buffalo learning guide, 114–116
Will and Ariel Durant: A Dual Autobiography, 185n, 278n
Wizardry of Words unit, 175–177
Women's Bureau, 5n
"Wondering If Children Are Necessary," 5
Workman, Brooke, 286, 288n
Writing About Ourselves and Others, 170
Writing skills, 140, 180–181, 306, 523–528

Zito, Genevieve P., 425n